THIS HYMNAL HAS BEEN REVISED IN KEEPING
WITH THE RESOLUTION:

"...it is the policy of this church
that the language used in our services
shall be inclusive..."

> By unanimous vote of the
> University Unitarian Church
> Board of Trustees
> November, 1976

# Hymns for the Celebration of Life

# HYMNS
# FOR THE
# CELEBRATION
# OF LIFE

THE UNITARIAN UNIVERSALIST ASSOCIATION, BOSTON

# Preface

Religion is a present reality; it is also an inheritance from the past. *Hymns for the Celebration of Life* is edited in the conviction that a vital faith must be a singing faith and that each generation needs to express itself freshly in its own idiom through song and the spoken word. Hence, to a solid core of songs and readings that have proved to have enduring significance have been added new materials—things old rediscovered, others newly fashioned. The title comes from Von Ogden Vogt's definition of worship as "the celebration of life." This book presents a wide gamut of life's varied experience, since no part of life may be excluded from our religious concern. Here are utterances representing differing minds, differing approaches to and interpretations of religion and life. Here we celebrate our recognition that truth for living is in all religious traditions. We bring together from diverse times and cultures texts and music that have meaning for us. Included are writings from the past which many modern minds can use by recognizing their non-literal validity and meaning; for example, Frederic Henry Hedge's translation of Luther's "A Mighty Fortress Is Our God," a wide selection from the King James Version of the Psalms, and our many Christmas carols.

As new texts to be sung as hymns, we have sought modern poetry of distinction having the regularity of verse form and clarity of expression which are necessary to our mode of group singing. We express our gratitude to authors who have permitted or suggested changes making it possible to include their work, through providing a more singable rhythm, or a phraseology more widely acceptable to people for whom this collection is designed.

In choosing tunes we have been guided by the belief that a vital religion calls for fresh, as well as for familiar, musical expression, including tunes which, if unfamiliar, deserve to be learned. The search for fresh material has repeatedly led to the rich repertory of American folk hymnody, and one of the distinctive features of this book is the large number of these tunes employed. Our substantial use of classic hymn tunes, particularly those of the Lutheran and Calvinist traditions, as well as folk music from many lands, is consonant with the best musical standards of current hymnody. Recognizing a widespread desire for a smaller and lighter volume than most past collections, we have given only one tune for each hymn with one exception.

We believe that any hymnbook worth publishing must be to some extent experimental, and we recognize that not everything in this one will be useful everywhere, nor will it necessarily stand the test of time. But we hope that the initial enthusiasm of a few, matched by the open-mindedness of the many, will lead to full use of this collection in that venturesome attitude which allows the new to become familiar.

Both texts and tunes often involve multiple authorship, including minor adjustments, abridgements, and thoroughgoing adaptations. We have sought to respect the integrity of authorship, either by employing original readings, or by noting carefully where changes have been made. "From" before the name of author or composer indicates relatively slight changes; "arranged" or "adapted" indicates greater changes. We have also sought to record the most accurate information available about text and tune sources, including date of composition, copyright, or publication. Further information as to the origin and history of texts, including readings, and of tunes, with biographical details concerning authors and composers, will be found in the "Notes on Hymns, Tunes, and Readings."

Single-stanza hymns have been included with several uses in mind: as responses sung regularly in the services of some churches following responsive reading, prayer or meditation, or benediction; as special responses to give variety to the development of particular topics; on occasions when a brief hymn would be appropriate.

With the hymns are readings for congregational utterance, responsive or unison, of various patterns and for diverse uses in the service. In the main, these passages are wholes or entities, sometimes centos or abstracts, seldom compilations from a variety of sources. Rather than trying to provide orders of service filled out in considerable detail, we leave it for those who are responsible for the conduct of worship to arrange orders of service which seem appropriate locally, and to contribute from other sources the materials which will be spoken by a leader alone. The exception is a brief collection of introductory, offertory, and closing words provided for reference as desired. With few exceptions, we have preferred to use the King James Version for biblical passages, deeming its stately rhythms and classical quality more important than any loss in literal accuracy; its mistranslations, indeed, are sometimes better religion than the original sense. The many and diverse sources of the readings will be evident upon the pages themselves.

We acknowledge with gratitude the answers by a large number of ministers, musicians, and lay people to an extensive questionnaire. While we did not regard the knowledge of preferences and use thus gained as binding, we did rely heavily upon it in forming our judgments. Decisions by the Commission were often not unanimous. Not included are many texts submitted to us, which, while expressing ideas and values important to religious liberalism, none the less seemed lacking in durability or in lyrical quality.

So many sources have been helpful in the shaping of this collection that to name them all would be impossible. We think it important, however, to note the following sources of information for the section, "Notes on Hymns, Tunes, and Readings." These have been John Julian's classic, *A Dictionary of Hymnology*, originally published in 1892 and frequently revised and reprinted since; Percy Dearmer's *Songs of Praise Discussed*, 1933; *The Hymnal 1940 Companion*, 1949 (Protestant Episcopal); E. Harold Geer's *Hymnal for Colleges and Schools*, 1956; Nicolas Slonimsky's edition of *Baker's Biographical Dictionary of Musicians*, 1958; and Henry Wilder Foote's *American Unitarian Hymn Writers and Hymns*, 1959, and *American Universalist Hymn Writers and Hymns*, 1959.

UNITARIAN UNIVERSALIST HYMNBOOK COMMISSION

### Arthur Foote II, Chairman

| | |
|---|---|
| Lorraine W. Bays | Kenneth Munson |
| Henry Leland Clarke | Kenneth L. Patton |
| Ida M. Folsom | Robert L. Sanders |
| Christopher Moore | Vincent B. Silliman |

# Contents

## HYMNS

| | | | |
|---|---|---|---|
| Celebration and Praise | 1–45 | Our World-wide Heritage | 245–251 |
| The Life That Maketh All Things New | 46–60 | Church of the Free Spirit | 252–261 |
| | | Christening or Naming | 262–263 |
| ~~Man~~ *Human* | 61–71 | Morning | 264–267 |
| Transience and Ongoing Life | 72–82 | Evening | 268–274 |
| Hours of Insight | 83–93 | Autumn and Harvest | 275–278 |
| The Life of Integrity | 94–113 | Hanukkah | 279 |
| Prayer and Aspiration | 114–134 | Advent | 280–284 |
| The Arts ~~of Man~~ | 135–140 | Christmas | 285–299 |
| Love and Human ~~Brotherhood~~ *Harmony* | 141–166 | Epiphany | 300 |
| | | Winter | 301–302 |
| Freedom | 167–173 | The Changing Year | 303–308 |
| Here and Now | 174–188 | Palm Sunday | 309–310 |
| In Time to Come | 189–210 | Maundy Thursday and Good Friday | 311–314 |
| Commitment and Action | 211–226 | Easter | 315–318 |
| Prophets, Exemplars, Pioneers | 227–237 | Spring | 319–325 |
| Nation and Nations | 238–244 | Summer | 326–327 |

## READINGS

| | | | |
|---|---|---|---|
| Responsive Readings and Litanies | 328–467 | Affirmations | 486–511 |
| Unison Readings and Prayers | 468–485 | Opening, Offering, and Closing Words | 512–558 |

**NOTES ON HYMNS, TUNES, AND READINGS**     *page 415*

# ACKNOWLEDGMENTS *page* 475

# INDEXES

First Phrases and Titles of Readings                                      *page* 478

Topical Index of Responsive Readings                                     *page* 482

Authors, Translators, and Sources of Responsive Readings       *page* 488

Authors and Sources of Unison Readings and Affirmations       *page* 489

Authors, Translators, and Sources of Hymns                           *page* 489

Composers, Arrangers, and Sources of Hymns                         *page* 495

Alphabetical Index of Tunes                                                    *page* 497

Metrical Index of Tunes                                                          *page* 498

Topical Index of Hymns                                                          *page* 501

First Lines and Titles of Hymns                                               *page* 510

# Hymns for the Celebration of Life

# 1 The Morning Hangs a Signal

MEIRIONYDD 7.6.7.6.D.

William Channing Gannett, 1886; recast, 1934 — William Lloyd, 1840

1. The morn-ing hangs a sig-nal Up-on the moun-tain crest, While
2. A-bove the gen-er-a-tions The lone-ly proph-ets rise, While
3. The soul hath lift-ed mo-ments, A-bove the drift of days, When

all the sleep-ing val-leys In si-lent dark-ness rest. From
truth flings dawn and day-star With-in their glow-ing eyes; And
life's great mean-ing break-eth In sun-rise on our ways. Be-

peak to peak it flash-es, It laughs a-long the sky, Till
oth-er eyes, be-hold-ing, Are kin-dled from that light; And
hold the ra-diant to-ken Of faith a-bove all fear; Night

glo-ry of the sun-light On all the land shall lie.
dawn be-comes the morn-ing, The dark-ness put to flight.
shall be lost in splen-dor And morn-ing shall ap-pear.

CELEBRATION AND PRAISE

# O Source of Life

ADAM'S SONG 10.10.10.10.10.

Ridgely Torrence, 1941
Based on Psalm 104

Robert L. Sanders, 1961

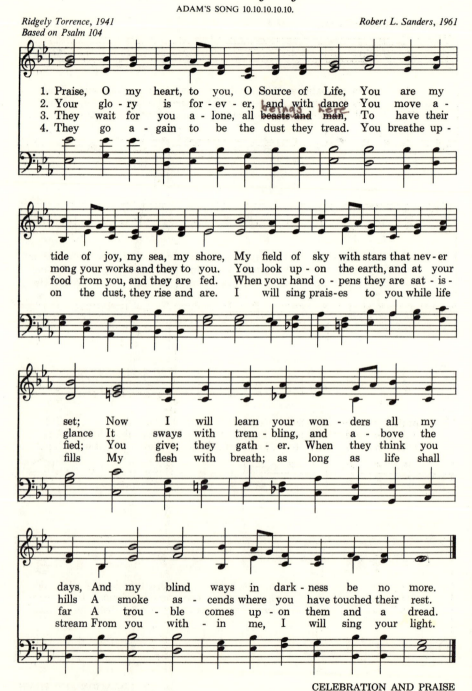

1. Praise, O my heart, to you, O Source of Life, You are my
tide of joy, my sea, my shore, My field of sky with stars that nev-er
set; Now I will learn your won-ders all my
days, And my blind ways in dark-ness be no more.

2. Your glo-ry is for-ev-er, and with dance You move a-
mong your works and they to you. You look up-on the earth, and at your
glance It sways with trem-bling, and a-bove the
hills A smoke as-cends where you have touched their rest.

3. They wait for you a-lone, all beasts and man, To have their
food from you, and they are fed. When your hand o-pens they are sat-is-
fied; You give; they gath-er. When they think you
far A trou-ble comes up-on them and a dread.

4. They go a-gain to be the dust they tread. You breathe upon the dust, they rise and are. I will sing prais-es to you while life
fills My flesh with breath; as long as life shall
stream From you with-in me, I will sing your light.

CELEBRATION AND PRAISE

# 3 Praise from Depth and Height

FARLEY CASTLE 10.10.10.10.

Ridgely Torrence, 1941
Based on Psalm 104

Henry Lawes, 1638

1. Praise, O my heart, with praise from depth and height, To
2. You laid the deep foun - da - tions of the earth Not
3. The cloud you made your car - rier as it streams Up -

you, O Source of Life. How ver - y great The
to be moved for a - ges from their place. You
on the wings of winds; at your de - sire Life

glo - ries are that beat up - on my sight, So
raised the sea to cov - er all its girth; The
woke and made the dark - ness glo - ri - ous, And

robed are you with hon - or and with light.
wa - ters lay a - broad its gleam - ing face.
man earth rose up - ward from the at - om - fire.

**CELEBRATION AND PRAISE**

# 4 Holy, Holy, Holy

NICAEA 11.12.12.10. Irregular

*Reginald Heber, 1826; arranged*

*John Bacchus Dykes, 1861*

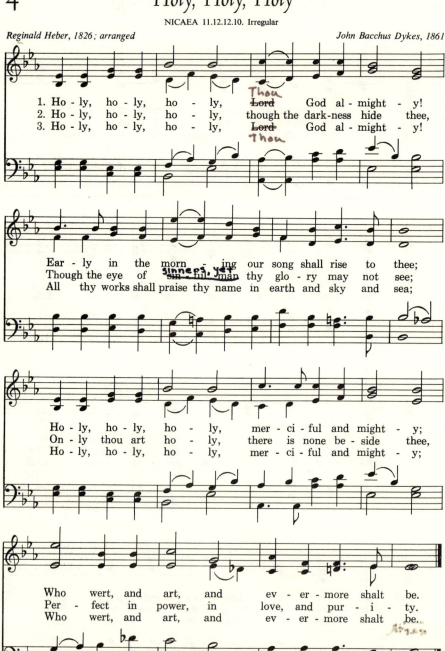

1. Ho - ly, ho - ly, ho - ly, ~~Lord~~ *Thou* God al - might - y!
2. Ho - ly, ho - ly, ho - ly, though the dark-ness hide thee,
3. Ho - ly, ho - ly, ho - ly, ~~Lord~~ *Thou* God al - might - y!

Ear - ly in the morn - ing our song shall rise to thee;
Though the eye of ~~sin - ful man~~ *sinners, yet* thy glo - ry may not see;
All thy works shall praise thy name in earth and sky and sea;

Ho - ly, ho - ly, ho - ly, mer - ci - ful and might - y;
On - ly thou art ho - ly, there is none be - side thee,
Ho - ly, ho - ly, ho - ly, mer - ci - ful and might - y;

Who wert, and art, and ev - er - more shalt be.
Per - fect in power, in love, and pur - i - ty.
Who wert, and art, and ev - er - more shalt be.

CELEBRATION AND PRAISE

# 5 Bring, O Morn, Thy Music

NICAEA 12.13.12.10.

William Channing Gannett, 1893

John Bacchus Dykes, 1861

1. Bring, O morn, thy mu - sic! night, thy star - lit si - lence!
2. Life and death, thy crea - tures, praise thee, might-y Giv - er!
3. "Light us! lead us! love us!" cry thy grop-ing na - tions,
4. Life nor death can part us, O thou Love e - ter - nal,

O - ceans, laugh the rap - ture to the storm-winds cours-ing free!
Praise and prayer are ris - ing in thy beast and bird and tree:
Plead-ing in the thou-sand tongues, but nam-ing on - ly thee,
Shep - herd of the wan-dering star and souls that way - ward flee!

Suns and plan - ets cho - rus, "Thou art our Cre - a - tor"—
Lo! they praise and van - ish, van - ish at thy bid - ding—
Weav-ing blind - ly out thy ho - ly, hap - py pur - pose—
Home-ward draws the spir - it to thy Spir - it yearn - ing—

Who wert, and art, and ev - er - more shalt be!

CELEBRATION AND PRAISE

# 6

# Yigdal

LEONI 6.6.8.4.D.

Daniel Ben Judah, 14th century
Translated by Newton Mann and
William Channing Gannett, 1910

*Synagogue melody*
*Adapted by Meyer Lyon (1751–1797)*

1. Praise to the liv-ing God! All prais-ed be his name, Who
2. Form-less, all love-ly forms De-clare this love-li-ness; Ho-
3. His spir-it flow-eth free, High surg-ing where it will: In
4. E-ter-nal life hath he Im-plant-ed in the soul; His

was, and is, and is to be, For aye the same. The
ly, no ho-li-ness of earth Can his ex-press. Lo,
proph-et's word he spoke of old; He speak-eth still. Es-
love shall be our strength and stay While a-ges roll. Praise

one e-ter-nal God Ere aught that now ap-pears: The
he is Lord of all; Cre-a-tion speaks his praise, And
tab-lished is his law, And change-less it shall stand, Deep
to the liv-ing God! All prais-ed be his name Who

first, the last, be-yond all thought His time-less years.
ev-ery-where, a-bove, be-low, His will o-beys.
writ up-on the hu-man heart, On sea or land.
was, and is, and is to be, For aye the same.

**CELEBRATION AND PRAISE**

# 7 Praise to the Lord, the Almighty

LOBE DEN HERREN 14.14.4.7.8.

Joachim Neander, 1680
Translation based on Catherine Winkworth, 1863

Erneuertes Gesangbuch, II, Stralsund, 1665
Version of Catherine Winkworth's
Chorale Book for England, 1863

1. Praise to the Lord, the Al-might-y, the King of cre - a - tion!
O my soul, praise him, for he is thy health and sal - va - tion.
Join the great throng, Wake harp and psal - tery and song,
Sound forth thy glad ad - o - ra - tion.

2. Praise to the Lord, who o'er all things so won-drous-ly reign - eth,
Who, as on wings of an ea - gle up - lift - ed, sus - tain - eth.
Hast thou not seen How what thou need - est hath been
Grant - ed in what he or - dain - eth?

3. Praise to the Lord, who doth pros-per thy work and de - fend thee;
Sure - ly his good-ness and mer - cy here dai - ly at - tend thee.
Pon - der a - new What the Al - might - y can do,
Who with his love doth be - friend thee.

4. Praise to the Lord! O let all that is in me a - dore him;
All that hath life and breath, come now with prais-es be - fore him.
Let the A - men Sound from his peo - ple a - gain;
Glad - ly for aye we a - dore him.

CELEBRATION AND PRAISE

# The Lark Ascending

FILLMORE 8.8.8.8.8.8.

*George Meredith, 1881; arranged*

*William Walker's* Southern Harmony, *1835*

1. In singing till the heaven fills, 'Tis love of earth the
   lark instills, And ever winging up and up, Our
   valley is his golden cup, And he the wine which
   overflows To lift us with him as he goes.

2. The woods and brooks, the sheep and kine He is — the hills, the
   human line, The meadows green, the fallows brown, The
   dreams of labor in the town; He sings the sap, the
   quickened veins, The wedding song of sun and rains.

3. He is the dance of children, thanks Of sowers, shout of
   primrose banks, And you shall hear the herb and tree, The
   better heart of men shall see, Shall feel celestial-
   ly, as long As you crave nothing save the song.

CELEBRATION AND PRAISE

**9**

# O ~~Lord~~ God of Stars and Sunlight

PAEAN 7.6.7.6.D.

*John Holmes, 1948*                                        *Frederic Weber, 1857*

1. O ~~Lord~~ God of stars and sun - light, Whose wind lifts up a bird, In
2. O ~~Lord~~ of cloud and moun - tain, Whose rain on rock is art, Thy
3. O ~~Lord~~ of root and shad - ing Of boughs a - bove our head, We

march - ing wave and leaf - fall We hear thy pa - tient word. The
plan and care and mean - ing Re - new the head and heart. Thy
breathe in thy long breath - ing Our spir - it spir - it - ed. We

col - or of thy sea - sons Goes gold a - cross the land. By
word and col - or spo - ken, Thy sum - mer noons and showers — By
walk be - neath thy bless - ing, Thy sea - sons and thy way, O

green up - on the tree - tops We know thy mov - ing hand.
these and by thy day - shine, We know thy world is ours.
~~Lord~~ of stars and sun - light, O God of this year's day.

CELEBRATION AND PRAISE

# Let the Whole Creation Cry

10

ST. GEORGE'S WINDSOR 7.7.7.7.D.

From Stopford Augustus Brooke, 1881
Based on Psalm 148

George Job Elvey, 1858

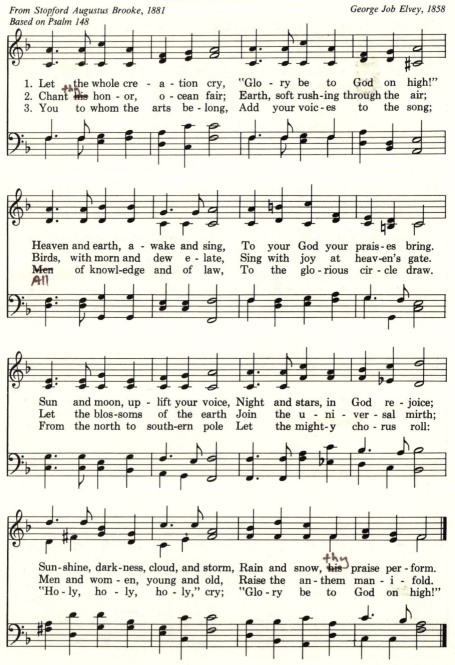

1. Let the whole cre - a - tion cry, "Glo - ry be to God on high!"
2. Chant thy hon - or, o - cean fair; Earth, soft rush-ing through the air;
3. You to whom the arts be - long, Add your voic - es to the song;

Heaven and earth, a - wake and sing, To your God your prais - es bring.
Birds, with morn and dew e - late, Sing with joy at heav-en's gate.
All of knowl-edge and of law, To the glo - rious cir - cle draw.

Sun and moon, up - lift your voice, Night and stars, in God re - joice;
Let the blos-soms of the earth Join the u - ni - ver - sal mirth;
From the north to south-ern pole Let the might - y cho - rus roll:

Sun-shine, dark-ness, cloud, and storm, Rain and snow, thy praise per - form.
Men and wom - en, young and old, Raise the an - them man - i - fold.
"Ho - ly, ho - ly, ho - ly," cry; "Glo - ry be to God on high!"

CELEBRATION AND PRAISE

# 11 Joyful, Joyful, We Adore Thee

HYMN TO JOY 8.7.8.7.D.

*Henry Van Dyke, 1908*　　　　　　　　　　　*Ludwig van Beethoven, 1823; adapted*

1. Joy - ful, joy - ful, we a - dore thee, God of glo - ry, Lord *[God]* of love;
2. All thy works with joy sur-round thee, Earth and heaven re - flect thy rays,
3. Thou art giv - ing and for - giv - ing, Ev - er bless - ing, ev - er blest,
4. Mor - tals, join the might-y cho - rus, Which the morn - ing stars be - gan;

Hearts un - fold like flowers be - fore thee, Hail thee as the sun a - bove.
Stars and an - gels sing a - round thee, Cen - ter of un - bro - ken praise;
Well-spring of the joy of liv - ing, O - cean-depth of hap - py rest.
Fa - ther-love is reign-ing o'er us, Broth-er love binds man to man. *[Divine] [Human] [each] [each]*

Melt the clouds of sin and sad - ness; Drive the dark of doubt a - way;
Field and for - est, vale and moun-tain, Blos-soming mead-ow, flash-ing sea,
Thou our Fa - ther, Christ our broth-er, All who live in love are thine; *[Parent]*
Ev - er sing - ing march we on - ward, Vic - tors in the midst of strife;

Giv - er of im - mor - tal glad - ness, Fill us with the light of day.
Chant-ing bird, and flow - ing foun - tain Call us to re - joice in thee.
Teach us how to love each oth - er, Lift us to the joy di - vine.
Joy - ful mu - sic lifts us sun - ward In the tri - umph song of life.

CELEBRATION AND PRAISE

# For the Beauty of the Earth

DIX 7.7.7.7.7.7.

*From Folliott Sandford Pierpoint, 1864*

*Conrad Kocher, 1838; abridged*

1. For the beau-ty of the earth, For the splen-dor of the skies,
2. For the joy of ear and eye, For the heart and mind's de-light,
3. For the won-der of each hour Of the day and of the night,

For the love which from our birth O-ver and a-round us lies:
For the mys-tic har-mo-ny Link-ing sense to sound and sight:
Hill and vale and tree and flower, Sun and moon and stars of light:

*Source*
Lord of all, to thee we raise This, our hymn of grate-ful praise.

# 13  From All That Dwell

OLD HUNDREDTH L.M. Modern form

*Composite*
*Based on Isaac Watts, 1719*

*Genevan Psalter, 1551*

From all that dwell be-low the skies Let songs of hope and faith a-rise; Let

CELEBRATION AND PRAISE

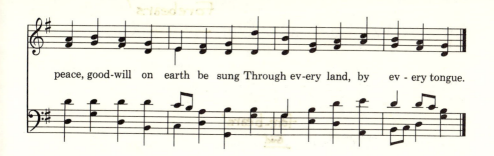

peace, good-will on earth be sung Through ev-ery land, by ev-er-y tongue.

## 14 *Morning, So Fair to See*

SCHÖNSTER HERR JESU 6.6.9.6.6.8.

*Vincent B. Silliman, 1934*

*A. H. Hoffmann von Fallersleben's*
*Schlesische Volkslieder, 1842*

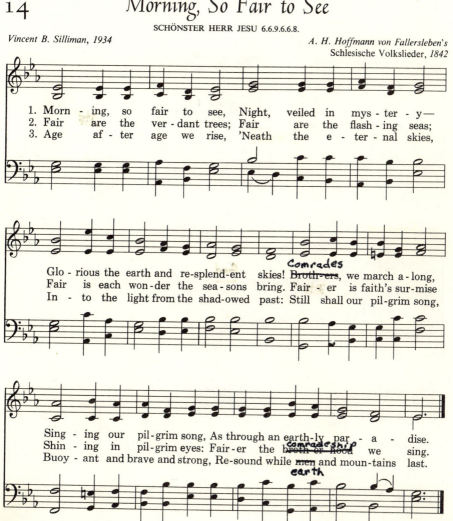

1. Morn - ing, so fair to see, Night, veiled in mys - ter - y—
2. Fair are the ver - dant trees; Fair are the flash - ing seas;
3. Age af - ter age we rise, 'Neath the e - ter - nal skies,

Glo - rious the earth and re-splend-ent skies! Broth-ers, we march a - long,
Fair is each won-der the sea-sons bring. Fair - er is faith's sur-mise
In - to the light from the shad-owed past: Still shall our pil-grim song,

Sing - ing our pil-grim song, As through an earth-ly par - a - dise.
Shin - ing in pil-grim eyes: Fair-er the broth-er-hood we sing.
Buoy - ant and brave and strong, Re-sound while men and moun-tains last.

CELEBRATION AND PRAISE

# 15 We Come unto Our Forebears' God

MIT FREUDEN ZART 8.7.8.7.8.8.7.

*Thomas Hornblower Gill, 1868*

*Bohemian Brethren, Kirchengeseng, 1566*

1. We come un-to our forebears' God; Their rock is our sal-va-tion; The e-ter-nal arms, their dear a-bode, We make our hab-i-ta-tion. We bring thee, God, the praise they brought, We seek thee as thy saints have sought In ev-er-y gen-er-a-tion.

2. Their joy un-to their God we bring; Their song to us de-scend-eth; The Spir-it who in them did sing, To us His mu-sic lend-eth. His song in them, in us, is one; We raise it high, we send it on— The song that nev-er end-eth.

# A Mighty Fortress

16

EIN' FESTE BURG 8.7.8.7.6.6.6.6.7.

Martin Luther, 1529
Translated by Frederic Henry Hedge, 1853

Martin Luther, 1529

1. A might-y for-tress is our God, A bul-wark nev-er fail - ing; Our
2. God's word a-bove all earth-ly powers, No thanks to them, a-bid - eth; The

help-er *thee* a - mid the flood Of mor-tal ills pre-vail - ing. For
spir - it and the gifts are ours, Through *him* *thee* who with us sid - eth. Let

still our an-cient foe Doth seek to work us woe; *Its* His craft and power are
goods and kin-dred go, This mor-tal life al - so; The bod-y they may

great; And, armed with cru-el hate, On earth is not *its* his e - qual.
kill, God's truth a-bid-eth still; *Thy reign is thus* His king-dom is for-ev - er.

CELEBRATION AND PRAISE

## 17 Now Let Every Tongue Adore Thee

WACHET AUF 8.9.8.8.9.8.6.6.4.8.8.

*Philipp Nicolai, 1599*
*Translated by Paul English, 1921*

*Philipp Nicolai, 1599*
*Harmonized by J. S. Bach, ca. 1731*

Now let ev - ery tongue a - dore thee; Let men with an - gels sing be - fore thee; Let harps and cym - bals now u - nite. All thy gates with pearl are glo - rious, Where we par - take through faith vic - to - rious, With an - gels round thy throne of light. No

CELEBRATION AND PRAISE

mor - tal eye hath seen, No mor - tal ear hath heard Such won-drous things; There-

fore with joy our song shall soar In praise to God for - ev - er - more.

## 18    All People That on Earth Do Dwell

OLD HUNDREDTH L.M. Original form

*William Kethe, 1561*
*Paraphrase of Psalm 100*

Genevan Psalter, *1551*

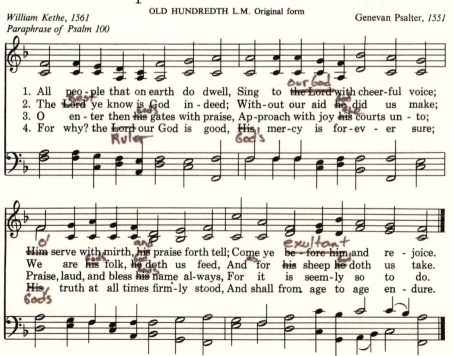

1. All peo-ple that on earth do dwell, Sing to the Lord with cheer-ful voice;
2. The Lord ye know is God in - deed; With-out our aid he did us make;
3. O en - ter then his gates with praise, Ap-proach with joy his courts un - to;
4. For why? the Lord our God is good, His mer-cy is for-ev - er sure;

Him serve with mirth, his praise forth tell; Come ye be - fore him and re - joice.
We are his folk, he doth us feed, And for his sheep he doth us take.
Praise, laud, and bless his name al-ways, For it is seem-ly so to do.
His truth at all times firm-ly stood, And shall from age to age en - dure.

CELEBRATION AND PRAISE

# 19 Now Thank We All Our God

NUN DANKET ALLE GOTT 6.7.6.7.6.6.6.6.

*Martin Rinkart, ca. 1636*
*Translated by Catherine Winkworth, 1858*

*Johann Crüger, 1648*

1. Now thank we all our God With heart and hands and voic - es, Who
2. O may this boun-teous God Through all our life be near us, With

won - drous things hath done, In whom his world re - joic - es; Who
ev - er joy - ful hearts And bless - ed peace to cheer us; The

from our moth - ers' arms Hath blessed us on our way With
one e - ter - nal God, Whom earth and heaven a - dore, For

count - less gifts of love, And still is ours to - day.
thus it was, is now, And shall be ev - er - more.

CELEBRATION AND PRAISE

# God Is My Strong Salvation

20

ST. THEODULPH 7.6.7.6.D.

*James Montgomery, 1822*

*Melchior Teschner, 1615*
*Adapted and harmonized by J.S. Bach, 1723*

1. God is my strong sal - va - tion: What foe have I to fear? In
2. Place on the Lord re - li - ance; My soul, with cour - age wait;

dark - ness and temp - ta - tion, My light, my help is near. Though
truth be thine af - fi - ance, When faint and des - o - late. His

hosts en - camp a - round me, Firm to the fight I stand: What
might thine heart shall strength - en, His love thy joy in - crease; Mer -

ter - ror can con - found me With God at my right hand?
cy thy days shall length - en; The Lord will give thee peace.

# Give Thanks

FOUNDATION 11.11.11.11.

*Anonymous, 1904 or earlier; recast, 1955*  　　　　　　　　*William Caldwell's* Union Harmony, *1837*

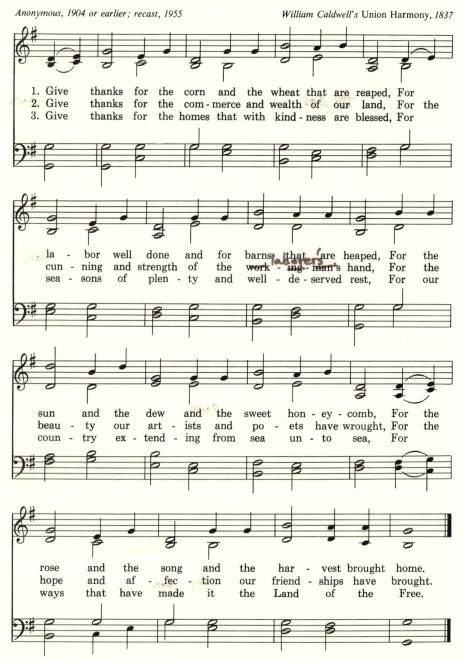

1. Give thanks for the corn and the wheat that are reaped, For
2. Give thanks for the com-merce and wealth of our land, For the
3. Give thanks for the homes that with kind-ness are blessed, For

la - bor well done and for barns that are heaped, For the
cun - ning and strength of the work-ing-man's hand, For the
sea - sons of plen - ty and well - de - served rest, For our

sun and the dew and the sweet hon - ey - comb, For the
beau - ty our art - ists and po - ets have wrought, For the
coun - try ex - tend - ing from sea un - to sea, For

rose and the song and the har - vest brought home.
hope and af - fec - tion our friend - ships have brought.
ways that have made it the Land of the Free.

CELEBRATION AND PRAISE

# Song of Thanksgiving

KREMSER 12.11.13.12.

*Edwin T. Buehrer, 1956*

*Adrian Valerius'* Nederlandtsch Gedenckclanck, *1626*
*Arranged by Edward Kremser (1838–1914)*

1. We sing now to - geth - er our song of thanks-giv - ing, Re -
2. We sing of the free - doms which mar - tyrs and he - roes Have
3. We sing of the proph - ets, the teach - ers, the dream - ers, De -
4. We sing of earth's broth - er - hood, now in the mak - ing In

joic - ing in goods which the a - ges have wrought, For
won by their la - bor, their sor - row, their pain; The op-
sign - ers, cre - a - tors, and work - ers, and seers; Our
ev - ery far con - ti - nent, re - gion, and land; With

Life that en - folds us, and helps and heals and holds us, And
press - ed be - friend - ing, men's am - pler hopes de - fend - ing, Their
own lives ex - pand - ing, our grat - i - tude com-mand-ing, Their
men of all rac - es, all times and names and plac - es, We

leads be - yond the goals which our fa - thers once sought.
death be - comes our tri - umph, their loss is our gain.
deeds have made im - mor - tal their days and their years.
pledge our - selves in fel - low - ship firm - ly to stand.

CELEBRATION AND PRAISE

# 23 The Canticle of the Sun

LASST UNS ERFREUEN 8.8.4.4.8.8.3.3.4.4.4.

*Attributed to Francis of Assisi (1182–1226)*
*From paraphrase by W.H. Draper, 1926*

Ausserlesene catholische geistliche Kirchengesäng,
Cologne, 1623

LET GOD'S PRAISES RING

1. All crea-tures of our God and King, Lift up your voice and with us sing Al - le - lu - ia, Al - le - lu - ia! Thou burn-ing sun with gold-en beam, Thou sil - ver moon with soft-er gleam: O praise him, O praise him, Al - le -

2. Thou rush-ing wind that art so strong, Ye clouds that sail in heaven a - long, Al - le - lu - ia, Al - le - lu - ia! Thou ris - ing morn, in praise re - joice, Ye lights of eve-ning, find a voice:

3. Thou flow-ing wa - ter, pure and clear, Make mu - sic for thy Lord to hear, Al - le - lu - ia, Al - le - lu - ia! Thou fire so mas - ter - ful and bright, That giv - est man both warmth and light:

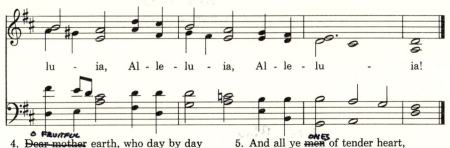

lu - ia, Al - le - lu - ia, Al - le - lu - ia!

4. ~~Dear mother~~ *O FRUITFUL* earth, who day by day
Unfoldest blessings on our way,
Alleluia, Alleluia!
The flowers and fruits that in thee grow,
Let them ~~his~~ *All* glory also show:
O praise ~~him~~ *All*, O praise ~~him~~ *All*,
Alleluia, Alleluia, Alleluia!

5. And all ye ~~men~~ *ONES* of tender heart,
Forgiving others, take your part,
Alleluia, Alleluia!
And thou, most kind and gentle death,
Waiting to hush our latest breath:
O praise ~~him~~ *All*, O praise ~~him~~ *All*,
Alleluia, Alleluia, Alleluia!

6. Let all things their Creator bless,
And worship ~~him~~ *All* in humbleness,
Alleluia, Alleluia!
Praise, praise ~~your Maker and your King~~ *TO GOD ALL PRAISES RING*,
Lift up your voice and with us sing:
O praise ~~him~~ *All*, O praise ~~him~~ *All*,
Alleluia, Alleluia, Alleluia!

## 24 The Abiding Presence

PELHAM STREET C.M.

*George Wallace Briggs, 1931*      *William King Covell, 1960*

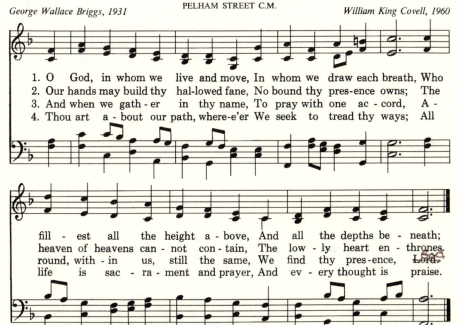

1. O God, in whom we live and move, In whom we draw each breath, Who
2. Our hands may build thy hal-lowed fane, No bound thy pres-ence owns; The
3. And when we gath-er in thy name, To pray with one ac - cord, A -
4. Thou art a - bout our path, where-e'er We seek to tread thy ways; All

fill - est all the height a - bove, And all the depths be - neath;
heaven of heavens can - not con - tain, The low - ly heart en - thrones.
round, with - in us, still the same, We find thy pres-ence, ~~Lord~~ *God*.
life is sac - ra - ment and prayer, And ev - ery thought is praise.

CELEBRATION AND PRAISE

## 25 O Worship the King

LYONS 10.10.11.11.

Robert Grant, 1833
Based on Psalm 104
and on William Kethe's paraphrase, 1561

*William Gardiner's* Sacred Melodies, *1815*

1. O wor-ship the King, all glo-rious a-bove; O
2. O tell of his might, O sing of his grace, Whose
3. The earth with its store of won-ders un-told, Al-

grate-ful-ly sing his power and his love— Our
robe is the light, whose can-o-py space. His
might-y, thy power hath found-ed of old, Hath

shield and de-fend-er, the An-cient of Days, Pa-
char-iots of wrath the deep thun-der-clouds form, And
stab-lished it fast by a change-less de-cree, And

vil-ioned in splen-dor, and gird-ed with praise.
dark is his path on the wings of the storm.
round it hath cast, like a man-tle, the sea.

4. Thy bountiful care what tongue can recite?
   It breathes in the air, it shines in the light;
   It streams from the hills, it descends to the plain,
   And sweetly distills in the dew and the rain.

5. Frail children of dust, and feeble as frail,
   In thee do we trust, nor find thee to fail;
   Thy mercies how tender, how firm to the end,
   Our maker, defender, redeemer, and friend.

**26**

*Let God's name Ring*

## Come, ~~Thou Almighty King~~

TRINITY 6.6.4.6.6.6.4.

Anonymous, before 1757
From version in S. Longfellow and S. Johnson, A Book of Hymns, 1848
*Felice Giardini, 1769; adapted*

1. Come, thou al-might-y King, Help us thy name to sing,
2. Come, thou cre-a-tive Word, With-in the si-lence heard,
3. Come, bless-ed Com-fort-er, Thy sa-cred wit-ness bear

Help us to praise! Sov-ereign all glo-ri-ous, O'er all vic-
Our prayer at-tend! Come and thy peo-ple bless; Give to thy
In this glad hour. Thou who al-might-y art, Rule now in

to-ri-ous, Come and reign o-ver us, An-cient of Days!
truth suc-cess; Spir-it of ho-li-ness, On us de-scend!
ev-ery heart, Nev-er from us de-part, Spir-it of power.

CELEBRATION AND PRAISE

# 27 God of Grace and God of Glory

CWM RHONDDA 8.7.8.7.4.4.7.7.

*Harry Emerson Fosdick, 1930*                    *John Hughes, 1907*

1. God of grace and God of glo - ry, On thy peo - ple
2. Cure thy chil - dren's war - ring mad - ness; Bend our pride to
3. Set our feet on loft - y plac - es; Gird our lives that

pour thy power; Crown thine an-cient church's sto - ry; Bring her bud to
thy con - trol; Shame our wan - ton, self - ish glad-ness, Rich in things and
they may be Ar - mored with all Christ-like grac-es In the fight to

glo - rious flower. Grant us wis - dom, Grant us cour - age,
poor in soul. Grant us wis - dom, Grant us cour - age,
set men free. Grant us wis - dom, Grant us cour - age,

For the fac - ing of this hour, For the fac - ing of this hour.
Lest we miss thy king-dom's goal, Lest we miss thy king-dom's goal.
That we fail not man nor thee, That we fail not man nor thee.

CELEBRATION AND PRAISE

# Brief Our Days

**28**

WERDE MUNTER, MEIN GEMÜTE 8.7.8.7.8.8.7.7.

*Kenneth L. Patton, 1956*

*Johann Schop, 1642; adapted and harmonized by J.S. Bach, 1716*

1. Brief our days, but long for sing-ing, When to sing is made our
2. Plan - et earth for men all a dwell-ing, Cool in wind and warm in

call, For a mil - lion stars now fling-ing Light up - on this
light, In its praise our song is swell-ing, Grate - ful for this

earth - ly ball. In a set - ting of what splen-dor
day and night. We, the cit - i - zens of heav - en,

Are we giv - en chance to ren - der Trib - ute for the
Rid - ing earth as it is driv - en Down the span - gled

whirl - ing sky Where we live and where we die.
course of space, Know the glo - ry of this place.

CELEBRATION AND PRAISE

# For All the Joys That Greet Us

STRUTHER 7.7.7.7.6.D.

*Jan Struther, 1931*

*Arthur Foote II, 1949*

1. We thank you, Lord ~~God~~ of heav - en, For all the joys that greet us, For
2. For swift and gal - lant hors - es, For lambs in pas - tures spring-ing, For
3. For home - ly dwell-ing plac - es Where child-hood's vi-sions lin - ger, For

all that you have giv - en To help us and de - light us In
dogs with friend - ly fac - es, For birds with mu - sic throng - ing Their
friends and kind - ly voic - es, For bread to stay our hun - ger And

earth and sky and seas; The sun-light on the mead - ows, The
chan - tries in the trees; For herbs to cool our fe - ver, For
sleep to bring us ease; For zeal and zest of liv - ing, For

rain-bow's fleet - ing won - der, The clouds with cool-ing shad - ows, The
flowers of field and gar - den, For bees a - mong the clo - ver With
faith and un - der - stand - ing, For words to tell our lov - ing, For

CELEBRATION AND PRAISE

stars that shine in splen - dor — We thank you, ~~Lord,~~ for these.
sto - len sweet - ness lad - en — We thank you, Lord, for these.
hope of peace un - end - ing — We thank you, ~~Lord,~~ for these.

## 30 *For Flowers That Bloom About Our Feet*

WAS GOTT THUT 8.8.8.8.7.

*Anonymous, 1904 or earlier; altered*      *Severus Gastorius, 1681; adapted*

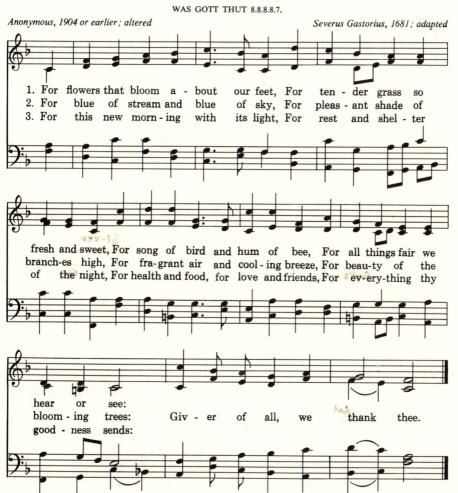

1. For flowers that bloom a - bout our feet, For ten - der grass so
2. For blue of stream and blue of sky, For pleas - ant shade of
3. For this new morn - ing with its light, For rest and shel - ter

fresh and sweet, For song of bird and hum of bee, For all things fair we
branch-es high, For fra - grant air and cool - ing breeze, For beau-ty of the
of the night, For health and food, for love and friends, For ev-ery-thing thy

hear or see: Giv - er of all, we thank thee.
bloom - ing trees:
good - ness sends:

# Praise Ye

**31**

AMHERST 6.6.7.7.8.8.

*Carrie Ward Lyon, 1960*

*William Billings, 1770; adapted*

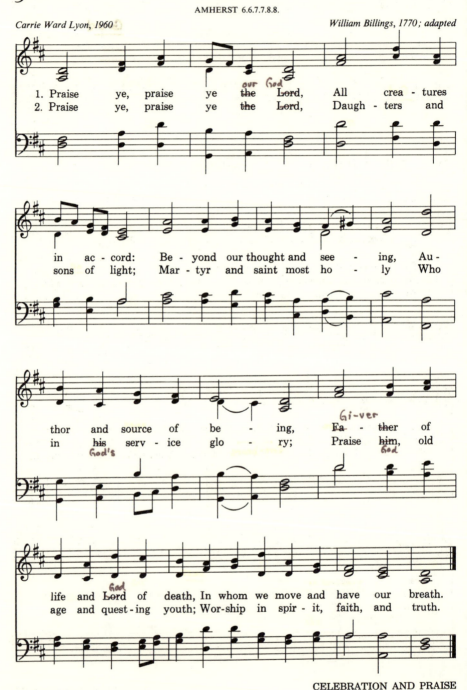

1. Praise ye, praise ye the Lord, *(our God)* All crea - tures in ac - cord: Be - yond our thought and see - ing, Au - thor and source of be - ing, Fa - ther of *(Gi-ver)* life and Lord *(God)* of death, In whom we move and have our breath.

2. Praise ye, praise ye the Lord, Daugh - ters and sons of light; Mar - tyr and saint most ho - ly Who in his serv - ice glo - ry; *(God's)* Praise him, *(God)* old age and quest - ing youth; Wor - ship in spir - it, faith, and truth.

CELEBRATION AND PRAISE

## 32 ~God~ Lord of All Majesty and Might

VATER UNSER 8.8.8.8.8.8.8.

*George Wallace Briggs, 1931*

*Valentin Schumann's Geistliche Lieder, 1539*
*Arranged from J.S. Bach, 1723*

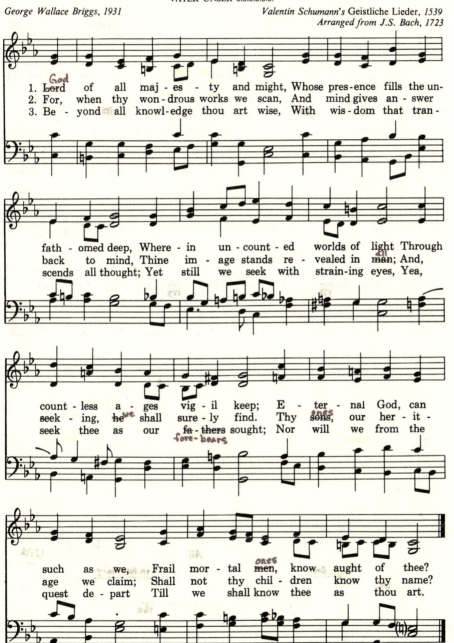

1. ~Lord~ God of all maj-es-ty and might, Whose pres-ence fills the un-
fath-omed deep, Where-in un-count-ed worlds of light Through
count-less a-ges vig-il keep; E - ter - nal God, can
such as we, Frail mor-tal ~men~ ones, know aught of thee?

2. For, when thy won-drous works we scan, And mind gives an - swer
back to mind, Thine im-age stands re-vealed in man; And,
seek-ing, he ~we~ shall sure-ly find. Thy ~sons~ ones, our her - it-
age we claim; Shall not thy chil-dren know thy name?

3. Be-yond all knowl-edge thou art wise, With wis-dom that tran-
scends all thought; Yet still we seek with strain-ing eyes, Yea,
seek thee as our ~fa-thers~ fore-bears sought; Nor will we from the
quest de-part Till we shall know thee as thou art.

**CELEBRATION AND PRAISE**

## 33 Heaven and Earth and Sea and Air

POSEN 7.7.7.7.

Joachim Neander, 1680
From translation by James Drummond Burns, 1869
Based on Acts 14:17

Georg Christoph Strattner, 1691
Version of J. A. Freylinghausen's Geistreiches
Gesangbuch, 1704

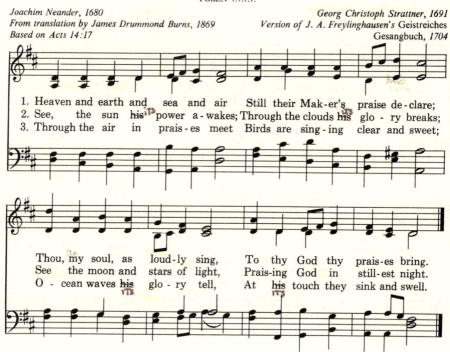

1. Heaven and earth and sea and air Still their Mak-er's praise de-clare;
2. See, the sun his power a-wakes; Through the clouds his glo-ry breaks;
3. Through the air in prais-es meet Birds are sing-ing clear and sweet;

Thou, my soul, as loud-ly sing, To thy God thy prais-es bring.
See the moon and stars of light, Prais-ing God in still-est night.
O-cean waves his glo-ry tell, At his touch they sink and swell.

4. See how God this rolling globe
   Swathes with beauty like a robe;
   Forest, field, and living thing
   Their Creator's glory sing.

5. Lo, my soul, what wonders lie
   Hid in this infinity;
   With creation take thy part,
   Praising God with all thy heart.

## 34 God Moves in a Mysterious Way

DUNDEE C.M.

William Cowper, 1774

Scottish Psalter, 1615

1. God moves in a mys-te-rious way His won-ders to per-form: He
2. Judge not the Lord by fee-ble sense, But trust him for his grace: Be-
3. His pur-pos-es will rip-en fast, Un-fold-ing ev-ery hour: The
4. Blind un-be-lief is sure to err, And scan his work in vain: God

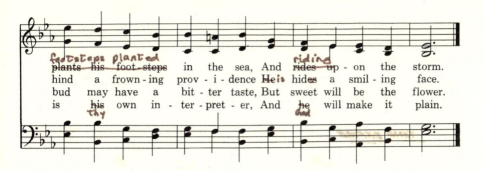

plants his foot-steps in the sea, And rides up-on the storm.
*(handwritten: footsteps planted ... riding)*
hind a frown-ing prov-i-dence He hides a smil-ing face.
bud may have a bit-ter taste, But sweet will be the flower.
is his own in-ter-pret-er, And he will make it plain.
*(handwritten: thy ... God)*

## 35    All My Hope on God Is Founded

MEINE HOFFNUNG STEHET FESTE 8.7.8.7.3.3.7.

Joachim Neander, 1680
Paraphrase, Robert Bridges, 1899

*Joachim Neander's* Glaub- und Liebesübung, *1680*
*Adapted by J.S. Bach (1685–1750)*

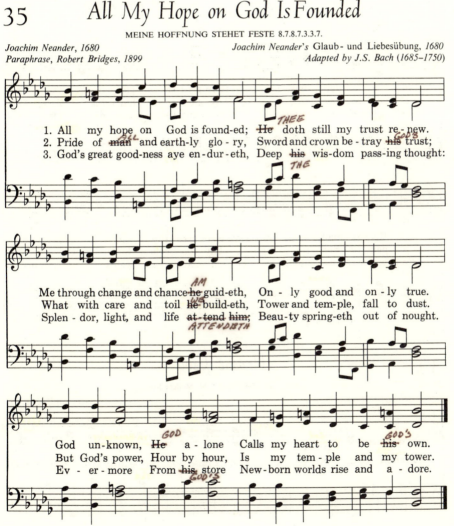

1. All my hope on God is found-ed; He doth still my trust re-new. *(handwritten: THEE)*
2. Pride of man and earth-ly glo-ry, Sword and crown be-tray his trust; *(handwritten: GOD'S)*
3. God's great good-ness aye en-dur-eth, Deep his wis-dom pass-ing thought: *(handwritten: THE)*

Me through change and chance he guid-eth, On-ly good and on-ly true. *(handwritten: AM)*
What with care and toil he build-eth, Tower and tem-ple, fall to dust. *(handwritten: WE)*
Splen-dor, light, and life at-tend him; Beau-ty spring-eth out of nought. *(handwritten: ATTENDETH)*

God un-known, He a-lone Calls my heart to be his own. *(handwritten: GOD ... GOD'S)*
But God's power, Hour by hour, Is my tem-ple and my tower.
Ev-er-more From his store New-born worlds rise and a-dore. *(handwritten: GOD'S)*

# 36 Our God, Our God, Thou Shinest Here

CORONATION 8.6.8.6.8.6.

Thomas Hornblower Gill, 1846

Oliver Holden, 1793

1. Our God, our God, thou shin-est here; Thine own this lat-ter day; To
2. The fa-thers had not all of thee; New births are in thy grace; All
3. Thou com-est near; thou stand-est by; Our work be-gins to shine; Thou

us thy ra-diant steps ap-pear; Here goes thy glo-rious way; To
o-pen to our souls shall be Thy glo-ry's hid-ing place; All
dwell-est with us might-i-ly—On come the years di-vine; Thou

us thy ra-diant steps ap-pear; Here goes thy glo-rious way.
o-pen to our souls shall be Thy glo-ry's hid-ing place.
dwell-est with us might-i-ly—On come the years di-vine.

# 37 Praise God

OLD HUNDREDTH L.M. Modern form

Charles H. Lyttle, 1919

Genevan Psalter, 1551

Praise God, the love we all may share; Praise God, the beau-ty ev-ery-where; Praise

CELEBRATION AND PRAISE

God, the hope of good to be; Praise God, the truth that makes us free.

**38  Lord ~~Lord~~ God of All Being**

TRANSYLVANIA L.M.

*Oliver Wendell Holmes, 1859*                    *Hungarian melody, 16th century; arranged*

1. ~~Lord~~ God of all be-ing, throned a-far, Thy glo-ry
2. Sun of our life, thy quick-ening ray Sheds on our
3. ~~Lord~~ God of all life, be-low, a-bove, Whose light is
4. Grant us thy truth to make us free, And kin-dling

flames from sun and star; Cen-ter and soul of ev-ery
path the glow of day; Star of our hope, thy sof-tened
truth, whose warmth is love, Be-fore thy ev-er-blaz-ing
hearts that burn for thee, Till all thy liv-ing al-tars

sphere, Yet to each lov-ing heart how near.
light Cheers the long watch-es of the night.
throne We ask no lus-ter of our own.
claim One ho-ly light, one heaven-ly flame.

CELEBRATION AND PRAISE

# 39

## Wonder

ERFYNIAD 10.10.10.10.

*Alfred Noyes, from* Watchers of the Sky, *1922*
*Recast 1959*

*Ieuan Gwyllt's* Llyfr Tonau Cynulleidfaol, *1859*
*Harmonized by David Evans, 1931*

1. Knowl - edge, they say, drives won - der from the world;
2. We seem like chil - dren wan - dering by the shore,

They'll say it still, though all the dust's a - blaze
Gath - er - ing peb - bles col - ored by the wave;

With mar - vels at their feet— while New - ton's laws
While the great sea of truth, from sky to sky

Fore - tell that knowl - edge one day shall be song.
Stretch - es be - fore us, bound -less, un - ex - plored.

# We Sing of Golden Mornings

COMPLAINER 7.6.7.6.D.

*Ralph Waldo Emerson, 1846; recast, 1925, 1950*     *William Walker's* Southern Harmony, *1835*

1. We sing of gold-en morn-ings, We sing of spar-kling seas, Of
2. We sing the heart cou-ra-geous, The youth-ful, ea-ger mind; We

prai-ries, val-leys, moun-tains, And state-ly for-est trees. We
sing of hopes un-daunt-ed, Of friend-ly ways and kind. We

sing of flash-ing sun-shine And life-be-stow-ing rain, Of
sing the ros-es wait-ing Be-neath the deep-piled snow; We

birds a-mong the branch-es, And spring-time come a-gain.
sing, when night is dark-est, The day's re-turn-ing glow.

CELEBRATION AND PRAISE

## 41

# Immortal, Invisible

ST. DENIO 11.11.11.11.

*From Walter Chalmers Smith, 1867*
*Based on I Timothy 1:17*

*John Roberts' Caniadau y Cyssegr, 1839*

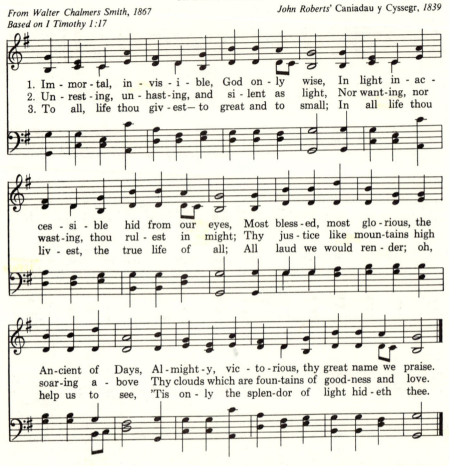

1. Im - mor - tal, in - vis - i - ble, God on - ly wise, In light in - ac -
2. Un - rest - ing, un - hast - ing, and si - lent as light, Nor want - ing, nor
3. To all, life thou giv - est— to great and to small; In all life thou

ces - si - ble hid from our eyes, Most bless - ed, most glo - rious, the
wast - ing, thou rul - est in might; Thy jus - tice like moun - tains high
liv - est, the true life of all; All laud we would ren - der; oh,

An - cient of Days, Al - might - y, vic - to - rious, thy great name we praise.
soar - ing a - bove Thy clouds which are foun - tains of good - ness and love.
help us to see, 'Tis on - ly the splen - dor of light hid - eth thee.

## 42

# Rejoice in Love We Know and Share

VOM HIMMEL HOCH L.M.

*Charles H. Lyttle, 1919; recast, 1955*

*Valentin Schumann's Geistliche Lieder, 1539*

Re - joice in love we know and share, In law and beau - ty ev - ery - where; Re -

CELEBRATION AND PRAISE

joice in truth that makes men free, And in the good that yet shall be.

# 43 God of the Earth, the Sky, the Sea

DUKE STREET L.M.

Samuel Longfellow, 1864                                        John Hatton, 1793

1. God of the earth, the sky, the sea, Mak-er of all a-bove, be-low, Cre-a-tion lives and moves in thee; Thy pres-ent life through all doth flow.

2. Thy love is in the sun-shine's glow, Thy life is in the quick-ening air; When light-nings flash and storm-winds blow, There is thy power, thy law is there.

3. We feel thy calm at eve-ning's hour, Thy gran-deur in the march of night; And when the morn-ing breaks in power, We hear thy word, "Let there be light."

4. But high-er far, and far more clear, Thee in man's spir-it we be-hold; Thine im-age and thy-self are there—In-dwell-ing God, pro-claimed of old.

# 44

## There's a Wideness in God's Mercy

CHARLESTON 8.7.8.7.

*Frederick William Faber, 1854*

*Amos Pilsbury's United States' Sacred Harmony, 1799*

1. There's a wide-ness in God's mer-cy Like the wide-ness of the sea;
2. But we make his love too nar-row By false lim-its of our own,
3. For the love of God is broad-er Than the meas-ures of man's mind,

There's a kind-ness in his jus-tice Which is more than lib-er-ty.
And we mag-ni-fy his strict-ness With a zeal he will not own.
And the heart of the E-ter-nal Is most won-der-ful-ly kind.

# 45

## God Makes a Path

DUNDEE C.M.

*From Roger Williams, 1643*

*Scottish Psalter, 1615*

1. God makes a path, pro-vides a guide, And feeds in wil-der-ness; His
2. Lost many a time, I had no guide, No house but hol-low tree; In
3. In him I found a house, a bed, A ta-ble, com-pa-ny; No

glo-rious name, while breath re-mains, O that I may con-fess.
storm-y win-ter night, no fire, No food, no com-pa-ny.
cup so bit-ter but made sweet, Where God shall sweet-en-ing be.

# Who Thou Art I Know Not

EINTRACHT 6.5.7.5.7.5.7.5. Irregular

*Harry Kemp, 1914*

*Franz Xaver Mathias (1871–1939)*
*Arranged by Sylvia Freeman and Raymond C. Robinson, 1934*

1. Who thou art I know not But this much I know;
2. Thou hast made the flowers to bloom And the stars to shine;

Thou hast set the Plei-a-des In a sil-ver row;
Hid rare gems of rich-est ore In the tun-neled mine; But

Thou hast sent the track-less winds Loose up-on their way;
chief of all thy won-drous works, Su-preme of all thy plan,

Thou hast reared a col-ored wall 'Twixt the night and day.
Thou hast put an up-ward reach In the heart of man.

THE LIFE THAT MAKETH ALL THINGS NEW

# 47 The Spacious Firmament on High

CREATION L.M.D.

Joseph Addison, 1712
Based on Psalm 19:1-6

Franz Joseph Haydn, 1798; adapted

1. The spa - cious fir - ma - ment on high, With all the
2. Soon as the eve - ning shades pre - vail The moon takes
3. What though in sol - emn si - lence all Move round the

blue e - the - real sky, And span - gled heavens, a
up the won - drous tale, And night - ly to the
dark ter - res - trial ball? What though no re - al

shin - ing frame, Their great O - rig - i - nal pro - claim.
lis - tening earth Re - peats the sto - ry of her *its* birth;
voice nor sound A - mid their ra - diant orbs be found?

claim. The un-wea - ried sun from day to day Does *the* Cre -
birth; Whilst all the stars that round *the* burn, And all the
found? In rea - son's ear they all re - joice, And ut - ter

THE LIFE THAT MAKETH ALL THINGS NEW

a - tor's power dis - play, And pub - lish - es to
plan - ets in their turn, Con - firm the ti - dings,
forth a glo - rious voice, For - ev - er sing - ing

ev - ery land The work of an al - might - y hand.
as they roll, And spread the truth from pole to pole.
as they shine, "The hand that made us is di - vine."

## 48 *Earth Arrayed in Wondrous Beauty*

GUTER HIRTE 8.7.8.7.

*Vincent B. Silliman, 1935*

*J.A. Freylinghausen's*
Geistreiches Gesangbuch, *1705*

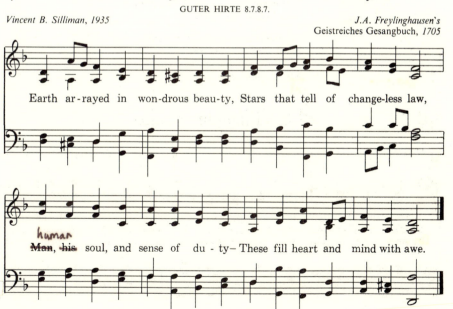

Earth ar-rayed in won-drous beau-ty, Stars that tell of change-less law,

human
~~Man, his~~ soul, and sense of du - ty— These fill heart and mind with awe.

THE LIFE THAT MAKETH ALL THINGS NEW

## 49

### ~~The Lord's~~ My Shepherd
*God Is*

DUNDEE C.M.

Scottish Psalter, *1650*
*Paraphrase of Psalm 23*

Scottish Psalter, *1615*

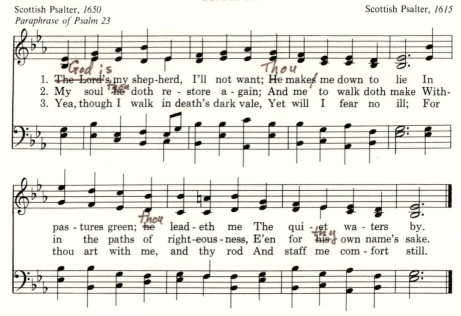

1. ~~The Lord's~~ my shep-herd, I'll not want; He makes me down to lie In
   *God is*
2. My soul ~~he~~ doth re-store a-gain; And me to walk doth make With-
   *Thou*
3. Yea, though I walk in death's dark vale, Yet will I fear no ill; For

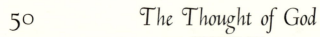

pas-tures green; ~~he~~ lead-eth me The qui-et wa-ters by.
*thou*  *thy*
in the paths of right-eous-ness, E'en for ~~his~~ own name's sake.
*thy*
thou art with me, and thy rod And staff me com-fort still.

4. My table thou hast furnishéd
   In presence of my foes;
   My head thou dost with oil anoint,
   And my cup overflows.

5. Goodness and mercy all my life
   Shall surely follow me;
   And in God's house forevermore
   My dwelling-place shall be.

## 50

### The Thought of God

ROCHESTER C.M.

*Frederick Lucian Hosmer, 1880*

*Aaron Williams'* Universal Psalmodist, *1764*

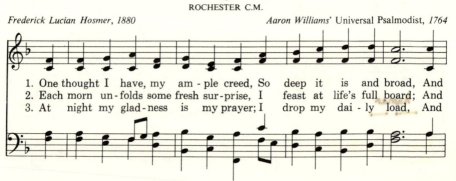

1. One thought I have, my am-ple creed, So deep it is and broad, And
2. Each morn un-folds some fresh sur-prise, I feast at life's full board; And
3. At night my glad-ness is my prayer; I drop my dai-ly load, And

THE LIFE THAT MAKETH ALL THINGS NEW

| e - qual | to | my | ev - ery | need— | It | is | the | thought of | God. |
| ris - ing | in | my | in - ner | skies | Shines forth the | | | thought of | God. |
| ev - ery | care | is | pil - lowed | there | Up - on | | the | thought of | God. |

4. I ask not far before to see,
   But take in trust my road;
   Life, death, and immortality
   Are in my thought of God.

5. To this their secret strength they owed
   The martyr's path who trod;
   The fountains of their patience flowed
   From out their thought of God.

6. Be still the light upon my way,
   My pilgrim staff and rod,
   My rest by night, my strength by day,
   O blessèd thought of God.

## 51 O God, Our Help in Ages Past

ST. ANNE C.M.

Isaac Watts, 1719
Paraphrase of Psalm 90

William Croft, 1708

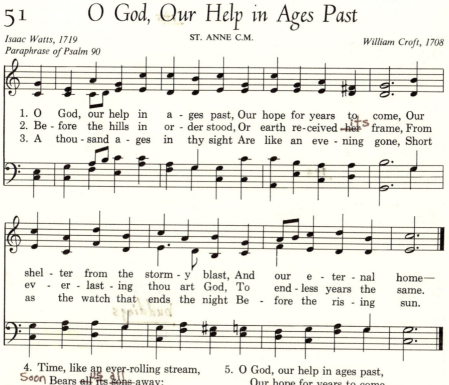

1. O God, our help in a - ges past, Our hope for years to come, Our
2. Be - fore the hills in or - der stood, Or earth re-ceived her frame, From
3. A thou - sand a - ges in thy sight Are like an eve - ning gone, Short

shel - ter from the storm - y blast, And our e - ter - nal home—
ev - er - last - ing thou art God, To end - less years the same.
as the watch that ends the night Be - fore the ris - ing sun.

4. Time, like an ever-rolling stream,
   Bears all its sons away:
   They fly forgotten, as a dream
   Dies at the opening day.

5. O God, our help in ages past,
   Our hope for years to come,
   Be thou our guard while troubles last,
   And our eternal home.

THE LIFE THAT MAKETH ALL THINGS NEW

# 52
# Roll on, Ye Stars

AINSWORTH 97  10.10.10.10.

*Erasmus Darwin, 1789*

Genevan Psalter, *1562*
*Version of Henry Ainsworth's Psalter, 1612*

1. Roll on, ye stars, ex - ult in youth - ful prime,
2. Star af - ter star from heaven's high arch shall rush;
3. Till o'er the wreck, e - merg - ing from the storm,

Mark with bright curves the print - less steps of time;
Suns sink on suns, and sys - tems sys - tems crush;
Im - mor - tal na - ture lifts her *its* change - ful form,

Flowers of the sky, ye too must age and yield,
Head - long, ex - tinct, to one dark cen - ter fall,
Mounts from her *its* fu - neral pyre on wings of flame,

Frail as your silk - en *buddings* sis - ters of the field.
And death and night and cha - os min - gle all;
And soars and shines, an - oth - er and the same.

THE LIFE THAT MAKETH ALL THINGS NEW

# 53 Unrest

SALVATION C.M.D.

Don Marquis, 1925

Ananias Davisson's Kentucky
Harmony, ca. 1815

1. A fierce un-rest seethes at the core Of all ex-ist-ing things: It
2. But for the urge of this un-rest These joy-ous spheres are mute; But
3. From deed to dream, from dream to deed, From dar-ing hope to hope, The

was the ea-ger wish to soar That gave the gods their wings. There
for the reb-el in his breast Had man re-mained as brutes. When
rest-less wish, the in-stant need, Still lashed him up the slope. Sing

throbs through all the worlds that are This heart-beat hot and strong, And
baf-fled lips de-mand-ed speech, Speech trem-bled in-to birth— One
we no gov-erned fir-ma-ment, Cold, or-dered, reg-u-lar— We

shak-en sys-tems, star by star, A-wake and glow in song.
day the lyr-ic word shall reach From earth to laugh-ing earth.
sing the sting-ing dis-con-tent That leaps from star to star.

THE LIFE THAT MAKETH ALL THINGS NEW

# 54 O Life That Maketh All Things New

TRURO L.M.

Samuel Longfellow, 1874

Thomas Williams' Psalmodia Evangelica, 1789

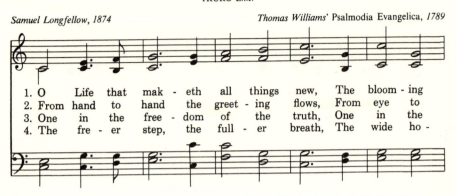

1. O Life that mak - eth all things new, The bloom - ing
2. From hand to hand the greet - ing flows, From eye to
3. One in the free - dom of the truth, One in the
4. The fre - er step, the full - er breath, The wide ho -

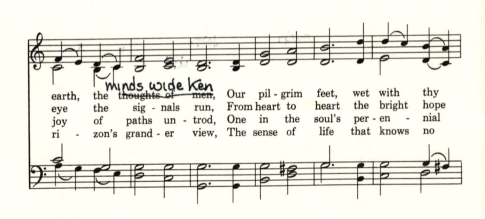

earth, the thoughts of men, Our pil - grim feet, wet with thy
eye the sig - nals run, From heart to heart the bright hope
joy of paths un - trod, One in the soul's per - en - nial
ri - zon's grand - er view, The sense of life that knows no

dew, In glad - ness hith - er turn a - gain.
glows; The seek - ers of the light are one.
youth, One in the larg - er thought of God;
death, The Life that mak - eth all things new.

THE LIFE THAT MAKETH ALL THINGS NEW

# 55

# In This Stern Hour

### INTERCESSOR 11.10.11.10.

*Josephine Johnson (1890-    )*                                                  *C. Hubert H. Parry, 1904*

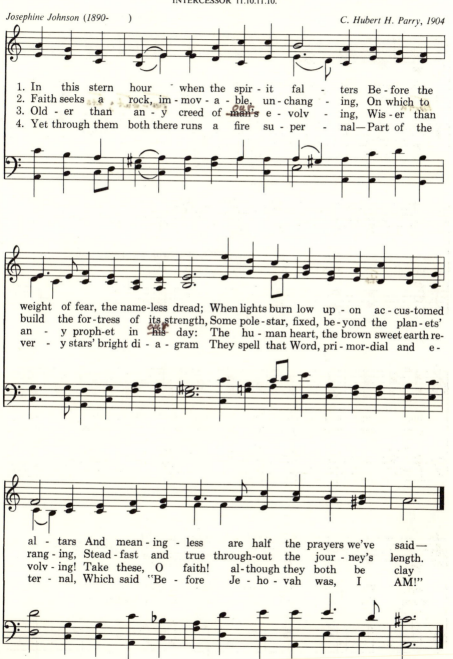

1. In this stern hour when the spir-it fal - ters Be-fore the
2. Faith seeks a rock, im-mov-a-ble, un-chang - ing, On which to
3. Old - er than an - y creed of man's e - volv - ing, Wis-er than
4. Yet through them both there runs a fire su - per - nal—Part of the

weight of fear, the name-less dread; When lights burn low up - on ac - cus-tomed
build the for-tress of its strength, Some pole-star, fixed, be-yond the plan-ets'
an - y proph-et in his day: The hu - man heart, the brown sweet earth re-
ver - y stars' bright di - a - gram They spell that Word, pri - mor-dial and e-

al - tars And mean - ing - less are half the prayers we've said—
rang - ing, Stead-fast and true through-out the jour - ney's length.
volv - ing! Take these, O faith! al-though they both be clay
ter - nal, Which said "Be - fore Je - ho - vah was, I AM!"

**THE LIFE THAT MAKETH ALL THINGS NEW**

# 56 The Earth Is Home

ST. PETERSBURG 9.8.9.8.9.9. Irregular

Kenneth L. Patton, 1956

Dmitri Bortniansky, 1825; arranged

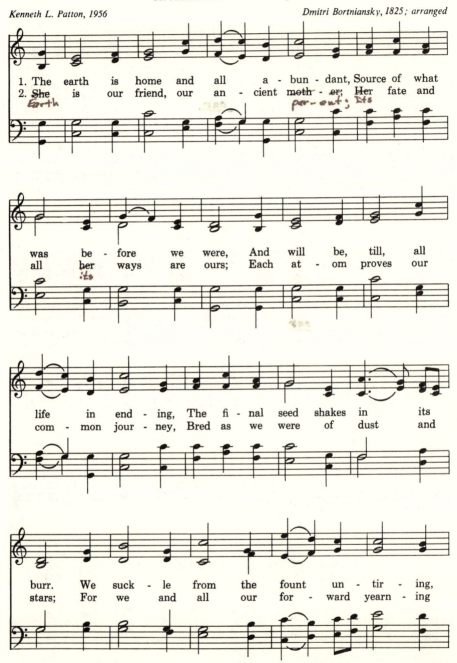

1. The earth is home and all a - bun - dant, Source of what
2. She is our friend, our an - cient moth - er; Her fate and

was be - fore we were, And will be, till, all
all her ways are ours; Each at - om proves our

life in end - ing, The fi - nal seed shakes in its
com - mon jour - ney, Bred as we were of dust and

burr. We suck - le from the fount un - tir - ing,
stars; For we and all our for - ward yearn - ing

THE LIFE THAT MAKETH ALL THINGS NEW

Chil - dren born of earth's de - sir - ing.
Are yet a spark in na - ture's burn - ing.

# 57 The World Stands Out on Either Side

HAMILTON L.M.

*Edna St. Vincent Millay, 1917*                    *Benjamin Franklin White, 1844*

1. The world stands out on ei - ther side No wid - er
2. The heart can push the sea and land Far - ther a -

than the heart is wide; A - bove the world is
way on ei - ther hand; The soul can split the

stretched the sky No high - er than the soul is high.
sky in two And let the face of God shine through.

THE LIFE THAT MAKETH ALL THINGS NEW

# 58 Divinity Is Round Us

ST. MARTIN 10.4.10.4.

*Sophia Lyon Fahs, 1952*         *George Wallace Briggs, 1931*

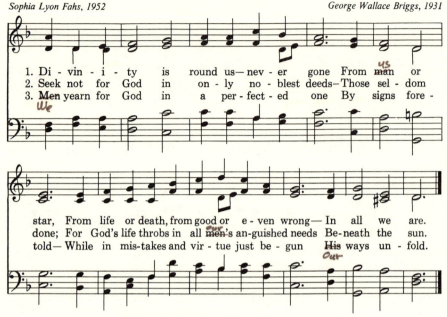

1. Di - vin - i - ty   is   round us— nev - er   gone  From man  or
2. Seek not for  God   in   on - ly  no - blest deeds— Those sel - dom
3. Men yearn for God   in   a  per - fect - ed  one  By signs fore -

star, From life or death, from good or  e - ven wrong— In  all  we  are.
done; For God's life throbs in all men's an-guished needs Be-neath the  sun.
told— While in mis-takes and vir - tue just be - gun His ways un - fold.

4. Wait not at last in truth and love made whole
Your God to see;
In every timid, false, or angered soul
There's love to free.

5. Then wake, O Soul, respect yourself today;
Create your part;
And look to find your life and truth and way
With honest art.

# 59 The Light, My Light

ILLINOIS L.M.

*Rabindranath Tagore, 1912; recast*      *Adapted from a tune in Thomas Hastings'*
*Based on Poem LVII, in Tagore's Gitanjali*      Manhattan Collection, *1837*

1. The   light,  my   light,  world - fill - ing  light,  The
2. The   but - ter - flies have spread  their  sails  To
3. Now  heav - en's riv - er drowns  its  banks,  And

THE LIFE THAT MAKETH ALL THINGS NEW

danc - ing cen - ter of my life; The sky breaks forth, the
glide up - on the seas of light; The lil - ies and the
floods of joy have run a - broad; Now mirth has spread from

wind runs wild, And laugh - ter pass - es o - ver earth.
jas - mine flowers Surge on the crest of waves of light.
leaf to leaf, And glad - ness with - out meas - ure comes.

## 60 Let Us Wander Where We Will

SAVANNAH 7.7.7.7.

Robert Louis Stevenson, 1879                    Herrnhut Manuscript, ca. 1740

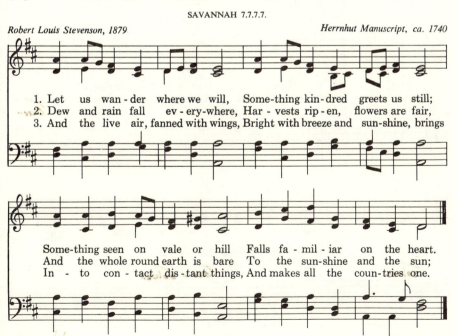

1. Let us wan - der where we will, Some-thing kin - dred greets us still;
2. Dew and rain fall ev - ery-where, Har - vests rip - en, flowers are fair,
3. And the live air, fanned with wings, Bright with breeze and sun-shine, brings

Some-thing seen on vale or hill Falls fa - mil - iar on the heart.
And the whole round earth is bare To the sun-shine and the sun;
In - to con - tact dis - tant things, And makes all the coun-tries one.

THE LIFE THAT MAKETH ALL THINGS NEW

# 61 The Fiery Element

WOODLANDS 10.10.10.10.

*John Holmes, 1943*                                        *Walter Greatorex, 1919*

1. Though man (*we*), the fi - ery el - ement, sink like fire With
2. His (*Ours*) is the burn - ing, va - ri - ous - ly bright, Now

win - ter on the world, and go out black, He flames a -
tall as love, and now as low as shame, That breaks earth's

gain, a new light leap - ing higher, A
shad - ow with a hu - man light, Him - (*Our-*)

hu - man warmth that drives the win - ter back.
self (*selves*) the fuel and ash, him - self (*our-selves*) the flame.

*Hu* MAN

# 62 ~~Man Is~~ We Are the Earth Upright and Proud

EIN' FESTE BURG 8.7.8.7.6.6.6.6.7.

Kenneth L. Patton, 1950

Martin Luther, 1529

1. ~~Man is~~ We are the earth up-right and proud; In ~~him~~ us the earth is know - ing. Its
2. Come, lift your voic-es, fill the skies With your ex-ult-ant sing - ing. Now

winds are mu-sic in ~~his~~ our mouths, In ~~him~~ us its riv-ers flow - ing. The
ded-i-cate your minds and hearts, Beau-ty and or-der bring - ing. Your

sun is ~~man's~~ our hearth-fire; Warm with the earth's de-sire, And with its pur-pose
la-bor is your strength; Your love will win at length; Your minds will ~~form a~~ reach the

strong, He sings earth's pil-grim song; In ~~man~~ us the earth is grow - ing.
~~plan~~ goal To draw ~~man~~ soul un-to ~~man~~ soul ~~His~~ Our day is just be-gin - ning.

Hu MAN

# 63 If We Think the Thought Eternal

LOBT DEN HERRN, DIE MORGENSONNE 8.7.8.7.

Johann Wolfgang von Goethe, 1828
Translated by Ludwig Lewisohn, 1949

J. F. Naue's Allgemeines evangelisches
Choralbuch, 1829

1. Wheth-er day my spir-it's yearn-ing Un-to far, blue hills has led,
2. Hours of light or hours noc-tur-nal Do I praise our mor-tal fate:

Or the night lit all the burn-ing Con-stel-la-tions at my head-
If we think the thought e-ter-nal We are ev-er fair and great.

# 64 From the First One to Climb the Hill

DISTRESS L.M.

Anonymous

William Walker's Southern Harmony, 1835

1. From the first one to climb the hill And seek a pros-pect wid-er still; From
2. From him who first from stub-born stone Wrought tool and weap-on of their own; From
3. From the first one to brave the sea, Un-scared by its im-men-si-ty; From

him who, con-quering crav-en fear, First found in fire a friend to cheer;
him, the first with pa-tient toil To break the clod and till the soil;
such as these, since men be-gan, We gain the strength that makes us hu-man.

HUMAN

# 65 I Am Part of All That I Have Met

WOODLANDS 10.10.10.10.

*Alfred Lord Tennyson, 1853; arranged, 1960*        *Walter Greatorex, 1919*

1. I am a part of all that I have met; Yet all ex-pe-rience is an arch, where-through Gleams that un-trav-eled world whose mar-gin fades, For-ev-er and for-ev-er when I move.

2. Life piled on life were all too lit-tle worth Were not our spir-its yearn-ing with de-sire To fol-low knowl-edge like a sink-ing star, Be-yond the ut-most bound of hu-man thought.

# 66 O Man, Acclaim Your Heritage

**CREATION L.M.D.**

*Kenneth L. Patton, 1949*

*Franz Joseph Haydn, 1798; arranged*

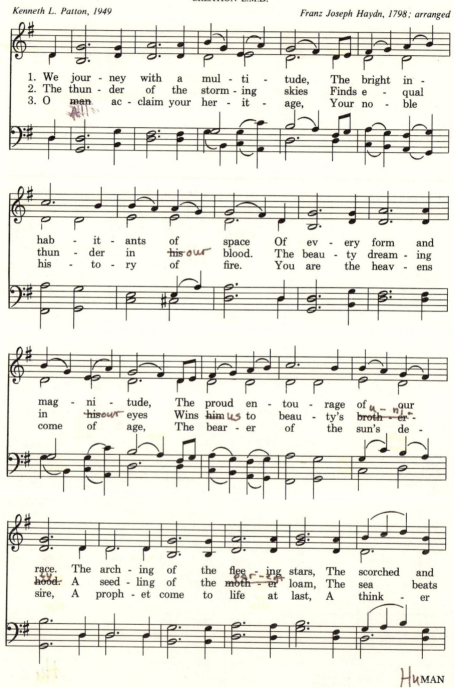

1. We jour - ney with a mul - ti - tude, The bright in -
2. The thun - der of the storm - ing skies Finds e - qual
3. O man, ac - claim your her - it - age, Your no - ble

hab - it - ants of space Of ev - ery form and
thun - der in his our blood. The beau - ty dream - ing
his - to - ry of fire. You are the heav - ens

mag - ni - tude, The proud en - tou - rage of our
in his our eyes Wins him us to beau - ty's broth - er -
come of age, The bear - er of the sun's de -

race. The arch - ing of the flee - ing stars, The scorched and
hood. A seed - ling of the moth - er loam, The sea beats
sire, A proph - et come to life at last, A think - er

freez - ing skies they span, The bru - tal wastes of
in his/our pulse a - gain; The plan - et earth his/our
from its mol - ten streams, A val - iant po - et

space and night— This is the dwell - ing place of man./all
na - tive home, A u - ni - ver - sal cit - i - zen.
of the vast To dream the u - ni - vers - e's dreams.

67   The Eternal

NUN KOMM, DER HEIDEN HEILAND 7.7.7.7.

*Dilys Bennett Laing, 1941*

*Melody based on "Veni Redemptor gentium"*
*Enchiridion, Erfurt, 1524*
*Harmonized by Seth Calvisius, 1594*

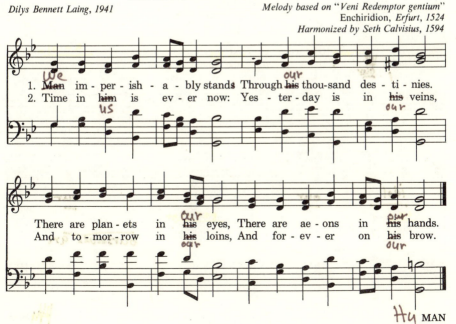

1. Man im - per - ish - a - bly stands Through his thou - sand des - ti - nies.
2. Time in him is ev - er now: Yes - ter - day is in his veins,

There are plan - ets in his eyes, There are ae - ons in his hands.
And to - mor - row in his loins, And for - ev - er on his brow.

HU MAN

# 68 The Middle State

CROSS OF CHRIST C.M.D.

Kenneth L. Patton, 1960

Leonard P. Breedlove, 1844

1. Be - fore the stars a man is small, Be - fore the at - om great; Be -
2. The size of man is not of flesh, Of meas-ure-ment or weight, Mu -
3. His po - ems fly a - bove all time, His songs be - wil - der test, And,

tween the two in - fin - i - ties He walks his mid - dle state. What
nif - i - cence of count or time, To ear - ly come or late. In
give or take a u - ni - verse, The lov - er has the best. Man

is this crea - ture, worm or god, All mean - ing, or in - ane, The
thought he stalks the u - ni - verse And walks the at - om's way, And
holds his own mag - nif - i - cence With - out a - pol - o - gy To

he - ro of his wish - ful hope, Or mi - ser of his pain?
makes e - ter - ni - ties to scale To han - dle day by day.
star or bird, to age or range, And in him - self is free.

# 69

# Affirmation

CONGLETON 10.10.10.10.

*From John Hall Wheelock, 1927*

*Michael Wise, 1684*

1. How lit - tle our true maj - es - ty is
2. Not by the mind shall we be judged a -
3. Through all our veins the flood of be - ing

shown In these proud minds by which we are con -
lone, Who are much more than in the mind is
roars; The gal - lant heart, a - gain and yet a -

fessed Trai - tors so of - ten, rec - re - ants at
guessed— By faith we live, the heart in ev - ery
gain— In sac - ra - men - tal af - fir - ma - tion,

best— Un - wor - thy of life's great - ness and our own:
breast La - bors, be - liev - ing, toward the end un - known.
pours Life's an - swer through the un - be - liev - ing brain.

H4 MAN

# Circular Secret

O MENTES PERFIDAS 6.6.6.6.D.

*John Hall Wheelock, 1955*                    *Theodoric Petri's* Piae Cantiones, *1582; adapted*

Leave star-ry heaven be-hind, En-ter the at-om, shrink Into the vast, and find You stand up-on the brink Of
star-ry heaven a-gain— There where you were you are, Full
cir-cle come a-gain Through at-om back to star.

# The Mind of Man

*(handwritten: Human)*

SURSUM CORDA 10.10.10.10.

*Edward Young, 1745; arranged*                    *Alfred Morton Smith, 1941*

71

When in ~~his~~ *our* thoughts the stars and plan-ets roll, How mar-vel-ous ap-pears the ~~mind of man,~~ *hu-man mind,* That, won-der-ful it-self, through won-der strays, Dis-cov-er-ing their gran-deur, finds its ~~own~~ *Kind*

*(handwritten: Human)*

# Fair Is Their Fame

DONNE SECOURS 11.10.11.10.

*Laurence Housman, 1919*

Genevan Psalter, *1551*

1. Fair is their fame who stand in earth's high plac - es,
2. These be our he - roes, hearts un - named in sto - ry,
3. They are the race— they are the race im - mor - tal,

Rul - ers of men, strong - armed to break and
Foot - firm that stood, and swerved not from the
Whose beams make broad the com - mon light of

bind. Fair - er the light which shines from com - rade fac - es,
right; Though in the world's eyes they at - tained no glo - ry,
day. Though time may dim, though death hath barred their por - tal,

Those we have loved, and lost, and kept in mind.
Girt to their goal they gained the wished - for height.
These we sa - lute, which name - less passed a - way.

TRANSIENCE AND ONGOING LIFE

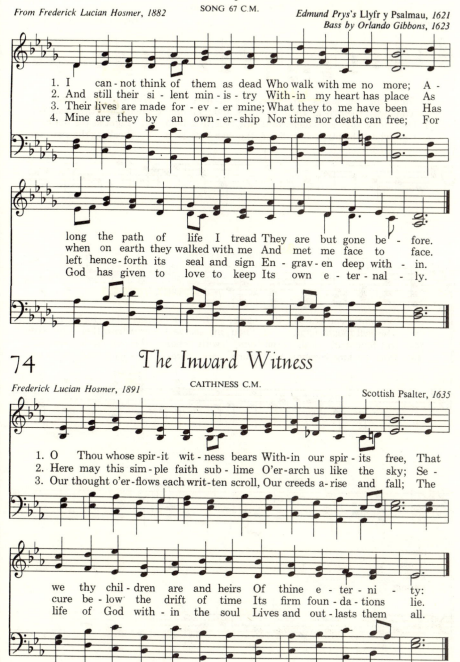

**73**  **I Cannot Think of Them as Dead**

SONG 67 C.M.

From Frederick Lucian Hosmer, 1882

Edmund Prys's Llyfr y Psalmau, 1621
Bass by Orlando Gibbons, 1623

1. I can-not think of them as dead Who walk with me no more; A-
2. And still their si - lent min - is - try With-in my heart has place As
3. Their lives are made for - ev - er mine; What they to me have been Has
4. Mine are they by an own-er-ship Nor time nor death can free; For

long the path of life I tread They are but gone be - fore.
when on earth they walked with me And met me face to face.
left hence-forth its seal and sign En - grav-en deep with - in.
God has given to love to keep Its own e - ter - nal - ly.

**74**  **The Inward Witness**

CAITHNESS C.M.

Frederick Lucian Hosmer, 1891

Scottish Psalter, 1635

1. O Thou whose spir-it wit - ness bears With-in our spir-its free, That
2. Here may this sim - ple faith sub - lime O'er-arch us like the sky; Se -
3. Our thought o'er-flows each writ-ten scroll, Our creeds a - rise and fall; The

we thy chil - dren are and heirs Of thine e - ter - ni - ty:
cure be - low the drift of time Its firm foun - da - tions lie.
life of God with - in the soul Lives and out - lasts them all.

TRANSIENCE AND ONGOING LIFE

# 75

# For All the Saints

SINE NOMINE 10.10.10.4.

*William Walsham How, 1864*

*Ralph Vaughan Williams, 1906*

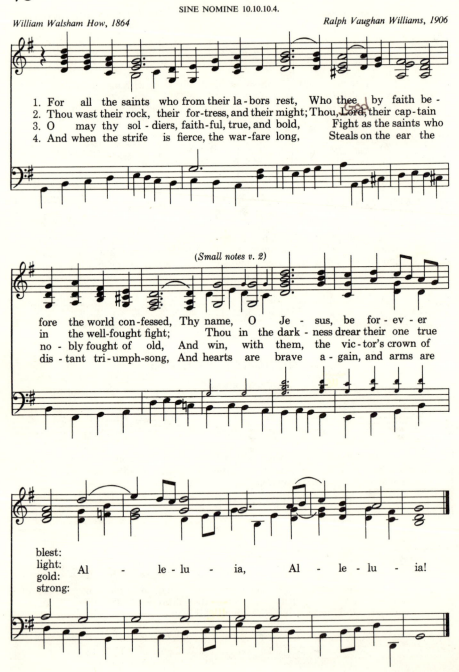

1. For all the saints who from their la-bors rest, Who thee by faith be-
2. Thou wast their rock, their for-tress, and their might; Thou, Lord, their cap-tain
3. O may thy sol-diers, faith-ful, true, and bold, Fight as the saints who
4. And when the strife is fierce, the war-fare long, Steals on the ear the

*(Small notes v. 2)*

fore the world con-fessed, Thy name, O Je - sus, be for - ev - er
in the well-fought fight; Thou in the dark - ness drear their one true
no - bly fought of old, And win, with them, the vic-tor's crown of
dis - tant tri-umph-song, And hearts are brave a - gain, and arms are

blest:
light: Al - le - lu - ia, Al - le - lu - ia!
gold:
strong:

TRANSIENCE AND ONGOING LIFE

# 76 Say Not They Die

DAS NEUGEBORNE KINDELEIN L.M.

Malcolm Quin, 1882

Melchior Vulpius, 1609
Harmonized by J.S. Bach, ca. 1742

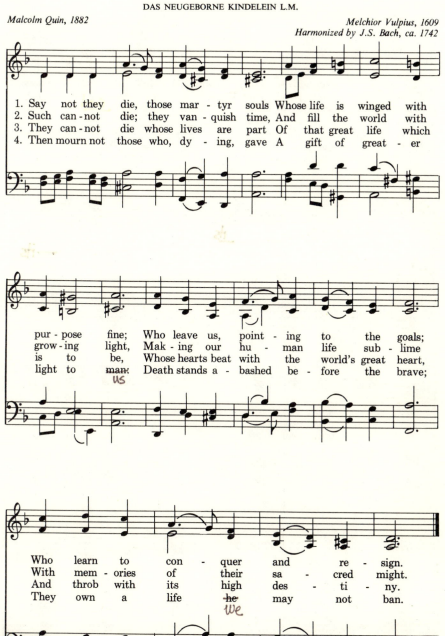

1. Say not they die, those mar - tyr souls Whose life is winged with
2. Such can - not die; they van - quish time, And fill the world with
3. They can - not die whose lives are part Of that great life which
4. Then mourn not those who, dy - ing, gave A gift of great - er

pur - pose fine; Who leave us, point - ing to the goals;
grow - ing light, Mak - ing our hu - man life sub - lime,
is to be, Whose hearts beat with the world's great heart,
light to man. Death stands a - bashed be - fore the brave;
     us

Who learn to con - quer and re - sign.
With mem - ories of their sa - cred might.
And throb with its high des - ti - ny.
They own a life he may not ban.
                        We

TRANSIENCE AND ONGOING LIFE

# Transience

DONNE SECOURS 11.10.11.10.

*From Sarojini Naidu, 1912*                                 Genevan Psalter, *1551*

1. Nay, do not grieve though life be full of sad - ness,
2. Nay, do not pine though life be dark with trou - ble,
3. Nay, do not weep; new hopes, new dreams, new fac - es,

Dawn will not veil her splen - dor for your
Time will not pause or tar - ry on his
Joy yet un - spent of all the un - born

grief, Nor spring de - ny their bright, ap - point - ed beau - ty
way; To - day, that seems so long, so strange, so bit - ter,
years, Will prove your heart a trai - tor to its sor - row,

To lo - tus blos - som and a - sho - ka leaf.
Will soon be some for - got - ten yes - ter - day.
And make your eyes un - faith - ful to their tears.

TRANSIENCE AND ONGOING LIFE

# Away, O Soul

**MAGDA 10.10.10.10.**

Walt Whitman, 1870; arranged, 1956

Ralph Vaughan Williams, 1925

1. A - way, O soul, hoist up the an - chor now;
2. Great-er than stars, O soul, you jour - ney forth;
3. Joy - ous we too launch out on track - less seas,

Cut haw - sers, haul out, shake out ev - ery sail;
What love than ours could wid - er am - pli - fy?
For we are bound where none has dared to go;

Sail forth, steer on - ly for the deep - er parts, With
What plans of pu - ri - ty, per - fec - tion, strength, What
And we will risk the ship, our - selves, and all; O

me ex - plor - ing, soul, and I with you.
as - pi - ra - tions ours out - vie, O soul?
my brave soul! oh, far - ther, far - ther sail.

TRANSIENCE AND ONGOING LIFE

# 79

## Abide with Me

EVENTIDE 10.10.10.10.

*Henry Francis Lyte, 1847*

*William Henry Monk, 1861*

1. A - bide with me, fast falls the e - ven - tide; The dark-ness
2. Swift to its close ebbs out life's lit - tle day; Earth's joys grow
3. I fear no foe, with thee at hand to bless; Ills have no

deep - ens; Lord, with me a - bide. When oth - er help - ers
dim, its glo - ries pass a - way; Change and de - cay in
weight, and tears no bit - ter - ness. Where is death's sting? where,

fail, and com - forts flee, Help of the help-less, oh, a - bide with me.
all a - round I see: O thou who chang-est not, a - bide with me.
grave, thy vic - to - ry? I tri-umph still if thou a - bide with me.

# 80    He That Dies Shall Not Die Lonely

LOBT DEN HERRN, DIE MORGENSONNE 8.7.8.7.

*From William Morris, 1884*

*J.F. Naue's* Allgemeines evangelisches
Choralbuch, *1829*

1. He that dies shall not die lone - ly, Many a one has gone be - fore.
2. Named and name-less all live in us; One and all they lead us yet,
3. Though our names be all for - got - ten And the tale of how we died,

TRANSIENCE AND ONGOING LIFE

He that lives shall bear no bur-den Heav-ier than the life they bore.
Ev-ery pain to count for noth-ing, Ev-ery sor-row to for-get.
In the world one day new-build-ed Shall our earth-ly deeds a-bide.

# 81 *The Sense of Death*

VATER UNSER 8.8.8.8.8.8.

Helen Hoyt, 1924

*Valentin Schumann's* Geistliche Lieder, *1539*
*Arranged from J.S. Bach, 1723*

1. Since I have felt the sense of death, Since I have borne its dread and fear— Oh,
2. Since I have felt the sense of death, Since I have looked on black-est night—My

how my life has grown more dear Since I have felt the sense of death. Sor-
in-most brain is fierce with light Since I have felt the sense of death. O

rows are good and cares are small, Since I have known the loss of all.
dark, that made my eyes to see! O death, that gave my life to me!

TRANSIENCE AND ONGOING LIFE

# Now I Recall My Childhood

SURSUM CORDA 10.10.10.10.

*Rabindranath Tagore, 1918; recast*
*Based on poem LXXI, in Tagore's* Crossing

*Alfred Morton Smith, 1941*

1. Now I re-call my child-hood when the sun Burst
2. Look-ing up-on the world with sim-ple joy, On
3. Now when I turn to think of com-ing death, I

to my bed-side with the day's sur-prise; Faith in the mar-velous
in-sects, birds, and beasts, and com-mon weeds, The grass and clouds had
find life's song in star-songs of the night, In rise of cur-tains

bloomed a-new each dawn, Flowers burst-ing fresh with-in my heart each day.
full-est wealth of awe; My moth-er's voice gave mean-ing to the stars.
and new morn-ing light, In life re-born in fresh sur-prise of love.

TRANSIENCE AND ONGOING LIFE

# 83 Light

CLIFF TOWN 10.10.10.10.

*S. R. Lysaght, 1911; arranged*                                        *Erik Routley, 1951*

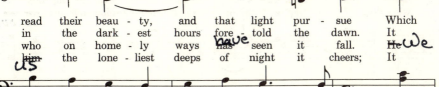

1. Let us be faith - ful to our pass - ing hours And
2. Our he - roes have be - held it and our seers, Who
3. The vast, the in - fi - nite, no more ap - pall Him
4. And all the beau - ty that his dreams re - call. For

read their beau - ty, and that light pur - sue Which
in the dark - est hours fore - told the dawn. It
who on home - ly ways has seen it fall. He
him the lone - liest deeps of night it cheers; It

gives the dawn its rose, the noon its blue, And
flash - es on the sword for free - dom drawn; It
trusts the far, hope dow - ers the un - known With
gath - ers in its folds the count - less spheres, And

tells its se - cret to the way - side flowers.
makes a rain - bow of a peo - ple's tears.
all the love that earth has made her own,
makes a con - stant home - light for them all.

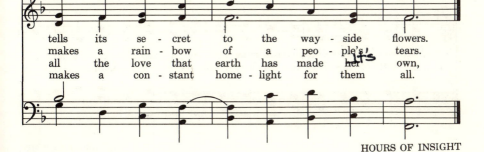

HOURS OF INSIGHT

# 84 From All the Fret and Fever of the Day

COOLINGE 10.10.10.10.

*Monroe Beardsley, 1958*                    *Cyril V. Taylor (1907–    )*

1. From all the fret and fe - ver of the day, Let there be
2. In qui - et - ness and sol - i - tude we find The sound - less

mo - ments when we turn a - way, And, deaf to all con - fus - ing out - er
wis - dom of the deep - er mind; With clear har - mo - nious pur - pose ~~let us~~ *as our*

din, In - tent - ly lis - ten for the voice with - in.
~~then~~ Bring rich - er mean - ing to the world of ~~men.~~ *all,*
*call,*

# 85 Calm Soul of All Things

TALLIS' CANON L.M.

*Matthew Arnold, 1852*                    *Thomas Tallis, ca. 1561*

1. Calm soul of all things, make it mine To feel, a - mid the cit - y's jar, That
2. The will to nei - ther strive nor cry, The power to feel with oth - ers, give. Calm,

**HOURS OF INSIGHT**

there a-bides a peace of thine we did not make, and can-not mar.
calm me more; nor let me die Be - fore I have be - gun to live.

## 86    Hours of Insight

LEICESTER 8.8.8.8.8.8.

*Matthew Arnold, 1852*                                      *John Bishop, ca. 1700*

1. We can-not kin-dle when we will The fire which in the heart re-sides; The
2. With ach-ing hands and bleed-ing feet We dig and heap, lay stone on stone; We

spir - it blow-eth and is still; In mys-ter - y our soul a - bides: But
bear the bur - den and the heat Of the long day, and wish 'twere done. Not

tasks in hours of in-sight willed Can be through hours of gloom ful-filled.
till the hours of light re - turn, All we have built do we dis-cern.

HOURS OF INSIGHT

# The Still, Small Voice

O GOTT, DU FROMMER GOTT 6.7.6.7.6.6.6.6.

*From James Martineau, 1873*

*Ahasuerus Fritsch, 1679*
*Harmonized by J.S. Bach, 1735*

1. Where is your God? they say; Give an-swer, Lord [God] most ho - ly. Re-
2. Come not in flash-ing storm Or burst-ing frown of thun - der, But

veal thy se - cret way Of vis - it - ing the low - ly. In
in the view-less form Of wak-ening love and won - der. To

du - ty grown di - vine The rest - less spir - it still— In
ev - ery wait - ing soul Speak in thy still, small voice, Till

sor - rows taught to shine As shad - ows of thy will.
bro - ken love be whole And sad - dened hearts re - joice.

**HOURS OF INSIGHT**

# 88

## The Indwelling God

OLD 137th C.M.D.

*Frederick Lucian Hosmer, 1879*　　　　　　　　　　　　One and fiftie Psalms, *Geneva, 1556*

1. Go not, my soul, in search of God, Thou wilt not find him there — Or
2. Thought an-swer-eth a-lone to thought, And Soul with soul hath kin; The

in the depths of shad-ow dim, Or heights of up-per air. For
out-ward God he find-eth not Who finds not God with-in. And

not in far-off realms of space The Spir-it hath its throne; In
if the vi-sion come to thee Re-vealed by in-ward sign, Earth

ev-ery heart it find-eth place And wait-eth to be known.
will be full of De-i-ty And with his glo-ry shine.

HOURS OF INSIGHT

# 89 In Quietude the Spirit Grows

WINDSOR C.M.

*Anonymous 1845; recast, 1960*　　　　　　　　　　*William Damon's* Psalmes, *1591*

1. Noise - less the morn - ing flings its gold, And
2. Night moves in si - lence round the pole, The
3. In qui - e - tude the spir - it grows In
4. At - tend, O soul; and hear at length The

still is eve - ning's pace; All si - lent - ly the
stars sing on un - heard; Their mu - sic pierc - es
man from hour to hour; In calm e - ter - nal
spir - it's si - lent voice: In still - ness la - bor;

earth is rolled A - mid the vast of space.
to the soul, Yet bor - rows not a word.
on - ward flows Its all - re - deem - ing power.
wait in strength; And, con - fi - dent, re - joice.

HOURS OF INSIGHT

# Not Always on the Mount

DANBY L.M.

*From Frederick Lucian Hosmer, 1882*

*English melody*
*Arranged by Ralph Vaughan Williams, 1925*

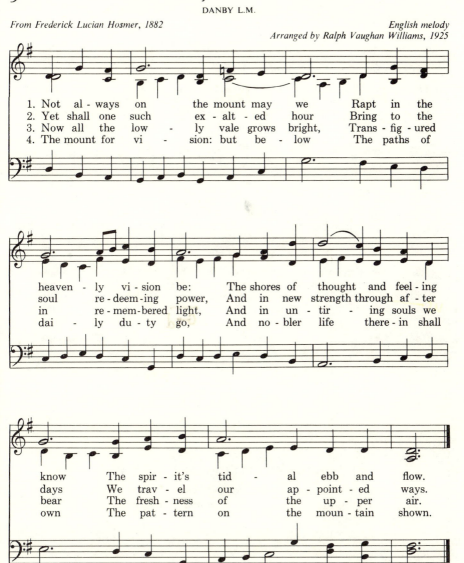

1. Not al - ways on the mount may we Rapt in the
heaven - ly vi - sion be: The shores of thought and feel - ing
know The spir - it's tid - al ebb and flow.

2. Yet shall one such ex - alt - ed hour Bring to the
soul re - deem - ing power, And in new strength through af - ter
days We trav - el our ap - point - ed ways.

3. Now all the low - ly vale grows bright, Trans - fig - ured
in re - mem - bered light, And in un - tir - ing souls we
bear The fresh - ness of the up - per air.

4. The mount for vi - sion: but be - low The paths of
dai - ly du - ty go, And no - bler life there - in shall
own The pat - tern on the moun - tain shown.

HOURS OF INSIGHT

91

# The Soul's Sincere Desire

WINDSOR C.M.

James Montgomery, 1818

William Damon's Psalmes, 1591

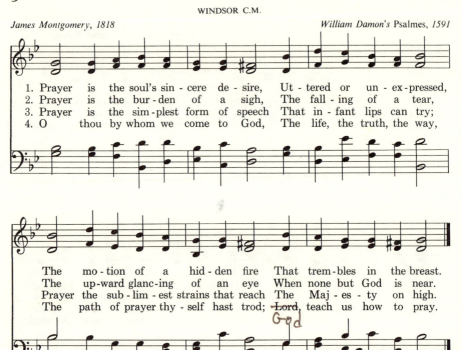

1. Prayer is the soul's sin - cere de - sire, Ut - tered or un - ex - pressed,
2. Prayer is the bur - den of a sigh, The fall - ing of a tear,
3. Prayer is the sim - plest form of speech That in - fant lips can try;
4. O thou by whom we come to God, The life, the truth, the way,

The mo - tion of a hid - den fire That trem - bles in the breast.
The up - ward glanc - ing of an eye When none but God is near.
Prayer the sub - lim - est strains that reach The Maj - es - ty on high.
The path of prayer thy - self hast trod; Lord, teach us how to pray.

92

# The Soul Wherein God Dwells

MARIA JUNG UND ZART 6.6.6.6.

Johann Scheffler, 1657
Translator unknown

Geistliche Kirchengesäng, Cologne, 1623; adapted

1. The soul where-in God dwells—What church could ho - lier be?— Be-
2. Though Christ a thou-sand times In Beth - le - hem be born, If
3. O would thy heart but be A man - ger for his birth, God

comes a walk-ing tent Of heaven-ly maj-es-ty.
he's not born in thee, Thy soul is still for-lorn.
would once more be-come A child up-on this earth.

# 93 The Harp at Nature's Advent Strung

BYZANTIUM C.M.

John Greenleaf Whittier, 1867

Thomas Jackson, 1780

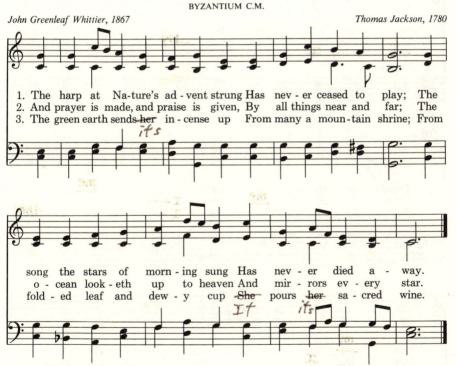

1. The harp at Na-ture's ad-vent strung Has nev-er ceased to play; The
2. And prayer is made, and praise is given, By all things near and far; The
3. The green earth sends her in-cense up From many a moun-tain shrine; From

song the stars of morn-ing sung Has nev-er died a-way.
o-cean look-eth up to heaven And mir-rors ev-ery star.
fold-ed leaf and dew-y cup She pours her sa-cred wine.

4. The blue sky is the temple's arch,
   Its transept, earth and air;
   The music of its starry march,
   The chorus of a prayer.

5. So Nature keeps the reverent frame
   With which her years began;
   And all her signs and voices shame
   The prayerless heart of man.

HOURS OF INSIGHT

# 94 *Who Would True Valor See*

MONKS GATE 6 5.6.5.6.6.6.5.

*From John Bunyan, 1684*

*English melody*
*Arranged by Ralph Vaughan Williams, 1906*

1. Who would true val - or see, Let him come hith - er;
2. Who - so be - set him round With dis - mal sto - ries,
3. No word of foe or friend Can daunt his spir - it;

One here will con - stant be, Come wind, come weath - er;
Do but them-selves con - found; His strength the more is.
He knows he at the end Shall life in - her - it.

There's no dis - cour - age - ment Shall make him once re -
No li - on can him fright, He'll with a gi - ant
Then fan - cies fly a - way; He'll not fear what men

lent His first a - vowed in - tent To be a pil - grim.
fight, But he will have a right To be a pil - grim.
say; He'll la - bor night and day To be a pil - grim.

THE LIFE OF INTEGRITY

# 95

## Hold Fast Thy Loyalty

CAITHNESS C.M.

Frederick Lucian Hosmer, 1881

Scottish Psalter, 1635

1. When cour-age fails and faith burns low And men are tim-id grown, Hold
2. The race is not un-to the swift, The bat-tle to the strong, When
3. And more than thou canst do for truth Can she on thee con-fer, If
4. Who fol-low her though men de-ride, In her strength shall be strong; Shall

fast thy loy-al-ty, and know That truth still mov-eth on.
dawn her judg-ment days that sift The claims of right and wrong.
thou, O heart, but give thy youth And man-hood un-to her.
see their shame be-come their pride, And share her tri-umph song.

# 96

## Wisdom Has Treasures

GRÄFENBURG C.M.

From Scotch Paraphrases, 1781; recast, 1952
Based on Proverbs 3: 13–18

Johann Crüger, 1653

1. Wis-dom has treas-ures great-er far Than east or west un-fold,
2. She guides the young with in-no-cence In pleas-ure's path to tread;
3. A tree of life she is to men; Their years she shall in-crease;

And her re-wards more pre-cious are Than is the gain of gold.
A crown of glo-ry she be-stows Up-on the hoar-y head.
Her ways are ways of pleas-ant-ness, And all her paths are peace.

THE LIFE OF INTEGRITY

# 97 Say Not, "The Struggle Nought Availeth"

LES COMMANDEMENS 9.8.9.8.

Arthur Hugh Clough, 1861

Louis Bourgeois' Pseaulmes, 1547

1. Say not, "The strug - gle nought a - vail - eth, The la - bor and the
2. If hopes were dupes, fears may be li - ars; It may be, in yon
3. For while the tired waves, vain - ly break - ing, Seem here no pain - ful
4. And not by east - ern win - dows on - ly, When day-light comes, comes

wounds are vain, The en - e - my faints not nor
smoke con - cealed, Your com - rades chase e'en now the
inch to gain, Far back, through creeks and in - lets
in the light; In front the sun climbs slow, how

fail - eth, And as things have been they re - main."
fli - ers, And, but for you, pos - sess the field.
mak - ing, Comes si - lent, flood - ing in, the main.
slow - ly, But west - ward, look, the land is bright.

# 98 Not Gold, but Only Men

ST. MAGNUS C.M.

Anonymous

Attributed to Jeremiah Clark, 1707

1. Not gold, but on - ly men can make A peo - ple great and strong—Men
2. Brave men who work while oth - ers sleep, Who dare while oth - ers fly— They

THE LIFE OF INTEGRITY

who for truth and hon-or's sake Stand fast and suf-fer long.
build a na-tion's pil-lars deep; They lift them to the sky.

99 The Man of Integrity (People)

WAREHAM L.M.

Henry Wotton, ca. 1616      William Knapp, 1738

1. How hap-py is he born or taught Who serv-eth (are they)
2. Whose pas-sions not his mas-ters are; Whose souls is (their) (are)
3. Who hath his life from ru-mors freed, Whose con-science (Their lives)
4. This man is freed from serv-ile bands Of hope to (A spir-it loosed)

not an-oth-er's will; Whose ar-mor is his (their)
still pre-pared for death, Un-tied un-to the (their)
is his strong re-treat, Whose state can nei-ther
rise, or fear to fall; Lord of him-self, though (rul-er of)

hon-est thought, And sim-ple truth his high-est skill; (Their)
world by care Of pub-lic fame or pri-vate breath;
flat-terers feed, Nor ru-in make op-pres-sors great.
not of lands, And hav-ing noth-ing, yet hath all.

THE LIFE OF INTEGRITY

# 100 To Suffer Woes Which Hope Thinks Infinite

CONGLETON 10.10.10.10.

*From Percy Bysshe Shelley, 1819*

*Michael Wise, 1684*

1. To suf - fer woes which hope thinks in - fi -
nite, For - giv - ing wrongs more dark than death or
night; To love and bear; to hope till hope cre -
ates From its own wreck the thing it con - tem - plates;

2. Nei - ther to change, nor fal - ter, nor re -
pent, De - fy - ing power which seems om - nip - o -
tent— Good, great and joy - ous, beau - ti - ful and
free, This is life, em - pire, joy, and vic - to - ry.

THE LIFE OF INTEGRITY

# It Is Something to Have Wept

KEITH 11.10.11.10.

*From Gilbert Keith Chesterton, 1915*                    *Robert L. Sanders, 1958*

1. It is some-thing to have wept as we have wept, And
2. It is some-thing to have smelt the mys - tic rose, Al -
3. To have known the things that from the weak are furled, The
4. Lo, and bless - ed are our ears for they have heard; Yea,

some - thing to have done as we have done; It is
though it break and leave the thorn - y rods; It is
fear - ful an - cient pas - sions, strange and high; It is
bless - ed are our eyes for they have seen: Let the

some - thing to have watched when all men slept, And
some - thing to have hun - gered once as those Must
some - thing to be wis - er than the world, And
thun - der break on man and beast and bird, And

seen the stars which nev - er see the sun.
hun - ger who have ate the bread of gods:
some - thing to be old - er than the sky.
light - ning. It is some - thing to have been.

THE LIFE OF INTEGRITY

# What Makes a City Great

LEICESTER 8.8.8.8.8.8.

*Anonymous*                                                    *John Bishop, ca. 1700*

1. What makes a cit-y great and strong? Not ar-chi-tec-ture's grace-ful strength, Not
2. What makes a cit-y men can love? Not things that charm the out-ward sense, Not
3. This is a cit-y that shall stand, A light up-on a na-tion's hill, A

fac-to-ries' ex-tend-ed length, But we who see the civ-ic wrong, And
gross dis-play of op-u-lence, But right that wrong can-not re-move, And
voice that e-vil can-not still, A source of bless-ing to the land; Its

give their lives to make it right, And turn its dark-ness in-to light.
truth that fac-es civ-ic shame To ban-ish it in hon-or's name.
strength not brick, nor stone, nor wood, But jus-tice, love, and neigh-bor-hood.

# 103        Human-making

ST. MAGNUS C M.

*Edwin Markham, ca. 1920*                              *Attributed to Jeremiah Clark, 1707*

1. We are all blind, un-til we see That in the hu-man plan Noth-
2. Why build these cit-ies glo-ri-ous If man un-build-ed goes? In

THE LIFE OF INTEGRITY

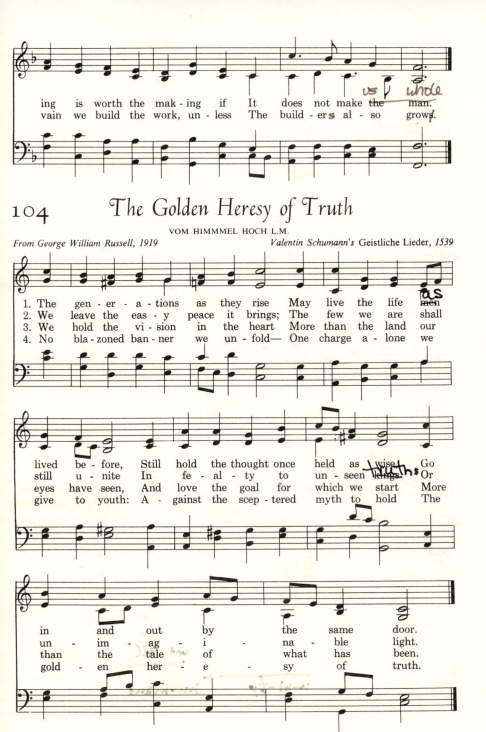

# 105 Truth Is the Trial of Itself

ROCHESTER C.M.

*Ben Jonson, 1624*

*Aaron Williams'* Universal Psalmodist, *1764*

1. Truth is the tri - al of it - self, And needs no oth - er touch; And
2. It is the life and light of love, The sun that ev - er shines, And
3. It is the war - rant of the word That yields a scent so sweet As

pur - er than the pur - est gold, Re - fine it ne'er so much.
spir - it of that spe - cial grace That faith and love de - fines.
gives a power to faith to tread All false - hood un - der feet.

# 106 A Noble Life

LANCASTER C.M.

*A. S. Isaacs, 1914*

*Samuel Howard, 1762*

1. A no - ble life, a sim - ple faith, An o - pen heart and hand—These
2. These are the firm - knit bonds of grace, Though hid - den to the view, Which

are the love - ly lit - a - nies Which all men un - der - stand;
bind in sa - cred broth - er - hood All men the whole world through.

THE LIFE OF INTEGRITY

## 107 The Man of Life Upright

*HUMANS* (handwritten)

CAMPIAN 2 6.6.6.6.

*From Thomas Campian, ca. 1613*          *Thomas Campian, ca. 1613*

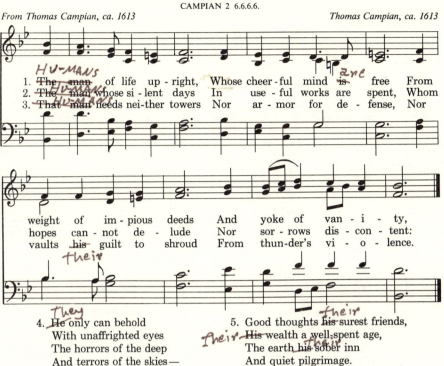

1. The man [*HUMANS*] of life up-right, Whose cheer-ful mind is [*are*] free From
2. The man [*HUMANS*] whose si-lent days In use-ful works are spent, Whom
3. That man [*HUMANS*] needs nei-ther towers Nor ar-mor for de-fense, Nor

weight of im-pious deeds And yoke of van-i-ty,
hopes can-not de-lude Nor sor-rows dis-con-tent:
vaults his [*their*] guilt to shroud From thun-der's vi-o-lence.

4. He [*They*] only can behold
With unaffrighted eyes
The horrors of the deep
And terrors of the skies—

5. Good thoughts his [*their*] surest friends,
His [*Their*] wealth a well-spent age,
The earth his [*their*] sober inn
And quiet pilgrimage.

## 108 Since What We Choose Is What We Are

VOM HIMMEL HOCH L.M.

*William De Witt Hyde, 1903*          *Valentin Schumann's Geistliche Lieder, 1539*

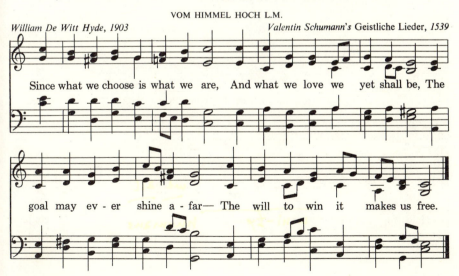

Since what we choose is what we are, And what we love we yet shall be, The

goal may ev-er shine a-far— The will to win it makes us free.

**THE LIFE OF INTEGRITY**

## 109 · What Else Is Wisdom?

GENEVA 51 11.10.10.11.

Euripides, The Bacchae, *ca. 407 B.C.*
*From translation by Gilbert Murray, 192-?*

Genevan Psalter, *1551; adapted*

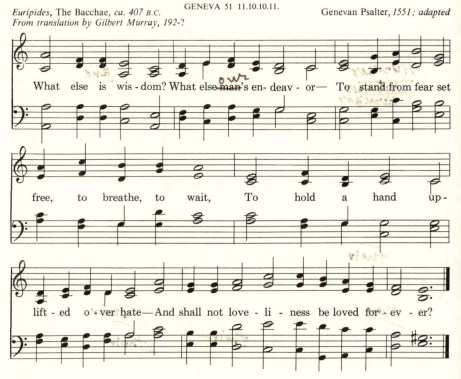

What else is wis-dom? What else man's en-deav-or— To stand from fear set free, to breathe, to wait, To hold a hand up-lift-ed o-ver hate—And shall not love-li-ness be loved for-ev-er?

## 110 · Be Ye Lamps unto Yourselves

LUMINA Irregular

*Attributed to Gautama Buddha, 5th century B.C.*
*Translation anonymous*

*From a melody in the* Sarum Antiphonal

Be ye lamps un-to your-selves; Be your own con - fi - dence; Hold to the truth with-in your-selves As to the on - ly lamp.

THE LIFE OF INTEGRITY

# They Cast Their Nets in Galilee

GEORGETOWN C.M.

*From William Alexander Percy, 1924*　　　　　　　　　*David McKinley Williams, 1941*

1. They cast their nets in Gal - i - lee Just off the hills of brown; Such hap - py, sim - ple fish - er - folk, Be - fore the Lord came down.
2. Con - tent - ed, peace - ful fish - er - men, Be - fore they ev - er knew The peace of God that filled their hearts Brim - ful, and broke them too.
3. Young John, who trimmed the flap - ping sail, Home - less in Pat - mos died. Pe - ter, who hauled the teem - ing net, Head - down was cru - ci - fied.
4. The peace of God, it is no peace, But strife closed in the sod. Yet, broth - ers, pray for but one thing— The mar - velous peace of God.

*Let us*

THE LIFE OF INTEGRITY

# 112 Heart's Remembering

### PART I
#### CROSS OF CHRIST C.M.D.

*Archibald MacLeish, 1915*  *Leonard P. Breedlove, 1844*

1. The peo-ple of the earth go down, Each with his wealth of dream, To
2. They sell their treas-ur-ies of dreams For dreams' re-al-i-ties, Their
3. They buy and pass no more that way; Their eyes for-get the star, For-

bar-ter in the mar-ket town A star for a torch'-s gleam; To
wealth of fair-y quin-que-remes For ships of salt-er seas, Their
get the mys-ter-ies of May, For-get the dim and far; They

bar-ter hope for cer-ti-tude, And mys-ter-ies of love For
gods for shapes of tor-tured stone, Their faith for shrines that fall, The
build them tow-er and high wall To bolt a-gainst the spring, To

pas-sion's lit-tle in-ter-lude; And joy for the laugh there-of.
un-known for the touched and known, Life at the liv-ing's call.
shut-ter out the ma-vis' call, And heart's re-mem-ber-ing.

THE LIFE OF INTEGRITY

# Heart's Remembering

PART II
CROSS OF CHRIST C.M.D.

Archibald MacLeish, 1915                    Leonard P. Breedlove, 1844

1. Yet when the splen-dor of the earth Is fall-en in-to dust, When
2. Old-er than time, with a-ges shod, The mat-ins of a thrush; Deep-

plow and sword, and fame and worth Are rot-ted with black rust, The
er than rev-er-ence of God, The sum-mer eve-ning's hush. Than

dream, still death-less, still un-born, Blows in the hearts of men, The
tram-pling death is grief more strong, Love than its av-a-tars, And

*A ris-es live and true.*

star, the mys-ter-y, the morn Bloom age-less-ly a-gain. *new*
ech-o of an ech-oed song Shall shake the e-ter-nal stars.

THE LIFE OF INTEGRITY

## 114   Prayer

KEDRON L.M.

*Louis Untermeyer, 1914*       *Amos Pilsbury's* United States' Sacred
Harmony, *1799*

1. God, though this life is but a wraith, Al - though we know not
2. Ev - er in - sur -gent let me be, Make me more dar - ing
3. O - pen my eyes to vi - sions girt With beau - ty, and with

what we use, Al - though we grope with lit - tle faith, Give
than de - vout; From sleek con - tent - ment keep me free, And
won - der lit— But let me al - ways see the dirt, And

me the heart to fight— and lose.
fill me with a buoy - ant doubt.
all that spawn and die in it.

4. Open my ears to music; let
   Me thrill with Spring's first flutes and drums—
   But never let me dare forget
   The bitter ballads of the slums.

5. From compromise and things half-done,
   Keep me, with stern and stubborn pride;
   And when, at last, the fight is won,
   God, keep me still unsatisfied.

PRAYER AND ASPIRATION

# O Star of Truth

NYLAND 7.6.7.6.D

*Minot Judson Savage, 1883*

*Finnish melody*
*Adapted by David Evans, 1927; arranged*

1. O star of truth, down shin - ing Through clouds of doubt and fear, I
2. I know thy bless-ed ra - diance Can nev - er lead a - stray, Though

ask be-neath thy guid - ance My path - way may ap - pear: How-
an - cient creed and cus - tom May point an - oth - er way; Or

ev - er long the jour - ney, How - ev - er hard it be, Though
through the un - trod des - ert, Or o - ver track-less sea, Though

I be lone and wea - ry, Lead on, I fol - low thee.

PRAYER AND ASPIRATION

# 116     *Past, Present, Future*

LONDON L.M.D.

Frederick May Eliot, 1916           John Sheeles, ca. 1720

1. O thou, to whom the fa - thers built *[fore-bears]* Their al - tars in the
an - cient days, Up - on our wor - ship we in - voke The ben - e - dic - tion of their praise; As then their rev - erent hearts re - ceived The Spir - it's gift of flame from thee, So

2. Thou liv - ing, ra - diant, in - ward Light, Whom we to - day, though dim - ly, see— Our guide a - mid the world we know, Our hope for what is yet to be— Break now, in great - er maj - es - ty, Up - on the minds and hearts that crave With

3. God of the a - ges yet un - born, Whose clear - er pres - ence then shall shine, When man with man shall live in peace, *[hu-man-kind]* And hu - man life be - come di - vine; O touch our lips that we may be The mes - sen - gers of thy swift word, And

PRAYER AND ASPIRATION

# 118 Dear ~~Lord and~~ Father of ~~Mankind~~

*God, Parent* *Human*

LOBT GOTT, IHR CHRISTEN 8.6.8.8.6. (First tune)

John Greenleaf Whittier, 1872

Nikolaus Herman, 1554
Harmonized by J. S. Bach, ca. 1740

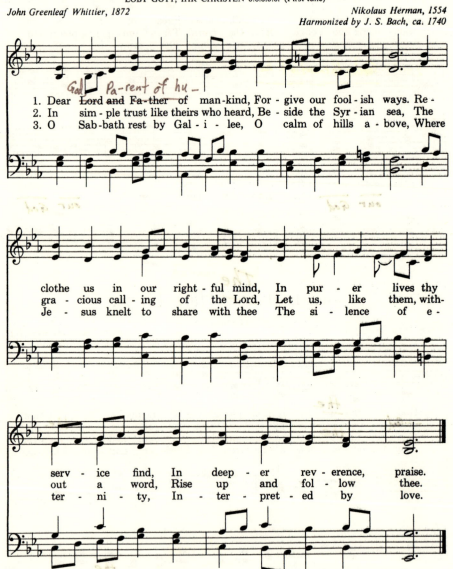

1. Dear ~~Lord and~~ Fa-ther of man-kind, For - give our fool - ish ways. Re -
*God Pa-rent of hu-*
2. In sim - ple trust like theirs who heard, Be - side the Syr - ian sea, The
3. O Sab-bath rest by Gal - i - lee, O calm of hills a - bove, Where

clothe us in our right - ful mind, In pur - er lives thy
gra - cious call - ing of the Lord, Let us, like them, with-
Je - sus knelt to share with thee The si - lence of e -

serv - ice find, In deep - er rev - erence, praise.
out a word, Rise up and fol - low thee.
ter - ni - ty, In - ter - pret - ed by love.

4. With that deep hush subduing all
Our words and works that drown
The tender whisper of thy call,
As noiseless let thy blessing fall
As fell thy manna down.

5. Drop thy still dews of quietness,
Till all our strivings cease;
Take from our souls the strain and stress,
And let our ordered lives confess
The beauty of thy peace.

PRAYER AND ASPIRATION

**119** *Dear ~~Lord and Father of~~ Mankind*

REST 8.6.8.8.6. (Second tune)

*John Greenleaf Whittier, 1872*                    *Frederick Charles Maker, 1887*

1. Dear ~~Lord and Fa-ther  of~~ man-kind, For - give our fool - ish ways. Re -
2. In   sim - ple trust like theirs who heard, Be - side the Syr - ian  sea, The
3. O    Sab-bath rest by  Gal - i - lee, O  calm  of hills  a - bove, Where

clothe  us   in   our   right - ful mind, In  pur - er lives  thy
gra - cious call - ing   of   the Lord, Let  us,  like them, with-
Je - sus knelt  to  share  with thee  The  si - lence of   e -

serv - ice  find,  In  deep - er  rev - erence,  praise.
out   a   word,  Rise  up   and  fol - low   thee.
ter - ni - ty,  In - ter - pret - ed   by   love.

4. With that deep hush subduing all
   Our words and works that drown
   The tender whisper of thy call,
   As noiseless let thy blessing fall
   As fell thy manna down.

5. Drop thy still dews of quietness,
   Till all our strivings cease;
   Take from our souls the strain and stress,
   And let our ordered lives confess
   The beauty of thy peace.

PRAYER AND ASPIRATION

# 120 O Thou Great Friend

AINSWORTH 97  10.10.10.10.

*From Theodore Parker, 1846*

*Genevan Psalter, 1562*
*Version of Henry Ainsworth's Psalter, 1612*

1. O thou great friend to all the sons of men, [*gen-er-a-tions*]
   Who once ap-peared in hum-blest guise be-low,
   Sin to re-buke, to break the cap-tive's chain,
   And call thy breth - ren [*peo-ple*] forth from want and woe!

2. We look to thee: thy truth is still the light
   Which guides the na - tions, grop-ing on their way,
   Stum - bling and fall - ing in dis - as - trous night,
   Yet hop - ing ev - er for the per - fect day.

3. Yes, thou art still the life, thou art the way
   The ho - liest know— light, life, and way of heaven;
   And they who dear - est hope and deep - est pray
   Toil by the light, life, way which thou hast given.

PRAYER AND ASPIRATION

# 121 Our Friend, Our Brother, and Our Lord

LORD, FOR THY TENDER MERCIES' SAKE C.M.

*John Greenleaf Whittier, 1866*                                  *Adapted from the 16th century anthem*

1. Our friend, our broth-er, and our lord, What may thy serv-ice be? Nor
2. We faint-ly hear, we dim-ly see, In dif-fering phrase we pray; But,
3. To do thy will is more than praise, As words are less than deeds; And

name, nor form, nor rit-ual word, But sim-ply fol-lowing thee.
dim or clear, we own in thee The light, the truth, the way.
sim-ple trust can find thy ways We miss with chart of creeds.

# 122 O Light of Light

ST. MAGNUS C.M.

*Washington Gladden, 1897*                                  *Attributed to Jeremiah Clark, 1707*

O Light of light, with-in us dwell, Through us thy ra-diance pour; That

word and life thy truths may tell, And praise thee ev-er-more.

PRAYER AND ASPIRATION

**123** Come, My Way, My Truth, My Life

George Herbert, 1633

THE CALL 7.7.7.7.

Ralph Vaughan Williams, 1911; adapted

1. Come, my way, my truth, my life: Such a
2. Come, my light, my feast, my strength: Such a
3. Come, my joy, my love, my heart: Such a

way as gives us breath, Such a truth as ends all
light as shows a feast, Such a feast as mends in
joy as none can move, Such a love as none can

strife, Such a life as kill - eth death.
length, Such a strength as makes This guest.
part, Such a heart as joys in love.

**124** Send Down Thy Truth

Edward Rowland Sill, 1867

ST. THOMAS S.M.

Aaron Williams' Universal Psalmodist, 1763

1. Send down thy truth, O God, Too long the shad-ows frown; Too
2. Send down thy spir - it free, Till wil - der-ness and town One
3. Send down thy love, thy life, Our less - er lives to crown, And
4. Send down thy peace, O Lord; God; Earth's bit - ter voic - es drown In

PRAYER AND ASPIRATION

long    the   dark-ened   way   we've trod:   Thy   truth,   O   ~~Lord~~, *God* send   down.
tem - ple   for   thy   wor - ship   be:   Thy   spir - it,   O   send   down.
cleanse them   of   their   hate   and   strife:   Thy   liv - ing   love   send   down.
one   deep   o - cean   of   ac - cord:   Thy   peace,   O   God,   send   down.

## 125     *Communion Hymn*

*Marion Franklin Ham, 1912*     PUER NOBIS NASCITUR L.M.     *Latin carol, 15th century*
*Adapted by Michael Praetorius, 1609*

1. O   thou whose   gra - cious   pres - ence   shone   A   light   to
2. Thy   grace   and   truth,   thy   life   that   shed   Un - dy - ing
3. And   lo,   a - gain   we   seem   to   hear   Thy   bless - ing
4. Our   less - er   lives,   thus   touch - ing   thine,   Are   joined,   with

bless   thy   fel - low   ~~men~~, *all hu-man-kind*   To   thee   we   fond - ly
ra - diance through   all   time,   Thy   ten - der   love,   thy
on   the   loaf   and   cup—   The   pres - ence   that   was   *in Thee*
all   the   pure   and   ~~good~~,   In   tru - er,   no - bler

turn   a - gain,   As   to   a   friend   that   we   have known.
faith   sub - lime—   Re - mem - bering these,   we   break   the   bread.
lift - ed   up   A - gain   to   lov - ing   hearts   brought   near.
~~broth - er - hood~~ *u-ni-ty*   That   lifts   the   world   to   realms   di - vine.

PRAYER AND ASPIRATION

# 126 Nearer, My God, to Thee

BETHANY 6.4.6.4.6.6.6.4.

*Sarah Flower Adams, 1841*

*Lowell Mason, 1856*

1. Near - er, my God, to thee, Near - er to thee! E'en though it
be a cross That rais - eth me; Still all my song shall be,
Near - er, my God, to thee, Near - er, my God, to thee, Near - er to thee!

2. Though like the wan - der - er, The sun gone down, Dark - ness be
o - ver me, My rest a stone; Yet in my dreams I'd be
Near - er, my God, to thee, Near - er, my God, to thee, Near - er to thee.

3. There let the way ap-pear Steps un - to heaven; All that thou
send - est me In mer - cy given; An - gels to beck - on me
Near - er, my God, to thee, Near - er, my God, to thee, Near - er to thee.

4. Then, with my waking thoughts
Bright with thy praise,
Out of my stony griefs
Bethel I'll raise;
So by my woes to be
Nearer, my God, to thee,
Nearer, my God, to thee,
Nearer to thee.

5. Or if on joyful wing
Cleaving the sky,
Sun, moon, and stars forgot,
Upwards I fly,
Still all my song shall be,
Nearer, my God, to thee,
Nearer, my God, to thee,
Nearer to thee!

PRAYER AND ASPIRATION

# Sovereign and Transforming Grace

SPANISH HYMN 7.7.7.7.D.

*Frederic Henry Hedge, 1829*

*Arranged by Benjamin Carr, 1824*

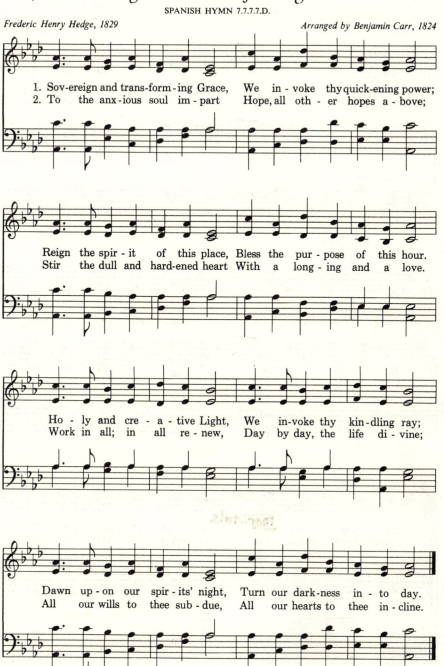

1. Sov-ereign and trans-form-ing Grace, We in - voke thy quick-ening power;
2. To the anx-ious soul im - part Hope, all oth - er hopes a - bove;

Reign the spir - it of this place, Bless the pur - pose of this hour.
Stir the dull and hard-ened heart With a long - ing and a love.

Ho - ly and cre - a - tive Light, We in-voke thy kin-dling ray;
Work in all; in all re - new, Day by day, the life di - vine;

Dawn up - on our spir - its' night, Turn our dark-ness in - to day.
All our wills to thee sub - due, All our hearts to thee in - cline.

PRAYER AND ASPIRATION

# 128 O Thou Whose Power

ADORO TE DEVOTE 10.10.10.10.

Boëthius (ca. 475–525)
Translated by Samuel Johnson, 1750

*Solesmes version of the plainsong melody; adapted*

1. O Thou whose power o'er mov - ing worlds pre - sides,
2. 'Tis thine a - lone to calm the pi - ous breast

Whose voice cre - at - ed, and whose wis - dom guides,
With si - lent con - fi - dence and ho - ly rest:

On dark - ling man in pure ef - ful - gence shine,
From thee, great God, we spring, to thee we tend—

PRAYER AND ASPIRATION

And cheer the cloud - ed mind with light di - vine.
Path, mo - tive, guide, o - rig - i - nal, and end.

## 129 Hard Is Now the Constant Woe

HOPE 7.7.7.7.

G. W. Fox

John Antes (1740–1811)

In Stanton Coit's Social Worship, II, 1913

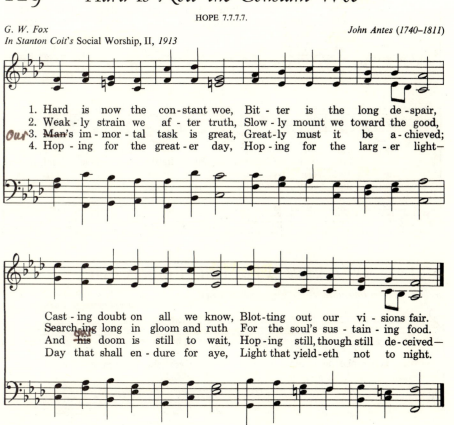

1. Hard is now the con-stant woe, Bit - ter is the long de -spair,
2. Weak - ly strain we af - ter truth, Slow - ly mount we toward the good,
3. Man's im - mor - tal task is great, Great-ly must it be a - chieved;
4. Hop - ing for the great-er day, Hop-ing for the larg - er light—

Cast - ing doubt on all we know, Blot-ting out our vi - sions fair.
Search-ing long in gloom and ruth For the soul's sus - tain - ing food.
And his doom is still to wait, Hop-ing still, though still de-ceived—
Day that shall en - dure for aye, Light that yield-eth not to night.

**PRAYER AND ASPIRATION**

## 130 Mysterious Presence, Source of All

*From Seth Curtis Beach, 1866*   WAREHAM L.M.   *William Knapp, 1738*

1. Mys - te - rious Pres - ence, source of all— The world with-
2. Thou breath - est in the rush - ing wind, Thy spir - it
3. Thy hand un - seen to ac - cents clear A - woke the
4. That touch di - vine still, ~~Lord,~~ *God* im - part, Still give the

out, the soul with - in— Thou fount of life, O
stirs in leaf and flower; Nor wilt thou from the
psalm - ist's trem - bling lyre, And touched the lips of
proph - et's burn - ing word; And vo - cal in each

hear our call, And pour thy liv - ing wa - ters in.
will - ing mind With - hold thy light and love and power.
ho - ly seer With flame from thine own al - tar fire.
wait - ing heart Let liv - ing psalms of praise be heard.

## 131 We Give Thee But Thine Own

*William Walsham How, 1858*   SWABIA S.M.   *Johann Martin Spiess, 1745*
*Arranged by W. H. Havergal, 1847*

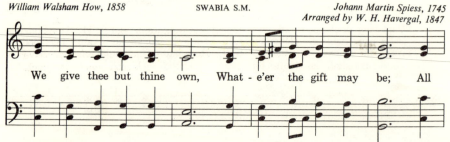

We give thee but thine own, What - e'er the gift may be; All

PRAYER AND ASPIRATION

that we have is thine a-lone, A trust, O Lord, from thee.
*(handwritten: God)*

**132**     *Mercy, Pity, Peace, and Love*
LOBT GOTT, IHR CHRISTEN C.M.
*William Blake, 1789*                                   *Nikolaus Herman, 1554*
*Harmonized by J. S. Bach, ca. 1740*

1. To Mer-cy, Pit-y, Peace, and Love All pray in their dis-tress, And
2. For Mer-cy, Pit-y, Peace, and Love Is God our Fa-ther dear; And
3. For Mer-cy has a hu-man heart, Pit-y, a hu-man face; And
4. Then ev-ery man, of ev-ery clime, That prays in his dis-tress, Prays

*(handwritten: all-peo-ple)*   *(handwritten: pa-rent)*   *(handwritten: their)*

to those vir-tues of de-light Re-turn their thank-ful-
Mer-cy, Pit-y, Peace, and Love Is man, his child and
Love, the hu-man form di-vine, And Peace, the hu-man
to the hu-man form di-vine— Love, Mer-cy, Pit-y,

*(handwritten: are we the)*

ness, Re-turn their thank-ful-ness.
care, Is man, his child and care.
dress, And Peace, the hu-man dress.
Peace, Love, Mer-cy, Pit-y, Peace.

*(handwritten: are we the)*

PRAYER AND ASPIRATION

## 133 The Universal Prayer

TALLIS' ORDINAL C.M.

*Alexander Pope, 1715*                                    *Thomas Tallis, ca. 1561*

1. Fa - ther *pa-rent* of all, in ev - ery age, In ev - ery clime a - dored, By
2. If I am right, thy grace im - part Still in the right to stay; If
3. Save me a - like from fool - ish pride, Or im - pious dis - con - tent, At

saint, by sav - age, and by sage, Je - ho - vah, Jove, or Lord: *God*
I am wrong, thy grace im - part To find the bet - ter way.
aught thy wis - dom has de - nied, Or aught thy good - ness lent.

4. Teach me to feel another's woe,
   To hide the fault I see.
   That mercy I to others show,
   That mercy show to me.

5. To thee, whose temple is all space,
   Whose altar, earth, sea, skies,
   One chorus let all being raise,
   All nature's incense rise.

## 134 Give Me Your Whole Heart

COLE 5.5.5.5.5. Irregular

*From the Bhagavad-Gita, 5th to 2nd centuries B.C.*          *Kenneth Munson, 1961*
*Translated by Swami Prabhavananda*
*and Christopher Isherwood, 1944*

1. Give me your whole heart, Love and a - dore me, Wor-ship me
2. This is my prom - ise, Who love you dear - ly. Fear no

al - ways, Bow to me on - ly, and you shall find me:
long - er For I will save you from sin and bond - age.

PRAYER AND ASPIRATION

# 135 All Things Are Doubly Fair

ART 6.6.2.6.

Théophile Gautier (1811–1872)
From translation by George Santayana, ca. 1922

Henry Leland Clarke, 1959

1. All things are dou - bly fair If pa - tience
2. Now chis - el, carve, and file, Till thy vague
3. Oft doth the plough-man's heel, Break - ing an
4. The gods too die, a - las! But death - less

fash - ion them And care— E - nam - el, mar - ble, gem.
dream im - print Its smile Up - on un - yield - ing flint.
an - cient clod, Re - veal A Cae - sar or a god.
and more strong Than brass Re - mains the sov-ereign song.

# 136 Truly the Light Is Sweet

GANADOR 6.6.6.6.6.

From Josephine Preston Peabody, 1911

Robert L. Sanders, 1958

1. Tru - ly the light is sweet; Yea, and a pleas-ant thing It is to see the
2. That he should take and keep, Aft - er his la - bor-ing, His bread that he hath

sun; And that a man should eat His bread that he hath won;
won; Yea, and in qui - et, sleep When all his work is done.

THE ARTS OF MAN

## 137 I Love All Beauteous Things

PONT NEUF Irregular

Robert Bridges, 1890

Robert L. Sanders, 1961

1. I love all beau-teous things, I seek and a - dore them; God
2. I too will some-thing make And joy in the mak - ing; Al-

hath no bet - ter praise, And we [man] in our [his] hast - y
though to - mor - row it seem Like the emp - ty words of a

days are [Is] hon - ored for them.
dream Re - mem - bered on wak - ing.

## 138 Ours Be the Poems of All Tongues

TALLIS' CANON L.M.

Kenneth L. Patton, 1956

Thomas Tallis, ca. 1561

Ours be the po-ems of all tongues, All things of love - li - ness and worth, All

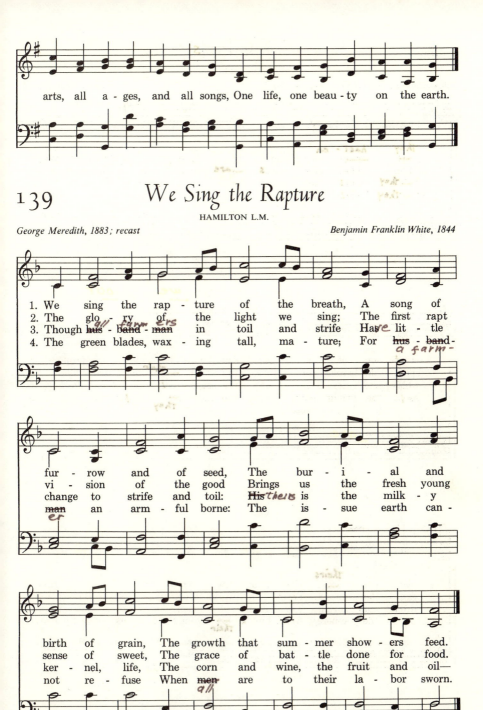

arts, all a-ges, and all songs, One life, one beau-ty on the earth.

## 139     *We Sing the Rapture*

HAMILTON L.M.

*George Meredith, 1883; recast*        *Benjamin Franklin White, 1844*

1. We sing the rap - ture of the breath, A song of
2. The glo - ry of the light we sing; The first rapt
3. Though hus - band - man in toil and strife Have lit - tle
4. The green blades, wax - ing tall, ma - ture; For hus - band -

fur - row and of seed, The bur - i - al and
vi - sion of the good Brings us the fresh young
change to strife and toil: His is the milk - y
man an arm - ful borne: The is - sue earth can -

birth of grain, The growth that sum - mer show - ers feed.
sense of sweet, The grace of bat - tle done for food.
ker - nel, life, The corn and wine, the fruit and oil—
not re - fuse When men are to their la - bor sworn.

THE ARTS OF MAN

# The Poets

O SALUTARIS L.M.

*Edwin Markham, 1899, 1900; arranged, 1961*    *Abbé Duguet?, ca. 1767*

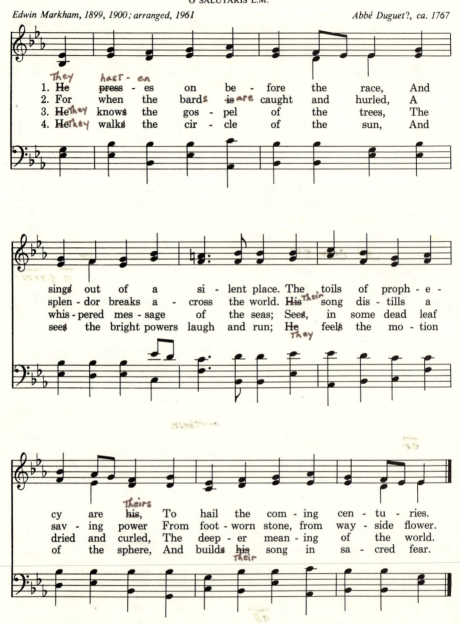

1. He presses on before the race, And
sings out of a si - lent place. The toils of proph - e -
cy are his, To hail the com - ing cen - tu - ries.

2. For when the bards are caught and hurled, A
splen - dor breaks a - cross the world. His song dis - tills a
sav - ing power From foot - worn stone, from way - side flower.

3. He knows the gos - pel of the trees, The
whis - pered mes - sage of the seas; Sees, in some dead leaf
dried and curled, The deep - er mean - ing of the world.

4. He walks the cir - cle of the sun, And
sees the bright powers laugh and run; He feels the mo - tion
of the sphere, And builds his song in sa - cred fear.

## 141 — Sing Notes of Love

BOHEMIA 8.8.8.

*Christina Georgina Rossetti, 1859*

*Bohemian Brethren, Kirchengeseng, 1566*

1. O ye who taste that love is sweet, Set way-marks
for the doubt-ful feet That stum-ble on in search of it.

2. Sing hymns of love; that some who hear Far off, in
pain, may lend an ear, Rise up and won - der and draw near.

3. Lead lives of love; that oth - ers who Be - hold your
lives may kin - dle too With love, and cast their lot with you.

## 142 — Immortal Love

DUNDEE C.M.

*John Greenleaf Whittier, 1866*

Scottish Psalter, *1615*

1. Im - mor - tal Love, for - ev - er full, For - ev - er flow - ing free, For -
ev - er shared, for - ev - er whole, A nev - er - ebb - ing sea!

2. Our out-ward lips con - fess the name All oth - er names a - bove; But
love a - lone knows whence it came, And com - pre - hend - eth love.

3. Blow, winds of God, a - wake and blow The mists of earth a - way; Shine
out, O Light di - vine, and show How wide and far we stray.

4. The let - ter fails, the sys - tems fall, And ev - ery sym - bol wanes: The
Spir - it o - ver - brood-ing all, E - ter - nal Love, re - mains.

LOVE AND HUMAN BROTHERHOOD

# 143 The Crest and Crowning of All Good

WER DA WONET L.M.D.

*Edwin Markham, 1899*

*Michael Vehe's* New Gesangbüchlin, *1537; adapted*

1. The crest and crown-ing of all good, Life's fi - nal star, is
2. Come, clear the way, then, clear the way; Blind creeds and kings have

*har - mo - ny*

*am - i - ty*     *ITS*

broth - er-hood; For it will bring a - gain to earth Her
had their day. Break the dead branch - es from the path; Our

long - lost po - e - sy and mirth; Will send new light on ev - ery face, A
hope is in the af - ter-math; Our hope is in he - ro - ic men, Star-

*the*     *few*

king - ly power up - on the race. And till it comes, we
led to build the world a - gain. To this e - vent the

*lov - ing*

*new*

LOVE AND HUMAN BROTHERHOOD

*HARMONY*

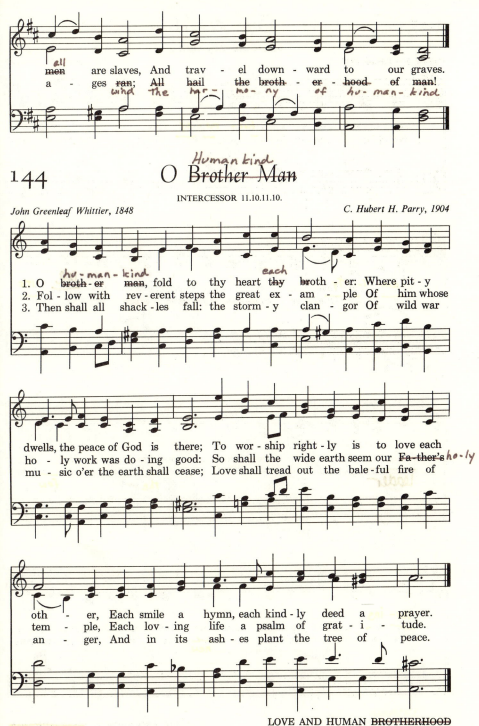

men    are slaves, And    trav - el    down - ward    to    our graves.
*all*
a - ges ~~ran~~; All    hail    the ~~broth - er - hood~~    of    man!
*wind    the    har - mo - ny    of    hu - man - kind*

144    O ~~Brother Man~~
*Human kind*

INTERCESSOR 11.10.11.10.

*John Greenleaf Whittier, 1848*                    *C. Hubert H. Parry, 1904*

1. O ~~broth - er    man~~, fold    to    thy    heart ~~thy~~    broth - er: Where pit - y
   *hu - man - kind*    *each*
2. Fol - low with    rev - erent steps the    great ex - am - ple Of    him whose
3. Then shall all    shack - les    fall: the storm - y    clan - gor Of    wild war

dwells, the peace of God is    there; To wor - ship right - ly    is    to love each
ho - ly work was do - ing    good: So shall the    wide earth seem our ~~Fa - ther's~~ *ho - ly*
mu - sic o'er the earth shall cease; Love shall tread out    the    bale - ful fire of

oth - er, Each smile a    hymn, each kind - ly    deed    a    prayer.
tem - ple, Each lov - ing    life a psalm of    grat - i - tude.
an - ger, And in    its    ash - es plant the    tree of    peace.

LOVE AND HUMAN ~~BROTHERHOOD~~
*HARMONY*

# 145 One World

SCHMÜCKE DICH 8.8.8.8.D.

*Vincent B. Silliman, 1947*                                                      *Johann Crüger, 1649*

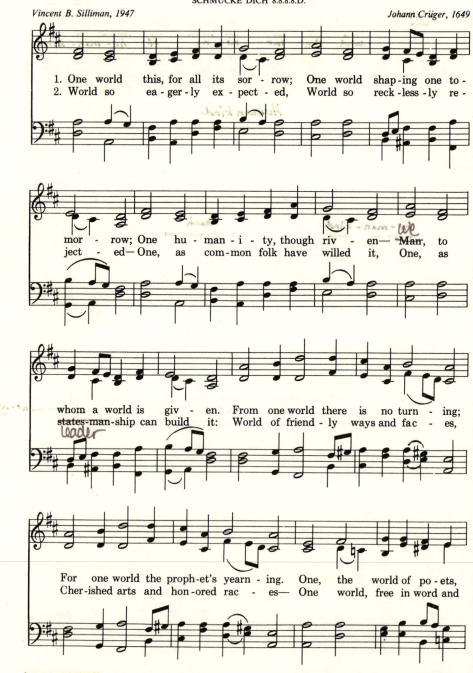

1. One world this, for all its sor-row; One world shap-ing one to-
2. World so ea-ger-ly ex-pect-ed, World so reck-less-ly re-

mor - row; One hu-man-i-ty, though riv-en— Man, to
ject - ed— One, as com-mon folk have willed it, One, as

whom a world is giv - en. From one world there is no turn - ing;
states-man-ship can build it: World of friend-ly ways and fac - es,

For one world the proph-et's yearn - ing. One, the world of po - ets,
Cher-ished arts and hon-ored rac - es— One world, free in word and

sag - es; One world, goal of all the a - ges.
sci - ence; Man - hood free, its firm re - li - ance.
*li-ber-ty*

# 146    *Spirit of Truth, of Life, of Power*

HAMBURG L.M.

*Horace Westwood, 1922*        *Lowell Mason, 1824*

Spir - it of truth, of life, of power, We bring our-

selves as gifts to thee: Oh, bind our hearts this

sa - cred hour In faith and hope and char - i - ty.

LOVE AND HUMAN BROTHERHOOD

*Harmony*

**147**

# This Is the Charge I Keep

ROCKBRIDGE L.M.

*Leslie Pinckney Hill (1880–1959)*                    *Amzi Chapin, 1813*

1. This is the charge I keep as mine, The goal of ev - ery
2. That so for me all fear shall end Save this— that I may
3. Though par - lia - ments may rise and fall, I hold to this e -

hope and plan, To can - cel the di - vid - ing line Be -
fail to see My neigh - bor as a need - ed friend, Or
ter - nal good, This death - less truth— that men are all One

tween me and my fel - low man:
sense my neigh - bor's need of me.
earth - en - cir - cling broth - er - hood.

*(handwritten annotations: pace, play, key, the, hu-man race, fa-mi-ly, love)*

**148**

# Man's Comradeship

*(handwritten: Our)*

LISLE C.M.

*Florence Kiper Frank, 1914*                    *Brethren Hymnal, 1901*

1. Man's com - rade - ship is ver - y wide, A large and no - ble throng By
2. The vast de - moc - ra - cy of earth, The fel - low - ship of man— Who
3. The com - mon lot of hu - man - kind, Its glad - ness and its woe, This

*(handwritten: our, hu-man fa-mi-ly)*

LOVE AND HUMAN BROTHERHOOD

*(handwritten: Harmony)*

toil and tears and faith al - lied, By suf - fer - ing and song.
asks for an - y no - bler birth Than son to *human* clan? *com-rade-ship*
mor - tal bond all lives shall bind And broth - er - hood be - stow.

## 149 My Country Is the World

TRINITY 6.6.4.6.6.6.4.

*Robert Whitaker, 1899*                     *Felice Giardini, 1769; adapted*

1. My coun-try is the world; My flag, with stars im - pearled,
2. Mine are all lands and seas, All flow - ers, shrubs, and trees,
3. And all men are *ev-ery one is* my kin, Since ev - er man *we have* has been

Fills all the skies. All the round earth I claim; Peo - ples of
All life's de - sign; My heart with - in me thrills For all up -
Blood of my blood; I glo - ry in the grace And strength of

ev - ery name, And all in - spir - ing fame, My heart would prize.
lift - ed hills, And for all streams and rills; The world is mine.
ev - ery race, And joy in ev - ery trace Of *neighbor* broth - er - hood.

LOVE AND HUMAN BROTHERHOOD *Harmony*

# 150 Let Not Young Souls Be Smothered Out

CONGLETON 10.10.10.10.

*Vachel Lindsay, 1914*                                                                 *Michael Wise, 1684*

1. Let not young souls be smoth - ered out be -
2. Not that they starve, but starve so dream - less -

fore They do quaint deeds and ful - ly flaunt their
ly; Not that they sow, but that they sel - dom

pride. It is the world's one crime its babes grow
reap; Not that they serve, but have no gods to

dull, Its poor are ox - like, limp, and lead - en eyed.
serve; Not that they die, but that they die like sheep.

LOVE AND HUMAN *Harmony* ~~BROTHERHOOD~~

## 151 ~~Man~~ We Live~~s~~ Not for ~~Himself~~ Ourselves Alone

BETRACHT'N WIR HEUT ZU DIESER FRIST 8.8.8.

*Henry Cary Shuttleworth, 1898*                     *Bohemian Brethren, Gesangbuch, 1544*

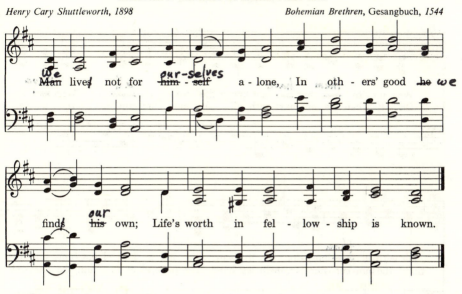

We / Man lives not for ~~him~~ our-selves a - lone, In oth - ers' good ~~he~~ we

finds ~~his~~ our own; Life's worth in fel - low - ship is known.

## 152 For Mercy, Courage, Kindness, Mirth

LYNE 7.7.7.7. Irregular

*From Laurence Binyon, 1920*                     *Magdalen Chapel, Hymns, ca. 1760*

1. For mer - cy, cour-age, kind-ness, mirth, There is no meas-ure on the earth;
2. O - ver-brim and o - ver-flow, If your own heart you would know:

Nay, they with - er, root and stem, If an end be set to them.
For the spir - it, born to bless, Lives but in its own ex - cess.

LOVE AND HUMAN ~~BROTHERHOOD~~ Harmony

# 153

## Woe unto ~~Him~~ *Them*

BINYON 12.12.12.12.12.12.

*Laurence Binyon, 1913*                    *Robert L. Sanders, 1961*

1. Woe un-to ~~him~~ *them* that ~~has~~ *have* not known the woe of ~~man~~ *all*, Who ~~has~~ *have* not
2. On-ly when we are hurt with all the hurt un-told— In us the

felt with-in ~~him~~ *them* burn-ing all the want Of des-o-lat-ed bos-oms, since the
thirst, the hun-ger—ours the help-less hands, The pal-sied ef-fort vain, the dark-ness

world be-gan; Felt, as ~~his~~ *their* own, the bur-den of the fears that daunt;
and the cold— Then, on-ly then, the spir-it knows and un-der-stands,

Who ~~has~~ *have* not eat-en fail-ure's bit--ter bread, and been A-
And finds in ev-ery sigh breathed out be-neath the sun The

LOVE AND HUMAN ~~BROTHERHOOD~~ *Harmony*

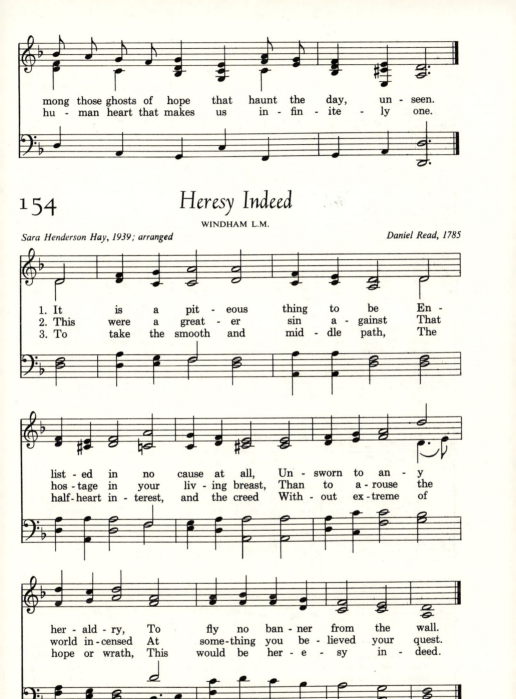

mong those ghosts of hope that haunt the day, un - seen.
hu - man heart that makes us in - fin - ite - ly one.

**154**  *Heresy Indeed*

WINDHAM L.M.

*Sara Henderson Hay, 1939; arranged*          *Daniel Read, 1785*

1. It is a pit - eous thing to be En -
2. This were a great - er sin a - gainst That
3. To take the smooth and mid - dle path, The

list - ed in no cause at all, Un - sworn to an - y
hos - tage in your liv - ing breast, Than to a - rouse the
half - heart in - terest, and the creed With - out ex - treme of

her - ald - ry, To fly no ban - ner from the wall.
world in - censed At some - thing you be - lieved your quest.
hope or wrath, This would be her - e - sy in - deed.

LOVE AND HUMAN BROTHERHOOD

## 155 Knight Without a Sword

*Jan Struther, 1931*
*Based on Acts 7*

SALVATION C.M.D.

*Ananias Davisson's* Kentucky
Harmony, *ca. 1815*

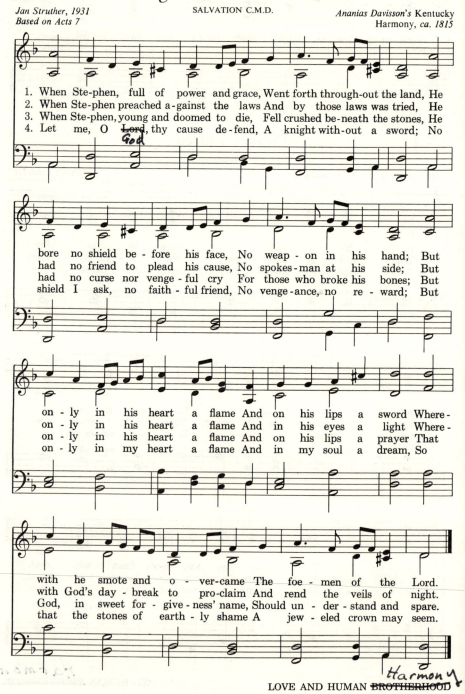

1. When Ste-phen, full of power and grace, Went forth through-out the land, He
2. When Ste-phen preached a-gainst the laws And by those laws was tried, He
3. When Ste-phen, young and doomed to die, Fell crushed be-neath the stones, He
4. Let me, O God, thy cause de-fend, A knight with-out a sword; No

bore no shield be - fore his face, No weap - on in his hand; But
had no friend to plead his cause, No spokes-man at his side; But
had no curse nor venge - ful cry For those who broke his bones; But
shield I ask, no faith - ful friend, No venge-ance, no re - ward; But

on - ly in his heart a flame And on his lips a sword Where-
on - ly in his heart a flame And in his eyes a light Where-
on - ly in his heart a flame And on his lips a prayer That
on - ly in my heart a flame And in my soul a dream, So

with he smote and o - ver-came The foe - men of the Lord.
with God's day - break to pro-claim And rend the veils of night.
God, in sweet for - give - ness' name, Should un - der - stand and spare.
that the stones of earth - ly shame A jew - eled crown may seem.

LOVE AND HUMAN BROTHERHOOD

# 156 The Compass

MACH'S MIT MIR, GOTT 8.8.8.8.8.8.

*John Hall Wheelock, 1955*

*Johann Hermann Schein, 1628*
*Harmonized by J. S. Bach (1685–1750)*

1. Put down your foot and you shall feel What long was there be -
2. She draws them toward her if they fall, She too is drawn, is
3. On earth be - low, in heaven a - bove, One truth, and in the

fore your birth, The faith - ful ground be - neath your heel, The
fall - ing, she Serves the one law that gov - erns all— The
world of men One truth; the truth of man is love. Look

stead - fast and en - dur - ing earth That bears up all things,
truth, the prime ne - ces - si - ty, Which all the star - ry
for the com - pass in the heart— That nee - dle points true

great or small, Re - gard - less of their weight or worth.
or - bits prove, Em - brac - ing which the worlds are free.
north— and know The truth from which you may not part.

LOVE AND HUMAN BROTHERHOOD

## 157 The Law of Love

SONG 67 C.M.

*From Richard Chenevix Trench, 1838*

*Edmund Prys's Llyfr y Psalmau, 1621*
*Bass by Orlando Gibbons, 1623*

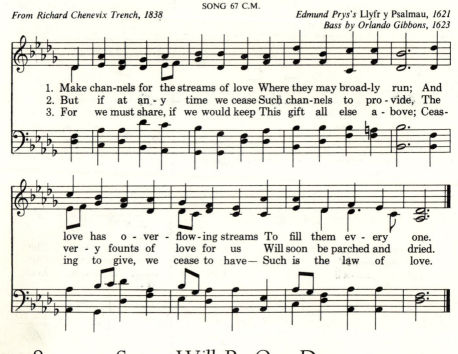

1. Make chan-nels for the streams of love Where they may broad-ly run; And
2. But if at an-y time we cease Such chan-nels to pro-vide, The
3. For we must share, if we would keep This gift all else a-bove; Ceas-

love has o-ver-flow-ing streams To fill them ev-ery one.
ver-y founts of love for us Will soon be parched and dried.
ing to give, we cease to have— Such is the law of love.

## 158 Serene Will Be Our Days

MELCOMBE L.M.

*William Wordsworth, 1807*

*Samuel Webbe, 1782*

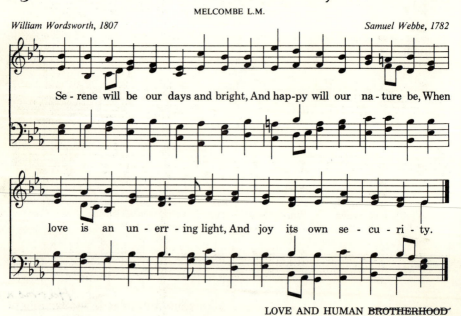

Se-rene will be our days and bright, And hap-py will our na-ture be, When

love is an un-err-ing light, And joy its own se-cu-ri-ty.

LOVE AND HUMAN ~~BROTHERHOOD~~ Harmony

**159**

# Prayer for This House

OLDBRIDGE 8.8.8.4.

*Louis Untermeyer, 1923*

*Robert N. Quaile, 1903*

1. May noth - ing e - vil cross this door,
2. By faith made strong, the raft - ers will
3. Peace shall walk soft - ly through these rooms,
4. With laugh - ter drown the rau - cous shout

And may ill - for - tune nev - er pry A - bout these
With-stand the bat - tering of the storm. This hearth, though
Touch-ing our lips with ho - ly wine, Till ev - ery
And, though these shel - tering walls are thin, May they be

win - dows; may the roar And rain go by.
all the world grow chill Will keep you warm.
cas - ual cor - ner blooms In - to a shrine.
strong to keep hate out And hold love in.

**160**

# Shalom Havayreem

SHALOM Irregular

*Anonymous*

*Jewish melody*

Sha - lom, ha - vay - reem; sha - lom, ha - vay - reem; sha - lom, sha -
*(Translation: Peace, Friends.)*

lom. Sha - lom, ha - vay - reem; sha - lom, ha - vay - reem; sha - lom, sha - lom.

LOVE AND HUMAN ~~BROTHERHOOD~~ Harmony

**161** *All Within Four Seas*

FOUR SEAS 6.6.5.6.5.

*Confucius (551–479 B.C.)*
*From translation by James Legge, 1861*

*Ieuan Gwyllt, 1859*

Let ~~him~~ *them* who would ex - cel Tend ~~his~~ *their* own con-duct well, Re-spect-ing

oth - ers; Then all with-in four seas Will be ~~his~~ *their* ~~broth~~ - ~~ers.~~ *part-ners.*

**162** *Love Can Tell*

LYNE 7.7.7.7.

*Robert Bridges, 1899; arranged*

*Magdalen Chapel, Hymns, ca. 1760*

1. Love can tell, and love a - lone, Whence the mil-lion stars were strewn.
2. Love can tell, and love a - lone, Why each at - om knows its own,

Love, from whom the world be - gun, Hath the se - cret of the sun.
How, in spite of woe and death, Gay is life, and sweet is breath.

LOVE AND HUMAN ~~BROTHERHOOD~~ *Harmony*

# 163 Can I See Another's Woe?

ACH, WANN WERD ICH 7.7.7.7.

*From William Blake, 1794*

*C. F. Witt's Psalmodia Sacra, 1715*

1. Can a fa - ther see his child Weep, nor be with sor - row filled?
2. Can I see an - oth - er's woe, And not be in sor - row too?
3. Can I see an - oth - er's grief, And not seek for kind re - lief?

Can a moth - er sit and hear In - fant groan, an in - fant fear?
Can I see a fall - ing tear, And not feel my sor - row's share?
No, no! nev - er can it be! Nev - er, nev - er can it be!

# 164 The Night Has a Thousand Eyes

BOURDILLON 7.5.8.5. Irregular

*Francis William Bourdillon, 1890*

*Orlando Gibbons, 1623; adapted*

1. The night has a thou - sand eyes, And the day but one; Yet the
2. The mind has a thou - sand eyes, And the heart but one; Yet the

light of the bright world dies With the dy - ing sun.
light of a whole life dies When love is done.

LOVE AND HUMAN ~~BROTHERHOOD~~ *Harmony*

## 165 "Remember Me," the Master Said

DUNDEE C.M.

*From Nathaniel Langdon Frothingham, 1855*

Scottish Psalter, *1615*

1. "Re-mem-ber me," the Mas-ter said, On that for-sak-en night, When
2. Through all the fol-lowing a-ges' track The world re-mem-bers yet; With
3. But who of us has seen his face, Or heard the words he said? And
4. We hear his word a-long our way; We see his light a-bove; Re-

from his side the near-est fled, And death was close in sight.
love and wor-ship gaz-es back, And nev-er can for-get.
none can now his look re-trace In break-ing of the bread.
mem-ber when we strive and pray, Re-mem-ber when we love.

## 166 For No Sect Elect

MEADOW COVE 5.5.5.5.5.

*Algernon Charles Swinburne, 1868*

Genevan Psalter, *1551*
Psalm 47; abridged

1. For no sect e-lect Is the soul's wine poured And ~~her~~ *its*
2. ~~Broth-er-hood~~ *Cer-ti-Tude* of good, E-qual laws and rights, Free-dom,

ta-ble decked; Whom should *we* ~~man~~ re-ject From ~~man's~~ *our* com-mon board?
whose sweet food Feeds the mul-ti-tude All their days and nights.

LOVE AND HUMAN ~~BROTHERHOOD~~ *Harmony*

# 167   *Eternal Spirit of the Chainless Mind*

SONG 24   10.10.10.10.

*George Gordon, Lord Byron, 1816*        *Orlando Gibbons, 1623*

1. E - ter - nal spir - it of the chain - less
2. And when thy ~~sons~~ *heirs* to fet - ters are con -

mind! Bright - est in dun - geons, Lib - er - ty! thou
signed— To fet - ters, and the damp vault's day - less

art, For there thy hab - i - ta - tion is the
gloom— Their coun - try con - quers with their mar - tyr -

heart— The heart which love of thee a - lone can bind;
dom, And Free - dom's fame finds wings on ev - ery wind.

**FREEDOM**

# 168 When a Deed Is Done for Freedom

*From James Russell Lowell, 1845*

AN DIE FREUDE 8.7.8.7.D.

*German melody for Schiller's*
*"Hymn to Joy," 1799*

1. When a deed is done for free-dom, through the broad earth's ach-ing
2. New oc-ca-sions teach new du-ties; time makes an-cient good un-
3. For man-kind are one in spir-it, and an in-stinct bears a-

breast Runs a thrill of joy pro - phet-ic, trem-bling
couth; We must up-ward still and on - ward, who would
long, Round the earth's e - lec-tric cir - cle, the swift

on from east to west; And the slaves, where-e'er they
keep a-breast of truth— Launch our ves - sel, and steer
flash of right or wrong; All earth's o - cean - sun - dered

cow - ers, feels the soul with - in them climb To the
bold - ly through the des - perate win - ter sea, Nor at -
fi - bers feel the gush of joy or shame; In the

FREEDOM

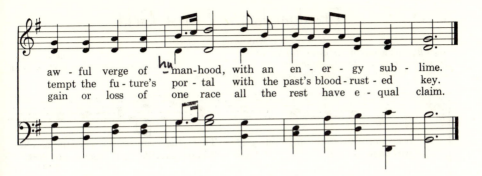

aw - ful verge of human-hood, with an en - er - gy sub - lime.
tempt the fu - ture's por - tal with the past's blood - rust - ed key.
gain or loss of one race all the rest have e - qual claim.

## 169 Through All the Long Dark Night

ACH GOTT UND HERR 8.7.8.7.

Gerald Massey, ca. 1854

As Hymnodus Sacer, Leipzig, 1625
Harmonized by J. S. Bach (1685–1750)

1. Through all the long dark night of years The peo-ple's cry as-
2. When driv - en back, for our next fray A new - er strength we
3. The world is roll - ing free-dom's way And rip-ening with her

cend - eth, And earth is wet with blood and tears, But
bor - row, And where the van - guard camps to - day The
sor - row. It is the mar - tyr - dom to - day Brings

our meek suf - ferance end - eth.
ranks shall rest to - mor - row.
vic - to - ry to - mor - row.

FREEDOM

# 170 Freedom Is the Finest Gold

ACH WAS SOLL ICH 7.7.6.D.

*From Bishop Thomas of Strängnäs, Sweden, 1439*
*Translated or arranged by Elias Gordon*
*In W. R. Benét and N. Cousins' The Poetry of Freedom, 1945*

*Johann Flitner's*
*Himmlisches Lustgärtlein, 1661; adapted*

1. Free-dom is the fin-est gold That the sun strews o'er the mould—
2. Free-dom is a cit-y blest Whose calm life no hates mo-lest;

Treas-ure it for-ev-er. From the free-dom-lov-ing heart
Neigh-bor there loves neigh-bor. Though each loves his for-bears' name,
*all    their*

Hon-or can-not live a-part: None the twain can sev-er.
He lets oth-ers do the same. Each for all there la-bor.
*They*

# 171 Let All Who Live in Freedom

MELCOMBE L.M.

*Kenneth L. Patton, 1956*

*Samuel Webbe, 1782*

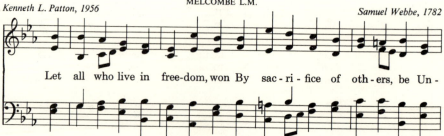

Let all who live in free-dom, won By sac-ri-fice of oth-ers, be Un-

FREEDOM

tir - ing in the task be - gun Till ev - ery *one* ~~man~~ on earth is free.

# 172 The People's Liberty

VIENNA 7.7.7.7.

Samuel Johnson, 1864

Justin Heinrich Knecht, 1799

1. Life of a - ges, rich - ly poured, Love of God, un - spent and free,
2. Nev - er was to cho - sen race That un - stint - ed tide con - fined;
3. Breath-ing in the think-er's creed, Puls - ing in the he - ro's blood,

Flow - ing in the proph-et's word And the peo - ple's lib - er - ty—
Thine is ev - ery time and place, Foun-tain sweet of heart and mind.
Nerv - ing sim - plest thought and deed, Fresh-ening time with truth and good,

4. Consecrating art and song,
   Holy book and pilgrim track,
   Hurling floods of tyrant wrong
   From the sacred limits back—

5. Life of ages, richly poured,
   Love of God, unspent and free,
   Flow still in the prophet's word
   And the people's liberty!

FREEDOM

# 173 True Freedom

SALZBURG 7.7.7.7.D.

*James Russell Lowell, 1844*

*Jacob Hintze, 1678*
*Harmonized by J. S. Bach (1685–1750)*

1. Men, whose boast it is that ye Come of fa-thers brave and free,
2. Is true free-dom but to break Fet-ters for our own dear sake,
3. They are slaves who fear to speak For the fall-en and the weak;

If there breathe on earth a slave, Are ye tru-ly free and brave?
And with leath-ern hearts for-get That we owe man-kind a debt?
They are slaves who will not choose Ha-tred, scoff-ing, and a-buse,

If ye do not feel the chain When it works a broth-er's-pain,
No, true free-dom is to share All the chains our broth-ers wear,
Rath-er than in si-lence shrink From the truth they needs must think.

Are ye not base slaves in-deed, Slaves un-wor-thy to be freed?
And, with heart and hand, to be Ear-nest to make oth-ers free.
They are slaves who dare not be In the right with two or three.

FREEDOM

# 174 Seek Not Afar for Beauty

CLIFF TOWN 10.10.10.10.

*From Minot Judson Savage, 1883*

*Erik Routley, 1951*

1. Seek not a - far for beau - ty; lo, it glows In
2. Go not a - broad for hap - pi - ness; be - hold It
3. Dream not of no - ble serv - ice else - where wrought; In
4. In won - der - work - ings, or some bush a - flame, ~~Men~~ We

dew - wet grass - es all a - bout your feet, In
is a flow - er bloom - ing at your door. Bring
sim - ple du - ties that a - wait your hand God's
look for God ~~and fan - cy him~~ con - cealed; But
who there - in is

birds, in sun - shine, child - ish fac - es sweet, In
love and laugh - ter home, and ev - er - more Joy
voice is speak - ing ~~his~~ the di - vine com - mand: Life's
in earth's com - mon things ~~he~~ stands re - vealed, While
then

stars and moun - tain sum - mits topped with snows.
shall be yours as chang - ing years un - fold.
com - mon deeds build all that saints have taught.
grass and flowers and stars spell out ~~his~~ name.
God's

HERE AND NOW

# 175 All Are Architects

*Henry Wadsworth Longfellow, 1846*

HASIDIM 7.7.7.7.

*From a Hasidic tune in*
*The Songs We Sing, 1950*

1. All are ar-chi-tects of fate, Work-ing in these walls of time;
2. For the struc-ture that we raise Time is with ma-te-rials filled;
3. Build to-day, then, strong and sure, With a firm and am-ple base;

Some with mas-sive deeds and great, Some with or-na-ments of rhyme.
Our to-days and yes-ter-days Are the blocks with which we build.
And as-cend-ing and se-cure Shall to-mor-row find its place.

# 176 Only We Earns Life and Freedom

LES COMMANDEMENS 9.8.9.8.

*Johann Wolfgang von Goethe, 1831*
*From translation by Florence Melian Stawell, 1929*

*Louis Bourgeois' Pseaulmes, 1547*

This thought shall have our whole al-le-giance, These words of wis-dom

know for true, That on-ly we earns life and

HERE AND NOW

## 177 O Sometimes Gleams upon Our Sight

HAMBURG L.M.

*From John Greenleaf Whittier, 1851*                   *Lowell Mason, 1824*

1. O some-times gleams up - on our sight, Through pres - ent wrong, the e - ter - nal right; And step by step, since time *com-menced*, We see the stead - y gain of *Sense:*

2. That all of good the past hath had Re - mains to make our own time glad, Our com - mon, dai - ly life di - vine, And ev - ery land a Pal - es - tine.

3. Through the harsh nois - es of our day A low, sweet prel - ude finds its way; Through clouds of doubt and creeds of fear A light is break - ing calm and clear.

4. Hence - forth my heart shall sigh no more For old - en time and ho - lier shore; God's love and bless - ing, then and there, Are now and here and ev - ery - where.

HERE AND NOW

# 178 Now Give Heart's Onward Habit Brave Intent

FARLEY CASTLE 10.10.10.10.

*John Holmes, 1937*  *Henry Lawes, 1638*

1. Now give heart's on - ward hab - it brave in - tent: Ham -
   mer the gold - en day un - til it lies A
   glim - mering plate to heap with mem - o - ry; Sa -
   lute ar - riv - ing mo - ments with your eyes.

2. We live, we are e - lect - ed now by time, Few
   out of man - y not yet come to birth, And
   man - y dead, to use the day - light now, To
   stand be - neath the sun up - on the earth.

3. Then break the si - lence with a voice of praise Be -
   fore we fall a - sleep, be - fore we die; Press
   mind and bod - y hard a - gainst this world; O -
   pen the door that o - pens toward the sky.

HERE AND NOW

# 179 The People's Peace

SURSUM CORDA 10.10.10.10.

John Holmes, 1937

Alfred Morton Smith, 1941

1. Peace is the mind's old wil - der - ness cut down— A
2. Not schol - ar's calm, nor gift of church or state, Nor
3. The peace not past our un - der - stand - ing falls Like
4. Days in - to years, the door - ways worn at sill, Years

wid - er na - tion than our fa - thers dreamed. Peace is the main street
ev - er - last - ing date of death's re - lease; But care - less noon, the
light up - on the soft white ta - ble - cloth At win - ter sup - per
in - to lives, the plans for long in - crease Come true at last for

in a coun - try town; Our chil - dren named; our fa - thers' lives re - deemed.
hous - es light - ed late, Har - vest and hol - i - day: the peo - ple's peace.
warm be - tween four walls, A thing too sim - ple to be tried as truth.
men of God's good will: These are the things we mean by say - ing, Peace.

HERE AND NOW

# 180 Earth Is Enough

FILLMORE 8.8.8 8.8.8.

*From Edwin Markham, ca. 1913*                    *William Walker's* Southern Harmony, *1835*

1. Here on the paths of ev - ery - day— Here on the com - mon
2. We need no oth - er stones to build The tem - ple of the

hu - man way— Is all the stuff the gods would take To
un - ful - filled— No oth - er i - vory for the doors— No

build a heaven, to mould and make New E - dens. Ours the
oth - er mar - ble for the floors— No oth - er ce - dar

task sub - lime To build e - ter - ni - ty in time.
for the beam And dome of man's. im - mor - tal dream.

HERE AND NOW

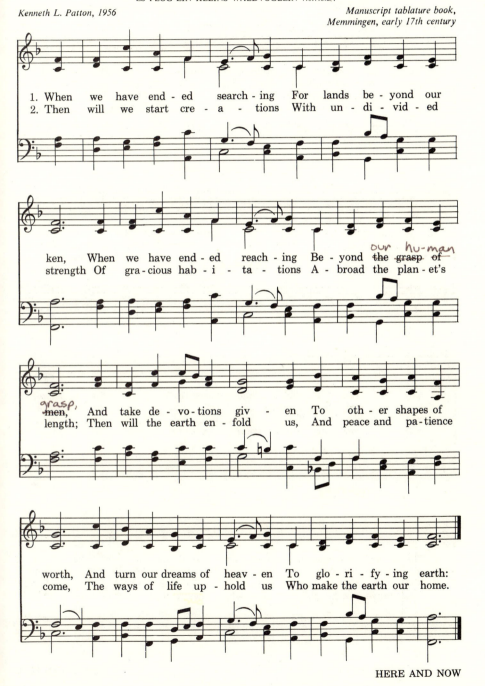

# 181 When We Have Ended Searching

ES FLOG EIN KLEINS WALDVÖGLEIN 7.6.7.6.D.

Kenneth L. Patton, 1956

*Manuscript tablature book,*
*Memmingen, early 17th century*

1. When we have end - ed search - ing For lands be - yond our
2. Then will we start cre - a - tions With un - di - vid - ed

ken, When we have end - ed reach - ing Be - yond the grasp of *our hu-man*
strength Of gra - cious hab - i - ta - tions A - broad the plan - et's

*grasp,*
men, And take de - vo - tions giv - en To oth - er shapes of
length; Then will the earth en - fold us, And peace and pa - tience

worth, And turn our dreams of heav - en To glo - ri - fy - ing earth:
come, The ways of life up - hold us Who make the earth our home.

HERE AND NOW

## 182 The Amplitude of Space

WHEELOCK 12.12.12.12.12.

*From John Hall Wheelock, 1911*  ·  *Robert L. Sanders, 1961*

1. The am - pli - tude of space comes down to your own door, And,
2. Not in some world be - yond lies won - der, nor a - bove, Nor
3. Be - tween your birth and death, here in this womb of race, A -
4. While with your gen - er - a - tion you go hurry - ing by, Have

e - qual with the stars, the com - mon and the street Are
throned a - mong the spheres, nor set for days to be; But
cross this field of world, from you to far - thest end, And
you no word for all, of pure and val - orous breath? Oh,

part of beau - ty's light that shines from shore to shore.
o - ver and be - neath, or if you rest or move,
scat - tered like the flowers, the myr - iad face on face,
how the com - mon doom trans - fig - ures des - ti - ny!

The u - ni - verse di - vine lies round us at our feet— All
Ex - tends the shin - ing fact, star - ry in - fin - i - ty, And
The lives, like to your fate, of lov - er and of friend— Have
How brave the thought of all who pass through life and death, How

HERE AND NOW

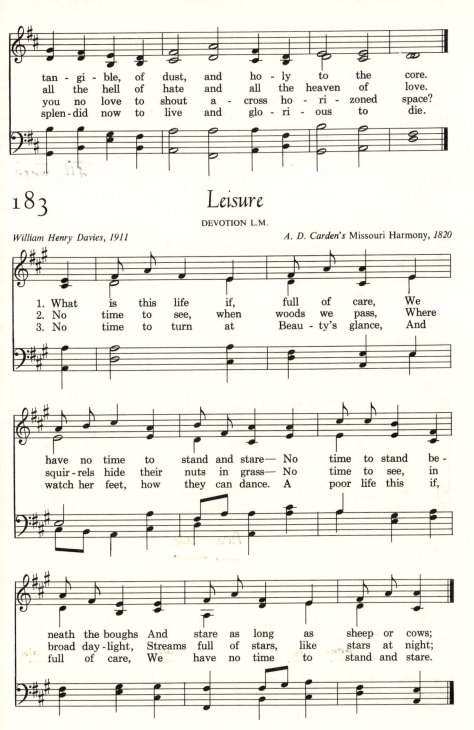

tan - gi - ble, of dust, and ho - ly to the core.
all the hell of hate and all the heaven of love.
you no love to shout a - cross ho - ri - zoned space?
splen - did now to live and glo - ri - ous to die.

## 183 *Leisure*

### DEVOTION L.M.

*William Henry Davies, 1911*

*A. D. Carden's* Missouri Harmony, *1820*

1. What is this life if, full of care, We
2. No time to see, when woods we pass, Where
3. No time to turn at Beau - ty's glance, And

have no time to stand and stare— No time to stand be -
squir - rels hide their nuts in grass— No time to see, in
watch her feet, how they can dance. A poor life this if,

neath the boughs And stare as long as sheep or cows;
broad day - light, Streams full of stars, like stars at night;
full of care, We have no time to stand and stare.

HERE AND NOW

## 184 Every Night and Every Morn

THE CALL 7.7.7.7.

*William Blake, ca. 1803*

*Ralph Vaughan Williams, 1911; adapted*

1. Ev - ery night and ev - ery morn Some to
2. Joy and woe are wo - ven fine, Cloth - ing
3. It is right it should be so: ~~Man was~~ *All were*

mis - er - y are born; Ev - ery morn and ev - ery
for the soul di - vine: Un - der ev - ery grief and
made for joy and woe; And when this we right - ly

night Some are born to sweet de - light.
pine Runs a joy with silk - en twine.
know, Safe - ly through the world we go.

## 185 Happy *Are We* ~~the~~ Man

ALDWINKLE 10.8.8.12.

*Horace (65–8 B.C.), Ode III, 29*
*From paraphrase by John Dryden, 1685*

*Wolfgang Wessnitzer, 1665; adapted*

Hap - py ~~the~~ *are* ~~man~~ *we,* and hap - py ~~he~~ *we* a - lone, ~~He~~ *We*

HERE AND NOW

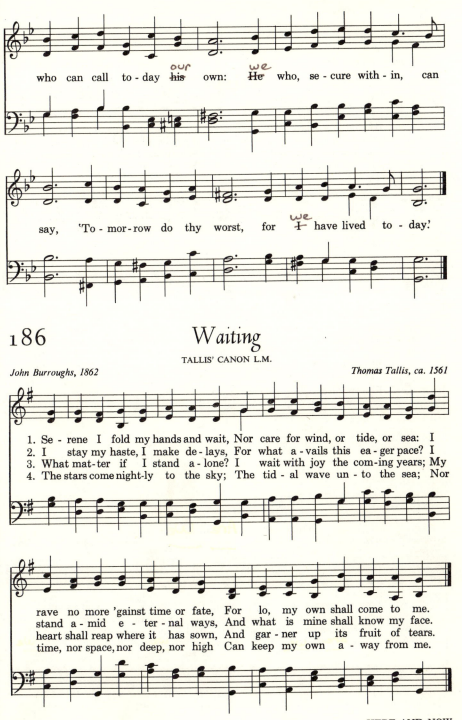

who can call to-day our own: We who, se-cure with-in, can say, 'To-mor-row do thy worst, for we have lived to-day.'

**186** ## Waiting

TALLIS' CANON L.M.

*John Burroughs, 1862*

*Thomas Tallis, ca. 1561*

1. Se - rene I fold my hands and wait, Nor care for wind, or tide, or sea: I
2. I stay my haste, I make de - lays, For what a - vails this ea - ger pace? I
3. What mat - ter if I stand a - lone? I wait with joy the com-ing years; My
4. The stars come night-ly to the sky; The tid - al wave un - to the sea; Nor

rave no more 'gainst time or fate, For lo, my own shall come to me.
stand a - mid e - ter - nal ways, And what is mine shall know my face.
heart shall reap where it has sown, And gar - ner up its fruit of tears.
time, nor space, nor deep, nor high Can keep my own a - way from me.

HERE AND NOW

## 187 Now and Here

ST. MAGNUS C.M.

*John Greenleaf Whittier, 1859*                                          *Attributed to Jeremiah Clark, 1707*

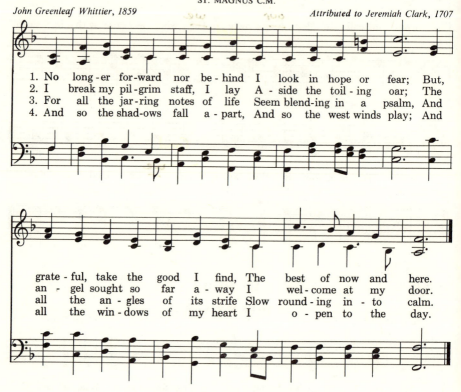

1. No long-er for-ward nor be-hind I look in hope or fear; But,
2. I break my pil-grim staff, I lay A-side the toil-ing oar; The
3. For all the jar-ring notes of life Seem blend-ing in a psalm, And
4. And so the shad-ows fall a-part, And so the west winds play; And

grate-ful, take the good I find, The best of now and here.
an - gel sought so far a - way I wel-come at my door.
all the an-gles of its strife Slow round-ing in - to calm.
all the win-dows of my heart I o - pen to the day.

## 188 The Larger Faith

CHRISTUS DER IST MEIN LEBEN C.M.

*Frederick Lucian Hosmer, 1879*                                          *Melchior Vulpius, 1609; adapted*

1. We pray no more, made low-ly wise, For mir - a - cle and sign; A -
2. "Lo here! lo there!" no more we cry, Di - vid - ing with our call The
3. We turn from seek-ing thee a - far, And in un-wont-ed ways, To
4. And no - bler yet shall du - ty grow, And more shall wor-ship be, When

HERE AND NOW

noint our eyes to see with-in The com-mon, the di - vine.
man - tle of thy pres - ence, Lord *(God)*, That seam - less cov - ers all.
build from out our dai - ly lives The tem - ples of thy praise.
thou art found in all our life, And all our life in thee.

**189**     The Son of ~~Man~~ *God*

MEIN' SEEL', O GOTT L.M.

*Frank Mason North, 1903*        *Bartholomäus Gesius, 1603*

1. Where cross - the crowd - ed ways of life, Where
2. In haunts of wretch - ed - ness and need, On
3. O Mas - ter, from the moun - tain - side, Make

sound the cries of race and clan, A - bove the noise of
shad - owed thresh-olds dark with fears, From paths where hide the
haste to heal these hearts of pain; A - mong these rest - less

self - ish strife, We hear thy voice, O Son of ~~Man~~. *God*
lures of greed, We catch the vi - sion of thy tears.
throngs a - bide, O tread the cit - y's streets a - gain.

IN TIME TO COME

# 190 These Things Shall Be

TRURO L.M.

*John Addington Symonds, 1880*                    *Thomas Williams'* Psalmodia Evangelica, *1789*

1. These things shall be: a loft - ier race Than e'er the
2. They shall be gen - tle, brave, and strong To spill no
3. They shall be sim - ple in their homes, And splen - did

world hath known shall rise, With flame of free - dom in their
drop of blood, but dare All that may plant man's lord - ship
in their pub - lic ways, Fill - ing the man - sions of the

souls, And light of sci - ence in their eyes.
earth and fire and sea and air.
state With mu - sic and with hymns of praise.

4. Nation with nation, land with land,
   Unarmed shall live as comrades free;
   In every heart and brain shall throb
   The pulse of one fraternity.

5. New arts shall bloom of loftier mould,
   And mightier music thrill the skies,
   And every life shall be a song
   When all the earth is paradise.

IN TIME TO COME

# 191 Wonders Still the World Shall Witness

IN BABILONE 8.7.8.7.D.

*Jacob Trapp, 1932*

Oude en nieuwe Hollantse Boerenlities
en Contradanseu, *ca. 1710*

1. Won - ders still the world shall wit - ness Nev - er known by *those* men of old,
2. *They* Men shall rule with wing - ed free - dom Worlds of health and hu - man good,
3. For a spir - it then shall move them We but vague - ly ap - pre - hend—

Nev - er dreamed by an - cient sag - es, How - so - ev - er free and bold.
Worlds of com - merce, worlds of sci - ence, All made one and un - der - stood.
Aims mag - nif - i - cent and ho - ly, Mak - ing joy and la - bor friend.

Sons and daugh - ters shall in - her - it Won - drous arts to us un - known,
They shall know a world trans - fig - ured, Which our eyes but dim - ly see;
Then shall bloom in song and fra - grance Har - mo - ny of thought and deed,

When the dawn of peace its splen - dor O - ver all the world has thrown.
They shall make its towns and wood - lands Beau - ti - ful from sea to sea.
Fruits of peace and love and jus - tice— Where to - day we plant the seed.

IN TIME TO COME

## 192 Hail the Glorious Golden City

HYFRYDOL 8.7.8.7.D.

*From Felix Adler, 1878*

*Rowland Hugh Prichard, 1855*

1. Hail the glo-rious gold-en cit-y, Pic-tured by the
2. We are build-ers of that cit-y. All our joys and
3. And the work that we have build-ed, Oft with bleed-ing

seers of old: Ev-er-last-ing light shines o'er it,
all our groans Help to rear its shin-ing ram-parts;
hands and tears, Oft in er-ror, oft in an-guish,

Won-drous things of it are told. Wise and right-eous men and
All our lives are build-ing-stones. Wheth-er hum-ble or ex-
Will not per-ish with our years: It will live and shine trans-

wom-en Dwell with-in its gleam-ing wall; Wrong is
alt-ed, All are called to task di-vine;
fig-ured In the fi-nal reign of right: It will

IN TIME TO COME

ban - ished from its bor - ders, Jus - tice reigns su - preme o'er all.
aid a - like to car - ry For - ward one sub - lime de - sign.
pass in - to the splen - dors Of the cit - y of the light.

# 193     *Children of Tomorrow*

VOM HIMMEL HOCH L.M.

*Zona Gale, 1931*          *Valentin Schumann's* Geistliche Lieder, *1539*

1. Come, chil - dren of to - mor - row, come! New glo - ry dawns up -
2. From plain and field and town there sound The stir - ring ru - mors
3. Di - vid - ed we have long with-stood The love that is our

on the world; The war - ring ban - ners must be furled, The
of the day; Old wrongs and bur - dens must make way For
com - mon speech. The com - rade cry of each to each Is

earth be - come our com - mon home.
men us to tread the com - mon ground.
call - ing us to hu - man - hood.

IN TIME TO COME

# 194 Hear, Hear, O Ye Nations

MILTON 11.11.11.11.

*From Frederick Lucian Hosmer, 1909*

*Jacob Kimball, 1793*

1. Hear, hear, O ye na-tions, and hear-ing o-bey The cry from the past and the call of to-day. Earth wea-ries and wastes with her fresh life out-poured, The glut of the can-non, the spoil of the sword.

2. Lo, dawns a new e-ra, tran-scend-ing the old, The po-et's rapt vi-sion, by proph-et fore-told. From war's grim tra-di-tion it mak-eth ap-peal To serv-ice of all in a world's com-mon-weal.

3. The home, school, and al-tar, the mill and the mart, The work-ers in sci-ence, the mak-ers of art, Peace-cir-cled and shel-tered, shall join to cre-ate The man-i-fold life of the firm-build-ed state.

4. Then, then shall the em-pire of right o-ver wrong Be shield to the weak and a curb to the strong; Then jus-tice pre-vail and, the bat-tle-flags furled, The high court of na-tions give law to the world.

IN TIME TO COME

195

The Parliament of ~~Man~~ Peace

HYMN TO JOY 8.7.8.7.D.

*Alfred Lord Tennyson, 1842*

*Ludwig van Beethoven, 1823; adapted*

1. Not in vain the dis-tance bea-cons. For-ward, for-ward let us range.
2. Oh, we see the cres-cent prom-ise of ~~man's~~ our spir-it has not set;
3. Yea, we dip in-to the fu-ture, far as hu-man eye can see,

Let the great world spin for-ev-er down the ring-ing grooves of change;
An-cient founts of in-spi-ra-tion well through all ~~his~~ our fan-cy yet;
See the vi-sion of the world, and all the won-der that shall be,

Through the shad-ow of the globe we sweep a-head to heights sub-lime—
And we doubt not through the a-ges one in-creas-ing pur-pose runs,
Hear the war-drum throb no long-er, see the bat-tle flags all furled,

We, the heirs of all the a-ges, in the fore-most files of time.
And the thoughts of all are wid-ened with the pro-cess of the suns.
In the par-lia-ment of ~~man~~ peace, the fed-er-a-tion of the world.

IN TIME TO COME

# 196

## Turn Back, O Friend ~~Man~~

OLD 124th 10.10.10.10.10.10.

*Clifford Bax, 1916*                      *Genevan Psalter, 1551*

1. Turn back, O Friend ~~man~~, for-swear thy fool-ish ways. Old now is
2. Earth might be fair and all ~~men~~ the glad and wise. Age aft-er
3. Earth shall be fair, and all the peo-ple one; Nor till that

earth, and none may count its ~~her~~ days; Yet thou, a ~~her~~ child, whose
age their trag-ic em-pires rise, Built while they dream, and
hour shall God's whole will be done. Now, e-ven now, once

head is crowned with flame, Still wilt not hear thine in-ner God pro-
in that dream-ing weep; Would they ~~them~~ but wake from out their haunt-ed
more from earth to sky, Peals forth in joy that ~~man's~~ old un-daunt-ed

claim— "Turn back, O Friend ~~man~~, for-swear thy fool-ish ways."
sleep, Earth might be fair, and all be ~~men~~ glad and wise.
cry— "Earth shall be fair, and all the ~~her~~ folk be one."

IN TIME TO COME

# 197 The World-tree

YGDRASIL 10.10.10.10.

Ridgely Torrence, 1952

Henry Leland Clarke, 1960

1. The sky has gath - ered the flowers of sun - set. The earth is red with the dew of slaugh - ter. The shores are ringed with the steel of on - set. And dark - ness cov - ers the weap - oned wa - ter.

2. The world - tree sick - ens be - yond all know - ing. The worm is wast - ing the leaves that wreath it. The bough is dry - ing; the sap is slow - ing; For ha - treds gnaw in their hells be - neath it.

3. On one sole ground will the world - tree flour - ish, On earth un - ar - mored a - gainst its bear - ing, Its glo - ries free and its strength to nour - ish The world - wide lands in a com - mon shar - ing.

4. In kin - ship on - ly, with all earth gar - dened, The rav - ished leaf may be stayed in thin - ning, The ston - y ground at the root un - hard - ened, The boughs be green for a new be - gin - ning.

IN TIME TO COME

# 198 *Years Are Coming*

PLEADING SAVIOR 8.7.8.7.D.

Adin Ballou, 1849

*Joshua Leavitt's* Christian Lyre, *1830*

1. Years are com-ing—speed them on - ward, When the sword shall gath-er rust,
2. Years are com-ing when for - ev - er War's dread ban-ner shall be furled,

And the hel - met, lance, and fal-chion Sleep at last in si - lent dust.
And the an - gel Peace be wel-comed, Re - gent of a hap - py world.

Earth has heard too long of bat - tle, Heard the trump-et's voice too long;
Hail with song that glo - rious e - ra When the sword shall gath-er rust,

But an - oth - er age ad - vanc - es, Seers fore-told in an - cient song.
And the hel - met, lance, and fal - chion Sleep at last in si - lent dust.

IN TIME TO COME

# 199 The Time Shall Come

WINDSOR FOREST 10.10.10.10.

*From Alexander Pope, 1713*

*Henry Leland Clarke, 1960*

1. The time shall come when, free as seas of wind, Un - bound - ed life shall flow for *hu-* ~~all~~ man - kind, Whole na - tions en - ter with each swell - ing tide, And seas but join the re - gions they di - vide.

2. O stretch thy reign, fair Peace, from shore to shore, Till con - quest cease, and slav - ery be no more. Earth's dis - tant ends one glo - ry shall be - hold, And the new world launch forth to seek the old.

IN TIME TO COME

200    # We Move in Faith

MERTHYR TYDVIL L.M.D.

*Malcolm Quin, 1882*                                        *Joseph Parry, 1870*

1. We move in faith to un - seen goals; We strive in pa - tience
2. But, e - ven as we fail, our aim Grows larg - er from our

through the night, Which weighs up - on our doubt - ing souls,
high at - tempt; And while we suf - fer love's large blame,

To some great realm of love and light. For still the ig - no -
And rea - son's most au - gust con - tempt, We grow in great - ness

rance that kills, And still the ha - treds that di - vide, And still the
of de - sign, In high - er powers of pa - tient toil, In hopes that

IN TIME TO COME

strife of war - ring wills Sub-due our strength, and check our pride.
seize the se - cret sign Of far - off joys which nought may foil.

**201**

# Let There Be Light

TRANSYLVANIA L.M.

*William Merrill Vories, 1911*

*Hungarian melody, 16th century; arranged*

1. Let there be light, Lord God of Hosts; Let there be
2. With - in our pas - sioned hearts in - still The calm that
3. Give us the peace of vi - sion clear To see our in
4. Let woe and waste of war - fare cease, That use - ful

wis - dom on the earth; Let broad hu - man - i - ty have
end - eth dead - ly strife; Make us thy min - is - ters of
broth-ers' good our own, To joy and suf - fer not a -
la - bor yet may build Its homes with love and laugh - ter

birth; Let there be deeds, in - stead of boasts.
life; Purge us from lusts that curse and kill.
lone: The love that cast - eth out all fear.
filled. God, give thy way - ward chil - dren peace.

IN TIME TO COME

# 202
## Sound over All Waters

**FOUR WINDS** 11.11.11.11.11.11.11.

*From John Greenleaf Whittier, 1873*　　　　　　　　　　　　　　　*Arthur Foote II, 1958*

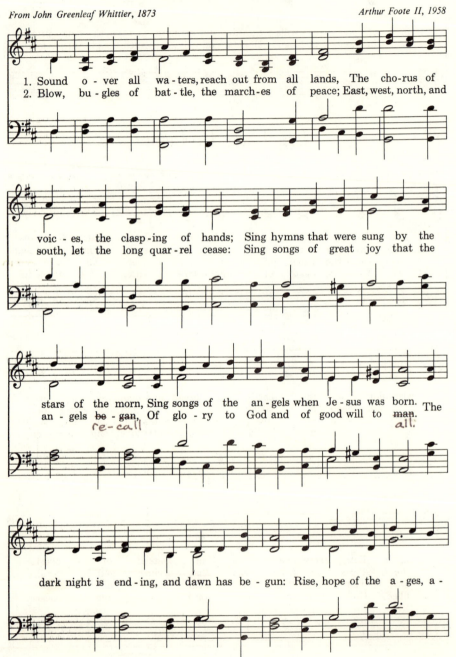

1. Sound o-ver all wa-ters, reach out from all lands, The cho-rus of
2. Blow, bu-gles of bat-tle, the march-es of peace; East, west, north, and

voic-es, the clasp-ing of hands; Sing hymns that were sung by the
south, let the long quar-rel cease: Sing songs of great joy that the

stars of the morn, Sing songs of the an-gels when Je-sus was born. The
an-gels be-gan, Of glo-ry to God and of good will to man. The
*re-call* ... *all.*

dark night is end-ing, and dawn has be-gun: Rise, hope of the a-ges, a-

IN TIME TO COME

rise like the sun, All speech flow to mu-sic, all hearts beat as one!

**203**

# Quest of the Ages

CONSOLATION 8.6.8.6.8.6.

*Kenneth L. Patton, 1956*

*John Wyeth's*
*Repository of Sacred Music, Part Second, 1813*

1. Quest of the a - ges, goal of *all* men, Where life and good-ness thrive, Where
2. Heirs of the a - ges, *we have* man has seen The gold - en e - ras spill; A

peace and eq - ui - ty shall reign, And all be free to strive; This
thou - sand cen - tu - ries have been The test - ing of *our* his will; A

quest will be *our* man's ache and gain As long as *we* men shall live.
thou - sand cen - tu - ries to come Will find *us* him work-ing still.

IN TIME TO COME

# 204 The City of our God

ICH DANK' DIR SCHON 8.7.8.7.

William George Tarrant, 1914      Michael Praetorius' Musae Sionae, VIII, 1610

PART I

1. I saw the cit - y of our God, E - ter - nal
2. Four-square to all the lands it stood, And, through its
3. There princes came on pil - grim - age With mil - lion -
4. At peace with - in those man - sions fair They dwelt with

its foun - da - tion, On high its gleam - ing
por - tals wend - ing; The true, the brave, the
hand - ed la - bor; There came the sim - ple
one an - oth - er, And ev - ery one was

tur - rets soared, The joy of ev - ery na - tion.
wise, the good Flowed on, a stream un - end - ing.
and the sage, Each hap - py with his neigh - bor.
wel - come there Each sister and Each broth - er.

PART II

5. A temple of our God I saw,
   All beautiful and holy,
   Its light was love, its highest law
   Compassion for the lowly.

6. And thence arose a mighty voice
   Of countless voices blended,
   The song of singers that rejoice,
   Their night of sorrow ended.

7. I saw that city from afar,
   A city of salvation,
   And still it shineth like a star
   To every generation.

8. And I, a pilgrim too, would press
   Where God the host is guiding,
   To reach the gates of righteousness,
   A citizen abiding.

IN TIME TO COME

# 205 The Pageant of the Years

O JESU, WARUM LEGST DU MIR 8.6.8.6.8.8.

*John Haynes Holmes, 1921*                    *Johann Balthasar Reimann, 1747*

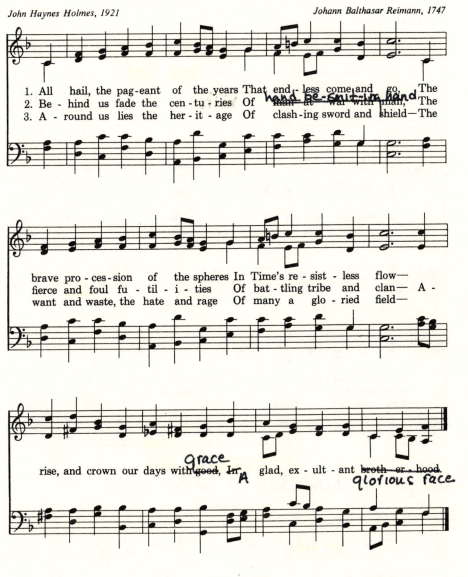

1. All hail, the pag-eant of the years That end-less come and go, The
2. Be-hind us fade the cen-tu-ries Of man at war with man, The
3. A-round us lies the her-it-age Of clash-ing sword and shield—The

brave pro-ces-sion of the spheres In Time's re-sist-less flow—
fierce and foul fu-til-i-ties Of bat-tling tribe and clan— A-
want and waste, the hate and rage Of many a glo-ried field—

rise, and crown our days with good, In glad, ex-ult-ant broth-er-hood.

4. Behold, there looms the mystery
   Of love diviner far,
   There speaks the steadfast prophecy
   Of nations freed from war—
   Arise, and crown our days with good,
   In glad, exultant brotherhood.

5. The aeons come, the aeons go,
   The stars nor pause nor cease;
   On wings of silence, soft as snow,
   Shall come the boon of peace.
   Arise, and crown our days with good,
   In glad, exultant brotherhood.

IN TIME TO COME

## 206 Between Midnight and Morning

*From Owen Seaman, 1914*  PEACE 10.10.10.6.  *Revivalist, 1869*
*Adapted by George Brandon, 1958*

1. You that have faith to look with fear-less eyes Be-
2. Re-joice, what-ev-er an-guish rend your heart, That
3. That you may tell your sons (heirs) who see the light High

yond this trag-e-dy, a world at strife, And trust that out of
God has given you, for a price-less dower, To live in these great
in the heaven, their her-it-age to take: "I saw the powers of

death and night shall rise The dawn of am-pler life;
times and have your part In free-dom's crown-ing hour;
dark-ness put to flight; I saw the morn-ing break."

## 207 Bend Back the Lance's Point

FESTAL SONG S.M.

*From John Ruskin, ca. 1865*  *William H. Walter, 1872*

1. Bend back the lance-'s point, And break the hel-met's bar; A
2. Put off your mail, ye kings (soldiers), And beat your brands to dust; A
3. The time for wrath is past, And near the time for rest; Let

IN TIME TO COME

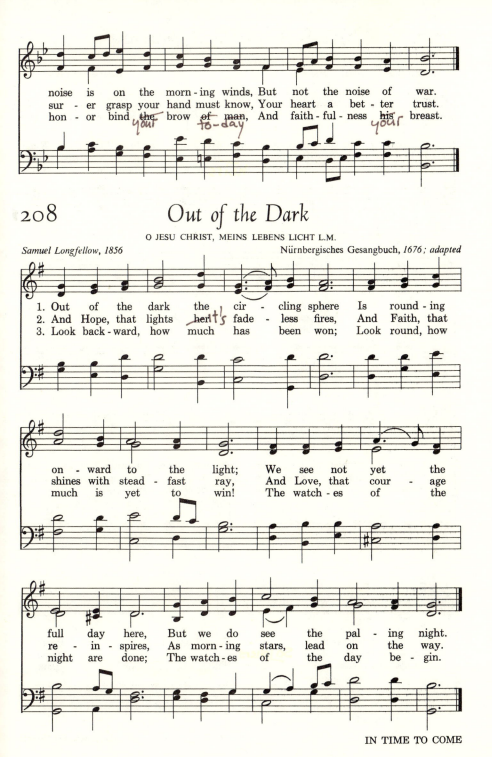

# Now Is the Time Approaching

WEBB 7.6.7.6.D.

*From Jane Laurie Borthwick, 1859*　　　　　　　　　　　　　　*George James Webb, 1837*

1. Now is the time ap-proach - ing, By proph-ets long fore - told, When
2. Let all that now di - vides us Re - move and pass a - way, Like
3. O long - ex-pect-ed dawn - ing, Come with thy cheer - ing ray! Yet

all shall dwell to - geth - er, One shep-herd and one fold. Let
shad-ows of the morn - ing Be - fore the blaze of day. Let
shall the morn-ing bright - en, The shad-ows flee a - way. O

war be learned no long - er, Let strife and tu - mult cease, All
all that now u - nites us More sweet and last - ing prove, A
sweet an-tic - i - pa - tion! It cheers the watch-ers on, To

earth his bless-ed king - dom, The Lord and Prince of Peace.
clos - er bond of un - ion, In a blest land of love.
pray, and hope, and la - bor, Till the dark night be gone.

IN TIME TO COME

210 Thy Kingdom Come *(Glory)*

MEIN SCHÖPFER, STEH' MIR BEI 6.6.6.6.D.

*Frederick Lucian Hosmer, 1905*

*Franz Heinrich Christoph Meyer, 1741; adapted*

1. Thy king-dom come *(glory)*, O Lord *(God)*, Wide cir-cling as the sun; Ful-
2. Speed, speed the longed-for time Fore-told by rap-tured seers— The

fill thine an-cient word And make the na-tions one— One
proph-e-cy sub-lime, The hope of all the years— Till

in the bond of peace, The serv-ice glad and free Of
rise at last, to span Its firm foun-da-tions broad, The

truth and right-eous-ness, Of love and eq-ui-ty.
com-mon-wealth *(the plan)* of man, The cit-y of our God.

IN TIME TO COME

**211**

# Pioneers, O Pioneers!

PIONEERS Irregular

*From Walt Whitman, 1865*

*Irving Lowens, 1955*

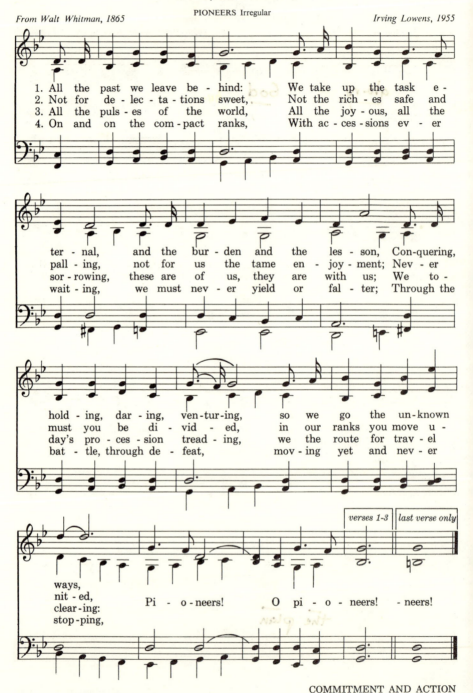

1. All the past we leave be - hind: We take up the task e -
2. Not for de - lec - ta - tions sweet, Not the rich - es safe and
3. All the puls - es of the world, All the joy - ous, all the
4. On and on the com - pact ranks, With ac - ces - sions ev - er

ter - nal, and the bur - den and the les - son, Con-quering,
pall - ing, not for us the tame en - joy - ment; Nev - er
sor - rowing, these are of us, they are with us; We to -
wait - ing, we must nev - er yield or fal - ter; Through the

hold - ing, dar - ing, ven-tur-ing, so we go the un-known
must you be di - vid - ed, in our ranks you move u -
day's pro - ces - sion tread - ing, we the route for trav - el
bat - tle, through de - feat, mov - ing yet and nev - er

*verses 1-3* | *last verse only*

ways,
nit - ed, Pi - o - neers! O pi - o - neers! - neers!
clear - ing:
stop - ping,

COMMITMENT AND ACTION

# 212 Gird on Thy Sword, O ~~Man~~ *Human*

ERFYNIAD 10.10.10.10.

Robert Bridges, 1898

*Ieuan Gwyllt's* Llyfr Tonau Cynulleidfaol, *1859*
Harmonized by David Evans, 1931

1. Gird on thy sword, O hu-man, thy strength en - due,
   In fair de - sire thine earth - born joy re - new.
   Live thou thy life be - neath the mak - ing sun
   Till beau - ty, truth, and love in thee are one.

2. Through thou-sand a - ges hath thy child - hood run:
   On time - less ru - in hath thy glo - ry been:
   From the for - got - ten night of loves for - done
   Thou ris - est in the dawn of hopes un - seen.

3. High - er and high - er shall thy thoughts as - pire,
   Un - to the stars of heaven, and pass a - way,
   And earth re - new the buds of thy de - sire
   In fleet - ing blooms of ev - er - last - ing day.

4. Thy work with beau - ty crown, thy life with love;
   Thy mind with truth up - lift to God a - bove:
   For whom all is, from whom was all be - gun,
   In whom all beau - ty, truth, and love are one.

COMMITMENT AND ACTION

## 213 God's Trumpet Wakes

ALL SAINTS NEW C.M.D.

*From Samuel Longfellow, 1864*  
*Henry Stephen Cutler, 1872*

1. God's trump-et wakes the slum-ber-ing world: Now, each man to his post! The
2. He who, no an-ger on his tongue, Nor an-y i-dle boast, His
3. He who is read-y for the cross, The cause de-spised loves most, Who

glo-rious ban-ner is un-furled: Who joins the might-y host? He
wit-ness bears a-gainst the wrong—He joins the sa-cred host. He
shuns not pain or shame or loss—He joins the mar-tyr host. God's

who, in feal-ty to the truth, And count-ing all the cost, Doth
who, with calm, un-daunt-ed will, Counts not the bat-tle lost, But,
trump-et wakes the slum-ber-ing world: Now, each man to his post! The

con-se-crate his gen-erous youth—He joins the no-ble host.
though de-feat-ed, bat-tles still—He joins the faith-ful host.
glo-rious ban-ner is un-furled: Who joins the might-y host?

COMMITMENT AND ACTION

# 214 The Voice of God

KING'S LYNN 7.6.7.6.D.

*John Haynes Holmes, 1913*

*English melody*
*Arranged by Ralph Vaughan Williams, 1906*

1. The voice of God is call - ing Its sum-mons un - to men; As
2. I hear my peo - ple cry - ing In cot and mine and slum; No
3. We heed, O Lord, thy sum - mons, And an-swer: Here are we! Send
4. From ease and plen - ty save us, From pride of place ab - solve; Purge

once he spake in Zi - on, So now he speaks a - gain. Whom
field or mart is si - lent, No cit - y street is dumb. I
us up - on thine er - rand, Let us thy serv - ants be! Our
us of low de - si - re, Lift us to high re - solve. Take

shall I send to suc - cor My peo - ple in their need? Whom
see my peo - ple fall - ing In dark-ness and de - spair. Whom
strength is dust and ash - es, Our years a pass - ing hour; But
us, and make us ho - ly, Teach us thy will and way. Speak,

shall I send to loos - en The bonds of shame and greed?
shall I send to shat - ter The fet - ters which they bear?
thou canst use our weak - ness To mag - ni - fy thy power.
and, be - hold! we an - swer, Com - mand, and we o - bey!

COMMITMENT AND ACTION

## 215 Forward Through the Ages

ST. GERTRUDE 6.5.6.5. Triple

*Frederick Lucian Hosmer, 1908*                    *Arthur Seymour Sullivan, 1871*

1. For-ward through the a - ges, In un - bro - ken line, Move the faith-ful
2. Wid - er grows the king - dom, Reign of love and light; For it we must
3. Not a - lone we con - quer, Not a - lone we fall; In each loss or

spir - its At the call di - vine: Gifts in dif-fering meas - ure,
la - bor, Till our faith is sight. Proph-ets have pro -claimed it,
tri - umph Lose or tri-umph all. Bound by God's far pur - pose

Hearts of one ac - cord, Man - i - fold the serv - ice, One the sure re-ward.
Mar - tyrs tes - ti - fied, Po - ets sung its glo - ry, He-roes for it died.
In one liv-ing whole, Move we on to - geth - er To the shin-ing goal.

For - ward through the a - ges, In un - bro - ken line,

COMMITMENT AND ACTION

Move the faith-ful spir - its At the call di - vine.

## 216 When Abraham Went Out of Ur

CONGLETON 10.10.10.10.

*Nancy Byrd Turner, 1935*            *Michael Wise, 1684*

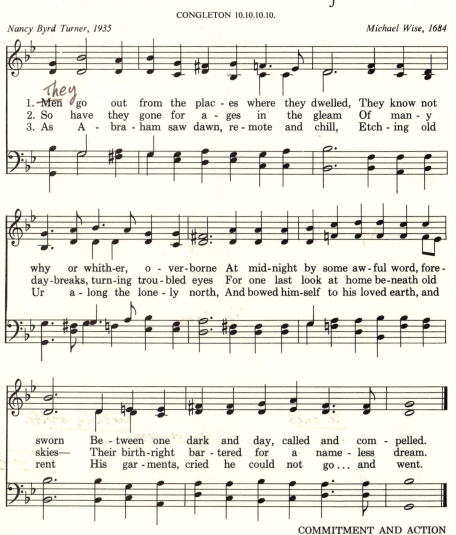

1. *They* Men go out from the plac - es where they dwelled, They know not
2. So have they gone for a - ges in the gleam Of man - y
3. As A - bra - ham saw dawn, re - mote and chill, Etch - ing old

why or whith-er, o - ver-borne At mid-night by some aw-ful word, fore-
day-breaks, turn-ing trou - bled eyes For one last look at home be-neath old
Ur a - long the lone - ly north, And bowed him-self to his loved earth, and

sworn Be - tween one dark and day, called and com - pelled.
skies— Their birth-right bar - tered for a name - less dream.
rent His gar - ments, cried he could not go ... and went.

COMMITMENT AND ACTION

**217** **God Send Us ~~Men~~** All

WAYLAND L.M.

*From Frederick John Gillman, 1909*  George Blackburn Holsinger, 1902

1. God send us ~~men~~ all whose aim will be, Not to de-fend some
2. God send us ~~men~~ a - lert and quick These loft - y pre - cepts
3. God send us ~~men~~ of stead - fast will, Pa - tient, cou - ra - geous,
4. God send us ~~men~~ with hearts a - blaze, All truth to love, all

an - cient creed, But to live out the laws of right
to trans - late, Un - til the laws of right be - come
strong, and true; With vi - sion clear, and mind e - quipped
wrong to hate; These are the pa - triots na - tions need,

In ev - ery thought and word and deed.
The laws and hab - its of the state.
~~His~~ Thy will to learn, ~~his~~ thy work to do.
These are the bul - warks of the state.

**218** **Rise Up, ~~O Men~~ Ye Ones of God**

FESTAL SONG S.M.

*William Pierson Merrill, 1911*  *William H. Walter, 1872*

1. Rise up, ~~O men~~ Ye ones of God: Have done with ~~less - er things~~ earthly strife; Give
2. Rise up, ~~O men~~ of God: ~~His~~ The king - dom tar - ries long; Bring
3. Rise up, ~~O men~~ of God: The church for you doth wait, Her

COMMITMENT AND ACTION

heart and soul and mind and strength To serve the ~~King~~ *Source* of ~~kings~~ *life*.
in the day of ~~broth-er-hood~~ And end the night of wrong.
strength un - e - qual to ~~her~~ *its* task: Rise up, and make ~~her~~ *it* great.

**219**

# The Open Way

FESTUS L.M.

John Coleman Adams, 1911

J. A. Freylinghausen's
Neues geistreiches Gesangbuch, 1714; adapted

1. We praise thee, God, for har - vests earned, The
2. We praise thee for the har - bor's lee, For
3. We praise thee for the jour - ney's end, The

fruits of la - bor gar - nered in; But praise thee more for
moor - ings safe in wa - ters still; But more the leagues of
inn, all warmth and light and cheer; But more for length - ening

soil un - turned From which the yield is yet to win.
o - pen sea, Where fa - voring gales our can - vas fill.
roads that wend Through dust and heat and hill - tops clear.

COMMITMENT AND ACTION

220 Once to Every ~~Man~~ Soul and Nation

EBENEZER 8.7.8.7.D.

*From James Russell Lowell, 1844*

*Thomas John Williams, 1890*

1. Once to ev-ery ~~man~~ Soul and na-tion comes the mo-ment to de-cide,
2. Though the cause of e - vil pros-per, yet 'tis truth a - lone is strong;

In the strife of truth with false-hood, for the good or
Though, ~~her~~ Truth's por - tion be the scaf-fold, and up - on the

e - vil side: Then to stand with truth is no - ble,
throne be wrong. Then it is the brave ~~man~~ one choos - es,

when we share ~~her~~ the wretch-ed crust; Ere ~~her~~ the cause bring
while the cow - ard stands a - side, Till the mul - ti -

COMMITMENT AND ACTION

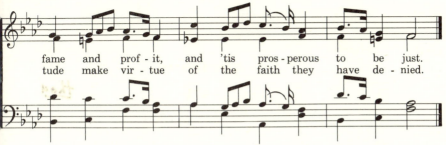

fame and prof - it, and 'tis pros - perous to be just.
tude make vir - tue of the faith they have de - nied.

# 221 Creation's Lord, We Give Thee Thanks

VOM HIMMEL HOCH L.M.

William De Witt Hyde, 1903

Valentin Schumann's Geistliche Lieder, 1539

1. Cre - a - tion's Lord, we give thee thanks That this thy world is
2. That thou hast not yet finished man, That we are in the
3. Be - yond the pres - ent sin and shame, Wrong's bit - ter, cru - el,

in - com - plete, That bat - tle calls our mar - shaled ranks, That
mak - ing still— As friends who share the Mak - er's plan; As
scorch - ing blight, We see the beck - oning vi - sion flame, The

work a - waits our hands and feet;
sons who know the Fa - ther's will.
bless - ed King - dom of the Right.

4. What though the Kingdom long delay,
   And still with haughty foes must cope?
   It gives us that for which to pray,
   A field for toil and faith and hope.

5. Since what we choose is what we are,
   And what we love we yet shall be,
   The goal may ever shine afar—
   The will to win it makes us free.

COMMITMENT AND ACTION

## 222 Abide Not in the Realm of Dreams

DUKE STREET L.M.

*From William Henry Burleigh (1812-1871)*    *John Hatton, 1793*

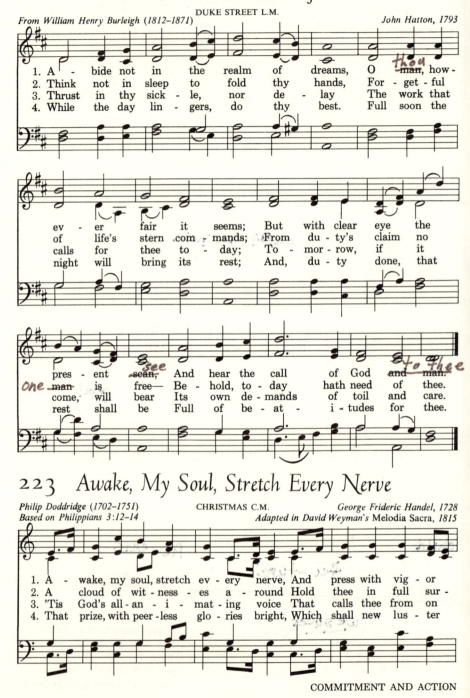

1. A - bide not in the realm of dreams, O man, how- *(thou)*
2. Think not in sleep to fold thy hands, For - get - ful
3. Thrust in thy sick - le, nor de - lay The work that
4. While the day lin - gers, do thy best. Full soon the

ev - er fair it seems; But with clear eye the
of life's stern com - mands; From du - ty's claim no
calls for thee to - day; To - mor - row, if it
night will bring its rest; And, du - ty done, that

pres - ent scan, *(one man, see)* And hear the call of God and man. *(to thee)*
is free— Be - hold, to - day hath need of thee.
come, will bear Its own de - mands of toil and care.
rest shall be Full of be - at - i - tudes for thee.

## 223 Awake, My Soul, Stretch Every Nerve

*Philip Doddridge (1702-1751)*    CHRISTMAS C.M.    *George Frideric Handel, 1728*
*Based on Philippians 3:12-14*    *Adapted in David Weyman's* Melodia Sacra, 1815

1. A - wake, my soul, stretch ev - ery nerve, And press with vig - or
2. A cloud of wit - ness - es a - round Hold thee in full sur -
3. 'Tis God's all - an - i - mat - ing voice That calls thee from on
4. That prize, with peer - less glo - ries bright, Which shall new lus - ter

COMMITMENT AND ACTION

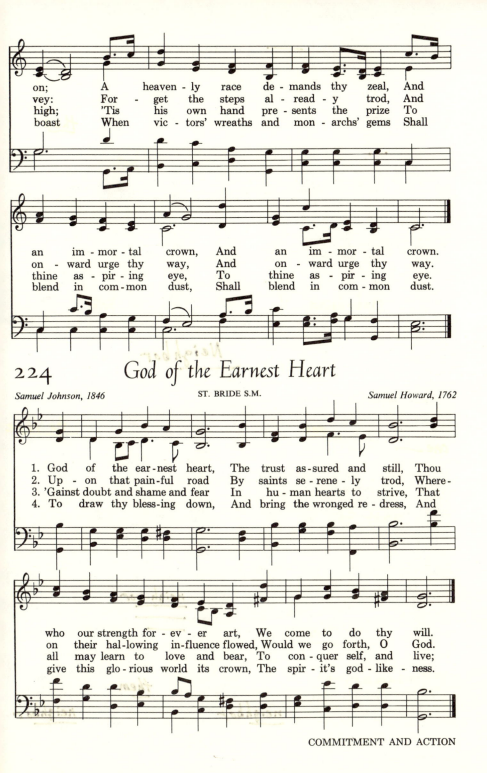

on; A heaven - ly race de - mands thy zeal, And
vey: For - get the steps al - read - y trod, And
high; 'Tis his own hand pre - sents the prize To
boast When vic - tors' wreaths and mon - archs' gems Shall

an im - mor - tal crown, And an im - mor - tal crown.
on - ward urge thy way, And on - ward urge thy way.
thine as - pir - ing eye, To thine as - pir - ing eye.
blend in com - mon dust, Shall blend in com - mon dust.

**224** *God of the Earnest Heart*

*Samuel Johnson, 1846*  ST. BRIDE S.M.  *Samuel Howard, 1762*

1. God of the ear - nest heart, The trust as - sured and still, Thou
2. Up - on that pain - ful road By saints se - rene - ly trod, Where -
3. 'Gainst doubt and shame and fear In hu - man hearts to strive, That
4. To draw thy bless - ing down, And bring the wronged re - dress, And

who our strength for - ev - er art, We come to do thy will.
on their hal - lowing in - fluence flowed, Would we go forth, O God.
all may learn to love and bear, To con - quer self, and live;
give this glo - rious world its crown, The spir - it's god - like - ness.

COMMITMENT AND ACTION

**225** *Let All ~~Men~~ Living in All Lands*

VOM HIMMEL HOCH L.M.

*Kenneth L. Patton, 1956*    *Valentin Schumann's* Geistliche Lieder, *1539*

Let all ~~men~~ liv-ing in all lands De-clare that fear and war are done—Joined

by the la-bor of their hands, In love and un-der-stand-ing, one.

**226** *Thy* ~~Brother~~ Neighbor

WOODLAWN 8.5.8.3.

*Theodore Chickering Williams, 1891*    *Robert L. Sanders, 1934*

1. When thy heart, with joy o'er-flow-ing, Sings a thank-ful
2. When the har-vest sheaves in-gath-ered Fill thy barns with
3. If thy soul, with power up-lift-ed, Yearn for glo-rious

prayer, In thy joy, O let thy ~~broth-er~~ neighbor With thee share.
store, To thy God and to thy ~~broth-er~~ Give the more.
deed, Give thy strength to serve thy ~~broth-er~~ In his need.

4. Hast thou borne a secret sorrow
In thy lonely breast?
Take to thee thy sorrowing ~~brother~~ neighbor
For a guest.

5. Share with ~~him~~ them thy bread of blessing,
Sorrow's burden share;
When thy heart enfolds a ~~brother~~ neighbor,
God is there.

COMMITMENT AND ACTION

# O'er Continent and Ocean

LLANGLOFFAN 7.6.8.6.D.

*John Haynes Holmes, 1917*

*Daniel Evans'* Hymnau a Thônau, *1865*

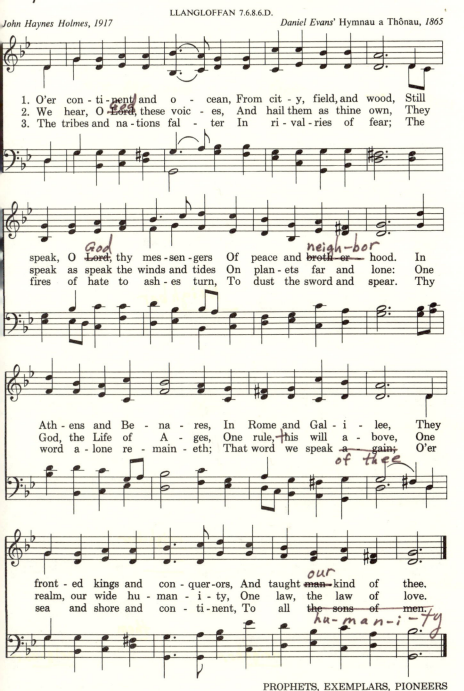

1. O'er con-ti-nent and o - cean, From cit - y, field, and wood, Still
2. We hear, O Lord, these voic - es, And hail them as thine own, They
3. The tribes and na-tions fal - ter In ri - val-ries of fear; The

*God (over Lord)*
*Sea (over Lord)*

speak, O Lord, thy mes-sen-gers Of peace and broth-er — hood. In
speak as speak the winds and tides On plan - ets far and lone: One
fires of hate to ash - es turn, To dust the sword and spear. Thy

*God (over Lord)*
*neigh-bor (over broth-er)*

Ath - ens and Be - na - res, In Rome and Gal - i - lee, They
God, the Life of A - ges, One rule, this will a - bove, One
word a - lone re - main - eth; That word we speak a - gain; O'er

*of thee (over a gain)*

front - ed kings and con - quer-ors, And taught man-kind of thee.
realm, our wide hu - man - i - ty, One law, the law of love.
sea and shore and con - ti-nent, To all the sons of men.

*our (over man)*
*hu-man-i-ty (over the sons of men)*

PROPHETS, EXEMPLARS, PIONEERS

# 228 Obedient They But to a Dream

FARLEY CASTLE 10.10.10.10.

*George Dillon, 1931; adapted*                    *Henry Lawes, 1638*

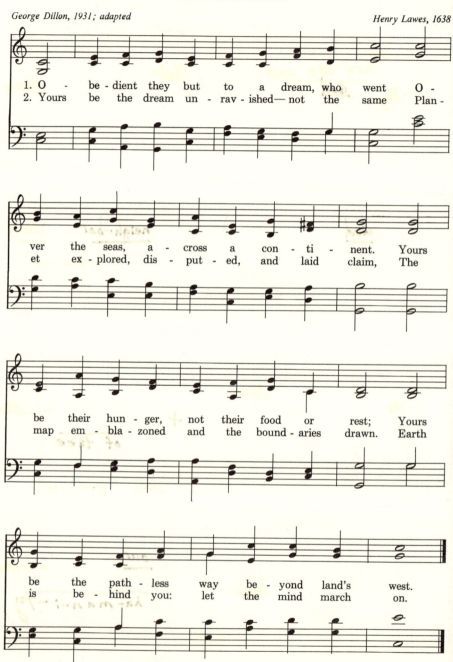

1. O - be - dient they but to a dream, who went O -
2. Yours be the dream un - rav - ished— not the same Plan -

ver the seas, a - cross a con - ti - nent. Yours
et ex - plored, dis - put - ed, and laid claim, The

be their hun - ger, not their food or rest; Yours
map em - bla - zoned and the bound - aries drawn. Earth

be the path - less way be - yond land's west.
is be - hind you: let the mind march on.

PROPHETS, EXEMPLARS, PIONEERS

# 229

**Blest ~~Is that Man~~** *Are the Ones*

GENEVA 119 11.11.11.11. Irregular

*Joseph Auslander, 1950*

*Genevan Psalter, 1551; adapted*

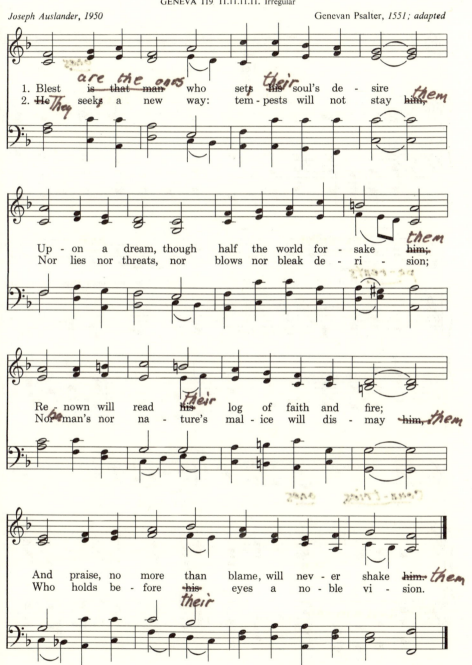

1. Blest ~~is that man~~ *are the ones* who sets ~~his~~ *their* soul's de - sire
2. ~~He~~ *They* seeks a new way: tem - pests will not stay ~~him,~~ *them*

Up - on a dream, though half the world for - sake ~~him;~~ *them*
Nor lies nor threats, nor blows nor bleak de - ri - sion;

Re - nown will read ~~his~~ *Their* log of faith and fire;
Nor ~~man's~~ nor na - ture's mal - ice will dis - may ~~him,~~ *them*

And praise, no more than blame, will nev - er shake ~~him.~~ *them*
Who holds be - fore ~~his~~ *their* eyes a no - ble vi - sion.

PROPHETS, EXEMPLARS, PIONEERS

# 230 Let Us Now Praise Famous Men *Ones*

*Ecclesiasticus 44:1–14; abridged*

FAMOUS MEN Irregular

*Ralph Vaughan Williams, 1923*

Let us now praise fa-mous men, *ones* and our pa-rents fa-thers that be-gat us: Such as did bear rule in their coun-tries king-doms, *ones* men re-nown-ed for their power:

**PROPHETS, EXEMPLARS, PIONEERS**

PROPHETS, EXEMPLARS, PIONEERS

hon-ored in their gen - er - a -tions, and were the glo - ry of their

times. And some there be which have

no me-mo - ri - al; who are per-ished as though they had nev-er

been. Their bod - ies are bur - ied in peace;
but their name liv - eth for - ev - er -
more.

PROPHETS, EXEMPLARS, PIONEERS

**231**

# From Age to Age

CHRISTUS DER IST MEIN LEBEN C.M.

*Frederick Lucian Hosmer, 1899*

*Melchior Vulpius, 1609; adapted*

1. From age to age how grand-ly rise The proph-et souls in line; A-
2. They wit-ness to one her-it-age, One Spir-it's quick-ening breath, One
3. Their kin-dling power our souls con-fess; Though dead they speak to-day: How
4. Through ev-ery race, in ev-ery clime, One song shall yet be heard: Move

bove the pass-ing cen-tu-ries Like bea-con-lights they shine.
wid-ening reign from age to age Of free-dom and of faith.
great the cloud of wit-ness-es En-com-pass-ing our way!
on-ward in thy course sub-lime, O ev-er-last-ing Word.

**232**

# The Pioneer

BRIDGEWATER 8.8.8.8.8.8.

*Kenneth L. Patton, 1956*

*Lewis Edson, 1782*

1. Feet of the ur-gent pi-o-neer— Whose for-ward jour-ney
2. Stir in us hun-ger to ex-plore To-mor-row's un-dis-

quells our fear, Whose vi-sions, nev-er rest-ing, drive The race to won-der
cov-ered shore. In coun-tries won we may not rest, But start from them our

PROPHETS, EXEMPLARS, PIONEERS

and    to strive, Ad - vance our trail and    mark   it         clear—
fur - ther quest, And   so   move on - ward   ev - er  -    more.

## 233 O Prophet Souls of All the Years

GRÄFENBURG C.M.

*From Frederick Lucian Hosmer, 1893*                              *Johann Crüger, 1653*

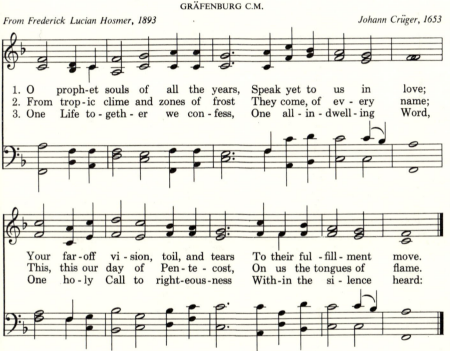

1. O    proph-et souls of    all  the years,  Speak yet to   us   in      love;
2. From trop-ic clime and zones of  frost  They come, of  ev - ery   name;
3. One  Life to - geth - er   we con - fess,  One  all - in - dwell-ing  Word,

Your   far - off   vi - sion, toil, and tears  To their ful - fill - ment   move.
This, this our  day of   Pen - te - cost,  On  us  the tongues of   flame.
One   ho - ly  Call  to  right-eous-ness  With-in the  si - lence  heard:

4. One Law that guides the shining spheres
   As on through space they roll,
   And speaks in flaming characters
   On Sinais of the soul:

5. One Love, unfathomed, measureless,
   An ever-flowing sea,
   That holds within its vast embrace
   Time and eternity.

PROPHETS, EXEMPLARS, PIONEERS

## 234

# Prayer of the Pilgrims

L'OMNIPOTENT 11.10.11.10.

*Le Baron Russell Briggs, 1920*  Genevan Psalter, *1551*

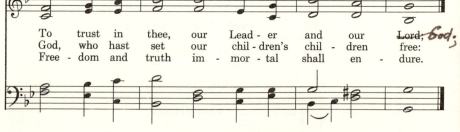

1. God of our *fore-bears*, who hast safe - ly brought us
2. God, who hast sent thy truth to shine be - fore us,
3. Free - dom a free - born na - tion still shall cher - ish;

Through seas and sor - rows, fam - ine, fire, and sword;
A fi - ery pil - lar, bea - coning on the sea;
Be this our cov - e - nant, un - chang - ing, sure—

Who, in thy mer - cies man - i - fold, hast taught us
God, who hast spread thy wings of mer - cy o'er us;
Earth shall de - cay, the fir - ma - ment shall per - ish,

To trust in thee, our Lead - er and our *God;*
God, who hast set our chil - dren's chil - dren free:
Free - dom and truth im - mor - tal shall en - dure.

PROPHETS, EXEMPLARS, PIONEERS

# 235

## The Pilgrims

DUKE STREET L.M.

Leonard Bacon, 1838

John Hatton, 1793

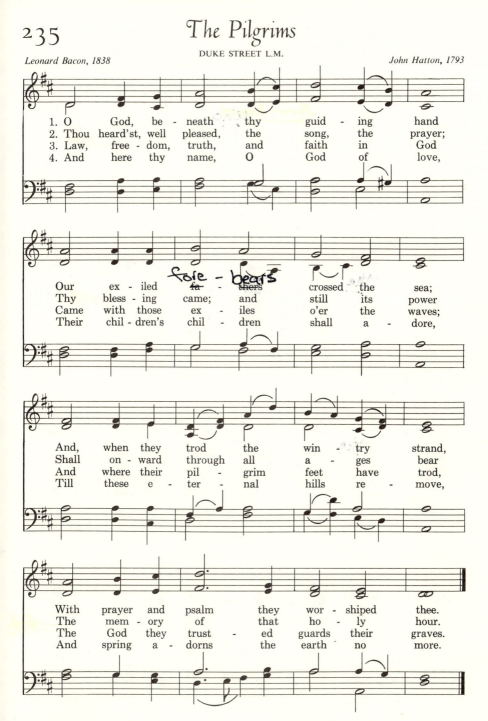

1. O God, be - neath thy guid - ing hand
2. Thou heard'st, well pleased, the song, the prayer;
3. Law, free - dom, truth, and faith in God
4. And here thy name, O God of love,

Our ex - iled fore - bears crossed the sea;
Thy bless - ing came; and still its power
Came with those ex - iles o'er the waves;
Their chil - dren's chil - dren shall a - dore,

And, when they trod the win - try strand,
Shall on - ward through all a - ges bear
And where their pil - grim feet have trod,
Till these e - ter - nal hills re - move,

With prayer and psalm they wor - shiped thee.
The mem - ory of that ho - ly hour.
The God they trust - ed guards their graves.
And spring a - dorns the earth no more.

PROPHETS, EXEMPLARS, PIONEERS

# 236 Behold a Sower

**ELLACOMBE C.M.D.**

*Washington Gladden, 1897*

*X. L. Hartig's* Vollständige Sammlung, *ca. 1833*

1. Be - hold a Sow - er! from a - far He goeth forth with might; The
2. O Lord of life, to thee we lift Our hearts in praise for those, Thy
3. Shine forth, O Light, that we may see, With hearts all un - a - fraid, The
4. Light up thy word; the fet-tered page From kill - ing bond-age free: Light

roll - ing years his fur-rows are, His seed the grow-ing light; For
proph-ets, who have shown thy gift Of grace that ev - er grows, Of
mean-ing and the mys-ter - y Of things that thou hast made: Shine
up our way; lead forth this age In love's large lib - er - ty. O

all the just his word is sown, It spring-eth up al - way; The
truth that spreads from shore to shore, Of wis - dom's wid - ening ray, Of
forth, and let the dark-ling past Be - neath thy beam grow bright; Shine
Light of light! with - in us dwell, Through us thy ra - diance pour, That

ten - der blade is hope's young dawn, The har - vest, love's new day.
light that shin-eth more and more Un - to thy per - fect day.
forth, and touch the fu - ture vast With thine un - trou - bled light.
word and life thy truths may tell, And praise thee ev - er - more.

PROPHETS, EXEMPLARS, PIONEERS

## 237 We Met Them on the Common Way

SALVATION C.M.D.

*Elizabeth C. Cardozo, 1914*                                   *Ananias Davisson's* Kentucky Harmony, *ca. 1815*

1. We met them on the com-mon way, They passed and gave no sign, The
2. Here are earth's splen-did fail-ures, come From glo-rious fought-en fields; Some

he - roes that had lost the day, The fail - ures half di - vine. Ranged
bear the wounds of com - bat, some Are prone up - on their shields. To

in a qui - et place we see Their might - y ranks con - tain Fig -
us that still do bat - tle here, If we in aught pre - vail, Grant,

ures too great for vic - to - ry, Hearts too un-spoiled for gain.
God, a tri - umph not too dear, Or strength, like theirs, to fail!

PROPHETS, EXEMPLARS, PIONEERS

# 238    O God of Earth and Altar

KING'S LYNN 7.6.7.6.D.

*Gilbert Keith Chesterton, 1906*

*English melody*
*Arranged by Ralph Vaughan Williams, 1906*

1. O God of earth and al - tar, Bow down and hear our cry, Our
2. From all that ter - ror teach - es, From lies of tongue and pen, From
3. Tie in a liv - ing teth - er The priest and prince and thrall, Bind

earth - ly rul - ers fal - ter, Our peo - ple drift and die; The
all the eas - y speech - es That com - fort cru - el men, From
all our lives to - geth - er, Smite us and save us all; In

walls of gold en - tomb us, The swords of scorn di - vide, Take
sale and prof - a - na - tion Of hon - or and the sword, From
ire and ex - ul - ta - tion, A - flame with faith, and free, Lift

not thy thun - der from us, But take a - way our pride.
sleep and from dam - na - tion, De - liv - er us, good God.
up a liv - ing na - tion, A sin - gle sword to thee.

NATION AND NATIONS

# 239 Not Alone for Mighty Empire

*William Pierson Merrill, 1909*

IN BABILONE 8.7.8.7.D.

Oude en nieuwe Hollantse Boernlietes
en Contradanseu, *ca. 1710*

1. Not a-lone for might-y em - pire, Stretch-ing far o'er land and sea,
2. Not for bat - tle - ship and for-tress, Not for con - quests of the sword,
3. God of jus - tice, save the peo - ple From the war of race and creed;

Not a - lone for boun-teous har-vests, Lift we up our hearts to thee:
But for con-quests of the spir - it Give we thanks to thee, O ~~Lord;~~ *God*
From the strife of class and fac - tion, Make our na - tion free in - deed;

Stand-ing in the liv - ing pres - ent, Mem - o - ry and hope be - tween,
For the her - it - age of free-dom, For the home, the church, the school,
Keep ~~her~~ *its* faith in sim - ple ~~man-hood~~ *cour-age* Strong as when ~~her life be-gan,~~ *it came to be*

~~Lord,~~ *God* we would with deep thanks-giv-ing Praise thee more for things un - seen.
For the o - pen door to ~~man-hood~~ *hu-man* In a land the peo - ple rule.
Till it find its full fru - i - tion In ~~the broth-er-hood of man.~~ *our hu-man u-ni-ty*

NATION AND NATIONS

240 # O Beautiful, Our Country

THE SPIRITUAL SAILOR 7.6.7.6.D.

*From Frederick Lucian Hosmer, 1884*　　　　*William Walker's* Southern Harmony, *1835*

1. O  beau - ti - ful, my  coun - try!  Be  thine  a  no - bler  care  Than
2. For  thee  our  fa - thers  suf - fered;  For  thee  they toiled and prayed;  Up -
3. O  beau - ti - ful, our  coun - try!  Round thee  in  love  we  draw;  Thine

all thy wealth of  com - merce, Thy  har - vests  wav - ing  fair;  Be
on thy ho - ly  al - tar  Their  will - ing  lives they  laid.  Thou
is the grace of  free - dom, The  maj - es - ty  of  law.  Let

it  thy pride to  lift  up  The  man - hood  of  the  poor;  Be
hast no com - mon birth - right, Grand mem - ories  on  thee  shine;  The
jus - tice be  thy scep - ter, The  right thy  di - a - dem;  And

thou  to the op - press - ed  Fair  free - dom's  o - pen  door.
blood  of pil - grim  na - tions Com - min - gled  flows in  thine.
on  thy shin - ing  fore - head Be  peace the  crown - ing  gem.

NATION AND NATIONS

# 241 America the Beautiful

MATERNA C.M.D.

*Katharine Lee Bates, 1893, 1904*                    *Samuel Augustus Ward, 1882*

1. O beau-ti-ful for spa-cious skies, For am-ber waves of grain, For
2. O beau-ti-ful for pil-grim feet, Whose stern, im-pas-sioned stress A
3. O beau-ti-ful for he-roes proved In lib-er-at-ing strife, Who
4. O beau-ti-ful for pa-triot dream That sees be-yond the years Thine

pur - ple moun-tain maj - es-ties A - bove the fruit - ed plain! A-
thor-ough-fare for free-dom beat A - cross the wil - der - ness! A-
more than self their coun-try loved, And mer - cy more than life! A-
al - a-bas-ter cit - ies gleam Un-dimmed by hu - man tears! A-

mer - i - ca! A - mer - i - ca! God shed *love's* ~~his~~ grace on thee, And
mer - i - ca! A - mer - i - ca! God mend thine ev - ery flaw, Con-
mer - i - ca! A - mer - i - ca! May God thy gold re - fine, Till
mer - i - ca! A - mer - i - ca! God shed *love's* ~~his~~ grace on thee, ~~And~~ *Thy*

~~crown~~ *bless days in Godly ways* thy ~~good with broth - er-hood~~ From sea to shin - ing sea.
firm thy soul in self - con-trol, Thy lib - er - ty in law.
all suc-cess be no - ble-ness, And ev - ery gain di - vine.
~~crown~~ thy ~~good with broth - er-hood~~ *mission done, thy people one* From sea to shin - ing sea.

NATION AND NATIONS

242 My Country, 'Tis of Thee

AMERICA 6.6.4.6.6 6.4.

Samuel Francis Smith, 1832

Thesaurus Musicus, ca. 1740–45

1. My coun - try, 'tis of thee, Sweet land of lib - er - ty,
2. My na - tive coun - try, thee, Land of the no - ble free,
3. Let mu - sic swell the breeze, And ring from all the trees
4. Our fa - thers' founders God, to thee, Au - thor of lib - er - ty,

Of thee I sing: Land where my fore-bears died,
Thy name I love; I love thy rocks and rills,
Sweet free - dom's song. Let mor - tal tongues a - wake;
To thee we sing: Long may our land be bright

Land of the pil - grims' pride, From ev - ery
Thy woods and 'tem - pled hills; My heart with
Let all that breathe par - take; Let rocks their
With free - dom's ho - ly light; Pro - tect us

moun - tain side Let free - dom ring.
rap - ture thrills Like that a - bove.
si - lence break, The sound pro - long.
by thy might, Great God, our King. Thy bless—ings bring!

NATION AND NATIONS

# The New Patriot

TRURO L.M.

*Frederick Lawrence Knowles, 1904*       *Thomas Williams' Psalmodia Evangelica, 1789*

1. Who is the pa - triot? They who lights The
2. Who is the pa - triot? It is They Who
3. The soil that bred the pi - o - neers He
4. Who is the pa - triot? On - ly they Whose

torch of war from hill to hill? Or
knows no bound - ary, race or creed, Whose
loves and guards, yet loves the more That
busi - ness is the gen - eral good, Whose

they who kin - dles on the heights The
na - tion is hu - man - i - ty, Whose
larg - er land with - out fron - tiers, Those
keen - est sword is sym - pa - thy, Whose

bea - con neighbors are of men, a world's good will?
wid - er seas with - out a shore.
dear - est flag is neighbor - hood.

NATION AND NATIONS

## 244 God Save the Queen

*Anonymous, ca. 1743, 1745*

GOD SAVE THE QUEEN 6.6.4.6.6.6.4.

*Thesaurus Musicus, ca. 1740–45*

1. God save our gra-cious Queen, Long live our no - ble Queen, God save the
2. Thy choic-est gifts in store On her be pleased to pour, Long may she

Queen! Send her vic - to - ri - ous, Hap - py, and glo - ri - ous,
reign; May she de - fend our laws, And ev - er give us cause

Long to reign o - ver us; God save the Queen!
To sing with heart and voice, God save the Queen!

## 245 Heir of All the Ages

NUREMBERG 7.7.7.7.

*From Julia Caroline Ripley Dorr, 1879 or earlier*

*Johann Rudolph Ahle, 1664; adapted*

1. Heir of all the a - ges, I— Heir of all that they have wrought,
2. Ev - ery gold - en deed of theirs Sheds its lus - ter on my way;
3. Heir of all that they have earned By their pas - sion and their tears;
4. As - pi - ra - tions pure and high, Strength to do and to en - dure:

NATION AND NATIONS/OUR WORLD-WIDE HERITAGE

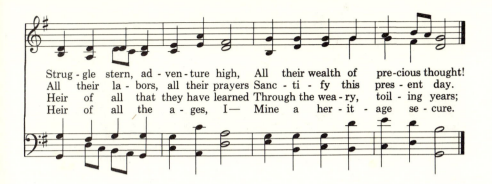

Strug-gle stern, ad-ven-ture high, All their wealth of pre-cious thought!
All their la-bors, all their prayers Sanc-ti-fy this pres-ent day.
Heir of all that they have learned Through the wea-ry, toil-ing years;
Heir of all the a-ges, I— Mine a her-it-age se-cure.

## 246 The Growing Light

WINCHESTER NEW L.M.

*From Samuel Longfellow, 1875*  Musicalisch Hand-buch, *Hamburg, 1690; adapted*

1. With joy we claim the grow-ing light, Ad-vanc-ing thought, and
2. With wid-er view, come loft-ier goal; With full-er light, more

wid-ening view, The larg-er free-dom, clear-er sight, Which
good to see; With free-dom, tru-er self-con-trol; With

from the old un-fold the new.
knowl-edge, deep-er rev-erence be.

OUR WORLD-WIDE HERITAGE

# 247 It Sounds Along the Ages

FAR OFF LANDS 7.6.7.6.D.

*From William Channing Gannett, 1894*

*Melody of the Bohemian Brethren*
*Hemlandssånger,*
*Rock Island, Illinois, 1892; arranged*

1. It sounds a-long the a - ges, Soul an-swer-ing to soul; It
2. From Si - nai's cliffs it ech - oed, It breathed from Bud-dha's tree, It
3. It calls—and lo, new jus - tice! It speaks—and lo, new truth! In

kin - dles on the pag - es Of ev - ery Bi - ble scroll; The
charmed in Ath-ens' mar - ket, It hal-lowed Gal - i - lee; The
ev - er no - bler stat - ure And un - ex - haust-ed youth. For -

psalm - ist heard and sang it, From mar - tyr lips it broke, And
ham - mer stroke of Lu - ther, The Pil-grims' sea - side prayer, The
ev - er on re - sound-ing, And know-ing nought of time, Our

proph - et tongues out - rang it Till sleep - ing na - tions woke.
or - a - cles of Con - cord One ho - ly word de - clare.
laws but catch the mu - sic Of its e - ter - nal chime.

OUR WORLD-WIDE HERITAGE

# 248   Light of Ages and of Nations

AUSTRIA 8.7.8.7.D.

Samuel Longfellow, 1860

Franz Joseph Haydn, 1797

1. Light of a - ges and of na - tions, Ev - ery race and ev - ery time
2. Rea - son's no - ble as - pi - ra - tion Truth in grow-ing clear - ness saw;
3. Lord, that word a - bid - eth ev - er; Rev - e - la - tion is not sealed;

Has re-ceived thine in - spi - ra - tions, Glimps-es of thy truth sub-lime.
Con-science spoke its con-dem - na - tion, Or pro-claimed the e - ter - nal law.
An-swering now to our en - deav-or, Truth and right are still re - vealed.

Al - ways spir-its in rapt vi - sion Passed the heaven-ly veil with - in,
While thine in-ward rev - e - la-tions Told thy saints their prayers were heard,
That which came to an-cient sag-es, Greek, Bar - ba - rian, Ro-man, Jew,

Al-ways hearts bowed in con - tri-tion Found sal - va - tion from their sin.
Proph-ets to the guilt - y na-tions Spoke thine ev - er - last-ing word.
Writ-ten in the soul's deep pag-es, Shines to - day, for - ev - er new.

OUR WORLD-WIDE HERITAGE

# 249

## Gather Us In

AINSWORTH 97 10.10.10.10.

*George Matheson, 1890*

*Genevan Psalter, 1562*
*Version of Henry Ainsworth's Psalter, 1612*

1. Gath - er us in, thou Love that fill - est all;
2. Gath - er us in: we wor - ship on - ly thee;
3. Some seek a Fa - ther in the heavens a - bove;

Gath - er our ri - val faiths with - in thy fold;
In va - ried names we stretch a com - mon hand;
Some ask a hu - man im - age to a - dore;

Rend each one's tem - ple veil, and bid it fall,
In di - verse forms a com - mon soul we see;
Some crave a Spir - it vast as life and love:

That we may know that thou hast been of old.
In man - y ways we seek one prom - ised land.
With - in thy man - sions we have all and more.

OUR WORLD-WIDE HERITAGE

# Heritage

O JESU CHRIST, MEINS LEBENS LICHT L.M.

*Jacob Trapp, 1958*

Nürnbergisches Gesangbuch, *1676; adapted*

1. The art, the sci - ence, and the lore Of those men through
2. From Si - nai and from Beth - le - hem, From Chi - na,
3. The gold - en splen - dor of the sun, The beau - ty

a - ges long since dust, Their hard - won wis - dom,
In - dia, Greece, and Rome, Their mu - sic, sym - bols,
of the liv - ing earth, The far - flung gal - ax -

slow - ly grown, Come down to us a sa - cred trust.
songs, and prayers En - rich and beau - ti - fy our home.
ies of stars, Man's need to love, at - tend our birth;
Our

4. And all our men's hopes and prophecies
   Of freedom, peace, the coming day
   Of life more deeply, grandly lived,
   Shine luminous upon our way.

5. Ours for the present, to increase,
   Ours for the future and its care,
   A heritage of growing light,
   To live, transmit, and greatly share.

OUR WORLD-WIDE HERITAGE

## 251
# From Heart to Heart

GRAFTON C.M.

*William Channing Gannett, 1875*                    *Attributed to Thomas Clark (1775–1859)*

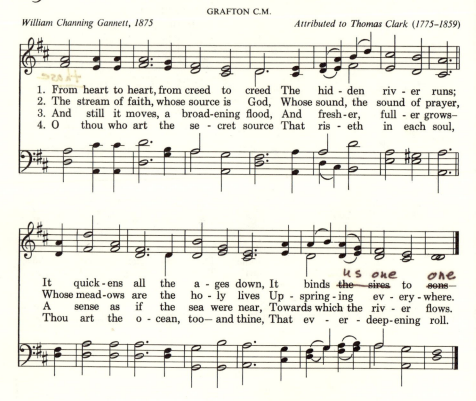

1. From heart to heart, from creed to creed The hid-den riv-er runs;
2. The stream of faith, whose source is God, Whose sound, the sound of prayer,
3. And still it moves, a broad-ening flood, And fresh-er, full-er grows—
4. O thou who art the se-cret source That ris-eth in each soul,

It quick-ens all the a-ges down, It binds the sires to sons (us one / one)
Whose mead-ows are the ho-ly lives Up-spring-ing ev-ery-where.
A sense as if the sea were near, Towards which the riv-er flows.
Thou art the o-cean, too— and thine, That ev-er-deep-ening roll.


## 252
# Unto Thy Temple, Lord (God), We Come

DUKE STREET L.M.

*Robert Collyer, 1873*                    *John Hatton, 1793*

1. Un-to thy tem-ple, Lord (God), we come With thank-ful hearts to wor-ship thee;
2. The com-mon home of rich and poor, Of bond and free, and great and small;
3. May thy whole truth be spo-ken here; Thy gos-pel light for-ev-er shine;

OUR WORLD-WIDE HERITAGE/CHURCH OF THE FREE SPIRIT

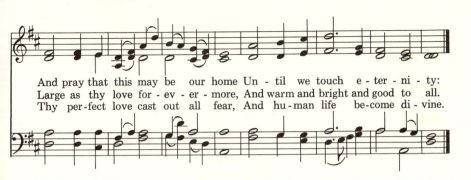

And pray that this may be our home Un - til we touch e - ter - ni - ty:
Large as thy love for - ev - er - more, And warm and bright and good to all.
Thy per - fect love cast out all fear, And hu - man life be - come di - vine.

**253** *Our Kindred Fellowships*

WINCHESTER NEW L.M.

*From Marion Franklin Ham, 1933* Musicalisch **Hand**-buch, *Hamburg, 1690; adapted*

1. As tran - quil streams that meet and merge And
2. Free from the bonds that bind the mind To
3. A free - dom that re - veres the past, But
4. Pro - phet - ic Church, the fu - ture waits Thy

flow as one to seek the sea, Our kin - dred fel - low -
nar - row thought and life - less creed; Free from a so - cial
trusts the dawn - ing fu - ture more; And bids the soul, in
lib - er - at - ing min - is - try; Go for - ward in the

ships u - nite To build a church that shall be free —
code that fails To serve the cause of hu - man need;
search of truth, Ad - ven - ture bold - ly and ex - plore.
power of love, Pro - claim the truth that makes men free.

CHURCH OF THE FREE SPIRIT

254 Church of the Free Spirit

NICAEA 12.13.12.10.

Charles H. Lyttle, 1942

John Bacchus Dykes, 1861

1. Bring, O Past, your hon - or; bring, O Time, your har - vest,
2. Ring, in glad thanks - giv - ing, bell of grief and glad - ness,
3. Shrine of fron - tier cour - age, Si - nai of its vi - sion,
4. Church of pure re - form - ers, pi - o - neers un - daunt - ed,

Gold - en sheaves of hal-lowed lives and minds by Truth made free;
Forth to town and prai - rie let our fes - tal greet - ing go.
Home and hearth of com - mon quest for life's im - mor - tal good,
Biv - ou - ac of com-rades sworn to keep our spir - it free;

Come, you faith - ful spir - its, build - ers of this tem - ple:
Voic - es long de - part - ed in your tones re - ech - o:
Stand, in years on - com - ing, sen - ti - nel of con - science,
Long o'er life's swift riv - er preach the e - ter - nal gos - pel:

"To Ho - li - ness, to Love, and Lib - er - ty."
"Praise to the High - est, Peace to all be - low."
As through the past your stal - wart walls have stood.
Faith, hope, and love for all hu - man - i - ty.

CHURCH OF THE FREE SPIRIT

# 255 Faith's Freer Shrine

### ST. MATTHEW C.M.D.

*Frederick Lucian Hosmer, 1890*                    *William Croft?, 1708*

1. O Light, from age to age the same, For - ev - er liv - ing Word, Here
2. What vi - sions rise a - bove the years, What ten - der mem-ories throng, To
3. O not in vain their toil who wrought To build faith's fre - er shrine, Nor

have we felt thy kin - dling flame, Thy voice with - in have heard. Here
fill the eye with hap - py tears, The heart with grate-ful song! Then
theirs whose stead-fast love and thought Have watched the fire di-vine. Burn,

ho - ly thought and hymn and prayer Have winged the spir - it's powers, And
van - ish mists of time and sense; They come, the loved of yore, And
ho - ly fire, and shine more wide, While sys - tems rise and fall; Faith,

made these walls di - vine - ly fair, Thy tem - ple, ~~Lord~~, God and ours.
one en - cir - cling Prov - i - dence Holds all for - ev - er - more.
hope, and char - i - ty a - bide, The heart and soul of all.

CHURCH OF THE FREE SPIRIT

# 256 Our Friendly House

FILLMORE 8.8.8.8.8.8.

Kenneth L. Patton, 1951

William Walker's Southern Harmony, 1835

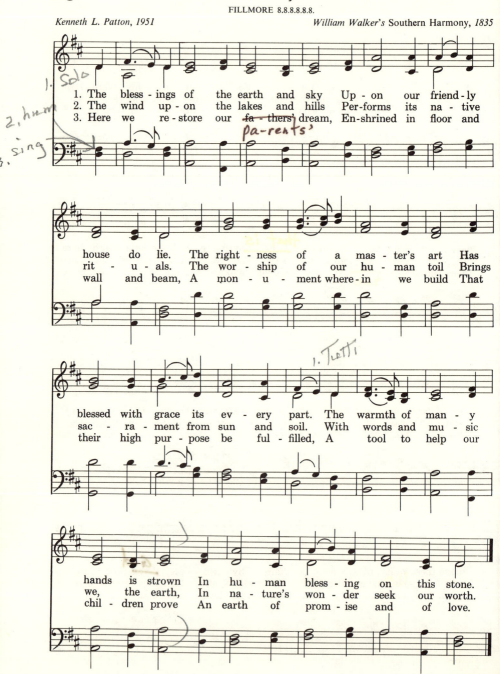

1. The bless - ings of the earth and sky Up - on our friend - ly
2. The wind up - on the lakes and hills Per - forms its na - tive
3. Here we re - store our fa - thers' dream, En - shrined in floor and

house do lie. The right - ness of a mas - ter's art Has
rit - u - als. The wor - ship of our hu - man toil Brings
wall and beam, A mon - u - ment where - in we build That

blessed with grace its ev - ery part. The warmth of man - y
sac - ra - ment from sun and soil. With words and mu - sic
their high pur - pose be ful - filled, A tool to help our

hands is strown In hu - man bless - ing on this stone.
we, the earth, In na - ture's won - der seek our worth.
chil - dren prove An earth of prom - ise and of love.

CHURCH OF THE FREE SPIRIT

# 257 Faith of the Free

MIT FREUDEN ZART 8.7.8.7.8.8.7.

Vincent B. Silliman, 1944

Bohemian Brethren, Kirchengeseng, 1566

1. Faith of the larg - er lib - er - ty, Source of the light ex -
2. He - roes of faith in ev - ery age, Far - see - ing, self - de -
3. Faith for the peo - ple ev - ery - where, What - ev - er their op -

pand - ing, Law of the church that is to be, Old bond-age not - with -
ny - ing, Wrought an in - creas - ing her - it - age, Mon - arch and priest de -
pres - sion, Of all who make the world more fair, Liv - ing their faith's con -

stand - ing: Faith of the free! By thee we live— By all thou giv - est
fy - ing. Faith of the free! In thy dear name The cost - ly her - it -
fes - sion: Faith of the free! What-e'er our plight, Thy law, thy lib - er -

and shalt give Our loy - al - ty com - mand - ing.
age we claim: Their liv - ing and their dy - ing.
ty, thy light Shall be our blest pos - ses - sion.

CHURCH OF THE FREE SPIRIT

# 258 Rank by Rank Again We Stand

REUNION 7.8.7.8.7.7.7.7.

*John Huntley Skrine, 1884*

*University of Wales,*
*A Students' Hymnal, 1923*

1. Rank by rank again we stand,
From the four winds gath-ered hith-er. Loud the hal-lowed
walls de-mand Whence we come, and how, and whith-er.

2. Ours the years' me-mo-rial store,
He-ro days and names we reck-on, Days of com-rades
gone be-fore, Lives that speak and deeds that beck-on.

CHURCH OF THE FREE SPIRIT

From their still - ness break - ing clear,     Ech - oes wake to
One   in name, in   hon - or one,              Guard we well the

warn or   cheer;  High - er truth *good* and   *truth to see* ho - lier good
crown they won;   What they dreamed be ours to do,

Call     our   mus - tered     broth *com - pan - y* - er - hood.
Hope   their  hopes,    and    seal    them   true.

CHURCH OF THE FREE SPIRIT

## 259 Where Is Our Holy Church?

ST. MICHAEL S.M.

*Edwin Henry Wilson, 1928*

*Genevan Psalter, 1551*
*Adapted by William Crotch, 1836*

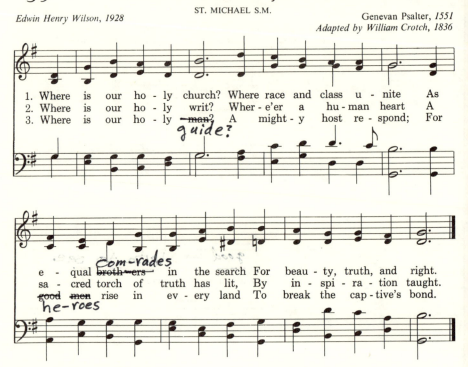

1. Where is our ho-ly church? Where race and class u-nite As
2. Where is our ho-ly writ? Wher-e'er a hu-man heart A
3. Where is our ho-ly ~~man?~~ *guide?* A might-y host re-spond; For

e-qual ~~broth-ers~~ *Com-rades* in the search For beau-ty, truth, and right.
sa-cred torch of truth has lit, By in-spi-ra-tion taught.
~~good men~~ *he-roes* rise in ev-ery land To break the cap-tive's bond.

4. Where is our holy land?
   Within the human soul,
   Wherever ~~strong men~~ *people* truly seek
   With character the goal.

5. Where is our paradise?
   In aspiration's sight,
   Wherein we hope to see arise
   Ten thousand years of light.

## 260 Here Be No *One* ~~Man~~ a Stranger

CHRISTUS DER IST MEIN LEBEN 7.6.7.6.

*William Channing Gannett, 1888*

*Melchior Vulpius, 1609*

1. To clois-ters of the spir-it These aisles of qui-et lead; Here
2. Here be no ~~man~~ *one* a stran-ger; No ho-ly cause be banned; No

CHURCH OF THE FREE SPIRIT

shall the vi - sion glad - den, The voice with - in us plead.
good for one be count - ed, Not good for all the land.

# 261 One Holy Church

ST. STEPHEN C.M.

*Samuel Longfellow, 1860*                    *William Jones, 1789*

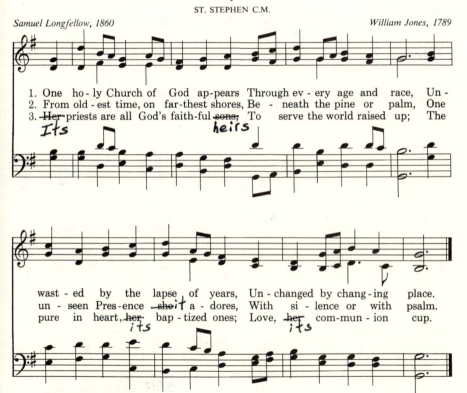

1. One ho - ly Church of God ap-pears Through ev - ery age and race, Un -
2. From old - est time, on far-thest shores, Be - neath the pine or palm, One
3. Her priests are all God's faith-ful sons, To serve the world raised up; The

*Its*                                *heirs*

wast - ed by the lapse of years, Un - changed by chang - ing place.
un - seen Pres - ence she a - dores, With si - lence or with psalm.
pure in heart, her bap - tized ones; Love, her com - mun - ion cup.

*its*        *it*                    *its*

4. The truth is her prophetic gift,
   The soul, her sacred page;
   And feet on mercy's errands swift
   Do make her pilgrimage.

*its*

5. O living Church, thine errand speed;
   Fulfill thy task sublime;
   With bread of life earth's hunger feed;
   Redeem the evil time.

CHURCH OF THE FREE SPIRIT

# 262 For Ceremony of Naming

**WER DA WONET L.M.D.**

*Ridgely Torrence, 1925*

*Michael Vehe's* New Gesangbüchlin, *1537; adapted*

1. Con - sid - er well your ways and lives, You gar - deners of the
2. Will you be mind - ful of your care, Know-ing you are, through
3. And who shall say what he must be Who by your fol - ly

pre - cious seed. As brief at - tend - ers of the need, Draw
*her* ~~him,~~ of those Who leave their col - ors in the air When
may not fly, Or long be hin - dered from the sky, Or

hon - ey from the up - per hives. Make sweet the weath - er
you are dust and *s*he a rose? Will you take thought be -
shore-bound nev - er know the sea? Make him the keep - er

for the flower; With - draw the bonds and set it free. You
fore you find The words to curb *his* long - ing will, And
of the key To lock or hold in stern ar - ray The

CHRISTENING OR NAMING

shall be watch-ers for an hour, But it shall nev - er cease to be.
from com-mands a - while be still, Con - sid-er-ing which of you is blind?
ur - gent fi - ber of his clay, And send his rang - ing spir - it free!

## 263     A Blessing

ROCKBRIDGE L.M.

*Siegfried Sassoon, 1940*     *Amzi Chapin, 1813*

1. Your lit - tle flame of life we guard For the long night that
2. Bright be your flame, my soul, my *Child* Whose pil - grim - age I

must be hard: Your eyes we teach to know the day That
see be - gun: And when these guid - ing hands are gone, In

shall make won - der - ful your way.
love of all things good go on.

CHRISTENING OR NAMING

## 264    Morning Chorale

George Gascoigne, 1573; adapted    LOBT GOTT, IHR CHRISTEN C.M.    Nikolaus Herman, 1554
Harmonized by J. S. Bach, ca. 1740

1. Ye that have spent the si - lent night In sleep and qui - et rest, And
2. Now lift your hearts, your voic - es raise, Your morn - ing trib - ute bring; All

joy to see the cheer - ful light That ris - eth in the
na - ture join in grate - ful praise— Re - joice, give thanks, and

east,    That ris - eth in the east,
sing,    Re - joice, give thanks, and sing.

## 265    Thomas Ken's Morning Hymn

MORNING HYMN L.M.

Thomas Ken, 1695, 1709    François Hippolyte Barthélemon, 1785

1. A - wake, my soul, and with the sun Thy dai - ly stage of du - ty run, Shake
2. Shine on me, Lord, new life im - part; Fresh ar - dors kin - dle in my heart: One
3. Di - rect, con - trol, sug - gest this day All I de - sign, or do, or say—That
4. Lord, I my vows to thee re - new: Dis - perse my sins as morn - ing dew, Guard

**MORNING**

off dull sloth, and joy - ful rise To pay thy morn-ing sac - ri - fice.
ray of thine all - quick-ening light Dis - pels the sloth and clouds of night.
all my powers, with all their might, In thy sole glo - ry may u - nite.
my first springs of thought and will, And with thy-self my spir - it fill.

## 266 Morning Has Broken

BUNESSAN 5.5.5.4.D.

Eleanor Farjeon, 1931

Gaelic melody
Arranged by Martin Shaw, 1931

1. Morn-ing has bro - ken Like the first morn-ing, Black-bird has spo - ken
2. Sweet the rain's new fall Sun - lit from heav-en, Like the first dew - fall
3. Mine is the sun - light; Mine is the morn-ing Born of the one light

Like the first bird. Praise for the sing - ing; Praise for the morn-ing;
On the first grass. Praise for the sweet - ness Of the wet gar - den,
E - den saw play. Praise with e - la - tion, Praise ev - ery morn-ing,

Praise for them, spring - ing Fresh from the Word.
Sprung in com - plete - ness Where my feet pass.
God's re - cre - a - tion Of the new day.

MORNING

# 267 High o'er the Lonely Hills

DAWN 6.4.6.4.6.6.6.4.

*Jan Struther, 1931*

*T. H. Ingham, 1931*

1. High o'er the lone - ly hills Black turns to gray;
2. So, o'er the hills of life, Storm - y, for - lorn,
3. Bid then fare - well to sleep: Rise up and run.

Bird - song the val - ley fills, Mists fold a - way;
Out of the cloud and strife Sun - rise is born;
What though the hill be steep? Strength's in the sun.

Gray wakes to green a - gain, Beau - ty is seen a - gain;
Swift grows the light for us; End - ed is night for us;
Now shall you find at last Night's left be - hind at last,

Gold and se - rene a - gain Dawn - eth the day.
Sound - less and bright for us Break - eth God's morn.
And for man kind at last Day has be - gun.
ouv

MORNING

## 268    Now All the Heavenly Splendor

INNSBRUCK 7.7.6.7.7.8.

Paul Gerhardt, 1648
Paraphrase by Robert Bridges, 1899

Attributed to Heinrich Isaak (ca. 1450–1517)
Harmonized by J. S. Bach, 1729

Now all the heaven-ly splen - dor Breaks forth in star-light ten - der From myr - iad worlds un - known; And we man, the mar - vel see - ing, For - gets our his self - ish be - ing, For joy of beau - ty not our his own.

EVENING

# 269 Now While the Day in Trailing Splendor

RENDEZ À DIEU 9.8.9.8.D.

Frederick Lucian Hosmer, 1902

Genevan Psalter, 1543

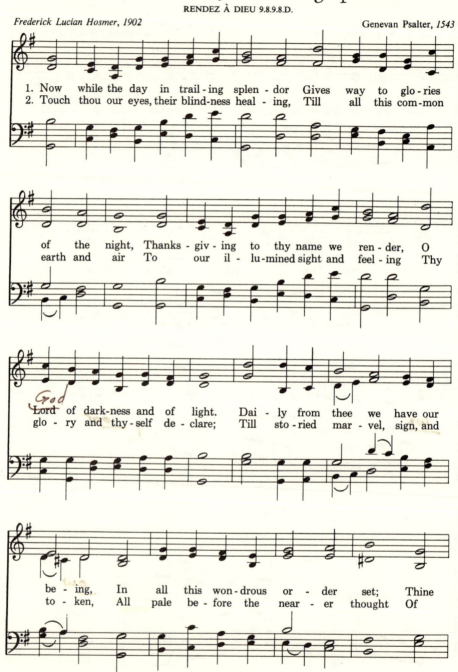

1. Now while the day in trail-ing splen-dor Gives way to glo-ries of the night, Thanks-giv-ing to thy name we ren-der, O God of dark-ness and of light. Dai-ly from thee we have our be-ing, In all this won-drous or-der set; Thine

2. Touch thou our eyes, their blind-ness heal-ing, Till all this com-mon earth and air To our il-lu-mined sight and feel-ing Thy glo-ry and thy-self de-clare; Till sto-ried mar-vel, sign, and to-ken, All pale be-fore the near-er thought Of

EVENING

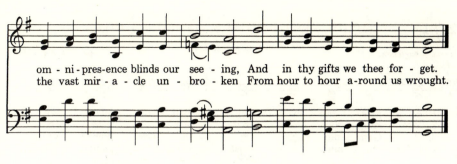

om - ni - pres-ence blinds our see - ing, And in thy gifts we thee for - get.
the vast mir - a - cle un - bro - ken From hour to hour a-round us wrought.

## 270 Thomas Ken's Evening Hymn

TALLIS' CANON L.M.

*From Thomas Ken, 1693, 1709*                    *Thomas Tallis, ca. 1561*

1. All praise to thee, my God, this night, For
2. When in the night I sleep - less lie, My
3. Teach me to live, that I may dread The
4. O may my soul on thee re - pose, And

all the bless - ings of the light; Keep me, O keep me,
soul with heaven - ly thoughts sup - ply; Let no ill dreams dis -
grave as lit - tle as my bed; That with the world, my -
may sweet sleep mine eye - lids close, Sleep that shall me more

King of kings, Be - neath thine own al - might - y wings.
turb my rest, No powers of dark - ness me mo - lest.
self, and thee, I, ere I sleep, at peace may be.
vig - orous make To serve my God when I a - wake.

EVENING

## 271 Again, As Evening's Shadow Falls

Samuel Longfellow, 1859     ROCKBRIDGE L.M.     Amzi Chapin, 1813

1. A - gain, as eve - ning's shad - ow falls, We
2. May strug - gling hearts that seek re - lease Here
3. O God, our light, to thee we bow; With -
4. Life's tu - mult we must meet a - gain; We

gath - er in these hal - lowed walls; And ves - per hymn and
find the rest of God's own peace; And, strength-ened here by
in all shad - ows stand - est thou; Give deep - er calm than
can - not at the shrine re - main; But in the spir - it's

ves - per prayer Rise min - gling on the ho - ly air.
hymn and prayer, Lay down the bur - den and the care.
night can bring; Give sweet - er songs than lips can sing.
se - cret cell May hymn and prayer for - ev - er dwell.

## 272 When the Gladsome Day Declineth

Minot Judson Savage, 1883     SHIPSTON 8.7.8.7.     Warwickshire melody
Arranged by Ralph Vaughan Williams, 1906

1. When the glad-some day de - clin - eth And the earth is wrapped in night,
2. So the night it - self, that hid - eth From our eyes the sun - ny sky,

**EVENING**

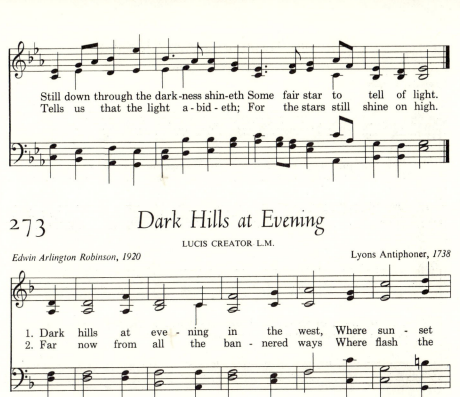

Still down through the dark-ness shin-eth Some fair star to tell of light.
Tells us that the light a - bid - eth; For the stars still shine on high.

## 273 Dark Hills at Evening

LUCIS CREATOR L.M.

*Edwin Arlington Robinson, 1920*                    Lyons Antiphoner, *1738*

1. Dark hills at eve - ning in the west, Where sun - set
2. Far now from all the ban - nered ways Where flash the

hov - ers like a sound Of gold - en horns that
le - gions of the sun, You fade — as if the

sang to rest Old bones of war - riors un - der ground,
last of days Were fad - ing, and all wars were done.

EVENING

## 274 Now, on Land and Sea Descending

VESPER HYMN 8.7.8.7.D.

Samuel Longfellow, 1859

Russian melody?
Arranged by J. A. Stevenson, 1818

1. Now, on land and sea de-scend-ing, Brings the night its peace pro-found;
2. Now, our wants and bur-dens leav-ing To this care who cares for all,

Let our ves-per hymn be blend-ing With the ho-ly calm a-round.
Cease we fear-ing, cease we griev-ing; At this touch our bur-dens fall.

Soon as dies the sun-set glo-ry, Stars of heaven shine out a-bove,
As the dark-ness deep-ens o'er us, Lo, e-ter-nal stars a-rise;

Tell-ing still the an-cient sto-ry—Their Cre-a-tor's change-less love.
Hope and faith and love rise glo-rious, Shin-ing in the spir-it's skies.

EVENING

# Harvest Festival

AFFECTION L.M.

*John Greenleaf Whittier, 1859*　　　*John Greenwood's* Psalmody Harmonized in Score, *1838*

1. Once　more　the　lib - eral　year　laughs　out　O'er
2. O　fa - vors　ev - ery　year　made　new!　O
3. We　shut　our　eyes,　the　flowers　bloom　on;　We
4. Now　let　these　al - tars, wreathed　with　flowers　And

rich - er　stores than　gems　or　gold; Once　more, with har - vest-
bless - ings　with　the　sun - shine　sent! The　boun - ty　o - ver-
mur - mur,　but　the　corn ears　fill; We　choose the shad - ow,
piled with　fruits, a - wake　a - gain Thanks - giv - ing　for　the

song　and　shout,　Is　na - ture's　blood - less　tri - umph　told.
runs　our　due,　The　full - ness　shames　our　dis - con - tent.
but　the　sun　That casts　it　shines　be - hind　us　still.
gold - en　hours,　The　ear - ly　and　the　lat - ter　rain.

AUTUMN AND HARVEST

# 276 Autumn Fields

CRADLE SONG 12.12.12.12.

*Elizabeth Madison, 1942*

*William James Kirkpatrick, 1895*
*Harmonized by Ralph Vaughan Williams, 1931*

1. In sweet fields of au - tumn the gold grain is fall - ing, The
2. The snows of De - cem - ber shall fill wind - y hol - low; The
3. The still - ness of death shall stoop o - ver the wa - ter, The

white clouds drift lone - ly, the wild swan is call - ing. A -
bleak rain trails aft - er, and March wind shall fol - low. The
plov - er sweep low where the pale stream - lets fal - ter; But

las for the dai - sies, the tall fern and grass - es, When
deer through the val - leys leave print of their go - ing; And
deep in the earth clod the black seed is liv - ing, When

wind - sweep and rain - fall fill low - lands and pass - es.
di - amonds of sleet mark the ridg - es of snow - ing.
spring sounds her bu - gles for rous - ing and giv - ing.

AUTUMN AND HARVEST

# 277

# I Walk the Unfrequented Road

CONSOLATION C.M.

From Frederick Lucian Hosmer
In Stanton Coit's Social Worship, II, 1913

John Wyeth's
Repository of Sacred Music, Part Second, 1813

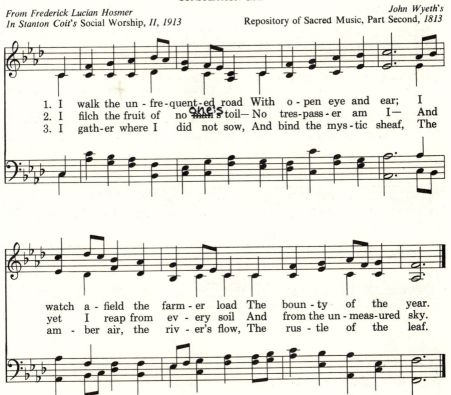

1. I walk the un-fre-quent-ed road With o-pen eye and ear; I
2. I filch the fruit of no one's toil— No tres-pass-er am I— And
3. I gath-er where I did not sow, And bind the mys-tic sheaf, The

watch a-field the farm-er load The boun-ty of the year.
yet I reap from ev-ery soil And from the un-meas-ured sky.
am-ber air, the riv-er's flow, The rus-tle of the leaf.

4. A beauty springtime never knew
Haunts all the quiet ways,
And sweeter shines the landscape through
Its veil of autumn haze.

5. I face the hills, the streams, the wood,
And feel with all akin;
My heart expands; their fortitude
And peace and joy flow in.

AUTUMN AND HARVEST

## 278 Come, Ye Thankful People

ST. GEORGE'S WINDSOR 7.7.7.7.D.

*Henry Alford, 1844*                                                      *George Job Elvey, 1858*

1. Come, ye thank-ful peo - ple, come, Raise the song of har - vest-home:
2. All the world is God's own field, Fruit un - to this praise to yield;

All is safe - ly gath - ered in Ere the win - ter storms be - gin;
Wheat and tares to - geth - er sown, Un - to joy or sor - row grown:

God, our Mak - er, doth pro - vide For our wants to be sup - plied;
First the blade, and then the ear, Then the full corn shall ap - pear;

Come to God's own tem - ple, come, Raise the song of har - vest-home.
Lord of har - vest, grant that we Whole-some grain and pure may be.

AUTUMN AND HARVEST

# 279 *Hanukkah Hymn*

MOOZ TSUR 7.6.7.6.6.6.3.3.6.

Leopold Stein, ca. 1860
Adapted from the German by
Marcus M. Jastrow and
Gustav Gottheil, 1897; altered

*German synagogue melody*

1. Rock of A-ges, let our song Praise thy sav-ing pow-er;
2. Kin-dling new the ho-ly lamps, Priests, ap-proved in suf-fering,
3. Chil-dren of a proph-et race, Wheth-er free or fet-tered,

Thou a-midst the rag-ing foes Wast our shel-tering tow-er.
Pu-ri-fied the na-tion's shrine, Brought to God their of-fering.
Wake the ech-oes of the songs Where ye may be scat-tered.

Fu-rious they as-sailed us, But thine arm a-vailed us,
And the courts sur-round-ing Hear, in joy a-bound-ing,
Yours the mes-sage cheer-ing That the time is near-ing

And thy word Broke their sword When our own strength failed us.
Hap-py throngs Sing-ing songs With a might-y sound-ing.
Which will see All men free, Ty-rants dis-ap-pear-ing.

HANUKKAH

# 280  O Come, O Come, Emmanuel

### VENI EMMANUEL 8.8.8.8.8.8.

*13th century hymn in*
Psalteriolum Cantionum Catholicarum, *1710*
*Translation composite, based on John Mason Neale, 1851*
*Third stanza by Vincent B. Silliman, 1928*

*Adapted from plainsong by*
*Thomas Helmore, 1854*

1. O come, O come, Em - man - u - el, And ran - som cap - tive
2. O come, thou Day-spring, come and cheer Our spir - its by thine
3. O come, O come, thou Lord of love, De - clare thy law all

Is - ra - el, That mourns in lone - ly ex - ile here Un-
ad - vent here; Dis - perse the gloom - y shades of night, Break
law a - bove; From dire op - pres - sions bring re - lease, And

til the Son of God ap - pear. Re - joice! Re - joice! Em-
through the clouds and bring us light. Re - joice! Re - joice! Em-
lead us in the way of peace.

man - u - el Shall come to thee, O Is - ra - el.

ADVENT

# 281

# People, Look East

BESANÇON CAROL 8.7.9.8.8.7.

*Eleanor Farjeon, 1928*

*French carol*
*Harmonized by John Stainer (1840-1901)*

1. Peo - ple, look East. The time is near Of the
2. Fur - rows, be glad. Though earth is bare, One more
3. Stars, keep the watch. When night is dim One more

crown - ing of the year. Make your house fair as you are
seed is plant - ed there: Give up your strength the seed to
light the bowl shall brim, Shin - ing be - yond the frost - y

a - ble, Trim the hearth, and set the ta - ble. Peo - ple, look
nour - ish, That in course the flower may flour - ish. Peo - ple, look
weath - er, Bright as sun and moon to - geth - er. Peo - ple, look

East, and sing to - day: Love, the Guest, is on the way.
East, and sing to - day: Love, the Rose, is on the way.
East, and sing to - day: Love, the Star, is on the way.

**ADVENT**

# 282 Hail to ~~the Lord~~ *our Gods* Anointed

WEBB 7.6.7.6.D.

*From James Montgomery, 1821*
*Based on Psalm 72*

*George James Webb, 1837*

1. Hail to ~~the Lord's~~ *our Gods* a-noint-ed, Great Da-vid's great-er son! Hail, in the time ap-point-ed, His reign on earth be-gun! He comes to break op-pres-sion, To set the cap-tive free, To take a-way trans-gres-sion, And rule in eq-ui-ty.

2. He shall come down like show-ers Up-on the fruit-ful earth, And joy and hope, like flow-ers, Spring in his path to birth: Be-fore him on the moun-tains Shall peace, the her-ald, go; And right-eous-ness in foun-tains From hill to val-ley flow.

3. He comes with suc-cor speed-y To those who suf-fer wrong; To help the poor and need-y, And bid the weak be strong. The tide of time shall nev-er His cov-e-nant re-move; His name shall stand for-ev-er: That name to us is love.

ADVENT

# 283 Watchman, Tell Us of the Night

WATCHMAN 7.7.7.7.D.

John Bowring, 1825

Lowell Mason, 1830

1. Watch-man, tell us of the night, What its signs of prom-ise are.
2. Watch-man, tell us of the night; High - er yet that star as-cends.
3. Watch-man, tell us of the night, For the morn - ing seems to dawn.

Trav - eler, o'er yon moun-tain's height See that glo - ry - beam - ing star.
Trav - eler, bless-ed - ness and light, Peace and truth its course por-tends.
Trav - eler, dark-ness takes its flight, Doubt and ter - ror are with-drawn.

Watch-man, doth its beau-teous ray Aught of hope or joy fore - tell?
Watch-man, will its beams a - lone Gild the spot that gave them birth?
Watch-man, let thy wan-derings cease, Hie thee to thy qui - et home.

Trav - eler, yes, it brings the day, Prom - ised day of Is - ra - el.
Trav - eler, a - ges are its own, See! it bursts o'er all the earth.
Trav - eler, lo! the Prince of Peace, Lo! the Son of God is come.

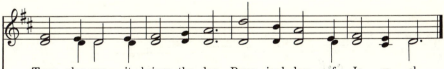

ADVENT

# 284 Veiled in Darkness Judah Lay

NICHT SO TRAURIG 7.7.7.7.7.7.

*Douglas LeTell Rights, 1915*  *Johann Georg Ebeling, 1666*

1. Veiled in dark-ness Ju-dah lay, Wait-ing for the
2. Still the earth in dark-ness lies. Up from death's dark
3. Light of light, we hum-bly pray, Shine up-on thy

prom-ised day, While a-cross the shad-owy night
vale a-rise Voic-es of a world in grief,
world to-day; Break the gloom of our dark night,

Streamed a flood of glo-rious light, Heaven-ly voic-es
Prayers of those who seek re-lief: Now our dark-ness
Fill our souls with love and light, Send thy bless-ed

chant-ing call, "Peace on earth, good-will to all,"
pierce a-gain,
word a-gain,

**ADVENT**

# The First Nowell

THE FIRST NOWELL Irregular, with refrain

*English carol*
*Davis Gilbert's* Ancient Christmas Carols, *1823*

*William Sandys'* Christmas
Carols Ancient and Modern, *1833*
*Harmonized by John Stainer, 1871*

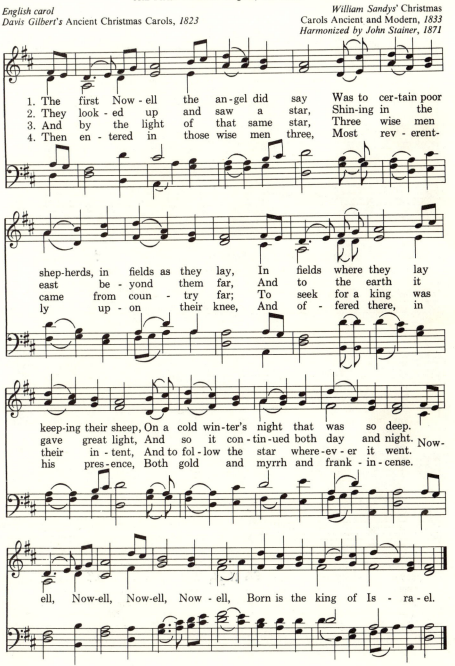

1. The first Now-ell the an-gel did say Was to cer-tain poor
2. They look-ed up and saw a star, Shin-ing in the
3. And by the light of that same star, Three wise men
4. Then en-tered in those wise men three, Most rev-erent-

shep-herds, in fields as they lay, In fields where they lay
east be-yond them far, And to the earth it
came from coun-try far; To seek for a king was
ly up-on their knee, And of-fered there, in

keep-ing their sheep, On a cold win-ter's night that was so deep.
gave great light, And so it con-tin-ued both day and night. Now-
their in-tent, And to fol-low the star where-ev-er it went.
his pres-ence, Both gold and myrrh and frank-in-cense.

ell, Now-ell, Now-ell, Now-ell, Born is the king of Is-ra-el.

CHRISTMAS

## 286 O Little Town of Bethlehem

ST. LOUIS 8.6.8.6.7.6.8.6.

*Phillips Brooks, 1868*         *Lewis H. Redner, 1868*

1. O    lit - tle town of  Beth - le - hem, How  still  we  see  thee  lie! A -
2. For Christ is  born  of  Ma  -  ry, And  gath - ered all  a - bove, While
3. How  si - lent - ly, how  si - lent - ly  The  won - drous gift  is  given! So
4. O    ho - ly Child  of  Beth - le - hem, De - scend  to  us,  we  pray; Cast

bove  thy deep and  dream - less sleep The   si - lent stars  go   by;  Yet
mor - tals sleep, the   an - gels keep  Their watch of  won - dering love. O
God  im - parts to   hu - man hearts The  bless - ings of  This heaven. No
out  our  sin and   en - ter  in;  Be  born in   us   to - day. We

in   thy dark streets shin - eth  The  ev - er - last - ing  light; The
morn-ing stars, to - geth - er  Pro - claim the  ho - ly  birth; And
ear  may hear his  com - ing, But  in  this world of  sin, Where
hear the Christ-mas  an - gels  The  great glad  ti - dings tell; O

hopes and fears  of   all   the years Are  met  in  thee  to - night.
prais - es sing  to  God the King, And  peace to  all  on  earth.
meek souls will  re - ceive him, still  The  dear Christ en - ters  in.
come  to  us,   a - bide with us,  Our  Lord Em - man - u - el!

**CHRISTMAS**

# 287 It Came upon the Midnight Clear

Edmund Hamilton Sears, 1849  CAROL C.M.D.  Richard Storrs Willis, 1850

1. It came up-on the mid-night clear, That glo-rious song of old, From
2. Still through the clo-ven skies they come, With peace-ful wings un - furled; And
3. But with the woes of sin and strife The world has suf-fered long; Be -
4. For, lo! the days are has-tening on By proph-et bards fore - told, When

an - gels bend-ing near the earth, To touch their harps of gold: "Peace
still their heaven-ly mu - sic floats O'er all the wea - ry world. A -
neath the an - gel-strain have rolled Two thou-sand years of wrong; And
with the ev - er - cir - cling years Comes round the age of gold: When

on the earth, good - will to men, From heaven's all-gra-cious King." The
bove its sad and low - ly plains They bend on hov-ering wing; And
War - ring his man - hear not The love song which they bring. O
peace shall o - ver all the earth Its an - cient splen-dors fling, And

world in sol - emn still - ness lay To hear the an - gels sing.
ev - er o'er its Ba - bel sounds The bless - ed an - gels sing.
hush the noise, ye men of strife, And hear the an - gels sing.
the whole world give back the song Which now the an - gels sing.

CHRISTMAS

# 288 O Come, All Ye Faithful

### ADESTE FIDELES Irregular

*Latin, 18th century*
*Translated by Frederick Oakeley, 1852, and others*

*John Francis Wade's*
*manuscript, ca. 1740–43*

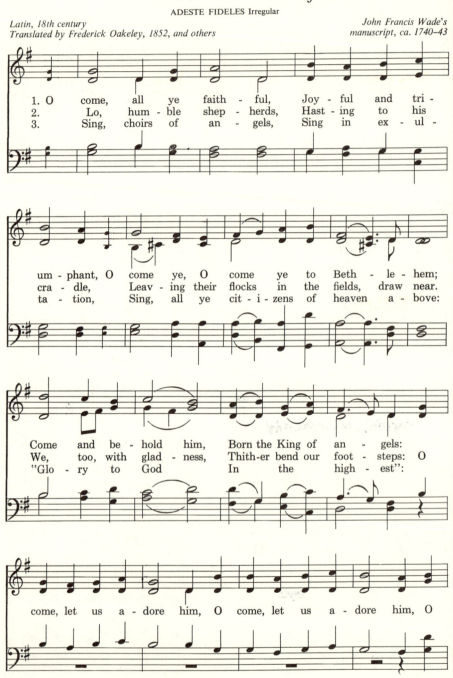

1. O come, all ye faith - ful, Joy - ful and tri -
2. Lo, hum - ble shep - herds, Hast - ing to his
3. Sing, choirs of an - gels, Sing in ex - ul -

um - phant, O come ye, O come ye to Beth - le - hem;
cra - dle, Leav - ing their flocks in the fields, draw near.
ta - tion, Sing, all ye cit - i - zens of heaven a - bove:

Come and be - hold him, Born the King of an - gels: 
We, too, with glad - ness, Thith-er bend our foot - steps: O
"Glo - ry to God In the high - est": 

come, let us a - dore him, O come, let us a - dore him, O

**CHRISTMAS**

come, let us a - dore him, Christ the Lord.

## 289 Silent Night, Holy Night

STILLE NACHT Irregular

*Joseph Mohr, 1818*
*Translation in C. L. Hutchins'*
Sunday School Hymnal, *1871*

*Franz Xaver Gruber, 1818*

1. Si - lent night, ho - ly night, All is calm, all is bright
2. Si - lent night, ho - ly night, Shep-herds quake at the sight,
3. Si - lent night, ho - ly night, Son of God, love's pure light

Round yon vir - gin moth-er and child. Ho - ly in - fant so ten - der and mild,
Glo - ries stream from heav-en a-far, Heaven-ly hosts sing "Al - le - lu - ia,
Ra - diant beams from thy ho-ly face, With the dawn of re - deem - ing grace,

Sleep in heav-en-ly peace, Sleep in heav - en - ly peace.
Christ, the Sav-ior, is born! Christ, the Sav - ior, is born!"
Je - sus, Lord, at thy birth, Je - sus, Lord, at thy birth.

**CHRISTMAS**

# 290 Thank We Now the Lord of Heaven

*(handwritten: God)*

**DIVINUM MYSTERIUM** 7.7.7.7.7.7.7.

*From Henry W. Hawkes, 1898*

*Plainsong, 12th century?*
*Theodoric Petri's* Piae Cantiones, *1582*

1. Thank we now the Lord of heaven   For the day-spring he has given, *(handwritten: God; we've been)*
2. Where our hearts through love are strong,   Still is heard the an - gel song.

For the light of truth and grace   Shin-ing from the Mas - ter's face. *(handwritten: Author's)*
"Glo-ry be to God on high,   Peace on earth, good-will to men": *(handwritten: all)*

Years   have   come   and   years   have   gone,
Sing,   ye   an - gels   from   the   sky;

CHRISTMAS

Still that light is shin-ing on, Ev - er - more and ev - er - more!
Mor-tals, raise the glad re - frain, Ev - er - more and ev - er - more!

# 291 *Ye Shepherd Plains of Bethlehem*

THIS ENDRIS NYGHT C.M.

*William Merriam Crane, 1937*

*English carol, 15th century*
*Arranged by Ralph Vaughan Williams, 1906*

1. Ye shep-herd plains of Beth - le - hem, That rest in si - lence long,
2. Ye shad-owed homes in lands op-pressed By cen - tu - ries of wrong,
3. Ye bus - y towns and cit - ies vast, With all your hur - ried throng,
4. Ye wid - er plains of neigh-bor lands, Ye hills and moun-tains strong,

Break forth your Christ-mas ech - oes, till Men hear the an - gel song.
Let heaven-ly glad - ness en - ter in For, hark, the an - gel song.
Calm now your noise and tu - mult, while Ye learn the an - gel song.
Take up the sound, and ev - ery-where Re - peat the an - gel song.

CHRISTMAS

## 292    In the Lonely Midnight

ADORO TE DEVOTE 6.5.6.5.D.

*From Theodore Chickering Williams, 1914*

*Solesmes version of the plainsong melody; adapted*

1. In the lone-ly mid-night, On the win-try hill, Shep-herds heard the an - gels
2. Though in Da-vid's cit - y An-gels sing no more, Love makes an-gel mu - sic
3. Though the child of Mar - y, Her-ald-ed on high, In his man-ger cra - dle

Sing-ing, "Peace, good will." Lis - ten, O ye wea - ry, To the
On earth's dark-est shore; Though no heaven - ly glo - ry Meet your
May no long - er lie, Love is king for - ev - er, Though the

an - gels' song, Un - to you the ti - dings Of great joy be - long.
won - dering eyes, Love can make your dwell - ing Bright as par - a - dise.
proud world scorn; If ye tru - ly seek him, Christ for you is born.

**CHRISTMAS**

# 293
## Heir of All the Waiting Ages

PICARDY 8.7.8.7.8.7.

*Marion Franklin Ham, 1937*

*French melody*
*English Hymnal, 1906*

1. Heir of all the wait - ing a - ges, Hope of a - ges yet to be,
2. Thou shalt be the great phy - si - cian For the sor-rows of human - kind;
3. An - gel voic - es in the heav - ens Joy - ful - ly pro - claim thy birth,

Light to them that sit in dark - ness, Liv-ing truth to make men *[us]* free:
Thou shalt heal the wound-ed spir - it, And give vi - sion to the blind —
Sing - ing of a prom - ised king - dom *[glo-ry]*, Reign of right-eous-ness and worth —

Strick-en souls shall know the com - fort Of thy gra-cious min - is - try.
Larg - er life for all who seek it In the child-like heart and mind.
Songs of proph-e - cy and prom - ise, Peace, good will to men *[all]* on earth.

**CHRISTMAS**

# 294 Angels We Have Heard on High

GLORIA 7.7.7.7. with refrain

*French carol*
*Version by Earl Marlatt, 1937*

*French carol*
Nouveau recueil de cantiques, *1855*

1. An - gels we have heard on high Sweet - ly sing - ing through the night,
2. Shep-herds, why this ju - bi - lee? Why these songs of hap - py cheer?
3. Come to Beth - le - hem and see Him whose birth the an - gels sing;

And the moun-tains in re - ply Ech - o - ing their brave de - light.
What great bright-ness did you see? What glad ti - dings did you hear?
Come, a - dore on bend - ed knee, Christ, the Lord, the new - born King.

Glo - - - - - - - - - - - - - ri - a

in ex - cel - sis De - o. De - o.

# 295 While Shepherds Watched

CHRISTMAS C.M.

*Nahum Tate, 1700*

*George Frideric Handel, 1728*
*Adapted in David Weyman's Melodia Sacra, 1815*

1. While shep-herds watched their flocks by night, All
2. "To you, in Da-vid's town this day, Is
3. "The heaven-ly babe you there shall find To

seat-ed on the ground, The an-gel of the Lord *our God* came down, And
born of Da-vid's line, The Sav-ior, who is Christ, the Lord, And
hu-man view dis-played, All mean-ly wrapped in swath-ing bands, And

glo-ry shone a-round, And glo-ry shone a-round.
this shall be the sign, And this shall be the sign:
in a man-ger laid, And in a man-ger laid."

4. Thus spake the seraph—and forthwith,
   Appeared a shining throng
   Of angels, praising God, who thus
   Addressed their joyful song:

5. "All glory be to God on high,
   And to the earth be peace; *all*
   Good will henceforth from heaven to ~~men~~
   Begin, and never cease!"

CHRISTMAS

# 296 On This Day Everywhere

PERSONENT HODIE 6.6.6.6.6.6. with refrain

Composite, 1958
Based on Theodoric Petri's Piae Cantiones, 1582

Theodoric Petri's Piae Cantiones, *1582*
Arranged by Gustav Holst, 1924

*Moderato maestoso*

1. On this day ev - ery - where
2. Sweet the babe, strange his bed,
3. Ma - gi three find their way

Chil - dren's songs fill the air, Greet the child,
Man - ger hay round his head, Cat - tle there
By a star's shin - ing ray To the child

new and fair, Christ - mas gift so ho - ly,
in the shed; Mar - y, Jo - seph by him,
in the hay; Give their won - drous pres - ents,

CHRISTMAS

Born in sta - ble low - ly.
Shep - herds draw - ing nigh him. Id - e - o -
Gold and myrrh and in - cense.

o - o, Id - e - o - o - o, Id - e - o

*D. C.*

glo - ri - a in ex - cel - sis De - o!

*D. C.*

CHRISTMAS

# 297 Break Forth, O Beauteous Light

ERMUNTRE DICH, MEIN SCHWACHER GEIST 8.7.8.7.8.8.7.7.

*Johann Rist, 1641*
*Translated by John Troutbeck (1832–1899)*

*Johann Schop, 1641*
*Harmonized by J. S. Bach, 1734*

Break forth, O beau-teous heaven-ly light, And ush-er in the morn-ing; Ye shep-herds, shrink not with af-fright, But hear the an-gels' warn-ing. This child, now weak in in-fan-cy, Our con-fi-dence and joy shall be, The power of Sa-tan break-ing, Our peace e-ter-nal mak-ing.

**CHRISTMAS**

# 298    Lo, How a Rose E'er Blooming

ES IST EIN' ROS' ENTSPRUNGEN 7.6.7.6.6.7.6.

*Brother Conrad of Mainz ? 1587/8*
*From translation by Theodore Baker (1851–1934)*

Alte catholische geistliche Kirchengeseng,
Cologne, 1599
*Harmonized by Michael Praetorius, 1609*

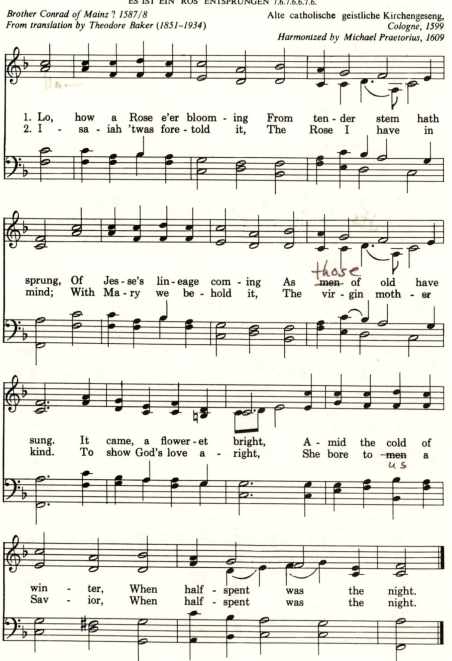

1. Lo, how a Rose e'er bloom - ing From ten - der stem hath
2. I - sa - iah 'twas fore - told it, The Rose I have in

sprung, Of Jes - se's lin - eage com - ing As those men of old have
mind; With Ma - ry we be - hold it, The vir - gin moth - er

sung. It came, a flower - et bright, A - mid the cold of
kind. To show God's love a - right, She bore to us men a

win - ter, When half - spent was the night.
Sav - ior, When half - spent was the night.

CHRISTMAS

# 299 Joy to the World

ANTIOCH C.M.

*From Isaac Watts, 1719*

*Lowell Mason, 1836*
*On a motive from Handel's Messiah, 1742*

1. Joy to the world! the Lord is come: Let earth re-
2. Joy to the earth! the Sav-ior reigns: Let men all their
3. No more let sins and sor-rows grow, Nor thorns in-
4. He rules the world with truth and grace, And makes the

ceive her king; Let ev-ery heart pre-pare him room, And
songs em-ploy, While fields and floods, rocks, hills, and plains Re-
fest the ground: He comes to make his bless-ings flow As
na-tions prove The glo-ries of his right-eous-ness And

heaven and na-ture sing, And heaven and na-ture
peat the sound-ing joy, Re-peat the sound-ing
far as sin is found, As far as sin is
won-ders of his love, And won-ders of his

And heaven and na-ture sing, And

sing, And heaven, and heaven and na-ture sing.
joy, Re-peat, re-peat the sound-ing joy.
found, As far, as far as sin is found.
love, And won-ders, won-ders of his love.

heaven and na-ture sing,

CHRISTMAS

# 300 We Three Kings of Orient Are

KINGS OF ORIENT Irregular

*From John Henry Hopkins, Jr., 1857*
*Fifth stanza by Vincent B. Silliman, 1935*

*John Henry Hopkins, Jr., 1857*

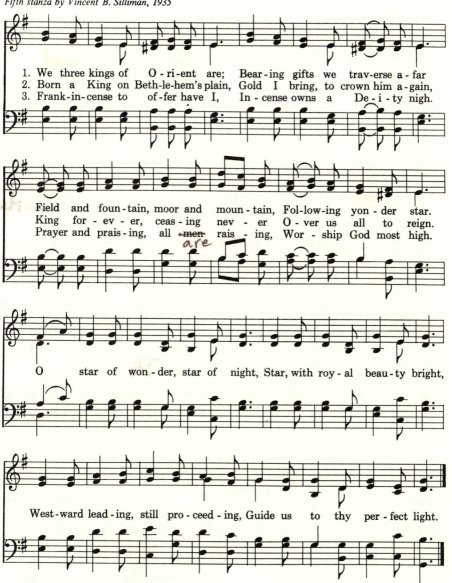

1. We three kings of O-ri-ent are; Bear-ing gifts we trav-erse a-far
2. Born a King on Beth-le-hem's plain, Gold I bring, to crown him a-gain,
3. Frank-in-cense to of-fer have I, In-cense owns a De-i-ty nigh.

Field and foun-tain, moor and moun-tain, Fol-low-ing yon-der star.
King for-ev-er, ceas-ing nev-er O-ver us all to reign.
Prayer and prais-ing, all men rais-ing, Wor-ship God most high.

O star of won-der, star of night, Star, with roy-al beau-ty bright,

West-ward lead-ing, still pro-ceed-ing, Guide us to thy per-fect light.

4. Myrrh is mine, its bitter perfume
   Breathes a life of gathering gloom—
   Sorrowing, sighing, bleeding, dying,
   Sealed in the stone-cold tomb.

5. See him now in power arise,
   Mighty through his sacrifice.
   Alleluia! Alleluia!
   Echo it, earth and skies.

EPIPHANY

# 301

## 'Tis Winter Now

PUER NOBIS NASCITUR L.M.

*Samuel Longfellow, 1859*

*Latin carol, 15th century*
*Adapted by Michael Praetorius, 1609*

1. 'Tis win - ter now; the fall - en snow Has left the
2. And though a - broad the sharp winds blow, And skies are

heavens all cold - ly clear; Through leaf - less boughs the
chill, and frosts are keen, Home clos - er draws her *its*

sharp winds blow, And all the earth lies dead and drear.
cir - cle now, And warm - er glows her *its* light with - in.

# 302

## Winter Is a Cold Thing

VALLEY FORGE 6.6.7.6. Irregular

*Barrows Dunham, 1954*

*Henry Leland Clarke, 1958*

1. Win - ter is a cold thing, But faith and hope are warm, And
   love has its de - fens - es Where win - ter can - not blow, And

**WINTER**

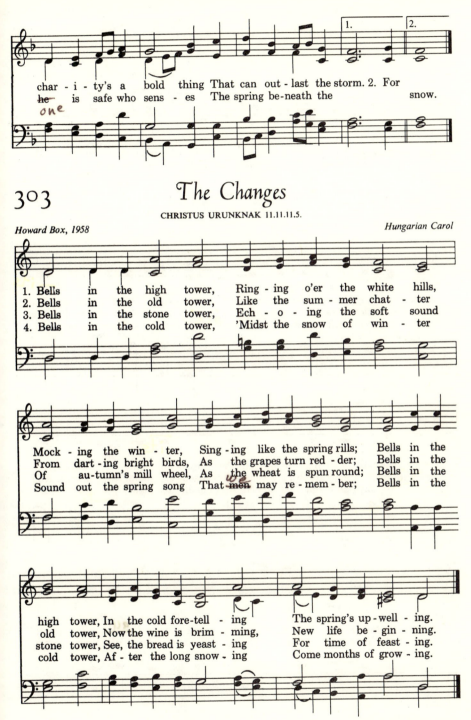

char - i - ty's a bold thing That can out - last the storm. 2. For
he is safe who sens - es The spring be-neath the snow.

*one*

## 303

# The Changes

CHRISTUS URUNKNAK 11.11.11.5.

Howard Box, 1958

Hungarian Carol

1. Bells in the high tower, Ring - ing o'er the white hills,
2. Bells in the old tower, Like the sum - mer chat - ter
3. Bells in the stone tower, Ech - o - ing the soft sound
4. Bells in the cold tower, 'Midst the snow of win - ter

Mock - ing the win - ter, Sing - ing like the spring rills; Bells in the
From dart - ing bright birds, As the grapes turn red - der; Bells in the
Of au - tumn's mill wheel, As the wheat is spun round; Bells in the
Sound out the spring song That men may re - mem - ber; Bells in the

high tower, In the cold fore-tell - ing The spring's up - well - ing.
old tower, Now the wine is brim - ming, New life be - gin - ning.
stone tower, See, the bread is yeast - ing For time of feast - ing.
cold tower, Af - ter the long snow - ing Come months of grow - ing.

**THE CHANGING YEAR**

# 304 All Beautiful the March of Days

FOREST GREEN C.M.D.

*Frances Whitmarsh Wile, ca. 1907*

*English melody*
*Arranged by Ralph Vaughan Williams, 1906*

1. All beau-ti-ful the march of days, As sea-sons come and go; The
2. O'er white ex-pans-es spar-kling pure The ra-diant morns un-fold; The
3. O Thou from whose un-fath-omed law The year in beau-ty flows, Thy-

hand that shaped the rose hath wrought The crys-tal of the snow; Hath
sol-emn splen-dors of the night Burn bright-er through the cold; Life
self the vi-sion pass-ing by In crys-tal and in rose, Day

sent the hoar-y frost of heaven, The flow-ing wa-ters sealed, And
mounts in ev-ery throb-bing vein, Love deep-ens round the hearth, And
un-to day doth ut-ter speech, And night to night pro-claim, In

laid a si-lent love-li-ness On hill and wood and field.
clear-er sounds the an-gel-hymn, "Good will to men on earth."
ev-er chang-ing words of light, The won-der of thy name.

THE CHANGING YEAR

# Ring Out, Wild Bells

**305**

DEUS TUORUM MILITUM L.M.

*From Alfred Lord Tennyson, 1850*

Grenoble Antiphoner, 1868; adapted

1. Ring out, wild bells, to the wild, wild sky, The fly - ing
2. Ring out the old, ring in the new, Ring, hap - py
3. Ring out the grief that saps the mind For those that

cloud, the frost - y light: The year is dy - ing
bells, a - cross the snow: The year is go - ing,
here we see no more; Ring out the feud of

in the night; Ring out, wild bells, and let him die.
let him go; Ring out the false, ring in the true.
rich and poor; Ring in re - dress to all *hu*-man - kind.

4. Ring out false pride in place and blood,
   The civic slander and the spite;
   Ring in the love of truth and right,
   Ring in the common love of good.

5. Ring in the valiant *Soul* and free,
   The larger heart, the kindlier hand;
   Ring out the darkness of the land;
   Ring in the light that is to be.

THE CHANGING YEAR

# 306 To Make This Earth, Our Hermitage

DEVOTION L.M.

Robert Louis Stevenson, 1879

A. D. Carden's Missouri Harmony, 1820

1. To make this earth, our her - mit - age, A cheer - ful and a change - ful page, God's bright and in - tri - cate de - vice Of days and sea - sons doth suf - fice.

2. Here shall the wiz - ard moon as - cend The heav - ens, in the crim - son end Of day's de - clin - ing splen - dor; here The ar - mies of the stars ap - pear.

3. The neigh - bor hol - lows, dry or wet, Spring shall with ten - der flowers be - set; And oft the morn - ing mus - er see Larks ris - ing from the broom - y lea.

4. When dai - sies go, shall win - ter time Sil - ver the sim - ple grass with rime; And when snow - bright the moor ex - pands, How shall your chil - dren clap their hands!

THE CHANGING YEAR

# 307 Thou, Earth, Art Ours

WAS GOTT THUT 8.8.8.8.8.8.

*Mary Howitt (1799–1888)*                    *Severus Gastorius, 1681; adapted*

1. Thou, earth, art ours, and ours to keep, That man (we) may la-bor
2. Thou, earth, art mine— thou sum-mer earth, Fresh with the dews, the
3. Thou, earth, art mine; when days are dim, And leaf-less stands the
4. The earth is yours and mine, O men (friends). Ours are all worlds, all

not in vain; Thou givest the grass, the corn, the tree; Seed-
sun-shine bright, With gold-en clouds in eve-ning hours, With
state-ly tree, When from the north the fierce winds blow, When
suns that shine; Dark-ness and light, and life and death, What-

time and har-vest come from thee, The ear-ly and the lat-ter rain.
sing-ing birds and fra-grant flowers, Crea-tures of beau-ty and de-light.
fall-eth fast the man-tling snow, Thou, earth, be-long-est still to me.
e'er all space in-hab-it-eth, All these are yours and all are mine.

THE CHANGING YEAR

# 308 Praise to God and Thanks We Bring

SPANISH HYMN 7.7.7.7.D.

*From William Channing Gannett, 1882*

*Arranged by Benjamin Carr, 1824*

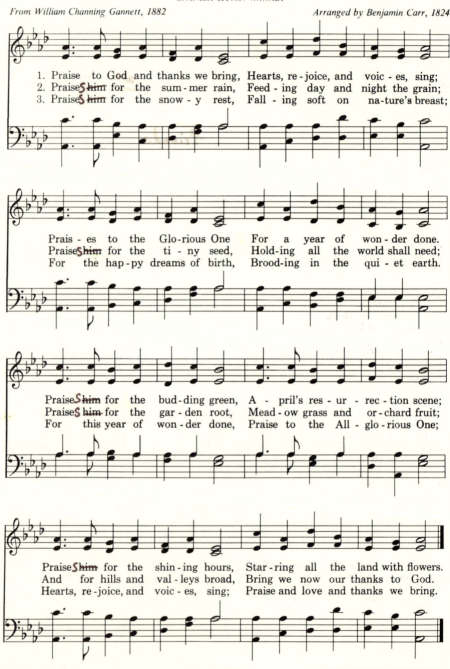

1. Praise to God and thanks we bring, Hearts, re-joice, and voic-es, sing;
2. Praise him for the sum-mer rain, Feed-ing day and night the grain;
3. Praise him for the snow-y rest, Fall-ing soft on na-ture's breast;

Prais-es to the Glo-rious One For a year of won-der done.
Praise him for the ti-ny seed, Hold-ing all the world shall need;
For the hap-py dreams of birth, Brood-ing in the qui-et earth.

Praise him for the bud-ding green, A-pril's res-ur-rec-tion scene;
Praise him for the gar-den root, Mead-ow grass and or-chard fruit;
For this year of won-der done, Praise to the All-glo-rious One;

Praise him for the shin-ing hours, Star-ring all the land with flowers.
And for hills and val-leys broad, Bring we now our thanks to God.
Hearts, re-joice, and voic-es, sing; Praise and love and thanks we bring.

THE CHANGING YEAR

# 309

# Hosanna in the Highest

ELLACOMBE 7.6.7.6.D.

*John Howland Lathrop, 1935*          *X. L. Hartig's* Vollständige Sammlung, *ca. 1833*

1. Ho - san - na in the high - est! Our ea - ger hearts ac - claim The
2. Long a - ges dim the mes - sage, And cus - tom has suf - ficed For
3. O first of man - y proph - ets Who come of sim - ple folk To

proph - et of the king - dom (*heav - ens*), Who bears Mes - si - ah's name. O
mer - chants and for pri - ces (*rul - ers*), To bow, and own him Christ. But
free us from our bond - age, To break op - pres - sion's yoke: Re -

bold, O fool - ish peas - ants, To deem that he (*another*) should reign! The
when a - broth - er spir - it A - ris - es from the plain, Then
store our eyes from blind - ness, Make clear the life, the way That

tem - ple and the pal - ace Look down in high dis - dain.
*those men in* of pow - er trem - ble, And cru - ci - fy a - gain.
leads through love and jus - tice Un - to the peace-crowned day.

PALM SUNDAY

# 310 Lift Up Your Heads, Ye Mighty Gates

MISSTRÖSTA EJ ATT GUD ÄR GOD 8.8.8.8.8.8.

*Georg Weissel, 1642; based on Psalm 24*
*Translated by Catherine Winkworth, 1855*
*Adapted, 1960*

Then Swenska Psalmboken, *Stockholm, 1697*

1. Lift up your heads, ye might-y gates, Be-hold the Prince of
2. Fling wide the por-tals of your heart; Make it a tem-ple

Peace a-waits. The Son of *God* is draw-ing near, The
set a-part, A-dorned with prayer, and love, and joy, Its

hope of long-ing hearts is here. An end to strife and
earth-ly powers in Heaven's em-ploy; So shall your sov-ereign

woe he brings, Where-fore the earth is glad and sings.
en-ter in, And new and no-bler life be-gin.

PALM SUNDAY

# 311 O Sacred Head, Now Wounded

PASSION CHORALE 7.6.7.6.D.

*Based on Latin attributed to Bernard of Clairvaux (1091–1153)*
*German version by Paulus Gerhardt, 1656*
*From translation by James Waddell Alexander, 1830*

Hans Leo Hassler, 1601
Harmonized by J. S. Bach, 1729

1. O  sa-cred head, now  wound-ed,  With  grief and shame bowed down, Now
2. What lan-guage shall I   bor-row  To  thank thee, dear-est  friend, For

scorn-ful-ly  sur-round-ed  With thorns, thy  on-ly   crown: How
this  thy  dy-ing   sor-row, Thy  pit-y  with-out   end?  Let

art  thou pale with   an  -  guish, With sore  a-buse and   scorn! How
me  be thine for  -  ev  -  er.  And, should I  faint-ing  be,  Oh,

does that  vis-age   lan-guish  Which  once was  bright as  morn!
let  me  nev-er,   nev-er,  Out-live my  love  to  thee.

MAUNDY THURSDAY AND GOOD FRIDAY

## 312   Beneath the Shadow of the Cross

DUNDEE C.M.

Samuel Longfellow, 1848

Scottish Psalter, 1615

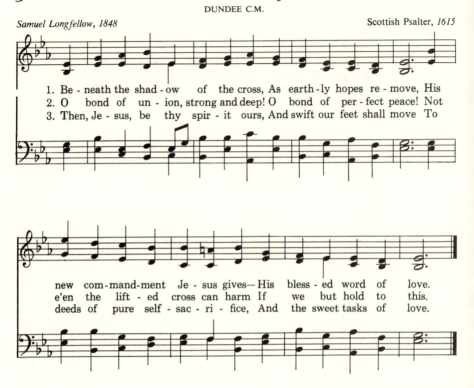

1. Be - neath the shad - ow of the cross, As earth - ly hopes re - move, His
2. O bond of un - ion, strong and deep! O bond of per - fect peace! Not
3. Then, Je - sus, be thy spir - it ours, And swift our feet shall move To

new com-mand-ment Je - sus gives—His bless - ed word of love.
e'en the lift - ed cross can harm If we but hold to this.
deeds of pure self - sac - ri - fice, And the sweet tasks of love.

## 313   Gethsemane and Calvary

CAMPIAN 5 7.7.7.7.

John Reynell Wreford, 1837
Samuel Longfellow, 1848

Thomas Campian, ca. 1613; arranged

1. When my love to God grows weak, When for deep - er faith I seek,
2. There I walk a - mid the shades, While the lin - gering twi - light fades;
3. When my love for man grows weak, When for strong - er faith I seek,

MAUNDY THURSDAY AND GOOD FRIDAY

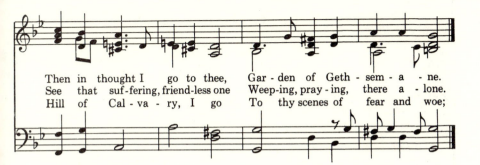

Then in thought I go to thee, Gar-den of Geth-sem-a-ne.
See that suf-fering, friend-less one Weep-ing, pray-ing, there a-lone.
Hill of Cal-va-ry, I go To thy scenes of fear and woe;

4. There behold his agony
   Suffered on the bitter tree;
   See his anguish, see his faith,
   Love triumphant still in death.

5. Then to life I turn again,
   Learning all the worth of pain,
   Learning all the might that lies
   In a full self-sacrifice.

314 *Now in the Tomb Is Laid*

LAMENT 6.6.6.6.

*Padraic Colum, 1926*                           *Vincent Persichetti, 1956*

1. Now in the tomb is laid, Who in the wide world walked, And
2. Now in the tomb is laid, Who told the spar-row's worth, The
3. Per-fect, no wound nor mark! By thine own dark-ened hour, Do

talked with one and all. Now in the tomb is laid.
lil-y's prais-es said. Now in the tomb is laid.
live with-in my heart. Per-fect, no wound nor mark!

Tune copyrighted by Elkan-Vogel Co., Inc.        MAUNDY THURSDAY AND GOOD FRIDAY

# 315 Past Are the Cross, the Scourge, the Thorn

O FILII ET FILIAE 8.8.8. with alleluias

*Alfred Charles Jewitt, 1879*

*French melody, 15th century?; adapted*
*Airs sur les hymnes sacrez, odes et noëls, 1623; adapted*

Al - le - lu - ia, Al - le - lu - ia, Al - le - lu - ia!

1. Past are the cross, the scourge, the thorn, The
2. Then let us raise the glo - rious strain, Love's

scoff - ing tongue, the gibe, the scorn, And bright - ly breaks the
tri - umph o - ver sin and pain, Faith's vic - tory o - ver

East - er morn. Al - le - lu - ia!
ter - ror's reign.

EASTER

# 316    O Day of Light and Gladness

LANCASHIRE 7.6.7.6.D.

*Frederick Lucian Hosmer, 1903*        *Henry Smart, 1836*

1. O day of light and glad - ness, Of proph - e - cy and song, What
thoughts with-in us wak - en, What hal-lowed mem-ories throng! The
soul's ho - ri - zon wid - ens, Past, pres - ent, fu - ture blend; And
ris - es on our vi - sion The life that hath no end.

2. Earth feels the sea-son's joy - ance; From moun-tain range to sea The
tides of life are flow - ing, Fresh, man - i - fold, and free. In
val - ley and on up - land, By for - est path-ways dim, All
na - ture lifts in cho - rus The res - ur - rec - tion hymn.

3. O Lord of life e - ter - nal, To thee our hearts up - raise The
East - er song of glad - ness, The Pass - o - ver of praise. Thine
are the man - y man-sions, The dead die not to thee, Who
fill - est from thy full - ness Time and e - ter - ni - ty.

EASTER

# 317 Lo, the Day of Days Is Here

LLANFAIR 7.7.7.7. with alleluias

*From Frederick Lucian Hosmer, 1890, 1914*

*Robert Williams, 1817*
*Harmonized by John Roberts, 1837*

1. Lo, the day of days is here,
2. Fields are smil-ing in the sun, Al - le - lu - ia!
3. Lo, the East-er-tide is here,

Fes - ti - val of hope and cheer!
Loos-ened stream-lets sea - ward run, Al - le - lu - ia!
Mu - sic thrills the at - mos-phere.

At the south-wind's gen - ial breath—
Ten - der blade and leaf ap - pear; Al - le - lu - ia!
Join, ye peo - ple all, and sing—

Na - ture wakes from seem - ing death.
'Tis the spring-tide of the year. Al - le - lu - ia!
Love and praise and thanks - giv - ing.

**EASTER**

# 318 Lo, the Earth Awakes Again

EASTER HYMN 7.7.7.7. with alleluias

*From Samuel Longfellow, 1887; arranged*

Lyra Davidica, *1708*
*Version of John Arnold's* Compleat Psalmodist, *1749*

1. Lo, the earth a - wakes a - gain—
2. Once a - gain the word comes true, Al - le - lu - ia!
3. Change, then, mourn-ing in - to praise,

From the win-ter's bond and pain.
All the earth shall be made new. Al - le - lu - ia!
And, for dirg - es, an - thems raise.

Bring we leaf and flower and spray—
Now the dark, cold days are o'er, Al - le - lu - ia!
How our spir - its soar and sing,

To a - dorn this hap - py day.
Light and glad-ness are be - fore. Al - le - lu - ia!
How our hearts leap with the spring!

**EASTER**

# 319
## Lift Your Hidden Faces

GRÂCE SOIT RENDUE 6.5.6.5.D. with refrain

*Rose Fyleman, 1928*

*French carol*
*L. E. Grinault's Noëls angevins, 1878*

1. Lift your hid-den fac-es, Ye who wept and prayed; Leave your cov-ert
2. Now from mead and spin-ney, Now from flood and foam, Feath-ered, furred, and

plac - es, Ye who were a - fraid. Here's a gold-en sto - ry,
fin - ny, All ye crea-tures come. Here ye shall dis - cov - er

Here is sil-ver news, Here be gifts of glo - ry For us all to choose:
That for which ye wait; Win-ter days are o - ver, Sing and cel - e - brate:

Al-le-lu-ia, al-le-lu-ia! Praise our God with thanks-giv-ing: Prais-es sing to God.

SPRING

# 320 Now Once Again the Heaven Turns

HAMILTON L.M.

Kenneth L. Patton, 1960

Benjamin Franklin White, 1844

1. Now once a - gain the heav - en turns To bring a-
2. A - non, a - non, the seeds will burst, From swell - ing
3. And, an - swer - ing, the heart of man Will wak - en
4. Then will the blos - soms of our hope, Ar - ranged with

gain the ver - dant year. And once a - gain the
in the warm - ing soil. The rains will quench the
from its old de - spair, And glo - ry in what
blos - soms of the year, So beau - ti - fy the

old sun burns To fresh - en up the earth to bear.
sea - son's thirst; The till - ers will re - sume their toil.
spring it can, To make the hu - man sea - son fair.
fes - tive scope, The heart will tri - umph o - ver fear.

**SPRING**

# 321 Spring Has Now Unwrapped the Flowers

TEMPUS ADEST FLORIDUM 7.6.7.6.D.

*Theodoric Petri's* Piae Cantiones, *1582*
*Translation in* The Oxford Book of Carols, *1928*

*Theodoric Petri's* Piae Cantiones, *1582*
*Harmonized by Martin Shaw, 1928*

1. Spring has now un-wrapped the flowers, Day is fast re - viv - ing;
2. All the world with beau - ty fills, Gold the green en - hanc - ing;

Life in all its grow - ing powers Towards the light is striv - ing:
Flowers make mer-ry on the hills, Set the mead - ows danc - ing.

Gone the i - ron touch of cold, Win - ter time and frost time;
Earth puts on its dress of glee; Flowers and grass - es hide it

Seed - lings, work - ing through the mold, Now make up for lost time.
Go we forth in char - i - ty, Equals all be - side it

**SPRING**

# 322

## Early Spring

Fan Cheng-ta, ca. 1186
Translated by Gerald Bullett, 1946; adapted, 1960

SURSUM CORDA 10.10.10.10.

Alfred Morton Smith, 1941

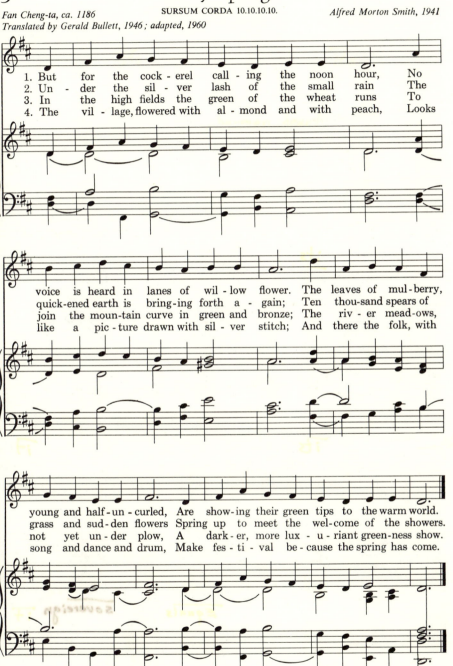

1. But for the cock-erel call-ing the noon hour, No
   voice is heard in lanes of wil-low flower. The leaves of mul-berry,
   young and half-un-curled, Are show-ing their green tips to the warm world.

2. Un-der the sil-ver lash of the small rain The
   quick-ened earth is bring-ing forth a-gain; Ten thou-sand spears of
   grass and sud-den flowers Spring up to meet the wel-come of the showers.

3. In the high fields the green of the wheat runs To
   join the moun-tain curve in green and bronze; The riv-er mead-ows,
   not yet un-der plow, A dark-er, more lux-u-riant green-ness show.

4. The vil-lage, flowered with al-mond and with peach, Looks
   like a pic-ture drawn with sil-ver stitch; And there the folk, with
   song and dance and drum, Make fes-ti-val be-cause the spring has come.

SPRING

# 323 Now the Spring Has Come Again

IN VERNALI TEMPORE 7.6.7.6.7.7.6.7.7.6.

*Theodoric Petri's Piae Cantiones, 1582*
*Translated by Steuart Wilson, 1928*

*Theodoric Petri's Piae Cantiones, 1582*
*Harmonized by Geoffrey Shaw, 1928*

1. Now the spring has come a - gain, Joy and warmth will fol - low;
2. All the woods are new in leaf, All the fruit is bud - ding;

Cold and wet are quite for - got, North-ward flies the swal - low;
Bees are hum-ming round the hive, Done with win-ter's brood - ing;

O - ver sea and land and air Spring's soft touch is ev - ery-where
Seas are calm and blue a - gain; Clouds no more fore-tell the rain;

And the world looks clean - er; All our sin - ews feel new strung;
Winds are soft and ten - der; High a - bove, the ~~king - ly~~ sovereign sun

SPRING

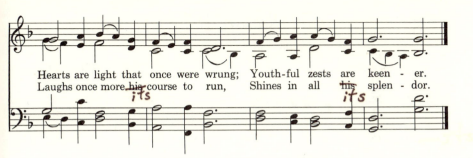

Hearts are light that once were wrung; Youth-ful zests are keen - er.
Laughs once more *its* course to run, Shines in all *its* splen - dor.

# 324 Oh, Give Us Pleasure in the Flowers Today

COOLINGE 10.10.10.10.

*Robert Frost, 1913*                                          *Cyril V. Taylor, 1951*

1. Oh, give us pleas - ure in the flowers to - day; And give us
2. Oh, give us pleas - ure in the or - chard white Like noth - ing
3. And make us hap - py in the dart - ing bird That sud - den -
4. For this is love and noth - ing else is love, The which it

not to think so far a - way As the un - cer - tain har - vest; keep us
else by day, like ghosts by night; And make us hap - py in the hap - py
ly a - bove the bees is heard, The me - teor that thrusts in with nee - dle
is re - served for God a - bove To sanc - ti - fy to what far ends *that true*

here All sim - ply in the spring - ing of the year.
bees, The swarm di - lat - ing round the per - fect trees.
bill, And off a blos - som in mid air stands still.
will, But which it on - ly needs that we ful - fill.

SPRING

# 325 Pleasure It Is

ES MUSS DIE GANZE CHRISTENSCHAR Irregular

William Cornish, d. 1523

Burkard Waldis, 1553; adapted

Pleas-ure it is To hear, I wis, The bird-es sing. The deer in the dale, The sheep in the vale, The corn spring-ing; God's pur-vey-ance For sus-te-nance It is for *man*. *u s* Then we al-ways To ~~him~~ *God* give praise, And thank ~~him~~ *God* then, And thank ~~him~~ *God* then.

SPRING

# 326

## June Days

FOREST GREEN C.M.D.

*Samuel Longfellow, 1859*

*English melody*
*Arranged by Ralph Vaughan Williams, 1906*

1. The sweet June days are come a - gain; Once more the glad earth yields Her *Its*
2. The sweet June days are come a - gain; The birds are on the wing; Bright

gold - en wealth of rip-ening grain, And breath of clo - ver fields, And
an - thems, in their mer-ry strain, Un - con-scious-ly they sing. Oh,

deep-ening shade of sum-mer woods, And glow of sum - mer air, And
how our cup o'er - brims with good These hap - py sum - mer days; For

wing - ing thoughts and hap - py moods Of love and joy and prayer.
all the joys of field and wood We lift our song of praise.

SUMMER

# 327 Thy Summer

COLCHESTER C.M.

*From Thomas Hornblower Gill, 1852*  *William Tans'ur's Compleat Melody, 1734*

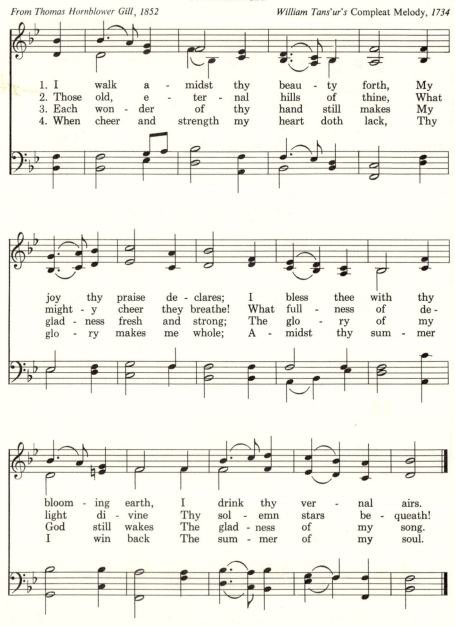

1. I walk a - midst thy beau - ty forth, My
2. Those old, e - ter - nal hills of thine, What
3. Each won - der of thy hand still makes My
4. When cheer and strength my heart doth lack, Thy

joy thy praise de - clares; I bless thee with thy
might - y cheer they breathe! What full - ness of de -
glad - ness fresh and strong; The glo - ry of my
glo - ry makes me whole; A - midst thy sum - mer

bloom - ing earth, I drink thy ver - nal airs.
light di - vine Thy sol - emn stars be - queath!
God still wakes The glad - ness of my song.
I win back The sum - mer of my soul.

**SUMMER**

# Readings

## RESPONSIVE READINGS

| | | | |
|---|---|---|---|
| Celebration and Praise | 328–338 | Love and Human Brotherhood | 406–418 |
| The Life That Maketh All Things New | 339–354 | Freedom | 419–423 |
| | | Here and Now | 424–426 |
| Man | 355–360 | In Time to Come | 427–434 |
| Transience and Ongoing Life | 361–370 | Commitment and Action | 435–439 |
| Hours of Insight | 371–375 | Prophets, Exemplars, Pioneers | 440–444 |
| The Life of Integrity and Wisdom | 376–389 | Nation and Nations | 445–451 |
| | | Our World-wide Heritage | 452–455 |
| Prayer and Aspiration | 390–397 | Church of the Free Spirit | 456–462 |
| The Arts of Man | 398–405 | Times and Seasons | 463–467 |

Opening of Service (Unison) — 468–479

Close of Service (Unison) — 480–485

Affirmation (Unison) — 486–511

Opening Words — 512–526

At the Offering — 527–534

Benedictions, Closing Words — 535–558

# Celebration and Praise

## 328

### I

O all ye things of tenderness and grace! Bless ye our minds and lift us up forever.

Beautiful is the blue weather that follows after rain; beautiful the brimming river that slides through meadows, with whispering reeds.

Beautiful is the flying moon that gleams and hides in the dappled sky. Beautiful are the salt pools locked in by bars of sand with seas beyond.

Beautiful is the wheat where crimson poppies burn; beautiful the brown waves of ripening grain, the glory of forest leaves, and orchards hung with fruit.

Beautiful is the return of the swallow, the cooing of doves in the treetops; beautiful is the skylark throwing down his shower of melody.

Beautiful is the labor of the bee, and that of parent birds with their nestlings.

Beautiful are the mist and the rain, the sere woods, the troubled clouds and the storm, and the hoarfrost and the clean snow.

O all ye things of tenderness and grace! Bless ye our minds and lift us up forever.

### II

O all ye works of strength! Bless ye our minds and lift us up forever.

Beautiful is the work of man, though black with smoke and slag.

Beautiful are the city streets with their carnival of eagerness and joy.

Beautiful is the sea of roofs and spires and drifting smoke at sunset.

Beautiful is fine machinery with gleaming steel and brass and whirling shafts, the perfect brotherhood of part with part.

Beautiful is the form of a ship on the sea, the red sail of the fisher, and the great liner.

Beautiful are the granite wharves, the water gates and stalwart bridges.

Beautiful is the flow of commerce, the ceaseless traffic of oils and fruits and fibers.

Beautiful are the smelting fires that blaze from their towers a gush of glory into the night.

O all ye works of strength!

Bless ye our minds and lift us up forever.

### III

O all ye memories of love! Bless ye our minds and lift us up forever.
Beautiful is the sight of many children at play; beautiful the croon of a mother over her babe; beautiful are the feet and hands of the new-born.

Beautiful is the love of the strong for the helpless, beautiful is the love born of gratitude, and still more beautiful is the love that knows not how it arose.

Beautiful is suffering when it flowers into the purity of a soul transfigured. Beautiful are the dreams that visit lovers of mankind.

Beautiful is heroism that does not see itself. Beautiful is the humility of a strong man.

O all ye memories of love! Bless ye our minds and lift us up forever.

HARRY YOULDEN

# 329

## GOD IN NATURE

### I

Bless the Lord, O my soul.
O Lord, my God, thou art very great:
Thou art clothed with honor and majesty:

Who coverest thyself with light as with a garment;
Who stretchest out the heavens like a curtain;

Who layeth the beams of his chambers in the waters;
Who maketh the clouds his chariot;
Who walketh upon the wings of the wind;

Who maketh winds his messengers,
His ministers a flaming fire;

Who laid the foundations of the earth,
That it should not be removed forever.

Thou coveredst it with the deep as with a garment;
The waters stood above the mountains.

At thy rebuke they fled;
At the voice of thy thunder they hasted away.

He sendeth the springs into the valleys,
Which run among the hills.

They give drink to every beast of the field;
The wild asses quench their thirst.

By them shall the fowls of the heaven have their habitation,
Which sing among the branches.

He watereth the hills from his chambers:
The earth is satisfied with the fruit of thy works.

He causeth the grass to grow for the cattle,
And herb for the service of man,
That he may bring forth food out of the earth;
And wine that maketh glad the heart of man,
And oil to make his face to shine,
And bread which strengtheneth man's heart.

He appointed the moon for seasons;
The sun knoweth his going down.
Thou makest darkness, and it is night:
Wherein all the beasts of the forest do creep forth.

The young lions roar after their prey,
And seek their meat from God.
The sun ariseth, they gather themselves together,
And lay them down in their dens.

Man goeth forth unto his work,
And to his labor until the evening.

II

O Lord, how manifold are thy works!
In wisdom hast thou made them all;
The earth is full of thy riches.

So is this great and wide sea,
Wherein are things creeping innumerable,
Both small and great beasts.

There go the ships;
There is that leviathan whom thou hast made to play therein.

These wait all upon thee,
That thou mayest give them their meat in due season.
That thou givest them they gather;
Thou openest thine hand, they are filled with good.

Thou hidest thy face, they are troubled;
Thou takest away their breath, they die, and return to their dust.
Thou sendest forth thy spirit, they are created;
And thou renewest the face of the earth.

The glory of the Lord shall endure for ever;
The Lord shall rejoice in his works.
He looketh on the earth, and it trembleth;
He toucheth the hills and they smoke.

I will sing unto the Lord as long as I live;
I will sing praise to my God while I have my being.

My meditation of him shall be sweet;
I will be glad in the Lord.

Bless thou the Lord, O my soul.
Praise ye the Lord.

## 330

### AN ACCOUNTING OF GRATITUDE

Who can make an accounting of his gratitude?

For the universe we give thanks, a room of life to stretch us with wonder.

For the earth we give thanks, fragment of the stars that is our home, swathed with air and washed with waters, its skeleton of stone cushioned with the fat loam.

For life we give thanks, the burning of the stars ordered and tempered to the milder uses of blood and chlorophyll.

For the good will of men we give thanks, for their accustomed acts of consideration, for the order of society that enables us to live in dignity and freedom.

For parents we give thanks, whose patience has blessed all our days, passing to us in turn the honor of our children and the delicacy of their hands and feet.

For the co-workers of the world we give thanks, for the merging of our labors in which the goods of prosperity may be brought to all;

Our possessions made for us by another's hands establish us in our gratitude.

For growth we give thanks, and brotherhood, for all the forces that enrich us, ways past our knowing, power past our control;

For ages past our sojourn, for eternity in which our days are magnified in being lived therein, we give thanks.

KENNETH L. PATTON

## 331

### THE BEAUTY OF HOLINESS

O sing unto the Lord a new song:
Sing unto the Lord all the earth.

Sing unto the Lord, bless his name;
Show forth his salvation from day to day.

Declare his glory among the nations,
His wonders among all people.

For the Lord is great, and greatly to be praised:
He is to be feared above all gods.

For all the gods of the nations are idols;
But the Lord made the heavens.

Honor and majesty are before him;
Strength and beauty are in his sanctuary.

Give unto the Lord, O ye kindreds of the people,
Give unto the Lord glory and strength.

Give unto the Lord the glory due unto his name;
Bring an offering, and come into his courts.

O worship the Lord in the beauty of holiness:
Fear before him, all the earth.

Say among the nations that the Lord reigneth;

The world also shall be established that it shall not be moved;
He shall judge the people righteously.

Let the heavens rejoice, and let the earth be glad;
Let the sea roar, and the fullness thereof.

Let the field be joyful, and all that is therein.
Then shall all the trees of the wood rejoice
Before the Lord:

For he cometh,
For he cometh to judge the earth:

He shall judge the world with righteousness,
And the people with his truth.

PSALM 96

# 332

## THE MANIFOLD RICHNESS OF LIFE

Let us rejoice in the manifold richness of life, about us and within: within us as understanding and choice, about us as a fair and bountiful nature, and the works of generous men;

We rejoice in the abundant life:

In the immemorial story of humankind; of struggle and venture, of sowing and reaping, of mirth and zest, of rites and assemblies, of mating and feasting, of ordered custom and new liberties won;

We rejoice in the story of man:

In the finding of facts and in shapes of molded form, in motions of the dance and of melody, in storied images of grief and of ecstasy, in new visions of order;

We rejoice in the beauty of art and the power of knowledge.

For the rest of home, the comfort of friends, and the unending charm of persons; for the desire to work and to create, for the broad earth and the affairs of toil open before us:

> We are thankful for home and friends and life's labor.

For prophets and reformers who cry shame upon social wrong, for leaders of the people who are wise in the policies of state, for many forms of effort to build a commonwealth where every man may reach his highest good: we are thankful.

> Let us cherish the state that her mighty ends may be achieved.

For shrines of faith where goods are praised and evils faced, where sorrows are healed and high purposes kindled, where our spirits are brought to that accord with all things which is at once our noblest task and most sublime joy: we are thankful.

> Let us upbuild the church in strength to minister ever more abundant life and peace to all the world.

VON OGDEN VOGT

# 333

### THE GOODNESS OF THE EARTH

The heavens and the earth spread abroad before the eyes of men.

> Man grows up from the smallest seed, yet he has become a creator in his own power.

In the cattle roaming the earth there are warmth and many good uses.

> We eat of them; there is beauty in them when we drive them out to pasture and bring them home again in the evening.

They bear our burdens into far countries, which we could not else reach without much weariness.

There are horses and mules and asses for us to ride, and as an adornment.

The rain falls from the skies for us to drink, and to water our crops, and olives and vines, and all manner of fruit.

> The sun and moon and stars rise in order; we are under the rule of the night and day.

We are subject to the sea, that we may eat of its fish, and bring forth ornaments from it to wear.

> We watch the sails of the ships cutting through the waters.

The earth is firm under the heavy mountains; it does not tremble when we walk.

On the earth are rivers and ways whereby we are guided;

also the stars are above to lead us.

Nothing of all this have we created;
Thus is there no comeliness in the vain and proud man.

KORAN; freely rendered

# 334

## THE CANTICLE OF THE SUN

O Most High, Almighty, good Lord God,
To thee belong praise, glory, honor, and all blessing!

Praised be my Lord God with all his creatures,
And especially our brother the sun, who brings us the day and who brings us the light.

Fair is he, and shining with a very great splendor:
O Lord, to us he signifies thee!

Praised be my Lord for our sister the moon, and for the stars,
The which he has set clear and lovely in heaven.

Praised be my Lord for our brother the wind, and for air and cloud, calms and all weather,
By the which thou upholdest in life all creatures.

Praised be my Lord for our sister water, who is very serviceable unto us,
And humble and precious and clean.

Praised be my Lord for our brother fire, through whom thou givest us light in the darkness;
And he is bright and pleasant, and very mighty and strong.

Praised be my Lord for our mother the earth, the which doth sustain us and keep us,
And bringeth forth divers fruits, and flowers of many colors, and grass.

Praised be my Lord for all those who pardon one another for his love's sake,
And who endure weakness and tribulation.

Blessed are they who peaceably shall endure,
For thou, O Most Highest, shalt give them a crown!

Praised be my Lord for our sister the death of the body,
From whom no man escapeth.

Praise ye and bless ye the Lord, and give thanks unto him,
And serve him with great humility.

ST. FRANCIS OF ASSISI

## 335

### PRAISE YE THE LORD

Praise ye the Lord.
Praise ye the Lord from the heavens: praise him in the heights.

Praise ye him all his angels;
Praise him, all his hosts.

Praise ye him, sun and moon;
Praise him, all ye stars of light.

Praise him, ye heavens of heavens, and ye waters that be above the heavens.

Let them praise the name of the Lord, for he commanded and they were created.

He hath also stablished them for ever and ever;
He hath made a decree which shall not pass.

Praise the Lord from the earth:
Ye dragons, and all deeps;

Fire and hail, snow and vapor,
Stormy wind fulfilling his word;

Mountains and all hills,
Fruitful trees and all cedars;

Beasts and all cattle,
Creeping things and flying fowl;

Kings of the earth, and all people,
Princes, and all judges of the earth;

Both young men and maidens,
Old men and children:

Let them praise the name of the Lord, for his name alone is excellent;

His glory is above the earth and heaven.
Praise ye the Lord.

PSALM 148

## 336

### WE REJOICE

Let us rejoice in the light of day, in the glory and warmth of the sun, in the reawakening of life to duty and labor;

We rejoice in the light of day:

In the quiet night, with its rest from toil and its revelation of worlds beyond the dark;

We rejoice in the peace of night:

In the earth with its hills and valleys, its widespread fields of grain, its fruits, and hidden treasures;

We rejoice in the beauty of earth:

In the sea, changeless and yet forever changing, the ancient mother of renewing life;

We rejoice in the everlasting sea.

We rejoice in the strength to win our daily bread, and in our quiet homes, hallowed by love, where we find refuge from the cold and storm;

> We rejoice in the shelter of home:

In the love of fathers and mothers, who have nurtured our lives, with whose blessing we have gone forth to our own work in the world;

> We rejoice in the love of parents:

In the children who bless our homes, whose eager minds and hearts are the promise of tomorrow;

> We rejoice in our children:

In friends who share our sorrows and our joys, in the fullness of the abundant life, in the serenity of old age, and the peace which comes at the last:

> We rejoice, and will rejoice forevermore.

A NEW PRAYER BOOK; adapted

# 337

## LIFT UP YOUR HEADS, O YE GATES

The earth is the Lord's, and the fullness thereof;
The world, and they that dwell therein.

> For he hath founded it upon the seas,
> And established it upon the floods.

Who shall ascend into the hill of the Lord?
Or who shall stand in his holy place?

> He that hath clean hands and a pure heart;
> Who hath not lifted up his soul unto vanity,
> Nor sworn deceitfully.

He shall receive the blessing from the Lord,
And righteousness from the God of his salvation.

This is the generation of them that seek him,
That seek thy face, O God of Jacob.

Lift up your heads, O ye gates;
And be ye lifted up, ye everlasting doors;
And the King of glory shall come in.

> Who is this King of glory?
> The Lord, strong and mighty,
> the Lord, mighty in battle.

Lift up your heads, O ye gates;
Even lift them up, ye everlasting doors;
And the King of glory shall come in.

> Who is this King of glory?
> The Lord of hosts, he is the King of glory.

PSALM 24

# 338

## THE PRIDE OF THE HEIGHT

The pride of the height is the clear firmament,
The beauty of the heaven with its glorious show;
>Look upon the rainbow;
>It compasseth the heaven about with a glorious circle.

The sun when it appeareth, making proclamation at its rising,
Is a wonderful instrument.
>At noon it parcheth the country,
>And who can abide the burning heat thereof?

A man blowing a furnace is in works of heat,
But the sun burneth the mountains three times more.
>Breathing out fiery vapors, and sending forth bright beams,
>It dimmeth the eyes.

At the swift lightnings the treasuries are opened,
And clouds fly forth as fowls;
>The noise of the thunder maketh the earth to tremble;
>So doth the northern storm and the whirlwind.

The clouds are thick
And the hailstones are broken small.
>As birds flying the snow scattereth,
>And the falling down thereof is as the lighting of grasshoppers.

The eye marveleth at the beauty of the whiteness thereof,
And the heart is astonished at the raining of it.
>The hoarfrost also as salt is poured on the earth,
>And being congealed, it lieth on the top of sharp stakes.

When the cold north wind bloweth,
And the water is congealed into ice,
It abideth upon every gathering of water,
And clotheth the water as with a breastplate.
>It devoureth the mountains, and burneth the wilderness,
>And consumeth the grass as fire.

The moon also serveth in her season for a declaration of times,
And a sign of the world.
>From the moon is the sign of feasts,
>A light that waneth following her perfection.

The month is called after her name,
Increasing wonderfully in her changing;
>Being an instrument of the armies above,
>Shining in the firmament of heaven.

The beauty of heaven, the glory of the stars,
Is an ornament giving light in the highest places.
>They will stand in their order
>And never faint in their watches.

ECCLESIASTICUS 43; adapted

# 339

## GOD

God is the fact of the fact, the life
of the life, the soul of the soul,

> The incomprehensible, the
> sum of all contradictions, the
> unit of all diversity.

He who knows him, knows him not;

> He who is without him, is full
> of him.

God cannot be seen; but by him
all seeing comes.

He cannot be heard; yet by
him all hearing comes.

Turn your back upon him, then
turn your back upon gravity, upon
air, upon light.

> He is not a being, yet apart
> from him there is no being—
> there is no apart from him.

JOHN BURROUGHS

# 340

## I WILL LIFT UP MINE EYES

I will lift up mine eyes unto the
hills.
From whence cometh my help?

> My help cometh from the
> Lord,
> Which made heaven and
> earth.

He will not suffer thy foot to be
moved:
He that keepeth thee will not
slumber.

> Behold, he that keepeth Israel
> Shall neither slumber nor
> sleep.

The Lord is thy keeper;
The Lord is thy shade upon thy
right hand.

> The sun shall not smite thee
> by day,
> Nor the moon by night.

The Lord shall preserve thee from
all evil:
He shall preserve thy soul.

> The Lord shall preserve thy
> going out and thy coming in,
> From this time forth, and
> even forevermore.

PSALM 121

# 341

## THE INESCAPABLE GOD

O Lord, thou hast searched me, and known me.

Thou knowest my downsitting and mine uprising;
Thou understandest my thought afar off.

Thou compassest my path and my lying down,
And art acquainted with all my ways.

For there is not a word in my tongue,
But, lo, O Lord, thou knowest it altogether.

Thou hast beset me behind and before,
And laid thine hand upon me.

Such knowledge is too wonderful for me;
It is high, I cannot attain unto it.

Whither shall I go from thy spirit?
Or whither shall I flee from thy presence?

If I ascend up into heaven, thou art there:
If I make my bed in the grave, behold, thou art there.

If I take the wings of the morning,
And dwell in the uttermost parts of the sea:

Even there shall thy hand lead me,
And thy right hand shall hold me.

If I say, Surely the darkness shall cover me;
Even the night shall be light about me.

Yea, the darkness hideth not from thee;
But the night shineth as the day:
The darkness and the light are both alike to thee.

For thou didst form my inward parts:
Thou didst knit me together in my mother's womb.

I will praise thee, for I am fearfully and wonderfully made:
Marvelous are thy works; and that my soul knoweth right well.

How precious also are thy thoughts unto me, O God!
How great is the sum of them!

If I should count them, they are more in number than the sand;
When I awake, I am still with thee.

Search me, O God, and know my heart:
Try me, and know my thoughts:

And see if there be any wicked way in me,
And lead me in the way everlasting.

PSALM 139

# 342

## THE TAO

Before creation a presence existed,
Self-contained, complete,
Formless, voiceless, mateless,
Changeless,
Which yet pervaded itself
With unending motherhood.

> Though there can be no name
> for it,
> I have called it 'the way of
> life.'

Perhaps I should have called it 'the
fullness of life,'
Since fullness implies widening into
space,
Implies still further widening,
Implies widening until the circle is
whole.

In this sense
The way of life is fulfilled,
Heaven is fulfilled,
Earth is fulfilled,
And a fit man also is fulfilled.

These are the four amplitudes of
the universe
And a fit man is one of them:

> Man rounding the way of
> earth,
> Earth rounding the way of
> heaven,
> Heaven rounding the way of
> life
> Till the circle is full.

TAO-TEH-CHING

# 343

## THE SPIRIT OF GOD

The spirit of God is wonderful to
us;

> It is revealed in all the ways
> of creation:

In the ordered course of the stars
and in the unpredictable ways of
living things,

> In the heat of blazing suns
> and in the warmth of human
> affections.

His will is revealed in the majesty
of abiding law, in judgments that
are just,

> And in the mercy which re-

deems the penitent and up-
holds the humble of heart:

For his abode is not only in the
heavens; he dwells in the human
heart as his familiar home.

> The highways of history are
> his: but by the humble path
> of service we enter into his
> kingdom.

He surprises us in homely tasks, he
walks with us on lonely trails.

> His beauty is in our lives, and
> his spirit defines our right-
> eousness.

NAPOLEON W. LOVELY

## 344

### BRAHMAN

I am the Self that dwells in the heart of every mortal creature:
I am the beginning, the life span, and the end of all.

I am the radiant sun among the light-givers:
I am the mind; I am consciousness in the living.

I am death that snatches all;
I, also, am the source of all that shall be born.

I am time without end: I am the sustainer: my face is everywhere.

I am the beginning, the middle, and the end in creation:
I am the knowledge of things spiritual.

I am glory, prosperity, beautiful speech, memory, intelligence, steadfastness, and forgiveness.

I am the divine seed of all lives.
In this world nothing animate or inanimate exists without me.

I am the strength of the strong;
I am the purity of the good.

I am the knowledge of the knower. There is no limit to my divine manifestations.

Whatever in this world is powerful, beautiful, or glorious, that you may know to have come forth from a fraction of my power and glory.

BHAGAVAD-GITA

## 345

### OUT OF THE STARS

Out of the stars in their flight, out of the dust of eternity, here have we come,
Stardust and sunlight, mingling through time and through space.

Out of the stars have we come, up from time;
Out of the stars have we come.

Time out of time before time in the vastness of space, earth spun to orbit the sun,
Earth with the thunder of mountains newborn, the boiling of seas.

Earth warmed by sun, lit by sunlight: this is our home;
Out of the stars have we come.

Mystery hidden in mystery, back through all time;

Mystery rising from rocks in the storm and the sea.

Out of the stars, rising from rocks and the sea,
Kindled by sunlight on earth, arose life.

Ponder this thing in your heart; ponder with awe:
Out of the sea to the land, out of the shallows came ferns.

Out of the sea to the land, up from darkness to light,
Rising to walk and to fly, out of the sea trembled life.

Ponder this thing in your heart, life up from sea:

Eyes to behold, throats to sing, mates to love.

Life from the sea, warmed by sun, washed by rain,
Life from within, giving birth rose to love.

This is the wonder of time; this is the marvel of space;
Out of the stars swung the earth; life upon earth rose to love.

This is the marvel of life,
rising to see and to know;
Out of your heart, cry wonder: sing that we live.

ROBERT T. WESTON

# 346

## THE VOICE OF THE LORD

Give unto the Lord, O ye mighty,
Give unto the Lord glory and strength.

Give unto the Lord the glory due unto his name;
Worship the Lord in the beauty of holiness.

The voice of the Lord is upon the waters:
The God of glory thundereth:
The Lord is upon many waters.

The voice of the Lord is powerful;
The voice of the Lord is full of majesty.

The voice of the Lord breaketh the cedars;
Yea, the Lord breaketh the cedars of Lebanon.

He maketh them also to skip like a calf;
Lebanon and Sirion like a young unicorn.

The voice of the Lord divideth the flames of fire.

The voice of the Lord shaketh the wilderness;
The Lord shaketh the wilderness of Kadesh.

The Lord sitteth upon the flood;
Yea, the Lord sitteth King forever.

The Lord will give strength unto his people;
The Lord will bless his people with peace.

PSALM 29

# 347

### THE OVERSOUL

Let man learn the revelation of all nature and thought to his heart: that the Highest dwells within him, that the sources of nature are in his own mind.

> As there is no screen or ceiling between our heads and the infinite heavens, so there is no bar or wall in the soul where man, the effect, ceases, and God, the cause, begins.

I am constrained every moment to acknowledge a higher origin for events than the will I call mine.

> There is a deep power in which we exist and whose beatitude is accessible to us.

Every moment when the individual feels himself invaded by it is memorable.

> It comes to the lowly and simple; it comes to whosoever will put off what is foreign and proud; it comes as insight; it comes as serenity and grandeur.

The soul's health consists in the fullness of its reception.

> For ever and ever the influx of this better and more universal self is new and unsearchable.

Within man is the soul of the whole; the wise silence; the universal beauty, to which every part and particle is equally related; the eternal One.

> When it breaks through his intellect, it is genius; when it breathes through his will, it is virtue; when it flows through his affections, it is love.

RALPH WALDO EMERSON

# 348

### THE UNKNOWN GOD

God that made the world and all things therein, seeing he is Lord of heaven and earth, dwelleth not in temples made with hands;

> Neither is worshiped with men's hands, as though he needed any thing, seeing he giveth to all life, breath, and all things;

And hath made of one blood all nations of men for to dwell on all the face of the earth,

And hath determined the times before appointed, and the bounds of their habitation;

That they should seek the Lord, if haply they might feel after him, and find him, though he be not far from every one of us:

For in him we live, and move, and have our being.

ACTS 17

# 349

WHO HATH MEASURED THE WATERS?

Who hath measured the waters in the hollow of his hand,
And meted out heaven with the span,
And comprehended the dust of the earth in a measure,
And weighed the mountains in scales,
And the hills in a balance?

Who hath directed the Spirit of the Lord,
Or being his counselor hath taught him?

With whom took he counsel,
And who instructed him in the path of judgment,
And taught him knowledge,
And showed him the way of understanding?

Behold, the nations are as a drop of a bucket,
And are counted as the small dust of the balance:
Behold, he taketh up the isles as a very little thing.

And Lebanon is not sufficient to burn,
Nor the beasts thereof sufficient for a burnt offering.

All nations before him are as nothing;
And they are counted to him less than nothing, and vanity.

Hast thou not known? hast thou not heard?
The everlasting God, the Lord,
The Creator of the ends of the earth,
Fainteth not, neither is weary?
There is no searching of his understanding.

He giveth power to the faint;
And to them that have no might he increaseth strength.

Even the youths shall faint and be weary,
And the young men shall utterly fall:

But they that wait upon the Lord shall renew their strength;
They shall mount up with wings as eagles;
They shall run and not be weary;
They shall walk and not faint.

ISAIAH 40

# 350

## NATURE'S IMPARTIAL PROVIDENCE

I see the Nature Providence going its impartial way.

I see drought and flood, heat and cold, war and pestilence, defeat and death, besetting *us* man at all times, in all lands.

I see the elemental forces as indifferent toward *us* him as toward ants and fleas.

I see the righteous defeated and the ungodly triumphant —this and much more I see.

And yet I behold through the immense vista behind us the *human* race of man, slowly—oh, so slowly! —emerging:

From its brute and semihuman ancestry into the full estate of man, from blind instinct and savage passion into consciousness.

I see on an immense scale, and as clearly as in a demonstration in a laboratory, that good comes out of evil;

That the impartiality of the Nature Providence is best;

That we are made strong by what we overcome; that *we are human* man is man because *we are* he is as free to do evil as to do good;

That disease, wars, the unloosened, devastating elemental forces have each and all played their part in developing and hardening *us* man, and giving *us* him the heroic fiber.

JOHN BURROUGHS

# 351

## THE STREAM OF LIFE

I

The same stream of life that runs through my veins night and day runs through the world and dances in rhythmic measures.

It is the same life that shoots in joy through the dust of the earth in numberless blades of grass and breaks into tumultuous waves of leaves and flowers.

It is the same life that is rocked in the ocean-cradle of birth and death, in ebb and in flow.

I feel my limbs are made glorious by the touch of this world of life. And my pride is from the life-throb of ages dancing in my blood this moment.

II

Is it beyond thee to be glad with the gladness of this rhythm? to be tossed and lost and broken in the whirl of this fearful joy?

All things rush on, they stop not, they look not behind, no power can hold them back, they rush on.

Keeping step with that restless, rapid music, seasons come dancing and pass away—

Colors, tunes, and perfumes pour in endless cascades in the abounding joy that scatters and gives up and dies every moment.

III

How often, great Earth, have I felt my being yearn to flow over you, sharing the happiness of each green blade that raises its signal banner in answer to the beckoning blue of the sky!

I feel as if I had belonged to you ages before I was born.

That is why, in the days when the autumn light shimmers on the mellowing ears of rice, I seem to remember a past when my mind was everywhere, and even to hear voices as of play-fellows echoing from the remote and deeply veiled past.

When in the evening, the cattle return to their folds, raising dust from the meadow paths, as the moon rises higher than the smoke ascending from the village huts, I feel sad as for some great separation that happened in the first morning of existence.

RABINDRANATH TAGORE

# 352

## THE LORD IS MY SHEPHERD

The Lord is my shepherd;
I shall not want.

He maketh me to lie down in green pastures:
He leadeth me beside the still waters.

He restoreth my soul:
He leadeth me in the paths of righteousness for his name's sake.

Yea, though I walk through the valley of the shadow of death, I will fear no evil;

For thou art with me, thy rod and thy staff they comfort me.

Thou preparest a table before me in the presence of mine enemies:
Thou anointest my head with oil;
My cup runneth over.

Surely goodness and mercy shall follow me all the days of my life:
And I will dwell in the house of the Lord for ever.

PSALM 23

# 353

## GOD IS OUR REFUGE

God is our refuge and strength,
A very present help in trouble.

Therefore will not we fear,
though the earth be removed,
And though the mountains be
carried into the midst of the
sea;

Though the waters thereof roar
and be troubled,
Though the mountains shake with
the swelling thereof.

There is a river, the streams
whereof shall make glad the
city of God,
The holy place of the tabernacles of the Most High.

God is in the midst of her; she
shall not be moved:
God shall help her, and that right
early.

The Lord of hosts is with us;
The God of Jacob is our
refuge.

Come, behold the works of the
Lord,
What desolations he hath made in
the earth.

He maketh wars to cease unto
the end of the earth;
He breaketh the bow, and
cutteth the spear in sunder;
He burneth the chariot in the
fire.

Be still, and know that I am God:
I will be exalted among the nations,
I will be exalted in the earth.

The Lord of hosts is with us;
The God of Jacob is our
refuge.

PSALM 46

# 354

## THE HUMAN CALENDAR

The eternal past is the beginning
of man.

This is the statement of
theme by the violins, the announcement of the trumpets.

The pattern of time in the heavens
is the pattern of time on the earth.

For the earth is in the heavens, one planet circling one
star in one galaxy among
countless galaxies.

The time to come will be the day
of the manhood of man, the years
of human glory and greatness.

Tomorrow the universe will come into its own in the wisdom of its children.

The wild heavens have grown eyes for seeing in the sightless forehead of space.

The wordless wind has been trained to voice and speaking.

A purpose has evolved from fire and chemical habit.

From instinct and passion a mind has evolved for searching and design.

Write this upon the milestone that marks today upon the highway of cosmic history.

Mark this day upon the calendar of the universe, the calendar of man.

This day, a brief few thousand years of the human story, marks the coming of mind. On this day the universe, in man, began to think.

On this day the universe said: I know myself. I am. This is what I am going to be.

KENNETH L. PATTON

# Man

## 355

### THE DIGNITY OF HUMAN NATURE

Let us not disparage that nature which is common to all men, for no thought can measure its grandeur.

He who possesses the divine powers of the soul is a great being, let his place be what it may.

Though he make no show in the streets of a splendid city, a clear thought, a pure affection, and the resolute act of a virtuous will, have dignity of quite another kind.

You may clothe this man with rags, immure him in a dungeon, or chain him to slavish tasks, but he still is great.

The solemn conflicts of reason with passion, the victories of moral and religious principle, over urgent solicitations to self-indulgence, and the hardest sacrifices of duty:

These are of course unseen; so that the true greatness of human life is almost wholly out of sight.

I believe this greatness to be most common among the multitude, whose names are never heard.

We behold it in hardship borne manfully, in unvarnished truth, in religious trust, and in that generosity which gives what the giver needs himself.

Perhaps in this present the most heroic deed is done in some silent spirit: the loftiest purpose cherished, the most generous sacrifice made, and we do not suspect it.

A man is great as a man, be he where or what he may: the grandeur of his nature turns to insignificance all outward distinctions.

WILLIAM ELLERY CHANNING

## 356

### AWAKE, O MAN

Great and marvelous is man's progress on the earth,
He has discovered his strength,
He has wrought mighty works.

Rock of the earth he has turned into great towers;
With metal from the mine he has girded them.

Mountain torrent and waterfall serve him;
He has caused the thunderbolt to do his bidding.

The oceans are the highways of his ships;
He makes a path through the clouds;

He has weighed the sun in a balance,
And discerned the substance of the Pleiades;

That which was hidden he has uncovered,
The unseen he has brought to light;

His machines fill the earth with their thunder,
But his heart is heavy within him.

He has unlocked the force of the atom,
But has not learned the might of his own spirit.

Great as are his skill and power,
Yet he lives in uncertainty and fear.

Drunken with ambition and wealth,
He drives his soul to destruction;

He crushes his brothers to increase his riches;
His mills devour their bodies and souls.

A thousand battlefields proclaim his lust,
The place of burial his selfishness;

How long, how long will this madness prevail;
How long will man be slave of his own power?

He will not always turn from love,
He will come to himself and live.

EDWIN C. PALMER

# 357

ONE SPECIES

What does it mean to be creatures of thought and longing who live on this planet we have named the earth?

No other creature in all the universe is assembled and contained as we are.

Our history is our own, these few millions of years of evolution that have brought our conformation and countenance into being.

Only here has ensued this juncture of the dust and breath.

We are the end of a long and passionate working, a slow serenity and growth.

This is our captivity and emergence, our beginning and history.

This is the fact of human brotherhood, one species, one living kin.

How insignificant are the differences between us, against the mountainous identities of this one family of time and earth.

Sing the family of man. Sing the one home, the gentle earth, the grass, the sunlight, the eventide.

We will make this small plot of soil, this globe, a messenger of meaning and peace.

KENNETH L. PATTON

# 358

VISHNU — SHIVA

Man is the animal that most wearies himself, whose greatest source of fear and peril is himself.

Answers he has found in reason and science, but he has turned his answers into a danger of death.

Man himself is Vishnu and Shiva, sustainer and destroyer; his gods are but the reading of his own nature.

He lifts cities with pain and

patience, and then bombs and burns them to win bitter victories.

The world has much assurance of sustenance and security, despite storms and plagues and earthquakes.

The family of man has lived well enough in the garden of the earth; it has survived for a million years.

It is man who presents the ultimate peril to his kind.

The answer is simple, or seemingly so: to live and let live, to unmake the armies and withhold man's own hands from suicide.

Is man so willful and stupid that he cannot invent the answer to his own organizations of violence?

Is man so evil that he cannot bring his own nations under the constraint of law?

Can science, which brings the power of nature under our control, enable us to bring our own powers under control?

Thus we study ourselves and wonder, and seek wisdom and moral purpose;

For we have discovered that the Garden of Eden is in the hearts of men.

Adam is driven out of the garden only by the flaming sword he holds in his own hand.

Man is his own angel of judgment.

His sin is against himself, and whether he may return to the garden he himself will decide.

KENNETH L. PATTON

# 359

WHAT IS MAN?

O Lord, our Lord,
How excellent is thy name in all the earth!
Who hast set thy glory above the heavens.

When I consider thy heavens, the work of thy fingers,
The moon and the stars, which thou hast ordained;

What is man, that thou art mindful of him,
And the son of man, that thou visitest him?

For thou hast made him a little lower than the angels,

And hast crowned him with glory and honor.

Thou madest him to have dominion over the works of thy hands;
Thou hast put all things under his feet;

All sheep and oxen,
Yea, and the beasts of the field;

The fowl of the air, and the fish of the sea,
And whatsoever passeth through the paths of the seas.

O Lord, our Lord,
How excellent is thy name in all the earth!

PSALM 8

# 360

## THE WONDER OF ONE'S SELF

The soul is not more than the body,
And the body is not more than the soul,

And nothing, not God, is greater to one than one's self is,

And whoever walks a furlong without sympathy walks to his own funeral drest in his shroud,

And I or you pocketless of a dime may purchase the pick of the earth,

And to glance with an eye or show a bean in its pod confounds the learning of all times,

And there is no trade or employment but the young man following it can become a hero,

And there is no object so soft but it makes a hub for the wheeled universe,

And I say to any man or woman,
Let your soul stand cool and composed before a million universes.

WALT WHITMAN

# Transience and Ongoing Life

# 361

## LORD, THOU HAST BEEN OUR DWELLING PLACE

Lord, thou hast been our dwelling place
In all generations.

Before the mountains were brought forth,
Or ever thou hadst formed the earth and the world,
Even from everlasting to everlasting, thou art God.

Thou turnest man to destruction;
And sayest, Return, ye children of men.

For a thousand years in thy sight
Are but as yesterday when it is past,
And as a watch in the night.

Thou carriest them away as with a flood; they are as a sleep:
In the morning they are like grass which groweth up.

In the morning it flourisheth, and groweth up;

In the evening it is cut down,
and withereth.

For we are consumed by thine
anger,
And by thy wrath are we troubled.

Thou hast set our iniquities
before thee,
Our secret sins in the light of
thy countenance.

The days of our years are three-
score years and ten;
And if by reason of strength they
be fourscore years,
Yet is their strength labor and
sorrow;
For it is soon cut off, and we fly
away.

So teach us to number our
days,
That we may apply our hearts
unto wisdom.

Return, O Lord, how long?

And let it repent thee concerning
thy servants.

O satisfy us early with thy
mercy;
That we may rejoice and be
glad all our days.

Make us glad according to the days
wherein thou hast afflicted us,
And the years wherein we have
seen evil.

Let thy work appear unto thy
servants,
And thy glory unto their children.

And let the beauty of the Lord our
God be upon us:

And establish thou the work
of our hands upon us;
Yea, the work of our hands
establish thou it.

PSALM 90

# 362

### EPISTLE TO BE LEFT IN THE EARTH

. . . It is colder now, there are
many stars, we are drifting North
by the Great Bear, the leaves are
falling,
The water is stone in the scooped
rocks, to southward
Red sun grey air:

The crows are slow on their
crooked wings, the jays have
left us:
Long since we passed the
flares of Orion.

Each man believes in his heart he
will die,
Many have written last thoughts
and last letters.

None know if our deaths are
now or forever:
None know if this wandering
earth will be found.

We lie down and the snow covers
our garments.
I pray you, you (if any open this
writing)

Make in your mouths the words
that were our names.

> I will tell you all we have
> learned, I will tell you every-
> thing:

The earth is round, there are
springs under the orchards,
The loam cuts with a blunt knife,

> Beware of elms in thunder,
> the lights in the sky are
> stars—

We think they do not see, we think
also
The trees do not know nor the
leaves of the grasses hear us:
The birds too are ignorant.

> Do not listen. Do not stand
> at dark in the open windows.

We before you have heard this:
they are voices:

They are not words at all but
the wind rising.
Also none among us has seen
God.

(. . . We have thought often
The flaws of the sun in the late
and driving weather
Pointed to one tree but it was not
so.)

> As for the nights I warn you
> the nights are dangerous:
> The wind changes at night
> and the dreams come.

It is very cold, there are strange
stars near Arcturus,

> Voices are crying an unknown
> name in the sky.

ARCHIBALD MACLEISH

# 363

## THE TRAVAIL OF MAN

Great travail is created for every
man,
And an heavy yoke is upon the
sons of Adam,
From the day they go out of their
mother's womb,
Till the day that they return to
the mother of all things.

> Their imagination of things to
> come,
> And the day of death,
> Trouble their thoughts,
> And cause fear of heart.

From him that sitteth on a throne
of glory,
Unto him that is humbled in earth
and ashes;

> From him that weareth purple
> and a crown,
> Unto him that is clothed with
> a linen frock:

There is wrath, and envy, trouble,
unquietness,
Fear of death, and anger, and
strife;

And in the time of rest upon
his bed
His night sleep doth change
his knowledge.

A little or nothing is his rest,
And afterward he is in his sleep,
As in a day of keeping watch,
Troubled in the vision of his heart,
As if he had escaped out of a battle.

When all is safe, he awaketh,
And marveleth that the fear
was nothing.

All things that are of the earth
Shall turn to the earth again:

And that which is of the
waters
Doth return into the sea.

ECCLESIASTICUS 40

# 364

## THE SOULS OF THE RIGHTEOUS

The souls of the righteous are in
the hand of God,
And there shall no torment touch
them.

In the sight of the unwise
they seemed to die:
And their departure is taken
for misery,
And their going from us to
be utter destruction:

But they are in peace.
For though in the sight of men
they are punished,
Yet is their hope full of immortality.

They that put their trust in
God shall understand the
truth:
And such as be faithful shall
abide with him in love.

The memory of virtue is immortality:
Because it is known with God, and
with men.

When it is present, men take
example at it;

And when it is gone, they desire it:

It weareth a crown, and trium-
pheth for ever,
Having gotten the victory, striving
for undefiled rewards.

A righteous man, though he
die before his time, shall be at
rest.

For honorable age is not that
which standeth in length of time,
Nor that is measured by number
of years;

But wisdom is grey hair unto
men,
And an unspotted life is old
age.

Glorious is the fruit of good labors:
And the root of understanding
shall never fall away.

God created man to be im-
mortal,
And made him in the image
of his own eternity.

THE WISDOM OF SOLOMON 3, 4, 2

# 365

## ABOVE THE NAME OF MAN

The fellowship of nature is our shape and fabrication, witnessing the brotherhood of all things.

The same wind and rain are within us and upon us, and the same loam is gathered in our flesh.

We will put above the name of man the larger name of nature.

We will possess the friendly pride of oneness with all that moves and breathes, with all that moves and does not breathe.

Each man is as large in person as the gathering over which his thought and love preside.

He is as large as the city, the nation, the race of his discovery and settlement.

He can burgeon, if he will, beyond cultures and continents, the echoes of the common emergence sounding in his blood.

We are seekers of the fellowship of life and of death, which measures its ever-changing content and shape, breeding the laughter and hunger of our escaping years.

KENNETH L. PATTON

# 366

## THE YOUNG DEAD SOLDIERS

The young dead soldiers do not speak.

Nevertheless, they are heard in the still houses: who has not heard them?

They have a silence that speaks for them at night and when the clock counts.

They say: We were young. We have died. Remember us.

They say: We have done what we could but until it is finished it is not done.

They say: We have given our lives but until it is finished no one can know what our lives gave.

They say: Our deaths are not ours; they are yours; they will mean what you make them.

They say: Whether our lives and our deaths were for peace and a new hope or for nothing we cannot say; it is you who must say this.

They say: We leave you our deaths. Give them their meaning.

We were young, they say. We have died. Remember us.

ARCHIBALD MACLEISH

# 367

## THE LORD IS MERCIFUL

Bless the Lord, O my soul,
And all that is within me, bless his
holy name.

Bless the Lord, O my soul,
And forget not all his benefits:

Who forgiveth all thine iniquities;
Who healeth all thy diseases;

Who redeemeth thy life from
destruction;
Who crowneth thee with lov-
ing-kindness and tender mercies;

Who satisfieth thy mouth with
good things;
So that thy youth is renewed like
the eagle's.

The Lord executeth righteousness and judgment
For all that are oppressed.

The Lord is merciful and gracious,
Slow to anger, and plenteous in
mercy.

He hath not dealt with us
after our sins;
Nor rewarded us according to
our iniquities.

For as the heaven is high above the
earth,
So great is his mercy toward them
that fear him.

As far as the east is from the
west,

So far hath he removed our
transgressions from us.

Like as a father pitieth his children,
So the Lord pitieth them that fear
him.

For he knoweth our frame;
He remembereth that we are
dust.

As for man, his days are as grass:
As a flower of the field so he flourisheth.

For the wind passeth over it,
and it is gone;
And the place thereof shall
know it no more.

But the mercy of the Lord is from
everlasting to everlasting,
And his righteousness unto children's children;

To such as keep his covenant,
And to those that remember
his commandments to do
them.

Bless ye the Lord, all ye his hosts;
Ye ministers of his, that do his
pleasure.

Bless the Lord, all his works,
In all places of his dominion:
Bless the Lord, O my soul.

PSALM 103

# 368

## MY DAYS AS AN HANDBREADTH

I said, I will take heed to my ways,
That I sin not with my tongue:
I will keep my mouth with a bridle,
While the wicked is before me.

I was dumb with silence,
I held my peace, even from
good;
And my sorrow was stirred.

My heart was hot within me;
While I was musing, the fire
burned:
Then spake I with my tongue,

Lord, make me to know mine
end,
And the measure of my days
what it is;
That I may know how frail I
am.

Behold, thou hast made my days
as an handbreadth;
And mine age is as nothing before
thee:
Verily every man at his best state
is altogether vanity.

Surely every man walketh in
a vain show:
Surely they are disquieted in
vain:
He heapeth up riches,
And knoweth not who shall
gather them.

And now, Lord, what wait I for?
My hope is in thee.

Deliver me from all my transgressions:
Make me not the reproach of
the foolish.

I was dumb, I opened not my
mouth;
Because thou didst it.

Remove thy stroke away from
me:
I am consumed by the blow of
thine hand.

When thou with rebukes dost cor-
rect man for iniquity,
Thou makest his beauty to consume away like a moth:
Surely every man is vanity.

Hear my prayer, O Lord,
And give ear unto my cry;
Hold not thy peace at my
tears:

For I am a stranger with thee,
And a sojourner,
As all my fathers were.

O spare me, that I may re-
cover strength,
Before I go hence, and be no
more.

PSALM 39

# 369

## THE WAY

Friend, I have lost the way.
    The way leads on.
Is there another way?
    The way is one.
I must retrace the track.
    It's lost and gone.
Back, I must travel back!
    None goes there, none.
Then I'll make here my place—
    The road runs on—
Stand still and set my face—

    The road leaps on.
Stay here, for ever stay.
    None stays here, none.
I cannot find the way.
    The way leads on.
Oh, places I have passed!
    That journey's done.
And what will come at last?
    The way leads on.

EDWIN MUIR

# 370

## SOME THINGS WILL NEVER CHANGE

Some things will never change.
    Some things will always be the same.
The voice of forest water in the night, a woman's laughter in the dark, the clean, hard rattle of raked gravel, the cricketing stitch of midday in hot meadows, the delicate web of children's voices in bright air—
    These things will never change.
The glitter of sunlight on roughened water, the glory of the stars, the innocence of morning, the smell of the sea in harbors—
    These things will always be the same.

The feathery blur and smoky buddings of young boughs, and something there that comes and goes and never can be captured, the thorn of spring, the sharp and tongueless cry—
    These things will never change.
The leaf, the blade, the flower, the wind that cries and sleeps and wakes again, the trees, whose stiff arms clash and tremble in the dark, and the dust of lovers long since buried in the earth—
    All things belonging to the earth will never change.
All things proceeding from the earth to seasons, all things that

lapse and change and come again upon the earth, these come up from the earth that never changes, they go back into the earth that lasts forever.

Only the earth endures, but it endures forever.

The tarantula, the adder, and the asp will also never change.

Pain and death will always be the same.

But under the pavements trembling like a pulse, under the buildings trembling like a cry, under the waste of time, under the hoof of the beast above the broken bones of cities, there will be something growing like a flower—

Something bursting from the earth again, forever deathless, faithful, coming into life again like April.

THOMAS WOLFE

# Hours of Insight

## 371

### THE VOICE OF GOD IN THE SOUL

Blessed is the soul that heareth the Lord speaking within her,
And receiveth from his mouth the word of consolation.

Blessed are the ears that gladly receive the pulses of the divine whisper,
And heed not the loud clamors of the world.

Blessed indeed are those ears which listen not after the voices sounding without,
But to the truth teaching inwardly.

Blessed are they that enter far into inward things,
And endeavor to prepare themselves for the receiving of heavenly secrets.

The children of Israel in times past said unto Moses,

'Speak thou unto us, and we will hear;
Let not the Lord speak unto us lest we die.'

Not so, Lord, not so, we beseech thee; but rather do we humbly and earnestly entreat, 'Speak, Lord, for thy servant heareth.'

Do thou speak, O Lord God, the Inspirer and Enlightener of all the prophets.
Thou alone canst perfectly instruct, but they without thee can profit nothing.

They indeed sound forth words,
But they cannot give the spirit.

Most beautifully do they speak,
But if thou be silent they inflame not the heart,

> They teach the letter, but thou openest the sense;
> Thou unlockest the meaning of sealed things.

They point out the way,
But thou givest strength to walk in it.

> What they can do is only without,

But thou instructest and enlightenest the heart.

Speak, therefore, Lord, for thy servant heareth.
Thou hast the words of eternal life.

> Speak thou unto us, to the comfort of our souls, to the amendment of our whole life,
> And to thy praise and glory and honor everlasting.

THOMAS A KEMPIS

# 372

## LET US WORSHIP

Let us worship with our eyes and ears and fingertips; let us love the world through heart and mind and body.

> The rushing of the wind and the pouring of the sun gather us together with blessing and comfort.

The colors flowing in the field and sky, light over eyes, over faces, the windy colors and the colors of warm, tideless gardens, heal our spirits and feed our hungers.

> The lifting sounds of trees and grasses, the noises of men and women eddy into songs of human togetherness.

The purity of birds singing, the music of throat and brass and wood, these are golden to the ear lonely for beauty.

We feed our eyes upon the mystery and revelation in the faces of our brothers and sisters.

We seek to know the wistfulness of the very young and the very old, the wistfulness of men in all times of life.

> We seek to understand the shyness behind arrogance, the fear behind pride, the tenderness behind clumsy strength, the anguish behind cruelty.

We live a thousand lives as we walk through the city.

> All life flows into a great common life, if we will only open our eyes to our companions.

We listen to the secret voices of poetry and know that all men share our yearning.

All are lonely as we are lonely, and all men need the sure presence of those who love and are loved.

Let us worship, not in bowing down, not with closed eyes and stopped ears.

Let us worship with the opening of all the windows of our beings, with the full out-stretching of our spirits.

Life comes with singing and laughter, with tears and confiding, with a rising wave too great to be held in the mind and heart and body, to those who have fallen in love with life.

Let us worship, and let us learn to love.

KENNETH L. PATTON

# 373

## THE LORD IS MY LIGHT

The Lord is my light and my salvation; whom shall I fear?
The Lord is the strength of my life; of whom shall I be afraid?

Though an host should encamp against me,
My heart shall not fear:
Though war should rise against me,
In this will I be confident.

One thing have I desired of the Lord,
That will I seek after:
That I may dwell in the house of the Lord all the days of my life,
To behold the beauty of the Lord
And to inquire in his temple.

For in the time of trouble he shall hide me in his pavilion:
In the secret of his tabernacle shall he hide me.

When thou saidst, Seek ye my face:
My heart said unto thee, Thy face, Lord, will I seek.

Hide not thy face far from me;
Leave me not, neither forsake me, O God of my salvation.

When my father and mother forsake me,
Then the Lord will take me up.

Teach me thy way, O Lord,
And lead me in a plain path.

I had fainted, unless I had believed to see
The goodness of the Lord in the land of the living.

Wait on the Lord:
Be of good courage, and he shall strengthen thine heart:
Wait, I say, on the Lord.

PSALM 27

# 374

### THE ACCEPTANCE OF MYSTERY

There are questions which come to every man in feelings of wastelands and loneliness beyond the healing of known companions.

> For these he has sung a sad song in the day and night and written stories of slaughter and agony.

For want of answers his mind has splintered and he has wandered off into the ecstasy of madness.

> He has sought answers in the arguments of wine and the wisdom of opium.

Many have stifled the voices, drowning them in hurry and noise.

> Many have listened unwillingly, and turned away as soon as they could.

Some listen again and again, until the yearning unknown is itself known and familiar:

> The quandaries become remembered faces without names, and the mysteries, silent companions.

To them the unanswerables are no longer pools of terrible drowning.

> These become the depth and body of the sea, the lifting presence beneath the keels of their vessels.

They make of the mysteries a song and a story; they are taught the ways of acceptance and peace.

> Having known the wonder and been wedded unto it, they are secure and unconquerable.

KENNETH L. PATTON

# 375

### INVITATION TO SERENITY

When we are tired with the work we have to do or feel unequal to it;
When we dully wonder about its being worthwhile;
When our pleasures, so easily taken, communicate no happiness to the heart;
When we are fretting about our own faults or the faults of other people;
When one day repeats another and we pine for some change we know not what:

> Then may the voices of our own hearts' courage and of age-long wisdom call us to their hospitality.

When there is sound and fury all around, signifying little or nothing;
When the past derides us with re-

membered failures and we think we are never to be quit of them; When the future seems more a menace than a hope; When we feel that at our worst it will not matter much and at our best it will not really count; When we are a prey to fears because we cannot guard against a chance, and a slight thing happening would lay us low:

Then may we receive, each for oneself, the comforting assurance: 'In quietness and confidence shall be your strength.'

VIVIAN T. POMEROY

# The Life of Integrity and Wisdom

## 376

### IT MATTERS WHAT WE BELIEVE

Some beliefs are like walled gardens. They encourage exclusiveness, and the feeling of being especially privileged.

Other beliefs are expansive and lead the way into wider and deeper sympathies.

Some beliefs are like shadows, darkening children's days with fears of unknown calamities.

Other beliefs are like sunshine, blessing children with the warmth of happiness.

Some beliefs are divisive, separating the saved from the unsaved, friends from enemies.

Other beliefs are bonds in a universal fellowship, where sincere differences beautify the pattern.

Some beliefs are like blinders, shutting off the power to choose one's own direction.

Other beliefs are like gateways opening wide vistas for exploration.

Some beliefs weaken a person's selfhood. They blight the growth of resourcefulness.

Other beliefs nurture self-confidence and enrich the feeling of personal worth.

Some beliefs are rigid, like the body of death, impotent in a changing world.

Other beliefs are pliable, like the young sapling, ever growing with the upward thrust of life.

SOPHIA LYON FAHS

# 377

### THE COUNSEL OF THINE OWN HEART

My son, if thou wilt, thou shalt be taught;
And if thou wilt apply thy mind, thou shalt be prudent.

If thou love to hear, thou shalt receive understanding;
And if thou bow thine ear, thou shalt be wise.

Stand in the assembly of the elders;
And cleave unto him that is wise.

Be willing to listen to every godly discourse;
And let not the parables of understanding escape thee.

And if thou seest a man of understanding, get thee betimes unto him,

And let thy foot wear the steps of his door.

Accept no man against thine own soul,
And let not reverence for any man cause thee to fall;

And let the counsel of thine own heart stand:
For there is no man more faithful unto thee than it;

For a man's mind is sometime wont to tell him more than seven watchmen,
That sit above in an high tower.

ECCLESIASTICUS 6, 4, 37

# 378

### THE PARABLE OF THE SOWER

And when much people were gathered together, and were come to him out of every city, Jesus spake by a parable:

A sower went out to sow his seed: and as he sowed, some fell by the wayside; and it was trodden down, and the fowls of the air devoured it.

And some fell upon a rock; and as soon as it was sprung up, it withered away, because it lacked moisture.

And some fell among thorns; and the thorns sprang up with it, and choked it.

And other fell on good ground, and sprang up, and bare fruit a hundredfold.

And when he had said these things, he cried, He that hath ears to hear, let him hear.

And his disciples asked him, saying, What might this parable be?

And he said, Unto you it is given to know the mysteries

of the kingdom of God: but to others in parables; that seeing they might not see, and hearing they might not understand.

Now the parable is this: The seed is the word of God. Those by the wayside are they that hear;

Then cometh the devil, and taketh away the word out of their hearts, lest they should believe and be saved.

They on the rock are they, which, when they hear, receive the word with joy;

And these have no root, which for a while believe, and in time of temptation fall away.

And that which fell among thorns are they, which, when they have heard, go forth, and are choked with cares and riches and pleasures of this life, and bring no fruit to perfection.

But that on the good ground are they, which in an honest and good heart, having heard the word, keep it, and bring forth fruit with patience.

No man, when he hath lighted a candle, covereth it with a vessel, or putteth it under a bed; but setteth it on a candlestick, that they which enter in may see the light.

For nothing is secret, that shall not be made manifest; neither any thing hid, that shall not be known and come abroad.

Take heed therefore how ye hear: for whosoever hath, to him shall be given;

And whosoever hath not, from him shall be taken even that which he seemeth to have.

LUKE 8

# 379

## SELF-CONQUEST

If one man conquer in battle a thousand times a thousand men, And if another conquer himself, he is the greatest of conquerors.

One's own self conquered is better than all other people conquered; Not even a God could change into defeat the victory of a man who has vanquished himself.

We live happily indeed, not hating those who hate us! Among men who hate us we dwell free from hatred!

We live happily indeed, free from greed among the greedy! Among men who are greedy let us dwell free from greed!

We live happily indeed, though we call nothing our own!

We shall be like the bright gods,
feeding on happiness!

Victory breeds hatred, for the
conquered is unhappy.
He who has given up both
victory and defeat,
He is contented and happy.

'He abused me, he beat me, he
defeated me, he robbed me' —

In those who harbor such thoughts
hatred will never cease.
'He abused me, he beat me, he
defeated me, he robbed me' —
In those who do not harbor such
thoughts hatred will cease.

For hatred does not cease by
hatred at any time;
Hatred ceases by love.

DHAMMAPADA 8, 15, 1

# 380

## THE SUPERIOR MAN

The superior man is universally
minded and no partisan.

When he goes abroad, he be-
haves toward others as though
he were receiving a distinguished guest.

The superior man thinks of his
character; the inferior man thinks
of his position.

The superior man desires justice; the inferior man desires
favor.

The superior man makes demands
upon himself; the inferior man
makes demands upon others.

The superior man thinks of
virtue; the inferior man
thinks of comfort.

The superior man thinks of what
is right; the inferior man thinks of
what will pay.

The superior man regrets not

knowing; the inferior man
regrets not being known.

The superior man is not concerned
that he has no place, but rather
how he may fit himself for one.

The superior man ranks the
effort above the prize, and
worthiness to be known above
being known.

Small men never think they are
small; great men never think they
are great.

The men of old were reserved
in speech, lest they should fall
short in deed.

Is there any one maxim which
ought to be acted upon throughout
one's life?

Surely the maxim of loving
kindness is such: Do not unto
others what you would not
have them do unto you.

THE ANALECTS OF CONFUCIUS

# 381

THE FIRST LESSON IN CHARITY

Not until a man has helped himself can he help another; not until he has made himself strong can he lift his brother;

Not until he has enlightened his own understanding can he teach;

Not until his discipline is rewarded with artistry can he be a donor of beauty and service;

Not until he has established himself in goodness and mercy can he be a welcome hand;

Not until he has made justice the habit of himself can he bestow justice upon the world.

Each man must be his own support.

Let him care well for himself lest he burden another.

Let him nurse his own health and build his own prosperity.

Let him who would give mercy, to himself be merciful.

The man who is lost must himself be found before he can find a lost brother.

Let each man labor for the goodness of what he makes, to clothe and shelter his body and to feed his mouth.

Let each man live for the goodness of his own life, rich in his own laughter, strong in his own strength.

Let each man be sufficient in his own labor, upright in his own dignity, confident in his own skill, steady in his own honor, warm in his own love.

For he who lives fully within himself is a promise and a hope for his fellow man.

KENNETH L. PATTON

# 382

ACCEPTANCE

Be utterly humble
And you shall hold to the foundation of peace.

Be at one with all these living things which, having arisen and flourished,

Return to the quiet whence they came,
Like a healthy growth of vegetation
Falling back upon the root.

Acceptance of this return to the

root has been called 'quietism,'
Acceptance of quietism has been
condemned as 'fatalism.'

>But fatalism is acceptance of
>destiny
>And to accept destiny is to
>face life with open eyes,
>Whereas not to accept destiny
>is to face death blindfold.

He who is open-eyed is open-
minded,

He who is open-minded is open-
hearted,

>He who is open-hearted is
>kingly,
>He who is kingly is godly,

He who is godly is useful,
He who is useful is infinite,

>He who is infinite is immune,
>He who is immune is immor-
>tal.

TAO-TEH-CHING

# 383

## THE WAYS OF THE DEDICATED MAN

What are the ways of the dedicated
man and the virtues of his life?

>He controls his hands and
>feet; he controls his speech.

He is well controlled and he delights inwardly; he is collected and
solitary and content.

>He controls his mouth, speak-
>ing wisely and calmly; he
>teaches the meaning and the
>law, and his words are pleas-
>ing.

He will not despise what he has
received, nor envy others; and
thus he finds his peace of mind.

>Without knowledge there is
>no meditation; without med-
>itation there is no knowledge:
>he who has knowledge and
>meditation finds enlighten-
>ment.

When he has fulfilled his restraint
and contemplation, all bondage
falls from him who has gotten
knowledge.

>Knowing the end of his own
>suffering, having put down
>his burdens, he is unshackled.

He does no injury to other creatures, whether feeble or strong; he
neither kills nor causes slaughter.

>He is tolerant with the intol-
>erant, calm with the violent,
>and generous among the
>greedy.

Anger and hatred, pride and hypocrisy, have fallen from him.

>He utters true speech, in-
>structive and free from ran-
>cor; and he offends no one.

He takes nothing in the world that
is not given to him, whether long
or short, large or small, good or
bad.

He harbors no desires for this world or the next, has no inclinations, and is unshackled.

He has left all bondage to men, and risen above all bondage to the gods; he is free from every bondage.

He calls nothing his own, whether before, or behind, or between, and is free from the love of the world.

He is manly and good and wise, master of himself, accomplished and awakened.

Having knowledge of what has been, and foreseeing what he will become, he is enlightened and fulfilled.

DHAMMAPADA; freely rendered

# 384

## HE THAT MEDITATETH

He that giveth his mind to the law of the Most High,
And is occupied in the meditation thereof,
Will seek out the wisdom of all the ancients,
And be occupied in prophecies.

He will keep the sayings of the renowned men:
And where subtle parables are, he will be there also.

He will seek out the secrets of grave sentences,
And be conversant in dark parables.

He will travel through strange countries;
For he hath tried the good and the evil among men.

He will give his heart to resort early to the Lord that made him,
And will pray before the most High;

He will open his mouth in prayer,
And make supplication for his sins.

When the great Lord will,
He shall be filled with the spirit of understanding:

He shall pour out wise sentences,
And give thanks unto the Lord in his prayer.

He shall direct his counsel and knowledge,
And in his secrets shall he meditate.

He shall show forth that which he hath learned,
And shall glory in the law of the covenant of the Lord.

Many shall commend his understanding;
And so long as the world endureth, it shall not be blotted out.

Nations shall show forth his wisdom, and the congregation shall declare his praise.

ECCLESIASTICUS 39

# 385

### THE MASTERY OF SELF

The moral life of a man may be likened to traveling to a distant place: one must start from the nearest stage.

It may also be likened to ascending a height: one must begin from the lowest step.

When wives and children and their sires are one,
'Tis like a harp and lute in unison.

When brothers live in concord and at peace
The strain of harmony shall never cease.

The lamp of happy union lights the home,
And bright days follow when the children come.

In such a state of things, what more satisfaction can parents have?

The moral man conforms himself to his life circumstances; he does not desire anything outside his position.

Finding himself in a position of wealth and honor, he lives as becomes one living in a position of wealth and honor.

Finding himself in a position of poverty and humble circumstances, he lives as becomes one living in a position of poverty and humble circumstances.

The moral man can find himself in no situation in life in which he is not master of himself.

In a high position he does not domineer over his subordinates.

In a subordinate position he does not court the favors of his superiors.

He puts in order his own personal conduct and seeks nothing from others; hence he has no complaint to make.

He complains not against God, nor rails against men.

THE GOLDEN MEAN OF TSESZE

# 386

### MAN AT HIS BEST

I

The breath of life moves through a deathless valley
Of mysterious motherhood

Which conceives and bears the universal seed,

The seeming of a world never to end,

Breath for men to draw from
as they will:
And the more they take from
it, the more remains.

## II

The universe is deathless,
Is deathless because, having no
finite self,
It stays infinite.

> A sound man by not advancing himself
> Stays the further ahead of
> himself,

By not confining himself to himself
Sustains himself outside himself:

> By never being an end in
> himself
> He endlessly becomes himself.

## III

Man at his best, like water,
Serves as he goes along:

> Like water he seeks his own
> level,
> The common level of life,

Loves living close to the earth,
Living clear down in his heart,

> Loves kinship with his neighbors,
> The pick of words that tell
> the truth,
> The even tenor of a well-run
> state,

The fair profit of able dealing,
The right timing of useful deeds;

> And for blocking no man's
> way,
> No one blames him.

TAO-TEH-CHING 6, 7, 8

# 387

KEEP THY HEART WITH DILIGENCE

Happy is the man that findeth
wisdom,
And the man that getteth understanding;

> For the merchandise of it is
> better than the merchandise
> of silver,
> And the gain thereof than fine
> gold.

She is more precious than rubies;
And all the things thou canst desire are not to be compared unto
her.

Length of days is in her right
hand,
And in her left hand riches
and honor.

Her ways are ways of pleasantness,
And all her paths are peace.

> She is a tree of life to them
> that lay hold upon her,
> And happy is every one that
> retaineth her.

Get wisdom and she shall preserve
thee,

Love her and she shall keep thee:
For wisdom is the principal
thing, therefore get wisdom;
And with all thy getting get
understanding.

She shall give to thine head an
ornament of grace:

A crown of glory shall she deliver
to thee.
Keep thy heart with all diligence;
For out of it are the issues of
life.

PROVERBS 3, 4

# 388

### THE LORD GIVETH WISDOM

My son, if thou wilt receive my
words,
So that thou incline thine ear unto
wisdom,
And apply thine heart to under-
standing;
Yea, if thou criest after knowl-
edge,
And liftest up thy voice for
understanding;
If thou seekest her as silver,
And searchest for her as for hid
treasures;
Then shalt thou understand
the fear of the Lord,
And find the knowledge of
God.

For the Lord giveth wisdom;
Out of his mouth cometh knowledge and understanding.
He layeth up sound wisdom
for the righteous;
He is a buckler to them that
walk uprightly.

He keepeth the paths of judgment,

And preserveth the way of his
saints.
Then shalt thou understand
righteousness, and judgment,
and equity:
Yea, every good path.

My son, forget not my law;
But let thine heart keep my com-
mandments:
For length of days, and long
life, and peace,
Shall they add to thee.

Let not mercy and truth forsake
thee:
Bind them about thy neck;
Write them upon the table of thine
heart.
My son, let not them depart
from thine eyes;
Keep sound wisdom and dis-
cretion:
So shall they be life unto thy soul,
And grace to thy neck.
Then shalt thou walk in thy
way safely,

And thy foot shall not stumble.

When thou liest down, thou shalt not be afraid:
Yea, thou shalt lie down, and thy sleep shall be sweet,

For the Lord shall be thy confidence,
And shall keep thy foot from being taken.

PROVERBS 2, 3

# 389

## OVERCOME EVIL WITH GOOD

Let love be without hypocrisy. Abhor that which is evil; cleave to that which is good.

Be kindly affectioned one to another with brotherly love; in honor preferring one another;

Not slothful in business; fervent in spirit; serving the Lord.

Rejoicing in hope; patient in tribulation; continuing steadfastly in prayer;

Distributing to the necessity of saints; given to hospitality.

Bless them which persecute you: bless, and curse not.

Rejoice with them that do rejoice, and weep with them that weep.

Recompense to no man evil for evil. Provide things honest in the sight of all men.

If it be possible, as much as lieth in you, live peaceably with all men.

Dearly beloved, avenge not yourselves, but rather give place unto wrath.

Therefore if thine enemy hunger, feed him; if he thirst, give him drink: for in so doing thou shalt heap coals of fire on his head.

Be not overcome of evil, but overcome evil with good.

ROMANS 12

# Prayer and Aspiration

## 390

### RELIGION

Let religion be to us life and joy.

Let it be a voice of renewing challenge to the best we have and may be; let it be a call to generous action.

Let religion be to us a dissatisfaction with things that are, which bids us serve more eagerly the true and right.

Let it be the sorrow that opens for us the way of sympathy, understanding, and service to suffering humanity.

Let religion be to us the wonder and lure of that which is only partly known and understood:

An eye that glories in nature's majesty and beauty, and a heart that rejoices in deeds of kindness and of courage.

Let religion be to us security and serenity because of its truth and beauty, and because of the enduring worth and power of the loyalties which it engenders;

Let it be to us hope and purpose, and a discovering of opportunities to express our best through daily tasks:

Religion, uniting us with all that is admirable in human beings everywhere;

Holding before our eyes a prospect of the better life for humankind, which each may help to make actual.

VINCENT B. SILLIMAN

## 391

### THE MIND WITHOUT FEAR

I

Let me not pray to be sheltered from dangers, but to be fearless in facing them.

Let me not beg for the stilling of my pain, but for the heart to conquer it.

Let me not look for allies in life's battlefield, but to my own strength.

Let me not crave in anxious fear to be saved, but hope for the patience to win my freedom.

II

Give me the strength lightly to bear my joys and sorrows.

Give me the strength to make my love fruitful in service.

Give me the strength never to disown the poor, or bend my knees before insolent might.

Give me the strength to raise my mind high above daily trifles.

### III

Where the mind is without fear and the head is held high;

Where knowledge is free;

Where the world has not been broken up into fragments by narrow domestic walls;

Where words come out from the depth of truth;

Where tireless striving stretches its arms towards perfection;

Where the clear stream of reason has not lost its way into the dreary desert sand of dead habit;

Where the mind is led forward by thee into ever-widening thought and action—

Into that heaven of freedom, my Father, let my country awake.

RABINDRANATH TAGORE

# 392

## A STOIC'S PRAYER

May I be no man's enemy, and may I be the friend of that which is eternal and abides.

May I never quarrel with those nearest me; and if I do may I be reconciled quickly.

May I never devise evil against any man; and if any devise evil against me may I escape uninjured and without the need of hurting him.

May I love, seek, and attain only that which is good.

May I wish for all men's happiness, and envy none. May I never rejoice in the ill fortune of one who has wronged me.

When I have done or said what is wrong, may I never wait for the rebuke of another, but always rebuke myself until I make amends.

May I win no victory that harms either me or my opponent.

May I reconcile friends who are wroth with one another.

May I, to the extent of my power, give all needful help to my friends, and to all who are in want.

May I never fail a friend in danger.

When visiting those in grief may I be able by gentle and healing words to soften their pain.

May I respect myself. May I always keep tame that which rages within me.

May I accustom myself to be gentle, and never to be angry with people because of circumstances.

May I never discuss who is wicked and what wicked things he has done, but know good men and follow in their footsteps.

EUSEBIUS, a Stoic

# 393

## OUT OF THE DEPTHS

Out of the depths have I cried unto thee, O Lord.

> Lord, hear my voice:
> Let thine ears be attentive to the voice of my supplications.

If thou, Lord, shouldest mark iniquities,
O Lord, who shall stand?

> But there is forgiveness with thee,

That thou mayest be feared.

I wait for the Lord, my soul doth wait,
And in his word do I hope.

> My soul waiteth for the Lord
> More than they that watch for the morning:
> I say, more than they that watch for the morning.

PSALM 130

# 394

## THE HEAVENS DECLARE THE GLORY OF GOD

### I

The heavens declare the glory of God,
And the firmament showeth his handiwork.

> Day unto day uttereth speech,
> And night unto night showeth knowledge.

There is no speech nor language,
Where their voice is not heard.

> Their line is gone out through all the earth,
> And their words to the end of the world.

In them hath he set a tabernacle for the sun,
Which is as a bridegroom coming out of his chamber,
And rejoiceth as a strong man to run a race.

His going forth is from the end of the heaven,
And his circuit unto the ends of it;
And there is nothing hid from the heat thereof.

### II

The law of the Lord is perfect, converting the soul;
The testimony of the Lord is sure, making wise the simple.

> The statutes of the Lord are right, rejoicing the heart;
> The commandment of the Lord is pure, enlightening the eyes.

The fear of the Lord is clean, enduring for ever;
The judgments of the Lord are true and righteous altogether.

More to be desired are they
than gold,
Yea, than much fine gold:
Sweeter also than honey and
the honeycomb.

Moreover by them is thy servant
warned,
And in the keeping of them there
is great reward.

Who can understand his errors?
Cleanse thou me from secret
faults.

Keep back thy servant also from
presumptuous sins;
Let them not have dominion over
me;
Then shall I be upright,
And I shall be innocent from the
great transgression.

Let the words of my mouth,
and the meditation of my
heart,
Be acceptable in thy sight, O
Lord, My strength, and my
redeemer.

PSALM 19

# 395

### TO LIVE DELIBERATELY

We must learn to awaken and keep
ourselves awake by an infinite ex-
pectation of the dawn, which does
not forsake us in our soundest sleep;

For we are encouraged that
a man can elevate his life by
his own conscious endeavor.

It is something to be able to paint
a picture, or to carve a statue, and
so to make a few objects beautiful;

But it is far more glorious to
carve and paint the very
atmosphere and medium
through which we look, which
morally we can do.

To affect the quality of the day,
that is the highest of arts.

It is the task of every man
to make his life, even in its

details, worthy of the contemplation of his most elevated and critical hour.

Why should we live in such a hurry
and waste of life?

We are determined to be
starved before we are hungry.

I wish to live deliberately, to front
only the essential facts of life.

I wish to learn what life has
to teach, and not, when I
come to die, discover that I
have not lived.

I do not wish to live what is not
life, living is so dear.

Nor do I wish to practice
resignation, unless it is quite
necessary.

I wish to live deep and suck out all the marrow of life, to live so sturdily and Spartan-like as to put to rout all that is not life;

> I want to cut a broad swath and shave close, to drive life into a corner, and reduce it to its lowest terms.

If it proves to be mean, then to get the whole and genuine meanness of it, and publish its meanness to the world;

> Or if it is sublime, to know it by experience, and to be able to give a true account of it.

HENRY DAVID THOREAU

## 396

### HOPE THOU IN GOD

I

As the hart panteth after the water brooks,
So panteth my soul after thee, O God.

> My soul thirsteth for God, for the living God:
> When shall I come and appear before God?

My tears have been my meat day and night,
While they continually say unto me, Where is thy God?

> When I remember these things, I pour out my soul in me:
> For I had gone with the multitude, I went with them to the house of God,
> With the voice of joy and praise, with a multitude that kept holyday.

Why art thou cast down, O my soul?
And why art thou disquieted within me?

Hope thou in God:
For I shall yet praise him for the help of his countenance.

Deep calleth unto deep at the noise of thy waterspouts;
All thy waves and thy billows are gone over me.

> Yet the Lord will command his loving-kindness in the daytime;
> And in the night his song shall be with me,
> And my prayer unto the God of my life.

Why art thou cast down, O my soul?
And why art thou disquieted within me?

> Hope thou in God:
> For I shall yet praise him, who is the health of my countenance,
> And my God.

II

O send out thy light and thy truth, let them lead me:

Let them bring me unto thy holy hill, and to thy tabernacles.

Then will I go unto the altar of God, unto God my exceeding joy:
Yea, upon the harp will I praise thee,
O God my God.

Why art thou cast down, O my soul?

And why art thou disquieted within me?

Hope in God:
For I shall yet praise him, who is the health of my countenance,
And my God.

PSALMS 42, 43

# 397

## THE LIFE OF THE SPIRIT

For the holiness of every place where light is found, for the healing of nature and the understanding of our fellow men, for the insights of toil, and for the sanctities of birth and death:

For the ennobling graces of life we offer praise.

For this place and hour, where we leave behind old cares and pleasures, outgrown faiths and customs, and where all things meet and change and are renewed:

For temples and tabernacles, and their celebrations, we give thanks.

For the revival of zest in living, for tides of life about us and within, for present happiness and strong desire, and for the songs of our ascending way:

For all that renews and strengthens our spirits we are grateful.

For the bright procession of memory and new images of hope, for our relationships of privilege and duty, for those long gone and for those near whose virtues bless us, for school and church and state, and for all worthful concerns of our days and years:

For history past, and for this history in which we live, we give our thanks.

For the urgence in us to do and dare, to alter and effect, and for deep impulses of heart and hand, to work in the earth and recreate ourselves and the common life of men and nations, after patterns of righteousness beheld in mounts of vision:

For the dreams that arise in men, and for ever-renewing purposes and prophecies: our works and our dedications speak our gratitude.

*Services of Religion*

# The Arts of Man

## 398

Let us sing for the arts of man.
Let us sing for singing and dance
for dancing.

This is our thanksgiving, that
man is a creature fashioned of
delight and enabled with passion.

Forms and shapes are for him a
ready wisdom.

He brings forth an offspring
of loveliness from the mating
of mind and emotion.

The creatures of his inner landscape are weird and graceful beyond the creatures of the earth.

The arts of man are keys unto
doors; they are wings for the
flying of unmarked skies.

Poems are feet for running; they
break open a path through the
valley of questions.

The brush of the painter is
lightning, opening to the eyes
the awful mountains of the
night.

Sculpture reveals a secret in the
fullness of sunlight and shadow.

Dancing is the narration of a
dream; the dancer is the
moving body of a vision.

Play and story tell the history of
people in uncreated worlds.

The wordless voice of music
calls a greeting from beyond
the doorways of the unknown.

Would you meet your brother and
walk along his hidden places?

Then listen to his songs of
tongue and viol, for he will
tell you more than he knows
to tell.

KENNETH L. PATTON

## 399

### I HEAR AMERICA SINGING

I hear America singing, the varied
carols I hear:

Those of mechanics—each one
singing his, as it should be,
blithe and strong;

The carpenter singing his, as he
measures his plank or beam,

The mason singing his, as he
makes ready for work, or
leaves off work;

The boatman singing what belongs to him in his boat—the deck-hand singing on the steamboat deck;

The shoemaker singing as he sits on his bench—the hatter singing as he stands;

The wood-cutter's song—the ploughboy's, on his way in the morning, or at noon intermission, or at sundown;

The delicious singing of the mother—or of the young wife at work—or of the girl sewing or washing;

At night, the party of young fellows, robust, friendly—singing, with open mouths, their strong melodious songs:

Each singing what belongs to him or her, and to none else— The day what belongs to the day, and the night what belongs to it.

WALT WHITMAN

# 400

### A NEW SONG

#### I

Rejoice in the Lord, O ye righteous: For praise is comely for the upright.

Praise the Lord with harp: Sing unto him with the psaltery of ten strings.

Sing unto him a new song; Play skillfully with a loud noise.

For the word of the Lord is right; And all his works are done in truth.

He loveth righteousness and justice: The earth is full of the goodness of the Lord.

By the word of the Lord were the heavens made, And all the host of them by the breath of his mouth.

He gathereth the waters of the sea together as a heap: He layeth up the depth in storehouses.

Let all the earth fear the Lord: Let all the inhabitants of the world stand in awe of him.

#### II

Make a joyful noise unto the Lord, all ye lands.

Serve the Lord with gladness: Come before his presence with singing.

Know ye that the Lord he is God: It is he that hath made us, and not we ourselves;

We are his people and the sheep of his pasture.

Enter into his gates with thanksgiving, And into his courts with praise. Be thankful unto him, and bless his name. -

For the Lord is good; his mercy is everlasting; And his truth endureth to all generations.

PSALMS 33, 100

## 401

### THEN BUILD TEMPLES

Our breath vanishes among the winds; our words are lost in a tempest named yesterday.

We try to make our words endure by loud shouting, but this only shoves the echoes back a moment longer.

Speak softly; your words will be recalled for their melodies and proportions.

If you would speak for the hearing of children in ages to come, train your words to rhythm and resonance.

The moment will not tarry, but its making will linger if you color it and clothe it in shapeliness.

Age is the end of a wild wandering; if you carve figures for mile-posts and heap stone cairns into temples, their beauty will lure others to follow your likely path.

Would you make a mark on the face of the world, beauty is your only implement.

Would you make yesterday worth remembering, only songs will equip time with immortality.

Leave your journeying to build temples, and adorn them with intimations of longer journeys you cannot take, and images of countries you may never enter.

In far-off times others will put their carvings beside yours, and light candles where long ago yours burned away.

In their celebrations there will be a lingering of your questions and solicitations.

The rafters and pillars will remember your dreams, and your children will discover the beauty of your ancient hands.

KENNETH L. PATTON

## 402

### WHY DOES A MAN WORK?

Why does a man work and what is it he works for? These are the things:

A table of food and his family healthy, a house with grass and flowers, and warmth in winter;

A chance to stand as a man among men, with his children about him and the woman he loves beside him.

These are enough to drive him on, to give him reason for living.

Man desires work to do, bridges to build across streams, roads to lay across mountains;

Buildings to raise in the cities, and cottages on the roadsides; machines to invent whose swift-working powers can make life rich in things and leisure;

Homes to tend, for it is good to keep a home; fields to till, for it is good to farm and to eat;

Music to sing and the time to sing it and the time to listen; thoughts to be written and the time to write and to read;

The searching of man and his universe for knowledge, and the using of knowledge for the good of all;

The freedom to dream new dreams, and leaders to weave the dreams of the many into projects for the people.

A man would live in a countryside that is clean and honest; he would have his small domain set among the domains of his fellow workers, with peace and justice between them;

He would live in a commonwealth of free men, where his single voice has its hearing, and the voice of the people holds power.

KENNETH L. PATTON

# 403

## THE HANDIWORK OF THEIR CRAFT

The wisdom of a learned man cometh by opportunity of leisure; And he that hath little business shall become wise.

How can he get wisdom that holdeth the plow, And that glorieth in the goad,

That driveth oxen, and is occupied in their labors; And whose talk is of bullocks?

He giveth his mind to make furrows; And is diligent to give the kine fodder.

So every carpenter and workmaster, that laboreth night and day;

And they that cut and grave seals, And are diligent to make great variety;

And give themselves to preserve likeness in imagery, And watch to finish a work.

The smith also sitting by the anvil, And considering the unwrought iron:

The vapor of the fire wasteth his flesh, And he fighteth with the heat of the furnace;

The noise of the hammer and anvil
is ever in his ears,
And his eyes look still upon the pattern of the thing that he maketh;

>He setteth his mind to finish
>his work,
>And watcheth to polish it
>perfectly.

So doth the potter sitting at his
work,
And turning the wheel about with
his feet;

>Who is alway carefully set at
>his work,
>And maketh all his work by
>number;

He fashioneth the clay with his
arm,
And boweth down his strength before his feet;

>He applieth himself to finish
>the glazing;
>And he is diligent to make
>clean the furnace.

All these trust to their hands,
And every one is wise in his work.

>Without these cannot a city
>be established,
>And men can neither sojourn
>nor walk up and down therein.

They shall not be sought for in
public counsel,
Nor sit high in the congregation;

>They shall not sit on the
>judges' seat,
>Nor understand the sentence
>of judgment;

They cannot expound justice and
judgment;
And they shall not be found where
parables are spoken.

>But they will maintain the
>fabric of the world,
>And in the handiwork of their
>craft is their prayer.

ECCLESIASTICUS 38

# 404

## THE MAKER OF POEMS

All this time, and at all times,
wait the words of true poems;
The words of true poems do not
merely please.

>The maker of poems settles
>justice, reality, immortality;
>His insight and power encircle
>things and the human race.

He is the glory and extract thus
far, of things, and of the human
race.

>The true poets are not fol-
>lowers of beauty, but the
>august masters of beauty.

The words of poems are the tuft
and final applause of science.
The words of true poems give you
more than poems.

They give you to form for yourself, poems, religions, politics, war, peace, behavior, histories, essays, romances, and everything else.

They balance ranks, colors, races, creeds, and the sexes;
They do not seek beauty—they are sought.

They prepare for death—yet are they not the finish, but rather the outset;

They bring none to his or her terminus, or to be content and full.

Whom they take, they take into space, to behold the birth of stars, to learn one of the meanings:

To launch off with absolute faith—to sweep through the ceaseless rings, and never be quiet again.

WALT WHITMAN

# 405

## PRAISE GOD IN HIS SANCTUARY

Praise ye the Lord.
Praise God in his sanctuary;
Praise him in the firmament of his power.

Praise him for his mighty acts;
Praise him according to his excellent greatness.

Praise him with the sound of the trumpet;
Praise him with the psaltery and harp.

Praise him with the timbrel and dance;
Praise him with stringed instruments and organs.

Praise him upon the loud cymbals;
Praise him upon the high sounding cymbals.

Let every thing that hath breath praise the Lord.
Praise ye the Lord.

PSALM 150

# Love and Human Brotherhood

## 406

### LOVE

Though I speak with the tongues of men and of angels, and have not love, I am become as sounding brass or a tinkling cymbal.

And though I have the gift of prophecy and understand all mysteries and all knowledge; and though I have all faith, so that I could remove mountains, and have not love, I am nothing.

And though I bestow all my goods to feed the poor, and though I give my body to be burned, and have not love, it profiteth me nothing.

Love suffereth long and is kind; love envieth not; love vaunteth not itself, is not puffed up;

Doth not behave itself unseemly, seeketh not her own, is not easily provoked, thinketh no evil;

Rejoiceth not in iniquity, but rejoiceth in the truth;

Beareth all things, believeth all things, hopeth all things, endureth all things.

Love never faileth, but whether there be prophecies, they shall fail;

Whether there be tongues, they shall cease; whether there be knowledge, it shall vanish away.

And now abideth faith, hope, love, these three; but the greatest of these is love.

I CORINTHIANS 13

## 407

### LET A MAN LEAVE ANGER

Let a man leave anger, let him forsake pride, let him overcome all bondage.

He who holds back rising anger like a rolling chariot, him I call a real driver; other people are but holding the reins.

Beware of bodily anger, and control your body. Leave the sins of the body, and with your body practice virtue.

Beware of the anger of your tongue, and control your tongue.
Leave the sins of the tongue, and practice virtue with your tongue.

Beware of the anger of the mind, and control your mind. Leave the sins of the mind, and practice virtue with your mind.

> The wise who control their body, who control their tongue, the wise who control their mind, are indeed well-controlled.

The fault of others is easily perceived, but that of one's self is difficult to perceive;

> A man winnows his neighbor's faults like chaff, but his own fault he hides, as a cheat hides an unlucky cast of the die.

Speak the truth; do not yield to anger; give, if you are asked, even though it be a little: by these three steps you will come near the gods.

> Let a man overcome anger by love, let him overcome evil by good; let him overcome the greedy by liberality, the liar by truth.

DHAMMAPADA 17, 18

# 408

## BUDDHA'S PITY

The Enlightened One, because he saw mankind drowning in the great sea of birth, death, and sorrow, longed to save them; for this he was moved to pity.

> Because he saw the men of the world straying in false paths, and none to guide them; for this he was moved to pity.

Because he saw them doing evil with hand, heart, and tongue, and many times receiving the bitter fruits of sin, yet ever yielding to their desires; for this he was moved to pity.

> Because he saw them living in an evil time, subjected to tyrannous kings and suffering many ills, yet helplessly following after pleasure; for this he was moved to pity.

Because he saw them living in a time of wars, killing and wounding one another; and knew that for the riotous hatred that had flourished in their hearts they were doomed to pay an endless retribution; for this he was moved to pity.

> Because some had great riches that they could not bear to give away; for this he was moved to pity.

Because he saw the men of the world ploughing their fields, sowing the seed, trafficking, huckstering, buying, and selling, and at the end winnowing nothing but bitterness;

> For this he was moved to pity.

UPĀSAKA SĪLA SŪTRA

## 409

### OUR COMMON BONDS

Know the bonds by which we are bound to one another, for we are not alone.

A man is a road where his brothers may walk.

His body is the bed of a stream through which flow the many waters of his world and his race.

His heart is a city where his brothers may build their dwelling.

A man is many wires strung in the wind, and he must sing the song of the air that flows over him.

Tears awaken tears and laughter awakens laughter; another man's sorrow takes up lodging within us.

When the stranger weeps at the death of one he loves, we too must weep.

For the death of one is the symbol of the death of all men, and no man can escape its meaning.

When one baby is born it is a symbol of all birth and life.

Therefore all men must rejoice, and all men must lose their hearts to a child.

Hunger bites all men, and desire afflicts us all alike.

All men are opened by love and moved by the ecstasy of another.

One enveloping air gives breath to the men of all continents, and one sun shines on us all.

From the same river of time has come all the water of life.

All men smile with their lips and weep with their eyes. A smile disregards the color of the face, and the moaning of grief is alike in all tongues.

Pity and compassion are the deep working of man; they speak forth the completeness of his being.

KENNETH L. PATTON

## 410

### THE GOOD SAMARITAN

And, behold, a certain lawyer stood up, and tempted him saying, Master, what shall I do to inherit eternal life?

And he said unto him, What is written in the law? how readest thou?

And he answering said, Thou shalt love the Lord thy God with all thy heart, and with all thy soul, and with all thy strength, and with all thy mind; and thy neighbor as thyself.

And he said unto him, Thou hast answered right: this do, and thou shalt live.

But he, willing to justify himself, said unto Jesus, And who is my neighbor?

And Jesus answering said, A certain man went down from Jerusalem to Jericho, and fell among thieves, which stripped him of his raiment, and wounded him, and departed, leaving him half dead.

And by chance there came down a certain priest that way; and when he saw him, he passed by on the other side.

And likewise a Levite, when he was at the place, came and looked on him, and passed by on the other side.

But a certain Samaritan, as he journeyed, came where he was; and when he saw him, he had compassion on him,

And went to him, and bound up his wounds, pouring in oil and wine, and set him on his own beast, and brought him to an inn, and took care of him.

And on the morrow when he departed, he took out two pence, and gave them to the host, and said unto him, Take care of him: and whatsoever thou spendest more, when I come again, I will repay thee.

Which now of these three, thinkest thou, was neighbor unto him that fell among the thieves?

And he said, He that showed mercy on him.

Then Jesus said unto him, Go, and do thou likewise.

LUKE 10

## 411

### GOD IS LOVE

This is the message which ye heard from the beginning, that we should love one another.

We know that we have passed from death unto life, because we love the brethren.

But whoso hath this world's goods and beholdeth his brother in need,

and shutteth up his compassion from him, how doth the love of God abide in him?

Let us not love in word, neither with the tongue, but in deed and truth.

Beloved, let us love one another, for love is of God, and every one that loveth is born of God, and knoweth God.

> He that loveth not knoweth not God, for God is love.

No man hath seen God at any time: if we love one another, God abideth in us, and his love is perfected in us.

God is love, and he that abideth in love abideth in God, and God abideth in him.

I JOHN 3, 4

# 412

## PITY

Pity, more than any other feeling,
Is a learned emotion.

> A child will have it least of all.

Pity comes
From the infinite accumulations of ~~man~~'s memory,
From the anguish, pain, and suffering of life,
From the full deposit of experience,

> From the forgotten faces, the lost ~~men~~ contacts,
> And from the million strange and haunting visages
> Of time.

Pity comes upon the nick of time
And stabs us like a knife.

> Its face is thin and dark and burning,
> And it has come before we know it,
> Gone before we can grasp or capture it;

It leaves a shrewd, deep wound,
But a bitter, subtle one,
And it always comes most keenly
From a little thing.

> It comes, without a herald or a cause we can determine,

And how, why, where it comes
We cannot say. . . .

Then pity is there, is there at once
With its dark face and sudden knife,
To stab us with an anguish that we cannot utter,
To rend us with its agony
Of intolerable and wordless regret,
To haunt us with the briefness of our days,
And to tear our hearts with anguish and wild sorrow.

> And for what? For what?
> For all we want, that never may be captured,

For all we thirst for, that never may be found,
For love, that must grow old and be forever dying,

> For all the bone, brain, passion, marrow, sinew
> Of our lives, our hearts, our youth,
> That must grow old and bowed and barren,
> Wearied out!

And oh! for beauty,
That wild, strange song of magic,
aching beauty,
The intolerable, unutterable, un-
graspable
Glory, power, and beauty of the
world,

> This earth, this life, that is,
> And is everywhere around us,
> That we have seen and known
> At ten thousand moments of
> our lives,

That has broken our hearts, mad-
dened our brains,
And torn the sinews of our lives
asunder
As we have lashed and driven sav-
agely
In quest of it,

> Unresting in our frenzied hope
> That some day we shall find
> it, hold it, fix it,
> Make it ours forever — . . .

And beauty swells
Like a wild song in our heart,
Beauty, bursting like a great grape
in our throat,

Beauty aching, rending, word-
less, and unutterable,
Beauty in us, all around us,
Never to be captured —
And we know that we are
dying
As the river flows!

Oh, then will pity come,
To stab us
With a thousand wordless, lost,
forgotten,
Little things!

> And how, where, why it came
> We cannot say,
> But we feel pity now
> For all those who have ever
> lived upon the earth.

And it is night, now,
Night, and we are living, hoping,
fearing,
While the great stars shine upon us
As they have shone on all beings
dead and living
On this earth,

> On all those yet unborn, and
> yet to live
> Who will come after us!

THOMAS WOLFE

# 413

## HONOR THY PARENTS

Honor thy father with thy whole
heart,
And forget not the sorrows of thy
mother.

> Remember that thou wast be-
> gotten of them;
> And how canst thou recom-
> pense them the things that
> they have done for thee?

Whoso honoreth his father shall
have joy in his own children;

> And he that honoreth his
> mother is as one that layeth
> up treasure.

Honor thy father and mother both
in word and deed,
That a blessing may come upon
thee from them.

For the blessing of the father
establisheth the houses of
children,
But the curse of the mother
rooteth out foundations.

Glory not in the dishonor of thy
father;
For thy father's dishonor is no
glory unto thee.

For the glory of a man is from
the honor of his father;
And a mother in dishonor is
a reproach to her children.

My son, help thy father in his age,
And grieve not him as long as he
liveth.

And if his understanding fail,
have patience with him;

And despise him not when
thou art in thy full strength.

Despise not the discourse of the
wise,
But acquaint thyself with their
proverbs;

For of them thou shalt learn
instruction,
And how to serve great men
with ease.

Miss not the discourse of the elders,
For they also learned of their
fathers;

And of them thou shalt learn
understanding,
And to give answer as need
requireth.

ECCLESIASTICUS 7, 3, 8

# 414

## YOUR CHILDREN

Your children are not your children.
They are the sons and daughters
of Life's longing for itself.

They come through you but
not from you,
And though they are with
you yet they belong not to
you.

You may give them your love but
not your thoughts,
For they have their own thoughts.

You may house their bodies
but not their souls,
For their souls dwell in the
house of tomorrow, which you
cannot visit, not even in your
dreams.

You may strive to be like them,
but seek not to make them like you.
For life goes not backward nor
tarries with yesterday.

You are the bows from which
your children as living arrows
are sent forth.

The Archer sees the mark upon the
path of the infinite, and he bends
you with his might that his arrows
may go swift and far.

Let your bending in the Archer's hand be for gladness;
For even as he loves the arrow
that flies, so he loves also the
bow that is stable.

KAHLIL GIBRAN

# 415

## A FAITHFUL FRIEND

Sweet language will multiply friends;
And a fair-speaking tongue will increase kind greetings.

Be in peace with many:
Nevertheless have but one counselor of a thousand.

If thou wouldst get a friend, prove him first,
And be not hasty to credit him.

For some man is a friend for his own occasion,
And will not abide in the day of thy trouble.

And there is a friend, who being turned to enmity and strife
Will discover thy reproach.

A faithful friend is a strong defense;
And he that hath found such an one hath found a treasure.

Nothing doth countervail a faithful friend;
And his excellency is invaluable.

A faithful friend is the medicine of life.

ECCLESIASTICUS 6

# 416

## LOVE AND UNDERSTANDING

What more have we to give to one another than love and understanding?

We will gather a store of love for our children, and marry love to wisdom, that the needs and thoughts of the child may be known to us.

We will make a world for the gladness of children, bringing to them the conviction of their worth and beauty which their beings crave.

We will gather a store of love for youth, troubled in the rising turbulence of life, to guide them into maturity with less of loneliness and torture.

We will find useful tasks for their hands, that they may learn to create with clean joy.

We will gather a store of love for parents, for if the homes of the land are stark and brutal, then are we indeed poor.

Our chief labor is the building of homes, and our knowledge will be increased to set the seasons of childhood and parenthood in the ways of goodness.

We will gather a store of love for the aged, whose days have been wrung with our follies and hurts. Our land will be a large home for the elders.

Their strength shall be restored in the vigor of their grandchildren.

Their loneliness shall be forestalled in the companionship of their children, who in their own parenthood have met their fathers and mothers coming toward them across the years.

We will turn our whole persons to the use of love and understanding, for the one without the other is a fumbling hand, and ignorant mercy is a plague of death.

Wisdom must be made the ready implement of love, and love the guide and repairer of knowledge.

KENNETH L. PATTON

# 417

### A VIRTUOUS WOMAN

Who can find a virtuous woman?
For her price is far above rubies.

The heart of her husband doth safely trust in her;
She will do him good and not evil all the days of her life.

She seeketh wool, and flax,
And worketh willingly with her hands.

She layeth her hands to the spindle,
And her hands hold the distaff.

She stretcheth out her hand to the poor;
Yea, she reacheth forth her hands to the needy.

She is not afraid of the snow for her household,
For all her household are clothed with scarlet.

Her husband is known in the gates,
When he sitteth among the elders of the land.

Strength and honor are her clothing;

And she shall rejoice in time to come.

She openeth her mouth with wisdom;
And in her tongue is the law of kindness.

She looketh well to the ways of her household,
And eateth not the bread of idleness.

Her children arise up, and call her blessed;
Her husband also, and he praiseth her:

Many daughters have done virtuously,
But thou excellest them all.

Favor is deceitful, and beauty is vain:
But a woman that feareth the Lord, she shall be praised.

Give her of the fruit of her hands;
And let her own works praise her in the gates.

PROVERBS 31

# 418

## MAKE NOT A BOND OF LOVE

Love one another, but make not a bond of love:
Let it rather be a moving sea between the shores of your souls.

> Fill each other's cup but drink not from one cup.
> Give one another of your bread but eat not from the same loaf.

Sing and dance together and be joyous, but let each one of you be alone,
Even as the strings of a lute are alone though they quiver with the same music.

> Give your hearts, but not into each other's keeping.

For only the hand of Life can contain your hearts.

And stand together yet not too near together:

> For the pillars of the temple stand apart,
> And the oak tree and the cypress grow not in each other's shadow.

But let there be spaces in your togetherness,
And let the winds of the heavens dance between you.

> Love one another, but make not a bond of love.

KAHLIL GIBRAN

# Freedom

# 419

## IN PRAISE OF LIBERTY

Our faith and knowledge thrive by exercise, as well as our limbs and complexion.

> If the waters of truth flow not in a perpetual progression, they sicken into a muddy pool of conformity and tradition.

We boast our light; but if we look not wisely on the sun itself it smites us into darkness.

> The light which we have gained was given us not to be ever staring on, but by it to discover onward things more remote from our knowledge.

Where there is much desire to

learn, there of necessity will be much arguing, much writing, many opinions;

> A little generous prudence, a little forbearance of one another, and some grain of charity, might win all these diligences to join, and unite in one general and brotherly search after truth.

Give me liberty to know, to utter, and to argue freely according to conscience, above all liberties.

And though all the winds of doctrine were let loose to play upon the earth, so truth be in the field, we do injuriously to misdoubt her strength.

For who knows not that truth is strong, next to the Almighty; she needs no policies, no stratagems to make her victorious.

> Let her and falsehood grapple; whoever knew truth put to the worse in a free and open encounter.
>
> JOHN MILTON

# 420

## THE FREE MIND

I call that mind free which masters the senses,
And which recognizes its own reality and greatness:

> Which passes life, not in asking what it shall eat or drink,
> But in hungering, thirsting, and seeking after righteousness.

I call that mind free which jealously guards its intellectual rights and powers,
Which does not content itself with a passive or hereditary faith:

> Which opens itself to light whencesoever it may come;
> Which receives new truth as an angel from heaven.

I call that mind free which is not passively framed by outward circumstance,

And is not the creature of accidental impulse:

> Which discovers everywhere the radiant signatures of the Infinite Spirit,
> And in them finds helps to its own spiritual enlargement.

I call that mind free which protects itself against the usurpations of society,
And which does not cower to human opinion:

> Which refuses to be the slave or tool of the many or of the few,
> And guards its empire over itself as nobler than the empire of the world.

I call that mind free which resists the bondage of habit,
Which does not mechanically copy

the past, nor live on its old virtues:

> But which listens for new and higher monitions of conscience,
> And rejoices to pour itself forth in fresh and higher exertions.

I call that mind free which sets no bounds to its love,
Which, wherever they are seen, delights in virtue and sympathizes with suffering:

> Which recognizes in all human beings the image of God and the rights of his children,
> And offers itself up a willing sacrifice to the cause of mankind.

I call that mind free which has cast off all fear but that of wrong-doing,
And which no menace or peril can enthrall:

> Which is calm in the midst of tumults,
> And possesses itself, though all else be lost.

WILLIAM ELLERY CHANNING

## 421

### CHERISH YOUR DOUBTS

Cherish your doubts, for doubt is an instruments the handmaiden of truth.

> Doubt is the key to the door of knowledge; it is the servant of discovery.

A belief which may not be questioned binds us to error, for there is incompleteness and imperfection in every belief.

> Doubt is the touchstone of truth; it is an acid which eats away the false.

Let no one man fear for the truth, that doubt may consume it; for doubt is a testing of belief.

> The truth stands boldly and unafraid; it is not shaken by the testing:

For truth, if it be truth, arises from each testing stronger, more secure.

> Whoever He that would silence doubt is filled with fear; the house of his spirit is built on shifting sands.

But whoever he that fears not doubt, and knows its use, is founded on a rock.

> They He shall walk in the light of growing knowledge; the work of those his hands shall endure.

Therefore let us not fear doubt, but let us rejoice in its help:

> It is to the wise as a staff to the blind; doubt is the servant handmaiden of truth.

ROBERT T. WESTON

# 422

## THE FREE SPIRIT

The free spirit is the spirit of joy. It delights to create beauty. It is unafraid; it knows no fear.

The free spirit declares the earth to be its home, and the fragrance of the earth to be its inspiration.

It is strong, it is mighty in beneficence. It views its powers with emotions of adventure.

It dreams a civilization like unto itself. It would create such a world for ~~mankind~~. It has the strength. humankind

The free spirit sees the strength of the fertile earth, the strength of the mountains, the valleys, the far-spreading plains,

The vast seas, the rivers, the great sky as a wondrous dome, the sun in its rising, its zenith, and its setting, and the night.

It glories in these powers of earth and sky as in its own.

It affirms itself one with them all.

The free spirit sees Life at work everywhere—Life the mysterious, the companionable, the ineffable, the immensest and gentlest of powers:

Clothing the earth in a pattern of radiance, of tenderness, of fairy delicacy—ceaselessly at work.

Thus the free spirit feels itself to be likewise clothed.

Thus ~~is man~~, the wonder-worker, bound up in friendship with the wonder-worker—Life. *are we*

LOUIS H. SULLIVAN

# 423

## THE FAITH OF DOUBT

To doubt is a valorous and necessary faith, for to doubt is to believe in the intelligence and inventive imagination of humanity.

A man doubts because he believes there is an error which his doubt should uncover, and he believes that the searching

eye of his doubt can discover the error.

He believes that when the error is discovered he will be able to find an answer less faulty than the one he has.

Doubt is the necessary machinery whereby our satisfaction with what we have is prodded and disturbed.

To doubt is to exercise an exemplary humility; we doubt our own assumptions and creations.

We doubt that what man has created is the best that can be created; we doubt that human beings as yet know everything.

To doubt is to declare that, lovely as the creations of our fathers have been, they are not sufficient for their sons.

It is to declare that there is an upward sweep to history, and that the only way we can justify the inheritance from the past is to improve upon it.

Doubting is but the forefront of faith, a faith in the inexhaustibility of growth and the illimitable extent and wonder of the universe.

A doubting age is an age in the restlessness and discontent of growth; a doubt is an idea that is still alive.

To doubt that the past has uncovered all things is to express faith that many things are still to be uncovered.

To doubt that we have grown to our full stature and knowledge is to express faith that we may develop into beings of such power and dignity that we cannot as yet imagine what we shall be.

KENNETH L. PATTON

# Here and Now

## 424

### SONG OF THE OPEN ROAD

Afoot and light-hearted, I take to the open road,
Healthy, free, the world before me.

Henceforth I ask not good-fortune —
I myself am good-fortune;
Strong and content, I travel the open road.

I inhale great draughts of space;
The east and the west are mine, and the north and the south are mine.

All seems beautiful to me;
I can repeat over to men and women, You have done such good to me,
I would do the same to you.

Whoever you are, come travel with me!
However sweet these laid-up stores

—however convenient this dwelling, we cannot remain here;

> However sheltered this port, and however calm these waters, we must not anchor here;

Together! the inducements shall be greater;
We will sail pathless and wild seas;

> We will go where winds blow, waves dash, and the Yankee clipper speeds by under full sail.

Forward! after the Great Companions! and to belong to them! They too are on the road!

> Onward! to that which is endless, as it was beginningless, To undergo much, tramps of days, rests of nights,

To see nothing anywhere but what you may reach it and pass it, To look up or down no road but it stretches and waits for you—

> To know the universe itself as a road—as many roads—as roads for traveling souls.

WALT WHITMAN

# 425

### THE GLORY OF LIFE IS UPON ME

How beautiful is the morning, All light in its tranquillity.

> Clear blue is the depth of the heavens, And the earth is silent and calm.

The bloom is purple on the mountains;
The waters are transparent in the valley.

> The sweet grass is an emerald floor; The vesture of earth is aglow with rejoicing life.

The encircling sea, the breaking waves upon the rocks:
The serenity of inland calm:

> The friendly trees of the forest, Their noble forms, the quiet glades:

The flowers of hill and valley, The swelling downs, the hamlet that nestles below:

> The country, mine own people, unutterably beloved, Whose future I long to know:

The children, most precious, most to be revered,
Born of heaven to be soldiers of life and light:

> The glory of life is upon me; The vision of a pure delight.

The people shall be as one family, The happiness of each shall be sought by all.

> Fear will fall from our dwellings, And the night shall be safe with open doors.

ROLLO RUSSELL

# 426

## FOR YOU

The sum of all known reverence I
add up in you, whoever you are;
The men who govern are
there for you, it is not you
who are there for them;

All architecture is what you do to
it when you look upon it;

All music is what awakes
from you when you are re-
minded by the instruments;

The sun and stars that float in the
open air;
The apple-shaped earth and we
upon it;

The endless pride and out-
stretching of man; unspeak-
able joys and sorrows;

The wonder everyone sees in everyone else, he sees, and the wonders
that fill each minute of time forever;

It is for you whoever you are

—it is no farther from you
than your hearing and sight
are from you;
It is hinted by nearest, com-
monest, readiest.

We consider bibles and religions
divine —
I do not say they are not divine;
I say they have all grown out of
you, and may grow out of you still;

It is not they who give the
life—it is you who give the
life.

Will you seek afar off? you surely
come back at last,
In things best known to you, finding the best, or as good as the
best—

Happiness, knowledge, not in
another place, but this place
—not for another hour, but
this hour.

WALT WHITMAN

# In Time to Come

# 427

## GOOD TIDINGS OF GOOD

How beautiful upon the mountains
are the feet of him that bringeth
good tidings;

That publisheth peace, that

bringeth good tidings of good.

The cruel shall be turned to mercy,
and the unthankful shall open his
heart.

Let justice dwell in far-off isles, and righteousness among the people.

The judgments of peace shall be made among all peoples and shall rebuke strong nations afar off.

They shall beat their swords into plowshares, and their spears into pruning hooks;

Nation shall not lift up sword against nation, neither shall they learn war any more.

But they shall sit every man under his vine and under his fig tree, and none shall make them afraid.

Speak ye every man the truth to his neighbor; execute the judgment of truth and peace in your gates.

And let none of you imagine evil in your hearts against his neighbor.

We will make our officers peace, and our exactors righteousness.

Violence shall be no more heard in the land, wasting nor destruction within its borders.

Let goodwill speed from nation to nation;

Let the voice of friendship prevail in distant lands.

And the melody of righteousness shall be as the new song of them that are redeemed.

So shall all hearts be filled with rejoicing, and sorrow and sighing shall flee away.

COMPOSITE

# 428

## HOW BEAUTIFUL UPON THE MOUNTAINS

How beautiful upon the mountains are the feet of him that bringeth good tidings,
That publisheth peace;
That bringeth good tidings of good,
That publisheth salvation;
That saith unto Zion, thy God reigneth!

Thy watchmen shall lift up the voice;
With the voice together shall they sing:
For they shall see eye to eye,
When the Lord shall bring again Zion.

Break forth into joy, sing together,
Ye waste places of Jerusalem:
For the Lord hath comforted his people,
He hath redeemed Jerusalem.

The Lord hath made bare his holy arm in the eyes of all the nations;
And all the ends of the earth
Shall see the salvation of our God.

And it shall come to pass in the last days,
That the mountain of the Lord's

house shall be established in the top of the mountains,
And shall be exalted above the hills;
And all nations shall flow unto it.

And many people shall go and say,
Come ye, and let us go up to the mountain of the Lord,
To the house of the God of Jacob;
And he will teach us of his ways,
And we will walk in his paths:
For out of Zion shall go forth the law,

And the word of the Lord from Jerusalem.

And he shall judge among the nations,
And shall rebuke many people:
And they shall beat their swords into plowshares,
And their spears into pruning hooks:

Nation shall not lift up sword against nation,
Neither shall they learn war any more.

ISAIAH 52, 2

# 429

## ANNOUNCEMENT

I announce natural persons to arise;
I announce justice triumphant;

I announce uncompromising liberty and equality;

I announce the justification of candor, and the justification of pride.

I announce that the identity of These States is a single identity only;

I announce the Union more and more compact, indissoluble;

I announce splendors and majesties to make all the previous politics of the earth insignificant.

I announce adhesiveness—I say it shall be limitless, unloosened;

I say you shall yet find the friend you were looking for.

I announce a man or woman coming—perhaps you are the one.

I announce the great individual, fluid as Nature, chaste, affectionate, compassionate, fully armed.

I announce a life that shall be copious, vehement, spiritual, bold;

I announce an end that shall lightly and joyfully meet its translation.

I announce myriads of youths, beautiful, gigantic, sweet-blooded;

I announce a race of splendid and savage old men.

WALT WHITMAN

# 430

## A NEW HEAVEN AND EARTH

Behold, I create new heavens and a new earth:
And the former shall not be remembered, nor come into mind.

But be ye glad and rejoice for ever in that which I create:
For, behold, I create Jerusalem a rejoicing,
And her people a joy.

And I will rejoice in Jerusalem, and joy in my people:
And the voice of weeping shall be no more heard in her,
Nor the voice of crying.

There shall be no more thence an infant of days,
Nor an old man that hath not filled his days:
For the child shall die a hundred years old.

And they shall build houses, and inhabit them;
And they shall plant vineyards, and eat the fruit of them.

They shall not build, and another inhabit;
They shall not plant, and another eat:
For as the days of a tree are the days of my people;
And mine elect shall long enjoy the work of their hands.

They shall not labor in vain, nor bring forth for trouble;
For they are the seed of the blessed of the Lord,
And their offspring with them.

And it shall come to pass, that before they call, I will answer;
And while they are yet speaking, I will hear.

The wolf and the lamb shall feed together,
And the lion shall eat straw like the bullock:

They shall not hurt nor destroy in all my holy mountain, saith the Lord.

ISAIAH 65

# 431

## PARABLES OF THE KINGDOM

A parable put he forth unto them, saying, The kingdom of heaven is likened unto a man which sowed good seed in his field:

But while men slept, his enemy came and sowed tares among the wheat, and went his way.

But when the blade was sprung up, and brought forth fruit, then appeared the tares also.

So the servants of the householder came and said unto him, Sir, didst not thou sow good seed in thy field? from whence then hath it tares?

He said unto them, An enemy hath done this.
The servants said unto him,
Wilt thou then that we go and gather them up?

But he said, Nay; lest while ye gather up the tares, ye root up also the wheat with them.

Let them both grow together until the harvest:

And in the time of harvest I will say to the reapers, Gather ye together first the tares, and bind them in bundles to burn them: but gather the wheat into my barn.

Another parable put he forth unto them, saying, The kingdom of heaven is like to a grain of mustard seed, which a man took, and sowed in his field:

Which indeed is the least of all seeds: but when it is grown, it is the greatest among herbs, and becometh a tree, so that the birds of the air come and lodge in the branches thereof.

Another parable spake he unto them: The kingdom of heaven is like unto leaven, which a woman took, and hid in three measures of meal, till the whole was leavened.

Again, the kingdom of heaven is like unto a treasure hid in a field; the which when a man hath found, he hideth, and for joy thereof goeth and selleth all that he hath, and buyeth that field.

Again, the kingdom of heaven is like unto a merchantman, seeking goodly pearls:

Who, when he had found one pearl of great price, went and sold all that he had, and bought it.

MATTHEW 13

## 432

### COMFORT YE MY PEOPLE

Comfort ye, comfort ye my people, Saith your God,

Speak ye comfortably to Jerusalem, and cry unto her That her warfare is accomplished, that her iniquity is pardoned.

The voice of him that crieth in the wilderness,
Prepare ye the way of the Lord,
Make straight in the desert a highway for our God.

Every valley shall be exalted, And every mountain and hill

shall be made low;
And the crooked shall be made straight,
And the rough places plain:
And the glory of the Lord shall be revealed,
And all flesh shall see it together:
For the mouth of the Lord hath spoken it.

The voice said, Cry.
And he said, What shall I cry?
All flesh is grass,

And all the goodliness thereof is as the flower of the field:

The grass withereth, the flower fadeth;
Because the spirit of the Lord bloweth upon it:
Surely the people is grass.

The grass withereth, the flower fadeth:
But the word of our God shall stand forever.

ISAIAH 40

# 433

## THE PEOPLE SHALL DWELL IN PEACE

Peace to him that is far off, and to him that is near.

The work of righteousness shall be peace, and the effect of righteousness, quietness and assurance forever.

The voice of weeping shall be no more heard in the land, nor the voice of crying.

The city shall be full of boys and girls playing in the streets thereof.

There shall be no more thence an infant of days, nor an old man that hath not filled his days.

And they shall build houses and inhabit them; and they

shall plant vineyards and eat the fruit of them.

They shall not build, and another inhabit; they shall not plant, and another eat:

For as the days of a tree shall be the days of the people; they shall long enjoy the work of their hands.

They shall not labor in vain, nor bring forth for trouble; they shall not hurt nor destroy.

The people shall dwell in a peaceable habitation, and in sure dwellings, and in quiet resting places.

ISAIAH, ZECHARIAH; arranged

# 434

## IN PRAISE OF PEACE

Peace means the beginning of a new world;
Peace means a whole world like one country.

It means that nations are friends;
It means joy to the world.

Peace is quiet and calm; it is rest;
It is silence after a storm.

It is love and friendship;
It is the world's dream of dreams.

It means that the strong respect the weak,
The great respect the small, the many respect the few.

Peace brings comfort and happiness;
It brings bread to the hungry;
It brings prosperity to nations.

Peace is like a mother to those who have suffered;
Peace after war is like sleep after a long journey.

It is like spring after winter;
It brings sunshine into the world;
It is like sweet music after harsh sounds.

PUPILS OF THE LINCOLN SCHOOL,
NEW YORK; arranged

# Commitment and Action

# 435

## RIGHTEOUSNESS AS A MIGHTY STREAM

Ye who turn judgment to wormwood,
And leave off righteousness in the earth,

Seek him that maketh the seven stars and Orion,
And turneth the shadow of death into the morning,

And maketh the day dark with night:

And calleth for the waters of the sea,
And poureth them out upon the face of the earth:
The Lord is his name:

That strengtheneth the

spoiled against the strong,
So that destruction cometh upon the fortress.

They hate him that rebuketh in the gate,
And they abhor him that speaketh uprightly.

Forasmuch therefore as your treading is upon the poor,
And ye take from him burdens of wheat:
Ye have built houses of hewn stone, but ye shall not dwell in them;
Ye have planted pleasant vineyards, but ye shall not drink wine of them.

Hear this, O ye that swallow up the needy,
Even to make the poor of the land to fail,

Saying, When will the new moon be gone, that we may sell corn?
And the Sabbath, that we may set forth wheat,

Making the ephah small, and the shekel great,

And falsifying the balances by deceit?

That we may buy the poor for silver,
And the needy for a pair of shoes;
Yea, and sell the refuse of the wheat?

I hate, I despise your feast days,
And I take no delight in your solemn assemblies.

Though ye offer me burnt offerings and your meat offerings,
I will not accept them;
Neither will I regard the peace offerings of your fat beasts.

Take thou away from me the noise of thy songs;
For I will not hear the melody of thy viols.

But let judgment run down as waters,
And righteousness as a mighty stream.

AMOS 5, 8

# 436

## GEOGRAPHY OF THIS TIME

What is required of us is the recognition of the frontiers between the centuries.

And to take heart: to cross over.

Those who are killed in the place

between out of ignorance, those who wander like cattle and are shot, those who are shot and are left in the stone fields between histories—these *people* may be pitied as the victims of accidents are pitied but their deaths do not signify.

They are neither buried nor otherwise remembered but lie in the dead grass in the dry thorn in the worn light. Their years have no monuments.

There are many such in the sand here—many who did not perceive, who thought the time went on, the years went forward,

the history was continuous— who thought tomorrow was of the same nation as today.

There are many who came to the frontiers between the times and did not know them—who looked for the sentry-box at the stone bridge, for the barricade in the pines and the declaration in two languages—the warning and the opportunity to turn.

They are dead there in the down light, in the sheep's barren.

What is required of us is the recognition with no sign, with no word, with the roads raveled out into ruts and the ruts into dust and the dust stirred by the wind—the roads from behind us ending in the dust.

What is required of us is the recognition of the frontiers where the roads end.

We are very far. We are past the place where the light lifts and farther on than the relinquishment of leaves—farther even than the persistence in the east of the green color. Beyond are the confused tracks, the guns, the watchers.

What is required of us, Companions, is the recognition of the frontiers across this history, and to take heart: to cross over—

To persist and to cross over and survive

But to survive
To cross over.

ARCHIBALD MACLEISH

# 437

## HO, EVERY ONE THAT THIRSTETH

Ho, every one that thirsteth, come ye to the waters,
And he that hath no money, come ye, buy, and eat;
Yea, come, buy wine and milk without money and without price.

Wherefore do ye spend money for that which is not bread?
And your labor for that which satisfieth not?

Incline your ear, and come unto me;
Hear, and your soul shall live.

Seek ye the Lord while he may be found,
Call ye upon him while he is near:

Let the wicked forsake his way,
And the unrighteous man his thoughts:

And let him return unto the Lord, and he will have mercy upon him;
And to our God, for he will abundantly pardon.

For my thoughts are not your thoughts,
Neither are your ways my ways, saith the Lord.

For as the heavens are higher than the earth,
So are my ways higher than your ways, and my thoughts than your thoughts.

For as the rain cometh down, and the snow from heaven,
And returneth not thither, but watereth the earth, and maketh it bud,

That it may give seed to the sower, and bread to the eater:

So shall my word be that goeth forth out of my mouth:
It shall not return unto me void,
But it shall accomplish that which I please,
And it shall prosper in the thing whereto I sent it.

For ye shall go out with joy, and be led forth with peace:
The mountains and the hills shall break forth before you into singing,
And all the trees of the field shall clap their hands.

Instead of the thorn shall come up the fir tree,
And instead of the brier shall come up the myrtle tree:
And it shall be to the Lord for a name,
For an everlasting sign that shall not be cut off.

ISAIAH 55

# 438

## THIS IS TRUE RELIGION

This and this alone
Is true religion—
To serve thy brethren.

This is sin above all other sin—
To harm thy brethren.

In such a faith is happiness,

In lack of it is misery and pain.

Blessed is he who swerveth not aside
From this strait path:

Blessed is he whose life is lived
Thus ceaselessly in serving God.

Bearing others' burdens,
And so alone,
Is life, true life, to be attained:

Nothing is hard to him who, casting self aside,
Thinks only this—
How may I serve my fellow-men?

TULSĪ DĀS; translated
by MOHANDAS K. GANDHI

# 439

## ON THE VERGE OF MASTERY

We have set ourselves over many things; we have gathered terrible powers into our hands.

> We have made ourselves masters of the planet, users of its stores, governors of its teeming life, exploiters of its energies of fire and fission.

We have built and we have torn down; we have created and we have despoiled.

> We have chosen ourselves to be the leaders; but where are we leading the earth and its creatures?

To retreat from our election is to fall into creeping death.

> The man who has taken his cares upon him cannot be washed free of them as an infant; nor can our race, in weak longing, return to the childhood of life.

We have laid hold on much knowledge; our only cure lies in the increase of our science.

> We must proceed from the government of nations that live unto themselves, to the government of a united world.

The age of the pioneer is upon us; for we stand on the verge of self-mastery, and the mastery of the world.

> Lands stretch unexplored before us; our feet will break open new continents of hope, to enlarge the plenty and peace of the people.

We will advance each day, each generation, upon those horizons our eyes have come to behold.

> Whether our cities are builded afar off will be the measurement of man; for there is nothing to bar us from our leave-takings and our arrivals except ourselves.

KENNETH L. PATTON

# Prophets, Exemplars, Pioneers

## 440

### I THINK CONTINUALLY OF THOSE

I think continually of those who
were truly great.
> Who, from the womb, remem-
> bered the soul's history
> Through corridors of light
> where the hours are suns,
> Endless and singing.

Whose lovely ambition
Was that their lips, still touched
with fire,
Should tell of the spirit clothed
from head to foot in song.
> And who hoarded from the
> spring branches
> The desires falling across their
> bodies like blossoms.

What is precious is never to forget
The essential delight of the blood
drawn from ageless springs
Breaking through rocks in worlds
before our earth;
> Never to deny its pleasure in
> the simple morning light,

Nor its grave evening demand
for love;
Never to allow gradually the traffic
to smother
With noise and fog the flowering
of the spirit.
> Near the snow, near the sun,
> in the highest fields
> See how these names are fêted
> by the waving grass
> And by the streamers of white
> cloud
> And whispers of wind in the
> listening sky:

The names of those who in their
lives fought for life,
Who wore at their hearts the fire's
center.
> Born of the sun they traveled
> a short while towards the sun
> And left the vivid air signed
> with their honor.

STEPHEN SPENDER

## 441

### SERVANTS OF GOD

O Thou Eternal Light, towards
whose quickening dawn have
moved the peoples that walked in
darkness, rise with thy radiance
upon the souls which here await
thee. By the vision of ancient
seers, who beheld thy power moving within the veil of earthly things,

Teach us to live as seeing the invisible.

By the voices of prophets, who discerned the signs of their times and foretold the doom that follows wrong,

Arouse us to see and overcome the evils of today.

By the mind that was in Jesus, compassionate, free in thought, steadfast in purpose, stayed on thee,

Awaken in us also a generous mind and a bold vision.

By the self-sacrifice of saints and apostles, martyrs and missioners, who counted not the cost to themselves if they might testify of thy grace,

Inspire us to find in common life the paths of high devotion.

By the joy and praise of the church universal, by every prayer for light in shrines of whatsoever faith,

Kindle in our hearts the faith that shall be a light upon our way and a song upon our lips.

By the labors of all who show forth thy wonderful works, searching out thy law in nature, fashioning forms of beauty, skillful in industry, wise in statecraft, gentle in parenthood, gifted with insight,

Enlarge all our being with the fullness of thy life, that in thy light we may see light and become ministers of thy love brought near.

*Services of Religion*

# 442

### THE PROPHETS

It is no foretelling that engages the prophets; it is not some future day or condition that the prophets announce.

What they tell is not hidden; it faces any man with eyes to see it.

The prophets' complaint and the prophets' elation are the budding of the body of humanity.

Unfolding within them is the new flowering of knowledge of the people.

Roots lie deep in the soil to send up strange shoots, but men walk unknowingly over their hidden places.

Seeds are breaking in the soil of the race that men have not yet discovered.

High in the trees fruit has formed

and ripened that men have not climbed to nor eaten.

Men trample berries of goodness, neglected in the tall grass of their unconcern.

Within men are skills and arts which they have not used; men are creatures of greatness not yet discovered to themselves.

Plans sleep on paper and models gather dust which could uplift the faces of the cities.

The foundations are laid for building that men cannot see; learning is entombed in books that could unlock ages of peace.

All these neglected and unknown possessions are now with us; the prophets have found their hiding places.

They have wedded the unused to the undiscovered, and brought forth an offspring of vision.

Prophecy is the sharpened edge of already; it will cut out the shape of becoming.

KENNETH L. PATTON

# 443

## THE HUMAN FELLOWSHIP

Let us sing of the men and women who have cherished their hearths and gardens on this earth, our homestead.

For they have turned the forests and the wilderness into farms and villages and cities.

Their coming and going have worn paths across the world and made friendly ways for our feet.

They have plied the roads of the seas, and taught us to escape the reefs and the weather.

No longer need we wander, to gather nuts and berries, to find roots and apples.

No longer do we lie cold and hungry to trap the wandering hare and the antelope.

No longer do we huddle in thickets and crouch in caves to escape the wind and the sleet.

Our cities are mild and fraternal places when seen against the jungles that our fathers and mothers roamed for a million years.

It is easy to give thanks to one god, to imagine his single presence, to speak to his one ear.

It is not easy to give thanks to five hundred generations, from whom we have received our customs and our arts, our laws and our learning and our civility.

Our gratitude will be known as we become one with them, and in our turn leave benefits to five hundred generations that follow us,

To generations beyond end, if man can make his peace with himself, and establish his security in the universe.

KENNETH L. PATTON

# 444

## LET US NOW PRAISE FAMOUS MEN

Let us now praise famous men,
And our fathers that begat us.

Such as did bear rule in their kingdoms,
Men renowned for their power,
Giving counsel by their understanding,
And declaring prophecies:

Leaders of the people by their counsels,
And by their knowledge of learning meet for the people,
Wise and eloquent in their instructions:

Such as found out musical tunes,
And recited verses in writing:

Rich men furnished with ability,
Living peaceably in their habitations.

All these were honored in their generations,
And were the glory of their times.

There be of them, that have left a name behind them,
That their praises might be reported.

And some there be, which have no memorial;
Who are perished as though they had never been;
And their children after them.

But these were merciful men,
Whose righteousness hath not been forgotten.

With their seed shall continually remain a good inheritance,
And their children are within the covenant.

Their bodies are buried in peace;
And their glory shall not be blotted out.

The people will tell of their wisdom,
And the congregation will show forth their praise.

ECCLESIASTICUS 44

# Nation and Nations

## 445

God, who hast made us one nation out of many peoples, amid our diversities of race and tradition, unite us in a common love of freedom and in a high ambition for our national life.

> Continue in us the pioneering spirit which led our fathers across the estranging sea and upheld them in the wilderness.

Deepen in the people of this land a devotion to the common weal, so that we may open new doors of hope to the neglected and oppressed; cleanse our hearts from the greed which preys upon others; and deliver our politics from corruption.

> Help us to establish this land in righteousness.

Endue with the spirit of wisdom those entrusted with authority, that there may be peace within our borders, and that we may stand among the nations of the earth an example of justice and a power of good will.

> Let thy peace, O God, rule in all our hearts.

To every council where nations bring their hopes and fears, grant wisdom and mutual understanding, that distrust and hatred may be diminished, and a common law of justice be established.

> Let peace, O God, prevail throughout the earth.

*Services of Religion*

## 446

Open ye the gates, that the righteous nation, even the nation which keepeth faith, may enter in.

> Cast up, cast up the highway; gather out the stones; lift up a standard for the nations.

Go through, go through the gates;

prepare ye the way of the people.

> Behold, peace shall extend to thee like a river, and glory among nations like an overflowing stream.

Thine officers also shall be Peace, and thy magistrates Righteousness.

Violence shall no more be heard in thy land, desolation nor destruction within thy borders.

Then justice shall dwell in the wilderness, and righteousness shall abide in the fruitful field.

The wilderness and the parched land shall be glad;

and the desert shall rejoice, and blossom as the rose.

Then the eyes of the blind shall be opened, and the ears of the deaf shall be unstopped.

And they shall sit every man under his vine and under his fig tree; and none shall make them afraid.

ISAIAH, MICAH; adapted

# 447

## THE BULWARK OF OUR LIBERTY

What constitutes the bulwark of our own liberty and independence? It is not our frowning battlements, our bristling seacoasts, our army and navy.

Our reliance is in our love for liberty; our defense is in the spirit which prizes liberty as the heritage of all men in all lands everywhere.

Destroy this spirit and we have planted the seeds of despotism at our own doors.

Those who deny freedom to others deserve it not for themselves, and cannot long retain it.

The country with its institutions belongs to the people who inhabit it.

Why should there not be a patient confidence in the ulti-

mate justice of the people? Is there any better or equal hope in the world?

Let us have faith that right makes might, and in that faith let us to the end dare to do our duty as we understand it.

Passion has helped us, but can do so no more; reason must furnish the materials for our future support and defense.

With malice toward none, with charity for all, with firmness in the right as God gives us to see the right, let us strive on to finish the work we are in:

To do all which may achieve and cherish a just and lasting peace among ourselves and with all nations.

ABRAHAM LINCOLN

# 448

### THE GREAT CITY

A great city is that which has the greatest men and women;

> If it be a few ragged huts, it is still the greatest city in the whole world.

Where the city stands with the brawniest breed of orators and bards;

> Where the city stands that is beloved by these, and loves them in return, and understands them;

Where no monuments exist to heroes, but in the common words and deeds;

> Where thrift is in its place, and prudence is in its place;

Where the populace rise at once against the never-ending audacity of elected persons;

> Where outside authority enters always after the precedence of inside authority;

Where women enter the public assembly and take places the same as the men;

> Where children are taught to be laws to themselves, and to depend on themselves;

Where the city of the healthiest fathers stands;
Where the city of the best-bodied mothers stands;

> Where the city of the faithfulest friends stands;
> There the great city stands.

WALT WHITMAN

# 449

### FORCE AND THE WAY OF LIFE

#### I

Those who have power in the government of the world, and who follow the way of life, will oppose the use of armies for conquest.

> Those who use weapons will have weapons turned against them.

The places where armies are encamped will become a wilderness of briars and thorns.

> Raising a multitude of men for warfare will be followed by years of scarcity; bad times and disorders follow after war.

The wise ruler will curb his ambitions and refrain from using force.

His only aim will be to relieve the needs of the land; he will not exert his power over others.

He resolutely fulfills his purposes, but not for glory.

He does what must be done, but not for show.

He makes use of his power only as a last resort.

He prefers to achieve his goals without the use of violence.

It is the nature of things to grow to their full strength, and then to fall away.

Force and violence are not the way of life; those who do not live by the way of life will soon perish.

II

The way of life is not the way of actions and assertions.

Yet through the way of life all things achieve their being.

If those who govern the world would follow the way of life, then all things would unfold according to their own nature.

If the people are beset by troublesome desires, they should be taught the unnameable simplicity at the core of life.

When men have ceased from covetousness they will become serene.

Among such people peace will come of its own accord.

TAO-TEH-CHING; paraphrased

# 450

## SALUT AU MONDE!

What rivers are these? what forests and fruits are these?
What are the mountains called that rise so high in the mists?

What climes? what persons and lands are here?
What myriads of dwellings are they, filled with dwellers,
Each answering all—each sharing the earth with all?

I see a great round wonder rolling through the air;

I see the shaded part on one side, where the sleepers are sleeping—and the sun-lit part on the other side;
I see the curious silent change of the light and shade,

I see distant lands, as real and near to the inhabitants of them, as my land is to me.

Within me latitude widens, longitude lengthens;
Asia, Africa, Europe, are to the east—America is provided for in the west;

Banding the bulge of the earth winds the hot equator; curiously north and south turn the axis-ends;

I hear the workmen singing,
and the farmer's wife singing;
I hear in the distance the
sounds of children, and of
animals early in the day;

I see the battlefields of the earth—
grass grows upon them, and blos-
soms and corn;
I see the tracks of ancient and
modern expeditions.

I see the nameless masonries,
venerable messages of the
unknown events, heroes, rec-
ords of the earth.

What cities the light or warmth
penetrates, I penetrate those cities
myself;
All islands to which birds wing
their way, I wing my way myself.

Toward all,
I raise high the perpendicular
hand—I make the signal,
To remain after me in sight
forever, for all the haunts and
homes of men.

WALT WHITMAN

# 451

## ON WAR

One who would guide a leader of
people in the uses of life
Will warn us against the use of
arms for conquest.

Weapons often turn upon the
wielder,
An army's harvest is a waste
of thorns,
Conscription of a multitude
of people
Drains the next year dry.

Even the finest of arms are an instrument of evil,
A spread of plague;

And the way for a vital person
to go
Is not the way of a soldier.

But in time of war people civilized
in peace
Turn from their higher to their
lower nature.

Arms are an instrument of
evil,
No measure for thoughtful
people
Until there fail all other choice
But sad acceptance of it.

Triumph is not beautiful.
One who thinks triumph beautiful
Is one with a will to kill,
And one with a will to kill
Shall never prevail upon the world.

The death of a multitude is
cause for mourning:
Conduct your triumph as a
funeral.

TAO-TEH-CHING 30, 31

# Our World-wide Heritage

## 452

### OWNER OF THE SPHERE

There is one mind common to all individual men. Every man is an inlet to the same and to all of the same.

He that is once admitted to the right of reason, is made a freeman of the whole estate.

What Plato thought, he may think; what a saint has felt, he may feel; what at any time has befallen any man, he can understand.

Who hath access to this universal mind is a party to all that is or can be done.

Without hurry, without rest, the human spirit goes forth from the beginning to embody every faculty, every thought, every emotion, in appropriate events.

This human mind wrote history, and this must read it.

We, as we read, must become Greeks, Romans, Turks, priest and king, martyr and executioner; must fasten these images to some reality in our secret experience, or we shall learn nothing rightly.

This remedies the defect of our too great nearness to ourselves: it is the universal nature which gives forth to particular men and events.

All that Shakespeare says of the king, yonder slip of a boy that reads in the corner feels to be true of himself.

Law was enacted, the sea was searched, the land was found, the blow was struck, for us, as we ourselves in that place would have done or applauded.

I can find Greece, Asia, Italy, Spain, and the Islands—the genius and creative principle of each and all eras—in my own mind.

Every mind must know the whole lesson for itself. What it does not see, what it does not live, it will not know.

I am owner of the sphere,
Of the seven stars and the solar year,

Of Caesar's hand, and Plato's brain,
Of Lord Christ's heart, and Shakespeare's strain.

RALPH WALDO EMERSON

# 453

## A NEW SHAPE OF FELLOWSHIP

Let us indicate a new shape of fellowship; let us demonstrate a new kind of unity.

We have learned that men work together in consideration and loyalty while still seeking after truth.

Discoverers have a common purpose in their adventures; they can be joined together in becoming.

Disagreement among those seeking the truth is a blessing greater than the agreement of the assured.

We have been warned against leaving the temples of our upbringing;

But we have discovered that every temple in which men have worshiped is also our temple, if we enter it in the spirit of a common search for the goodness of life.

The search for goodness is a human search; it rings with the same resonance of purpose and longing whatever the local dialect and the tribal speech.

All the people of mankind are our family, and the cohorts of our common faith.

We have not left our homeland, for all the earth is our country, and all the roads are streets of one town.

If all men will search together for the truth in freedom and respect, they will not only find the truth, they will also discover one another.

KENNETH L. PATTON

# 454

## MAN IN TIME

Rich is the man who lives in today, filled with the problems and promises of his own times.

Richer is the man who lives in his own times, but sees in them the admixture of all the times that have been.

This earth is our present garden and a path for our feet, but each grain of soil is also a history and a romance.

Could it speak it would tell of being many times the flesh of plant and animal, lifted high in leaf, swift in muscle.

The smoothness of the stone is the story of many waters.

The stars are very old, although they seem to have changed hardly at all in the brief moment men have looked upon them.

Time and death, the great gatherers, are ancient dwellers of this place.

Fruitful is the life of him who sinks his roots deep in the soil of culture laid down by the generations.

Man too is a rich soil gathered from many centuries.

Man too is a romance and a history.

Rich is the man who sees things newly as if eyes had never before looked upon the earth.

Richer is he who learns to look through the eyes of men who have gone before, and adds to their vision the freshness of his own sight.

We live this day within all the years of the past.

Only seasoned by the memory of yesterday is the bread and meat of today tasted in its full flavor.

KENNETH L. PATTON

# 455

## UNIVERSAL RELIGION

All men are brothers, though we have grown strangers to one another.

Though we are born here and now, yet we are countrymen of the universe and all eternity is gathered in the days of our life.

Though we are citizens of but one country, yet fellow-feeling opens us to citizenship in all nations.

Though we speak but one tongue, yet all the words of the race are contrived for our understanding.

We are ignorant of the story of other lands, unmoved by their arts and aspirations; we are blind to beauties our eyes are not trained to discover.

We call only that good which we have named good, and announce the other people's righteousness an evil-doing.

We consume in small talk and menial concerns the days that might be invested in attaining the means of universal sympathy and understanding.

Yet we have glimpsed the whole in that fragment which we have seen; we know the dream of a united human family, all the greatness of mankind gathered into one glory;

All the yearning of men welded into one unconquerable desire;

All the law and morality of the race gathered into one ethic and jurisprudence;

All the prophets of all faiths installed in one pantheon of spiritual heroes;

All the poetry and prophecy canonized in a single bible;

All the scattered tribes and nations, citizens of one commonwealth.

In this universal faith, in which all wisdom and goodness are made one, we find a home for the human spirit, the adequacy of generous desires, the farthest dimensions of our aspiration.

KENNETH L. PATTON

# Church of the Free Spirit

## 456

### AN ETERNAL VERITY

Ancient as the home is the temple; ancient as the work-bench is the altar.

Ancient as the sword is the sacrificial faggot; ancient as the soldier is the priest.

Older than written language is spoken prayer; older than painting is the thought of a nameless one.

Religion is the first and last — the universal language of the human heart.

Differing words describe the outward appearance of things; diverse symbols represent that which stands beyond and within.

Yet each man's hunger is the same, and heart communicates with heart.

Ever the vision leads on, with many gods or with one, with a holy land washed by ocean waters, or a holy land within the heart.

In temperament we differ, yet we are dedicated to one august destiny; creeds divide us, but we share a common quest.

Because we are human, we shall ever build our altars; because each has his yearning, we offer everywhere our prayers and anthems.

For an eternal verity abides beneath diversities; we are children of one great love, and brethren one of another.

W. WALDEMAR W. ARGOW

# 457

## FOR GENERATIONS TO COME

Give ear, O my people, to my law:
Incline your ears to the words of
my mouth.

> I will open my mouth in a
> parable;
> I will utter dark sayings of old:

Things that we have heard and
known,
And our fathers have told us.

> We will not hide them from
> their children,
> Showing to the generation to
> come the praises of the Lord,
> And his strength, and his won-
> derful works that he hath
> done.

For he established a testimony in
Jacob, and appointed a law in
Israel,

Which he commanded our fathers,
That they should make them
known to their children;

> That the generation to come
> might know them,
> Even the children which
> should be born,
> Who should arise and declare
> them to their children;

That they might set their hope in
God,
And not forget the works of God,
But keep his commandments:

> And remember that God was
> their rock,
> And the high God their re-
> deemer.

PSALM 78

# 458

## HOW AMIABLE ARE THY TABERNACLES

How amiable are thy tabernacles,
O Lord of hosts.

> My soul longeth, yea, even
> fainteth for the courts of the
> Lord;
> My heart and my flesh crieth
> out for the living God.

Yea, the sparrow hath found an
house,
And the swallow a nest for herself,
where she may lay her young,

Even thine altars, O Lord of hosts,
my king, and my God.

> Blessed are they that dwell in
> thy house:
> They will be still praising
> thee.

Blessed is the man whose strength
is in thee;
In whose heart are the ways of
them:

Who passing through the valley of Baca make it a well;
The rain also filleth the pools.

They go from strength to strength;
Every one of them in Zion appeareth before God.

O Lord God of hosts, hear my prayer;
Give ear, O God of Jacob.

Behold, O God our shield,
And look upon the face of thine anointed.

For a day in thy courts is better than a thousand;

I had rather be a doorkeeper in the house of my God,
Than to dwell in the tents of wickedness.

For the Lord God is a sun and shield;
The Lord will give grace and glory;
No good thing will he withhold from them that walk uprightly.

O Lord of hosts,
Blessed is the man that trusteth in thee.

PSALM 84

# 459

### THE CHURCH OF TOMORROW

The church of tomorrow will not strive to save men from the world; it will save men in the world.

It will make honest and whole the cravings and appetites of men, leading to the joys of fullness and self-realization.

The church will seek to serve the whole man and the whole community; from it will come the hopes and ideals for a better world.

From the church will come the challenge of free minds to the evils of every age. It will fight all men and all groups who prey on their fellows.

No one shall be too mighty, too rich, or too famous; no tradition shall be too revered, no shrine too sanctified;

All shall be weighed in the scale of human values, for this is the church of men, and them alone it will serve.

There will the mother come with her infant and there will the child be introduced to his world;

There will he learn the meanings man has found in the skies, the fields, the hills and the valleys, and the cities of men.

There will he learn to weigh the meaning of his days, to gather into his mind the wisdom of his ancestors,

To know why men call one thing right and another wrong, and to treasure beauty, mercy, and justice in the deep places of his being.

As common as life itself, as strange as the air he breathes, as reasonable as his own mind, the friendly companion of his days:

> Such will be the church when it is free from the magic and the darkness of the centuries.

It will be the hub, the center of our life together, weaving the strands of our business into a pattern, a design, a meaning —

> Uniting us with our companions of the journey, helping us in our pilgrimage along the road between the cities of birth and death.

KENNETH L. PATTON

## 460

### A LIBERAL CHURCH

Let this church ever seek the oneness of God, and never turn from that venture, to the dark byways of quarrels and competitive struggles which interrupt the pilgrimage of man.

> We aspire to be catholic and to take into account all men.

We reject that which scatters men into ghettos, or forces upon them an ultimate loneliness.

> Ours is a church which holds the dead in sacred memory, and the living in a goodly fellowship.

We desire to live together in such affection as will not allow us to feel threatened by our differences —

> Happy in the liberty which encourages each to make his words correspond with his thought, his acts with his conscience.

Ours is a non-creedal church — not because we have no beliefs, but because we will not be restrained in our beliefs.

Ours is a church of conscience — not because we hold that conscience is infallible, but because it is the meeting place of man and God.

Ours is a church of reason — not because the mind of man is free of errors, but because the dialogue of mind with mind, and mind with itself, refines religious thought.

> Ours is a church of moral work — not because we think morality is a sufficient religion, but because we know no better way of showing our gratitude to God, and our confidence in one another.

We dare not fence the spirit, nor close off the sincerity of conversation with which souls must meet in religious association.

> As others have their ways of religion, so do we have this faith; and, in honest difference, we order our lives together.

WALLACE W. ROBBINS

# 461

### THIS HOUSE

This is a house for the ingathering of nature and of man in nature.

It is a house of friendship, a haven in trouble, an open room for the encouragement of our struggle.

It is a house of freedom, guarding the dignity and worth of each man's person.

It offers a platform for the free voice, for declaring, both in times of security and danger, the full and undivided conflict of opinion.

It is a house of truth-seeking, where the scientist can encourage the devotion of his quest, and the mystic can abide in the brotherhood of searchers.

It is a house of art, adorning its celebrations with the melodies and handiwork of man.

It is a house of prophecy, outrunning times past and times present in visions of growth and progress.

This house is a cradle for our dreams and the workshop of our common endeavor.

KENNETH L. PATTON

# 462

### THE GREAT END IN RELIGIOUS INSTRUCTION

The great end in religious instruction is not to stamp our minds upon the young, but to stir up their own;

Not to make them see with our eyes, but to look inquiringly and steadily with their own;

Not to give them a definite amount of knowledge, but to inspire a fervent love of truth;

Not to form an outward regularity, but to touch inward springs;

Not to bind them by ineradicable prejudices to our particular sect or peculiar notions, but to prepare them for impartial, conscientious judging of whatever subjects may be offered to their decision;

Not to burden the memory, but to quicken and strengthen the power of thought;

Not to impose religion upon them in the form of arbitrary rules, but to awaken the conscience, the moral discernment.

In a word, the great end is to awaken the soul; to bring understanding, conscience, and heart into earnest, vigorous action on religious and moral truth, to excite and cherish spiritual life.

WILLIAM ELLERY CHANNING

## Times and Seasons

# 463

### THE NEW YEAR

The days of the year have stiffened in ice, and darkness has grown upon the land.

The season of cold and early dusk is upon us.

The sun has retreated down the sky, the living green has forsaken the earth, and the leaves have fallen.

No longer do the flowers bloom, and the birds have fled to the south.

But men approach the shortened days with gladness, and the ancient fear is no longer on their faces.

From darkness will come light, and out of the cold will be born the flaming sun.

The frozen soil is no enduring danger, and the heavy death upon the earth is no lasting peril.

For seed is stored in the bins, and the roots in the soil are only sleeping a long sleep.

Men hold the turning of the year as a promise, and the renewing of life is their solid hope.

The time of the new year is known, and they ready their houses for the celebration.

Now the sun will again climb the heavens, and henceforth the darkness will be pushed back each day.

And the months of snow will give way to the months of leaves, and petals will fall upon the earth.

The young will be brought from the womb, and the shoot will burst from the seed.

Men will walk upon the greening grass, and their plowshares will divide the warming soil.

In the midst of winter the promise is given of the summer season, and in the midst of darkness there comes the assurance of the light.

In the midst of cold comes a messenger of warmth, and in the days of death there is heard the good news of life.

KENNETH L. PATTON

# 464

## CHRISTMAS BEATITUDES

On this blessed day let us worship at the altar of joy, for to miss the joy of Christmas is to miss its holiest secret.

Let us enter into the spiritual delights which are the natural heritage of childlike hearts.

Let us withdraw from the cold and barren world of prosaic fact, if only for a season:

That we may warm ourselves by the fireside of fancy, and take counsel of the wisdom of poetry and legend.

Blessed are they who have vision enough to behold a guiding star in the dark mystery which girdles the earth;

Blessed are they who have imagination enough to detect the music of celestial voices in the midnight hours of life;

Blessed are they who have faith enough to contemplate a world of peace and justice in the midst of present wrong and strife;

Blessed are they who have greatness enough to become as little children;

Blessed are they who have zest enough to take delight in simple things;

Blessed are they who have wisdom enough to know that the kingdom of heaven is very close at hand, and that all may enter in who have eyes to see and ears to hear and hearts to understand.

DAVID RHYS WILLIAMS

# 465

## THE COMING OF SPRING

Soon shall the winter's foil be here;
Soon shall these icy ligatures unbind and melt—

A little while, and air, soil, wave, suffused shall be in softness, bloom, and growth—
A thousand forms shall rise

from these dead clods and chills, as from low burial graves.

Thine eyes, ears—all thy best attributes—all that takes cognizance of natural beauty, shall wake and fill.

Thou shalt perceive the simple shows, the delicate miracles of earth,
Dandelions, clover, the emerald grass, the early scents and flowers;

The arbutus under foot, the willow's yellow-green, the blossoming plum and cherry;

With these the robin, lark, and thrush, singing their songs — the flitting bluebird: such are the scenes the annual play brings on.

WALT WHITMAN

# 466

## RANGE ON RANGE OF LIFE

Bright joy, bright joy: the joy of flowers and shining sun, the joy of smiles and play and dancing.

We rejoice in the good of nature.

Lovely things, beautiful shapes and sounds: the shapes of houses and carven stones, the shapes of words together, the sounds of songs and sounds of many woven voices, winding, rhythmic.

We rejoice in the artifice of man.

Darkness and night: the dark of pain, the fret of baffling malady, the last dark, the dark of death.

We know the perils and pains of nature's body.

Gloom and deeper gloom: the dim dark of knowledge never known, of spirits unillumined, the darker gloom of light denied, the dark of mercy quenched and fellowman contemned.

We acknowledge the shame and evil within.

Mighty man, inventive man: the man of tools and wheels, the man of dynamos and wings, the man of computation.

We rejoice in the masteries of man.

Noble man, stately man: the man of order and device, man painting designs of thought, man welding citizen hearts in the state.

We rejoice in the order that is, and nobler orders dreamed.

Folly, wasteful folly: the folly of war and greed, the ruin of bodies, the waste of brains, the folly of riches that stifle alike him who has not and him who has.

We acknowledge our share of guilt in the wastage of life.

Feeble life, futile life: the life of pride, pride of place and pride of learning, life falsely free that draws away from common songs and common prayers.

We seek the fellowships that order all men's hopes.

Man generous, man uplifted: man that lays down his life for his friends, man giving his body to the tomb that new spirit may rise on the world.

We also would walk in newness of life.

Sublime truth, healing truth: light that is light, and darkness turned to light, joy that is joy, and sorrow turned to joy.

We rejoice in wondrous good received and good performed, and we commit ourselves with trust and zeal to that enfolding life that holds us all.

VON OGDEN VOGT

## 467

### UNTO US A CHILD IS BORN

The people that walked in darkness have seen a great light:
They that dwelt in the land of the shadow of death,
Upon them hath the light shined.

For unto us a child is born, unto us a son is given;
And the government shall be upon his shoulder:

And his name shall be called Wonderful Counselor, Mighty God, Everlasting Father, Prince of Peace.

Of the increase of his government and of peace there shall be no end,
Upon the throne of David,
To establish it with judgment and with righteousness from henceforth even for ever.

And there shall come forth a shoot out of the stock of Jesse;
And a branch out of his roots shall bear fruit:

And the spirit of the Lord shall rest upon him,
The spirit of wisdom and understanding,

The spirit of counsel and might,
The spirit of knowledge and of the fear of the Lord;

And his delight shall be in the fear of the Lord:
And he shall not judge after the sight of his eyes,
Neither reprove after the hearing of his ears:

But with righteousness shall he judge the poor,
And reprove with equity for the meek of the earth.

And righteousness shall be the girdle of his loins,
And faithfulness the girdle of his reins.

And the wolf shall dwell with the lamb;
And the leopard shall lie down with the kid;
And the calf and the young lion and the fatling together;
And a little child shall lead them.

And the cow and the bear shall feed;
Their young ones shall lie down together:
And the lion shall eat straw like the ox.

They shall not hurt nor destroy in all my holy mountain:
For the earth shall be full of the knowledge of the Lord,
As the waters cover the sea.

ISAIAH 9, 11

# Opening of Service (Unison)

## 468

### INTO THIS HOUSE OF LIGHT WE COME

Into this house of light we come to seek that which is just and to find that which is good, and here we remember those whose lives are darkened by the greed and wrong of others. We have not purged the commerce of our times of those harsh ways that thwart the hopes and dreams of many. In this house of peace we remember wars and rumors of wars; we have made but feeble effort to understand the peoples of the world and to foster peace among the nations. In this house of joy we remember all sorrowing and troubled folk. Let us here be gathered into a common power of good will which shall issue in lasting peace and larger right.

VON OGDEN VOGT

## 469

### TAKE US NOW TO SERVE THEE

Source of all good, day by day are thy blessings renewed to us, and again we come with thankful hearts to seek the sense of thy presence. O that we could be reborn like the morning! For even as we seek to commune with thee, shadows from our past dim the joy of our aspiration. We remember our thoughtless lives, our impatient tempers, our selfish aims; and yet we know that thou hast neither made us blind like the creatures that have no sin, nor left us without holy guidance — thy still, small voice speaking in our inmost conscience, and thine open word, having dwelt among us full of grace and truth, appealing to us to choose the better part. Take us now to serve thee in newness of spirit, and sweep away every dust of care, every trace of fear, every taint of an uncharitable mind. Amen.

JAMES MARTINEAU

## 470

### WE ARRIVE OUT OF MANY SINGULAR ROOMS

We arrive out of many singular rooms, walking over the branching streets.

We come to be assured that our friends surround us, to restore their images upon our eyes.

We enlarge our voices in common speaking and singing.

We try again that solitude found in the midst of those who with us seek their hidden reckonings.

Our eyes reclaim the remembered faces; their voices stir the surrounding air.

The warmth of their hands assures us, and the gladness of our spoken names.

This is the reason of cities, of homes, of assemblies in the houses of fellowship.

It is good to be with one another.

KENNETH L. PATTON

## 471

### ALMIGHTY GOD, UNTO WHOM ALL HEARTS ARE OPEN

Almighty God, unto whom all hearts are open, all desires known, and from whom no secrets are hid, cleanse the thoughts of our hearts by the inspiration of thy holy Spirit, that we may perfectly love thee, and worthily magnify thy holy name. Amen.

BOOK OF COMMON PRAYER

## 472

### THE EXHORTATION OF THE DAWN

Look to this day!
For it is life, the very life of life.
In its brief course lie all the verities
and realities of your existence:
The bliss of growth,
The glory of action,
The splendor of beauty;
For yesterday is but a dream,
And tomorrow is only a vision;
But today, well lived, makes every
yesterday a dream of happiness

And every tomorrow a vision of hope.
Look well, therefore, to this day.

ATTRIBUTED TO KĀLIDĀSA

## 473

### BEFORE THE WONDERS OF LIFE

Before the wonders of life we acknowledge our failures to see and to revere;

Before the sanctities of life we are ashamed of our disrespects and indignities;

Before the gifts of life we own that we have made choices of lesser goods, and here today seek the gifts of the spirit;

Before the heroisms of life we would be enlarged to new devotion.

VON OGDEN VOGT

## 474

### EVEN AS OF OLD

O Eternal, thy spirit hath not changed its ways, nor hath the human heart forgotten its speechless longing for thy presence.

Even as of old thy secret place is in the humble, contrite heart.

Even as of old thy spirit listeneth more to our hearts than to our lips.

In this quiet hour and silent place come thou to us and touch our hearts with thine unutterable love. Amen.

FRANK CARLETON DOAN

## 475

### OUT OF DARKNESS, INTO LIGHT

We rejoice this day in the unquenchable and eternal light that lighteth every ~~man~~ soul that cometh into the world. In that light we are ashamed of those greeds within us that have darkened our own souls, and those selfish customs among us that have shadowed the lives and spirits of others. We seek thy presence here, O Thou Most High, not alone for our joy today, but to illumine the ways of all our doings, until every child of ~~man~~ earth shall be brought out of darkness into thy marvelous light. Amen.

VON OGDEN VOGT

## 476

### A PRAYER AT HARVEST TIME

We bring today our joyful thanksgiving for all the increase that the fertile earth has yielded. Whether we toil or rest, whether we wake or sleep, we are upheld by a life that forever makes all things new and by a law that never fails.

We remember all those who plow the fields and sow the seed, who cultivate the rows of growing herbs and garner in the harvest. We would be mindful of the mutual dependence of all ~~the members of the family of man,~~ the human family, and would take a useful part in the world's life.

May we never be satisfied to enjoy plenty so long as any are in want.

May we express our gratitude for nature's gifts not in words alone, but also in the purposes for which we live and in the kindliness of our deeds.

VINCENT B. SILLIMAN

## 477

### NUMBERLESS ARE THY WITNESSES

Numberless are thy witnesses, O God,
And the manifestations of thine invisible presence:

In the light of the stars thou shinest;
In the life of earth's creatures thou livest;
In the words of the wise thou dost speak;
In the deeds of the brave thou dost act;
Where self-forgetting love is, there art thou.

In the full beauty of thy holiness we would worship thee. Amen.

ROBERT FRENCH LEAVENS

## 478

### CONFIRM THE BONDS OF MUTUAL TRUST

Almighty God, who hast made of one blood all nations to dwell on all the face of the earth, deepen among us the spirit of understanding and good will. Take from the hearts of people and rulers all partial aims, unhallowed ambitions, jealousies, covetousness, and fears. Confirm the bonds of mutual trust, and subdue the rivalries of race and power. Unite us in the things that make for peace, in the exchanges of merchandise, the pursuit of knowledge, the spread of liberty and good government, till the reign of justice be securely established, and law and order prevail throughout the earth. Amen.

MANCHESTER COLLEGE, OXFORD

## 479
### THOU ART THE PATH

Thou art the path and the goal that paths never reach.
Thou feedest and sustainest all that man sees, or seems.
Thou art the trembling grass and the tiger that creeps under it.
Thou art the light in sun and moon, the sounds fading into silence, and the sanctity of sacred books.
Thou art the good that destroys evil.

FROM INDIA

# Close of Service (Unison)

## 480
### IN THE SPIRIT OF ST. FRANCIS

Where hate rules, let us bring love; where sorrow, joy.

Let us strive more to comfort others than to be comforted,
to understand others, than to be understood,
to love others more than to be loved.

For it is in giving that we receive, and in pardoning that we are pardoned.

ATTRIBUTED TO
ST. FRANCIS OF ASSISI

## 481
### LET BROTHERLY LOVE CONTINUE

Let brotherly love continue.

If we agree in brotherly love, there is no disagreement that can do us any injury; but if we do not, no other agreement can do us any good.

Let us keep a secret guard against the enemy that sows discord among the brethren.

Let us endeavor to keep the unity of the spirit in the bonds of peace.

HOSEA BALLOU

## 482

### OUR SEARCH TOGETHER

Unto the goodness in the heart of every man, and the truth in the mind of every man, we make appeal, by whatever name it is known, in whatever land it is found,

For in our search together for goodness of life is universal religion established.

KENNETH L. PATTON

## 483

### IN OUR HEARTS MAY THERE BE LOVE

In our hearts may there be the love which seeketh not its own, suffereth long, hopeth, believeth, endureth all things.

By the power of that love may the dissensions of earth be reconciled, and the children of earth be drawn together into unity of purpose.

May we live as members of one family, with one heart and mind to serve the commonwealth of men and nations.

ROBERT FRENCH LEAVENS;
arranged

## 484

### THE HORIZON OF OUR MINDS

Let the horizon of our minds include all men people!
The great family here on earth with us;
Those who have gone before and left to us the heritage of their memory and of their work;
And those whose lives will be shaped by what we do or leave undone.

SAMUEL McCHORD CROTHERS;
adapted

## 485

### MAY WE GO FORTH

May we go forth to the duties of our days, with willing hands and honest minds, with faith in the power of good over evil, ready to take our places in the world of men;

Expecting to be forgiven only as we forgive others;

Working and hoping for that day when ties of brotherhood shall bind together every member of the human family.

GEORGE RUDOLPH FREEMAN

# Affirmation (Unison)

## 486

### THE EFFORTS OF FAITH

We are united in the efforts of faith:

Faith in truth, in the growth of knowledge and understanding;

Faith in love, in the labors and rewards of friendly living;

Faith in people, in the power of men to build an earthly commonwealth of freedom and of peace;

Faith in life, the life of all things that is the life of God,

Whose service is perfect freedom, whose presence is fullness of joy.

VON OGDEN VOGT

## 487

### UNTO THE CHURCH UNIVERSAL

Unto the church universal, which is the depository of all ancient wisdom and the school of all modern thought;

Which recognizes in all prophets a harmony, in all scriptures a unity, and through all dispensations a continuity;

Which abjures all that separates and divides, and always magnifies brotherhood and peace;

Which seeks truth in freedom, justice in love, and individual discipline in social duty;

And which shall make of all sects, classes, nations, and races, one fellowship of men—

Unto this church and unto all its members, known and unknown throughout the world,

We pledge the allegiance of our hands and hearts.

KESHAB CHANDRA SEN;
arranged by
JOHN HAYNES HOLMES

## 488

### THE BEATITUDES

Blessed are the poor in spirit, for theirs is the kingdom of heaven.

Blessed are they that mourn, for they shall be comforted.

Blessed are the meek, for they shall inherit the earth.

Blessed are they which do hunger and thirst after righteousness, for they shall be filled.

Blessed are the merciful, for they shall obtain mercy.

Blessed are the pure in heart, for they shall see God.

Blessed are the peacemakers, for they shall be called the children of God.

Blessed are they which are persecuted for righteousness' sake, for theirs is the kingdom of heaven.

Blessed are ye when men shall revile you, and persecute you, and shall say all manner of evil against you falsely, for my sake.

Rejoice, and be exceeding glad, for great is your reward in heaven; for so persecuted they the prophets which were before you.

MATTHEW 5

## 489

### THE POWER OF LOVE

Nor can that endure which has not its foundations upon love;

For love alone diminishes not but shines with its own light:

Makes an end to discord,
Softens the fires of hate,
Restores peace in the world,
Brings together the sundered,
Redresses wrongs and injures none.

And whoso invokes its aid will find peace and safety,
And have no fear of future ill.

ACT OF HORODLO (Poland, 1413 A.D.)

## 490

### CHURCH COVENANT

In the freedom of the truth,
And the spirit of Jesus,
We unite for the worship of God
And the service of man.

CHARLES GORDON AMES

## 491

### WE AVOW OUR FAITH

We avow our faith:

In God as eternal and all-conquering love,

In the spiritual leadership of Jesus,

In the supreme worth of every human personality,

In the authority of truth known or to be known,

And in the power of men of good will and sacrificial spirit to overcome all evil, and progressively to establish the kingdom of God.

THE WASHINGTON DECLARATION, 1935

## 492

### THE FELLOWSHIP OF FREE SOULS

We believe in a fellowship that shall unite men, not in the bonds of Confucian, or Moslem, or Christian love, but in the holier bonds of human love;

Going down, beneath all that separates and estranges, to the principles of freedom and understanding;

Below religions to religion; beneath all sacraments to the universal impulse that bends the soul in reverence and awe;

Beneath all forms to the faith that strives to express itself in and through them:

Thus touching common foundations and securing a common fellowship,

Each helping the other by whatsoever his deeper insights may reveal—

A union not of religious systems, but of free souls,

United to build on the basis of truth, justice, and love, the commonwealth of man.

ALFRED W. MARTIN

# 493

## THE NONCONFORMIST

Society everywhere is in conspiracy against the manhood of every one of its members.

The virtue in most request is conformity; self-reliance is its aversion.

It loves not realities and creators, but names and customs.

Whoso would be a man must be a nonconformist.

He who would gather immortal palms must not be hindered by the name of goodness, but must explore if it be goodness.

Nothing is at last sacred but the integrity of your own mind.

RALPH WALDO EMERSON

# 494

## LOVE IS THE SPIRIT OF THIS CHURCH

Love is the spirit of this church, and service its law.

This is our great covenant:

To dwell together in peace,

To seek the truth in love,

And to help one another.

JAMES VILA BLAKE

# 495

## YOU SHALL POSSESS

You shall possess the origin of all poems,

You shall possess the good of the earth and sun—there are millions of suns left—

You shall no longer take things at second or third hand, nor look through the eyes of the dead, nor feed on specters in books,

You shall not look through my eyes either, nor take things from me,

You shall listen to all sides and filter them from yourself.

WALT WHITMAN

# 496

## TO OUTGROW THE PAST

To outgrow the past but not to extinguish it;

To be progressive but not raw,

Free but not mad, critical but not sterile, expectant but not deluded;

To be scientific but not to live on formulas that cut us off from life;

To hear amidst clamor the pure, deep tones of the spirit;

To seek the wisdom that liberates and a loyalty that consecrates;

To turn both prosperity and adversity into servants of character;

To master circumstances by the power of principle,

And to conquer death by the splendor of loving trust:

This is to attain peace,

This is to invest the lowliest life with magnificence.

WILLIAM L. SULLIVAN

## 497

### WE, THE PEOPLES OF THE UNITED NATIONS

We, the peoples of the United Nations,

Determined to save succeeding generations from the scourge of war,

To reaffirm faith in fundamental human rights, in the dignity and worth of the human person, in the equal rights of men and women, and of nations large and small,

To promote social progress and better standards of life in larger freedom,

And for these ends to practice tolerance and to live together in peace as good neighbors,

To unite our strength to maintain international peace and security,

To insure that armed force shall not be used, save in the common interest,

To employ international machinery in the promotion of the economic and social advancement of all people,

Have resolved to combine our efforts to accomplish these aims.

CHARTER OF THE UNITED NATIONS

## 498

### A COVENANT FOR LIBERALS

Mindful of truth ever exceeding our knowledge
And brotherhood ever exceeding our practice,

Reverently we covenant together, beginning with ourselves as we are,

To share the strength of integrity and the heritage of the spirit

In man's unending quest for reality and love.

WALTER ROYAL JONES, JR.

## 499

### IDEAL AND QUEST

Religion is the vision of something which stands beyond, behind, and within the passing flux of immediate things:

Something which is real, and yet waiting to be realized;

Something which is a remote possibility, and yet the greatest of present facts;

Something that gives meaning to all that passes, and yet eludes apprehension;

Something whose possession is the final good, and yet is beyond all reach;

Something which is the ultimate ideal, and the hopeless quest.

ALFRED NORTH WHITEHEAD

## 500

### INDIVIDUALITY

It is not by wearing down into uniformity all that is individual in themselves, but by cultivating it and calling it forth, within the limits imposed by the rights and interests of others, that human beings become a noble and beautiful object of contemplation. And as the works partake the character of those who do them, by the same process human life also becomes rich, diversified, and animating, furnishing more abundant aliment to high thoughts and elevated feelings, and strengthening the tie which binds every individual to the race, and making the race infinitely better worth belonging to.

JOHN STUART MILL

## 501

### THE CENTER OF ALL DAYS, ALL RACES

I know that the past was great and the future will be great,

And I know that both curiously conjoint in the present time,

And that where I am, or you are, this present day, there is the center of all days, all races,

And there is the meaning, to us, of all that ever has come of races and days, or ever will come.

WALT WHITMAN

## 502

### THIS IS THE GREATEST BLESSING

This is the greatest blessing:

Not to serve the foolish, but to serve the wise; to honor those worthy of honor—

To dwell in a pleasant land, with right desires in the heart—

Self-control and pleasant speech, and whatever word be well spoken—

To live righteously, to give help to kindred, to follow a peaceful calling—

To abhor and cease from evil, not to be weary in well doing—

To be long-suffering and meek, to associate with the peaceable—

Beneath the stroke of life's changes, the mind that shaketh not, without grief or passion, and secure—

On every side they are invincible who do acts like these, on every side they walk in safety—

And theirs is the greatest blessing.

BUDDHIST

## 503

### THE COURAGE TO BELONG

There is no choice but to immerse oneself in the stream of history, accept one's time-location,

breathe in—with shared memories and hopes—the contamination of tradition, become defined as the *people* of this cause, this party, this emergency.

Failure to accept responsibility, refusal to take a stand on vital issues, timid rejection—as one must reject false tags—of the ties of a true belonging, these are denials of life —in effect they are deeds of death.

To understand the times in which we live, to add our weight to the scales on the side of *Brotherhood* and equality within valid difference, this is 'life with shape and character'—the one eternity worth having.

WILLIAM ERNEST HOCKING

## 504

### A BOND OF FELLOWSHIP

Our bond of fellowship is the common purpose of producing a more abundant life for all mankind.

To that end we avow faith in:

The orderliness of nature,

The goodness of life,

The equality of every person,

The use of intelligence and the self-correcting method of science,

The power of men of goodwill and sacrificial spirit to overcome difficulties in themselves and in their world, to establish progressively a democratic commonwealth of humankind.

KENNETH L. PATTON

## 505

### I BELIEVE

I believe in myself.

I believe in my neighbor.

I believe in the unity of myself and my neighbor.

I believe in the progressive achievement of a universal community of human co-operation and fellowship.

I believe in love and intelligence as the most potent agents for developing the ideal world within the actual.

I believe in my universe as a kind of place that brings into existence all the values, purposes, and possibilities of human life.

I believe that human life is a growing point in the universe.

I believe that my life finds significance only as I identify myself with the creative process.

E. BURDETTE BACKUS

## 506

### A COVENANT FOR FREE WORSHIP

Love is the doctrine of this church,
The quest of truth is its sacrament,
And service is its prayer.

To dwell together in peace,
To seek knowledge in freedom,
To serve mankind in fellowship,
To the end that all souls shall grow into harmony with the Divine —

Thus do we covenant with each other and with God.

Arranged by
L. GRISWOLD WILLIAMS

## 507

### A STATEMENT OF BELIEFS

We believe in God, Father of our spirits, life of all that is; infinite in power, wisdom, and goodness, and working everywhere for righteousness and peace and love.

We believe in the ideal of human life which reveals itself in Jesus as love to God and love to man.

We believe that we should be ever growing in knowledge and ever aiming at a higher standard of character.

We believe in the growth of the kingdom of God on earth, and that our loyalty to truth, to righteousness, and to our fellow men, is the measure of our desire for its coming.

We believe that the living and the dead are in the hands of God; that underneath both are his everlasting arms.

*Services of Religion*

## 508

### WE BELIEVE

We believe in the goodness of life, realizable in this present world, available to all the children of men who seek the masteries of the spirit in every condition.

We believe in man and the worth of all persons.

We believe in labor, in the duty of all to bring forth in their several callings the fruits of useful living, and in the right of each to the just rewards of his industry.

We believe in society, in the ordered life of church and state, of school and home, of the arts and sciences.

And we rejoice in this present hour of communion with one another and with the common hopes of all men.

VON OGDEN VOGT

## 509

### AROUND THE WHOLE EARTH

My spirit has passed in compassion and determination around the whole earth;

I have looked for equals and lovers, and found them ready for me in all lands;

I think some divine rapport has equalized me with them.

I see cities of the earth and make myself at random a part of them;

I see ranks, colors, barbarisms, civilizations—

I go among them—I mix indiscriminately,

And I salute all the inhabitants of the earth.

WALT WHITMAN

## 510

### THE GATES OF FREEDOM

Though our knowledge is incomplete, our truth partial, and our love imperfect,

We believe that new light is ever waiting to break through individual hearts and minds to enlighten the ways of ~~men~~ all,

That there is mutual strength in willing co-operation,

And that the bonds of love keep open the gates of freedom.

NAPOLEON W. LOVELY

## 511

### OURS, O ~~MEN~~ PEOPLE

Ours, O ~~men~~ people, has been yesterday, and ours will be today and tomorrow.

Ours is the world, the universe, and life, if we will make it ours by the largeness and strength of our love.

Ours is the commonwealth of ~~man~~ all people, now and tomorrow, building and yet to be builded.

KENNETH L. PATTON

# Opening Words

## 512

The hour cometh and now is, when the true worshipers shall worship the Father in spirit and in truth; for the Father seeketh such to worship him.

God is spirit, and they that worship him must worship him in spirit and in truth.

JOHN 4

## 513

Why dost thou wonder, O man, at the height of the stars or the depth of the sea?

Enter into thine own soul, and wonder there.

FRANCIS QUARLES

## 514

Holy and beautiful the custom which brings us together,
In the presence of the Most High:

To face our ideals,
To remember our loved ones in absence,
To give thanks, to make confession, to offer forgiveness,
To be enlightened, and to be strengthened.

Through this quiet hour breathes the worship of ages,
The cathedral music of history.

Three unseen guests attend,
Faith, hope, and love:

Let all our hearts prepare them place.

ROBERT FRENCH LEAVENS

## 515

O worship the Lord in the beauty of holiness:
Let the whole earth stand in awe of him.

PSALM 96

## 516

Surely the Lord is in this place.
This is none other but the house of God,
And this is the gate of heaven.

GENESIS 28

## 517

The Lord is nigh unto all them that call upon him,
To all that call upon him in truth.

PSALM 145

## 518

The place where men meet to seek the highest is holy ground.

FELIX ADLER

## 519

Separate not thyself from the congregation and its concerns, nor postpone thought for thy spirit until the day of thy death. Say not, 'By and by, when I have leisure, I will care for my soul,' lest perchance thou never find leisure.

HILLEL

## 520

Whoever you are! you are he or she for whom the earth is solid and liquid,
You are he or she for whom the sun and moon hang in the sky;
For none more than you are the present and the past,
For none more than you is immortality.

WALT WHITMAN

## 521

Choose you this day whom ye will serve;
But as for me and my house we will serve the Lord.
The Lord our God will we serve
And his voice will we obey.

JOSHUA 24

## 522

It is above all other joys to be with men and women and children. Their companionship is the meaning of the working hours of the day, the comfort of our memories in solitude, and the peace and security of our sleeping.

KENNETH L. PATTON

## 523

Two things fill the mind with ever-increasing awe and admiration:
The starlit heavens above, and the moral law within.

IMMANUEL KANT

## 524

Why should not we enjoy an original relation to the universe?

Why should not we have a poetry and philosophy of insight and not of tradition, and a religion by revelation to us, and not the history of theirs?

The sun shines also today. There are new lands, new men, new thoughts.

Let us demand our own works and law and worship.

RALPH WALDO EMERSON

## 525

Wherewith shall I come before the Lord,
And bow myself before the high God?
He hath showed thee, O man, what is good;
And what doth the Lord require of thee,
But to do justly, and to love mercy,
And to walk humbly with thy God?

MICAH 6

## 526

Come into the circle of love and justice,
Come into the brotherhood of pity,
Of holiness and health—
Come, and ye shall know peace and joy.

Let what ye desire of the universe penetrate you,
Let lovingkindness and mercy pass through you,
And truth be the law of your mouth.

ISRAEL ZANGWILL

# At the Offering

## 527

If thou bring thy gift to the altar, and there rememberest that thy brother hath aught against thee; leave there thy gift before the altar, and go thy way; first be reconciled to thy brother, and then come and offer thy gift.

MATTHEW 5

## 528

Say to thyself, 'If there is any good thing that I can do, or any kindness that I can show to any human being, let me do it now; let me not defer it or neglect it, for I may not pass this way again.'

ANONYMOUS

## 529

Whatsoever ye do, do it heartily:

He that giveth, let him do it with liberality;

He that showeth mercy, with cheerfulness.

COLOSSIANS 3, ROMANS 12

## 530

Whatsoever ye would that men should do to you, do ye even so to them, for this is the law and the prophets.

MATTHEW 7

## 531

Wherewith shall I come before the Lord,
And bow myself before the high God?

He hath showed thee, O man, what is good;
And what doth the Lord require of thee,
But to do justly,
And to love mercy,
And to walk humbly with thy God?

MICAH 6

## 532

O God, we would render unto thee all that we have and all that we are, that we may praise thee not with our lips only but with our whole lives. Amen.

*Services of Religion*

## 533

To the service of truth and the increase of righteousness, we dedicate our lives, and this our offering.

ARTHUR FOOTE II

## 534

Freely have we received of gifts that minister to our needs of body and spirit. Gladly we bring to our church and its wide concerns a portion of this bounty.

ARTHUR FOOTE II

# Benedictions, Closing Words

## 535

Whether there be tongues, they shall cease; whether there be knowledge, it shall vanish away.

And now abideth faith, hope, love, these three: and the greatest of these is love.   I CORINTHIANS 13

## 536

The blessing of God be upon us, his truth direct us and his love sustain us; and may he preserve our going out and our coming in from this time forth and even for evermore.

*Orders of Worship*

## 537

Go your ways,
knowing not the answers to all things,
yet seeking always the answer
to one more thing than you know.

Be searchers with your fellow men;
be adventurers in ways untrod.

Hold the hope of discovery high within you —
sharing the hope,
and whatever discovery may come,
with others.   JOHN W. BRIGHAM

## 538

May peace dwell within our hearts, and understanding in our minds;

May courage steel our wills, and love of truth forever guide us.

ARTHUR FOOTE II

## 539

The Lord bless us and keep us;

The Lord make his face to shine upon us and be gracious unto us;

The Lord lift up his countenance upon us,

And give us peace.   NUMBERS 6

## 540

Whatsoever things are true,
Whatsoever things are honorable,
Whatsoever things are just,
Whatsoever things are pure,
Whatsoever things are lovely,
Whatsoever things are of good report;
If there be any virtue,
And if there be any praise,
Think on these things.

PHILIPPIANS 4

## 541

Let us have faith that right makes might, and in that faith let us to the end dare to do our duty as we understand it.   ABRAHAM LINCOLN

## 542

Thou canst not, even if thou wouldst, separate thy life from that of humanity.

Thou livest in it, by it, and for it.

Thy soul cannot separate itself from the elements amongst which it moves.   GIUSEPPE MAZZINI

## 543

If the day and the night are such that you greet them with joy, and life emits a fragrance like flowers and sweet-scented herbs, is more elastic, more starry, more immortal—that is your success. All nature is your congratulation, and you have cause momentarily to bless yourself.

HENRY DAVID THOREAU

## 544

May the life that is God
    animate our frames;
May the truth that is God
    illumine our minds;
And may the love that is God
    fill our hearts
    and govern our lives.

ROBERT FRENCH LEAVENS

## 545

Now, therefore, since the struggle deepens,
Since evil abides and good does not yet prosper,

Let us gather what strength we have, what confidence, and valor,
That our small victories may end in triumph,
And the world awaited be a world attained.

BARROWS DUNHAM

## 546

The courage of the early morning's dawning,

And the strength of the eternal hills,

And the peace of the evening's ending,

And the love of God,

Be in our hearts.

ANONYMOUS

## 547

Nothing else matters much—not wealth, nor learning, nor even health—without this gift: the spiritual capacity to keep zest in living.

This is the creed of creeds, the final deposit and distillation of all man's important faiths:

That he should be able to believe in life.

HARRY EMERSON FOSDICK

## 548

Be ours a religion which, like sunshine, goes everywhere; its temple, all space; its shrine, the good heart; its creed, all truth; its ritual, works of love; its profession of faith, divine living.

THEODORE PARKER

## 549

One thought ever at the fore—

That in the Divine Ship, the World, breasting Time and Space,

All people of the globe together sail, sail the same voyage, are bound to the same destination.

WALT WHITMAN

## 550

Go forth into the world in peace; be of good courage;

Prove all things, and hold fast that which is good.

COMPOSITE

## 551

Be ye lamps unto yourselves; be your own confidence.

Hold to the truth within yourselves as to the only lamp.

BUDDHIST

## 552

Let the human heart be secure in its many seasons,

In the unfinished tasks waiting to be done tomorrow.

In its own nature let the human heart be secure,

In its being, in itself.

KENNETH L. PATTON

## 553

Let thy work, O Lord, appear unto thy servants,

And thy glory unto their children;

And let the beauty of the Lord our God be upon us;

And establish thou the work of our hands upon us;

Yea, the work of our hands establish thou it.

PSALM 90

## 554

It is provided in the essence of things that from the fruition of success, no matter what, shall come forth something to make greater struggle necessary.

WALT WHITMAN

## 555

The peace which passeth understanding,

The peace of God,

Which the world can neither give nor take away,

Be among us, and abide in our hearts.

COMPOSITE

## 556

Tomorrow is unto men as a door to be opened or closed, as a journey, an adventure.

Tomorrow is a springtime and a harvest time, and the grain to be gathered is life, and the flowers and fruit are brotherhood and mercy.

KENNETH L. PATTON

## 557

The spirit that was in Jesus be in us also, enabling us to know the truth, to do the will of God, and to abide in his peace.

WILLIAM WALLACE FENN

## 558

From the murmur and subtlety of suspicion with which we vex one another, give us rest.

Make a new beginning,

And mingle again the kindred of the nations in the alchemy of love;

And with some finer essence of forbearance temper our minds.

ARISTOPHANES

# Notes and Indexes

NOTES ON HYMNS, TUNES, AND READINGS      *page* 415

ACKNOWLEDGMENTS      *page* 475

INDEXES

First Phrases and Titles of Readings      *page* 478

Topical Index of Responsive Readings      *page* 482

Authors, Translators, and Sources of Responsive Readings      *page* 488

Authors and Sources of Unison Readings and Affirmations      *page* 489

Authors, Translators, and Sources of Hymns      *page* 489

Composers, Arrangers, and Sources of Hymns      *page* 495

Alphabetical Index of Tunes      *page* 497

Metrical Index of Tunes      *page* 498

Topical Index of Hymns      *page* 501

First Lines and Titles of Hymns      *page* 510

# NOTES ON HYMNS, TUNES, AND READINGS

1. **THE MORNING HANGS A SIG-NAL.** William Channing Gannett (1840–1923), Unitarian minister, served churches in St. Paul, Minn., and Rochester, N. Y., among others, and briefly as secretary of the Western Unitarian Conference. In 1880, with Frederick Lucian Hosmer (*see No. 50*) and James Vila Blake, he published *Unity Hymns and Chorals*, which he and Hosmer revised in 1911. He and Hosmer published collections titled *The Thought of God in Hymns and Poems* in 1885, 1894, and 1918. The present text, arranged about 1930 by Curtis Reese, first appeared in *Love to God and Love to Man*, ca.1885, liberal texts adapted to popular "revival" tunes, this one to "The Crowning Day." It was recast by Vincent B. Silliman (*see No. 14*) in 1934 and set to this tune for *The Beacon Song and Service Book*. There are further slight revisions here.

William Lloyd (1786–1852), composer of MEIRIONYDD, was a Welsh farmer who held singing classes in his home. Called "Berth" in *Caniadau Seion*, a manuscript tune book of 1840, the tune takes this name from Merionethshire, just south of Lloyd's county, Caernarvon.

2. **O SOURCE OF LIFE.** Ridgely Torrence (1875–1950), an American poet and playwright, was an editor of the *New Republic* (1920–34). This hymn and its companion, No. 3, are drawn from "Adam's Song of the Visible World," a poem clearly reminiscent of Psalm 104.

ADAM'S SONG was composed for this book by one of its compilers, Robert L. Sanders (1906–    ). Mr. Sanders received two degrees from the Bush Conservatory in his native Chicago, Ill. In 1925 he studied with Respighi as a fellow of the American Academy in Rome. While teaching at Chicago Conservatory, the University of Chicago, and Meadville Theological School, he was organist-director of the First Unitarian Society. In 1937 he was cosigner of the music preface of *Hymns of the Spirit*. In 1938 he became dean of the School of Music at

Indiana University, and since 1947 he has been professor of music at Brooklyn College. He received a Guggenheim Fellowship in 1954–55. Among his compositions, of particular interest here is the cantata for soprano solo, chorus, and chamber orchestra, *A Celebration of Life*, 1956.

3. **PRAISE FROM DEPTH AND HEIGHT.** Ridgely Torrence. *See No. 2.*

FARLEY CASTLE is the tune for Psalm 72 in George Sandys' *Paraphrase upon the Psalmes of David*, 1638. Its composer, Henry Lawes (1596–1662), Gentleman of the Chapel Royal, is the subject of Milton's sonnet beginning, "Harry, whose tuneful and well-measured song."

4. **HOLY, HOLY, HOLY.** Reginald Heber (1783–1826) was an Anglican clergyman, hymn writer, hymnbook compiler, who became bishop of Calcutta, with all India as his diocese, in 1823. American Unitarian use of arrangements of this text which omitted Heber's reference to the Trinity dates at least to 1848. The words, "holy, holy, holy," as an address to God, appear in Isa. 6:3, Rev. 4:8, and in the traditional eucharistic prayer of the Christian church from early times.

NICAEA was composed for *Hymns Ancient and Modern*, 1861. Appropriate to Bishop Heber's original text, the name refers to the ecumenical council at Nicaea, Asia Minor, in 325, when the doctrine of the Trinity became a recognized dogma. John Bacchus Dykes (1823–76), a Yorkshireman, was precentor of Durham Cathedral and a founder of the University Musical Society at Cambridge.

5. **BRING, O MORN, THY MUSIC.** William Channing Gannett. *See No. 1.* Written in 1892, this appeared in *A Chorus of Faith*, being an account and resumé of the 1893 World Parliament of Religions in Chicago. The author's title, "Who Wert and Art and Evermore Shalt Be," relates the hymn to Heber's "Holy, holy, holy," for which the tune NICAEA was composed. *See No. 4.*

6. YIGDAL. The Yigdal, named for its first Hebrew word, sung antiphonally by precentor and congregation at the close of Jewish worship on the eve of the Sabbath and other festivals, is a versification, probably by Daniel ben Judah Dayyan between 1396 and 1404, of the thirteen articles of Jewish faith drawn up by Moses ben Maimon (1130–1205). A Christian hymn based on the Yigdal, written by Thomas Olivers, an English Methodist preacher, about 1770, was used in England and the United States. In the 1880's Rabbi Max Landsberg of Temple Berith Kodesh in Rochester, N. Y., asked Newton Mann, minister of the Unitarian church there, to make a more exact translation. Later, Rabbi Landsberg asked Mann's successor, Dr. Gannett (*see No. 1*) to recast Mann's version in the traditional meter; that version, omitting one stanza, appears here.

LEONI, one of seven traditional tunes for the Yigdal, has been the accepted Friday evening tune in England for two centuries. It is named for Meyer Lyon (1751–97), cantor at the Great Synagogue, London, who transcribed it for Olivers.

7. PRAISE TO THE LORD, THE ALMIGHTY. Joachim Neander (1650–80) was a German pietistic preacher, a scholar, teacher, poet, and musician. Discharged as headmaster of the Reformed Grammar School at Düsseldorf, he lived for some time in a cave on the Rhine, still known as Neander's Cave. In Neanderthal, the valley of that cave, were found the skeletal remains of Neanderthal Man in 1856. Neander was for a brief time a controversial second preacher at St. Martin's in Bremen. He wrote sixty hymns with tunes which were published the year he died. This version of Catherine Winkworth's (*see No. 19*) translation of Neander's text beginning, *"Lobe den Herren, den mächtigen König der Ehren!"* is from *Hymns of the Spirit*, 1937. The text is based on Psalm 103:1–6 and Psalm 150.

Originally used for *"Hast du denn, Liebster"* in the *Ander Theil des Erneuerten Gesangbuchs*, Stralsund, 1665, LOBE DEN HERREN has been associated with Neander's text since 1680. This version accompanies Catherine Winkworth's translation (*see No. 19*) in *The Chorale Book for England*, 1863.

8. THE LARK ASCENDING. George Meredith (1828–1909), English novelist and poet, was one of the "Great Victorians." An early twentieth-century critic says of him, "Where other writers appeal to the Christian divinities or to humanity, he speaks somewhat insistently of the Earth, a term to which he attaches his own mystic meaning.... Life is an adjustment and realization of the inward forces that Earth generates, and love it is that both tasks and rewards most completely our power of controlling these forces." This text was arranged by Kenneth L. Patton (*see No. 28*) from a longer poem of the same title.

FILLMORE is called "Parting Hand" in *The Southern Harmony* (New Haven, 1835), one of the most famous shape-note hymnals, with noteheads of four different shapes indicating specific degrees of the scale. Its compiler, William Walker (1809–75) of Spartanburg, S. C., conducted singing schools with it through the southeastern states, where it is still in use. FILLMORE was later widely ascribed to Jeremiah Ingalls (1764–1828). Kenneth Munson (*see No. 134*) provided this harmonization.

9. O LORD OF STARS AND SUNLIGHT. John Holmes (1904–62), a Unitarian, was a poet and, from 1934 a professor of English at Tufts University in Medford, Mass. Author of several volumes of poetry, and of *Writing Poetry*, he was Phi Beta Kappa poet at Tufts, William and Mary, and Harvard, and editor of several collections of poetry. This hymn was written for the 1948 meeting of the American Unitarian Association.

PAEAN by Frederic Weber (1819– ?) first appeared in his *Church of England Chorale Book*, 1857. Born in Württemberg, Germany, Weber became music master at the Pestalozzian Institute for boys, Worksop, Nottinghamshire, England, in 1841 and organist at the German Royal Chapel, St. James's Palace, in 1849. It was thus harmonized for this book.

10. LET THE WHOLE CREATION CRY. Stopford Augustus Brooke (1832–

1916), a prominent preacher, was born at Letterkenny, Donegal, Ireland, educated at Trinity College, Dublin, and ordained in London. In 1872 he was appointed chaplain to Queen Victoria, who offered him a canonry of Westminster, although his liberal views made that impossible. In 1880 he resigned from the Anglican ministry, and officiated at Bedford Chapel, Bloomsbury, as a Unitarian, until 1894. These stanzas are arranged and adapted from a longer text. New to American Unitarian Universalist hymnody is the stanza beginning, "Ye to whom the arts belong."

Sir George Job Elvey (1816–93) was a choirboy at Canterbury Cathedral, England, a pupil of Dr. William Crotch (see No. 259) at the Royal Academy of Music, a Doctor of Music from Oxford, 1840, and a teacher of Sir Hubert Parry (see No. 55). From 1835 to 1882 organist and master of the boys at St. George's Chapel, Windsor, he contributed ST. GEORGE'S WINDSOR to A Selection of Psalm and Hymn Tunes, 1858. Since the first musical edition of Hymns Ancient and Modern, 1861, the tune has been associated with "Come, ye thankful people, come" (No. 278).

11. JOYFUL, JOYFUL, WE ADORE THEE. Henry Van Dyke (1852–1933) was an American Congregational and Presbyterian minister, professor, and diplomat. He was chairman of committees which prepared the American Presbyterian Book of Common Worship, 1905, and which revised it in 1932. This hymn was written during a visit at Williams College: Dr. Van Dyke said to President Garfield, "Here is a hymn for you. Your mountains were my inspiration. It must be sung to the music of Beethoven's 'Hymn to Joy.'"

HYMN TO JOY was adapted from Beethoven's Ninth Symphony as a hymn tune by Edward Hodges (1796–1867), an Englishman who settled in 1839 in New York, where he became organist of St. John's Episcopal Chapel and Trinity Church.

12. FOR THE BEAUTY OF THE EARTH. Folliott Sandford Pierpoint (1835–1917) was an English classicist and poet. The main point of the text originally was a refrain beginning, "Christ, our God, to thee we raise," now replaced often, as here, in many de-nominations. The refrain alluded to one of the earliest secular references to Christians, in a letter by Pliny the Younger to the Roman Emperor Trajan, which mentioned their gathering before daybreak to repeat in turn "a hymn to Christ as to a god. . . ." This nature hymn originally had eight stanzas and was written for Anglican communion services.

Conrad Kocher (1786–1872), director of music in the collegiate church at Stuttgart, Germany, in his Stimmen aus dem Reiche Gottes, 1838, published his setting of Zeller's "Treuer Heiland, wir sind hier." This became the tune, DIX, as we know it when the third phrase was omitted to accommodate William Chatterton Dix's "As with gladness men of old" in the first musical edition of Hymns Ancient and Modern, 1861.

13. FROM ALL THAT DWELL. Isaac Watts. See No. 51. This text utilizes part of the first stanza of Watts's paraphrase of Psalm 117, adds phrases from the angelic song of Luke 2:14. It appeared in We Sing of Life, 1955.

The tune OLD HUNDREDTH appears here in the even time-values familiar to modern congregations. For its original rhythm and a note on its history, see No. 18.

14. MORNING, SO FAIR TO SEE. Vincent B. Silliman (1894– ) is an American Unitarian Universalist minister, one of the compilers of this book. Born in Hudson, Wis., he has served in Brooklyn, Buffalo, and Hollis, N. Y.; Portland, Me.; and Chicago, Ill. He now serves the First Universalist Church in Yarmouth, Me. He was an editor of The Beacon Song and Service Book, 1935; he edited We Sing of Life, 1955, with Irving Lowens (see No. 211), and We Speak of Life, 1955. This text was prepared for The Beacon Song and Service Book and is based on a lyric by Bernhardt Severin Ingemann (1789–1862), Danish poet and professor, a Lutheran. The English translation by S. D. Rodholm begins, "Beauty around us. . . ."

SCHÖNSTER HERR JESU is a Silesian folk melody, used for a pre-existent text in A. H. Hoffmann von Fallersleben's Schlesische Volkslieder, 1842. Franz Liszt, who used the melody in his oratorio *The Legend of St. Elizabeth,* 1862, made the fanciful assertion that it was "an old pilgrim song apparently from the Crusades."

**15. WE COME UNTO OUR FA-THERS' GOD.** Thomas Hornblower Gill (1819–1906) was born into an English Unitarian family, but later associated himself with the Evangelical and Protestant section of the Church of England. He wrote nearly 200 hymns, many still in common use. Of this text he wrote, "The birthday of this hymn, Nov. 22, 1868 (St. Cecilia's Day), was almost the most delightful day of my life. Its production employed the whole day and was a prolonged rapture." It is based on Psalm 90:1 and originally had seven stanzas.

MIT FREUDEN ZART is from the Bohemian Brethren's *Kirchengeseng darinnen die Heubtartickel des christlichen Glaubens gefasset,* 1566. It is reminiscent of the tune used for Psalm 138 in the Genevan Psalter of 1543 and of "*Une pastourelle gentille,*" a chanson published by Attaignant (1529–30).

**16. A MIGHTY FORTRESS.** Martin Luther (1483–1546) was the dominating figure of the Reformation, whose translation of the Bible has a classical quality for the German language comparable to that of the King James Version for English. A hymn writer and musician, he was primarily responsible for the important place of congregational song in Protestant churches. Thomas Carlyle said that this "Battle Hymn of the Reformation" based on Psalm 46 was "like the sound of Alpine avalanches, or the first murmur of earthquakes." This translation by Frederic Henry Hedge (*see No. 127*) has been used widely in American Protestant churches.

EIN' FESTE BURG, also credited to Luther, was first published in Joseph Klug's *Geistliche Lieder,* 1529.

**17. NOW LET EVERY TONGUE ADORE THEE.** The text and tune of WACHET AUF were written by Pastor Philipp Nicolai (1556–1608) in Unna, Westphalia, Germany, during an epidemic in which over 1,300 of his parishioners died. First published in Nicolai's *Frewden-Spiegel des ewigen Lebens,* 1599,

the melody was embellished and harmonized by J. S. Bach when used as the basis of his Cantata 140, ca. 1731. This translation by Paul English (died 1932) was based on one by Catherine Winkworth (*see No. 19*) in *Lyra Germanica,* Second Series, 1858.

**18. ALL PEOPLE THAT ON EARTH DO DWELL.** William Kethe, said to be of Scottish origin, appeared on the Continent as a refugee from Marian persecution; he was a clergyman of the Church of England for over thirty years. Psalm 100, of which this is the first stanza, was among twenty-five of his psalm versions in the Anglo-Genevan Psalter, 1561. The word "mirth" comes from the Scottish Psalter, 1650, in place of Kethe's "fear." While all of Kethe's paraphrases were adopted in the Scottish Psalter, fewer than half appeared in the English Psalter (Old Version). Among them was Psalm 100 and the tune with it, therefore now called OLD HUNDREDTH. This melody was the setting for Psalm 134 in the Genevan Psalter, 1551. Although its first phrase suggests a folk origin, it owes much to Louis Bourgeois, Calvin's leading psalmodist. This is the original rhythm. For the modern rhythm, *see Nos. 13 and 37.*

**19. NOW THANK WE ALL OUR GOD.** Martin Rinkart (1586–1649) was a German pastor, poet, and musician. This text consists of the first stanza, the first quatrain of the second stanza, and second quatrain of the third stanza of Catherine Winkworth's translation of the original, based on Ecclus. 50:22–24, which began, "*Nun danket alle Gott.*" Miss Winkworth (1829–78), an Anglican, an educator, a feminist, is best known for her translations of German hymns into English. This text is from her *Lyra Germanica,* Second Series, 1858.

Johann Crüger (1598–1662), for forty years cantor at the St. Nicholas Church, Berlin, Germany, first published his setting of NUN DANKET ALLE GOTT in *Praxis Pietatis Melica,* 1648. That collection, of which he was an editor, ran through forty editions by 1724.

**20. GOD IS MY STRONG SALVA-TION.** James Montgomery (1771–1854), an Englishman, the son of a

Moravian minister, was a bookseller and printer. In 1796 he began thirty-one years as editor of the *Sheffield Iris*, where he twice suffered fines and imprisonment in York Castle—once for printing a song on the fall of the Bastille, once for an article on a political riot in Sheffield. He wrote 400 hymns, most of them in early life. This text appeared in Montgomery's *Songs of Zion* and was based on Psalm 27.

Melchior Teschner (1584–1635), cantor at Fraustadt, Silesia, composed two settings of *"Valet will ich dir geben"* in *Ein andächtiges Gebet*, 1615. J. S. Bach adapted one of the settings (as here) for the third stanza of this hymn in Part II of his *St. John Passion*, 1723. ST. THEODULPH refers to the use of this tune for John Mason Neale's translation of *"Gloria, laus, et honor"* by the eighth-century Bishop of Orleans.

21. GIVE THANKS. The original, which begins, "For the hay and the corn and the wheat that is reaped," has been appearing for over fifty years, with no indication of origin. As revised here, it first was published in *We Sing of Life*, 1955.

FOUNDATION is the setting for "How firm a foundation" in William Caldwell's *Union Harmony*, Maryville, Tenn., 1837, and in White and King's *Sacred Harp*, Philadelphia, 1844. The former calls it "Protection"; the latter, "Bellevue" and attributes it to "Z. Chambless" (Chambers?). Some later editors, by error, ascribe it to the poet, Anne Steele.

22. SONG OF THANKSGIVING. Edwin T. Buehrer (1894–     ), an American Unitarian Universalist minister, was ordained into the Methodist ministry in 1921. He became minister of Third Unitarian Church of Chicago in 1941. He was editor of the *Journal of Liberal Religion*, 1944–47, and president of the Western Unitarian Conference, 1953–59.

KREMSER, a Netherlands folk tune, first was published in Adrian Valerius' *Nederlandtsch Gedenckclanck*, 1626, with the text, *"Wilt heden nu treden,"* celebrating the sixteenth-century liberation from Spain. Edward Kremser (1838–1914), director of the Vienna *Männergesangverein*, arranged it for

men's chorus and orchestra; and the American edition of his *Sechs altniederländische Volkslieder*, Milwaukee, 1895, introduced it to this country.

23. THE CANTICLE OF THE SUN. St. Francis of Assisi (1182–1226). Following a serious illness, Francis was converted in 1206 from his gay youth to a life of ascetic devotion, ministering to the neglected, and preaching. He founded the Franciscan order of friars in 1210. His joyousness and love of nature are reflected in "The Canticle of Brother Sun," reputedly composed by him in the Umbrian dialect in his last year. That would make him among the first to adapt the Provençal troubadour style to religious use and to the Italian language. This text by William Henry Draper (1855–1933), Church of England clergyman and hymn writer, was composed for school children while the author was rector of Adel, Leeds, Yorkshire. Here, four lines are omitted, and in the last line a reference to the Trinity, not in Francis' text, is removed.

LASST UNS ERFREUEN is from *Auserlesene catholische geistliche Kirchgesäng* printed by Peter von Brachel in Cologne, Germany, 1623. It bears a strong resemblance to the Genevan tune used for Psalms 36 and 68 (*Strassburger Kirchenamt*, 1525), which in England became "Old 113th." It was thus harmonized for this book.

24. THE ABIDING PRESENCE. George Wallace Briggs (1875–1959), an Anglican, graduated from Cambridge and served as rector of Loughborough and canon of Leicester. He wrote hymns and composed fine tunes. This communion hymn was written for *Songs of Praise*, 1931.

PELHAM STREET was contributed to this book by William King Covell (1904–     ), a Unitarian, for many years secretary of the Board of Trustees of Channing Memorial Church, Newport, R. I. He studied music at Harvard University with Walter Raymond Spalding and shared in designing the Harvard Memorial Church organ.

25. O WORSHIP THE KING. Sir Robert Grant (1779–1834) was born in India, educated at Oxford, served in

Parliament, and was appointed Governor of Bombay in 1934. Many of his hymns were published in India the year after his death; of them, this hymn based on Psalm 104 survives in wide use.

LYONS first appeared in Volume II of *Sacred Melodies from Haydn, Mozart, and Beethoven*, 1815, edited by William Gardiner (1770–1853), who introduced Beethoven's music into England. A successful hosiery manufacturer, he tells of sending Haydn stockings with the recipient's melodies, including "Austria" (No. 248), woven into the design. He credits Haydn with the subject of "Lyons," actually a phrase of common currency. A number of minuets by Joseph or Michael Haydn begin with it, but so does William Croft's "Hanover," 1708, often sung to this same text.

## 26. COME, THOU ALMIGHTY KING.

Anonymous. The earliest known appearance of this text is in a tract bound up with George Whitefield's *Collection*, 1757, titled "An Hymn to the Trinity." The version in *Hymns of the Spirit*, 1937, which omits references to the Trinity, was compiled from four of the original five stanzas and appeared in Unitarian hymnbooks from 1844 or earlier; it is objectionable to many. Another text, "Come thou Almighty Will," based on a different original and meeting some of the objections, has failed to win acceptance. The version here is essentially that in *A Book of Hymns*, 1848, by Samuel Longfellow and Samuel Johnson.

TRINITY, named for this text, was published in *The Collection of Psalm and Hymn Tunes Sung at the Chapel of the Lock Hospital*, 1769. The composer, Felice de Giardini (1716–96), a native of Italy, was a leading violinist and opera conductor in London from 1752 to 1784 who died penniless in Moscow. This widely used version differs slightly from the original. The tune is often, if incorrectly, called "Italian Hymn" or "Moscow."

## 27. GOD OF GRACE AND GOD OF GLORY.

Harry Emerson Fosdick (1878– ) is an American Baptist minister and author of many books. Originally a Presbyterian, after a heresy trial he became minister of what is now Riverside Church, New York City, and was radio minister to Protestants through the country. This hymn was written in 1930 for the dedication of the Riverside Church.

CWM RHONDDA, named for the chief coal town in Glamorganshire, Wales, was composed in 1907 by John Hughes (1873–1932). Within twenty-five years of its introduction in the annual Baptist Singing Festival at Capel Rhondda, Pontypridd, the tune was used on more than five thousand festival programs. Hughes rose from being a doorboy at Glyn Colliery to being a traffic official of the Great Western Railway.

## 28. BRIEF OUR DAYS.

Kenneth L. Patton (1911– ), one of the compilers of this book, has been minister of the Charles Street Universalist Meeting House, Boston, since 1949. A graduate of Eureka College, Ill., and the University of Chicago, he has held pastorates in Disciples of Christ churches, and the First Unitarian Society, Madison, Wis. He is the author of six volumes of poetry; of *Beyond Doubt*, 1946; *Man's Hidden Search*, 1954; and editor of *Readings for the Celebration of Life*, 1957. This text was published in *Man Is the Meaning*, 1956.

In his *Himmlische Lieder*, 1642, Johann Schop (died ca. 1665), municipal music director in Hamburg, Germany, included WERDE MUNTER, MEIN GEMÜTE among his many settings of hymns by Johann Rist. Much altered, this form is that used twice in J. S. Bach's Cantata 147, "Herz und Mund und That und Leben," 1716. The melody became known as "Jesu, joy of man's desiring."

## 29. FOR ALL THE JOYS THAT GREET US.

Jan Struther (1901–53), the pseudonym of Mrs. A. K. Placzek, was formed from her maiden name, Anstruther. The popular British author wrote *Mrs. Miniver*, 1939, and several volumes of poetry. This hymn was written for *Songs of Praise, Enlarged*, 1931.

STRUTHER was composed by Arthur Foote II (1911– ), chairman of the commission that compiled this volume. Born in Ann Arbor, Mich., he was educated at Harvard University and at Meadville Theological School, Chicago, of whose Board of Trustees he is chairman. From 1936 to 1945 he served concurrently the Unitarian churches of Stockton and Sacramento, Cal.; since 1945 he has been minister of Unity Church of St. Paul, Minn. He is the son of Henry Wilder Foote, (1875– ), an editor of *The New Hymn and Tune Book*, 1914, and *Hymns of the Spirit*, 1937. He is named for his great-uncle, Arthur Foote, the American composer. His grandfather, Henry Wilder Foote (1838–89), minister of King's Chapel, Boston, edited *Hymns of the Church Universal*, 1893, which was completed by his sister, Mary Wilder Tileston, and his brother, Arthur.

### 30. FOR FLOWERS THAT BLOOM ABOUT OUR FEET. Anonymous.

This text, in circulation for over fifty years, is often attributed erroneously to Ralph Waldo Emerson.

The original of WAS GOTT THUT appeared in *Auserlesenes Weimarisches Gesangbuch*, 1681. S. Rodigast wrote a text beginning, "*Was Gott thut*" for his sick friend, Severus Gastorius, cantor at Jena, Germany; after his recovery Gastorius composed this tune for it.

### 31. PRAISE YE. Carrie Ward Lyon

(1879– ) is a lifelong Unitarian, a member of the Unitarian Church in Summit, N. J. This hymn appears for the first time here.

AMHERST is adapted from the tune by William Billings, (1746–1800) in *The New England Psalm Singer*, 1770. A Boston tanner and singing-school organizer, Billings was the leading native-American composer in the eighteenth century. This harmonization is by Robert L. Sanders (*see No. 2*).

### 32. LORD OF ALL MAJESTY AND MIGHT. George Wallace Briggs. *See No. 24.* This hymn first appeared in *Songs of Praise, Enlarged*, 1931. Numbers 1, 4, and 2, of its five stanzas are included here. Canon Briggs wrote it, "to provide a Christian expression of our thought about God in an age of scientific knowledge."...

Revised by Luther to fit his text, VATER UNSER, in Valentin Schumann's *Geistliche Lieder*, 1539, this tune by 1560 reached England, where it became known as "Old 112th." This setting is J. S. Bach's harmonization in his first version of the *St. John Passion*, 1723.

### 33. HEAVEN AND EARTH AND SEA AND AIR. Joachim Neander. *See No. 7.* This hymn, based on Acts 14:17, was translated by James Drummond Burns, 1869, and is considerably revised here.

*Vermehrte Glaub- und Liebes-übung*, Frankfurt and Leipzig, Germany, 1691, with words by Neander (*see No. 7*) and music by Georg Christoph Strattner (1650–1705), assistant choirmaster at Weimar, includes a setting of this text in 12/8 meter. The tune, later known as POSEN, received its present, even note-values in J. A. Freylinghausen's *Geistreiches Gesangbuch*, 1704 (*see No. 48*).

### 34. GOD MOVES IN A MYSTERIOUS WAY. William Cowper (1731–1800) was an English poet. This hymn remains in wide use, having been translated into Latin and several other languages. We include Stanzas 1, 4, 5, and 6 of the original.

DUNDEE, the English title, is called "French tune" in the Scottish Psalter of 1615, where it is one of the twelve common tunes. Another tune known in Scotland by this name, appears here (No. 89) under its English title, WINDSOR.

### 35. ALL MY HOPE ON GOD IS FOUNDED. Joachim Neander. *See No. 7.* This hymn was paraphrased by Robert Bridges (*see No. 137*) for his *Yattendon Hymnal*, 1899.

Neander refers to this tune, the setting of his text MEINE HOFFNUNG STEHET FESTE in *Glaub- und Liebesübung*, 1680, as a melody already known.

### 36. OUR GOD, OUR GOD, THOU SHINEST HERE. Thomas Hornblower Gill. *See No. 15.*

Composed for "All hail the power of Jesus' Name" in the first volume of *The Union Harmony*, 1793, CORONATION is the oldest tune in continuous use in the American urban northeast. The composer, Oliver Holden (1765–1844), was a carpenter and realtor, as well as a leading church musician. He served Charlestown in the Massachusetts House of Representatives.

### 37. PRAISE GOD. Charles H. Lyttle (1884– ) is James Freeman Clarke Professor of Church History, Emeritus,

at Meadville Theological School, Chicago, Ill., having joined its faculty in 1925, following Unitarian pastorates in Brooklyn, N. Y. and Omaha, Neb. He is minister of The First Unitarian Society, Geneva, Ill., and author of *The Liberal Gospel*, 1925, and *Freedom Moves West*, 1952. He conceived this doxology as a bridge between theists and humanists at the height of their controversy in the late nineteen-twenties.

OLD HUNDREDTH appears here in its modern form. For its original rhythm and a historical note, see *No. 18*.

**38. LORD OF ALL BEING.** Oliver Wendell Holmes (1809–94) was an American physician, a Unitarian, whose fame rests upon his essays and other writings. This hymn was included in *The Professor at the Breakfast Table* as "A Sun - day Hymn."

Originally a Hungarian chorale tune believed to date from the sixteenth century, TRANSYLVANIA was provided with new words by Marton Palfi in his *Unitarius Egyhazazi Ekeneskönyv, Cluj-Koloszvar*, 1924. It is very popular among Unitarians in Transylvania and Hungary. This arrangement by Robert L. Sanders (*see No. 2*) appeared in *Hymns of the Spirit*, 1937.

**39. WONDER.** Alfred Noyes (1880–1958) was an English poet who from 1914–23 taught at Princeton University. This text has been arranged from his *Watchers of the Sky*, by Kenneth L. Patton (*see No. 28*). Reared a Protestant, influenced by Thomas H. Huxley's agnosticism, Noyes became a Roman Catholic in 1925. Mr. Hugh Noyes, the poet's son, has graciously consented to this adaptation.

ERFYNIAD is a Welsh hymn melody from *Llyfr Tonau Cynulleidfaol* (Book of Congregational Tunes), 1859. That year the editor of that Calvinistic Methodist tune book, John Roberts, also known as Ieuan Gwyllt, (1822–77) initiated a long series of Welsh singing festivals for the encouragement of writing new hymns and tunes. The harmonization is by David Evans (1874–1948), professor at the University of Wales, for *Songs of Praise*, 1925.

**40. WE SING OF GOLDEN MORN-INGS.** Ralph Waldo Emerson. *See*

*Note 347*. This text is based on a hymn in *Free Religious Hymns*, London, 1925, edited by Walter Walsh as "a hymnal of Universal Religion." Vincent B. Silliman (*see No. 14*) rewrote Walsh's adaptation in this form for *We Sing of Life*, 1955. A poem titled "The World Soul," in Emerson's *Poems*, 1846, will be seen to be the original text.

COMPLAINER is from *The Southern Harmony*, New Haven, 1835, compiled by William Walker (*see No. 8*). The harmonization is by Henry Leland Clarke (*see No. 135*).

**41. IMMORTAL, INVISIBLE.** Walter Chalmers Smith (1824–1908) was a minister of the Free High Church of Edinburgh and moderator of the Assembly of the Free Church of Scotland. This hymn, based on a verse in I Tim., first appeared in Dr. Smith's *Hymns of Christ and the Christian Life*, 1867. We have omitted four lines of the original, combining Stanzas 3 and 4.

ST. DENIO, known in Wales as "Joanna," is closely related to several Welsh ballad tunes, notably *"Can Mlynedd i 'nawr"* ("A Hundred Years from Now"). It became a hymn tune, "Palestrina," in *Caniadau y Cyssegr*, Denbigh, North Wales, 1839, edited by John Roberts (Henllan), not John Roberts (Ieuan Gwyllt, *see No. 39*).

**42. REJOICE IN LOVE WE KNOW AND SHARE.** This revision of the quatrain by Charles H. Lyttle (No. 37) appeared in *We Sing of Life*, 1955, the work of Edwin C. Palmer (*see No. 356*) and Vincent B. Silliman (*see No. 14*).

Martin Luther contributed two prefaces to Valentin Schumann's *Geistliche Lieder*, 1539, which introduced this setting of Luther's text, *"Vom Himmel hoch."* It has been suggested without proof that Luther also wrote the tune VOM HIMMEL HOCH.

**43. GOD OF THE EARTH, THE SKY, THE SEA.** Samuel Longfellow (1819–92) was the younger brother of Henry Wadsworth Longfellow (*see No. 175*). Reared in the First Parish Society in Portland, Me., he became a Unitarian minister, serving churches in Fall River, Mass.; Brooklyn, N. Y.; and Germantown, Pa. While still in the Harvard Divinity School, he edited *A Book of*

*Hymns for Public and Private Devotion,* 1846, with Samuel Johnson (*see No. 172*), a classmate. Joseph May believes that Theodore Parker, who promptly adopted the book at the Boston Music Hall, was first to call it the "Book of Sams." Revised in 1848, it ran to twelve editions. Other hymnbooks followed, most notably *Hymns of the Spirit,* 1864, also with Samuel Johnson. The author of fifty or more hymns, he also wrote several biographies, including a *Life of Henry Wadsworth Longfellow,* 1886. This fine definition of God, reminiscent of Wordsworth's "Tintern Abbey"—"I have felt a presence that disturbs me with the joy of elevated thoughts"—was printed anonymously in *Hymns of the Spirit,* 1864.

DUKE STREET in the district of St. Helens in the township of Windle, England, was the residence of John Hatton (died 1793), composer of the tune of that name. Born at Warrington, near Liverpool, Hatton is said to have been killed in a stagecoach accident. He is not to be confused with another composer, John Liptrott Hatton (1809–86).

## 44. THERE'S A WIDENESS IN GOD'S MERCY.

Frederick William Faber (1814–63), an Anglican who turned Roman Catholic, helped found a community called "Brothers of the Will of God," which later joined the Oratory of St. Philip Neri. Author of many theological books, he is best known for his 150 hymns. We have kept Stanzas 1, 5, and 4 of the original six.

Amos Pilsbury of Charleston, S. C., published CHARLESTON in his *United States' Sacred Harmony,* Boston, 1799. Here old English ballad melody of the "Lord Lovel" type is applied to the text, "Come, thou fount of every blessing." This harmonization is by Henry Leland Clarke (*see No. 135*).

## 45. GOD MAKES A PATH.

Roger Williams (1604?–83) was the Welshborn founder of Rhode Island, the first pure democracy in America, and a pioneer of religious liberty. He immigrated to Boston in 1631 as a Puritan divine, but was banished four years later. In 1636, on land purchased from the Indians on the shores of Narragansett Bay, he founded Providence. There he

helped found the first Baptist church in America; soon he withdrew from the Baptists to become a "seeker," or independent Christian. This text is one of several bits of poetry concluding chapters in Williams' *A Key into the Language of America,* 1643.

For DUNDEE see No. 34.

## 46. WHO THOU ART I KNOW NOT.

Harry Kemp (1883–1960), American vagabond, poet, and dramatist, born in Youngstown, Ohio, resident of Provincetown, Mass., stated: "I wrote the poem under great stress when attending the Unitarian church in Lawrence, Kansas, when studying at the university in that state." Its first appearance as a hymn was in *The Beacon Song and Service Book,* 1935, set to this tune. The author's title is "God, the Architect."

EINTRACHT is a melody by Franz Xaver Mathias (1871–1939), Alsatian church composer and musicologist, director of the Catholic academic choir at Strasbourg, and editor of *Cäcilia.* Found in *Elsässicher Liederkranz,* fifth edition, 1927, the tune was arranged by Sylvia Freeman of Portland, Me., and Raymond C. Robinson, organist of King's Chapel, Boston, for *The Beacon Song and Service Book,* 1935. It was thus harmonized for this book.

## 47. THE SPACIOUS FIRMAMENT ON HIGH.

Joseph Addison (1672–1719) was an English poet, politician, public official, and essayist, major contributor to *The Spectator,* 1711–12, for which he furnished 274 of the 555 daily issues. This hymn appeared first in *The Spectator,* No. 465, at the close of the essay, "Faith and Devotion." Thomas Paine in *The Age of Reason,* 1794, recognized it as among "true *deistical* compositions," with approval. It has been in all editions of the Protestant Episcopal Hymnal, since 1789. American Unitarians and Universalists have been singing it for generations, although it is missing from the hymnbooks of 1846, 1848, and 1864 of Samuel Longfellow and Samuel Johnson.

CREATION, an adaptation of the chorus, "The heavens are telling," from Franz Joseph Haydn's *The Creation,* 1798, is the responsibility of Benjamin F. Baker and Isaac B. Woodbury, who published it in *The Choral*, Boston, 1845. Haydn (1732–1809) was born in Rohrau, Lower Austria, became a choirboy at St. Stephen's, Vienna, and for many years served the Esterhazy family as composer and director of music. Greatly honored in England, he received the degree of Doctor of Music from Oxford in 1791. One of the giants of Viennese classical music, he composed over one hundred symphonies and a whole literature of chamber music. Yet, outside of this American arrangement, his one permanent contribution to hymnody is the magnificent national anthem, "AUSTRIA" (*see No. 248*).

**48. EARTH ARRAYED IN WONDROUS BEAUTY.** Vincent B. Silliman. *See No. 14*. This response was written for *The Beacon Song and Service Book*, 1935, and is based upon Immanuel Kant's famous saying in *The Critique of Practical Reason*: "*Two things fill the mind with ever new and increasing/admiration and awe, the oftener and the more steadily/we reflect upon them: the starry heavens above and/the moral law within.*"

GUTER HIRTE was added to the second edition of the *Geistreiches Gesangbuch*, 1705, compiled by Johann August Freylinghausen (1670–1739), the poet of the Pietist movement and preacher at Halle, Germany. That song book was subsequently expanded to contain 1,588 hymns and 327 tunes and was widely used by immigrants to this country. It was thus harmonized for this book.

**49. THE LORD'S MY SHEPHERD.** Scottish Psalter, 1650. This metrical version of Psalm 23 evolved gradually between 1640 and 1650 and cannot be ascribed to any one author. The Psalter of 1650 has survived all proposals to modernize it and remains to this day the only version used by Presbyterian Scotland. This text has won wide usage in England and America also.

For DUNDEE *see No. 34*.

**50. THE THOUGHT OF GOD.** Frederick Lucian Hosmer (1840–1929) was an American Unitarian minister, serving in Cleveland, Ohio; St. Louis, Mo.; and Berkeley, Calif. Beginning in 1875, for nearly four decades he and William Channing Gannett worked together,

making a contribution to hymnody comparable to that of the "two Sams," Longfellow and Johnson, a generation earlier. It has been said, "Gannett was the better poet, Hosmer the better hymn writer." This is one of fifty-six poems Hosmer contributed to their *The Thought of God*, 1885; it first appeared in *Unity Hymns and Chorals*, Chicago, 1880.

ROCHESTER appeared in the second edition of Aaron Williams' *Universal Psalmodist*, London, 1764, and in the same year in *A New and Compleat Introduction to the Grounds and Rules of Music*, published in Newburyport, Mass., by Daniel Bayley (1725?–99). Bayley drew his material chiefly from English sources, notably Aaron Williams (*see No. 124*) and William Tans'ur (*see No. 327*). This harmonization is by Robert L. Sanders (*see No. 2*).

**51. O GOD, OUR HELP IN AGES PAST.** Isaac Watts (1674–1748), an English Independent or Congregationalist minister, in verse paraphrased biblical psalms so that they became Christian hymns and thus was a pioneer in emancipating English-speaking churches from a hymnody consisting almost exclusively of psalms in rhyme. His psalms and freely composed hymns became immensely popular in England and America. Many would call this paraphrase of Psalm 90 the greatest hymn in English. A liberal, for his time, Watts wrote: "*I hate these shackles of the mind./ Forg'd by the haughty wise;/ Souls were not born to be confin'd,/ And led, like Samson, blind and bound. . . .*"

ST. ANNE was first published anonymously in the sixth edition of the *Supplement to the New Version of Psalms*, 1708, prepared by William Croft (1676–1727), organist of St. Anne's, Soho. Subsequent collections by Croft's associates, Philip Hart and John Church, leave no doubt that Croft composed this tune. The hardy first phrase is a stock melody used by Henry Lawes and by Handel. The Bach fugue beginning with that phrase is known in England as the "St. Anne's Fugue." The leading Anglican musician of his generation, Dr. Croft succeeded his master, Dr. John Blow, as organist of Westminster Abbey and master of the children and composer at the Chapel Royal.

52. ROLL ON, YE STARS. Erasmus Darwin (1731–1802) was an English poet and author and also a physician and biologist. The grandfather of Charles Darwin, he taught a kind of evolution. This text is from his poem, *The Botanic Garden*, Canto 4, in "The Loves of the Plants," published anonymously in 1789.

AINSWORTH 97 was the setting of Psalm 97 and others in *The Book of Psalmes, Englished Both in Prose and Metre*, 1612, translated by Henry Ainsworth for the English Separatists in Holland. Brought to Plymouth, Mass., on the *Mayflower*, this was the first hymnal used in New England. The tune was adapted from the setting of Psalm 74 in the Genevan Psalter, 1562, and the harmony is based on that attributed to Claude Le Jeune (1528–1600), Parisian composer of vocal music.

53. UNREST. Don Marquis (1878–1937) was an American journalist and humorist, best known for the satirical *Archy and Mehitabel*. He also wrote serious poetry and drama, and left an uncompleted autobiography, *Sons of the Puritans*, published in 1939. This poem, found in many anthologies, may be the most quoted of his serious verse.

SALVATION appears in *Kentucky Harmony*, Harrisonburg, Va., ca. 1815, compiled by Ananias Davisson (1780–1857), elder of the Presbyterian church and a teacher of sacred music. Very close to a number of English ballad tunes, the melody is ascribed by Davisson to "Boyd,"—James M. Boyd, compiler of *The Virginia Sacred Musical Repository*, Winchester, 1818. This harmonization is by Kenneth Munson (*see No. 134*).

54. O LIFE THAT MAKETH ALL THINGS NEW. Samuel Longfellow. *See No. 43.* This text, then titled "The Light that Lighteth Every Man," was first sung at the second Social Festival of the Free Religious Association in 1874. Longfellow and Samuel Johnson devised memorable phrases synonymous with the word *God* and explanatory of their thought of God: "O Life that maketh all things new," "Light of ages and of nations" (Longfellow); and "Life of ages, richly poured" (Johnson).

TRURO, a setting of "Now to the Lord a noble song" in Thomas Williams' *Psalmodia Evangelica*, 1789, is sometimes ascribed without evidence to Charles Burney (1726–1814).

55. IN THIS STERN HOUR. Josephine Johnson (1890–    ) is an Episcopalian living in Norfolk, Va. Her poetry has appeared in anthologies and magazines and in her volume, *The Unwilling Gypsy*.

INTERCESSOR was composed for *Hymns Ancient and Modern*, 1904, by Sir Charles Hubert Hastings Parry (1848–1918), director of the Royal College of Music, London, England.

56. THE EARTH IS HOME. Kenneth L. Patton. *See No. 28.* This hymn was first published in *Man Is the Meaning*, 1956, as one of a group of "Anthems of Humanity."

ST. PETERSBURG by Dmitri Stepanovitch Bortniansky (1751–1825), court choir director at St. Petersburg, accompanies the Russian hymn *"Kol slaven"* in No. 116 of the Tchaikovsky edition of Bortniansky's sacred works. In Protestant hymnody it was first applied to a stanza by Tersteegen, *"Ich bete an die Macht der Liebe"* in Tscherlitzky's *Choralbuch*, 1825.

57. THE WORLD STANDS OUT ON EITHER SIDE. Edna St. Vincent Millay (1892–1950) was an American writer of poetry, short stories, and verse plays. From the closing section of her poem, "Renascence," comes this hymn, which appears for the first time in this hymnbook. *Renascence and Other Poems* was published in 1917.

HAMILTON is from *The Sacred Harp*, compiled in the town of Hamilton, Ga., by B. F. White and E. J. King and published in Philadelphia in 1844. This tune is claimed by the principal editor of the collection, Benjamin Franklin White (1800–79). A native of Spartanburg, S. C., White assisted his brother-in-law, William Walker (*see No. 8*), in preparing *The Southern Harmony*, 1835. *The Sacred Harp* soon outstripped the earlier collection of shape-note tunes and to this day is widely used in the southeastern states. This harmonization is by Robert L. Sanders (*see No. 2*).

**58. DIVINITY IS ROUND US.** Sophia Lyon Fahs (1876–      ) is an American educator, ordained to the Unitarian ministry in 1959. A pioneer in religious education, she worked with Harry Emerson Fosdick at Riverside Church, New York City, before becoming editor of religious education materials for the American Unitarian Association and the Council of Liberal Churches. Among her books are *Exploring Religion with Eight Year Olds*, *Consider the Children*, and *Today's Children and Yesterday's Heritage*. This text first was published in *We Sing of Life*, 1955.

ST. MARTIN was composed by George Wallace Briggs (1875–1959) for his text, "Lord, who thyself hast bidden us to pray," in the enlarged *Songs of Praise*, 1931. See No. 24.

**59. THE LIGHT, MY LIGHT.** Rabindranath Tagore (or Ravindranatha Thakura) (1861–1941) was a Hindu poet, dramatist, musician, painter, and author of religious and philosophic writings. He was awarded the Nobel Prize for literature in 1913 and was active in educational and social reform in India. Knighted by the British in 1915, he renounced the honor in 1919, in protest against repressive measures by the British. This hymn has been arranged by Kenneth L. Patton (*see No. 28*) from Poem 57 in *Gitanjali*.

The tune is an adaptation of ILLINOIS, a "Western melody" in *The Manhattan Collection*, 1837, compiled by Thomas Hastings (1784–1872). A native of Washington, Conn., Hastings went to New York City after pioneering in music education at Utica, N. Y., where he had edited a religious paper, *The Western Recorder*. He wrote a thousand or more hymn tunes, including "Rock of Ages, cleft for me." Later Methodist hymnals attribute ILLINOIS to the Rev. Jonathan Spilman (1835), "arr. by Thomas Hastings." The harmonization was adapted for this book by Robert L. Sanders (*see No. 2*).

**60. LET US WANDER WHERE WE WILL.** Robert Louis Stevenson (1850–94) was a Scottish novelist, essayist, and poet. Leisurely travels in France by canoe and on foot, passage in the steerage of an emigrant ship to America, and across it in an immigrant train, and

final years in Samoa, provided material for such books as *Treasure Island*, *Kidnapped*, and *A Child's Garden of Verses*. This text is from Stanzas 2 and 3 of Poem 17 in *Poems 1869–1879*.

SAVANNAH (or HERRNHUT) is from a manuscript *Choralbuch*, ca. 1740, at Herrnhut, Saxony, where Count von Zinzendorf had founded his Moravian Brethren. John Wesley published it in the *Collection of Tunes as They Are Sung at the Foundery*, 1742.

**61. THE FIERY ELEMENT.** John Holmes. See No. 9. This hymn consists of the last eight lines from the title poem in *Map of My Country*, 1943.

WOODLANDS, first published in the *Public School Hymn Book*, 1919, was named by its composer, Walter Greatorex (1877–1949), after a house at Gresham's School, Norfolk, England, where he was director of music.

**62. MAN IS THE EARTH UPRIGHT AND PROUD.** Kenneth L. Patton. See No. 28. This hymn, already in wide usage, was first published in *Man Is the Meaning*, 1956, where the opening line reads "We are the earth upright and proud."

For EIN' FESTE BURG see No. 16.

**63. IF MAN THINK THE THOUGHT ETERNAL.** Johann Wolfgang von Goethe (1749–1832) was a German poet and playwright, the author of *Faust*. This text is translated as one eight-line stanza in Ludwig Lewisohn's *The Story of a Man*, 1949, which gives the life of Goethe in his own words and those of his contemporaries.

LOBT DEN HERRN, DIE MORGENSONNE first appeared in *Allgemeines evangelisches Choralbuch*, 1829, edited by Johann Friedrich Naue (1787–1858), music director of the united universities of Halle and Wittenberg, Germany.

**64. FROM THE FIRST MAN TO CLIMB THE HILL.** Anonymous. We cannot trace the source of this text.

DISTRESS appears in *The Southern Harmony* (*see No. 8*) The harmonization is by Robert L. Sanders (*see No. 2*).

**65. I AM PART OF ALL THAT I HAVE MET.** Alfred Lord Tennyson (1809–92) was England's poet laureate forty-two years. This text, drawn from "Ulysses," was arranged by Kenneth L. Patton (*see No. 28*).

For WOODLANDS *see No. 61*.

### 66. O MAN, ACCLAIM YOUR HERITAGE. Kenneth L. Patton. *See No. 28*. This hymn, written in 1949, first appeared in *Man Is the Meaning*, 1956.

For CREATION *see No. 47*.

### 67. THE ETERNAL. Dilys Bennett Laing (1906–60), a Welsh-born poet, became a naturalized American after marrying Alexander Laing, a novelist and poet. These stanzas, her first to appear in a hymnbook, are from *Another England*, 1941.

The tune of NUN KOMM, DER HEIDEN HEILAND derives from the plain-song melody of its Latin original, "*Veni Redemptor gentium*." It was published with Martin Luther's translation in the Erfurt *Enchiridion*, 1524, and harmonized in 1594 by Seth Calvisius (1556–1615), a predecessor of Schein and Bach as cantor of St. Thomas's School, Leipzig, Germany.

### 68. THE MIDDLE STATE. Kenneth L. Patton. *See No. 28*. This text was written at Ocean Point, Me., for this book.

CROSS OF CHRIST bears a close family resemblance to ballad tunes such as "James Harris." *The Sacred Harp*, Philadelphia, 1844, compiled by B. F. White and E. J. King, credits it to Leonard P. Breedlove (died ca. 1879) who actively assisted Major White in distributing his *Sacred Harp* to states adjoining Georgia. The harmonization is by Robert L. Sanders (*see No. 2*).

### 69. AFFIRMATION. John Hall Wheelock (1886– ) is an American poet and an editor at Charles Scribner's Sons. This hymn appears as a sonnet in *The Bright Doom*, 1927. Mr. Wheelock graciously consented to the omission of two lines, and himself amended Stanza 3 for its use as a hymn.

CONGLETON, the setting of Psalm 67 in Robert Goodridge's *Psalms of David*, 1684, was composed by Michael Wise (ca. 1648–87), organist of Salisbury Cathedral, England, and Gentleman of the Chapel Royal.

### 70. CIRCULAR SECRET. John Hall Wheelock. *See No. 69*. This poem, "Circular Secret," is in *Poems Old and New*, 1956. The poet has allowed omission of one line of the original.

O MENTES PERFIDAS is an abridged version of a tune in *Piae Cantiones* (*see No. 323*).

### 71. THE MIND OF MAN. Edward Young (1683–1765) was an Anglican clergyman and poet, who gained popularity with a classic series of poems, *The Complaint: or, Night Thoughts on Life, Death and Immortality*, 1742–45. Our text is a cento arranged by Kenneth L. Patton (*see No. 28*) from that work.

SURSUM CORDA, composed in 1941, appeared in *The Hymnal 1940* as the setting of " 'Lift up your hearts!' We lift them, Lord, to thee," written by Henry Montagu Butler, headmaster of the Harrow School, England. The composer, Alfred Morton Smith (1879– ), was born in Jenkintown, Pa., and educated at the University of Pennsylvania and the Philadelphia Divinity School. A chaplain in World War I and later, he served from 1919 on the staff of the Episcopal City Mission of Philadelphia.

### 72. FAIR IS THEIR FAME. Laurence Housman (1865–1959) was an English Quaker, artist, and author of several novels and volumes of poetry, who illustrated other poets' works before writing poetry himself. His *An Englishwoman's Love Letters*, published anonymously, made a great sensation. After World War I he supported the Life and Liberty movement for international understanding and peace. This text was in *The Heart of Peace*, 1919. Its first use as a hymn was in *The Beacon Song and Service Book*, 1935, with this tune.

DONNE SECOURS replaced in the 1551 edition the tune used for Psalm 12 in the Genevan Psalter of 1542.

### 73. I CANNOT THINK OF THEM AS DEAD. Frederick Lucian Hosmer. *See No. 50*. This poem, written in 1882, appeared in *The Thought of God*, 1885, as "My Dead."

Among the most songlike of hymn tunes are those conventionally designated by the word *Song* followed by a number. These are melodies provided for George Wither's *Hymnes and Songs of the Church*, 1623, by Orlando Gibbons (1583–1625). Gibbons took the tune of SONG 67 from Edmund Prys's Welsh Psalter, *Llyfr y Psalmau*, 1621, and added the bass underlying this harmonization. He was a chorister at King's College, Cambridge, during the reign of Elizabeth I and the outstanding organist of James I's reign, serving at the Chapel Royal and also at Westminster Abbey.

74. THE INWARD WITNESS. Frederick Lucian Hosmer. *See No. 50.* This was written for the dedication of the First Unitarian Church, Omaha, Neb., 1891, and published in *The Thought of God*, Second Series, 1894.

CAITHNESS is one of the thirty-one common tunes set in four parts in the Scottish Psalter of 1635.

75. FOR ALL THE SAINTS. William Walsham How (1823–97), an Anglican clergyman, Bishop of Wakefield, England, edited three hymnals and wrote numerous hymns. This, his most famous, was published with eleven stanzas in Earl Nelson's *Hymns for Saints' Days*, 1864, as "For all thy saints."

Ralph Vaughan Williams (*see No. 78*) composed the admired SINE NOMINE for *The English Hymnal*, 1906, to replace Sir Joseph Barnby's *St. Philip*. At the time the latter was so well entrenched that a bishop, it is said, exclaimed on hearing SINE NOMINE, "Good gracious, they will change the tune of 'God save the King' next!"

76. SAY NOT THEY DIE. Malcolm Quin (1855–1944) wrote *Memoirs of a Positivist*, 1924. From 1882 to 1910 he was religious leader of the Positivist community in Newcastle upon Tyne, England—one of those societies established in France, England, and Brazil, embodying the religious ideas of Auguste Comte (1798–1857). This text, written in 1882, appeared in the Positivist Society's *Service of Man* and in the Ethical Society's *Hymns of Modern Thought*, ca. 1900.

DAS NEUGEBORNE KINDELEIN by Melchior Vulpius (ca. 1560–1615), cantor at Weimar, Germany, first appeared in *Ein schön geistlich Gesangbach*, 1609. This version is J. S. Bach's treatment in Cantata 122, ca. 1742, where the fourth stanza of the text forms the closing chorale.

77. TRANSIENCE. Sarojini Naidu (1879–1949), a Hindu poet and reformer, was the first woman president of the Indian National Congress, 1925. In 1908, she organized flood relief; in 1928 and 1929, she lectured in the United States. Her poetry has been translated into many of India's languages. This poem appeared in *The Bird of Time*, 1912.

For DONNE SECOURS *see No. 72.*

78. AWAY, O SOUL. Walt Whitman (1819–92), American poet, the bard of democracy, a visionary, a citizen extraordinary, his poems were published as *Leaves of Grass*, a collection gradually evolving through nine editions between 1855 and 1892. This hymn is freely arranged by Kenneth L. Patton (*see No. 28*) from "Passage to India," Parts 8 and 9. The poem appeared in the fifth edition of *Leaves of Grass*, 1872.

MAGDA is by Ralph Vaughan Williams (1872–1958), whose genius and enthusiasm for folk song brought new life to English hymnody and English music in general. A native of Gloucestershire, Vaughan Williams studied at the Royal College of Music and at Trinity College, Cambridge, where he received the degree of Doctor of Music in 1901. Among his teachers were Sir Hubert Parry (*see No. 55*) and Maurice Ravel. He was professor of composition at the Royal College of Music, musical editor of *The English Hymnal*, 1906, and co-editor of *The Oxford Book of Carols*, 1928, and *Songs of Praise*, 1925, for which he composed this tune.

79. ABIDE WITH ME. Henry Francis Lyte (1793–1847), born in Scotland, educated in Ireland, for twenty-four years was Anglican curate at Lower Brixham, Devonshire, England. Author of several volumes of poetry, he is chiefly remembered for this hymn of approaching death. Long supposed to have been written near the end of his own life, some scholars now believe it to have been written around 1820, after a visit to a dying friend, William A. Le Huntte, who had repeated the phrase, "Abide with me."

EVENTIDE, setting for this hymn in *Hymns Ancient and Modern*, 1861, was composed by William Henry Monk (1823–89) at the end of a committee meeting, according to one account, or at the end of a day, his widow asserted, as the two watched a sunset. A London organist and professor of vocal music, Monk was musical coadjutor for the first two editions of *Hymns Ancient and Modern* and musical editor of the enlarged edition of 1875. Durham University made him Doctor of Music in 1882.

80. HE THAT DIES SHALL NOT DIE LONELY. William Morris (1834–96), an Englishman, was a prolific poet, a translator of Icelandic sagas, and an artist. A founder of Morris and Company, manufacturers of artistic household and church furnishings, he was an idealistic and active Socialist, lecturing and writing for the Socialistic League. This hymn is from the poem, "All for the Cause," which appeared in *Justice*, organ of the Social Democratic Federation, April 19, 1884, and reprinted in *Chants for Socialists*, 1885; the hymn consists of Stanzas 2, 8, and 15, the last slightly adapted.

For LOBT DEN HERRN *see No. 63.*

81. THE SENSE OF DEATH. Helen Hoyt (1887–    ) is an American poet, formerly a New Englander, and now Mrs. W. W. Lyman of St. Helena, Calif. This poem was written in Chicago about 1915, when she was assisting Harriet Monroe in editing the magazine *Poetry*. It appears in her first book, *Apples Here in My Basket*, 1924. We omit one stanza.

For VATER UNSER *see No. 32.*

82. NOW I RECALL MY CHILD-HOOD. Rabindranath Tagore. *See No. 59.* This text is adapted from Poem 71, in *Crossing*, by Kenneth L. Patton *(see No. 28).*

For SURSUM CORDA *see No. 71.*

83. LIGHT. S. R. Lysaght (1870–1941) was an Irish author and poet. This text is a cento from the poem, "Beyond the Farthest Horizon," from *Horizons and Landmarks*, 1911.

CLIFF TOWN, appearing first in *Congregational Praise*, 1951, was composed by the Congregational minister, Erik Routley (1917–    ), member of the musical advisory committee for that volume and co-author of the *Companion to Congregational Praise*. Formerly at Mansfield College, Oxford, now in Edinburgh, Dr. Routley has produced several studies in hymnody from *I'll Praise My Maker*, 1951, to *Music, Sacred and Profane*, 1960.

84. FROM ALL THE FRET AND FEVER OF THE DAY. Monroe Beardsley (1915–    ) is an American Unitarian, a professor of philosophy at Swarthmore College, Pa. His most recent book is *Aesthetics*, 1958. He wrote these stanzas for a service designed to show the meaning of silence, for the Unitarian Church of Delaware County, Springfield, Pa.

COOLINGE. Cyril Vincent Taylor (1907–    ), English composer and musical editor, is warden of the Royal School of Church Music and author of *The Way to Heaven's Door*, 1955, and *A Chronicle of Carols*, 1957. He edited *The Botsford Book of Christmas Carols*, 1957.

85. CALM SOUL OF ALL THINGS. Matthew Arnold (1822–88) was an English poet and critic who exerted a wide influence on religion and morals by the nobility, grace, and power of his verse. Son of Dr. Thomas Arnold of Rugby, he was professor of poetry at Oxford, 1857–67. This text is from "Lines Written in Kensington Garden."

TALLIS' CANON has a long history from its appearance in Archbishop Parker's Psalter, ca. 1561, to its use for congregational participation in Benjamin Britten's miracle play, *Noye's Fludde*, 1957. Its strict canon between soprano and tenor is attractive to the learned and the unlearned. Thomas Tallis (ca. 1505–85), one of the first to set English words for Anglican use, was Gentleman of the Chapel Royal throughout the reigns of Henry VIII, Edward VI, Mary, and Elizabeth I. He was organist with William Byrd; together they held a monopoly for printing music and ruled music paper in England.

86. HOURS OF INSIGHT. Matthew Arnold. *See No. 85.* This text is the first two stanzas of the poem, "Morality."

John Bishop (1665-1737) composed LEICESTER as one of his *Sett of New Psalm Tunes in Four Parts*, ca. 1700. He was organist at Winchester College, England, succeeding Jeremiah Clark (*see No. 98*), and then at Winchester Cathedral.

## 87. THE STILL, SMALL VOICE.

James Martineau (1805-1900) was a dominating figure of the British Unitarian movement. Rejecting any label with doctrinal implication, like *Unitarian*, he attained wide renown as a theologian. Scholar, preacher, teacher, his *Common Prayer for Christian Worship*, 1862, embodying much of his own writing, is one of the noblest handbooks for congregational worship in English. Hymnbooks edited by him and published in 1831, 1840, and 1873 illustrated the catholicity and liberality of his spirit. This hymn is an abbreviated adaptation of one of three hymns which he originally published anonymously.

O GOTT, DU FROMMER GOTT (also "Darmstadt") is a melody by Ahasuerus Fritsch (1629-1701), chancellor of the University of Jena, Germany. It first appeared in *Himmels-Lust und Welt-Unlust*, 1679, with the text, "*Die Wollust dieser Welt.*" This version follows J. S. Bach's setting of the second stanza of "*O Gott, du frommer Gott,*" used for the closing number of his Cantata 45, "*Es ist dir gesagt, Mensch, was gut ist,*" ca. 1740.

## 88. THE INDWELLING GOD.

Frederick Lucian Hosmer. *See No. 50.* The hymn first appeared in *The Christian Register*, May 31, 1879, and then in *The Thought of God*, 1885. Here, the seven four-line stanzas are reduced to two eight-line stanzas.

OLD 137TH is from the Anglo-Genevan Psalter, *One and Fiftie Psalmes*, Geneva, 1556, published by refugees from the England of the Roman Catholic Queen Mary. The tune was retained for Psalm 137 in subsequent English and Scottish Psalters.

## 89. IN QUIETUDE THE SPIRIT GROWS.

Anonymous. The original four stanzas of this text appear first in a Unitarian hymnbook which was described thus in Louis F. Benson's *The English Hymn*, 1915: "George W. Briggs of Plymouth, like Martineau, cared only

for the Hymnology of the inner life, and in his *Hymns for Public Worship*, Boston, 1845, sought 'to bring together the most fervent expressions of a profound spiritual life.' " The hymn, beginning "Unheard the dews around me fall," appeared frequently in Unitarian hymnbooks, including James Martineau's 1873 collection. In *Christian Hymns*, 1881, edited by Stopford A. Brooke (*see No. 10*), it acquired the present third stanza. Here the text is rearranged and rewritten, with a suggestion from Jacob Trapp's *Songs and Readings*, 1937.

WINDSOR is the setting of Psalm 116 in *The Second Booke of the Musicke of William Damon . . . Conteining All the Tune of David's Psalmes, &c.*, 1591. Reminiscent of the third chapter of Christopher Tye's *Actes of the Apostles*, 1553, the melody later appears as "Dundie," one of the twelve common tunes in the Scottish Psalter of 1615.

## 90. NOT ALWAYS ON THE MOUNT.

Frederick Lucian Hosmer. *See No. 50.* This hymn, based on the Transfiguration, Matt. 17, was written in 1882 and published in *Unity*, Chicago, April 1, 1884. As revised by the author, it was included in *The Thought of God*, 1885, and *Hymns of the Spirit*, 1937. We have omitted the author's second stanza and have altered slightly Stanzas 2 and 3.

DANBY, an arrangement by Ralph Vaughan Williams (*see No. 78*) of a traditional English ballad air, appeared in *Songs of Praise*, 1925.

## 91. THE SOUL'S SINCERE DESIRE.

James Montgomery. *See No. 20.* This beloved definition of prayer first appeared in Edward Bickersteth's *Treatise on Prayer*, 1818.

For WINDSOR see No. 89.

## 92. THE SOUL WHEREIN GOD DWELLS.

Johann Scheffler (1624-77), German mystical poet and physician, was born in Breslau, Silesia, where he died in the monastery into which he had withdrawn. Reared a Lutheran, he became Roman Catholic in 1653 and a promoter of anti-Protestant propaganda. His *Geistreiche Sinn- und Schlussreime*, 1657, pseudonymously attributed to Angelus Silesius the "Cherubinic Wanderer," is a devotional work of rhymed epigrams of extraordinary insight and power; the first part was written in four days of religious ecstasy. Its mysticism resembles that of the Indian *Bhagavad-Gita* and that of Ralph Waldo Emerson. We cannot trace this English translation.

MARIA JUNG UND ZART, sometimes called "Hosmer," or "Mainz," first appeared in *Ausserlesene catholische geistliche Kirchengesäng*, printed by Peter von Brachel in Cologne, Germany, 1623; it appeared in this form in *Psalteriolum Harmonicum Sacrarum Cantilenarum*, Cologne, 1642.

93. THE HARP AT NATURE'S ADVENT STRUNG. John Greenleaf Whittier (1807–92) poet, Quaker, and abolitionist, was born on a farm near Haverhill, Mass. At least seventy-five centos have been drawn from his poetry for inclusion in hymnbooks. This hymn is from "The Worship of Nature."

BYZANTIUM, also called "Jackson," was composed by Thomas Jackson (ca. 1715–81), organist of St. Mary's Newark-on-Trent, England, master of the song-school there. It first appeared in *Twelve Psalm Tunes and Eighteen Double and Single Chants*, 1780, as "Byzantium" in Miller's *Sacred Music*, 1800. The harmonization is by Robert L. Sanders (*see No. 2*).

94. WHO WOULD TRUE VALOR SEE. John Bunyan (1628–88), the Baptist tinker of Bedford Gaol, was an English author, scripture student, and Nonconformist, who spent twelve years in jail for "the crime of preaching." He wrote prolifically, but is best remembered for *Pilgrim's Progress*, 1678. This hymn is in the chapter, "Mr. Valiant for Truth," in the 1684 edition. The last stanza substitutes "No word of foe or friend" for "Hobgoblin nor foul fiend." Thus modified, the text was first used as a hymn in *The Beacon Song and Service Book*, 1935.

MONKS GATE was collected from a folk singer at Monks Gate near Horsham, Sussex, England, by Ralph Vaughan Williams (*see No. 78*) who arranged it for *The English Hymnal*, 1906. The original text began, "Our captain calls all hands on board tomorrow."

95. HOLD FAST THY LOYALTY. Frederick Lucian Hosmer. *See No. 50.* This poem, "Loyalty," was written in 1881 and published in *The Thought of God*, 1885.

For CAITHNESS *see No. 74.*

96. WISDOM HAS TREASURES. Michael Bruce (1746–67), Scottish Presbyterian, taught school during university vacations. One of the hymns he wrote for his singing classes began, "O happy is the man who hears," a paraphrase of Prov. 3:13–17 which entered the Paraphrases of the Church of Scotland in 1781. Four stanzas of it, beginning "Wisdom hath treasures greater far," appeared in *Hymns of the Spirit*, 1937. Three of those, the third rewritten to include phraseology from Prov. 3:18, constitute the present hymn, from *We Sing of Life*, 1955.

GRÄFENBERG is the setting of *"Nun danket all und bringet Ehr"* by Johann Crüger in the fifth edition of *Praxis Pietatis Melica* (*see No. 19*).

97. SAY NOT, "THE STRUGGLE NOUGHT AVAILETH." Arthur Hugh Clough (1819–61), a brilliant Englishman who died of malaria in Florence, Italy, before approaching his apparent potential. This poem was his last. His poetry was collected and published by Francis Turner Palgrave, 1863.

Beginning like a secular chanson, LES COMMANDEMENS apparently was completed by Louis Bourgeois. The tune serves both the Decalogue and Psalm 140 in *Pseaulmes cinquante de David*, 1547, published by Bourgeois in Lyons. That psalter was the first with four-part harmonization, a practice of which Calvin disapproved.

98. NOT GOLD, BUT ONLY MEN. Anonymous. Though this hymn often is attributed to Ralph Waldo Emerson, a thorough check has failed to uncover its origin.

Before a series of four tunes, the second edition of Henry Playford's *Divine Companion*, 1707, states: "The three following psalms sett by Mr. Jer. Clark." Although ST. MAGNUS is the fourth tune, it also is generally attributed to Jeremiah Clark (ca. 1669–1707). Clark and William Croft (*see*

*No. 51)*, fellow pupils of John Blow as choristers in the English Chapel Royal, became joint organists there in 1704.

## 99. THE MAN OF INTEGRITY.
Sir Henry Wotton (1568–1639), English author and public servant, engaged for years in diplomatic missions on the Continent and later served as provost of Eton. This poem, published in *Reliquiae Wottonianae*, by Isaak Walton, 1651, was copied shortly after it was written in 1616 by Ben Jonson. Several phrases in this version are from Jonson's copy. Several stanzas are omitted.

WAREHAM by William Knapp (1698–1768) was in his *Sett of New Psalms and Anthems in Four Parts*, 1738. "A country psalm-singer," possibly of German extraction, he was born in Wareham, Dorsetshire, England, and served thirty-nine years as parish clerk of St. James's Church in Poole. There, a local rhymster placed "Will Knapp" as the ultimate terror from which he prayed to be delivered.

## 100. TO SUFFER WOES WHICH HOPE THINKS INFINITE.
Percy Bysshe Shelley (1792–1822), a sensitive boy, was "sent down" from Oxford for writing *The Necessity of Atheism*. Too early married, he left his wife and eloped to the Continent with Mary Godwin in 1814. After his wife's suicide, he married Mary and lived in Italy. He was drowned in the Gulf of Spezia. A social radical and a passionate believer in human perfectibility, his poetry reflects his fervent idealism. This text is a cento from "Prometheus Unbound."

For CONGLETON see *No. 69*.

## 101. IT IS SOMETHING TO HAVE WEPT.
Gilbert Keith Chesterton (1874–1936), controversial English journalist, novelist, and critic, became Roman Catholic in 1922. This text is four stanzas, with slight changes, from the six of "The Great Minimum," in *Poems by Gilbert Keith Chesterton*, 1915.

KEITH was composed for this book by Robert L. Sanders (*see No. 2*).

## 102. WHAT MAKES A CITY GREAT.
Anonymous. This poem is in James Dalton Morrison's *Masterpieces of Religious Verse*, 1948.

For LEICESTER see *No. 86*.

## 103. MAN–MAKING.
Edwin Markham (1852–1940) began as a teacher, principal, and superintendent in California schools. In 1899 he published *The Man with the Hoe and Other Poems* and moved to New York City to write. *Lincoln, and Other Poems*, followed in 1901, and other collections of poetry appeared until the final volume, *The Star of Araby*, 1937. This text appears in *The Gates of Paradise and Other Poems*, 1920.

For ST. MAGNUS see *No. 98*.

## 104. THE GOLDEN HERESY OF TRUTH.
George William Russell (1867–1935), Irish poet, signed his verse Æ. This text is from "On Behalf of Some Irishmen Not Followers of Tradition," which begins "They call us aliens." In his *Selected Poems*, 1935, it is grouped with "Poems, 1903–1920."

For VOM HIMMEL HOCH see *No. 42*.

## 105. TRUTH IS THE TRIAL OF ITSELF.
Ben Jonson (1573?–1637), English dramatist, friend of Shakespeare and Bacon, wrote *The Alchemist* and other plays, and the song, "Drink to Me Only with Thine Eyes." These stanzas are from his *The Touch-stone of Truth*, a book confuting "Papists," second impression, 1624.

For ROCHESTER see *No. 50*.

## 106. A NOBLE LIFE.
A. S. Isaacs. This hymn appeared in *Survey* magazine, January 3, 1914, and later in *Hymns of Brotherhood and Aspiration*, edited by Mabel Hay Barrows. We find no information about A. S. Isaacs.

LANCASTER, first called "St. Clement Danes" by the composer, Samuel Howard (1710–82), after the church where he was organist, is a setting of Psalm 1 in William Riley's *Parochial Harmony*, 1762. Howard was chorister in the Chapel Royal under William Croft (*see No. 51*), a pupil of Pepusch, and Doctor of Music, Cambridge, 1769. The harmonization is by Robert L. Sanders (*see No. 2*).

## 107. THE MAN OF LIFE UPRIGHT.
Thomas Campian (ca. 1566–1620) was a poet, musician, pioneer in English literary criticism, and a London physician. Forgotten for longer than

two centuries, his poems were republished in 1889 by A. H. Ballen, re-establishing him in the front rank of Elizabethan lyricists. This arrangement of one of his best-known poems alters the wording in our Stanzas 2 and 5 and omits the original Stanza 5.

CAMPIAN 2 follows Campian's own music in No. 2 of his *First Book of Airs*, ca. 1613.

**108. SINCE WHAT WE CHOOSE IS WHAT WE ARE.** William De Witt Hyde (1858–1917), Congregational minister and author, became president of Bowdoin College, Brunswick, Me. This stanza concludes his hymn, "Creation's Lord, we give thee thanks," No. 221 in this book. We print it separately for use as a short hymn or response.

For VOM HIMMEL HOCH *see No. 42.*

**109. WHAT ELSE IS WISDOM?** Euripides (480–406 B.C.) was one of the classical Greek tragedians. According to tradition he wrote ninety-two plays, but only eighteen survive. This text from *The Bacchae*, his last important play, is translated by Gilbert Murray (1866–1957), noted translator of Greek plays, a professor of Greek at Oxford, and a devoted worker for peace and the League of Nations. These lines are Nos. 877–881, omitting 878.

The four lines of GENEVA 51 were arranged from the eight-line setting of Psalm 51 in the Genevan Psalter, 1551, by Robert L. Sanders (*see No. 2*).

**110. BE YE LAMPS UNTO YOURSELVES.** Attributed to Gautama Buddha (fifth century B.C.). This, a most beloved Buddhist text, is from "Buddha's Farewell Address," which, like all texts attributed to the Buddha, was not committed to writing until centuries after his death. This passage, however, from the *Mahaparinibbana Suttanta* is believed to strike an authentic note. This translation resembles that of C. Rhys Davids from the Pali in *Sacred Books of the Buddhists*, Vol. III, Part 3, p. 128.

LUMINA is adapted by Kenneth Munson (*see No. 134*) from the plain-song setting of "*Splendor paternae gloriae*," in the *Sarum Antiphonal*, used in the liturgy of Salisbury Cathedral, England, before the Reformation.

**111. THEY CAST THEIR NETS IN GALILEE.** William Alexander Percy (1885–1942) was a Mississippi lawyer, a poet and outstanding citizen. Hodding Carter, in the *Reader's Digest*, August, 1952, wrote of him as "The Most Unforgettable Character I've Met." This hymn is from a poem in *Enzio's Kingdom and Other Poems*, 1924. Stanza 1 of the original is omitted here.

GEORGETOWN was composed for this text in 1941 by David McKinley Williams (1887– ), a native of Carnarvonshire, Wales, for twenty-seven years choirmaster of St. Bartholomew's, New York City. Organist and choirmaster of St. Peter's Church, Denver, Colo., at the age of thirteen, he headed the organ department at the Juilliard School in New York City, belonged to the music department of Union Theological Seminary, and the commission that produced *The Hymnal 1940*.

**112. HEART'S REMEMBERING** (PART I). Archibald MacLeish (1892– ), an American poet, soldier in World War I, lawyer, an editor of *Fortune*, Librarian of Congress, and winner of three Pulitzer prizes. MacLeish retired in 1962 after a dozen years as Boylston Professor of Rhetoric and Oratory at Harvard. Hymns 112 and 113 comprise a five-stanza lyric, part of his class poem at Yale graduation, 1915. Each of these groups of stanzas can stand by itself, though they may be used together, as before and after a reading or sermon.

For CROSS OF CHRIST *see No. 68.*

**113. HEART'S REMEMBERING** (PART II). Archibald MacLeish. *See No. 112.*

**114. PRAYER.** Louis Untermeyer (1885– ), American jewelry manufacturer, once vice-president of Untermeyer-Robbins Co., is far better known as an author. A poet, he is also noted for anthologies of modern British and American poetry. This prayer was included in his *Challenge*, 1914.

KEDRON first appears in *The United States' Sacred Harmony*, Boston, 1799, compiled by Amos Pilsbury of Charleston, S. C. Attributing it to his co-worker, the Rev. Elkanah Kelsay Dare (1782–1826), John Wyeth included the tune in *Repository of Sacred Music, Part Second*, 1813, thus transmitting to future generations of shape-note singers one of the most popular folk hymns.

**115. O STAR OF TRUTH.** Minot Judson Savage (1841–1918) was born of strictly orthodox Maine Congregationalists. After graduating from Bangor Theological Seminary, he served Congregational churches in California, Massachusetts, and Missouri. In 1872, having read Darwin and Spencer, he became Unitarian. After a brief ministry of Chicago's Third Unitarian Church, he had long pastorates at Boston's Unity Church and the Church of the Messiah (The Community Church), New York City. An early advocate of a religious interpretation of the doctrine of evolution, he wrote many books. In 1883 he published *Sacred Songs for Public Worship*, containing forty-two of his hymns; only a few survive in modern hymnbooks. This text is abridged and revised.

NYLAND, a Finnish folk melody from the village of Kuortane, became a Lutheran hymn tune in the appendix to the *Suomen Evankelis Luterilaisen Kirken Koraalikirja*, 1909. In the revised *Church Hymnary*, 1927, the tune was adapted to Anna Laetitia Waring's "In heavenly love abiding" by David Evans (1872–1948), professor at the University of Wales. Here its harmonization is simpler.

**116. PAST, PRESENT, FUTURE.** Frederick May Eliot (1890–1958), president of the American Unitarian Association from 1937 until his death, had served twenty years as minister of Unity Church of St. Paul, Minn. He wrote this hymn in 1916 for the centennial of the Harvard Divinity School, while assistant minister of the First Parish in Cambridge, Mass. The hymn appears in *Frederick May Eliot, an Anthology*, edited by Alfred M. Steirnotte, 1960.

The hymns from Addison's *Spectator* were set to music by John Sheeles in *The Skylark*, ca. 1720. LONDON, also known as "Addison's" or "Kettering," was his setting for "The spacious firmament on high" (*see No. 47*). Sheeles also published *Suites of Lessons for the Harpsicord or Spinnett*, ca. 1730.

**117. GOD IS IN HIS HOLY TEMPLE.** Anonymous. One line of this hymn is identical with an earlier hymn by Longfellow (*see No. 55*), suggesting that it is his, although in *Hymns of the Spirit*, 1864, it is cited as "anon."

STUTTGART was adapted for *Hymns Ancient and Modern*, 1861, from a tune composed or arranged by Christian Friedrich Witt (1660–1716), choirmaster at Altenburg, Germany, in his *Psalmodia Sacra*, 1715. The original text was "*Sollt es gleich bisweilen scheinen*."

**118. DEAR LORD AND FATHER OF MANKIND.** John Greenleaf Whittier. See No. 93. These are the concluding stanzas of "The Brewing of Soma," with a description of the East Indian drinking of intoxicating soma to commune with deity. Many Christians, he says, symbolically brew "the heathen soma still." Opening, "forgive our foolish ways," he sets forth a better and more natural way to converse with God.

LOBT GOTT, IHR CHRISTEN, first found in *Ein Christlicher Abentreien*, Leipzig, Germany, 1554, is by Nikolaus Herman (ca. 1480–1561), Meistersinger and friend of Luther's, who was cantor in Joachimstal, Bohemia. This version is the closing chorale in J. S. Bach's Cantata 151, "*Süsser Trost, mein Jesus kommt*," ca. 1740.

**119. DEAR LORD AND FATHER OF MANKIND.** See No. 118.

We provide a second tune, REST, by Frederick Charles Maker (1844–1927). The music reflects the mood of the text as sensed in 1887 by a Congregational organist who lived in Bristol, England. It was composed for the text and appeared in G. S. Barnett's *Congregational Hymnal*.

**120. O THOU GREAT FRIEND.** Theodore Parker (1810–60) was born in Lexington, Mass., grandson of Captain John Parker of the battle of Lexington, and died of consumption in Florence, Italy. He was a great American Unitarian preacher. After serving at the First Parish, West Roxbury, Mass., 1837–46, he became minister of the

Twenty-eighth Congregational Society, Boston, 1846–60. Inspired by Emerson's Transcendentalism and deeply mystical, he was considered heretical by most of his colleagues; nevertheless, he was widely popular. A social radical, an ardent Abolitionist, he wrote and published numerous treatises and a few poems. His South Boston sermon on "The Transient and the Permanent in Christianity," 1841, based religion and Christianity not on authority, but on the "self-authenticating" teachings of Jesus, a view prevailing later among Unitarians and Universalists. This text was a sonnet; by eliminating two lines, Longfellow and Johnson transformed it for their *Book of Hymns*, 1846.

For AINSWORTH 97 *see No. 52.*

**121. OUR FRIEND, OUR BROTHER, AND OUR LORD.** John Greenleaf Whittier. *See No. 93.* This text is one of several hymns made from "Our Master." In *Hymns of the Spirit*, 1937, it had five stanzas, beginning "O Love! O Life! our faith and sight."

LORD, FOR THY TENDER MERCIES' SAKE, commonly known as "Farrant," is adapted from the sixteenth-century anthem ascribed uncertainly to Richard Farrant (1530–81) or to John Hilton, the elder (died 1608), but probably by Christopher Tye (ca. 1500–72) or a contemporary of his.

**122. O LIGHT OF LIGHT.** Washington Gladden (1836–1918) was an American Congregational minister and author, a forthright preacher of the social gospel. A religious liberal, for thirty-two years he served the First Congregational Church, Columbus, Ohio. His most popular hymn was "O Master, let me walk with thee." This stanza is from "Behold a sower! from afar." *See No. 236.*

For ST. MAGNUS *see No. 98.*

**123. COME, MY WAY, MY TRUTH, MY LIFE.** George Herbert (1593–1633), English poet, a courtier under James I, took holy orders and in 1630 became rector of Bremerton in Wiltshire, England, where he died. His book of religious verse, *The Temple*, contained this hymn; his *Life*, was written by Izaak Walton.

For the Worcester Festival of 1911 Ralph Vaughan Williams (*see No. 78*) composed *Five Mystical Songs from George Herbert* for baritone, chorus, and orchestra. Two of these, including THE CALL, appear adapted to hymnody in the *Hymnal for Colleges and Schools*, 1956, edited by E. Harold Geer.

**124. SEND DOWN THY TRUTH.** Edward Rowland Sill (1841–87), professor of English literature at the University of California, wrote several books of poems. He wrote this hymn for Visitation Day, 1867, at Harvard Divinity School. It was published in *The Hermitage*. Although preparing for the Unitarian ministry, he never formally associated himself with any denomination. Today he is remembered for his poem, "The Fool's Prayer."

Aaron Williams (1731–76) published, and perhaps composed, ST. THOMAS. It was originally the second half of "Holborn" in his *Universal Psalmodist*, 1763. The abbreviated form soon appeared in collections, including the fifth edition of his own. Probably a native of London, England, Williams was a music teacher, engraver, and clerk at the Scottish Church in London Wall.

**125. COMMUNION HYMN.** Marion Franklin Ham (1867–1956) joined the Unitarian church in Chattanooga, Tenn., where he became a lay reader; he was ordained without a college education in 1898 as its minister. He later served Unitarian churches in Dallas, Tex., and Reading and Waverley, Mass. He published *The Golden Shuttle*, 1896, and several other books of poetry, including *Songs of a Lifetime*, 1953. This communion hymn, written in 1912, was in *The New Hymn and Tune Book*, 1914.

PUER NOBIS NASCITUR is a fifteenth-century carol adapted to "*Geborn ist Gottes Söhnelein*" in *Musae Sionae*, VI, 1609. That collection of over 1,200 choral works for Protestant use, was made by Michael Praetorius (1571–1621), choirmaster and private secretary to the Duke of Brunswick at Wolfenbüttel, Germany.

**126. NEARER, MY GOD, TO THEE.** Sarah Flower Adams (1805–48), an English Unitarian, wrote this beloved hymn (based on Gen. 28:10–22) for the Rev. W. H. Fox's *Hymns and*

*Anthems,* 1841. Fox was minister of the Unitarian South Place Chapel, London. This hymn is sung in translations throughout Christendom. Unfortunately, the deeply devotional character of the verse easily degenerates into mawkish sentimentality when sung draggingly to Mason's "Bethany."

Lowell Mason composed BETHANY for this text in 1856; it was published in the Andover *Sabbath Hymn and Tune Book,* 1859. The tune shares the harmonic scheme known for centuries as the *passamezzo moderno.* It resembles melodically some earlier tunes like a Scottish air, "The Auld House," or "Oft in the stilly night." Mason, himself, said that "one night" the melody came to him "through the stillness in the house." A native of Medfield, Mass., Lowell Mason (1792–1872) was the leading American church musician of his generation. With the active support of Mayor Samuel Eliot, he founded the Boston Academy of Music in 1832 and introduced music into the public schools in 1838.

**127. SOVEREIGN AND TRANSFORMING GRACE.** Frederic Henry Hedge (1805–90) was ready for Harvard College at twelve years of age, but he was sent to Germany for five years with George Bancroft, later a noted historian. Graduating from Harvard in 1825, he entered the Divinity School. He wrote this hymn for a friend's ordination in 1829, the year he was ordained minister of the First Congregational Parish, West Cambridge (now Arlington), Mass. He later served Unitarian parishes in Bangor, Me.; Providence, R. I.; and Brookline, Mass. He pioneered in acquainting this country with German literature and metaphysics. He ended his career as professor of German at Harvard.

Benjamin Carr performed his arrangement of SPANISH HYMN for the Musical Fund Society of Philadelphia, Pa., in 1824 and published it two years later, having copyrighted piano variations on the melody. Carr (1768–1831) was the first publisher of American compositions. It was reharmonized thus for this book.

**128. O THOU WHOSE POWER.** Anicius Manlius Severinus Boëthius (480?–524?), Roman philosopher and friend of Theodoric, Ostrogoth ruler of Rome, was made consul in 510. Later, accused of conspiracy, he was executed. *The Consolation of Philosophy* was written while he awaited his fate in prison at Pavia; this text, translated in the *Rambler,* April 10, 1750, by the English essayist, Samuel Johnson (1709–84), is from Book III, 9, of that work, and begins "*O qui perpetua mundum ratione.*"

ADORO TE DEVOTE was adapted for this book from the version of the plain-song melody used by the monks of Solesmes, France.

**129. HARD IS NOW THE CONSTANT WOE.** G. W. Fox is known only through Stanton Coit's *Social Worship,* 1913, Vol. 2, where this text appears as Hymn 73, titled "Hope."

HOPE was set to William Cowper's "Hark, my soul, it is the Lord" by John Antes (1740–1811). A leading Moravian composer, Antes was born in Frederick, Pa., became a missionary in Egypt, and died in England.

**130. MYSTERIOUS PRESENCE, SOURCE OF ALL.** Seth Curtis Beach (1837–1932) was a New England Unitarian minister. He wrote this hymn for Visitation Day at Harvard Divinity School in 1866, his graduation year.

*See No. 99* for WAREHAM.

**131. WE GIVE THEE BUT THINE OWN.** William Walsham How. *See No. 75.* This is Stanza 1 of a hymn by "the poor man's bishop."

SWABIA was set to Neander's "*Ach wachet! wachet auf!*" by Johann Martin Spiess in *Geistliche Liebes-Posaune,* Part II of his *David's Harpffen-Spiel,* 1745. Spiess (1696–1772) was cathedral organist in Bern, Switzerland. The original six-line melody (6.7.6.7.7.7.) was adapted for short meter in 1847 by William Henry Havergal (1793–1870), honorary canon of Worcester Cathedral, England.

**132. MERCY, PITY, PEACE, AND LOVE.** William Blake (1757–1827), mystic English poet and painter, called this "The Divine Image" in *Songs of Innocence,* 1789. This text first appeared in a hymnbook in *The English Hymnal,* 1906. We omit the final stanza.

For a note on LOBT GOTT, IHR CHRISTEN see *No. 118.*

133. THE UNIVERSAL PRAYER. Alexander Pope (1688–1744) was an English poet and satirist, the outstanding literary figure of his time. A Roman Catholic, his "Essay on Man" was alleged to be an apology for freethinkers; "The Universal Prayer," written as a conclusion to the essay to vindicate his orthodoxy, was in the spirit of the contemporary Deism, which helped shape both American liberties and Unitarian Universalism. Based upon the Lord's Prayer, the piece equates the Christian God with Jove, honors devout pagans along with Christians, and expresses "natural," rather than revealed, religion. Our hymn uses five of the poem's thirteen stanzas.

TALLIS' ORDINAL was originally a setting of the ordination hymn, "*Veni Creator*," and appeared in Archbishop Parker's Psalter, ca. 1561, as did TALLIS' CANON (*see No. 85*).

134. GIVE ME YOUR WHOLE HEART. The Bhagavad-Gita (500–200 B.C.) is the greatest Hindu classic, part of the *Mahabharata*. The title means "The Song of God." This text is from a translation by Swami Prabhavananda, senior minister of the Vedanta Society of Southern California, and Christopher Isherwood (1904– ), English-born novelist, now American, a student of the Hindu philosophy.

COLE was composed for this book by one of its compilers, Kenneth Munson (1916– ). He was born in Galesburg, Ill., and educated at Knox College. At the Eastman School of Music he wrote a Ph.D. dissertation on "The *Musicalische Seelenlust* of Tobias Michael," 1953. He is chairman of the department of music, St. Lawrence University, university organist, and organist-choirmaster of the First Presbyterian Church, Ogdensburg, N. Y.

135. ALL THINGS ARE DOUBLY FAIR. Théophile Gautier (1811–72) was a French poet, critic, and novelist. This poem, "Art," has fourteen stanzas; our cento is Stanzas 1, 14, 12, 13. The translation is by George Santayana (1863–1952), Spanish-born American philosopher, poet, novelist, and Harvard professor.

ART was composed for this book by one of its compilers, Henry Leland

Clarke (1907– ). A native of Dover, N. H., he studied music with Ruth Olive Roberts in Saco, Me., where his father, Rev. Ward R. Clarke, was Unitarian minister thirty-one years. He was educated at Harvard, studied composition with Nadia Boulanger, Gustav Holst, and Otto Luening, and taught at Bennington College, Westminster Choir College, Vassar College, and the University of California at Los Angeles. Associate professor of music at the University of Washington, he has served as music chairman and board member of the First Unitarian Church of Los Angeles, and the University Unitarian Church, Seattle.

136. TRULY THE LIGHT IS SWEET. Josephine Preston Peabody (1874–1922; Mrs. L. S. Marks), was an American dramatist and poet. This text is from "An Ode on the Portion of Labor," in *The Singing House*, 1911.

GANADOR was composed for this book by Robert L. Sanders (*See No. 2*).

137. I LOVE ALL BEAUTEOUS THINGS. Robert Bridges (1844–1930), an English physician, at the age of thirty-eight gave up his medical practice for literature. The *Yattendon Hymnal*, issued in installments and completed in 1899, is "easily the most distinguished of individual pioneer contributions to modern hymnody." He was appointed poet laureate in 1913. Among his dramas and poetry, *The Testament of Beauty*, 1929, stands out. This text, written in 1890, is in *Poetical Works of Robert Bridges*, 1936.

PONT NEUF was composed for this book by one of its compilers, Robert L. Sanders (*see No. 2*).

138. OURS BE THE POEMS OF ALL TONGUES. Kenneth L. Patton. *See No. 28*. This appears as a response in *Man Is the Meaning*, 1956.

*See No. 85 for* TALLIS' CANON.

139. WE SING THE RAPTURE. George Meredith. *See No. 8*. This text is arranged by Kenneth L. Patton (*see No. 28*) from "The Day of the Daughter of Hades," a poem about the daughter of Persephone and Pluto in Meredith's *Poems and Lyrics of the Joy of Earth*, 1883.

For HAMILTON *see No. 57*.

140. THE POET. Edwin Markham. *See No. 103.* This hymn is a cento from two early poems. Stanza 1 is from "The Poet," in *The Man with the Hoe, and Other Poems;* the others are from "Poet-Lore," in *Lincoln, and Other Poems.*

O SALUTARIS, a melody attributed to Abbé Duguet, ca. 1767, came into English usage in *The English Hymnal,* 1906.

141. SING NOTES OF LOVE. Christina Georgina Rossetti (1830–94), an English poet, was known for short, intense lyrics, like this. She was the daughter of the exiled Italian patriot and writer, Gabriele Rossetti. Miss Rossetti's two brothers also were distinguished men of letters, one being Dante Gabriel Rossetti, poet and painter. This hymn is the last three stanzas of "What Good Shall My Life Do to Me?"

BOHEMIA is the setting for *"O Mensch sieh, wie hie auf Erdreich"* in the Bohemian Brethren's *Kirchengeseng darinnen die Heubtartickel des christlichen Glaubens gefasset,* 1566.

142. IMMORTAL LOVE. John Greenleaf Whittier. *See No. 93.* This hymn consists of stanzas from "Our Master," in *Tent on the Beach and Other Poems,* 1867. When someone said, "But you, Sir, could never have been a Puritan and a Calvinist," the Quaker poet replied, "Nay, thee is right! the world is much too beautiful, and God much too good. I never was of that mind."

For DUNDEE see *No. 34.*

143. THE CREST AND CROWNING OF ALL GOOD. Edwin Markham. *See No. 103.* This text is in *The Man with the Hoe, and Other Poems.* Here, as in other hymnbooks, the last line of each stanza is abridged to fit the tune.

WER DA WONET is an adapted version in the St. Gall *Gesangbuch* of 1863. The original melody is a setting of Psalm 91 in *Ein New Gesangbüchlin,* Leipzig, 1537, compiled by Michael Vehe, regent of the Dominican house of studies at Heidelberg, Germany. The harmonization is by Robert L. Sanders (*see No. 2*).

144. O BROTHER MAN. John Greenleaf Whittier. *See No. 93.* These are the three final stanzas of "Worship." He was a friend of William Lloyd Garrison, and second only to James Russell Lowell as a poet of abolitionism. Union soldiers reportedly recited his "The Slave Mother's Lament" and "The Hunters of Men" by their camp-fires.

See *No. 55* for INTERCESSOR.

145. ONE WORLD. Vincent B. Silliman. *See No. 14.* This was written for the 1947 fall conference of the American Unitarian Association.

SCHMÜCKE DICH by Johann Crüger (*see No. 19*) appeared in *Geistliche kirchen Melodien,* 1649.

146. SPIRIT OF TRUTH, OF LIFE, OF POWER. Horace Westwood (1884–1956), born in Yorkshire, was a Methodist preacher in Great Britain and America before becoming a Unitarian minister in 1910. He served Unitarian churches in Toledo and Youngstown, Ohio; Winnipeg, Man.; and Berkeley, Calif.; as well as being mission preacher for the Unitarian Laymen's League. He wrote several books, including *Some Hymns and Verses.*

HAMBURG was composed by Lowell Mason (*see No. 126*) in Savannah, Ga., in 1824 and published in the third edition of the *Boston Handel and Haydn Society Collection of Church Music.*

147. THIS IS THE CHARGE I KEEP. Leslie Pinckney Hill (1880–1959), a poet, Virginia-born, and a Harvard graduate, taught at Tuskegee Institute, and was principal of the Cheyney Training School for Teachers, Pa. His magnum opus was a five-act play in blank verse, *Toussaint L'Ouverture—a Dramatic History,* based on the life of the great Haitian liberator.

According to Wyeth's *Sacred Repository,* Part II, Harrisburg, Pa., 1813, ROCKBRIDGE (also "Forest") is by "A. Chapin." No doubt, this is Amzi Chapin, a singing-master long active in Kentucky around 1800. The harmonization is by Robert L. Sanders (*see No. 2*).

148. MAN'S COMRADESHIP. Florence Kiper Frank (1886–    ), an

American poet, wrote *Three Plays for a Children's Theater*, 1926, and the sonnet, "The Jew to Jesus." The widow of Professor Jerome Frank of the Yale Law School, she lives in New Haven. This hymn, here slightly altered, appeared first in *Social Hymns of Brotherhood and Aspiration*, 1914.

LISLE is in the second *Brethren Hymnal* of the German Baptist Brethren, or "Dunkers," published in Elgin, Ill., 1901. The harmonization is by Robert L. Sanders (*see No. 2*).

149. MY COUNTRY IS THE WORLD. Robert Whitaker (1863–1944), an English-born American Baptist minister, was teacher, editor, missionary, evangelist, and field secretary for the American Civil Liberties Union. His books include collections of poetry.

For TRINITY see *No. 26*.

150. LET NOT YOUNG SOULS BE SMOTHERED OUT. Vachel Lindsay (1879–1931) was an American whose poetry is noted for its vivid imagery and dramatic auditory effects; he read it to audiences over the country. Among his best-known poems are "General William Booth Enters into Heaven," "The Congo," and "Abraham Lincoln Walks at Midnight." "Lindsay was a striking personality and lived an adventurous life, during the first years of his career lecturing on temperance and art in the winter and in the summer vagabonding about the country, frequently trading his poems for food and shelter."— William Rose Benét.

For CONGLETON see *No. 69*.

151. MAN LIVES NOT FOR HIM- SELF ALONE. Henry Cary Shuttleworth (1850–1900) was a Church of England clergyman and professor of pastoral and liturgical theology at King's College, London. Our text is Stanza 3 of his hymn beginning, "Father of men, in whom are one." It appeared as a response in *The Beacon Song and Service Book*, 1935.

BETRACHT'N WIR HEUT is from the songbook of the Bohemian Brethren, *Ein Gesangbuch der Brüder inn Behemen un Merherin, Die man auss hass und neyd Pickharden, Waldenses, 2c! nennt* (Nürnberg, 1544). It was har- monized by Henry Leland Clarke (*see No. 135*) for this text.

152. FOR MERCY, COURAGE, KINDNESS, MIRTH. Laurence Binyon. See *No. 153*. This poem is in *The Secret*, 1920.

LYNE is a setting of "Let us, with a gladsome mind" in *Hymns ... Used at the Magdalen Chapel*, ca. 1760.

153. WOE UNTO HIM. Laurence Binyon (1869–1943), English poet and historian, was in charge of oriental prints and drawings at the British Museum, 1913–32. Author of books on Japanese, Chinese, and East Indian art, and a translator of Dante, he edited *The Golden Treasury of Modern Lyrics*, a continuation of Palgrave's *Golden Treasury*. This poem, written in 1913, is in his *Collected Poems*, 1932.

BINYON was composed for this book by Robert L. Sanders (*see No. 2*).

154. HERESY INDEED. Sara Henderson Hay (1906–  ; Mrs. Nikolai Lopatnikoff) is an American poet. This text is from a poem of this title in *This, My Letter*, 1939. Miss Hay graciously allows us to use the first four lines of each of three six-line stanzas.

WINDHAM by Daniel Read (1757–1836), was published in his *American Singing Book*, New Haven, Conn., 1785. A native of Rehoboth, Mass., Read became a New Haven comb manufacturer, singing teacher, and publisher. It was harmonized thus for this book.

155. KNIGHT WITHOUT A SWORD. Jan Struther. See *No. 29*. Based on Acts 7, the story of the first Christian martyr, Stephen, this hymn was written for *Songs of Praise, Enlarged*, 1931.

For SALVATION see *No. 53*.

156. THE COMPASS. John Hall Wheelock. See *No. 69*. This hymn is part of a poem of this title, from the *Virginia Quarterly Review*, 1956.

Johann Hermann Schein (1586–1630), a predecessor of Bach as cantor of St. Thomas's School, Leipzig, Germany, composed MACH'S MIT MIR, GOTT and issued it in 1628 as a memorial tribute. This version is No. 44 of Bach's 371 chorale harmonizations.

**157. THE LAW OF LOVE.** Richard Chenevix Trench (1807–86), Dublin-born author and churchman, graduate of Cambridge, student of Spanish literature, became professor of divinity in King's College, dean of Westminster, and then Archbishop of Dublin in 1864. He wrote prolifically on history, literature, philology, the Bible, and theology. The poem from which this hymn, based on II Kings 4:1–7, is taken begins: "*Pour forth the oil—pour boldly forth;/It will not fail, until/Thou failest vessels to provide/ Which it may largely fill.*" Line 2 of Stanza 3 originally read, "That blessing from above."

For SONG 67 *see No. 73.*

**158. SERENE WILL BE OUR DAYS.** William Wordsworth (1770–1850) was an English poet laureate. This quatrain is from "Ode to Duty."

Appearing anonymously in the *Essay on the Church Plain Chant*, 1782, MELCOMBE later was acknowledged as the work of Samuel Webbe, as in his own *Collection of Motetts*, 1792. Webbe (1740–1816), a Londoner, won twenty-six prize medals from the Catch Club, whose secretary he was from 1784. The original Glee Club opened every meeting with his *Glorious Apollo.* He was chapel organist of the Portuguese and the Sardinian embassies.

**159. PRAYER FOR THIS HOUSE.** Louis Untermeyer. *See No. 114.* This poem is from *This Singing World*, 1923.

OLDBRIDGE, composed in 1903 and published in *The English Hymnal*, 1906, is by Robert N. Quaile (1867– ), a Methodist minister's son, a businessman in Mallow, Ireland.

**160. SHALOM HAVAYREEM.** The Hebrew words mean "Hail, comrades!" or "Peace, friends," and are a greeting or farewell. This song became popular in the colonies in Palestine after World War I.

SHALOM, a four-voice round, is from southeastern Europe, where Jewish and non-Jewish folk songs are practically identical. The original mode was Dorian.

**161. ALL WITHIN FOUR SEAS.** Confucius (551–479 B.C.) was the great Chinese sage whose humanism has dominated Chinese thought and life. This text is from James Legge's translation, in *The Texts of Confucianism; Sacred Books of the East*, Volume III.

FOUR SEAS, abridged for this text, is from "Moab," published in *Llyfr Tonau Cynulleidfaol*, 1870. Composed by Ieuan Gwyllt (*see No. 39*), "Moab" was acclaimed by Sir Henry Hadow as one of the world's greatest tunes.

**162. LOVE CAN TELL.** Robert Bridges. *See No. 137.* This text is arranged from "My Delight and Thy Delight" in *Poetical Works of Robert Bridges*, 1936.

For LYNE *see No. 152.*

**163. CAN I SEE ANOTHER'S WOE?** William Blake. *See No. 132.* In *Songs of Innocence* this is "On Another's Sorrow," with nine stanzas. Henry Hadow, in his *Oxford Treasury of English Literature*, commenting on Mozart, Burns, and Blake, says: "Blake exercised at the time the least influence. He was flouted as a madman . . . ; not until our own day has he come to his reputation and been acknowledged at his true value. His exquisite, sensitive genius is too delicate for the hand of cynicism; you must take it and be enriched or leave it and be impoverished."

Christian Friedrich Witt (1660–1716), choirmaster at Altenburg, Germany, either composed or arranged ACH, WANN WERD ICH.

**164. THE NIGHT HAS A THOUSAND EYES.** Francis William Bourdillon (1852–1921) was an English poet. This poem is in *Ailes d'Alouette* (Wings of Skylark), 1890.

BOURDILLON, based on "Song 46" by Orlando Gibbons (*see No. 73*), is adapted to this text by Robert L. Sanders (*see No. 2*).

**165. "REMEMBER ME," THE MASTER SAID.** Nathaniel Langdon Frothingham (1793–1870), a Unitarian, was for many years minister of the First Church in Boston. He published this communion hymn in *Metrical Pieces, Translated and Original*, 1855.

For DUNDEE *see No. 34.*

**166. FOR NO SECT ELECT.** Algernon Charles Swinburne (1837–1909), a controversial English poet, a "pagan," won early acclaim for *Atalanta in Calydon*, 1865. These stanzas, a hymn in Stanton Coit's *Social Worship*, 1913, Vol. II, are from Section III, "Beyond Church," of "Christmas Antiphones," in the poet's *Songs before Sunrise*, 1871.

MEADOW COVE consists of phrases from the latter two-thirds of the tune for Psalm 47 in the Genevan Psalter, 1551, arranged by Robert L. Sanders (*see No. 2*).

**167. ETERNAL SPIRIT OF THE CHAINLESS MIND.** George Gordon, Lord Byron (1788–1824) was an English poet and rebel against convention. This lyric is from "Sonnet on Chillon," the castle where François de Bonnivard (1493–1570) was held in the dungeon for six years as a political prisoner.

SONG 24 by Orlando Gibbons was in *Hymnes and Songs of the Church*, 1623 (*see No. 73*).

**168. WHEN A DEED IS DONE FOR FREEDOM.** James Russell Lowell (1819–91), a Unitarian, was a literary critic, poet, humorist, professor at Harvard, and first editor of the *Atlantic Monthly*. He was U. S. minister to Spain, 1877–80, and to England, 1880–85. His *Complete Poems* appeared in 1895. This contains Stanzas 1, 18, and 4 of *The Present Crisis*, a poem protesting the American war with Mexico.

AN DIE FREUDE is one of several settings of Schiller's *Hymn to Joy*, 1785, collected as *Schillers Ode an die Freude, in Musik gesetzt von Anonymus, Christmann, Müller, etc. etc.*, Berlin, 1799. This melody, thus, antedates Beethoven's in the *Ninth Symphony*, 1817–23 (*see No. 11*).

**169. THROUGH ALL THE LONG DARK NIGHT.** Gerald Massey (1828–1907) was a radical English poet, a member of the Christian Socialist Party, whose vigorous statements of aspiration for freedom and justice were considered obsolete and extreme toward the end of the nineteenth century, but which now are again seen as relevant. George Eliot based some features of *Felix Holt, the Radical*, 1866, on Massey's career. This hymn is part of his poem, "Today and Tomorrow."

Considerably altered since appearing in *As Hymnodus Sacer*, Leipzig, Germany, 1625, ACH GOTT UND HERR appears here as in No. 40 of J. S. Bach's 371 chorale harmonizations.

**170. FREEDOM IS THE FINEST GOLD.** Thomas Simonsson (died, 1443), Swedish prelate and poet of unknown origin, studied at the universities of Paris and Leipzig, and became bishop of Strängnäs in 1430. Following the suppression of a popular insurrection against King Erik of Pomerania, oppressor of the Swedes, Thomas wrote "The Song of Liberty," from which this text comes. A high point of Swedish medieval literature, the poem turns from contemporary conditions and, in the words of Professor Alrik Gustafson of the University of Minnesota, becomes ". . . a hymn which in the simple majesty of its utterance lifts the reader above the immediate political circumstances . . . singing finally the praise of freedom as the fundamental condition of the good life in all times and all climes." During World War II, three stanzas of the poem, including our first, became a popular patriotic song which was considered for adoption as the national anthem. Elias Gordon is known to us only as a translator into English of Scandinavian poetry.

ACH, WAS SOLL ICH, set to this text by Irving Lowens for *We Sing of Life*, 1955, is from *Suscitabulum musicum*, 1661, fifth part of *Himmlisches Lustgärtlein*, compiled by Johann Flitner (1618–78), cantor at Grimmen. The tune is a modification of the secular "*Silvius ging durch die Matten*," published by Enoch Gläser, Altdorf, Germany, 1653.

**171. LET ALL WHO LIVE IN FREEDOM.** Kenneth L. Patton. See *No. 28*. This response is in *Man Is the Meaning*, 1956.

For MELCOMBE see *No. 158*.

**172. THE PEOPLE'S LIBERTY.** Samuel Johnson (1822–82), an American minister, Unitarian in belief and closely associated with Unitarian churches, preferred not to be identified with any denomination. From 1853 to 1870 he served the Independent Church of Lynn, Mass., which he organized. With Samuel Longfellow (*see No. 43*) he compiled *A Book of Hymns*, 1846, which with the enlarged revision of 1848 makes "a notable contribution to American hymnody in its freshness of outlook and its inclusion of hymns by hitherto unrecognized writers, notably John Greenleaf Whittier." This hymn was one of seven of his in *Hymns of the Spirit*, 1864, also edited by him and Longfellow.

VIENNA was composed by Justin Heinrich Knecht (1752–1817), music director at Biberach, Württemberg, Germany, and director of opera and court concerts at Stuttgart. It was first published in *Vollständige Sammlung . . . für das neue wirtembergische Landgesangbuch*, Stuttgart, 1799, with the text, "*Ohne Rast und unverweilt.*"

173. TRUE FREEDOM. James Russell Lowell. *See No. 168*. This is Stanzas 1, 3, and 4 of his anti-slavery "Stanzas on Freedom," in *Poems*, 1844. This form was used first in a hymnbook in *A Book of Hymns*, 1846, edited by Samuel Longfellow and Samuel Johnson.

SALZBURG by Jacob Hintze (1622–1702), court musician to the Elector of Brandenburg at Berlin, Germany, appears with the text, "*Alle Menschen müssen sterben*" in *Praxis Pietatis Melica*, 1678, one of the editions edited by Hintze after Johann Crüger's death in 1662 (*see No. 19*). This version is No. 153 of J. S. Bach's 371 chorale harmonizations.

174. SEEK NOT AFAR FOR BEAUTY. Minot Judson Savage. *See No. 115*. Stanzas 2 and 3 have been revised by the editors.

For CLIFF TOWN *see No. 83*.

175. ALL ARE ARCHITECTS. Henry Wadsworth Longfellow (1807–82), popular American poet, was commemorated by a marble bust in Westminster Abbey. Professor of Modern Languages, at Bowdoin College and Harvard, he resigned in 1854 to write. In hymn writing he was outshone by his brother, Samuel (*see No. 43*), of whom he said, "I am the brother of a poet." This hymn is Stanzas 1, 3, and 8 of "The Builders."

HASIDIM takes its name from an eighteenth-century Jewish movement in eastern Europe which expressed religious feeling through joy, song, and dancing. The arrangement by Harry Coopersmith in *The Songs We Sing*, 1950, was adapted to this text by Irving Lowens in *We Sing of Life*, 1955. This harmonization is by Henry Leland Clarke (*see No. 135*).

176. ONLY HE EARNS LIFE AND FREEDOM. Johann Wolfgang von Goethe. *See No. 63*. This text is from Act V of *Faust*, 1831, and is believed to be from a translation by F. Melian Stawell and Nora Purtscher von Wydenbruch, which we have not been able to locate. A translation with many similarities is in F. M. Stawell and G. Lowes Dickinson, *Goethe and Faust*, 1929.

For LES COMMANDEMENS *see No. 97*.

177. O SOMETIMES GLEAMS UPON OUR SIGHT. John Greenleaf Whittier. *See No. 93*. This cento from "The Chapel of the Hermits," was made by Samuel Longfellow and Samuel Johnson for *Hymns of the Spirit*, 1864 (*see No. 43*).

HAMBURG is by Lowell Mason. For the tune *see No. 146*; for the composer, *No. 126*.

178. NOW GIVE HEART'S ONWARD HABIT BRAVE INTENT. John Holmes. *See No. 9*. This hymn is from "Address to the Living," from the volume of that name, 1937.

For FARLEY CASTLE *see No. 3*.

179. THE PEOPLE'S PEACE. John Holmes. *See No. 9*. This hymn is an arrangement, somewhat abbreviated, of a poem in *Map of My Country*, 1943.

For SURSUM CORDA *see No. 71*.

180. EARTH IS ENOUGH. Edwin Markham. *See No. 103*. This text is an arrangement of twelve lines of the poem beginning: "*We men of Earth have here the stuff/Of Paradise—we have enough!*" It was first published in a book in *The Shoes of Happiness and Other Poems*, 1916.

For FILLMORE *see No. 8*.

181. WHEN WE HAVE ENDED SEARCHING. Kenneth L. Patton. *See No. 28*. This text is from *Man Is the Meaning*, 1956.

ES FLOG EIN KLEINS WALDVÖGLEIN is the German folk song *"Der Ritter zum Besuch,"* first found in a manuscript tablature book from Memmingen of the early seventeenth century.

182. THE AMPLITUDE OF SPACE. John Hall Wheelock. *See No. 69.* This hymn is an adaptation of the poem, "Chant," 1911. The original version is in *Poems Old and New,* 1956.

WHEELOCK was composed for this book by Robert L. Sanders (*see No. 2*).

183. LEISURE. William Henry Davies (1871–1940) was a Welsh-born English poet of simple lyrics on nature, traditional in form. A hobo and peddler by choice as a young man, he shipped on cattle boats many times to America. After losing a foot under a Canadian freight train in 1901, he turned poet. *Collected Poems* appeared in 1916, 1923, and 1929; his *Autobiography of a Super-Tramp,* 1907, was called "splendid, rough, simple, direct prose."

Closely resembling certain English ballad tunes and Gaelic melodies, DEVOTION is anonymous in Allen D. Carden's *Missouri Harmony,* Cincinnati, Ohio, 1820. It was later ascribed to Americk Hall (1785–1827), a Massachusetts farmer who manufactured straw bonnets, kept a hotel, and taught a singing school. The harmonization is by Henry Leland Clarke (*see No. 135*).

184. EVERY NIGHT AND EVERY MORN. William Blake. *See No. 132.* This text is from "Auguries of Innocence."

For THE CALL *see No. 123.*

185. HAPPY THE MAN. Quintus Horatius Flaccus Horace (65–8 B.C.) was a Latin poet and satirist who professed adherence to the doctrines of Epicurus. John Dryden (1631–1700), the English poet, dramatist, and critic, paraphrased Horace's odes in Pindaric verse. Dryden, England's poet laureate, 1670–88, aroused bitter feelings by converting to Roman Catholicism in 1687. These lines were modified by Kenneth L. Patton (*see No. 28*) from Dryden's version of Ode 29, Book 3, by Horace.

ALDWINKLE is an adaptation by Henry Leland Clarke (*see No. 135*) from the *Vollständiges Gesang-Buch,* Lüneburg, Germany, 1665, where it is a setting of *"Wie gross ist dieser Freudentag,"* composed by Wolfgang Wessnitzer, seventeenth-century court organist at Celle.

186. WAITING. John Burroughs (1837–1921) was an American naturalist, author of many books. This poem, written in 1862, first appeared in the *Knickerbocker Magazine,* March, 1863. Here are four of the original six stanzas.

For TALLIS' CANON *see No. 85.*

187. NOW AND HERE. John Greenleaf Whittier. *See No. 93.* This is a cento from "My Psalm."

For ST. MAGNUS *see No. 98.*

188. THE LARGER FAITH. Frederick Lucian Hosmer. *See No. 50.* This hymn was published in *The Christian Register* March 22, 1879, and in *The Thought of God,* First Series, 1885.

Melchior Vulpius (ca. 1560–1615), cantor at Weimar, Germany, composer of chorale melodies and more elaborate choral works, published his tune CHRISTUS DER IST MEIN LEBEN in *Schön geistlich Gesangbuch,* 1609. The original meter, 7.6.7.6., is used here for Gannett's "To cloisters of the spirit" (*see No. 260*). It is here adapted to common meter.

189. THE SON OF MAN. Frank Mason North (1850–1935) directed the city missionary work of the Methodist church in New York City. This poem was published first in 1903 in *The Christian City,* a magazine which he edited. We use Stanzas 1, 2, and 5 of the original six. North was president of the Federal Council of Churches of Christ in America, 1916–20.

MEIN' SEEL', O GOTT by Bartholomäus Gesius (ca. 1555–1613), Lutheran cantor at Frankfurt-an-der-Oder, Germany, first appeared in *Enchiridion etlicher deutschen und lateinischen Gesengen,* 1603.

190. THESE THINGS SHALL BE. John Addington Symonds (1840–93) was an English critic and literary historian, student of Dante and of the Greek poets, author of a seven-volume

*History of the Italian Renaissance*, 1875–86. This hymn, from his *New and Old*, 1880, is part of the poem, "A Vista."

For TRURO see No. 54.

191. WONDERS STILL THE WORLD SHALL WITNESS. Jacob Trapp (1899–    ), a Unitarian Universalist minister, has served churches in Salt Lake City, Utah; Denver, Colo.; and since 1945, Summit, N. J. He is author of *The Word to Jesus*, 1950, and editor of "Thoughts for Meditation" in the *Unitarian Universalist Register-Leader*. He wrote this hymn in 1932, after a peace rally in Salt Lake City. It was included, with revisions, in *Hymns of the Spirit*, 1937.

IN BABILONE is from *Oude en nieuwe Hollantse Boernlities en Contradanseu* (Old and New Dutch Songs and Country Dances), ca. 1710. This harmonization, by Julius Röntgen (1855–1932), Dutch composer and conductor, is in *The English Hymnal*, 1906.

192. HAIL THE GLORIOUS GOLDEN CITY. Felix Adler (1851–1933), German-born author, the son of a rabbi, became professor of social and political ethics at Columbia University. In 1876, he founded the New York Society for Ethical Culture and was thereafter the central figure in the American Ethical Culture movement. This text has been slightly revised by J. Hutton Hynd, Ethical Leader.

Rowland Hugh Prichard (1811–87) composed HYFRYDOL about 1830, but it was first published by Griffith Roberts in *Haleliwiah Drachefn*, 1855. In the meantime, Prichard had published other original tunes in *Cyfaill y Cantorion*, 1844. When nearly seventy he left his birthplace at Graienyn, near Bala, Wales, to become a loom-tender's assistant for the Welsh Flannel Manufacturing Company in Holywell.

193. CHILDREN OF TOMORROW. Zona Gale (1874–1938), American novelist and short-story writer, spent most of her life in Portage, Wis. She was awarded the Pulitzer prize in 1921 for *Miss Lulu Bett*.

For VOM HIMMEL HOCH see No. 42.

194. HEAR, HEAR, O YE NATIONS. Frederick Lucian Hosmer.

See No. 50. This hymn, written in 1909, was in *Unity Hymns and Chorals*, 1911. The first half of Stanza 3 is revised here.

MILTON is from *Rural Harmony*, Boston, 1793, a collection of original tunes by Jacob Kimball (1761–1826), of Topsfield, Mass. Kimball was a graduate of Harvard College, taught music, and composed "fuguing pieces" in the style of William Billings. This harmonization was made by Irving Lowens (*see* No. 211) for *We Sing of Life*, 1955.

195. THE PARLIAMENT OF MAN. Alfred, Lord Tennyson. *See* No. 65. This text is an arrangement from "Locksley Hall."

For HYMN TO JOY see No. 11.

196. TURN BACK, O MAN. Clifford Bax (1886–    ), British dramatist and poet, once an art student, is the younger brother of the composer, Arnold Bax. Bax wrote this hymn for the English composer, Gustav Holst, who composed a motet on the tune, *Old 124th*, the tune generally associated with this text. In 1945 Bax stated that he was a Buddhist.

OLD 124TH is the tune for Psalm 124 in the Genevan Psalter, 1551, and in the English and Scottish Psalters.

197. THE WORLD–TREE. Ridgely Torrence. *See* No. 2. This poem, published first in the posthumous collection of his poetry, 1952, is based on the Norse myth of *Ygdrasil*, the world-tree.

YGDRASIL was composed for this book by Henry Leland Clarke (*see* No. 135).

198. YEARS ARE COMING. Adin Ballou (1803–90) was the founder of the Hopedale Community, 1842, an experiment in "practical Christianity." At nineteen he was minister in the Christian Connexion sect, but later entered the Universalist ministry, serving churches in New York City, and Milford, Mendon, and Hopedale, Mass. In 1849 was issued *The Hopedale Collection of Hymns and Songs for the Use of Practical Christians*, compiled by Adin Ballou, containing twenty pieces by him. In *The Gospel Psalmist*, 1861, prepared for Universalists, this text, titled "Reign of Christian Peace," and credited to "Hopedale Coll." is in the section, "Christian Philanthropy and Reform." After that

two syllables were added to Line 4 of each quatrain.

PLEADING SAVIOR, an anonymous setting of John Leland's "Now the Savior stands a-pleading," appears in *The Christian Lyre*, 1830, compiled by Joshua Leavitt (1794–1873), a New York lawyer, who later edited *The Evangelist* and *The Independent*. It was reharmonized for this book.

**199. THE TIME SHALL COME.** Alexander Pope. *See No. 133.* This text is adapted from the latter part of "Windsor Forest," 1713.

WINDSOR FOREST by Henry Leland Clarke *(see No. 135)* first appeared in *Songs of Faith in Man for Religious Liberals*, 1960, edited by Waldemar Hille for the First Unitarian Church of Los Angeles, Calif.

**200. WE MOVE IN FAITH.** Malcolm Quin. *See No. 76.* This hymn is found in the *Ethical Hymn Book*, London, 1905.

MERTHYR TYDVIL, from John Roberts' enlarged *Llyfr Tonau Cynulleidfaol*, 1870, is by Joseph Parry (1841–1903), named for his birthplace in Wales, where he worked in the puddling furnaces before he was ten. When he was seventeen and in Danbury, Pa., Welsh fellow workers started his musical education and then sent him to normal school at Geneseo, N. Y. He went to the Royal Academy of Music in London and Cambridge University (Mus.B., 1871; Mus.D., 1878). As a professor at Aberystwyth and Cardiff, he contributed to the advancement of Welsh music.

**201. LET THERE BE LIGHT.** William Merrill Vories (1880–    ), a native of Kansas, is a lay missionary in Japan. Before World War II he became a Japanese citizen, and since, has headed the architectural firm planning the campus of the International Christian University near Tokyo. This hymn was written for the American Peace Society, founded in 1828.

For TRANSYLVANIA *see No. 38.*

**202. SOUND OVER ALL WATERS.** John Greenleaf Whittier. *See No. 93.* This cento made by Arthur Foote II *(see No. 29)* is from Whittier's "A Christmas Carmen," in *Hazel-blossoms*, 1875.

FOUR WINDS was composed for this book by Arthur Foote II *(see No. 29).*

**203. QUEST CF THE AGES.** Kenneth L. Patton. *See No. 28.* This hymn was first published in *Man Is the Meaning*, 1956.

CONSOLATION first appears in Wyeth's *Repository of Sacred Music*, II, Harrisburg, Pa., 1813. A variant from Cambridge, Mass., John Wyeth (1770–1858) prepared Part II for the Methodists and Baptists to the west and south. His co-worker, Elkanah Kelsay Dare (1782–1826), a Methodist minister, who had been Dean of Boys at Wilmington College, Del., could have been the "Dean" credited with the tune in many shape-note tune books. The harmonization is by Henry Leland Clarke *(see No. 135).*

**204. THE CITY OF THE LORD.** William George Tarrant (1853–1928) was an English Unitarian minister. *Hymns for Worship, Revised*, 1962, the British Unitarian hymnbook, has twelve of his hymns. This is appropriate as a processional hymn; divided, either half may be used as a hymn in itself. The First Unitarian Society of Chicago, Ill., sings this as a hymn of urban renewal.

A variant of the melody, *"Ach, Herre Gott mich treibt die Not"* (*Cancyonal*, 1595), ICH DANK DIR SCHON was harmonized and published by Michael Praetorius *(see No. 125)* in *Musae Sionae*, VIII, 1610.

**205. THE PAGEANT OF THE YEARS.** John Haynes Holmes (1879–1964) was minister for over fifty years of The Community Church, New York City. He was a founder of the American Civil Liberties Union, of the National Association for the Advancement of Colored People, the Fellowship of Reconciliation, and the Unitarian Universalist Fellowship for Social Justice. He has written many books, including an autobiography, *I Speak for Myself*, 1959, and many hymns. This hymn appeared first in *The Beacon Song and Service Book*, 1935.

Johann Balthasar Reimann (1702–49), organist at Hirschberg in Schleswig, Germany, published O JESU, WARUM LEGST DU MIR in his *Sammlung alter und neuer Melodien evangelischer Lieder*, 1747.

206. BETWEEN MIDNIGHT AND MORNING. Sir Owen Seaman (1861–1936) was an English poet and satirist, joined the staff of *Punch* magazine in 1897 and was its editor 1906–32. This text was published in *Punch*, December 16, 1914.

PEACE, from *The Revivalist*, 1869, was adapted by George Brandon (1924–   ) for *The Pilgrim Hymnal*, 1958.

207. BEND BACK THE LANCE'S POINT. John Ruskin (1819–1900), English author, reformer, and art critic, was professor of art at Oxford. He wrote many books, notably *The Seven Lamps of Architecture*, and *The Stones of Venice*. This text is adapted from a poem beginning "Awake! Awake! the stars are pale."

FESTAL SONG is by William Henry Walter (1825–93), a native of Newark, N. J., and Doctor of Music, Columbia University, where he became organist in 1865. First published in *The Hymnal with Tunes Old and New*, New York, 1872, edited by J. Ireland Tucker, the tune became standard in the United States for "Rise up, O men of God" (*see No. 218*).

208. OUT OF THE DARK. Samuel Longfellow. *See No. 43.* This was written for the twenty-fifth anniversary of the American Anti-Slavery Society, titled "What of the Night?" Longfellow rewrote it in five stanzas for *Hymns of the Spirit*, 1864.

O JESU CHRIST, MEINS LEBENS LICHT is adapted from the tune in the *Nürnbergisches Gesangbuch*, 1676. The original is in duple time; the text begins, "*Herr Jesu Christ.*"

209. NOW IS THE TIME AP-PROACHING. Jane Laurie Borthwick (1813–97), a Scottish hymn writer, with her sister edited and published several collections of hymns. This text, originally beginning, "And is the time approaching," and here altered, first appeared in *Thoughts for Thoughtful Hours*, 1859, as "Anticipations." Now sung as a hymn of world brotherhood, this was originally a hymn of exclusively Christian ecumenicity.

WEBB, by George James Webb (1803–87), was a secular song, beginning " 'Tis dawn, the lark is singing"; it

was published in his *Odeon*, 1837. Born near Salisbury, England, Webb moved to Boston in 1830 and became organist of the Old South Church. A close associate of Lowell Mason (*see No. 126*), he helped organize the Boston Academy of Music. He became a conductor and was president of the Handel and Haydn Society, 1840. In 1870 he followed Mason to New York and died in Orange, N. J.

210. THY KINGDOM COME. Frederick Lucian Hosmer. *See No. 50.*

MEIN SCHÖPFER, STEH' MIR BEI is adapted from a florid melody by Franz Heinrich Christoph Meyer (1705–67), court organist at Hanover, Germany. The original is in Meyer's *Die unbekannte Melodeyen einiger Gesänge des neüen Hannöverischen Gesang-Buches*, 1741. It was reharmonized for this book.

211. PIONEERS, O PIONEERS! Walt Whitman. *See No. 78.* This is a cento made by Martin Shaw for *Songs of Praise*, 1925, from "Pioneers, O Pioneers," introduced in *Leaves of Grass*, 1865.

PIONEERS was composed for *We Sing of Life*, 1955, by its music editor, Irving Lowens (1916–   ), Assistant Head, Reference Section, Music Division, Library of Congress, and music critic of the Washington, D. C., *Evening Star*. A composition student of Edwin A. Stringham, Howard A. Murphy, and Quinto Maganini, Lowens holds degrees from Teachers College, New York City; Columbia University; and the University of Maryland. He is in charge of the American Music History Project of the Music Library Association.

212. GIRD ON THY SWORD, O MAN. Robert Bridges. *See No. 137.* This hymn is the last section of "A Hymn of Nature: an Ode Written for Music" in *Later Poems*, 1912. Sir Hubert Parry (*see No. 55*) composed the music, which was performed at the Gloucester Festival, 1898.

For ERFYNIAD *see No. 39.*

213. GOD'S TRUMPET WAKES. Samuel Longfellow. *See No. 43.* This hymn, a Unitarian counterpart to Bishop Heber's, "The Son of God goes forth to war," appeared anonymously

in *Hymns of the Spirit*, 1864, as "On the Lord's Side."

First published in J. Ireland Tucker's *Hymnal with Tunes Old and New*, 1872, ALL SAINTS NEW was composed as a setting of "The Son of God goes forth to war" by Henry Stephen Cutler (1824–1902). Born in Boston, Cutler studied music in Frankfurt, Germany, and in England, where he became interested in cathedral choirs. At the Church of the Advent, Boston, he established a choir of men and boys, the first surpliced choir in America, later doing the same at Trinity Church, New York City.

214. THE VOICE OF GOD. John Haynes Holmes. *See No. 205.* This hymn, based on Isa. 6:8, written on Holmes's first return voyage from Europe, appeared in *The New Hymn and Tune Book*, 1914. It has been translated into German, Spanish, and Japanese.

KING'S LYNN, an English traditional melody, was adapted by Ralph Vaughan Williams (*see No. 78*) for G. K. Chesterton's "O God of earth and altar" in *The English Hymnal*, 1906.

215. FORWARD THROUGH THE AGES. Frederick Lucian Hosmer. *See No. 50.*

Arthur Seymour Sullivan (1842–1909) composed ST. GERTRUDE, in the *Hymnary*, 1872, for "Onward, Christian soldiers," Sabine Baring-Gould's text for a children's festival. Chorister in the Chapel Royal under Thomas Helmore (*See No. 280*), Sullivan was the first to hold the Mendelssohn Scholarship at the Royal Academy of Music, where, after study in Leipzig, Germany, he became professor of music. He was knighted in 1883. His operettas, words by Sir William Gilbert, brought new life to English music, but his anthems and hymn tunes are what *The Hymnal 1940 Companion* calls "the small end of his career."

216. WHEN ABRAHAM WENT OUT OF UR. Nancy Byrd Turner (1880–     ) is a Virginian who has lived long in Boston. Formerly on the staffs of *The Youth's Companion* and *The Atlantic Monthly*, she has written volumes of stories and poetry for chil-

dren, among them *Star in a Well*, 1935, from which this text is taken.

For CONGLETON *see No. 69.*

217. GOD SEND US MEN. Frederick John Gillman (1866–1949), a leading hymn writer among the English Quakers, was an editor of the English Society of Friends' *The Fellowship Hymnbook*, 1910 and 1933. He wrote also *The Evolution of the English Hymn*, 1927. Small modifications in this text have been made for this book, with permission of the copyright owners. Line 3 of Stanza 1 and Line 2 of Stanza 2, long familiar in this form, substitute "right" for the original "Christ." The next-to-last line read originally, "These are the patriots Britain needs."

WAYLAND by George Blackburn Holsinger (1857–1908) appears in the *Mennonite Hymnary* of 1902. Holsinger, head of the music department at Bridgewater College, Va., contributed hymns to his own denomination, the German Baptist Brethren ("Dunkers"), and also to the Mennonites. The harmonization is by Henry Leland Clarke (*see No. 135*).

218. RISE UP, O MEN OF GOD. William Pierson Merrill (1867–1954), an American Presbyterian, was minister of the Brick Church, New York City. His many books included *Faith and Sight*, *Christian Internationalism*, and *Liberal Christianity*. Stanza 4, beginning "Lift high the cross of Christ," is omitted here.

For FESTAL SONG *see No. 207.*

219. THE OPEN WAY. John Coleman Adams (1849–1922) was an American Universalist minister who held pastorates at Newton and Lynn, Mass.; Chicago, Ill.; Brooklyn, N. Y.; and Hartford, Conn. Author of several hymns, he wrote this for a church anniversary. It appeared in *The New Hymn and Tune Book*, 1914, with five stanzas; these are the first three.

FESTUS is an adaptation of "O du Hüter Israel" from the *Neues geistreiches Gesangbuch*, compiled by Johann August Freylinghausen (*see No. 48*). The harmonization is by Kenneth Munson (*see No. 134*).

220. ONCE TO EVERY MAN AND NATION. James Russell Lowell. *See*

*No. 168.* Stanzas from "The Present Crisis," protesting the war with Mexico, were first published in a hymnbook by the English hymnologist, W. Garrett Horder, in *Hymns Supplemental*, 1896. Horder altered the text to make it regular enough to be sung.

EBENEZER, first published in *Llawlyfr Moliant* (Handbook of Praise), 1890, is by Thomas John Williams (1869–1944), native of Ynysmeudwy, Glamorganshire, Wales, pupil of David Evans of Cardiff (*see No. 39*), and organist and choirmaster at Llanelly. The tale improvised by a fun-loving youth at a party that it washed ashore in a bottle on the coast of Lleyn, did much to speed the tune through Wales and around the world as "Ton-y-Botel."

221. CREATION'S LORD, WE GIVE THEE THANKS. William De Witt Hyde. *See No. 108.*

For VOM HIMMEL HOCH *see No. 42.*

222. ABIDE NOT IN THE REALM OF DREAMS. William Henry Burleigh (1812–71), American abolitionist, editor, and publisher, became Harbor Master of New York in 1850. He was a member of the Second Unitarian Church in Brooklyn. His hymns and poems were collected in *Poems*, 1841, which was reprinted, enlarged, after his death. This hymn is a cento from "The Harvest-Call," of which four stanzas appeared in the Unitarian *Hymn and Tune Book*, 1877.

For DUKE STREET *see No. 43.*

223. AWAKE, MY SOUL, STRETCH EVERY NERVE. Philip Doddridge (1702–51), youngest son in a family of twenty, was an English Nonconformist who for twenty-two years ministered to a congregation in Northampton. Among his several theological works was *Rise and Progress of Religion in the Soul* which had many editions and was translated into other languages. In 1751, he took a voyage for his health, but died in Lisbon, Portugal. His hymns were published posthumously. This text is based on Phil. 3:12–14.

The soprano aria, *"Non vi piacque ingiusti Dei,"* in Handel's opera *Siroe*, 1728, was considerably adapted in

David Weyman's *Melodia Sacra*, 1815, to create CHRISTMAS, so called because of its early use with Nahum Tate's "While shepherds watched their flocks at night" (*see No. 295*). George Frideric Handel (1685–1759), the German who wrote Italian operas in England, overshadowed English church music for generations.

224. GOD OF THE EARNEST HEART. Samuel Johnson. *See No. 172.* This hymn was in Johnson and Longfellow's (*see No. 43*) *Book of Hymns*, 1848. It was written for his graduating exercises, 1846, at the Harvard Divinity School. Stanza 5 is omitted here.

ST. BRIDE, in William Riley's *Parochial Harmony*, 1762, is by Samuel Howard (*see No. 106*).

225. LET ALL MEN LIVING IN ALL LANDS. Kenneth L. Patton. *See No. 28.* This is a response in *Man Is the Meaning*, 1956.

For VOM HIMMEL HOCH *see No. 42.*

226. THY BROTHER. Theodore Chickering Williams (1855–1915) was an American Unitarian minister. Minister of The Unitarian Church of All Souls, New York City, 1883–96, he later served as headmaster of Hackley School, Tarrytown, N. Y., until 1905. He published a metrical translation of Virgil's *Aeneid* and edited with Velma C. Williams, his wife, *Hymnal: Amore Dei*, 1890. This text obviously is related to *I John*, especially Chapter 4.

WOODLAWN was composed by Robert L. Sanders (*see No. 2*) for *Hymns of the Spirit*, 1937.

227. O'ER CONTINENT AND OCEAN. John Haynes Holmes. *See No. 205.* This hymn was written for the Unitarian General Conference in Montreal, 1917; it was in *Hymns of the Spirit*, 1937.

LLANGLOFFAN is a Welsh melody from *Hymnau a Thônau* (Hymns and Tunes for the Service of the Church in Wales), 1865, edited by Canon Daniel Evans.

228. OBEDIENT THEY BUT TO A DREAM. George Dillon (1906– ) is an American poet whose book of poetry, *The Flowering Stone*, 1931, won the Pulitzer prize. This hymn is an

adaptation of a sonnet, "Address to the Doomed, IV," from that volume. Dillon is editor of *Poetry, A Magazine of Verse*.

For FARLEY CASTLE see No. 3.

229. BLEST IS THAT MAN. Joseph Auslander (1897–    ) is an American poet and editor of *The Winged Horse Anthology*, 1927, with Frank Ernest Hill. He was a lecturer on poetry at Columbia University and consultant on English poetry for the Library of Congress, 1937–44. The original title of this poem is "Columbus Day—1950." It first appeared as a hymn in *We Sing of Life*, 1955.

GENEVA 119 is adapted by Robert L. Sanders (see No. 2) from the six-line diatonic setting of Psalm 119 in the Genevan Psalter, 1551. The opening phrase derives ultimately from a secular chanson.

230. LET US NOW PRAISE FAMOUS MEN. This hymn is from *The Wisdom of Jesus the Son of Sirach*, or *Ecclesiasticus*, ca. 180 B.C., in Hebrew, and translated into Greek by his grandson, ca. 130 B.C. This text is an abridgment of Chapter 44, Verses 1, 3, 4a, 5, 7, 9a, and 14, King James Version, Old Testament Apocrypha.

FAMOUS MEN is eminently suitable for congregational use, although originally it appeared as a "canticle," a separate work, 1923. For Ralph Vaughan Williams, see No. 78.

231. FROM AGE TO AGE. Frederick Lucian Hosmer. See No. 50. Hosmer wrote this for the annual festival of the Free Religious Association, June 2, 1899, in Boston. It was published that year in *Souvenir Festival Hymns*.

For CHRISTUS DER IST MEIN LEBEN, C. M., see No. 188.

232. THE PIONEER. Kenneth L. Patton. See No. 28. This appeared as an "Anthem of Humanity," in *Man Is the Meaning*, 1956.

BRIDGEWATER by Lewis Edson (1748–1820) appears in Simeon Jocelin's *Chorister's Companion*, New Haven, Conn., 1782. It was originally a fuguing tune of the type popularized by William Billings. A blacksmith of Bridgewater, Mass., Edson became a music teacher, went to New York City

in 1776, and died in Woodstock, N. Y. This adaptation is by Kenneth Munson (see No. 134).

233. O PROPHET SOULS OF ALL THE YEARS. Frederick Lucian Hosmer. See No. 50. This hymn was written for the World Parliament of Religions, Chicago, 1893, and was included in *The Thought of God, Second Series*, 1894, as "One Law, One Life, One Love." Lines 2 and 4 of Stanza 1 ("Bend o'er us from above," and "Now to fulfillment move,") and Line 4 of Stanza 3 ("The Spirit's tongue of flame") are changed here.

For GRÄFENBURG see No. 96.

234. PRAYER OF THE PILGRIMS. Le Baron Russell Briggs (1855–1934) was the son of a Unitarian minister, George W. Briggs. After serving in the Harvard English department for some years, he was appointed dean of the college in 1891; he was president of Radcliffe College, 1903–23. These stanzas are from a poem written for the tercentenary of the 1620 landing of the Pilgrims at Plymouth, Mass.; they are included in a hymnbook for the first time here.

L'OMNIPOTENT is the tune for Psalm 110 in the Genevan Psalter, 1551.

235. THE PILGRIMS. Leonard Bacon (1802–81) was an American Congregationalist, for forty-one years minister at the Center Church, New Haven, Conn., then professor of theology at the Yale Divinity School. This hymn was written for the bicentennial of the founding of New Haven and of the Center Church. It was published, revised, in *Psalms and Hymns for Christian Use and Worship*, 1845, of which Bacon was an editor.

For DUKE STREET see No. 43.

236. BEHOLD A SOWER. Washington Gladden. See No. 122. This hymn associates the Parable of the Sower with Psalm 97:11: "Light is sown for the righteous, and gladness for the upright in heart."

ELLACOMBE is varied slightly from the setting of "*Der du im heil'gsten Sakrament*" in Xavier Ludwig Hartig's *Vollständige Sammlung der gewöhn-*

*lichen Melodien zum Mainzer Gesang-buche,* Mainz, Germany, ca. 1833. That, in turn, was much altered from an earlier melody in *Gesang-Buch . . . der herzogl. Wirtembergischen katholischen Hofkapelle,* 1784.

**237. WE MET THEM ON THE COMMON WAY.** Elizabeth C. Cardozo (1867–1918) was American. This poem first appeared in *The Survey,* Jan. 3, 1914, and later that year was published in *Hymns of Brotherhood and Aspiration,* edited by Mabel Hay Barrows.

For SALVATION see No. 53.

**238. O GOD OF EARTH AND ALTAR.** Gilbert Keith Chesterton. *See No. 101.* Printed in the British monthly, *The Commonwealth,* it was given by its author to the editors of *The English Hymnal,* 1906, who used it to KING'S LYNN *(see No. 214).*

**239. NOT ALONE FOR MIGHTY EMPIRE.** William Pierson Merrill. *See No. 218.* With reference to this text, Dr. Merrill states: "It came out of a Thanksgiving service in Chicago, at which Jenkin Lloyd Jones offered a prayer which impressed me greatly by its emphasis on the spiritual national blessings and assets. I went home and wrote a rather diffusive hymn about it, and later made it over into the present one." Jenkin Lloyd Jones (1843–1918) was a leader in Midwestern Unitarian missionary endeavor; he worked toward putting Unitarian fellowship on this continent upon a nondoctrinal basis; the 1893 World Parliament of Religions in Chicago was largely conceived and arranged by him. A Civil War veteran, he had become a pacifist by World War I. He was the founder and minister of All Souls' Unitarian Church, Chicago, Ill. He sought a religious fellowship embracing all the great religious traditions.

For IN BABILONE see No. 191.

**240. O BEAUTIFUL, OUR COUNTRY.** Frederick Lucian Hosmer. *See No. 50.* This hymn, here slightly altered, written in 1884 as "Our Country," was published April 1 in *Unity* magazine, Chicago, Ill., and the next year in *The Thought of God.*

THE SPIRITUAL SAILOR, in William Walker's *Southern Harmony,* 1835, is evidently a parody with religious words of a seafaring song. "I. Neighbours" must have been responsible in some way for the adaptation. The harmonization is by Henry Leland Clarke *(see No. 135).*

**241. AMERICA THE BEAUTIFUL.** Katharine Lee Bates (1859–1929), American author of several books of poems, was professor of English at Wellesley College, Mass., 1891–1925.

MATERNA was composed in 1882 by Samuel Augustus Ward (1848–1903) to set "O mother dear, Jerusalem." Fruitless efforts have been made to find a tune less restricted by the style of its period, yet equally suited to this text. In his native city, Newark, N. J., Ward conducted a retail music business and directed the Orpheus Club from its founding in 1889 until his death.

**242. MY COUNTRY, 'TIS OF THEE.** Samuel Francis Smith (1808–95), an American Baptist minister, wrote much religious verse and such books as *Knights and Sea Kings, Mythology and Early Greek History,* and *Poor Boys Who Became Great;* but he is remembered chiefly as the author, at the age of 24, of this national hymn.

The tune AMERICA is the English "God save the Queen," printed in *Thesaurus Musicus,* ca. 1740–45. Attempts to link it to various old tunes have been abetted by its opening with a rhythmic pattern typical of the sixteenth-century dance known as the galliard.

**243. THE NEW PATRIOT.** Frederick Lawrence Knowles (1869–1905) was an American poet, the son of a Methodist clergyman. He taught at Tilton Academy in New Hampshire, and later was a member of the editorial staff of *The Atlantic Monthly.* This poem is in *Love Triumphant,* 1904, and was revised four times after the poet's death. Our cento comprises Stanzas 1, 6, 8, and 10 of the original.

For TRURO see No. 54.

**244. GOD SAVE THE QUEEN.** Anonymous, although both words and music have been attributed without adequate evidence to Henry Carey, author of "Sally in Our Alley." A second stanza: *"O Lord our God, arise/ Scatter his enemies/ And make them fall!/ Confound their politics,/ Frustrate their knavish tricks,/ On him our hopes we fix,/ O, save us all!"* has long since dropped from usage.

For GOD SAVE THE QUEEN see No. 242.

245. HEIR OF ALL THE AGES. Julia Caroline Ripley Dorr (1825–1913) was an American whose poetry and prose were prominent in magazines in the second half of the last century. This text, used as a hymn by Curtis W. Reese at Abraham Lincoln Center, Chicago, Ill., ca. 1933, appeared in *The Beacon Song and Service Book*, 1935, with slight changes as here. It is a cento from "Heirship."

NUREMBERG by Johann Rudolf Ahle (1625–73), organist and later burgomaster of Mühlhausen, Germany, has the text, *"Ja, er ist's, das Heil der Welt,"* in his *Neue geistliche . . . Andachten*, 1664. Originally an aria in operatic style, the tune has been adapted in the direction of sobriety, first for *"Liebster Jesu, wir sind hier"* in the *Grosse Cantional*, Darmstadt, Germany, 1687, again by Bach, and once more as here.

246. THE GROWING LIGHT. Samuel Longfellow. *See No. 43*. These stanzas are adapted from Stanzas 3 and 4 of a five-stanza hymn beginning, "Eternal One, thou living God," written in 1875, possibly for the twenty-fifth anniversary of Preble Chapel, Portland, Me.

WINCHESTER NEW is adapted from a setting of *"Wer nur den lieben Gott,"* in *Musicalisch Hand-buch der geistlichen Melodien*, printed not by Georg Wittwe, but by the widow of Georg Rebenlein, Hamburg, Germany, 1690. The Rebenlein family had been printers in Hamburg since about 1630.

247. IT SOUNDS ALONG THE AGES. William Channing Gannett. *See No. 1*. The original four stanzas constitute a hymn titled, "The Word of God," in *Unity Hymns and Chorals, Revised*, 1911. Stanzas 1 and 2, with a new Stanza 3 made from the original 3 and 4, appeared in *Hymns of the Spirit*, 1937. Stanza 3 is in this form in *We Sing of Life*, 1955.

FAR OFF LANDS, originally a melody of the Bohemian Brethren, is named by its association with "Remember all the people," written for children by Percy Dearmer (*see No. 321*) in 1929. Swedish Lutherans in America were already familiar with the tune, which the Augustana Synod had published in *Hemlandssånger*, Rock Island, Ill., 1892, with the text *"Du ömma fadershjerta."* This version was made for this book by Robert L. Sanders (*see No. 2*).

248. LIGHT OF AGES AND OF NATIONS. Samuel Longfellow. *See No. 43*. Written in 1860, this hymn first appeared in *Hymns of the Spirit*, 1864, with the opening line, "God of ages." This hymn is one of the earliest to recognize fully other than Christian religious traditions. Compare Samuel Johnson's "Life of ages, richly poured," (No. 172), introduced in the same book; and Alexander Pope's "Father of all, in every age," (No. 133).

Franz Joseph Haydn (*see No. 47*) composed AUSTRIA, *"Gott erhalte Franz den Kaiser,"* in 1797 to give his nation an equivalent of "God Save the King." Close to German and non-German folk idioms of the Austrian Empire, the melody has a grand design which could only be the work of the master. Later he set it with variations as the slow movement of his "Emperor" quartet.

249. GATHER US IN. George Matheson (1842–1906) was a Scottish author and minister of St. Bernard's parish church, Edinburgh. This hymn, originally six stanzas, was first published in his *Sacred Songs*, 1890. We retain Stanzas 1, 2, and 6. This hymn, although its comparisons may slight other religions, may be the first in an orthodox Christian hymnbook to recognize truth in non-Christian religions.

For AINSWORTH 97 see No. 52.

250. HERITAGE. Jacob Trapp. *See No. 191*.

For O JESU CHRIST, MEINS LEBENS LICHT see No. 208.

251. FROM HEART TO HEART. William Channing Gannett. *See No. 1*. This was written for the one hundred and fiftieth anniversary of the First Religious

Society (Unitarian) in Newburyport, Mass., and published ten years later in *The Thought of God*, First Series, 1885.

GRAFTON is attributed to Thomas Clark (1775–1859), cobbler of Canterbury, England, and leader of psalmody in the Wesleyan church and later in a Unitarian church that had been originally Anabaptist. The tune is in the *Book of Psalms* published by the Reformed Presbyterian Church, Philadelphia, Pa., 1929. This harmonization is by Robert L. Sanders.

252. UNTO THY TEMPLE, LORD, WE COME. Robert Collyer (1823–1912) was a Yorkshire blacksmith with little formal education, who came to America in 1850 as a Methodist preacher. Drawn to Unitarian beliefs through friendship with Dr. W. H. Furness of the First Unitarian Church of Philadelphia, Pa., he left the Methodist church and in 1859 was called to the newly organized Unity Unitarian Church in Chicago, Ill., where he was twenty years before going to the Church of the Messiah (now The Community Church), New York, N. Y. This hymn was written for the dedication of the new building after the Unity Church building had been destroyed in the 1870 Chicago fire. Stanza 3 is omitted here.

For DUKE STREET *see No. 43.*

253. OUR KINDRED FELLOW-SHIPS. Marion Franklin Ham. *See No. 125.* This hymn was written in 1933 and was published in *Hymns of the Spirit*, 1937. It celebrates the growing closeness of the Unitarian and Universalist denominations through about a century, which resulted in consolidation as the Unitarian Universalist Association, May 15, 1961.

For WINCHESTER NEW *see No. 246.*

254. CHURCH OF THE FREE SPIRIT. Charles H. Lyttle. *See No. 37.* This hymn was written for the centennial of the first Unitarian Society, Geneva, Ill., which Dr. Lyttle has served since 1927. The hymn contains historical allusions: "Liberty, Holiness, and Love," the 1825 American Unitarian Association "motto," was incorporated in the Geneva church's constitution in 1842 and inscribed over its pulpit. The church bell is inscribed, "Praise to the Highest, peace to men below." The

building's field-stone walls—twenty inches thick—are, indeed, "stalwart."

For NICAEA *see No. 4.*

255. FAITH'S FREER SHRINE. Frederick Lucian Hosmer. *See No. 50.* Written for the fiftieth anniversary of The Unitarian Church of Quincy, Ill., in 1890, and included in the second series of *The Thought of God*, 1894, as "From Generation to Generation."

ST. MATTHEW, like "St. Anne," appears anonymously in the sixth edition of the supplement to the *New Version of the Psalms*, edited in 1708 by William Croft (*see No. 51*). According to later eighteenth-century collections, Croft composed both tunes. This version of "St. Matthew" is somewhat more florid than the original, in which the penultimate measure of many phrases consists solely of one short note and one long, a favorite pattern of Croft and other pupils of Dr. John Blow.

256. OUR FRIENDLY HOUSE. Kenneth L. Patton. *See No. 28.* This hymn was written in 1951, for the dedication of the meeting house designed by Frank Lloyd Wright for the First Unitarian Society of Madison, Wis. It was published first in *Man Is the Meaning*, 1956.

For FILLMORE *see No. 8.*

257. FAITH OF THE FREE. Vincent B. Silliman. *See No. 14.* This hymn was written for a 1944 institute of Middle Atlantic States Unitarian ministers. It was published in *We Sing of Life*, 1955.

For MIT FREUDEN ZART *see No. 15.*

258. RANK BY RANK AGAIN WE STAND. John Huntley Skrine (1848–1923) was a Church of England clergyman and an educator. This text appeared in his *Thirty Hymns for Public-School Singing*, 1899.

REUNION, appearing in *A Students' Hymnal*, University of Wales, 1923, is presumed to be by its editor, Sir Henry Walford Davies (1869–1941), English composer, professor of music at University College, Aberystwyth, an organist, teacher of music, and conductor in Wales and England, who often attributed his compositions to the institution he served.

## 259. WHERE IS OUR HOLY CHURCH?

Edwin Henry Wilson 1898– ), a Unitarian Universalist minister, has served in Chicago, Ill.; Schenectady, N. Y.; and Salt Lake City, Utah. He was executive director of the American Humanist Association, 1949–63. He is editor of the periodical, *Free Mind*. He wrote this hymn in the year of his ordination, 1928.

ST. MICHAEL was abridged from the 1551 Genevan setting of Psalm 101 and used in English and Scottish psalmody as "Old 134th." This version is in William Crotch's *Psalm Tunes*, 1836, as "St. Michael." Crotch (1775–1847) was the first principal of the Royal Academy of Music, London.

## 260. HERE BE NO MAN A STRANGER.

William Channing Gannett. *See No. 1.* Written for the dedication of The Unitarian Church of Hinsdale, Ill., in 1888, while he was minister there. This is a portion of the original, which began, "God laid his rocks in courses."

For CHRISTUS DER IST MEIN LEBEN, 7.6.7.6., *see No. 188.*

## 261. ONE HOLY CHURCH.

Samuel Longfellow. *See No. 43.* This hymn of the church universal was written in 1860 and included in *Hymns of the Spirit*, 1864.

ST. STEPHEN was originally a setting of Psalm 23 in *Ten Church Pieces for the Organ with Four Anthems in Score, Composed for the Use of the Church of Nayland in Suffolk*, 1789, by William Jones (1726–1800). Born in Lowick, Northamptonshire, England, he was called "Jones of Nayland," where he was perpetual vicar. He was Fellow of the Royal Society and author of *A Treatise on the Art of Musick*, 1784. Because his ancestor, Colonel John Jones, was one of the judges who condemned Charles I, he observed each anniversary of the execution as a day of humiliation.

## 262. FOR CEREMONY OF NAMING.

Ridgely Torrence. *See No. 2.* This poem, titled "Ceremony for Birth and Naming," whose opening section is omitted here, is a dedication service in verse. It was published in *Hesperides*, 1925, and is set to music for the first time here.

For WER DA WONET *see No. 143.*

## 263. A BLESSING.

Siegfried Sassoon (1886– ) is an English poet noted for anti-war lyrics and satires on the English upper classes. A hero of World War I who turned pacifist in 1918 and refused to fight further, he escaped court martial by being declared temporarily insane. Among his books are *Poems*, 1902; *Counter-Attack*, 1918; *The World of Youth*, 1942; and an autobiography.

For ROCKBRIDGE *see No. 147.*

## 264. MORNING CHORALE.

George Gascoigne (1540–77) was an English literary pioneer—law student, prodigal, member of Parliament, soldier, dramatist, satirist, and poet. Here are a stanza and a half from his poem, "Gascoigne's Good Morrowe," which in a later stanza rates our days on earth as "but hell to heavenly joy." The last lines of the text are original in this book.

For LOBT GOTT, IHR CHRISTEN *see No. 118.*

## 265. THOMAS KEN'S MORNING HYMN.

Thomas Ken (1637–1711), an English bishop, was one of seven sent to the Tower of London in 1688 for refusing to subscribe to James II's Declaration of Indulgence. He resigned his see in 1691, refusing to switch his allegiance to William of Orange. His magnum opus was *Hymns and Poems for the Holy Days and Festivals of the Church*.

MORNING HYMN first appeared in the supplement to *Hymns and Psalms Used at the Asylum for Female Orphans*, 1785. The tune is by François Hippolyte Barthélemon (1741–1808), born at Bordeaux, the son of a French officer and an Irish lady. Going to England as a professional violinist, he became director of the orchestra at Vauxhall Gardens. He was a close friend of Haydn and composed more music for theater than for church.

## 266. MORNING HAS BROKEN.

Eleanor Farjeon (1881– ) is a British writer, especially for children, who at the age of 70 was received into the Roman Catholic church. She wrote this hymn to fit this tune, on request for *Songs of Praise*.

BUNESSAN is an old Gaelic melody from Lachlan Macbean's *Songs and Hymns of the Gael*, 1900, arranged for the enlarged *Songs of Praise*, 1931, by Martin Shaw (1875–1958). Shaw was a prominent English church musician, editor, and composer.

267. HIGH O'ER THE LONELY HILLS. Jan Struther. See No. 29. Jan Struther wrote these words on request to fit T. H. Ingham's setting of "Hark! 'tis the watchman's cry" for the enlarged Songs of Praise, 1931. We omit Stanza 3.

At first called "Watchman," the tune has been renamed DAWN.

268. NOW ALL THE HEAVENLY SPLENDOR. Paul Gerhardt (1607–76) was a German Lutheran clergyman. Many of his hymns have been translated into English. He was removed from his post at St. Nicholas Cathedral, Berlin, in 1664 and forbidden to perform any ministerial functions when he refused to obey an edict of Elector Friedrich Wilhelm I which denied free speech on certain church disputes. Four years later, however, he was appointed archdeacon of Lübben. This stanza is a free translation by Robert Bridges (see No..137) for his Yattendon Hymnal, 1899, and is Stanza 2 of a four-stanza hymn beginning, "The duteous day now closeth"; Stanzas 3 and 4 are Bridges' own.

INNSBRUCK was published in Georg Forster's Ein Ausszug guter alter und newer teutscher Liedlein, 1539, with the secular words, "Innsbruck, ich muss dich lassen." Later associated with the texts, "O Welt, ich muss dich lassen" and "Nun ruhen alle Wälder," the melody is generally attributed to Heinrich Isaak (ca. 1450–1517), composer to Leonardo da Vinci in Florence, Italy, and Maximilian I in Vienna, Austria. It is harmonized here as in the first part of J. S. Bach's St. Matthew Passion, 1729.

269. NOW WHILE THE DAY IN TRAILING SPLENDOR. Frederick Lucian Hosmer. See No. 50. Written in 1902, this hymn was included in Louisa Loring's Hymns of the Ages, 1904.

RENDEZ À DIEU is the 1543 Genevan tune for Psalm 118 with a late harmonization.

270. THOMAS KEN'S EVENING HYMN. Thomas Ken. See No. 265. Our version is arranged from the original eleven stanzas.

For TALLIS' CANON see No. 85.

271. AGAIN, AS EVENING'S SHADOW FALLS. Samuel Longfellow. See No. 43. Originally this hymn was published in Vespers, 1859, a collection for use in services Longfellow instituted in Brooklyn, N. Y.

For ROCKBRIDGE see No. 147.

272. WHEN THE GLADSOME DAY DECLINETH. Minot Judson Savage. See No. 115.

SHIPSTON is the air of a Warwickshire ballad, "Bedlam City," arranged for The English Hymnal, 1906, by Ralph Vaughan Williams (see No. 78).

273. DARK HILLS AT EVENING. Edgar Arlington Robinson (1869–1935), American poet, thrice won Pulitzer prizes. He was famous for narrative poems in blank verse, portraying New England characters. "The Dark Hills" is in Collected Poems, 1944.

LUCIS CREATOR appears in a Lyons Antiphoner of 1738. It is one of the "church melodies," suggesting both plain-song and folk song antecedents, that grew out of the seventeenth-century French practice of substituting measured melodies for earlier plain-song settings of Latin hymns. In The English Hymnal, 1906, it is called an "Angers Church Melody."

274. NOW, ON LAND AND SEA DESCENDING. Samuel Longfellow. See No. 43. This vesper hymn, written in 1859, is in Hymns of the Spirit, 1864.

VESPER HYMN was published in 1818 as a glee for four voices in A Selection of Popular National Airs by Sir John Stevenson (1761–1833). Stevenson, an Irish musician, called it "Russian Air." It has been ascribed to Dmitri Bortniansky (see No. 56), but authoritative support for this is lacking. It was reharmonized for this book.

275. HARVEST FESTIVAL. John Greenleaf Whittier. See No. 93.

AFFECTION is from Psalmody Harmonized in Score, with Accompaniment for Organ and Pianoforte, 1838, published in Halifax, Yorkshire, England, by John Greenwood, a music teacher, who already had published two collections in his own city of Leeds.

276. AUTUMN FIELDS. Elizabeth Syle Madison (1883–    ) lives in Salinas, Calif.

William James Kirkpatrick (1832–1921) apparently accepted the fiction that "Away in a manger" was "composed by Martin Luther for his own children, and still sung by German mothers to their little ones." His setting of it, CRADLE SONG, which was published in *Around the World with Christmas*, 1895, was arranged for *Songs of Praise*, 1931, by Ralph Vaughan Williams (*see No. 78*). Kirkpatrick was an Irish-born carpenter, music director of Grace Methodist Episcopal Church, Philadelphia, Pa., and publisher of very popular gospel song collections.

277. I WALK THE UNFRE-QUENTED ROAD. Frederick Lucian Hosmer. *See No. 50.* It is not known when this poem was written; its publication in a hymnbook seems to have been in Stanton Coit's *Social Worship*, II, London, 1913.

For CONSOLATION *see No. 203.*

278. COME, YE THANKFUL PEO-PLE. Henry Alford (1810–71), an Anglican clergyman, became dean of Canterbury in 1857. He wrote *A Dissuasive against Rome*, *The Queen's English*, books of sermons, and poetry. He translated and wrote hymns. His magnum opus was a *Greek Testament*, a standard critical commentary of his time. This harvest hymn is his only one still widely used.

For ST. GEORGE'S WINDSOR *see No. 10.*

279. HANUKKAH HYMN. Leopold Stein (1810–82) was a scholar, liturgist, poet, dramatist, and leader in Reform Judaism, rabbi at Frankfurt-am-Main, Germany, for eighteen years. He wrote the German original of this text for a traditional Hanukkah tune to replace a thirteenth- or fourteenth-century Hebrew text, which also had an initial reference to a rock. This English adaptation is by Marcus Mordecai Jastrow (1829–1903) and Gustav Gottheil (1827–1903). Jastrow, born in Prussian Poland, educated in Germany, briefly a rabbi in Warsaw, was expelled from Poland for sympathizing with nationalistic rebels, and became a rabbi in Philadelphia, Pa.,

from 1866. He was a scholar, liturgist, teacher, and until 1903 editor-in-chief of the Jewish translation of the scriptures into English, published in 1917. Gottheil, born in Prussian Posen, served briefly in Manchester, England, and became assistant rabbi in 1873, then rabbi of Temple Emanu-El in New York City. In 1886 he prepared America's first Jewish hymnbook, basis of successive editions of the *Union Hymnal*. We have altered Stanza 3, Line 1, from "Children of the Martyr-race," to emphasize the prophetic role of Judaism. Hanukkah, a Jewish festival involving the lighting of 1 to 8 candles on successive December nights, commemorates the rededication of the Temple at Jerusalem, 165 B.C., under Judas Maccabaeus after its profanation three years before by Antiochus Epiphanes.

MOOZ TSUR, no less than some Lutheran chorales, draws on the phraseology of German folk song. Used in the synogogue with the Hebrew text, "*Mooz Tsur*," the tune is also sung by Jewish congregations with German and English texts.

280. O COME, O COME, EMMAN-UEL. This Latin hymn may well date to the ninth century or earlier. It is drawn from seven great Antiphons saluting the Messiah to come with as many symbolic names. This translation for Stanzas 1 and 2 is close to that of John Mason Neale (1818–66), a noted hymnologist who rendered many early Christian hymns into English. Stanza 3 was written by Vincent B. Silliman (*see No. 14*) for the Christmas pageant of the First Parish Society, Portland, Me., and was published in *The Beacon Song and Service Book*, 1935.

Thomas Helmore (1811–90), musical editor of *The Hymnal Noted*, 1854, provided the tune, VENI EMMANUEL, for Neale's translation of the Latin hymn. His exact plain-song source is undetermined, since his statement that the melody is from a French missal in the Lisbon, Portugal, national library is unconfirmed.

281. PEOPLE, LOOK EAST. Eleanor Farjeon. *See No. 266.* This Advent carol was written for *The Oxford Book of Carols*, 1928.

BESANÇON CAROL, a carol melody from Besançon in eastern France, was harmonized by Sir John Stainer (1840–1901), professor of music at Oxford University and organist at St. Paul's Cathedral, London, England.

282. HAIL TO THE LORD'S ANOINTED. James Montgomery. *See No. 20.* This highly esteemed hymn betrays Montgomery's strong feelings about slavery. He is considered one of the foremost social reformers of his time.

For WEBB *see No. 209.*

283. WATCHMAN, TELL US OF THE NIGHT. Sir John Bowring (1792–1872) was an English Unitarian, member of Parliament, a colonial official, an extraordinary linguist, who in 1854 became governor of Hong Kong. His numerous books include several of devotional poetry. This Advent dialogue first appeared in his *Hymns,* 1825; it is based on Isa. 21:11–12. He also wrote the well known "In the cross of Christ I glory."

WATCHMAN by Lowell Mason *(see No. 126)* was published first in the *Boston Handel and Haydn Society Collection of Church Music,* 1830. The original melody, while also in triple time, presented a variety of dotted rhythms.

284. VEILED IN DARKNESS JUDAH LAY. Douglas LeTell Rights (1891–1956) was an American Moravian minister.

NICHT SO TRAURIG is one of many settings of Paul Gerhardt's hymns composed by Johann Georg Ebeling (1637–76), music director at the St. Nicholas Church, Berlin, Germany, and professor of music at the Caroline Gymnasium, Stettin, Poland.

285. THE FIRST NOWELL. English carol of unknown origin, found in Davis Gilbert's *Ancient Christmas Carols,* 1823, and in William Sandys' *Christmas Carols Ancient and Modern,* 1833. The words are not scripturally accurate, for the shepherds saw no star. The carol presumably dates from no later than the seventeenth century.

THE FIRST NOWELL was first published in William Sandys' *Christmas Carols*

*Ancient and Modern,* 1833. The harmonization by Stainer *(see No. 281)* is from *Christmas Carols New and Old,* 1871.

286. O LITTLE TOWN OF BETHLEHEM. Phillips Brooks (1835–93), great preacher of the American Protestant Episcopal church, sometimes was likened to England's F. W. Robertson. As rector of Philadelphia's Holy Trinity Church, he wrote this Christmas hymn for his Sunday school in 1868, after a visit to the Holy Land. Next year Brooks became rector of Trinity Church, Boston, and in 1891, Bishop of Massachusetts.

Brooks's organist, Lewis H. Redner, at once composed a tune, ST. LOUIS, that closely fitted the sentiment of the words. Redner (1831–1908), a Philadelphian, was a real estate broker, organist, and Sunday school superintendent.

287. IT CAME UPON THE MIDNIGHT CLEAR. Edmund Hamilton Sears (1810–76), an American Unitarian minister, held pulpits in Wayland, Lancaster, and Weston, Mass. Author of many books, hymns, and poems, he is chiefly remembered for two Christmas hymns, this and "Calm on the listening ear of night." This hymn was written, reportedly, at the request of his friend, W. P. Lunt, minister in Quincy, Mass., where it was introduced at the 1849 Sunday school Christmas celebration. Percy Dearmer *(see No. 321)* in his *Songs of Praise Discussed,* 1933, notes "that most Victorian hymnbooks offered little or no application of the social message of Christmas—'Peace on earth, goodwill towards men.'. . . The hymns that began to express the teaching of Christ came from New England, and it is notable that this one was written by a Unitarian minister."

CAROL originally set "While shepherds watched their flocks by night" (No. 295), arranged by Richard Storrs Willis (1819–1900) from Study 23 of his *Church Chorals and Choir Studies,* 1850. Born in Boston, Willis was president of the Beethoven Society as a Yale undergraduate, a pupil of Mendelssohn and others during six years in Europe, and a prominent music critic and publisher in New York City. He died in Detroit, Mich.

288. O COME, ALL YE FAITHFUL.
John Francis Wade, an English Roman
Catholic, may have written this beloved
Christmas carol, ca. 1740–43. Wade, a
music copyist, when he was a politico-
religious refugee in Douai, France, made
hymn collections for Roman Catholic
family chapels. The earliest extant copies
of this text are in his script. This translation is based upon that of Frederick
Oakeley (1802–80), an English Anglican
who late in life converted to Roman
Catholicism.

ADESTE FIDELES is a "fuguing tune"
of the type common in England and
the United States in the eighteenth
century, the soprano being imitated
by the tenor in the refrain. It was
composed, or at least transcribed, by
John Francis Wade.

289. SILENT NIGHT, HOLY
NIGHT. Joseph Mohr (1792–1848),
an Austrian Roman Catholic priest, who,
when assistant priest of the parish
church at Oberndorf, collaborated with
the organist, Franz Xaver Gruber, on
this hymn for Christmas eve, 1818. The
translator of this familiar version is
unknown.

The composer of STILLE NACHT,
Gruber (1787–1863), the son of a poor
linen weaver, was born in Upper Austria. Later in life he was headmaster
at Berndorf and organist at Hallein,
near Salzburg.

290. THANK WE NOW THE LORD
OF HEAVEN. Henry Warburton
Hawkes (1843–1917), an English Unitarian minister, edited two hymnbooks
and wrote many hymns. This Christmas hymn was arranged to fit DIVINUM
MYSTERIUM for The Beacon Song and
Service Book, 1935. It is rearranged
here for the same tune. The original is
in The New Hymn and Tune Book, 1914.

DIVINUM MYSTERIUM, a melody found
in twelfth- to fifteenth-century Italian
and German manuscripts, derives
from a trope, or elaboration, of an
earlier plain-song Sanctus and was
printed in Piae Cantiones (see No. 323).
Canon Winfred Douglas made this
setting for The Hymnal 1940.

291. YE SHEPHERD PLAINS OF
BETHLEHEM. William Merriam
Crane (1880–1958), an American Con-

gregational minister, for many years
wrote a carol each year as a Christmas
greeting to his friends. The carols, of
which this was one, were collected pri-
vately into two books.

THIS ENDRIS NYGHT comes from a
three-voice setting of the carol, "Thys
endris nyght I saw a syght," in a
fifteenth-century manuscript (British
Museum, Royal Appendix 58). Ralph
Vaughan Williams (see No. 78) arranged it for The English Hymnal,
1906.

292. IN THE LONELY MIDNIGHT.
Theodore Chickering Williams. See
No. 226. This hymn first appeared in
The New Hymn and Tune Book, 1914.
Originals of Lines 2 and 8, Stanza 3, are
"Sent from heaven on high," and
"Christ your king is born."

For ADORO TE DEVOTE see No. 128.

293. HEIR OF ALL THE WAITING
AGES. Marion Franklin Ham. See No.
125. This was written for Hymns of the
Spirit, 1937, for the tune, PICARDY,
as an Advent hymn. This book uses
Stanzas 1, 3, and 2 of the original four.

PICARDY is a folk song from Picardy
as sung by Mme. Pierre Dupont and
published in Weckerlin's Chansons
populaires des provinces de France, IV,
1860. In The English Hymnal, 1906,
it was adapted to "Let all mortal
flesh keep silence."

294. ANGELS WE HAVE HEARD
ON HIGH. This French carol, with the
text, "Les anges dans nos campagnes,"
and its tune GLORIA, presumably dates
from the eighteenth century. It was
published in Nouveau recueil de cantiques,
1855. This English version, based on an
anonymous translation, is by Earl Bow-
man Marlatt (1892–    ), a Methodist
minister and a professor at Wellesley
College and at Boston University, where
he was dean of the School of Theology,
1938–45. He taught at Perkins Theological School, Southern Methodist
University, 1945–58.

295. WHILE SHEPHERDS WATCHED.
Nahum Tate (1652–1715) was born in
Dublin, Ireland, wrote much for the
stage, collaborated with Dryden on several occasions, and was appointed England's poet laureate in 1692. He wrote

the libretto for Henry Purcell's *Dido and Aeneas*, the oldest opera still in general use. He produced the *New Version of the Psalms of David*, 1696, in collaboration with Nicholas Brady. This hymn appeared in the Tate and Brady psalm book, 1700; it closely paraphrases Luke 2:8–15.

For CHRISTMAS see No. 223.

296. ON THIS DAY EVERY-WHERE. For Theodoric Petri's *Piae Cantiones see No. 323*. This version of the text was made by Rev. Christopher Moore, director of the children's choir, First Unitarian Society of Chicago, Ill., and Vincent B. Silliman (*see No. 14*).

PERSONENT HODIE, the original melody is here arranged by the composer, Gustav Holst (1874–1934). A native of Cheltenham, England, and a pupil of Sir Charles Stanford at the Royal College of Music, where he himself later taught, Holst directed music for over twenty-five years at St. Paul's School for Girls and Morley College, London. In 1931–32 he taught and performed his works at the University of Michigan and at Harvard.

297. BREAK FORTH, O BEAUTE-OUS LIGHT. Johann Rist (1607–67) was a German Lutheran pastor, patriot, and writer, during the Thirty Years' War. This is a translation by John Troutbeck (1832–99), Church of England clergyman and hymnbook editor, of Stanza 9 of Rist's *"Ermuntre dich, mein schwacher Geist,"* in Rist's *Himmlische Lieder*, 1641.

For Johann Schop see No. 28. The harmonization is from J. S. Bach's *Christmas Oratorio*, 1734.

298. LO, HOW A ROSE E'ER BLOOMING. Brother Conrad was, according to Luther Noss, contemporary American hymnologist, a monk of Mainz, Germany, whose name was signed to the original of this text in 1587/8, in a prayer book discovered in Trier in 1957. The translation is by Theodore Baker (1851–1934), music editor and scholar associated with the publishing house of G. Schirmer, New York City.

ES IST EIN' ROS' ENTSPRUNGEN, a traditional carol melody of the Rhineland, appeared in *Alte catholische geistliche Kirchengeseng*, 1599, published in Cologne for use in Speyer. The harmonization is from Praetorius' *Musae Sioniae*, VI, 1609 (*see No. 125*).

299. JOY TO THE WORLD. Isaac Watts. *See No. 51*. This is in part a paraphrase of Psalm 98.

ANTIOCH first appears in Lowell Mason's (*see No. 126*), *Occasional Psalm and Hymn Tunes*, No. 3, Boston, 1836, with the attribution, "arranged from Handel." Not an arrangement in the usual sense, the tune is a development of the four-note motive used for the opening syllables of the chorus, "Glory to God," in Handel's *Messiah*, 1742.

300. WE THREE KINGS OF ORIENT ARE. John Henry Hopkins, Jr. (1820–91), an American Episcopal clergyman, led in the development of hymnody in that denomination during the mid-nineteenth century. He created both text and tune, KINGS OF ORIENT, of this Epiphany carol in 1857; it appeared in his *Carols, Hymns and Songs*, 1863. The last stanza is by Vincent B. Silliman (*see No. 14*).

301. 'TIS WINTER NOW. Samuel Longfellow. *See No. 43*. Written in 1859, this hymn appeared in *Hymns of the Spirit*, 1864, in four stanzas; Stanzas 1 and 3 are used here.

For PUER NOBIS NASCITUR see No. 125.

302. WINTER IS A COLD THING. Barrows Dunham (1905–    ), an American Presbyterian, a professor of philosophy at Temple University, 1937–53. He is writing a history of heresy; his books are *Man Against Myth*, 1947, *Giant in Chains*, 1953, and *The Artist in Society*, 1961. He wrote this poem after a 1954 visit to Valley Forge.

VALLEY FORGE was composed for this book by Henry Leland Clarke (*see No. 135*).

303. THE CHANGES. Howard Box (1926–    ) is an American Unitarian Universalist minister and Ethical Culturist, Leader of the Brooklyn Society for Ethical Culture. Previous pastorates include Girard, Pa.; Newburgh, N. Y.; and Ottawa, Ont. This text was written for the Unitarian Church of Ottawa's Christmas Sunday, 1958, for a traditional Hungarian carol, CHRISTUS

URUNKNAK, arranged by Thomas La-grady, a refugee from the 1958 Hungarian uprising. The harmonization is by Robert L. Sanders (*see No. 2*).

304. ALL BEAUTIFUL THE MARCH OF DAYS. Frances Whitmarsh Wile (1878–1939) wrote this hymn about 1907, in consultation with the Rev. William Channing Gannett (*see No. 1*) in Rochester, N. Y. It was included in *Unity Hymns and Chorals*, 1911.

Ralph Vaughan Williams (*see No. 78*) recorded an English folk song, "The Plowboy's Dream," at Forest Green, Surrey, in 1903 and arranged it as FOREST GREEN for *The English Hymnal*, 1906.

305. RING OUT, WILD BELLS. Alfred Lord Tennyson. *See No. 65*. This text is five of the eight stanzas of Section 106 of "In Memoriam." In the last line "light" is substituted for "Christ."

DEUS TUORUM MILITUM was adapted from a Grenoble Antiphoner of 1868 for *The English Hymnal*, 1906. In place of the old unmeasured plainsong, measured melodies came into Roman Catholic use in several dioceses in seventeenth-century France. Here is one of the "church melodies," suggesting both plain-song and folk-song antecedents, that grew out of this practice.

306. TO MAKE THIS EARTH, OUR HERMITAGE. Robert Louis Stevenson. *See No. 60*. This text is arranged from "The House Beautiful," in *Travels with a Donkey*, 1879.

For DEVOTION *see No. 183*.

307. THOU, EARTH, ART OURS. Mary Botham Howitt (1799–1888), an English Quaker, who became Roman Catholic, wrote, often in collaboration with her husband, William. Her works include verse and tales for children. This altered text is from Stanton Coit's (1857–1944) *Social Worship*, II, 1913; we cannot locate the original.

For WAS GOTT THUT *see No. 30*.

308. PRAISE TO GOD AND THANKS WE BRING. William Channing Gannett. *See No. 1*. This was written for a harvest festival at Saint Paul, Minn., when he was minister of Unity Church. It was included in *The Thought of God*, First Series, 1885. Here, the text is revised considerably.

For SPANISH HYMN *see No. 127*.

309. HOSANNA IN THE HIGHEST. John Howland Lathrop (1880–    ), an American, for over forty years was minister of the First Unitarian Congregational Society in Brooklyn, N. Y. This hymn, here minus a stanza, was written at Senexet House, Woodstock, Conn. Dr. Lathrop writes: "At Senexet I went out for a tramp along a road covered with snow, beating the time with my foot, and the words came." It was used on Palm Sunday in Brooklyn, "where we always had a procession all around the church."

For ELLACOMBE *see No. 236*.

310. LIFT UP YOUR HEADS, YE MIGHTY GATES. Georg Weissel (1590–1635) was judge and later burgomaster at Domnau, near Königsberg, Prussia, where he was born. Educated at Königsberg and other universities, he was briefly rector of a school and then Lutheran pastor at Königsberg until his death. This text is an adaptation of Stanzas 1 and 4 of Catherine Winkworth's translation (*see No. 19*), in *Lyra Germanica*, 1855. It is based on Psalm 24 and begins, "*Macht hoch die Thür, das Thor macht weit.*"

The tune first appeared in the music edition of the Swedish hymnbook, *Then Swenska Psalmboken*, Stockholm, 1697, as an anonymous setting of Israel Kolmodin's text MISSTRÖSTA EJ ATT GUD ÄR GOD (Distrust not that God is good). The harmonization is by Kenneth Munson (*see No. 134*).

311. O SACRED HEAD, NOW WOUNDED. Bernard of Clairvaux (1091–1153) and Paul Gerhardt (1607–76). This Good Friday hymn is a free translation of "*Salve caput cruentatum*," the final section of "*Rhythmica Oratio*," attributed to St. Bernard. This English version was made in 1881 by James Waddell Alexander (1804–59), American clergyman who taught at Princeton University and later was minister of the Fifth Avenue Presbyterian Church, New York City.

Originally composed by Hans Leo Hassler (1564–1612) for the love song, "*Mein G'muth ist mir verwirret*," in his *Lustgarten neuer teutscher Gesäng*, 1601, the melody, applied to Christoph Knoll's "*Herzlich tut mich verlangen*," 1613, and to Paul Gerhardt's "*O Haupt voll Blut und Wunden*," 1656, became known as the PASSION CHORALE. This version is one of five given in J. S. Bach's *St. Matthew Passion*, 1729. A native of Nuremberg, Germany, Hassler studied with Andrea Gabrieli in Venice, Italy. He was organist to Octavian Fugger in Augsburg and Prince Christian II in Dresden.

312. BENEATH THE SHADOW OF THE CROSS. Samuel Longfellow. *See No. 43*. First published in the supplement to *A Book of Hymns*, second edition, 1848, titled "The New Commandment."

For DUNDEE, see *No. 34*.

313. GETHSEMANE AND CALVARY. John Reynell Wreford (1800–81) was an English Unitarian minister, who resigned his New Meeting, Birmingham, pastorate because of failing voice and became a schoolmaster. This was one of fifty-five hymns he contributed to J. R. Beard's *Collection of Hymns for Public and Private Worship*, 1837, a book described as "a protest against hymn-tinkering and as a novel effort to reconstruct Unitarian Hymnody out of materials exclusively Unitarian." This was rewritten by Samuel Longfellow (*see No. 43*) in 1848 for Samuel Johnson and his *A Book of Hymns*, enlarged.

CAMPIAN 5 derives from No. 5 in Thomas Campian's *First Book of Airs*, ca. 1613 (*see No. 107*).

314. NOW IN THE TOMB IS LAID. Padraic Colum (1881–     ), an Irish-born Roman Catholic poet, came to America in 1914. He received, among other honors, the Academy of American Poets' Award, 1952, and the Boston Arts Festival poet citation, 1961. He lives in New York City. This text is No. 14 of a series written for the stations of the cross in bronze, by Alfeo Faggi, sculptor, in St. Thomas' Roman Catholic Church, Chicago, Ill., published in the booklet, *The Way of the Cross*. Chicago, 1926.

LAMENT is from *Hymns and Responses for the Church Year*, 1956, by Vincent Persichetti (1915–     ). A native of Philadelphia, Pa., Persichetti studied piano with Alberto Jonás and Olga Samaroff, composition with Paul Nordoff and Roy Harris, and conducting with Fritz Reiner. He has distinguished himself as a composer and as a teacher at the Philadelphia Conservatory and the Juilliard School of Music. He has written *Twentieth-Century Harmony*, 1961.

315. PAST ARE THE CROSS, THE SCOURGE, THE THORN. Alfred Charles Jewitt (1845–1925) was an Englishman, said to be the author of *Lays and Legends*, London, 1879. Our text comprises Stanzas 1 and 5 of his five-stanza Easter hymn.

O FILII ET FILIAE is probably the original melody for the text written by Jean Tisserand, a Franciscan monk who died in Paris in 1494. The melody was first printed in *Airs sur les hymnes sacrez, odes et noëls*, Paris, 1623. It was harmonized thus for this book.

316. O DAY OF LIGHT AND GLADNESS. Frederick Lucian Hosmer. *See No. 50*. This Easter hymn was written in 1903, published in Louisa Loring's *Hymns of the Ages*, 1904, and, slightly revised, in *Unity Hymns and Chorals*, 1911.

LANCASHIRE was composed by Henry Smart (1813–79), organist at Blackburn, Lancashire, England, to fit the text, "From Greenland's icy mountains," for a missionary meeting in 1836. That year he returned to his native London, where he was long active as organist and designer of organs. The tune was introduced in *Psalms and Hymns for Divine Worship*, 1867.

317. LO, THE DAY OF DAYS IS HERE. Frederick Lucian Hosmer. *See No. 50*. We have taken portions of two of Hosmer's hymns to provide a new Easter text stressing the rebirth of nature for "Llanfair."

The melody of LLANFAIR, from a manuscript book dated 1817, is by Robert Williams (ca. 1781–1821), a blind basket maker of Anglesey, an island northwest of Wales. The harmony, from John Parry's *Peroriaeth*

*Hyfryd*, 1837, is by John Roberts, Henllan, *(see No. 41)* (not John Roberts, Ieuan Gwyllt, *see No. 39*).

**318. LO, THE EARTH AWAKES AGAIN.** Samuel Longfellow. *See No. 43.* This hymn originally began "Lo the earth again is risen." Longfellow later revised this to "Lo the earth is risen again," and otherwise improved the text. Here, set to alleluias, is a further revision by the editors of this book, chiefly a rearrangement of lines from Stanzas 3 and 4 into a new Stanza 3.

EASTER HYMN with its alleluias is the result of "a desire for a little freer air than the grand movement of the Psalm tunes," according to the unknown editor of *Lyra Davidica*, 1708, for the text, "Jesus Christ is risen today, Halle-halle-lujah." This form of the tune is from John Arnold's *Compleat Psalmodist*, second edition, 1749. The ascription to Dr. John Worgan is false; he was not born until 1724.

**319. LIFT YOUR HIDDEN FACES.** Rose Fyleman (1877–   ), English author and musician, who has published many books of plays, stories, and poems for children, contributes regularly to *Punch* magazine. This carol was written for *The Oxford Book of Carols*, 1928; the words are based upon a French original, and the refrain is from Psalm 147.

GRÂCE SOIT RENDUE is a French carol tune in L. Eugène Grinault's *Noëls angevins*, 1878. Variants of it are sung in Anjou, Champagne, and Burgundy. The harmonization is by Kenneth Munson *(see No. 134)*.

**320. NOW ONCE AGAIN THE HEAVEN TURNS.** Kenneth L. Patton. *See No. 28.* Written for a spring festival service in 1960 at the Charles Street Universalist Meeting House, Boston, the hymn appears here in a book for the first time.

For HAMILTON *see No. 57.*

**321. SPRING HAS NOW UNWRAPPED THE FLOWERS.** *Piae Cantiones. See No. 323.* This is a translation for *The Oxford Book of Carols*, 1928, of *"Tempus adest floridum."* "Unfortunately," writes Dearmer, "when that unique Swedish book [*Piae Cantiones*] was brought to England . . .

and given . . . to Dr. Neale, the latter wrote for it the words of 'Good King Wenceslas,' a poor ballad, difficult to understand, and unworthy of the writer of so many good carols. Habits are difficult to break, but we may hope that gradually the tune will become less associated with Christmas (for which there are so many glorious carols without it), and increasingly sung to its proper spring theme." To which the editors of this book add: Amen.

TEMPUS ADEST FLORIDUM is the original melody from *Piae Cantiones*, harmonized for *The Oxford Book of Carols*, 1928, by Martin Shaw *(see No. 266)*

**322. EARLY SPRING.** Fan Cheng-ta (1125–93), like other Chinese poets, spent much of his life in state service, having passed the highest literary examination in 1154. His talents were both military and diplomatic. As a governor, he gathered poets around him. He wrote the poem sequence from which this text is taken in his sixtieth year, a year of retirement for his health. Gerald Bullett (1894–1958), an Englishman, translated and published the sequence as *The Golden Year of Fan Cheng-ta*, 1946. Kenneth L. Patton *(see No. 28)*, with Mrs. Bullett's permission, adapted the stanzas for singing.

For SURSUM CORDA *see No. 71.*

**323. NOW THE SPRING HAS COME AGAIN.** *Piae Cantiones*, 1582, was a remarkable collection of medieval sacred and secular songs, gathered and edited by Theodoric Petri, a Finnish student at the University of Rostock, Denmark, then part of the Swedish kingdom. In 1591 Petri became secretary to King Sigismund; little else is known of him, save that he spent his late years in Poland. The single extant copy of Petri's collection was taken to England about 1852 by the British minister to Sweden. This spring carol was translated by Steuart Wilson (1889–   ), an English singer, who has edited several collections of songs and published translations of the songs of Schubert, Schumann, and Brahms.

The melody, IN VERNALI TEMPORE, from *Piae Cantiones* was harmonized for *The Oxford Book of Carols*, 1928, by Geoffrey Shaw (1879–1943), inspector of music in the London schools, and co-editor of many song books with his brother, Martin Shaw (*see No. 266*).

**324. OH, GIVE US PLEASURE IN THE FLOWERS TODAY.** Robert Lee Frost (1875–1963) was a New England poet of simple, colloquial verse. He was awarded the Pulitzer prize for *New Hampshire* in 1923 and for *A Further Range* in 1936. Two earlier books made his reputation: *A Boy's Will*, 1913 (containing this poem) and *North of Boston*, 1914. Other volumes include *In the Clearing*, 1962, and *Complete Poems*, 1949.

For COOLINGE *see No. 84.*

**325. PLEASURE IT IS.** William Cornish (or Cornysshe) (ca. 1465–1523) was pageant master, composer, and dramatist for England's Henry VIII. Much of his secular and sacred music survives, chiefly in manuscript in museums. "He had an especial gift for setting cheerful words."

ES MUSS DIE GANZE CHRISTENSCHAR is an elaboration of the melody composed by Burkard Waldis for Psalm 124 in his metrical version of the psalms, 1553. Born in Allendorf-an-der-Werra, Germany, he was associated with Hans Sachs in Nuremberg and is last heard of in 1557 when he resigned as parson in Abterode. The harmonization is by Robert L. Sanders (*see No. 2*).

**326. JUNE DAYS.** Samuel Longfellow. *See No. 43.* In *Hymns and Verses* by Samuel Longfellow, 1893, this poem is called "Summer Rural Gathering" and dated 1859; each stanza begins, "The sweet June days are come again." *Hymns of the Spirit*, 1864, includes Stanzas 2 and 3, with the stanzas beginning, "The summer days are come again," and the concluding quatrain rewritten. We have returned to the original opening line, but have kept the revised final quatrain.

For FOREST GREEN *see No. 304.*

**327. THY SUMMER.** Thomas Hornblower Gill. *See No. 15.* This text is Stanzas 3, 4, 2, 5, slightly changed, of "Joy in the Works of God," from *The Golden Chain of Praise Hymns*, 1894.

This is essentially the arrangement in W. C. Gannett (*see No. 5*) and F. L. Hosmer (*see No. 50*), *Unity Hymns and Chorals*, 1911.

COLCHESTER is in *A Compleat Melody; or, The Harmony of Sion*, London, 1734, compiled by William Tans'ur (1706?–83), whose publications became popular in pre-Revolutionary New England through reprints by Daniel Bayley of Newburyport, Mass. (*see No. 50*). We find no evidence to warrant attributing the tune to Henry Purcell.

**328. A ROSARY OF THINGS BEAUTIFUL.** Harry Youlden (1867–1916), an Englishman, was a Baptist minister at Norwich and then Liverpool. Gradually he moved toward the position of the Ethical Movement of Stanton Coit (*see Note 307*). He was dismissed from the pulpit in 1912 and then founded the Ethical Church, Liverpool, where he was resident lecturer until his death. This prose poem is substantially as it was in Coit's *Social Worship*, II, 1913. Youlden varied its form somewhat in his *A Manual of Ethical Devotion*, 1914, where the opening lines of Keats's "Endymion" are printed as its prelude. On occasion, only one or two sections of this passage need be used.

**329. GOD IN NATURE.** Sec. I: Psalm 104:1-7, 10-15, 19-23; Sec. II: Psalm 104:24-34, 35b; Verse 4 is from the English Revised Version. The cosmology is that of Gen. 1. Leviathan, a mythical beast, borrows features from crocodile and whale (see Job 40:15ff.). James H. Breasted in *The Dawn of Conscience*, 1934, holds that Psalm 104:20-26 is based on a hymn of Ikhnaton, Emperor of Egypt, fourteenth century B.C.

**330. AN ACCOUNTING OF GRATITUDE.** Kenneth L. Patton. *See Note 28.* This is in *Man Is the Meaning.*

**331. THE BEAUTY OF HOLINESS.** Psalm 96. The fine phrase, "O worship the Lord in the beauty of holiness," is a mistranslation of the Hebrew meaning, "Kneel before the Lord in sacred vestments." We follow the English Revised Version in substituting "nations" for "heathen" in Verses 3 and 10.

332. THE MANIFOLD RICHNESS OF LIFE. Von Ogden Vogt (1879– ), Unitarian Universalist minister, whose description of worship as "the celebration of life" provides the title for this book, was born in Altamont, Ill. Before becoming minister of the First Unitarian Society of Chicago, he served Congregational churches, including the Wellington Avenue Congregational Church, Chicago. His publications include *Art and Religion*, 1921, *Modern Worship*, 1927, and *The Primacy of Worship*, 1958. He was a member of the Unitarian and Universalist commission which produced *Hymns of the Spirit* and *Services of Religion*, 1937. This litany was in *Services of Religion*.

333. THE GOODNESS OF THE EARTH. The Koran, from which this passage has been freely rendered by Kenneth L. Patton (*see Note 28*), is the sacred scripture of Islam, allegedly revealed to Mohammed (ca. 568–632) through the intermediation of an angel.

334. THE CANTICLE OF THE SUN. St. Francis of Assisi. Hymn 23 is a paraphrase of "The Canticle of Brother Sun," of which this is Matthew Arnold's translation (*see Note 85*), abridged.

335. PRAISE YE THE LORD. Psalm 148; we omit most of Verse 14.

336. WE REJOICE. *A New Prayer Book*, London, 1923 (anonymous), proposing revisions of the *Book of Common Prayer*. Adapted in *Services of Religion*, 1937, it is further adapted here.

337. LIFT UP YOUR HEADS, O YE GATES. Psalm 24: "O God of Jacob," Verse 6, is from the English Revised Version. The cosmology is that of Gen. 1. This Psalm may have been written to celebrate the purification of the Temple, 165 B.C., the event commemorated by Hanukkah (*see Note 279*).

338. THE PRIDE OF THE HEIGHT. Ecclus. 43:1-21, adapted and arranged by Kenneth L. Patton (*see Note 28*). See No. 230.

339. GOD. John Burroughs. *See Note 186*. This passage, slightly arranged, is from *Accepting the Universe*, 1920.

340. I WILL LIFT UP MINE EYES. Psalm 121.

341. THE INESCAPABLE GOD. Psalm 139:1-14, 17, 18, 23, 24. "In the grave" is substituted for "in hell"; both refer to the Hebrew *sheol*, the dreary netherworld in which the dead reside; Verse 13 employs later translations.

342. THE TAO. The *Tao-teh-ching*, Chapter 25, attributed to Lao-tzu, sage of the fifth century B.C., legendary founder of Taoism, one of China's major religions. This translation, "an American version," is by Witter Bynner (1881– ) and is titled, *The Way of Life*, 1944.

343. THE SPIRIT OF GOD. Napoleon William Lovely (1907– ) is an American Unitarian Universalist minister, ordained in 1935, whose ministry included three years as an army chaplain; his latest assignment was at The People's Church (Unitarian), Cedar Rapids, Iowa. This passage is from his booklet, *The Liberal Meaning*, 1959.

344. BRAHMAN. *Bhagavad-Gita*, translated by Swami Prabhavananda and Christopher Isherwood. *See Note 134*.

345. OUT OF THE STARS. Robert Terry Weston (1898– ) is minister of the First Unitarian Church of Omaha, Neb., having previously served Unitarian churches in Schenectady, N.Y.; Lexington, Mass.; and Louisville, Ky.; and as a chaplain, U.S. Naval Reserve. He compiled *A Cup of Strength*, 1945, and wrote the Unitarian Universalist Association's Lenten manual, *Seasons of the Soul*, 1963.

346. THE VOICE OF THE LORD. Psalm 29 without Verse 9.

347. THE OVERSOUL. Ralph Waldo Emerson (1803–82), American Unitarian minister and writer, was educated at Harvard College and Divinity School. He served the Second Church in Boston (Unitarian), 1829–32, leaving because he was unwilling to use bread and wine at the Lord's Supper. His "Divinity School Address," 1838, marked the change in

American Unitarian thought from Bible and miracle to individual conscience as the final warrant in religion. This was arranged by Arthur Foote II (*see Note 29*) from "The Oversoul," *Essays, First Series,* 1841.

348. THE UNKNOWN GOD. Acts 17:24-28a. This passage, attributed to Paul, is more Stoic than Pauline.

349. WHO HATH MEASURED THE WATERS. Isa. 40:12-17; 28-31. Written ca. 540 B.C., this is by the "Second Isaiah."

350. NATURE'S IMPARTIAL PROVIDENCE. John Burroughs. *See Note 186.* This passage, slightly abridged, is from *Accepting the Universe,* 1920.

351. THE STREAM OF LIFE. Rabindranath Tagore. *See Note 59.* Poems 69 and 70 in *Gitanjali,* and Poem 3:7 in *The Fugitive, and Other Poems.*

352. THE LORD IS MY SHEPHERD. Psalm 23.

353. GOD IS OUR REFUGE. Psalm 46. We omit Verse 6 and substitute "nations" for "heathen" in Verse 10.

354. THE HUMAN CALENDAR. Kenneth L. Patton. *See Note 28.* This is from *Man Is the Meaning.*

355. THE DIGNITY OF HUMAN NATURE. William Ellery Channing (1780-1842), American Unitarian minister, reared a Congregationalist, was minister of the Federal Street Church (now the Arlington Street Church), Boston, 1803-42. His "Baltimore Sermon," 1819, on "Unitarian Christianity" polarized New England Congregational churches—a schism which resulted in the formation of the Unitarian denomination. Channing, "the great awakener," was, according to Van Wyck Brooks, "the father of half the reforms that characterized the Boston of his age." This passage was arranged by Vincent B. Silliman (*see Note 14*) from Channing's *Self Culture,* 1838.

356. AWAKE, O MAN. Edwin C. Palmer (1891-1956), after three years as minister of Congregational churches, served Unitarian churches in Lincoln,

Neb.; Bloomington, Ill.; and, for twenty-two years, Kalamazoo, Mich. His experiments in humanistic liturgy have had wide influence. This passage appeared in a somewhat different form in *Services of Religion,* 1937.

357. ONE SPECIES. Kenneth L. Patton. *See Note 28.* This is from *The Ground of Being.*

358. VISHNU-SHIVA. Kenneth L. Patton. *See Note 28.* This is from *The Ground of Being.*

359. WHAT IS MAN? Psalm 8. Verse 2 is omitted.

360. THE WONDER OF ONE'S SELF. Walt Whitman. *See Note 78.* This is from "Song of Myself," in *Leaves of Grass.*

361. LORD, THOU HAS BEEN OUR DWELLING PLACE. Psalm 90, without Verses 9 and 11.

362. EPISTLE TO BE LEFT IN THE EARTH. Archibald MacLeish. *See Note 112.* This was published in *New Found Land,* 1930.

363. THE TRAVAIL OF MAN. Ecclus. 40:1-7, 11. Verse 5a is from the English Revised Version.

364. THE SOULS OF THE RIGHTEOUS. *The Wisdom of Solomon,* far from being by the famous king, dates from around the beginning of the Christian era. Though written in Greek and influenced by Platonism and Stoicism, it is Alexandrian, possibly having more than one author. It is included in the Jewish Apocrypha. This passage, abstracted and arranged from Chapters 3, 4, and 2, employs wording from the English Revised Version.

365. ABOVE THE NAME OF MAN. Kenneth L. Patton. *See Note 28.* This is from *Man Is the Meaning.*

366. THE YOUNG DEAD SOLDIERS. Archibald MacLeish. *See Note 112.* This is in *Actfive and Other Poems,* 1948.

367. THE LORD IS MERCIFUL. Psalm 103, without Verses 7, 9, 19, and 20.

368. MY DAYS AS AN HAND-
BREADTH. Psalm 39.

369. THE WAY. Edwin Muir (1887–
1959), Scottish author and critic, published this poem first in *The Labyrinth*,
1949. It appears in his *Collected Poems,
1921–1951*.

370. SOME THINGS WILL NEVER
CHANGE. Thomas Wolfe (1900–38)
was an American novelist. This was
arranged from *The Web and the Rock* by
John S. Barnes in *A Stone, a Leaf, a
Door*, 1939.

371. THE VOICE OF GOD IN THE
SOUL. Thomas à Kempis (ca. 1380–
1471), originally Thomas Hammerken,
was born at Kempen, near Düsseldorf,
Germany, educated at Deventer, Holland, in a school maintained by the
pietistic and semi-monastic "Brothers
of the Common Life," and at St. Agnes'
Convent, Zwolle, Holland, where he
dwelt from 1399 to his death as an
Augustinian canon (monk) and a priest.
His writings include spiritual treatises,
tracts on monastic life, sermons, and the
*Imitatio Christi* (Imitation of Christ),
published anonymously, 1418, from
which this text comes. This translation
was "published at Oxford by Parker,"
not later than 1888. The *Imitatio* has
been "translated into more languages
than any other book save the Bible"—
*Encyclopaedia Britannica*. In one translation, this material is in Part III,
Chapters 1 and 2.

372. LET US WORSHIP. Kenneth
L. Patton. *See Note 28*. This is from
*Man Is the Meaning*.

373. THE LORD IS MY LIGHT.
Psalm 27, without Verses 2, 5b, 6, 7,
11b, and 12.

374. THE ACCEPTANCE OF MYS-
TERY. Kenneth L. Patton. *See Note
28*. This is from *Man Is the Meaning*.

375. INVITATION TO SERENITY.
Vivian Towse Pomeroy (1883–1961) was
born and educated in England, where
he was a Congregational minister,
1911–23. He served the First Congregational Parish in Milton, Mass. (Unitarian), 1924–61. His publications include sermons, children's books and
stories, and *New Prayers in Old Places*,
1955. This piece, arranged with his
permission, appeared in a Milton church
bulletin.

376. IT MATTERS WHAT WE BE-
LIEVE. Sophia Lyon Fahs. (*See Note
58*.) This is from *Today's Children and
Yesterday's Heritage*, 1952.

377. THE COUNSEL OF THINE
OWN HEART. Ecclus. 6:32-36; 4:22
(arranged); 37:13, 14.

378. THE PARABLE OF THE SOW-
ER. Luke 8:4-18.

379. SELF-CONQUEST. *Dhammapada* 8, 15, 1. This compendium of
Buddha's teachings is part of the *Sutta
Pitaka* and was in existence during the
reign of Emperor Asoka, ca. 250 B.C. Lin
Yutang calls it "a great spiritual testimony, one of the very few religious masterpieces of the world combining genu-
ineness of spiritual passion with a happy
gift of literary expression." The *Dhammapada* is widely assumed to contain the
actual teaching of the Buddha. The
translation is by Max Müller (1823–
1900), Vol. 10, *Sacred Books of the East*.

380. THE SUPERIOR MAN. Con-
fucius. *See Note 161*. Arranged by
Jacob Trapp (*see Note 191*) from *The
Analects of Confucius*, from *The Great
Scriptures of the East*.

381. THE FIRST LESSON IN
CHARITY. Kenneth L. Patton. *See
Note 28*. This is from *Readings for the
Celebration of Life*.

382. ACCEPTANCE. *Tao-teh-ching*
16. Attributed to Lao-tzu. From *The
Way of Life*, by Witter Bynner (*see No.
342*).

383. THE WAYS OF THE DEDI-
CATED MAN. *Dhammapada*. See
*No. 379*. This text is a free rendering
by Kenneth L. Patton (*see Note 28*)
based upon various translations.

384. HE THAT MEDITATETH.
Ecclus. 39:1-4b, 5-9a, 10. *See Note 230*.

385. THE MASTERY OF SELF.
*The Golden Mean* (ca. fourth century

B.C.) traditionally is attributed to Tsesze, a grandson of Confucius and teacher of Mencius. The book quotes often from Confucius. This translation is by Ku Hungming with revisions by Lin Yutang. In Lin's *The Wisdom of China and India*, 1942, it is called "The Humanistic Standard."

386. MAN AT HIS BEST. *Tao-teh-ching* 6, 7, 8, as rendered into English by Witter Bynner (*see Note 342*).

387. KEEP THY HEART WITH DILIGENCE. Prov. 3:13-18; 4:5, 7, 9, 23. *See No. 388*. For a paraphrase of Prov. 3:13-18, used as a hymn, *see Hymn 96*.

388. THE LORD GIVETH WISDOM. Prov. 2:1a, 2-9; 3:1-3, 22-24, 26. These verses come from a part of Proverbs which shows Greek influence and may be dated 300-250 B.C.

389. OVERCOME EVIL WITH GOOD. Rom. 12:9-21, without Verses 16 and 19b. "Steadfastly," Verse 12, is from the English Revised Version.

390. RELIGION. Vincent B. Silliman. *See Note 14*. This is from *We Speak of Life*.

391. THE MIND WITHOUT FEAR. Rabindranath Tagore. *See Note 59*. Sec. I is Poem 79, Verses 1-4, in *Fruit-Gathering*, 1916; Secs. II and III are Poem 36, Verses 2-5, and Poem 35 in *Gitanjali*, 1913.

392. A STOIC'S PRAYER. Eusebius, of unknown date, quoted by Stobaeus, a fifth-century anthologist of Greek authors. Of this passage Gilbert Murray (*see Note 109*), who translated it in *Five Stages of Greek Religion*, 1925, said, "How unpretending it is yet how searching! And in the whole there is no petition for any material blessing, and—most strikingly of all—it is addressed to no personal God. It is pure prayer." There are omissions in Murray's translation.

393. OUT OF THE DEPTHS. Psalm 130:1-6.

394. THE HEAVENS DECLARE THE GLORY OF GOD. Sec. I is Psalm 19:1-6 (part of a longer poem, on God in nature); Sec. II is Psalm 19:7-14 (an independent poem in praise of the divine law).

395. TO LIVE DELIBERATELY. Henry David Thoreau (1817-62). "I was born in the most favored spot on earth—and just in the nick of time, too," he said. The spot was Concord, Mass., where he lived and worked as handyman for his friend and neighbor, Ralph Waldo Emerson. His vocation was writing, and he gave mankind *Walden*, 1854, from which this reading comes, *Civil Disobedience, A Week on the Concord and Merrimack Rivers*, and other writings.

396. HOPE THOU IN GOD. Sec. I is Psalm 42:1-4, 6-8, 11. Sec. II is Psalm 43:3-5.

397. THE LIFE OF THE SPIRIT. This is in *Services of Religion*, 1937, and is partly rewritten here.

398. THE ARTS OF MAN. Kenneth L. Patton. *See Note 28*. This is from *Man Is the Meaning*.

399. I HEAR AMERICA SINGING. Walt Whitman. *See Note 78*. Our last two verses are arranged, the last phrase added; from *We Speak of Life*.

400. A NEW SONG. I, Psalm 33:1-8 (verse 2 from American Standard Revised Version); II, Psalm 100.

401. THEN BUILD TEMPLES. Kenneth L. Patton. *See Note 28*. This is from *The Ground of Being*.

402. WHY DOES A MAN WORK? Kenneth L. Patton. *See Note 28*. This is from *Man Is the Meaning*.

403. THE HANDIWORK OF THEIR CRAFT. Ecclus. 38:24-34; phrases are from the English Revised Version. *See Note 230*.

404. THE MAKER OF POEMS. Walt Whitman. *See Note 78*. This is from "Indications" in *Leaves of Grass*.

405. PRAISE GOD IN HIS SANCTUARY. Psalm 150.

406. LOVE. I Cor. 13:1-8, 13. We substitute "love" for "charity" to come closer to Paul's meaning.

407. LET A MAN LEAVE ANGER. *Dhammapada* 17, 18. *See Note 379.*

408. BUDDHA'S PITY. *Upāsaka Sīla Sūtra,* translated from Japanese by Arthur Waley (1889–    ) and arranged by Arthur Foote II (*see Note 29*) from *Buddhist Texts Through the Ages,* edited by E. Conze, 1954.

409. OUR COMMON BONDS. Kenneth L. Patton. *See Note 28.* This is from *Man Is the Meaning.*

410. THE GOOD SAMARITAN. Luke 10:25-37. Here a Jewish lawyer, not Jesus, singles out from Deut. 6:5 and Lev. 19:18 the "Great Commandments." The Samaritans were a religious sect disdained by Jews who accepted the Jewish law, but worshiped on Mt. Gerizim, Samaria, not in Jerusalem.

411. GOD IS LOVE. I John 3:11, 14a, 17, 18; 4:7, 8, 12, 16b. These beautiful verses come from a late, argumentative tract against the heretical and schismatic Gnostics. The translation is partly from the English Revised Version.

412. PITY. Thomas Wolfe. *See Note 370.* From *The Web and the Rock,* this was arranged in verse by John S. Barnes in *A Stone, a Leaf, a Door.*

413. HONOR THY PARENTS. Ecclus. 7:27, 28; 3:5a, 4, 8, 9-13; 8:8, 9. *See Note 230.*

414. YOUR CHILDREN. Kahlil Gibran (1883–1931), poet in Arabic and English and a painter, was born in Lebanon, moved to Boston in 1894, attended college at Beirut, studied painting in Paris, France, and died in New York City. *The Prophet,* written in Arabic, was published in English in 1923. This reading from it omits a few introductory words.

415. A FAITHFUL FRIEND. Ecclus. 6:5-9, 14-16a. *See Note 230.*

416. LOVE AND UNDERSTANDING. Kenneth L. Patton. *See Note 28.* This is from *Man Is the Meaning.*

417. A VIRTUOUS WOMAN. Prov. 31:10, 11a, 12, 13, 19-21, 23, 25-31. The only reference here to deity seems to be a scribe's substitution for the probable original, "a woman of intelligence," as in the Septuagint.

418. MAKE NOT A BOND OF LOVE. Kahlil Gibran. *See Note 414.* This is arranged from *The Prophet.*

419. IN PRAISE OF LIBERTY. John Milton (1608–74), English poet and pamphleteer, attacked the system of pre-publication licensing and censorship of the press in *Areopagitica,* 1644. This passage, arranged, appeared in *We Speak of Life.* A posthumous work, *De Doctrina Christiana,* showed Milton to be an anti-Trinitarian.

420. THE FREE MIND. William Ellery Channing. *See Note 355.* From the sermon, "Spiritual Freedom," preached before the Governor and legislature of Massachusetts, May 26, 1830: an "Election Sermon," this was arranged in *We Speak of Life.*

421. CHERISH YOUR DOUBTS. Robert Terry Weston. *See Note 345.*

422. THE FREE SPIRIT. Louis Henri Sullivan (1856–1924) was an American architect, artist, author, philosopher, and teacher. This text is from *The Autobiography of an Idea,* 1924.

423. THE FAITH OF DOUBT. Kenneth L. Patton. *See Note 28.* This is from *The Ground of Being.*

424. SONG OF THE OPEN ROAD. Walt Whitman. *See Note 78.* For Whitman's "*allons,*" are substituted "together," "forward," and "onward," as in *We Sing of Life,* 1955.

425. THE GLORY OF LIFE IS UPON ME. Francis Albert Rollo Russell (1849–1914) was an English Unitarian, educated at Oxford, fellow of the Royal Meteorological Society, whose hymns, including "Christian, rise and act thy creed," appeared in his *Break of Day,* London, 1893. He was a science writer and author of *Psalms of the West,* 1889 and 1897, from which this text comes.

426. FOR YOU. Walt Whitman. *See Note 78.* This text was arranged and adapted from "Carol of Occupations" by Jacob Trapp (*see Note 191*).

**427. GOOD TIDINGS OF GOOD.**
This composite text is adapted from
Mic. 4:3, 4; Isa. 60:18; Zech.
8:16, 17; and Rollo Russell (*see Note 425*).

**428. HOW BEAUTIFUL UPON THE
MOUNTAINS.** Isa. 52:7-10; 2:2-4.
Isa. 52, by the Second Isaiah, ca. 538
B.C., summoned exiled Israel to return
from Babylon; Isa. 2:2-4 is regarded as
a post-exilic interpolation.

**429. ANNOUNCEMENT.** Walt Whitman. *See Note 78.* This is a section of
"So Long!" from *Leaves of Grass.*

**430. A NEW HEAVEN AND
EARTH.** Isa. 65:17-25, omitting phrases
from Verses 20 and 25 (ca. 450 B.C.).

**431. PARABLES OF THE KING-
DOM.** Matt. 13:24-33, 44-46.

**432. COMFORT YE MY PEOPLE.**
Isa. 40:1, 2a, 3-8. The Second Isaiah
announces (ca. 540 B.C.) the end of the
Jewish exile in Babylonia.

**433. THE PEOPLE SHALL DWELL
IN PEACE.** This text is adapted from
Isa. 57:19; 32:17; 65:19; Zech. 8:5;
Isa. 65:20-25; 32:18; it appears in
*Readings for the Celebration of Life.*

**434. IN PRAISE OF PEACE.** Pupils
of the Lincoln School, New York, N.Y.
This text appeared in *Creative Expres-
sion*, 1932, by Gertrude Hartman and
Ann Schumacher and was arranged for
*We Speak of Life.*

**435. RIGHTEOUSNESS AS A
MIGHTY STREAM.** Amos 5:7-11;
8:4-6; 5:21-24 (ca. 760 B.C.). Amos is
the earliest of the known prophets who
revolutionized Hebrew religion by putting justice first. Amos 5:8 may be an
interpolation. We follow the English
Revised Version in 5:9 and 5:21.

**436. GEOGRAPHY OF THIS TIME.**
Archibald MacLeish. *See Note 112.*
This is from *Actfive and Other Poems*,
1948.

**437. HO, EVERY ONE THAT
THIRSTETH.** Isa. 55:1, 2a, 3a, 6-13.
The Second Isaiah (ca. 538 B.C.) portrays
to his fellow exiles in Babylon the glory
of the nation that shall be.

**438. THIS IS TRUE RELIGION.**
Tulsī Dās (1532–1623), influential
teacher and Hindu poet, was author of
an interpretation of the Ramayana. This
poem was translated into English by
Mohandas Gandhi (1869–1948), leader
of India's movement for national independence, in his *Songs from Prison.*

**439. ON THE VERGE OF MAS-
TERY.** Kenneth L. Patton. *See Note
28.* This is from *Readings for the Celebration of Life.*

**440. I THINK CONTINUALLY OF
THOSE.** Stephen Spender (1909–    )
is an English poet, writer, and critic.
This is from *Poems*, 1934.

**441. SERVANTS OF GOD.** This
text, slightly altered, is from *Services of
Religion*, 1937.

**442. THE PROPHETS.** Kenneth L.
Patton. *See Note 28.* This is from
*Readings for the Celebration of Life.*

**443. THE HUMAN FELLOWSHIP.**
Kenneth L. Patton. *See Note 28.* This
is from *The Ground of Being.*

**444. LET US NOW PRAISE FA-
MOUS MEN.** Ecclus. 44:1, 3-9a, 10, 11,
14a, 13b, 15. Hymn 230 sets part of
this text to music.

**445. FREE NATION AND FREE
WORLD.** This text, abridged and revised, is from *Services of Religion.*

**446. THE RIGHTEOUS NATION.**
This text is adapted in the *Beacon Song
and Service Book* from Isa. 26:2; 62:10;
66:12; 60:17b, 18; 32:16; 35:1, 5;
Mic. 4:4. The image is of returning
exiles; the goal is a commonwealth of
man prefigured in Jewish hopes for a
kingdom of God centering in a new
Jerusalem.

**447. THE BULWARK OF OUR
LIBERTY.** Abraham Lincoln (1809–
65) in life and undying words typifies the
American dream. These sentences, with
changes, are from speeches in Edwards-
ville and Springfield, Ill., at Cooper
Union, New York City, and from the
First and Second Inaugurals.

**448. THE GREAT CITY.** Walt Whitman. *See Note 78.* This is Sec. 5, "Song
of the Broad-Axe," in *Leaves of Grass.*

449. FORCE AND THE WAY OF LIFE. *Tao-teh-ching. See Note 342.* This text is a paraphrase by Kenneth L. Patton (*see Note 28*).

450. SALUT AU MONDE! Walt Whitman. (*See Note 78.*) This is an arrangement by Kenneth L. Patton (*see Note 28*) of "*Salut au Monde*" from *Leaves of Grass.*

451. ON WAR. *Tao-teh-ching* 30, 31. This text is translated by Witter Bynner. *See Note 342.*

452. OWNER OF THE SPHERE. Ralph Waldo Emerson. *See Note 347.* This was arranged by Arthur Foote II (*see Note 29*) from "History," one of the *Essays, First Series,* 1841.

453. A NEW SHAPE OF FELLOW-SHIP. Kenneth L. Patton. *See Note 28.* This is from *The Ground of Being.*

454. MAN IN TIME. Kenneth L. Patton. *See Note 28.* This is from *Man Is the Meaning.*

455. UNIVERSAL RELIGION. Kenneth L. Patton. *See Note 28.* This is from *Readings for the Celebration of Life.*

456. AN ETERNAL VERITY. W. Waldemar W. Argow (1891–1961), after four years as a Baptist minister, served Unitarian churches in Cedar Rapids, Iowa; Syracuse, N.Y.; and Baltimore, Md. His *Beyond,* 1931, consists of prose poems; his *Victorious Living* was the American Unitarian Association's 1941 Lenten manual. This is from *We Speak of Life.*

457. FOR GENERATIONS TO COME. Psalm 78:1-7, 35. The text is changed slightly.

458. HOW AMIABLE ARE THY TABERNACLES. Psalm 84. This is a pilgrim song; "sparrow" and "swallow" are pious Jewish pilgrims.

459. THE CHURCH OF TOMOR-ROW. Kenneth L. Patton. *See Note 28.* This is from *Man Is the Meaning.*

460. A LIBERAL CHURCH. Wallace W. Robbins (1910– ) is an American Unitarian Universalist minister who has served churches in Alton, Ill.; St. Paul, Minn.; and Worcester, Mass. He was president of Meadville Theological School, Chicago, Ill., 1944–56. This text is arranged from his response at his installation as eighth minister of the Second Parish, Town of Worcester, 1956.

461. THIS HOUSE. Kenneth L. Patton. *See Note 28.* This is from *Man Is the Meaning.*

462. THE GREAT END IN RE-LIGIOUS INSTRUCTION. William Ellery Channing. *See Note 355.* This is arranged from "The Sunday-School: Discourse Pronounced before the Sunday-School Society."

463. THE NEW YEAR. Kenneth L. Patton. *See Note 28.* This is from *Man Is the Meaning.*

464. CHRISTMAS BEATITUDES. David Rhys Williams (1890– ) entered the Unitarian ministry in 1924 after ten years as a Congregational minister. Since 1928 he has been with the First Unitarian Congregational Society, Rochester, N.Y. He wrote *World Religions and the Hope of Peace,* 1951, and arranged many popular responsive readings. He wrote this, which appeared in *We Speak of Life,* 1955.

465. THE COMING OF SPRING. Walt Whitman. *See Note 78.* This is from *Leaves of Grass,* 1888.

466. RANGE ON RANGE OF LIFE. Von Ogden Vogt. *See Note 332.* This is abridged from a text in *Services of Religion,* 1937.

467. UNTO US A CHILD IS BORN. Isa. 9:2, 6, 7; 11:1-4a, 5-7, 9. The text is from the English Revised Version. Verse 6, mistranslated here, describes a victorious hero, not an incarnate god.

468. INTO THIS HOUSE OF LIGHT WE COME. Von Ogden Vogt. *See Note 332.* This is from *Services of Religion,* 1937.

469. TAKE US NOW TO SERVE THEE. James Martineau. *See Note 87.* This text, arranged from *Home Prayers,* 1892, is in *Services of Religion,* 1937.

470. WE ARRIVE OUT OF MANY SINGULAR ROOMS. Kenneth L. Patton. *See Note 28.* This is in *Man Is the Meaning.*

471. ALMIGHTY GOD, UNTO WHOM ALL HEARTS ARE OPEN. This text from the Latin, probably of English origin, is in *The Booke of the Common Prayer,* 1549. The last phrase is omitted.

472. THE EXHORTATION OF THE DAWN. This is attributed to Kālidāsa, third-century A.D., Hindu poet, "the most illustrious name among the writers of the second epoch of Sanskrit literature."

473. BEFORE THE WONDERS OF LIFE. Von Ogden Vogt. *See Note 332.* This is in *Services of Religion,* 1937.

474. EVEN AS OF OLD. Frank Carleton Doan (1877–1927) was born of Quaker parents. In 1904, he became professor of the Philosophy of Religion at Meadville Theological School, Meadville, Pa., and in 1914 was ordained to the Unitarian ministry. He served churches in Summit, N.J.; Iowa City, Iowa; and Rochester, N.Y. These sentences (the last, adapted) are from *The Eternal Spirit and the Daily Round,* published posthumously in 1928.

475. OUT OF DARKNESS, INTO LIGHT. Von Ogden Vogt. *See Note 332.* This is from *Services of Religion,* 1937.

476. A PRAYER AT HARVEST TIME. This is from *The Beacon Song and Service Book,* 1935.

477. NUMBERLESS ARE THY WITNESSES. Robert French Leavens (1878–1961) was a Unitarian minister who served churches in Fitchburg, Mass.; Omaha, Neb.; and Berkeley, Calif. before becoming chaplain of Mills College, Oakland, Calif.; editor of *Great Companions,* Vol. I, 1927; and, with his sister, Mary, of Vol. II, 1941. This is from *Let Us Pray,* 1939.

478. CONFIRM THE BONDS OF MUTUAL TRUST. This is from *Orders of Public Worship for the Use of Manchester College,* Oxford University, 1915.

479. THOU ART THE PATH. Though thought and phrasing resemble the *Bhagavad-Gita,* we have not located the original of this Indian text.

480. IN THE SPIRIT OF ST. FRANCIS. Attributed to Francis of Assisi. *See Note 23.* This text was adapted for *We Speak of Life.* We find no evidence of the authorship.

481. LET BROTHERLY LOVE CONTINUE. Hosea Ballou (1771–1852), a great figure of American Universalism, was born in Richmond, N.H., son of a Baptist minister. Influenced by the Deism of Ethan Allen, he became a Universalist and was ordained informally in 1794. He founded and edited the *Universalist Magazine,* later *The Trumpet,* and the *Universalist Expositor.* After pastorates in Portsmouth, N.H., and Salem, Mass., he served the Second Society of Universalists of Boston from 1817 to his death. His influential *A Treatise on Atonement,* 1805, taught the invincible love of God and expressed a Unitarian view of Jesus that soon prevailed among Universalists. This text is from the concluding section of that book.

482. OUR SEARCH TOGETHER. Kenneth L. Patton. *See Note 28.* This is from *Readings for the Celebration of Life.*

483. IN OUR HEARTS MAY THERE BE LOVE. Robert French Leavens. *See Note 477.* This is adapted from *Let Us Pray,* 1939.

484. THE HORIZON OF OUR MINDS. Samuel McChord Crothers (1857–1927) was born in Oswego, Ill. After five years in the Presbyterian ministry, he served Unitarian churches in Brattleboro, Vt.; St. Paul, Minn.; and Cambridge, Mass. Crothers won early fame as an author, particularly for the insights and humor of his essays. This is an adaptation by Vincent B. Silliman (*see Note 14*) of a sentence from *Prayers,* 1928.

485. MAY WE GO FORTH. George Rudolph Freeman (1850–98), educated for the Lutheran ministry, began a distinguished scholarly career at Yale

Divinity School, then studied at Berlin, Germany. Becoming a Unitarian, he went to teach at Meadville Theological School, Meadville, Pa.. in 1890. This is adapted from *Chapel Prayers*, 1898.

486. THE EFFORTS OF FAITH. Von Ogden Vogt. *See Note 332.* This is in *We Speak of Life*, 1955.

487. UNTO THE CHURCH UNIVERSAL. Keshub Chandra Sen (1838–84). Joined in 1857 and then became a leader in the Brahmo Samaj, a Hindu reform movement founded by Rāmmohun Roy (ca. 1774–1833), which was in touch with British and American Unitarianism and devoted to understanding of and fellowship with all faiths. This text, arranged by John Haynes Holmes (*see Note 205*), is repeated congregationally each Sunday in The Community Church, New York, N.Y.

488. THE BEATITUDES. Matt. 5:3-12.

489. THE POWER OF LOVE. This remarkable statement from the Act of Horodlo, 1413 A.D., reputedly was inspired by Queen Jadwiga of Poland.

490. CHURCH COVENANT. Charles Gordon Ames (1828–1912), with little formal training, became a Free Baptist home missionary in Minnesota. In 1859, he gathered the Unitarian church in Bloomington, Ill., "the church of Lincoln's friends," and became a propagandist for Lincoln. He devised this text, ca. 1880, as the covenant for the Spring Garden Unitarian Society, Philadelpha, Pa., which he had founded. For twenty years he served the Church of the Disciples, Unitarian, in Boston.

491. WE AVOW OUR FAITH. This bond of fellowship and statement of faith, here abbreviated, was adopted at Washington, D.C., in 1935 by The Universalist Church of America. It was intended as a convenient summary of conclusions, not a binding creed.

492. THE FELLOWSHIP OF FREE SOULS. Alfred Wilhelm Martin (1862–1933). Born in Cologne, Germany, a graduate of McGill University, Montreal, he prepared for the Unitarian ministry at Harvard Divinity School, and was ordained in 1888. He left the Unitarian ministry and in 1908 became a Leader of the New York, N.Y., Society for Ethical Culture. Several of his books discuss world religions, but we cannot locate the source of this text.

493. THE NONCONFORMIST. Ralph Waldo Emerson. *See Note 347.* This is from "Self-Reliance," in *Essays, First Series*, 1841.

494. LOVE IS THE SPIRIT OF THIS CHURCH. James Vila Blake (1842–1925), an American Unitarian minister, served churches in Quincy, Chicago, and Evanston, Ill. His publications included *Unity Hymns and Chorals*, 1892, edited with W. C. Gannett (*see Note 1*), and F. L. Hosmer (*see Note 50*). This is from the covenant adopted by the Church of All Souls, Evanston, April 29, 1894.

495. YOU SHALL POSSESS. Walt Whitman. *See Note 78.* This is from "Song of Myself," *Leaves of Grass*, 1855.

496. TO OUTGROW THE PAST. William Laurence Sullivan (1872–1935) was born in East Braintree, Mass., of Irish Catholic immigrants and ordained as a Paulist father in 1899. A professor of theology at St. Thomas's College, Washington, D.C., he found himself unable to obey Pope Pius X's encyclical of 1907 which demanded unquestioning allegiance to medieval dogma. He left the Roman Catholic church in 1909 and three years later entered the Unitarian ministry. He served Unitarian churches in Schenectady and New York, N.Y.; St. Louis, Mo.; and Germantown, Pa. He was a mission preacher for the Unitarian Laymen's League, 1922–24. The autobiographical *Under Orders* was published posthumously in 1944. This passage, slightly abridged, is from *The Flaming Spirit*, 1961, edited by Rev. Max F. Daskam, minister of the Unitarian Society of Germantown, Pa.

497. WE, THE PEOPLES OF THE UNITED NATIONS. This is abridged from the preamble of the Charter of the United Nations which was adopted at San Francisco, Calif., June 26, 1945.

498. A COVENANT FOR LIBER-ALS. Walter Royal Jones, Jr. (1920– ), American Unitarian Universalist minister, is serving Thomas Jefferson Memorial Unitarian Church, Charlottesville, Va. He is on the Business Committee of the Unitarian Universalist Association.

499. IDEAL AND QUEST. Alfred North Whitehead (1861–1947), born in England, was lecturer on mathematics, science, and technology at Cambridge and later at the University of London. He was professor of philosophy at Harvard, 1924–36. This is from *Science and the Modern World*, 1926.

500. INDIVIDUALITY. John Stuart Mill (1806–73) was an English writer on political economy, philosophy, and religion. This is from *On Liberty*, 1859.

501. THE CENTER OF ALL DAYS, ALL RACES. Walt Whitman. *See Note 78*. From "With Antecedents."

502. THIS IS THE GREATEST BLESSING. Attributed to Gautama Buddha (fifth century B.C.). This is based on a translation by Robert C. Childers (1838–76), English Orientalist, of the *"Khuddaka Patha,"* in the *Fifth Nikaya*. See J. B. Pratt, *The Pilgrimage of Buddhism*, 1928, p. 48.

503. THE COURAGE TO BELONG. William Ernest Hocking (1873– ), an American philosopher at Harvard University, wrote this in an article "On Freedom and Belonging" for a 1939 volume honoring Gandhi on his seventieth birthday, which was edited by Radhakrishnan. Dr. Hocking developed the theme in *The Coming World Civilization*.

504. A BOND OF FELLOWSHIP. Kenneth L. Patton. *See Note 28*. This is from *Readings for the Celebration of Life*.

505. I BELIEVE. Edwin Burdette Backus (1888–1955) was an American Unitarian minister, son of a Unitarian minister, Wilson M. Backus. His longest pastorates were at Los Angeles, Calif., and Indianapolis, Ind.

506. A COVENANT FOR FREE WORSHIP. L. Griswold Williams (1893–1942) was an American Universalist minister in Reading, Pa.; Barre, Vt.; and Floral Park, N.Y. He was a member of the commission which produced *Hymns of the Spirit* and *Services of Religion*, 1937; he compiled *Antiphonal Readings for Free Worship*, 1933, containing this text.

507. A STATEMENT OF BELIEFS. This is from *Services of Religion*, 1937, based on a statement in *Four Services for Congregational Use*, 1915, which was compiled by W. Hanson Pulsford (1859–1934) for the First Unitarian Society of Chicago, Ill.

508. WE BELIEVE. Von Ogden Vogt. *See Note 332*. This was in *Services of Religion*, 1937.

509. AROUND THE WHOLE EARTH. Walt Whitman. *See Note 78*. This is arranged from *"Salut au Monde!"* in *Leaves of Grass*, 1856.

510. THE GATES OF FREEDOM. Napoleon William Lovely. *See Note 343*. This was written ca. 1957.

511. OURS, O MEN. Kenneth L. Patton. *See Note 28*. This is from *Hello, Man*, 1945.

512. John 4:23, 24. "God is spirit" is from the English Revised Version and the Revised Standard Version.

513. Francis Quarles (1592–1644) was an English poet. The source of this text is unknown.

514. Robert French Leavens. *See Note 477*. This text, abridged here, is from *Let Us Pray*.

515. Psalm 96:9. This beautiful mistranslation is from the *Great Bible*, 1539.

516. Gen. 28:16a, 17b.

517. Psalm 145:18.

518. Felix Adler. *See Note 192*. This is inscribed over the platform of the Society for Ethical Culture, New York, N.Y.

519. Hillel (ca. 70 B.C.–10 A.D.), president of the Jewish Sanhedrin, 30 B.C.–9 A.D., was a scholar, reformer, Pharisee, "particularly distinguished for his humility, gentleness, and liberal, humane spirit." The source of this text is unknown.

520. Walt Whitman. *See Note 78.* From "A Song of the Rolling Earth."

521. Josh. 24:15 (abridged).

522. Kenneth L. Patton. *See Note 28.* This is from *Readings for the Celebration of Life.*

523. Immanuel Kant (1724–1804). This is in the conclusion of *The Critique of Practical Reason,* 1788, as translated by Thomas Kingsmill Abbott.

524. Ralph Waldo Emerson. *See Note 347.* This is from *Nature.*

525. Mic. 6:6a, 8. These verses of unknown origin are thought to be from Micah's time, ca. 700 B.C. With the intervening text, they summarize prophetic religion superbly.

526. Israel Zangwill (1864–1926) was an English writer and Jewish leader. This is from "Jehovah," in *Blind Children,* 1903.

527. Matt. 5:23, 24.

528. This was quoted by Henry Drummond (1851–97) in *The Greatest Thing in the World,* 1890.

529. Col. 3:23; Rom. 12:8 (adapted).

530. Matt. 7:12. This is the Golden Rule.

531. Mic. 6:6a, 8. *See Note 525.*

532. The author is unknown.

533. Arthur Foote II. *See Note 29.*

534. Arthur Foote II. *See Note 29.*

535. I Cor. 13:8 (abridged), 13. *See Note 406.*

536. This is from W. Copeland Bowie's British Unitarian *Seven Services for Public Worship,* new edition, 1917, slightly adapted.

537. John Winthrop Brigham (1914–), American Unitarian Universalist minister, is Associate Director, Department of the Ministry, Unitarian Universalist Association. This was composed for a ministers' institute, Burlington, Iowa, 1959.

538. Arthur Foote II. *See Note 29.*

539. Num. 6:24-26; here changed to first person plural.

540. Phil. 4:8. This is from the English Revised Version.

541. Abraham Lincoln. *See Note 447.* This is from his address at Cooper Union, New York City, Feb. 27, 1860.

542. Giuseppe Mazzini (1805?–72), Italian republican, was a leader in the unification of Italy. This is from *The Duties of Man,* 1858, as quoted in Stanton Coit's *The Message of Man,* 1894 (*see Note 307*).

543. Henry David Thoreau. *See Note 395.*

544. Robert French Leavens. *See Note 477.* This is from *Let Us Pray.*

545. Barrows Dunham. *See Note 302.* This is from *Man against Myth,* 1947.

546. The source is unknown.

547. Harry Emerson Fosdick. *See Note 27.*

548. Theodore Parker. *See Note 120.*

549. Walt Whitman. *See Note 78.*

550. This biblical language includes I Thess. 5:21; it is from *A New Prayer Book,* London, 1923.

551. This is a Buddhist text. *See Note 110.*

552. Kenneth L. Patton. *See Note 28.* This is from *Readings for the Celebration of Life.*

553. Psalm 90:16, 17.

554. Walt Whitman. *See Note 78.*

555. This rearrangement of familiar phrases includes reminiscences from

John 14:27 and Phil. 4:7. It is based on the communion benediction in *The Booke of the Common Prayer* . . ., 1549.

556. Kenneth L. Patton. *See Note 28.*

557. William Wallace Fenn (1862–1932), American Unitarian, was minister of the First Unitarian Society of Chi-cago, Ill., 1890–1901, and dean of Harvard Divinity School, 1901–32. This text is a tablet honoring him in Divinity Hall, Harvard.

558. Aristophanes (ca. 448–380 B.C.), Greek comic poet, "clung to the old traditions of Athens with a sort of jovial, unreasoning toryism."

# Acknowledgments

We gratefully acknowledge our indebtedness to those individuals and publishers who have granted permission for use of their copyrighted materials. Every effort has been made to trace the ownership of all material believed to be under copyright, although in some instances exact ownership is obscure. If for this reason any omissions have been made, it is hoped that these will be brought to our attention, so that proper acknowledgment may be made in future editions of the book.

*Hymns and Tunes:*

2. Text, Justin E. Dunbar, literary executor, Tenants Harbor, Me.
3. Text, Justin E. Dunbar (*see No. 2*). Tune, arr. by Harold Geer for *Hymnal for Colleges and Schools*, Yale University Press
9. Text, author
10. Text, Henry Brooke
11. Text, reprinted with perm. of Charles Scribner's Sons from *The Poems of Henry Van Dyke*, © 1911; renewed © 1939, Tertius Van Dyke
12. Text, reprinted from *Enlarged Songs of Praise* by perm. of the Executors of the estate of the late F. S. Pierpoint and Oxford University Press
22. Text, author
23. Text translation, W. H. Draper, by J. Curwen and Sons
24. Text, Oxford University Press. Tune, composer
27. Text, author. Tune, G. D. Hughes and D. S. Webb
28. Text, Meeting House Press
29. Text, Oxford University Press
31. Text, author
32. Text, Oxford University Press
35. Text, reprinted from *The Yattendon Hymnal*, ed. by Robert Bridges, Oxford University Press
37. Text, author
39. Text, adapted for this use by perm. of Hugh Noyes, and J. B. Lippincott Co. Tune, harm. by Oxford University Press and Executors of the late Prof. Evans
40. Text, The American Ethical Union
42. Text, The American Ethical Union
46. Text, author's daughter, Mrs. Herman Tasha
53. Text, Doubleday & Company, Inc.
55. Text, author. Tune, The Proprietors of *Hymns Ancient and Modern*
56. Text, Meeting House Press
57. Text, an excerpt from "Renascence," from *Collected Poems*, Harper & Brothers, perm. by Norma Millay Ellis
58. Text, author and The American Ethical Union. Tune, Oxford University Press
59. Text, adapted from *The Collected Poems and Plays of Rabindranath Tagore*, with perm. of the Trustees of the Tagore Estate and The Macmillan Co.
61. Text, author. Tune, Oxford University Press
62. Text, The American Ethical Union
63. Text, Noonday Press, Farrar, Straus and Cudahy, Inc.
65. Tune, Oxford University Press
66. Text, Meeting House Press
67. Text, Alexander Laing
69. Text, "Affirmation" II, © 1927, Charles Scribner's Sons; renewed 1955. Adapted and reprinted with perm. of author and Charles Scribner's Sons from *Poems Old and New* © 1956 by John Hall Wheelock
70. Text, "Circular Secret," by the author and Charles Scribner's Sons from *Poems Old and New*, by John Hall Wheelock, © 1956. Tune, Oxford University Press
71. Tune, composer
72. Text, Jonathan Cape Ltd.
75. Tune, Oxford University Press
76. Text by the late Malcolm Quin, present owner untraceable
77. Text from *The Sceptered Flute* by Sarojini Naidu, © 1917, 1928, by perm. of Dodd, Mead & Co.
78. Tune, Oxford University Press
81. Text, Helen Hoyt Lyman (Mrs. W. W.)
82. Text, adapted from *The Collected Poems and Plays of Rabindranath Tagore*, with perm. of the Trustees of the Tagore Estate and The Macmillan Co. Tune, composer
83. Text, lines taken from *Horizon and Landmarks* by S. R. Lysaght, perm. by Macmillan and Co., Ltd. Tune, The Independent Press, Ltd. and the Congregational Union of England and Wales
84. Text, author. Tune, Oxford University Press
90. Tune, Oxford University Press
94. Tune, Oxford University Press
101. Text, from *The Collected Poems of G. K. Chesterton*, © 1932 by Dodd, Mead & Co.
103. Text, Virgil Markham
109. Text, George Allen and Unwin, Ltd., and Oxford University Press, N. Y.
111. Text, LeRoy Pratt Percy. Tune, The Church Pension Fund
112, 113. Text from *The Yale Book of Student Verse*, John M. Andrews et al, editors; Yale University Press
114. Text from *Challenge*, by Louis Untermeyer, © 1914 by Harcourt, Brace & World, Inc.; renewed 1942 by Mr. Untermeyer
116. Text, Mrs. Frederick M. Eliot
119. Tune, The Psalms and Hymns Trust
123. Tune, Stainer and Bell, Ltd., and Yale University Press
125. Text, by Mrs. Marion Franklin Ham
134. Text translation, The Vedanta Society of Southern California
135. Text, from *Poems* by George Santayana, © 1901, Charles Scribner's Sons
136. Text, Houghton Mifflin Company
137. Text, The Clarendon Press
138. Text, Meeting House Press
140. Text, Virgil Markham
144. Tune, The Proprietors of *Hymns Ancient and Modern*
145. Text, The American Ethical Union
146. Text, Mrs. Horace Westwood
147. Text, author's daughter, Hermione Hill Logan

476

ACKNOWLEDGMENTS

148. Text, author
150. Text from *Collected Poems* by Vachel Lindsay, © 1914 by The Macmillan Co.; renewed 1942 by Elizabeth Lindsay
152. Text, The Society of Authors and Mrs. Cicely Binyon
153. Text, The Society of Authors and Mrs. Cicely Binyon
154. Text, Sara Henderson Hay (Mrs. Nikolai Lopatnikoff)
155. Text, Oxford University Press
156. Text, author and Charles Scribner's Sons, from *Poems Old and New*, © 1956 by John Hall Wheelock and by *The Virginia Quarterly Review*, 1956
159. Text, from *This Singing World*, ed. by Louis Untermeyer, by Harcourt, Brace & World, Inc., © 1923; renewed 1951 by Louis Untermeyer
162. Text, The Clarendon Press
164. Text, Little, Brown & Co.
170. Tune, The American Ethical Union
171. Text, Meeting House Press
174. Tune, The Independent Press, Ltd., and the Congregational Union of England and Wales
176. Text from *Goethe and Faust*, perm. by G. Bell and Sons, Ltd., and The Dial Press, Inc.
178. Text, author. Tune, arr. by Harold Geer for *Hymnal for Colleges and Schools*, Yale University Press
179. Text, author. Tune, composer
180. Text, Virgil Markham
181. Text, Meeting House Press
182. Text, "Chant" by John Hall Wheelock, from *Poems Old and New*, © 1956 by perm. of Charles Scribner's Sons.
183. Text, Mrs. H. M. Davies and Jonathan Cape, Ltd.
184. Tune, Stainer and Bell, Ltd., and Yale University Press
191. Text, author
193. Text, Mrs. Thomas Curtis Clark
194. Tune, The American Ethical Union
196. Text, A. D. Peters
197. Text, Justin E. Dunbar, literary executor, Tenants Harbor, Me.
199. Tune, The Hodgin Press
200. Text by the late Malcolm Quin, present owner untraceable
201. Text, The American Peace Society
203. Text, Meeting House Press
204. Text, by author's daughter, Miss Dorothy Tarrant
205. Text, author
206. Text, *Punch* magazine and The Ben Roth Agency, Inc. Tune, Pilgrim Press
211. Tune, composer and The American Ethical Union
212. Text, Oxford University Press; reprinted from *The Yattendon Hymnal*, ed. by Robert Bridges. Tune, harm., © by the late Prof. David Evans, and reprinted by perm. of his executors and Oxford University Press (on behalf of Messrs. Gwilyn Treharne and Hopkins)
214. Text, author. Tune, Oxford University Press
216. Text, Dodd, Mead & Co. from *Star in a Well*, by Nancy Byrd Turner, © 1935
217. Text, the Trustees of the *Fellowship Hymn Book*
218. Text, *The Presbyterian Outlook*
219. Text, The Universalist Publishing House
220. Tune, Gwenlyn Evans, Ltd.
225. Text, Meeting House Press
227. Text, author

228. Text, adapted from *The Flowering Stone* by George Dillon, © 1931 by perm. of The Viking Press, Inc.; renewed 1959 by George Dillon. Tune, arr. by Harold Geer for *Hymnal for Colleges and Schools*, Yale University Press
229. Text, author
230. Tune, J. Curwen and Sons, Ltd.
232. Text, Meeting House Press
234. Text, by author's son, John deQ. Briggs
237. Text, by Harper & Brothers and *Hymns of the Christian Life*, ed. by Milton S. Littlefield
238. Text and tune, Oxford University Press
239. Text, by author's son, Ernest Merrill
243. Text, Mrs. Thomas Curtis Clark
250. Text, author
253. Text, Mrs. Marion Franklin Ham
254. Text, author
256. Text, Meeting House Press
258. Text by the late John H. Skrine, present owner untraceable. Tune, from *A Students' Hymnal*, by perm. of Oxford University Press
259. Text, author
262. Text, Justin E. Dunbar, literary executor, Tenants Harbor, Me.
263. Text from *Collected Poems* by Siegfried Sassoon, by perm. of The Viking Press, Inc.
266. Text, author. Tune, Oxford University Press
267. Text and tune, Oxford University Press
268. Text, reprinted from *The Yattendon Hymnal*, ed. by Robert Bridges, by perm. of Oxford Unversity Press
272. Tune, Oxford University Press
273. Text, Ruth Nivison
276. Text, "Autumn Fields," Octavo 1083, © 1942 by Hall and McCreary Co. Tune, Oxford University Press
281. Text, from *The Oxford Book of Carols*, by perm. of David Higham Associates, Ltd.
284. Text, by author's son, Burton J Rights
290. Tune, The Church Pension Fund
291. Text, Mrs. William Merriam Crane. Tune, from *The Oxford Book of Carols*, Oxford University Press
293. Text, Mrs. Marion Franklin Ham
294. Text, from *The New Church Hymnal*, by perm. of Fleming H. Revell Co.
296. Tune, J. Curwen and Sons, Ltd.
302. Text, author
303. Text, author
304. Tune, Oxford University Press
309. Text, author
314. Text, from *The Collected Poems of Padraic Colum*, by perm. of The Devin-Adair Co. Tune, from *Hymns and Responses for the Church Year* by Vincent Persichetti, © 1956, perm. of Elkan-Vogel Co., Inc.
319. Text, *The Oxford Book of Carols*, Oxford University Press
321. Text and tune, Oxford University Press
322. Text, adapted from *The Golden Year of Fan Cheng-ta*, trans. by Gerald Bullett; by perm. of Mrs. Gerald Bullett. Tune, composer
323. Text and tune, *The Oxford Book of Carols*, Oxford University Press
324. Text, from *Complete Poems of Robert Frost*, © 1935, perm. of Holt, Rinehart & Winston, Inc. Tune, Oxford University Press
326. Tune, Oxford University Press
The following hymns are copyright by Beacon Press: 1, 14, 31, 48, 68, 84, 89, 125, 191, 250, 257, 259, 280 (st. 8), 284, 291, 293, 296, 300 (st. 5), 309, 320.
The following tunes are copyright by Beacon Press: 2, 29, 101, 134, 135, 136, 137, 153, 182, 197, 202, 226, 302.

The following tune arrangements and harmonizations are copyright by Beacon Press: 8, 9, 14, 23, 31, 38, 40, 44, 46, 48, 50, 53, 57, 59, 64, 68, 93, 105, 106, 109, 110, 112, 113, 114, 115, 127, 128, 139, 143, 147, 148, 151, 154, 155, 161, 164, 166, 175, 180, 183, 185, 196, 198, 201, 203, 208, 210, 217, 219, 229, 232, 237, 240, 247, 250, 251, 256, 262, 263, 271, 273, 274, 277, 292, 293, 303, 306, 308, 310, 315, 319, 320, 325.

*Responsive Readings:*

330. Meeting House Press
332. Author
339. Houghton Mifflin Company
342. From *The Way of Life*, by Witter Bynner, © 1944, by perm. of The John Day Company, Inc.
343. Author
344. The Vedanta Society of Southern California
345. Author
350. Houghton Mifflin Company
351. From *Collected Poems and Plays of Rabindranath Tagore*, by perm. of the Trustees of the Tagore Estate and The Macmillan Co., N. Y. and Macmillan and Co., Ltd., London
354. Meeting House Press
356. By the author's daughter, Mrs. Bruce W. Ambrose
357. Meeting House Press
358. Meeting House Press
362. Houghton Mifflin Company
365. Meeting House Press
366. From *Actfive and Other Poems* by Archibald MacLeish, © 1948, by perm. of Random House, Inc.
369. From *Collected Poems 1921–1951* by Edwin Muir, © 1957, by perm. of Faber and Faber, Ltd. and Grove Press, Inc.
370. From *The Web and the Rock* by Thomas Wolfe, © 1939 by Maxwell Perkins as executor; as rearranged in verse by John S. Barnes; by perm. of Harper and Row, Publishers.
372. Meeting House Press
374. Meeting House Press
375. Mrs. Vivian T. Pomeroy
376. Author
381. Meeting House Press
382. From *The Way of Life* by Witter Bynner, © 1944; by perm. of The John Day Company, Inc.
385. From *The Wisdom of China and India*, ed. by Lin Yutang; by perm. of Random House, Inc.
386. From *The Way of Life* by Witter Bynner, © 1944; by perm. of The John Day Company, Inc.
391. From *Collected Poems and Plays of Rabindranath Tagore*, by perm. of the Trustees of the Tagore Estate and the Macmillan Co., N. Y., and Macmillan and Co., Ltd., London
392. From *Five Stages of Greek Religion* by Gilbert Murray; by perm. of Columbia University Press
398. Meeting House Press
401. Meeting House Press
402. Meeting House Press
408. From *Buddhist Texts Through the Ages*, ed. by Edward Conze, 1954; by perm. of Philosophical Library, Inc.
409. Meeting House Press
412. From *The Web and the Rock* by Thomas Wolfe, © 1939 by Maxwell Perkins as executor, as rearranged in verse by John S. Barnes, by perm. of Harper and Row, Publishers
414. From *The Prophet* by Kahlil Gibran, © 1923; renewed 1951 by Administrators C. T. A. of Kahlil Gibran Estate and Mary G. Gibran; by perm. of Alfred A. Knopf, Inc.
416. Meeting House Press
418. From *The Prophet* by Kahlil Gibran, © 1923; renewed 1951 by Administrators C. T. A. of Kahlil Gibran Estate and Mary G. Gibran; by perm. of Alfred A. Knopf, Inc.
421. Author
422. From *The Autobiography of an Idea* by Louis H. Sullivan, © 1924; republished 1956; by perm. of Dover Publications, Inc., and of Peter Smith, publisher
423. Meeting House Press
434. From *Creative Expression*, ed. by Gertrude Hartman and Ann Shumaker; by perm. of The John Day Company, Inc.
436. From *Actfive and Other Poems*, by Archibald MacLeish © 1948, by perm. of Random House, Inc.
438. From Gandhi's *Songs from Prison*, by perm. of George Allen and Unwin, Ltd.
439. Meeting House Press
440. From *Poems*, by Stephen Spender, © 1934 by Modern Library, Inc.; by perm. of Random House, Inc.
442. Meeting House Press
443. Meeting House Press
449. Meeting House Press
451. From *The Way of Life* by Witter Bynner, © 1944, by perm. of The John Day Company, Inc.
453. Meeting House Press
454. Meeting House Press
455. Meeting House Press
456. By the author's son, Waldemar Argow
459. Meeting House Press
460. Author
461. Meeting House Press
463. Meeting House Press
464. Author
466. Author
468. Author
470. Meeting House Press
473. Author
475. Author
477. Mrs. Robert French Leavens
478. From "Orders of Public Worship for Use in the Chapel of Manchester College, Oxford"; by perm. of the college and M. L. Jacks
482. Meeting House Press
483. Mrs. Robert French Leavens
486. Author
498. Author
499. From *Science and the Modern Mind* by Alfred North Whitehead, © 1925 by The Macmillan Co.; renewed 1953 by Evelyn Whitehead; perm. of Cambridge University Press and The Macmillan Co.
503. Author
504. Meeting House Press
505. Mrs. E. Burdette Backus
508. Author
510. Author
511. Meeting House Press
514. Mrs. Robert French Leavens
522. Meeting House Press
537. Author
544. Mrs. Robert French Leavens
545. Author
547. Author
552. Meeting House Press
556. Meeting House Press
557. Dan Huntington Fenn

# INDEX OF FIRST PHRASES AND TITLES OF READINGS

*(When they differ, a selection's title, as well as its first phrase, is listed. Titles, then, are in capital letters.)*

A BOND OF FELLOWSHIP (*unison*) 504
A COVENANT FOR FREE WORSHIP (*unison*) 506
A COVENANT FOR LIBERALS (*unison*) 498
A FAITHFUL FRIEND 415
A great city is that which has the greatest men or women 448
A LIBERAL CHURCH 460
A NEW HEAVEN AND EARTH 430
A NEW SHAPE OF FELLOWSHIP 453
A NEW SONG 400
A parable put he forth unto them 431
A PRAYER AT HARVEST TIME (*unison*) 476
A ROSARY OF THINGS BEAUTIFUL 328
A STATEMENT OF BELIEFS (*unison*) 507
A STOIC'S PRAYER 392
A VIRTUOUS WOMAN 417
ABOVE THE NAME OF MAN 365
ACCEPTANCE 382
ACCEPTANCE OF MYSTERY, THE 374
Afoot and light-hearted, I take to the open road 424
All men are brothers 455
All this time, and at all times, wait the words of true poems 404
Almighty God, unto whom all hearts are open (*unison*) 471
Almighty God, who hast made of one blood all nations (*unison*) 478
AN ACCOUNTING OF GRATITUDE 330
AN ETERNAL VERITY 456
Ancient as the home is the temple 456
And, behold, a certain lawyer stood up 410
And when much people were gathered 378
ANNOUNCEMENT 429
AROUND THE WHOLE EARTH (*unison*) 509
ARTS OF MAN, THE 398
As the hart panteth after the water brooks 396
AWAKE, O MAN 356

Be utterly humble 382
BEATITUDES, THE (*unison*) 488
BEAUTY OF HOLINESS, THE 331
Before creation a presence existed 342

Before the wonders of life (*unison*) 473
Behold, I create new heavens 430
Bless the Lord, O my soul, and all that is 367
Bless the Lord, O my soul. O Lord, My God 329
Blessed are the poor in spirit (*unison*) 488
Blessed is the soul that heareth the Lord 371
BRAHMAN 344
breath of life moves, The 386
Bright joy, bright joy 466
BUDDHA'S PITY 408
BULWARK OF OUR LIBERTY, THE 447

CANTICLE OF THE SUN, THE 334
CENTER OF ALL DAYS, ALL RACES, THE (*unison*) 501
Cherish your doubts 421
CHRISTMAS BEATITUDES 464
CHURCH COVENANT (*unison*) 490
church of tomorrow will not strive, The 459
Comfort ye, comfort ye my people 432
COMFORT YE MY PEOPLE 432
COMING OF SPRING, THE 465
CONFIRM THE BONDS OF MUTUAL TRUST (*unison*) 478
COUNSEL OF THINE OWN HEART, THE 377
COURAGE TO BELONG, THE (*unison*) 503

days of the year have stiffened in ice, The 463
DIGNITY OF HUMAN NATURE, THE 355
earth is the Lord's, and the fullness thereof, The 337
EFFORTS OF FAITH, THE (*unison*) 486
Enlightened One, because he saw, The 408
EPISTLE TO BE LEFT IN THE EARTH 362
eternal past is the beginning of man, The 354
EVEN AS OF OLD (*unison*) 474
EXHORTATION OF THE DAWN, THE (*unison*) 472

478

FAITH OF DOUBT, THE 423
FELLOWSHIP OF FREE SOULS, THE (unison) 492
fellowship of nature is our shape, The 365
FIRST LESSON IN CHARITY, THE 381
FOR GENERATIONS TO COME 457
For the holiness of every place 397
FOR YOU 426
FORCE AND THE WAY OF LIFE 449
FREE MIND, THE 420
FREE NATION AND FREE WORLD 445
free spirit is the spirit of joy, The 422
Friend, I have lost the way 369

GATES OF FREEDOM, THE (unison) 510
GEOGRAPHY OF THIS TIME 436
Give ear, O my people, to my law 457
Give unto the Lord, O ye mighty 346
GLORY OF LIFE IS UPON ME, THE 425
GOD 339
GOD IN NATURE 329
GOD IS LOVE 411
God is our refuge and strength 353
God is the fact of the fact 339
God that made the world and all things 348
God, who hast made us one nation 445
GOOD SAMARITAN, THE 410
GOOD TIDINGS OF GOOD 427
GOODNESS OF THE EARTH, THE 333
Great and marvelous is man's progress 356
GREAT CITY, THE 448
great end in religious instruction, The 462
Great travail is created for every man 363

HANDIWORK OF THEIR CRAFT, THE 403
Happy is the man that findeth wisdom 387
heavens and the earth spread abroad, The 333
heavens declare the glory of God, The 394
He that giveth his mind to the law 384
HE THAT MEDITATETH 384
Ho, every one that thirsteth 437
Honor thy father with thy whole heart 413
HONOR THY PARENTS 413
HOPE THOU IN GOD 396
HORIZON OF OUR MINDS, THE (unison) 484
How amiable are thy tabernacles 458
How beautiful is the morning 425
How beautiful upon the mountains 428

How beautiful upon the mountains are the feet of him 427
HUMAN CALENDAR, THE 354
HUMAN FELLOWSHIP, THE 443

I am the Self that dwells in the heart 344
I announce natural persons to arise 429
I believe in myself (unison) 505
I call that mind free 420
I hear America singing 399
I know that the past was great (unison) 501
I said, I will take heed to my ways 368
I see the Nature Providence going 350
I think continually of those 440
I will lift up mine eyes unto the hills 340
IDEAL AND QUEST (unison) 499
If one man conquer in battle 379
In our hearts may there be the love (unison) 483
IN PRAISE OF LIBERTY 419
IN PRAISE OF PEACE 434
In the freedom of the truth (unison) 490
IN THE SPIRIT OF ST. FRANCIS (unison) 480
INDIVIDUALITY (unison) 500
INESCAPABLE GOD, THE 341
Into this house of light we come (unison) 468
INVITATION TO SERENITY 375
It is colder now, there are many stars 362
It is no foretelling 442
It is not by wearing down into uniformity (unison) 500
IT MATTERS WHAT WE BELIEVE 376

KEEP THY HEART WITH DILIGENCE 387
Know the bonds by which we are bound 409

Let a man leave anger 407
Let brotherly love continue (unison) 481
Let love be without hypocrisy 389
Let man learn the revelation 347
Let me not pray to be sheltered 391
Let religion be to us life and joy 390
Let the horizon of our minds (unison) 484
Let this church ever seek the oneness 460
Let us indicate a new shape of fellowship 453
Let us not disparage that nature 355

Let us now praise famous men 444
Let us rejoice in the light of day 336
Let us rejoice in the manifold richness 332
Let us sing for the arts of man 398
Let us sing of the men and women 443
Let us worship with our eyes and ears 372
LIFT UP YOUR HEADS, O YE GATES 337
Look to this day! (*unison*) 472
LIFE OF THE SPIRIT, THE 397
LORD GIVETH WISDOM, THE 388
LORD IS MERCIFUL, THE 367
Lord is my light, The 373
Lord is my shepherd, The 352
Lord, thou hast been our dwelling place 361
LOVE 406
LOVE AND UNDERSTANDING 416
Love is the doctrine of this church (*unison*) 506
Love is the spirit of this church (*unison*) 494
Love one another, but make not a bond 418

MAKER OF POEMS, THE 404
MAKE NOT A BOND OF LOVE 418
MAN AT HIS BEST 386
MAN IN TIME 454
Man is the animal that most wearies himself 358
MANIFOLD RICHNESS OF LIFE, THE 332
MASTERY OF SELF, THE 385
May I be no man's enemy 392
May we go forth to the duties (*unison*) 485
MIND WITHOUT FEAR, THE 391
Mindful of truth ever exceeding (*unison*) 498
moral life of a man may be likened, The 385
MY DAYS AS AN HANDBREADTH 368
My son, if thou wilt receive my words 388
My son, if thou wilt, thou shalt be taught 377
My spirit has passed in compassion (*unison*) 509

NATURE'S IMPARTIAL PROVIDENCE 350
NEW YEAR, THE 463
NONCONFORMIST, THE (*unison*) 493
Nor can that endure which has not its foundations upon love (*unison*) 489
Not until a man has helped himself 381
Numberless are thy witnesses (*unison*) 477

O all ye things of tenderness and grace! 328
O Eternal, thy spirit hath not changed (*unison*) 474
O Lord, our Lord, how excellent is thy name 359
O Lord, thou has searched me 341
O Most High, Almighty, good Lord God 334
O sing unto the Lord a new song 331
O Thou Eternal Light 441
ON THE VERGE OF MASTERY 439
On this blessed day let us worship 464
ON WAR 451
ONE SPECIES 357
One who would guide a leader of men 451
Open ye the gates, that the righteous nation 446
Our bond of fellowship (*unison*) 504
Our breath vanishes among the winds 401
OUR COMMON BONDS 409
Our faith and knowledge thrive by exercise 419
OUR SEARCH TOGETHER (*unison*) 482
Ours, O men (*unison*) 511
OUT OF DARKNESS, INTO LIGHT (*unison*) 475
Out of the depths have I cried 393
Out of the stars in their flight 345
OVERCOME EVIL WITH GOOD 389
OVERSOUL, THE 347
OWNER OF THE SPHERE 452

PARABLE OF THE SOWER, THE 378
PARABLES OF THE KINGDOM 431
Peace means the beginning 434
Peace to him that is far off 433
PEOPLE SHALL DWELL IN PEACE, THE 433
people that walked in darkness, The 467
Pity, more than any other feeling 412
POWER OF LOVE, THE (*unison*) 489
PRAISE GOD IN HIS SANCTUARY 405
Praise ye the Lord 335
Praise ye the Lord . . . in his sanctuary 405
pride of the height, The 338
PROPHETS, THE 442

RANGE ON RANGE OF LIFE 466
Rejoice in the Lord, O ye righteous 400
RELIGION 390
Religion is the vision of something (*unison*) 499
Rich is the man who lives in today 454
RIGHTEOUS NATION, THE 446
RIGHTEOUSNESS AS A MIGHTY STREAM 435

SALUT AU MONDE! 450
same stream of life, The 351
SELF-CONQUEST 379
SERVANTS OF GOD 441
Society everywhere is in conspiracy
  (*unison*) 493
Some beliefs are like walled gardens 376
Some things will never change 370
SONG OF THE OPEN ROAD 424
Soon shall the winter's foil be here 465
soul is not more than the body, The 360
souls of the righteous, The 364
Source of all good, day by day
  (*unison*) 469
spirit of God is wonderful to us,
  The 343
STREAM OF LIFE, THE 351
sum of all known reverence, The 426
superior man is universally minded,
  The 380
Sweet language will multiply
  friends 415

TAKE US NOW TO SERVE THEE
  (*unison*) 469
TAO, THE 342
THEN BUILD TEMPLES 401
There are questions which come to
  every man 374
There is no choice but to immerse
  oneself (*unison*) 503
There is one mind common to all 452
This and this alone is true religion 438
THIS HOUSE 461
This is a house for the ingathering
  of nature 461
This is the greatest blessing (*unison*) 502
This is the message which ye heard 411
THIS IS TRUE RELIGION 438
Those who have power in the
  government 449
Thou art the path and the goal
  (*unison*) 479
Though I speak with the tongues
  of men and of angels 406
Though our knowledge is incom-
  plete (*unison*) 510
To doubt is a valorous and neces-
  sary faith 423
TO LIVE DELIBERATELY 395
To outgrow the past (*unison*) 496
TRAVAIL OF MAN, THE 363

UNIVERSAL RELIGION 455
UNKNOWN GOD, THE 348
Unto the church universal (*unison*) 487
Unto the goodness in the heart of
  every man (*unison*) 482
UNTO US A CHILD IS BORN 467

VISHNU—SHIVA 358
VOICE OF GOD IN THE SOUL, THE 371
VOICE OF THE LORD, THE 346

WAY, THE 369
WAYS OF THE DEDICATED MAN, THE 383
We are united in the efforts of
  faith (*unison*) 486
We arrive out of many singular
  rooms (*unison*) 470
We avow our faith (*unison*) 491
We believe in a fellowship that
  shall unite men (*unison*) 492
We believe in God, Father of our
  spirits (*unison*) 507
We believe in the goodness of life
  (*unison*) 508
We bring today our joyful thanks-
  giving (*unison*) 476
We have set ourselves over many
  things 439
We must learn to awaken 395
WE REJOICE 336
We rejoice this day in the un-
  quenchable (*unison*) 475
We, the peoples of the United
  Nations (*unison*) 497
What are the ways of the dedicated
  man 383
What constitutes the bulwark of
  our own liberty 447
What does it mean to be creatures
  of thought 357
WHAT IS MAN? 359
What is required of us is the
  recognition 436
What more have we to give to one
  another 416
What rivers are these? 450
When we are tired with the work
  we have to do 375
Where hate rules, let us bring love
  (*unison*) 480
Who can find a virtuous woman? 417
Who can make an accounting of
  his gratitude? 330
Who hath measured the waters 349
Why does a man work 402
wisdom of a learned man, The 403
WONDER OF ONE'S SELF, THE 360

Ye who turn judgment to wormwood 435
You shall possess the origin of all
  poems (*unison*) 495
young dead soldiers do not speak,
  The 366
Your children are not your children 414

# Topical Index of Responsive Readings

ANIMALS

Bless the Lord, O my soul 329
The heavens and the earth spread abroad 333
Praise ye the Lord . . . from the heavens 335
O Lord, our Lord, how excellent is thy name 359
The people that walked in darkness 467

THE ARTS OF MAN

O all ye things of tenderness and grace! 328
Let us rejoice in the manifold richness 332
Great and marvelous is man's progress 356
Let us worship with our eyes and ears and fingertips 372
There are questions which come 374
*The Arts of Man* 398–405
The sum of all known reverence 426
I think continually of those 440
Let us sing of the men and women 443
Let us now praise famous men 444
A great city 448
This is a house for the ingathering of nature 461
Bright joy, bright joy 466

AUTUMN AND HARVEST

O all ye things of tenderness and grace! 328
The same stream of life 351
A parable put he forth (Parables of the Kingdom) 431

BEAUTY

O all ye things of tenderness and grace! 328
Bless the Lord, O my soul 329
The pride of the height 338
Let us worship with our eyes and ears and fingertips 372
Pity, more than any other feeling 412
The free spirit is the spirit of joy 422

BUDDHISM

If one man conquer in battle 379
What are the ways of the dedicated man? 383
Let a man leave anger 407
The Enlightened One (Buddha's Pity) 408

CELEBRATION AND PRAISE

*Celebration and Praise* 328–338
Give unto the Lord, O ye mighty 346
O Lord, our Lord, how excellent is thy name 359
Bless the Lord, O my soul 367
Let us worship with our eyes and ears and fingertips 372
I hear America singing 399
Rejoice in the Lord, O ye righteous 400
Praise ye the Lord. Praise God in his sanctuary 405
The free spirit is the spirit of joy 422
How beautiful is the morning 425
The sum of all known reverence 426
I think continually of those 440
What rivers are these? (*Salut au Monde!*) 450

How amiable are thy tabernacles 458
Bright joy, bright joy 466

THE CHANGING YEAR

The pride of the height 338
The same stream of life 351
Some things will never change 370
The days of the year have stiffened in ice 463
Soon shall the winter's foil be here 465

CHILDREN

O all ye things of tenderness and grace! 328
Praise ye the Lord . . . from the heavens 335
Let us rejoice in the light of day 336
Some beliefs are like walled gardens 376
Our breath vanishes among the winds 401
Why does a man work? 402
Know the bonds by which we are bound 409
Your children are not your children 414
What more have we to give to one another 416
How beautiful is the morning 425
A great city 448
The great end in religious instruction 462
The people that walked in darkness 467

CHRISTMAS

O all ye things of tenderness and grace! 328
I think continually of those 440
The days of the year have stiffened in ice 463
On this blessed day 464
The people that walked in darkness 467

CHURCH OF THE FREE SPIRIT

Let us rejoice in the manifold richness 332
Some beliefs are like walled gardens 376
As the hart panteth after the water brooks 396
For the holiness of every place 397
Our breath vanishes among the winds 401
O thou Eternal Light (Servants of God) 441
Let us indicate a new shape of fellowship 453
*Church of the Free Spirit* 456–462

THE CITY

O all ye things of tenderness and grace! 328
Man is the animal that most wearies himself 358
Let us worship with our eyes and ears and fingertips 372
The wisdom of a learned man 403
Let us sing of the men and women 443
A great city 448

COMMITMENT AND ACTION

Let religion be to us life and joy 390
For the holiness of every place 397
And, behold, a certain lawyer (The Good Samaritan) 410
*Commitment and Action* 435–439

CONFUCIANISM

The superior man is universally minded 380
The moral life of a man 385

## THE COUNTRYSIDE
O all ye things of tenderness and grace! 328
The same stream of life 351
The Lord is my shepherd 352
Let us worship with our eyes and ears and fingertips 372
And when much people were gathered (The Parable of the Sower) 378
Why does a man work? 402
The wisdom of a learned man 403
How beautiful is the morning 425

## COURAGE
O all ye things of tenderness and grace! 328
Let us not disparage (The Dignity of Human Nature) 355
The Lord is my light and my salvation 373
When we are tired with the work 375
Let me not pray to be sheltered 391
I call that mind free 420
Cherish your doubts 421
The free spirit is the spirit of joy 422
What is required (Geography of This Time) 436

## DEDICATION OF CHURCH
O sing unto the Lord a new song 331
Let us rejoice in the manifold richness 332
The Lord is my light and my salvation 373
As the hart panteth after the water brooks 396
Our breath vanishes among the winds 401
Ancient as the home is the temple 456
The church of tomorrow 459
Let this church (A Liberal Church) 460
Bright joy, bright joy 466

## DEDICATION OF ORGAN
Let us sing for the arts of man 398
Rejoice in the Lord, O ye righteous 400
Our breath vanishes among the winds 401
Praise ye the Lord . . . in his sanctuary 405

## THE DEMOCRATIC WAY OF LIFE
(see Freedom; In Time to Come; Man; Nation and Nations)

## EASTER
O all ye things of tenderness and grace! 328
Out of the stars 345
The souls of the righteous 364
Some things will never change 370
Afoot and light-hearted, I take to the open road 424
The sum of all known reverence 426
How beautiful upon the mountains 428
I think continually of those 440
O Thou Eternal Light (Servants of God) 441
Bright joy, bright joy 466

## EVENING
Let us rejoice in the light of day 336
O Lord, thou hast searched me 341
The same stream of life 351
Pity, more than any other feeling 412

## EVOLUTION
Before creation a presence existed 342
Out of the stars in their flight 345
I see the Nature Providence going 350

The same stream of life 351
The eternal past is the beginning of man 354
What does it mean to be creatures of thought 357

## FAITH AND TRUST
I will lift up mine eyes unto the hills 340
Who hath measured the waters 349
The Lord is my shepherd 352
God is our refuge and strength 353
The Lord is my light and my salvation 373
There are questions which come 374
When we are tired with the work 375
My son, if thou wilt receive my words 388
As the hart panteth after the water brooks 396
How amiable are thy tabernacles 458

## FAMILY
O all ye things of tenderness and grace! 328
Who can make an accounting of his gratitude? 330
Let us rejoice in the manifold richness 332
Let us rejoice in the light of day 336
The moral life of a man 385
I hear America singing 399
Why does a man work? 402
Honor thy father with thy whole heart 413
Your children are not your children 414
What have we more to give 416

## FATHERS (see Mothers and Fathers)

## FORGIVENESS OF OTHERS
O Most High, Almighty, Good Lord God 334
If one man conquer in battle 379
Let love be without hypocrisy 389
May I be no man's enemy 392
Let a man leave anger 407

## FREEDOM
Let me not pray to be sheltered 391
Why does a man work? 402
Freedom 419–423
Afoot and light-hearted, I take to the open road 424
God, who hast made us one nation 445
What constitutes the bulwark of our own liberty 447
A great city 448
Let us indicate a new shape of fellowship 453
This is a house for the ingathering of nature 461

## FRIENDS
Let us rejoice in the manifold richness 332
Let us rejoice in the light of day 336
Sweet language will multiply friends 415
Afoot and light-hearted, I take to the open road 424
I announce natural persons to arise 429
A great city 448

## HERE AND NOW
The soul is not more than the body 360
The breath of life moves through a deathless valley 386
Here and Now 424–426
It is no foretelling (The Prophets) 442

HINDUISM
I am the Self that dwells                    344
The same stream of life                      351
Man is the animal that most wearies
  himself                                    358
This and this alone is true religion         438

HOURS OF INSIGHT
O Lord, thou hast searched me                341
The spirit of God is wonderful to us         343
Let man learn the revelation of all nature   347
  *Hours of Insight*                   371–375
He that giveth his mind to the law of the
  Most High                                  384
Ho, every one that thirsteth                 437

IN TIME TO COME
The eternal past is the beginning of man     354
Great and marvelous is man's progress        356
What does it mean to be creatures of
  thought                                    357
Let religion be to us life and joy           390
Our breath vanishes among the winds          401
  *In Time to Come*                    427–434
We have set ourselves over many things       439
All men are brothers                         455
The people that walked in darkness           467

ISLAM
The heavens and the earth spread abroad      333

JESUS
And when much people were gathered
  (The Parable of the Sower)                 378
And, behold, a certain lawyer (The Good
  Samaritan)                                 410
A parable put he forth (Parables of the
  Kingdom)                                   431
O Thou Eternal Light (Servants of God)       441

JOY AND SORROW
Let us rejoice in the manifold richness      332
Let us rejoice in the light of day           336
The same stream of life                      351
Lord, thou hast been our dwelling place      361
Great travail is created for every man       363
If one man conquer in battle                 379
Let me not pray to be sheltered              391
As the hart panteth after the water brooks   396
For the holiness of every place              397
The Enlightened One (Buddha's Pity)          408
Pity, more than any other feeling            412
The free spirit is the spirit of joy         422
How beautiful is the morning                 425
Behold, I create new heavens and a new
  earth                                      430
Bright joy, bright joy                       466

KINGDOM OF GOD (*see In Time to
  Come; Love and Human Brotherhood*)

LABOR
O all ye things of tenderness and grace!     328
Bless the Lord, O my soul                    329
Who can make an accounting of his
  gratitude?                                 330
Let us rejoice in the light of day           336
I hear America singing                       399
Why does a man work?                         402
The wisdom of a learned man                  403

What rivers are these? (*Salut au Monde!*)   450
Bright joy, bright joy                       466

LENT (*see Hours of Insight; Prayer and
  Aspiration; Wrong and Repentance*)

THE LIFE OF INTEGRITY
The earth is the Lord's, and the full-
  ness                                       337
O Lord, thou hast searched me                341
Let us not disparage (The Dignity of
  Human Nature)                              355
  *The Life of Integrity and Wisdom*   376–389
We must learn to awaken                      395
I call that mind free                        420

THE LIFE THAT MAKETH ALL
  THINGS NEW
Bless the Lord, O my soul                    329
Who can make an accounting of his
  gratitude?                                 330
O Most High, Almighty, Good Lord God         334
  *The Life That Maketh All Things
  New*                                 339–354
The soul is not more than the body           360
Lord, thou hast been our dwelling place      361
The breath of life moves through a death-
  less valley                                386
The heavens declare the glory of God         394
This is the message (God Is Love)            411
The free spirit is the spirit of joy         422
Ye who turn judgment to wormwood             435

LITANIES
Who can make an accounting of his
  gratitude?                                 330
Let us rejoice in the manifold richness      332
Let us rejoice in the light of day           336
When we are tired with the work              375
Let religion be to us life and joy           390
Let me not pray to be sheltered              391
May I be no man's enemy                      392
For the holiness of every place              397
O Thou Eternal Light (Servants of God)       441
God, who hast made us one nation             445
Bright joy, bright joy                       466

LOVE AND HUMAN
  BROTHERHOOD
O all ye things of tenderness and grace!     328
Who can make an accounting of his
  gratitude?                                 330
Out of the stars in their flight            345
God that made the world and all things       348
Great and marvelous is man's progress        356
What does it mean to be creatures of
  thought                                    357
Let us worship with our eyes and ears and
  fingertips                                 372
If one man conquer in battle                 379
The superior man is universally minded       380
Not until a man has helped himself           381
Let love be without hypocrisy                389
Let religion be to us life and joy           390
Let me not pray to be sheltered              391
May I be no man's enemy                      392
  *Love and Human Brotherhood*         406–418
I call that mind free                        420
How beautiful is the morning                 425

How beautiful upon the mountains 427
This and this alone is true religion 438
All men are brothers 455
Ancient as the home is the temple 456

MAN
O all ye things of tenderness and grace! 328
Let us rejoice in the manifold richness 332
Before creation a presence existed 342
Out of the stars in their flight 345
Let man learn the revelation of all nature 347
I see the Nature Providence going 350
The eternal past is the beginning of man 354
Man 355–360
The fellowship of nature is our shape 365
Know the bonds by which we are bound 409
The free spirit is the spirit of joy 422
I announce natural persons to arise 429
We have set ourselves over many things 439
Rich is the man who lives in today 454

MARRIAGE
Let us rejoice in the manifold richness 332
Why does a man work? 402
Who can find a virtuous woman? 417
Love one another, but make not a bond of love 418

MEMORIAL AND FUNERAL SERVICES
O Most High, Almighty, Good Lord God 334
The Lord is my shepherd 352
God is our refuge and strength 353
Lord, thou hast been our dwelling place 361
Though I speak with the tongues of men 406
I think continually of those 440
Let us now praise famous men 444

MORNING
Let us rejoice in the light of day 336
The heavens declare the glory of God 394
How beautiful is the morning 425

MOTHERS AND FATHERS
O all ye things of tenderness and grace! 328
I hear America singing 399
Honor thy father with thy whole heart 413
Your children are not your children 414
Who can find a virtuous woman? 417
A great city 448

NATION AND NATIONS
O sing unto the Lord a new song 331
Let me not pray to be sheltered 391
How beautiful upon the mountains 427
How beautiful upon the mountains 428
I announce natural persons to arise 429
Nation and Nations 445–451

NATURE
O all ye works of tenderness and grace! 328
Bless the Lord, O my soul 329
The heavens and the earth spread abroad 333
O Most High, Almighty, Good Lord God 334
Praise ye the Lord . . . from the heavens 335
Let us rejoice in the light of day 336
The pride of the height 338
Give unto the Lord, O ye mighty 346
I see the Nature Providence going 350
The same stream of life 351

O Lord, our Lord, how excellent is thy name 359
The fellowship of nature is our shape 365
Some things will never change 370
Let us worship with our eyes and ears and fingertips 372
Let religion be to us life and joy 390
The heavens declare the glory of God 394
How beautiful is the morning 425

NONVIOLENCE
If one man conquer in battle 379
What are the ways of the dedicated man? 383
The breath of life moves through a deathless valley 386
Let love be without hypocrisy 389
May I be no man's enemy 392
How beautiful upon the mountains 427
What constitutes the bulwark of our own liberty 447
Those who have power 449
One who would guide (On War) 451

OLD AGE
Praise ye the Lord . . . from the heavens 335
Let us rejoice in the light of day 336
Lord, thou hast been our dwelling place 361
Let us worship with our eyes and ears and fingertips 372
When we are tired with the work 375
Honor thy father with thy whole heart 413
What more have we to give to one another 416
I announce natural persons to arise 429

ORDINATION AND INSTALLATION
Pity, more than any other feeling 412
I call that mind free 420
The church of tomorrow 459
Let this church (A Liberal Church) 460
Bright joy, bright joy 466

OUR WORLD–WIDE HERITAGE
What rivers are these? (Salut au Monde!) 450
Our World-wide Heritage 452–455
Ancient as the home is the temple 456

PASSOVER (see Freedom; Prophets, Exemplars, Pioneers)

PATRIOTISM (see Nation and Nations)

PRAYER AND ASPIRATION
Prayer and Aspiration 390–397
Ancient as the home is the temple 456

PROPHETS, EXEMPLARS, PIONEERS
Let us rejoice in the manifold richness 332
Blessed is the soul that heareth the Lord 371
Afoot and light-hearted, I take to the open road 424
Ye who turn judgment to wormwood 435
What is required (Geography of This Time) 436
Prophets, Exemplars, Pioneers 440–444
There is one mind common to all 452

RELIGIOUS EDUCATION
Some beliefs are like walled gardens 376
My son, if thou wilt, thou shalt be taught 377
The heavens declare the glory of God 394

Your children are not your children 414
Cherish your doubts 421
Give ear, O my people, to my law 457
The church of tomorrow 459
This is a house for the ingathering of nature 461
The great end in religious instruction 462

REVELATION IS NOT SEALED
The spirit of God is wonderful to us 343
Let man learn the revelation of all nature 347
Blessed is the soul that heareth the Lord 371
Some beliefs are like walled gardens 376
For the holiness of every place 397
I call that mind free 420
Cherish your doubts 421
To doubt is a valorous and necessary faith 423
Afoot and light-hearted, I take to the open road 424
The sum of all known reverence 426
Ye who turn judgment to wormwood 435
All men are brothers 455

SCIENCE
Great and marvelous is man's progress 356
Man is the animal that most wearies himself 358
Cherish your doubts 421
To doubt is a valorous and necessary faith 423
We have set ourselves over many things 439
This is a house for the ingathering of nature 461

THE SEA
O all ye things of tenderness and grace! 328
Bless the Lord, O my soul 329
The heavens and the earth spread abroad 333
Let us rejoice in the light of day 336
Out of the stars in their flight 345
Give unto the Lord, O ye mighty 346
The same stream of life 351
Rejoice in the Lord, O ye righteous 400
Afoot and light-hearted, I take to the open road 424
How beautiful is the morning 425

SELF–CONTROL
If one man conquer in battle 379
The superior man is universally minded 380
Not until a man has helped himself 381
What are the ways of the dedicated man? 383
The moral life of a man 385
The breath of life moves through a deathless valley 386
Let me not pray to be sheltered 391
May I be no man's enemy 392
We must learn to awaken 395
Let a man leave anger 407
I call that mind free 420
We have set ourselves over many things 439

SERENITY
The Lord is my shepherd 352
When we are tired with the work 375
If one man conquer in battle 379
Be utterly humble 382
The moral life of a man 385

Let religion be to us life and joy 390
Let me not pray to be sheltered 391
Let a man leave anger 407
How beautiful is the morning 425
Those who have power 449

SOCIAL JUSTICE
O sing unto the Lord a new song 331
Let us rejoice in the manifold richness 332
Great and marvelous is man's progress 356
Let religion be to us life and joy 390
Let me not pray to be sheltered 391
How beautiful upon the mountains 427
Behold, I create new heavens and a new earth 430
Peace to him that is far off 433
Ye who turn judgment to wormwood 435
God, who hast made us one nation 445
Open ye the gates, that the righteous nation 446

SPRING
O all ye things of tenderness and grace! 328
Some things will never change 370
Soon shall the winter's foil be here 465
Bright joy, bright joy 466

SUKKOTH (see Autumn and Harvest; Thanksgiving Day)

TAOISM
Before creation a presence existed 342
Be utterly humble 382
The breath of life moves through a deathless valley 386
Those who have power 449
One who would guide (On War) 451

THANKSGIVING DAY
Who can make an accounting of his gratitude? 330
O Most High, Almighty, Good Lord God 334
Bless the Lord, O my soul 367
Rejoice in the Lord, O ye righteous 400

TIMES AND SEASONS
O all ye things of tenderness and grace! 328
The pride of the height 338
Times and Seasons 463–467

TRANSIENCE AND ONGOING LIFE
Bless the Lord, O my soul 329
O Most High, Almighty, Good Lord God 334
Let us rejoice in the light of day 336
O Lord, thou hast searched me 341
I am the Self that dwells 344
The same stream of life 351
The Lord is my shepherd 352
Transience and Ongoing Life 361–370
Be utterly humble 382
Our breath vanishes among the winds 401
All this time, and at all times 404
Though I speak with the tongues of men 406
The Enlightened One (Buddha's Pity) 408
Know the bonds by which we are bound 409
Pity, more than any other feeling 412
Afoot and light-hearted, I take to the open road 424
I announce natural persons to arise 429
Comfort ye, comfort ye my people 432

What is required (Geography of This
Time) 436
Rich is the man who lives in today 454
Give ear, O my people, to my law 457
Bright joy, bright joy 466

TRUTH
Let a man leave anger 407
Our faith and knowledge thrive by
exercise 419
Cherish your doubts 421
To doubt is a valorous and necessary
faith 423
Let us indicate a new shape of fellowship 453

VOCATIONS (see Ordination and Installation; The Arts of Man)

WINTER
O all ye things of tenderness and grace! 328
The pride of the height 338
The days of the year have stiffened in ice 463
Soon shall the winter's foil be here 465

WISDOM AND UNDERSTANDING
Man is the animal that most wearies
himself 358
There are questions which come 374
When we are tired with the work 375
My son, if thou wilt, thou shalt be taught 377
The superior man is universally minded 380
What are the ways of the dedicated man? 383
He that giveth his mind to the law of the
Most High 384
Happy is the man that findeth wisdom 387
My son, if thou wilt receive my words 388
What more have we to give to one another 416

WORLD PEACE
God is our refuge and strength 353
Great and marvelous is man's progress 356
What does it mean to be creatures of
thought 357

Man is the animal that most wearies
himself 358
The young dead soldiers do not speak 366
How beautiful upon the mountains 427
How beautiful upon the mountains 428
Comfort ye, comfort ye my people 432
Peace to him that is far off 433
Peace means the beginning 434
We have set ourselves over many things 439
It is no foretelling (The Prophets) 442
God, who hast made us one nation 445
Open ye the gates, that the righteous
nation 446
What constitutes the bulwark of our own
liberty 447
One who would guide (On War) 451
The people that walked in darkness 467

WRONG AND REPENTANCE
O Most High, Almighty, Good Lord God 334
O Lord, thou hast searched me 341
Great and marvelous is man's progress 356
Man is the animal that most wearies
himself 358
Bless the Lord, O my soul 367
I said, I will take heed to my ways 368
Out of the depths have I cried 393
The Enlightened One (Buddha's Pity) 408
Ho, every one that thirsteth 437
We have set ourselves over many things 439
Bright joy, bright joy 466

YOM KIPPUR (see Wrong and Repentance)

YOUTH
Praise ye the Lord ... from the heavens 335
The young dead soldiers do not speak 366
I hear America singing 399
What more have we to give to one another 416
I announce natural persons to arise 429

# INDEX OF AUTHORS, TRANSLATORS, AND SOURCES
# OF RESPONSIVE READINGS

Acts 348
Amos 435
Analects of Confucius, The 380
Argow, W. Waldemar W. 456

Bhagavad-Gita 344
Bible (see individual books)
  Composite 427
Buddhism (see Dhamma-
  pada, Upāsaka Sīla Sūtra)
Burroughs, John 339, 350
Bynner, Witter (trans.) 342,
  382, 386, 451

Channing, William Ellery 355,
  420, 462
I Corinthians 406

Dhammapada 379, 383, 407

Ecclesiasticus
  6 415
  6, 4, 37 377
  7, 3, 8 413
  38 403
  39 384
  40 363
  43 338
  44 444
Egan, Maurice F. (trans.) 334
Emerson, Ralph Waldo 347, 452
Eusebius 392

Fahs, Sophia Lyon 376
Francis of Assisi 334

Gandhi, Mohandas K.
  (trans.) 438
Gibran, Kahlil 414, 418
Golden Mean of Tsesze, The 385

Hinduism (see Bhagavad-
  Gita)

Isaiah
  9, 11 467
  40 349, 432
  52, 2 428
  55 437
  65 430
  Isaiah, Micah 446
  Isaiah, Zechariah 433

Isherwood, Christopher
  (trans.) 344
Islam (see Koran)

Jesus (see Luke, Matt.)
I John 411

Koran 333
Ku Hungming (trans.) 385

Lao-tzu (see Tao-teh-ching)
Lincoln, Abraham 447
Lincoln School, Pupils 434
Lovely, Napoleon W. 343
Luke
  8 378
  10 410

MacLeish, Archibald 362, 366,
  436
Matthew 431
Micah, Isaiah 446
Milton, John 419
Mohammedanism (see
  Koran)
Muir, Edwin 369

New Prayer Book, A 336

Palmer, Edwin C. 356
Patton, Kenneth L. 330, 354,
  357, 358, 365, 372, 374, 381, 398,
  401, 402, 409, 416, 423, 439, 442,
  443, 453, 454, 455, 459, 461, 463
Paul (see Corinthians,
  Romans)
Pomeroy, Vivian T. 375
Prabhavananda, Swami
  (trans.) 344
Proverbs
  2, 3 388
  3, 4 387
  31 417
Psalms
  8 359
  19 394
  23 352
  24 337
  27 373
  29 346
  33, 100 400
  39 368

42, 43 396
46 353
78 457
84 458
90 361
96 331
100 400
103 367
104 329
121 340
130 393
139 341
148 335
150 405
Pupils of the Lincoln School 434

Robbins, Wallace W. 460
Romans 389
Russell, Rollo 425

Services of Religion 397, 441, 445
Silliman, Vincent B. 390
Solomon, The Wisdom of 364
Spender, Stephen 440
Sullivan, Louis H. 422

Tagore, Rabindranath 351, 391
Tao-teh-ching 342, 382, 386,
  449, 451
Thomas a Kempis 371
Thoreau, Henry David 395
Tsesze, The Golden Mean of 385
Tulsī Dās 438

Upāsaka Sīla Sūtra 408

Vogt, Von Ogden 332, 466

Way of Life, The 342, 382, 386,
  451
Weston, Robert Terry 345, 421
Whitman, Walt 360, 399, 404,
  424, 426, 429, 448, 450, 465
Williams, David Rhys 464
Wisdom of Solomon, The 364
Wolfe, Thomas 370, 412

Youlden, Harry 328

Zechariah, Isaiah 433

# Index of Authors and Sources of Unison Readings and Affirmations

| | | | | | | |
|---|---|---|---|---|---|---|
| Act of Horodlo | 489 | Hocking, William Ernest | 503 | Patton, Kenneth L. | | 470, 482, |
| Ames, Charles Gordon | 490 | Holmes, John Haynes (arr.) | 487 | | | 504, 511 |
| | | Horodlo, Act of | 489 | | | |
| Backus, E. Burdette | 505 | | | Sen, Keshab Chandra | | 487 |
| Ballou, Hosea | 481 | India (passage from) | 479 | *Services of Religion* | | 507 |
| Blake, James Vila | 494 | | | Silliman, Vincent B. | | 476 |
| Book of Common Prayer, | | Jones, Walter Royal, Jr. | 498 | Sullivan, William L. | | 496 |
| The | 471 | | | | | |
| Buddhist | 502 | Kālidāsa (attrib. to) | 472 | United Nations, Charter | | 497 |
| Crothers, Samuel M. | 484 | Leavens, Robert French | 477, 483 | | | |
| | | Lovely, Napoleon W. | 510 | Vogt, Von Ogden | | 468, 473, |
| Doan, Frank Carleton | 474 | | | | | 475, 486, 508 |
| | | Manchester College | 478 | | | |
| Emerson, Ralph Waldo | 493 | Martin, Alfred W. | 492 | Washington Declaration | | 491 |
| | | Martineau, James | 469 | Whitehead, Alfred North | | 499 |
| Francis of Assisi | 480 | Matthew 5 | 488 | Whitman, Walt | | 495, 501, 509 |
| Freeman, George Rudolph | 485 | Mill, John Stuart | 500 | Williams, L. Griswold | | 506 |

# Index of Authors, Translators, and Sources of Hymns

| | | |
|---|---|---|
| *Adams, John Coleman* | 219 | We praise thee, God, for harvests earned |
| *Adams, Sarah Flower* | 126 | Nearer, my God, to thee |
| *Addison, Joseph* | 47 | The spacious firmament on high |
| *Adler, Felix* | 192 | Hail the glorious golden city |
| *Æ (George William Russell)* | 104 | The generations as they rise |
| *Alexander, James Waddell (trans.)* | 311 | O sacred head, now wounded |
| *Alford, Henry* | 278 | Come, ye thankful people, come |
| *Ancient Christmas Carols* | 285 | The first Nowell the angel did say |
| *Anonymous* | 21 | Give thanks for the corn |
| *Anonymous* | 26 | Come, thou almighty king |
| *Anonymous* | 30 | For flowers that bloom about our feet |
| *Anonymous* | 64 | From the first man to climb the hill |
| *Anonymous* | 89 | Noiseless the morning flings its gold |
| *Anonymous* | 98 | Not gold, but only men can make |
| *Anonymous* | 102 | What makes a city great and strong? |
| *Anonymous* | 160 | *Shalom havayreem* |
| *Anonymous* | 244 | God save our gracious Queen |
| *Anonymous* | 288 | O come, all ye faithful |
| *Anonymous* | 298 | Lo, how a Rose e'er blooming |
| *Arnold, Matthew* | 85 | Calm soul of all things |
| *Arnold, Matthew* | 86 | We cannot kindle when we will |
| *Auslander, Joseph* | 229 | Blest is that man who sets his soul's desire |
| *Bacon, Leonard* | 235 | O God, beneath thy guiding hand |
| *Baker, Theodore (trans.)* | 298 | Lo, how a Rose e'er blooming |
| *Ballou, Adin* | 198 | Years are coming—speed them onward |
| *Bates, Katharine Lee* | 241 | O beautiful for spacious skies |
| *Bax, Clifford* | 196 | Turn back, O man, forswear thy foolish ways |
| *Beach, Seth Curtis* | 130 | Mysterious Presence, source of all |
| *Beardsley, Monroe* | 84 | From all the fret and fever of the day |
| *Bernard of Clairvaux* | 311 | O sacred head, now wounded |
| *Bhagavad-Gita* | 134 | Give me your whole heart |
| *Binyon, Laurence* | 152 | For mercy, courage, kindness, mirth |
| *Binyon, Laurence* | 153 | Woe unto him that has not known the woe of man |
| *Blake, William* | 132 | To Mercy, Pity, Peace, and Love |
| *Blake, William* | 163 | Can a father see his child |
| *Blake, William* | 184 | Every night and every morn |
| *Boëthius* | 128 | O Thou whose power o'er moving worlds presides |
| *Borthwick, Jane Laurie* | 209 | Now is the time approaching |

| | | |
|---|---|---|
| Bourdillon, Francis William | 164 | The night has a thousand eyes |
| Bowring, John | 283 | Watchman, tell us of the night |
| Box, Howard | 303 | Bells in the high tower |
| Bridges, Robert (para.) | 35 | All my hope on God is founded |
| Bridges, Robert | 137 | I love all beauteous things |
| Bridges, Robert | 162 | Love can tell, and love alone |
| Bridges, Robert | 212 | Gird on thy sword, O man |
| Bridges, Robert (para.) | 268 | Now all the heavenly splendor |
| Briggs, George Wallace | 24 | O God, in whom we live and move |
| Briggs, George Wallace | 32 | Lord of all majesty and might |
| Briggs, Le Baron Russell | 234 | God of our fathers, who has safely brought us |
| Brooke, Stopford Augustus | 10 | Let the whole creation cry |
| Brooks, Phillips | 286 | O little town of Bethlehem |
| Buddha, Gautama (attrib.) | 110 | Be ye lamps unto yourselves |
| Buehrer, Edwin T. | 22 | We sing now together our song of thanksgiving |
| Bullett, Gerald | 322 | But for the cockerel calling the noon hour |
| Bunyan, John | 94 | Who would true valor see |
| Burleigh, William Henry | 222 | Abide not in the realm of dreams |
| Burns, James Drummond (trans.) | 33 | Heaven and earth and sea and air |
| Burroughs, John | 186 | Serene I fold my hands and wait |
| Byron, George Gordon, Lord | 167 | Eternal spirit of the chainless mind! |
| | | |
| Campian, Thomas | 107 | The man of life upright |
| Cardozo, Elizabeth C. | 237 | We met them on the common way |
| Chesterton, Gilbert Keith | 101 | It is something to have wept |
| Chesterton, Gilbert Keith | 238 | O God of earth and altar |
| Clough, Arthur Hugh | 97 | Say not, "The struggle nought availeth" |
| Collyer, Robert | 252 | Unto thy temple, Lord, we come |
| Colum, Padraic | 314 | Now in the tomb is laid |
| Confucius | 161 | Let him who would excel |
| Conrad of Mainz? | 298 | Lo, how a Rose e'er blooming |
| Cornish, William | 325 | Pleasure it is |
| Cowper, William | 34 | God moves in a mysterious way |
| Crane, William Merriam | 291 | Ye shepherd plains of Bethlehem |
| | | |
| Daniel Ben Judah Dayyan | 6 | Praise to the living God! |
| Darwin, Erasmus | 52 | Roll on, ye stars, exult in youthful prime |
| Davies, William Henry | 183 | What is this life if, full of care |
| Dearmer, Percy (trans.) | 321 | Spring has now unwrapped the flowers |
| Dillon, George | 228 | Obedient they but to a dream |
| Doddridge, Philip | 223 | Awake, my soul, stretch every nerve |
| Dorr, Julia Caroline Ripley | 245 | Heir of all the ages, I |
| Draper, W. H. (para.) | 23 | All creatures of our God and King |
| Dryden, John (para.) | 185 | Happy the man, and happy he alone |
| Dunham, Barrows | 302 | Winter is a cold thing |
| | | |
| Ecclesiasticus 44 | 230 | Let us now praise famous men |
| Eliot, Frederick May | 116 | O thou, to whom the fathers built |
| Emerson, Ralph Waldo | 40 | We sing of golden mornings |
| English Carol | 285 | The first Nowell the angel did say |
| English, Paul (trans.) | 17 | Now let every tongue adore thee |
| Euripides | 109 | What else is wisdom? |
| | | |
| Faber, Frederick William | 44 | There's a wideness in God's mercy |
| Fahs, Sophia Lyon | 58 | Divinity is round us—never gone |
| Fan Cheng-ta | 322 | But for the cockerel calling the noon hour |
| Farjeon, Eleanor | 266 | Morning has broken |
| Farjeon, Eleanor | 281 | People, look East |
| Fosdick, Harry Emerson | 27 | God of grace and God of glory |
| Fox, G. W. | 129 | Hard is now the constant woe |
| Francis of Assisi | 23 | All creatures of our God and King |
| Frank, Florence Kiper | 148 | Man's comradeship is very wide |
| French Carol | 294 | Angels we have heard on high |
| Frost, Robert | 324 | Oh, give us pleasure in the flowers today |
| Frothingham, Nathaniel L. | 165 | "Remember me," the Master said |
| Fyleman, Rose | 319 | Lift your hidden faces |
| | | |
| Gale, Zona | 193 | Come, children of tomorrow, come! |
| Gannett, William Channing | 1 | The morning hangs a signal |
| Gannett, William Channing | 5 | Bring, O morn, thy music! |
| Gannett, William Channing (trans.) | 6 | Praise to the living God! |
| Gannett, William Channing | 247 | It sounds along the ages |
| Gannett, William Channing | 251 | From heart to heart, from creed to creed |
| Gannett, William Channing | 260 | To cloisters of the spirit |

| | | |
|---|---|---|
| Gannett, William Channing | 308 | Praise to God and thanks we bring |
| Gascoigne, George | 264 | Ye that have spent the silent night |
| Gautier, Théophile | 135 | All things are doubly fair |
| Gerhardt, Paul | 268 | Now all the heavenly splendor |
| Gerhardt, Paul (trans.) | 311 | O sacred head, now wounded |
| Gill, Thomas Hornblower | 15 | We come unto our fathers' God |
| Gill, Thomas Hornblower | 36 | Our God, our God, thou shinest here |
| Gill, Thomas Hornblower | 327 | I walk amidst thy beauty forth |
| Gillman, Frederick John | 217 | God send us men whose aim will be |
| Gladden, Washington | 122 | O Light of light, within us dwell |
| Gladden, Washington | 236 | Behold a Sower! from afar |
| Goethe, Johann Wolfgang von | 63 | Whether day my spirit's yearning |
| Goethe, Johann Wolfgang von | 176 | This thought shall have our whole allegiance |
| Gordon, Elias (arr. or trans.) | 170 | Freedom is the finest gold |
| Gordon, George (Lord Byron) | 167 | Eternal spirit of the chainless mind! |
| Gottheil, Gustav | 279 | Rock of Ages, let our song |
| Grant, Robert | 25 | O worship the King |
| | | |
| Ham, Marion Franklin | 125 | O thou whose gracious presence shone |
| Ham, Marion Franklin | 253 | As tranquil streams that meet and merge |
| Ham, Marion Franklin | 293 | Heir of all the waiting ages |
| Hawkes, Henry W. | 290 | Thank we now the Lord of heaven |
| Hay, Sara Henderson | 154 | It is a piteous thing to be |
| Heber, Reginald | 4 | Holy, holy, holy, Lord God almighty |
| Hedge, Frederic Henry (trans.) | 16 | A mighty fortress is our God |
| Hedge, Frederic Henry | 127 | Sovereign and transforming Grace |
| Herbert, George | 123 | Come, my way, my truth, my life |
| Hill, Leslie Pinckney | 147 | This is the charge I keep as mine |
| Holmes, John | 9 | O Lord of stars and sunlight |
| Holmes, John | 61 | Though man, the fiery element, sink like fire |
| Holmes, John | 178 | Now give heart's onward habit brave intent |
| Holmes, John | 179 | Peace is the mind's old wilderness cut down |
| Holmes, John Haynes | 205 | All hail, the pageant of the years |
| Holmes, John Haynes | 214 | The voice of God is calling |
| Holmes, John Haynes | 227 | O'er continent and ocean |
| Holmes, Oliver Wendell | 38 | Lord of all being, throned afar |
| Hopkins, John Henry, Jr. | 300 | We three kings of Orient are |
| Horace | 185 | Happy the man, and happy he alone |
| Hosmer, Frederick Lucian | 50 | One thought I have, my ample creed |
| Hosmer, Frederick Lucian | 73 | I cannot think of them as dead |
| Hosmer, Frederick Lucian | 74 | O Thou whose spirit witness bears |
| Hosmer, Frederick Lucian | 88 | Go not, my soul, in search of him |
| Hosmer, Frederick Lucian | 90 | Not always on the mount may we |
| Hosmer, Frederick Lucian | 95 | When courage fails and faith burns low |
| Hosmer, Frederick Lucian | 188 | We pray no more, made lowly wise |
| Hosmer, Frederick Lucian | 194 | Hear, hear, O ye nations, and hearing obey |
| Hosmer, Frederick Lucian | 210 | Thy kingdom come, O Lord |
| Hosmer, Frederick Lucian | 215 | Forward through the ages |
| Hosmer, Frederick Lucian | 231 | From age to age how grandly rise |
| Hosmer, Frederick Lucian | 233 | O prophet souls of all the years |
| Hosmer, Frederick Lucian | 240 | O beautiful, my country! |
| Hosmer, Frederick Lucian | 255 | O Light, from age to age the same |
| Hosmer, Frederick Lucian | 269 | Now while the day in trailing splendor |
| Hosmer, Frederick Lucian | 277 | I walk the unfrequented road |
| Hosmer, Frederick Lucian | 316 | O day of light and gladness |
| Hosmer, Frederick Lucian | 317 | Lo, the day of days is here |
| Housman, Laurence | 72 | Fair is their fame |
| How, William Walsham | 75 | For all the saints who from their labors rest |
| How, William Walsham | 131 | We give thee but thine own |
| Howitt, Mary | 307 | Thou, earth, art ours, and ours to keep |
| Hoyt, Helen | 81 | Since I have felt the sense of death |
| Hyde, William De Witt | 108 | Since what we choose is what we are |
| Hyde, William De Witt | 221 | Creation's Lord, we give thee thanks |
| Hymns of the Spirit, 1864 | 117 | God is in his holy temple |
| | | |
| Isaacs, A. S. | 106 | A noble life, a simple faith |
| Isherwood, Christopher (trans.) | 134 | Give me your whole heart |
| | | |
| Jastrow, Marcus M. (trans.) | 279 | Rock of Ages, let our song |
| Jewitt, Alfred Charles | 315 | Past are the cross, the scourge, the thorn |
| Johnson, Josephine | 55 | In this stern hour when the spirit falters |
| Johnson, Samuel (1709–84) (trans.) | 128 | O Thou whose power o'er moving worlds presides |
| Johnson, Samuel (1822–82) (arr.) | 26 | Come, thou almighty King |

| Johnson, Samuel (1822–82) | 172 | Life of ages, richly poured |
| Johnson, Samuel (1822–82) | 224 | God of the earnest heart |
| Jonson, Ben | 105 | Truth is the trial of itself |
| Kemp, Harry | 46 | Who thou art I know not |
| Ken, Thomas | 265 | Awake, my soul, and with the sun |
| Ken, Thomas | 270 | All praise to thee, my God, this night |
| Kethe, William | 18 | All people that on earth do dwell |
| Knowles, Frederick Lawrence | 243 | Who is the patriot? |
| | | |
| Laing, Dilys Bennett | 67 | Man imperishably stands |
| Lathrop, John Howland | 309 | Hosanna in the highest! |
| Legge, James (trans.) | 161 | Let him who would excel |
| Lewisohn, Ludwig (trans.) | 63 | Whether day my spirit's yearning |
| Lindsay, Vachel | 150 | Let not young souls be smothered out |
| Longfellow, Henry Wadsworth | 175 | All are architects of fate |
| Longfellow, Samuel (arr.) | 26 | Come, thou almighty King |
| Longfellow, Samuel | 43 | God of the earth, the sky, the sea |
| Longfellow, Samuel | 54 | O Life that maketh all things new |
| Longfellow, Samuel | 208 | Out of the dark the circling sphere |
| Longfellow, Samuel | 213 | God's trumpet wakes the slumbering world |
| Longfellow, Samuel | 246 | With joy we claim the growing light |
| Longfellow, Samuel | 248 | Light of ages and of nations |
| Longfellow, Samuel | 261 | One holy Church of God appears |
| Longfellow, Samuel | 271 | Again, as evening's shadow falls |
| Longfellow, Samuel | 274 | Now, on land and sea descending |
| Longfellow, Samuel | 301 | 'Tis winter now; the fallen snow |
| Longfellow, Samuel | 312 | Beneath the shadow of the cross |
| Longfellow, Samuel | 313 | When my love to God grows weak |
| Longfellow, Samuel | 318 | Lo, the earth awakes again |
| Longfellow, Samuel | 326 | The sweet June days are come again |
| Lowell, James Russell | 168 | When a deed is done for freedom |
| Lowell, James Russell | 173 | Men, whose boast it is that ye |
| Lowell, James Russell | 220 | Once to every man and nation comes the moment to decide |
| Luther, Martin | 16 | A mighty fortress is our God |
| Lyon, Carrie Ward | 31 | Praise ye, praise ye the Lord |
| Lysaght, S. R. | 83 | Let us be faithful to our passing hours |
| Lyte, Henry Francis | 79 | Abide with me, fast falls the eventide |
| Lyttle, Charles H. | 37 | Praise God, the love we all may share |
| Lyttle, Charles H. | 42 | Rejoice in love we know and share |
| Lyttle, Charles H. | 254 | Bring, O Past, your honor; bring, O Time, your harvest |
| | | |
| MacLeish, Archibald | 112 | The people of the earth go down |
| MacLeish, Archibald | 113 | Yet when the splendor of the earth |
| Madison, Elizabeth | 276 | In sweet fields of autumn, the gold grain is falling |
| Mann, Newton (trans.) | 6 | Praise to the living God! |
| Markham, Edwin | 103 | We are all blind, until we see |
| Markham, Edwin | 140 | He presses on before the race |
| Markham, Edwin | 143 | The crest and crowning of all good |
| Markham, Edwin | 180 | Here on the paths of every day |
| Marlatt, Earl (arr.) | 294 | Angels we have heard on high |
| Martineau, James | 87 | Where is your God? they say |
| Marquis, Don | 53 | A fierce unrest seethes at the core |
| Massey, Gerald | 169 | Through all the long dark night of years |
| Matheson, George | 249 | Gather us in, thou Love that fillest all |
| Meredith, George | 8 | In singing till his heaven fills |
| Meredith, George | 139 | We sing the rapture of the breath |
| Merrill, William Pierson | 218 | Rise up, O men of God |
| Merrill, William Pierson | 239 | Not alone for mighty empire |
| Millay, Edna St. Vincent | 57 | The world stands out on either side |
| Mohr, Joseph | 289 | Silent night, holy night |
| Montgomery, James | 20 | God is my strong salvation |
| Montgomery, James | 91 | Prayer is the soul's sincere desire |
| Montgomery, James | 282 | Hail to the Lord's anointed |
| Morris, William | 80 | He that dies shall not die lonely |
| Murray, Gilbert (trans.) | 109 | What else is wisdom? |
| | | |
| Naidu, Sarojini | 77 | Nay, do not grieve though life be full of sadness |
| Neale, John Mason (trans.) | 280 | O come, O come, Emmanuel |
| Neander, Joachim | 7 | Praise to the Lord, the Almighty, the King of creation! |
| Neander, Joachim | 33 | Heaven and earth and sea and air |
| Neander, Joachim | 35 | All my hope on God is founded |

| | | |
|---|---|---|
| Nicolai, Philipp | 17 | Now let every tongue adore thee |
| North, Frank Mason | 189 | Where cross the crowded ways of life |
| Noyes, Alfred | 39 | Knowledge, they say, drives wonder from the world |
| Oakeley, Frederick (trans.) | 288 | O come, all ye faithful |
| Parker, Theodore | 120 | O thou great friend to all the sons of men |
| Patton, Kenneth L. | 28 | Brief our days, but long for singing |
| Patton, Kenneth L. | 56 | The earth is home and all abundant |
| Patton, Kenneth L. | 62 | Man is the earth upright and proud |
| Patton, Kenneth L. | 66 | We journey with a multitude |
| Patton, Kenneth L. | 68 | Before the stars a man is small |
| Patton, Kenneth L. | 138 | Ours be the poems of all tongues |
| Patton, Kenneth L. | 171 | Let all who live in freedom, won |
| Patton, Kenneth L. | 181 | When we have ended searching |
| Patton, Kenneth L. | 203 | Quest of the ages, goal of men |
| Patton, Kenneth L. | 225 | Let all men living in all lands |
| Patton, Kenneth L. | 232 | Feet of the urgent pioneer |
| Patton, Kenneth L. | 256 | The blessings of the earth and sky |
| Patton, Kenneth L. | 320 | Now once again the heaven turns |
| Peabody, Josephine P. | 136 | Truly the light is sweet |
| Percy, William Alexander | 111 | They cast their nets in Galilee |
| Piae Cantiones, Theodoric Petri, editor | 296 | On this day everywhere |
| Piae Cantiones, Theodoric Petri, editor | 321 | Spring has now unwrapped the flowers |
| Piae Cantiones, Theodoric Petri, editor | 323 | Now the spring has come again |
| Pierpoint, Folliott S. | 12 | For the beauty of the earth |
| Pope, Alexander | 133 | Father of all, in every age |
| Pope, Alexander | 199 | The time shall come when, free as seas of wind |
| Prabhavananda, Swami (trans.) | 134 | Give me your whole heart |
| Psalteriolum Cantionum Catholicarum, 1710 | 280 | O come, O come, Emmanuel |
| Quin, Malcolm | 76 | Say not they die, those martyr souls |
| Quin, Malcolm | 200 | We move in faith to unseen goals |
| Rights, Douglas LeTell | 284 | Veiled in darkness Judah lay |
| Rinkart, Martin | 19 | Now thank we all our God |
| Rist, Johann | 297 | Break forth, O beauteous heavenly light |
| Robinson, Edwin Arlington | 273 | Dark hills at evening in the west |
| Rossetti, Christina G. | 141 | O ye who taste that love is sweet |
| Ruskin, John | 207 | Bend back the lance's point |
| Russell, George William (Æ) | 104 | The generations as they rise |
| Santayana, George (trans.) | 135 | All things are doubly fair |
| Sassoon, Siegfried | 263 | Your little flame of life we guard |
| Savage, Minot Judson | 115 | O star of truth, down shining |
| Savage, Minot Judson | 174 | Seek not afar for beauty; lo, it glows |
| Savage, Minot Judson | 272 | When the gladsome day declineth |
| Scheffler, Johann | 92 | The soul wherein God dwells |
| Scotch Paraphrases | 96 | Wisdom has treasures greater afar |
| Scottish Psalter | 49 | The Lord's my shepherd, I'll not want |
| Seaman, Owen | 206 | You that have faith to look with fearless eyes |
| Sears, Edmund Hamilton | 287 | It came upon the midnight clear |
| Shelley, Percy Bysshe | 100 | To suffer woes which hope thinks infinite |
| Shuttleworth, Henry Cary | 151 | Man lives not for himself alone |
| Sill, Edward Rowland | 124 | Send down thy truth, O God |
| Silliman, Vincent B. | 14 | Morning, so fair to see |
| Silliman, Vincent B. | 48 | Earth arrayed in wondrous beauty |
| Silliman, Vincent B. | 145 | One world this, for all its sorrow |
| Silliman, Vincent B. | 257 | Faith of the larger liberty |
| Silliman, Vincent B. | 280 | O come, O come, Emmanuel (st. 3) |
| Silliman, Vincent B. | 300 | We three kings of Orient are (st. 5) |
| Skrine, John Huntley | 258 | Rank by rank again we stand |
| Smith, Samuel Francis | 242 | My country, 'tis of thee |
| Smith, Walter Chalmers | 41 | Immortal, invisible, God only wise |
| Stawell, Florence Melian (trans.) | 176 | This thought shall have our whole allegiance |
| Stein, Leopold | 279 | Rock of Ages, let our song |
| Stevenson, Robert Louis | 60 | Let us wander where we will |
| Stevenson, Robert Louis | 306 | To make this earth, our hermitage |
| Struther, Jan | 29 | We thank you, Lord of heaven |
| Struther, Jan | 155 | When Stephen, full of power and grace |
| Struther, Jan | 267 | High o'er the lonely hills |
| Swinburne, Algernon Charles | 166 | For no sect elect |
| Symonds, John Addington | 190 | These things shall be: a loftier race |

| | | |
|---|---|---|
| Tagore, Rabindranath | 59 | The light, my light, world filling light |
| Tagore, Rabindranath | 82 | Now I recall my childhood when the sun |
| Tarrant, William George | 204 | I saw the city of the Lord |
| Tate, Nahum | 295 | While shepherds watched their flocks by night |
| Tennyson, Alfred Lord | 65 | I am a part of all that I have met |
| Tennyson, Alfred Lord | 195 | Not in vain the distance beacons |
| Tennyson, Alfred Lord | 305 | Ring out, wild bells, to the wild, wild sky |
| Thomas, Bishop of Strängnäs | 170 | Freedom is the finest gold |
| Torrence, Ridgely | 2 | Praise, O my heart, to you, O Source of Life |
| Torrence, Ridgely | 3 | Praise, O my heart, with praise from depth and height |
| Torrence, Ridgely | 197 | The sky has gathered the flowers of sunset |
| Torrence, Ridgely | 262 | Consider well your ways and lives |
| Trapp, Jacob | 191 | Wonders still the world shall witness |
| Trapp, Jacob | 250 | The art, the science, and the lore |
| Trench, Richard Chenevix | 157 | Make channels for the streams of love |
| Troutbeck, John (trans.) | 297 | Break forth, O beauteous heavenly light |
| Turner, Nancy Byrd | 216 | Men go out from the places where they dwelled |
| | | |
| Untermeyer, Louis | 114 | God, though this life is but a wraith |
| Untermeyer, Louis | 159 | May nothing evil cross this door |
| | | |
| Van Dyke, Henry | 11 | Joyful, joyful, we adore thee |
| Vories, William Merrill | 201 | Let there be light, Lord God of Hosts |
| | | |
| Watts, Isaac | 13 | From all that dwell below the skies |
| Watts, Isaac | 51 | O God, our help in ages past |
| Watts, Isaac | 299 | Joy to the world! the Lord is come |
| Weissel, Georg | 310 | Lift up your heads, ye mighty gates |
| Westwood, Horace | 146 | Spirit of truth, of life, of power |
| Wheelock, John Hall | 69 | How little our true majesty |
| Wheelock, John Hall | 70 | Leave starry heaven behind |
| Wheelock, John Hall | 156 | Put down your foot and you shall find |
| Wheelock, John Hall | 182 | The amplitude of space comes down to your own door |
| Whitaker, Robert | 149 | My country is the world |
| Whitman, Walt | 78 | Away, O soul, hoist up the anchor now |
| Whitman, Walt | 211 | All the past we leave behind |
| Whittier, John Greenleaf | 93 | The harp at Nature's advent strung |
| Whittier, John Greenleaf | 118, 119 | Dear Lord and Father of mankind |
| Whittier, John Greenleaf | 121 | Our friend, our brother, and our Lord |
| Whittier, John Greenleaf | 142 | Immortal Love, forever full |
| Whittier, John Greenleaf | 144 | O brother man, fold to thy heart thy brother |
| Whittier, John Greenleaf | 177 | O sometimes gleams upon our sight |
| Whittier, John Greenleaf | 187 | No longer forward nor behind |
| Whittier, John Greenleaf | 202 | Sound over all waters, reach out from all lands |
| Whittier, John Greenleaf | 275 | Once more the liberal year laughs out |
| Wile, Frances Whitmarsh | 304 | All beautiful the march of days |
| Williams, Roger | 45 | God makes a path, provides a guide |
| Williams, Theodore Chickering | 226 | When thy heart, with joy o'erflowing |
| Williams, Theodore Chickering | 292 | In the lonely midnight |
| Wilson, Edwin Henry | 259 | Where is our holy church? |
| Wilson, Steuart (trans.) | 323 | Now the spring has come again |
| Winkworth, Catherine (trans.) | 7 | Praise to the Lord, the Almighty, the King |
| Winkworth, Catherine (trans.) | 19 | Now thank we all our God |
| Winkworth, Catherine (trans.) | 310 | Lift up your heads, ye mighty gates |
| Wordsworth, William | 158 | Serene will be our days and bright |
| Wotton, Henry | 99 | How happy is he born or taught |
| Wreford, John Reynell | 313 | When my love to God grows weak |
| | | |
| Young, Edward | 71 | When in his thoughts the stars and planets roll |

# INDEX OF COMPOSERS, ARRANGERS, AND SOURCES OF HYMNS

(Arrangements and harmonizations are indicated by italic numerals.)

Ahle, Johann Rudolph 245
Ainsworth, Henry, *The Book of Psalmes*, 1612 52, 120, 249
Anglo-Genevan Psalter, 1556 88
Antes, John 129
Arnold, John, *Compleat Psalmodist*, 1749 318

Bach, Johann Sebastian *17, 20, 28, 32, 35, 76, 81, 87, 118, 132, 156, 169, 173, 264, 268, 297, 311*
Barthélemon, François Hippolyte 265
Beethoven, Ludwig van 11, 195
Besançon carol 281
Billings, William 31
Bishop, John 86, 102
Bohemian Brethren, *Gesangbuch*, 1544 151
Bohemian Brethren, *Kirchengeseng*, 1566 15, 141, 257
Bortniansky, Dmitri 56
Bourgeois, Louis, *Pseaulmes cinquante de David*, 1547 97, 176
Brandon, George *206*
Breedlove, Leonard P. 68, 112, 113
*Brethren Hymnal*, 1901 148
Briggs, George Wallace 58

Caldwell, William, *Union Harmony*, 1837 21
Calvisius, Seth 67
Campian, Thomas 107, 313
Carden, A. D., *Missouri Harmony*, 1820 183, 306
Carr, Benjamin *127, 308*
Chapin, Amzi 147, 263, 271
Clark, Jeremiah 98, 103, 122, 187
Clark, Thomas 251
Clarke, Henry Leland *40, 44,* 135, *175, 183, 185,* 197, 199 *203, 217, 240, 277,* 302, *306*
Cologne, *Alte catholische geistliche Kirchengesäng*, 1599 298
Cologne, *Ausserlesene catholische geistliche Kirchengeseng*, 1623 23, 92
Coopersmith, Harry *175*
Covell, William King 24
Croft, William 51, 255
Crotch, William *259*
Crüger, Johann 19, 96, 145, 233
Cutler, Henry Stephen 213

Damon, William, *Psalmes*, 1591 89, 91
Davisson, Ananias, *Kentucky Harmony*, ca. 1815 53, 155, 237
Douglas, Winfred *290*
Duguet, Abbé 140
Dykes, John Bacchus 4, 5, 254

Ebeling, Johann Georg 284
Edson, Lewis 232
Elvey, George Job 10, 278
English carol 285, 291
*English Hymnal*, 1906 293
English melody 90, 94, 214, 238, 272, 304, 326
Erfurt, *Enchiridion*, 1524 67
Evans, Daniel, *Hymnau a Thônau*, 1865 227
Evans, David *39, 212*

Finnish melody 115
Flitner, Johann, *Himmlisches Lustgärtlein*, 1661 170
Foote, Arthur, II 29, 202
Freeman, Sylvia *46*
French carol 281, 294, 319
French melody 293, 315
Freylinghausen, J. A., *Geistreiches Gesangbuch*, 1704 33
1705 48
Freylinghausen, J. A., *Neues geistreiches Gesangbuch*, 1714 219
Fritsch, Ahasuerus 87

Gaelic melody 266
Gardiner, William, *Sacred Melodies*, 1815 25
Gastorius, Severus 30, 307
Genevan Psalter, 1543 269
1551 13, 18, 37, 72, 77, 109, 166, 196, 229, 234, 259
1562 52, 120, 249
German melody 168
German synagogue melody 279
Gesius, Bartholomäus 189
Giardini, Felice 26, 149
Gibbons, Orlando *73, 157,* 164, 167
Greatorex, Walter 61, 65
Greenwood, John, *Psalmody Harmonized in Score*, 1838 275
*Grenoble Antiphoner*, 1868 305
Gruber, Franz Xaver 289
Gwyllt, Ieuan 161
Gwyllt, Ieuan, *Llyfr Tonau Cynulleidfaol*, 1859 39, 212

Hamburg, *Musicalisch Hand-buch*, 1690 246, 253
Handel, George Frideric 223, 295, 299
Hartig, X. L., *Vollständige Sammlung*, ca. 1833 236, 309
Hasidic melody 175
Hassler, Hans Leo 311
Hastings, Thomas, *The Manhattan Collection*, 1837 59
Hatton, John 43, 222, 235, 252
Havergal, William Henry *131*
Haydn, Franz Joseph 47, 66, 248
Helmore, Thomas *280*
Hemlandssånger, Rock Island, Ill., 1892 247
Herman, Nikolaus 118, 132, 264
*Herrnhut Manuscript*, ca. 1740 60
Hintze, Jacob 173
Hodges, Edward *11*
Hoffmann von Fallersleben, A. H., *Schlesische Volkslieder*, 1842 14
Holden, Oliver 36
Holsinger, George Blackburn 217
Holst, Gustav *296*
Hopkins, John Henry, Jr. 300
Howard, Samuel 106, 224
Hughes, John 27
Hungarian melody 38, 201, 303
*Hymns Ancient and Modern*, 1861 117

Ingham, T. H. 267
Isaak, Heinrich 268

Jackson, Thomas 93
Jewish melody 160
Jones, William 261

Kentucky Harmony, ca. 1815 (See: Davisson)
Kimball, Jacob 194
Kirkpatrick, William James 276
Knapp, William 99, 130
Knecht, Justin Heinrich 172
Kocher, Conrad 12
Kremser, Edward 22

Latin carol 125, 301
Lawes, Henry 3, 178, 228
Leavitt, Joshua, Christian Lyre, 1830 198
Leipzig, As Hymnodus Sacer, 1625 169
Lloyd, William 1
Lowens, Irving 170, 194, 211
Luther, Martin 16, 62
Lyon, Meyer 6
Lyons Antiphoner, 1738 273
Lyra Davidica, 1708 318

Magdalen Chapel, Hymns, ca. 1760 152, 162
Maker, Frederick Charles 119
Mason, Lowell 126, 146, 177, 283, 299
Mathias, Franz Xaver 46
Memmingen, Manuscript tablature book, early
seventeenth century 181
Meyer, Franz Heinrich Christoph 210
Missouri Harmony, 1820 (See: Carden)
Monk, William Henry 79
Munson, Kenneth 8, 53, 110, 134, 155, 180, 219, 232,
237, 256, 310, 319

Naue, Johann Friedrich, Allgemeines
evangelisches Choralbuch, 1829 63, 80
Neander, Joachim, Glaub- und Liebesübung, 1680 35
Nicolai, Philipp 17
Nürnbergisches Gesangbuch, 1676 208, 250

Oude en niewe Hollantse Boernlities en
Contradanseu, ca. 1710 191, 239

Parry, C. Hubert H. 55, 144
Parry, Joseph 200
Persichetti, Vincent 314
Petri, Theodoric, Piae Cantiones, 1582 70, 290, 296,
321, 323
Piae Cantiones, 1582 (See: Petri, Theodoric)
Pilsbury, Amos, The United States' Sacred
Harmony, 1799 44, 114
Plainsong 110, 128, 280, 290, 292
Praetorius, Michael, Musae Sionae,
VI, 1609 125, 298, 301
VIII, 1610 204
Prichard, Rowland Hugh 192
Prys, Edmund, Llyfr y Psalmau, 1621 73, 157

Quaile, Robert N. 159

Read, Daniel 154
Redner, Lewis Henry 286
Reimann, Johann Balthasar 205
Revivalist, 1869 206
Roberts, John (Gwyllt) (See: Ieuan Gwyllt)
Roberts, John (Henllan) 317
Roberts, John (Henllan), Caniadau y
Cyssegr, 1839 41
Robinson, Raymond C. 46
Röntgen, Julius 191, 239
Routley, Erik 83, 174
Russian melody 274

Sanders, Robert L. 2, 31, 38, 50, 57, 64, 68, 93, 101,
105, 106, 109, 112, 113, 136, 137, 143, 147, 153,

164, 166, 182, 201, 210, 226, 229, 247, 251, 262,
263, 271, 303, 320, 325
Sandys, William, Christmas Carols Ancient and
Modern, 1833 285
Sarum Antiphonal 110
Schein, Johann Hermann 156
Schop, Johann 28, 297
Schumann, Valentin, Geistliche Lieder, 1539 32, 42,
81, 104, 108, 193, 221, 225
Scottish Psalter, 1615 34, 45, 49, 142, 165, 312
1635 74, 95
Shaw, Geoffrey 323
Shaw, Martin 266, 321
Sheeles, John 116
Smart, Henry 316
Smith, Alfred Morton 71, 82, 179, 322
Solesmes 128, 292
Southern Harmony, 1835 (See: Walker)
Spiess, Johann Martin 131
Stainer, John 281, 285
Stevenson, John Andrew 274
Stockholm, Then Swenska Psalmboken, 1697 310
Stralsund, Erneuertes Gesangbuch, II, 1665 7
Strattner, Georg Christoph 33
Sullivan, Arthur Seymour 215
Sussex melody 94
Swedish melody 310
Synagogue melody 6

Tallis, Thomas 85, 133, 138, 186, 270
Tans'ur, William, Compleat Melody, 1734 327
Taylor, Cyril V. 84, 324
Teschner, Melchior 20
Thesaurus Musicus, ca. 1740–45 242, 244
Tye, Christopher 121

Union Harmony, 1837 (See: Caldwell)
United States' Sacred Harmony, 1799 (See: Pilsbury)
University of Wales, A Students' Hymnal, 1923 258

Valerius, Adrian, Nederlandtsch Gedenckclanck,
1626 22
Vaughan Williams, Ralph 75, 78, 90, 94, 123, 184,
214, 230, 238, 272, 276, 291, 304, 326
Vehe, Michael, New Gesangbüchlin, 1537 143, 262
Vulpius, Melchior 76, 188, 231, 260

Wade, John Francis, Manuscript, ca. 1740–43 288
Waldis, Burkard 325
Walker, William, Southern Harmony, 1835 8, 40, 64,
180, 240, 256
Walter, William Henry 207, 218
Ward, Samuel Augustus 241
Warwickshire melody 272
Webb, George James 209, 282
Webbe, Samuel 158, 171
Weber, Frederic 9
Wessnitzer, Wolfgang 185
Weyman, David, Melodia Sacra, 1815 223, 295
White, Benjamin Franklin 57, 139, 320
Williams, Aaron, Universal Psalmodist,
1763 124
1764 50, 105
Williams, David McKinley 111
Williams, Robert 317
Williams, Thomas, Psalmodia Evangelica,
1789 54, 190, 243
Williams, Thomas John 220
Willis, Richard Storrs 287
Winkworth, Catherine et al., Chorale Book for
England, 1863 7
Wise, Michael 69, 100, 150, 216
Witt, Christian Friedrich, Psalmodia Sacra,
1715 117, 163
Wyeth, John, Repository of Sacred Music, II 203, 277

# ALPHABETICAL INDEX OF TUNES

Ach Gott und Herr 169
Ach, wann werd ich 163
Ach, was soll ich 170
Adam's Song 2
Adeste fideles 288
Adoro te devote 128, 292
Affection 275
Ainsworth 97 52, 120, 249
Aldwinkle 185
All Saints New 213
America 242
Amherst 31
An die Freude 168
Angel Voices (see Gloria)
Antioch 299
Art 135
Austria 248

Bartimeus (see Charleston)
Besançon Carol 281
Bethany 126
Betracht'n wir Heut zu dieser
Frist 151
Binyon 153
Bohemia 141
Bohemian Brethren (see Mit
Freuden zart)
Bohemian Brethren Hymn
(see Far Off Lands)
Bourdillon 164
Break forth, O Beauteous
Heavenly Light (see
Ermuntre dich)
Bridgewater 232
Bunessan 266
Byzantium 93

Caithness 74, 95
Call, The 123, 184
Campian 2 107
Campian 5 313
Carol 287
Charleston 44
Christian's Farewell (see
Foundation)
Christmas 223, 295
Christus der ist mein Leben
188, 231, 260
Christus Urunknak 303
Cliff Town 83, 174
Colchester 327
Cole 134
Complainer 40
Congleton 69, 100, 150, 216
Consolation 203, 277
Coolinge 84, 324
Coronation 36
Cradle Song 276
Creation 47, 66
Cross of Christ 68, 112, 113
Crusaders' Hymn (see
Schönster Herr Jesu)
Cwm Rhondda 27

Danby 90
Darmstadt (see O Gott, du
frommer Gott)

Das neugeborne Kindelein 76
Dawn 267
Deus tuorum militum 305
Devotion 183, 306
Distress 64
Divinum mysterium 290
Dix 12
Donne secours 72, 77
Duke Street 43, 222, 235, 252
Dundee 34, 45, 49, 142, 165, 312

Easter Hymn 318
Ebeling (see Nicht so traurig)
Ebenezer 220
Ein' feste Burg 16, 62
Eintracht 46
Ellacombe 236, 309
Erfurt (see Vom Himmel hoch)
Erfyniad 39, 212
Ermuntre dich, mein
schwacher Geist 297
Es flog ein kleins Waldvöglein 181
Es ist ein' Ros' entsprungen 298
Es muss die ganze
Christenschar 325
Eventide 79

Famous Men 230
Farley Castle 3, 178, 228
Far Off Lands 247
Farrant (see Lord, for Thy
Tender Mercies' Sake)
Festal Song 207, 218
Festus 219
Fillmore 8, 180, 256
First Nowell, The 285
Forest Green 304, 326
Forrest (see Rockbridge)
Foundation 21
Four Seas 161
Four Winds 202

Ganador 136
Geneva 47 (see Meadow Cove)
Geneva 51 109
Geneva 74 (see Ainsworth 97)
Geneva 119 229
Georgetown 111
Gloria 294
God Save the Queen 244
Grâce soit rendue 319
Gräfenburg 96, 233
Grafton 251
Guter Hirte 48

Hamburg 146, 177
Hamilton 57, 139, 320
Hasidim 175
Herzlich tut mich verlangen
(see Passion Chorale)
Holy Night (see Stille Nacht)
Hope 129
Hyfrydol 192
Hymn to Joy 11, 195

Ich dank' dir schon 204
Illinois 59
In Babilone 191, 239

Innsbruck 268
Intercessor 55, 144
In vernali Tempore 323
Italian Hymn (see Trinity)

Jesu, Joy of Man's Desiring
(see Werde munter, mein
Gemüte)
Jesu, meiner Seelen Wonne
(see Werde munter, mein
Gemüte)

Kedron 114
Keith 101
Kimball (see Milton)
King's Lynn 214, 238
Kings of Orient 300
Kremser 22

Lament 314
Lancashire 316
Lancaster 106
Lasst uns erfreuen 23
Leicester 86, 102
Leoni 6
Les commandemens 97, 176
Lisle 148
Llanfair 317
Llangloffan 227
Lobe den Herren 7
Lobt den Herrn, die
Morgensonne 63, 80
Lobt Gott, ihr Christen 118, 132,
264
L'Omnipotent 234
London 116
Lord, for Thy Tender Mer-
cies' Sake 121
Lucis Creator 273
Lumina 110
Lyne 152, 162
Lyons 25

Mach's mit mir, Gott 156
Magda 78
Mainz (see Maria jung und
zart)
Man of Grief (see Kedron)
Maria jung und zart 92
Materna 241
Mathias (see Eintracht)
Meadow Cove 166
Mein Leben (see Christus der
ist mein Leben)
Mein Schöpfer, steh' mir bei 210
Meine Hoffnung stehet feste 35
Mein' Seel', O Gott 189
Meirionydd 1
Melcombe 158, 171
Merthyr Tydvil 200
Milton 194
Missträsta ej att Gud är god 310
Mit Freuden zart 15, 257
Monks Gate 94
Mooz Tsur 279
Morning Hymn 265
Moscow (see Trinity)

Netherlands Folk Song (see
  Kremser)
Nicaea                          4, 5, 254
*Nicht so traurig*                    284
*Nun danket alle Gott*                 19
*Nun komm, der Heiden*
  *Heiland*                           67
Nuremberg                            245
Nyland                               115

*O filii et filiae*                   315
*O Gott, du frommer Gott*              87
*O Jesu Christ, meins Lebens*
  *Licht*                      208, 250
*O Jesu, warum legst du mir*          205
*O mentes perfidas*                    70
*O Salutaris*                         140
Oldbridge                            159
Old Hundredth              13, 18, 37
Old 112th (see *Vater unser*)
Old 124th                            196
Old 134th (see St. Michael)
Old 137th                             88

Paean                                  9
Passion Chorale                      311
Peace                                206
Pelham Street                         24
*Personent hodie*                     296
Picardy                              293
Pioneers                             211
Pleading Savior                      198
*Pont Neuf*                          137
Posen                                 33
*Puer nobis nascitur*            125, 301

*Rendez à Dieu*                      269
Rest                                 119
Reunion                              258
Rochester                        50, 105
Rockbridge                 147, 263, 271

St. Anne                              51
St. Bride                            224
St. Denio                             41
St. Elizabeth (see *Schönster*
  *Herr Jesu*)
St. George's Windsor           10, 278
St. Gertrude                         215
St. Louis                            286
St. Magnus         98, 103, 122, 187
St. Martin                            58
St. Matthew                          255
St. Michael                          259
St. Petersburg                        56
St. Stephen                          261
St. Theodulph                         20
St. Thomas                           124
Salvation              53, 155, 237
Salzburg                             173
Savannah                              60
*Schmücke dich*                      145
*Schönster Herr Jesu*                 14
Schop (see *Ermuntre dich*)
Shalom                               160
Shipston                             272
*Sine nomine*                         75
Song 24                              167
Song 67                          73, 157
Spanish Hymn                    127, 308
Spiritual Sailor, The                240
*Stille Nacht*                       289
Struther                              29
Stuttgart                            117
*Sursum Corda*       71, 82, 179, 322
Swabia                               131

Tallis' Canon      85, 138, 186, 270
Tallis' Ordinal                      133
*Tempus adest floridum*              321
This Endris Nyght                    291

Thou Man of Grief (see The
  Spiritual Sailor)
*Ton-y-Botel* (see Ebenezer)
Transylvania                     38, 201
Trinity                          26, 149
Truro                    54, 190, 243

Valley Forge                         302
*Vater unser*                     32, 81
*Veni Emmanuel*                      280
Vesper Hymn                          274
Vienna                               172
*Vom Himmel hoch*      42, 104, 108,
              193, 221, 225
Vulpius (see *Christus der ist*
  *mein Leben*)

*Wachet auf*                          17
Wareham                          99, 130
*Was Gott thut*                   30, 307
Watchman (Ingham) (see
  Dawn)
Watchman (Mason)                     283
Wayland                              217
Webb                         209, 282
*Wer da wonet*               143, 262
*Werde munter, mein Gemüte*           28
Wheelock                             182
Winchester New             246, 253
Windham                              154
Windsor                           89, 91
Windsor Forest                       199
Woodlands                         61, 65
Woodlawn                             226
Worgan (see Easter Hymn)

Yattendon 12 (see Leicester)
*Ygdrasil*                           197
*Yigdal* (see Leoni)

# Metrical Index of Tunes

**S.M. (6.6.8.6.  Iambic)**

FESTAL SONG                          207, 218
ST. BRIDE                                 224
ST. MICHAEL                               259
ST. THOMAS                                124
SWABIA                                    131

**C.M. (8.6.8.6.  Iambic)**

ANTIOCH (Particular)                      299
BYZANTIUM                                  93
CAITHNESS                             74, 95
CHRISTMAS                            223, 295
CHRISTUS DER IST MEIN LEBEN (see also
  7.6.7.6.)                      188, 231
COLCHESTER                                327
CONSOLATION (see also 8.6.8.6.8.6.)       277
DUNDEE           34, 45, 49, 142, 165, 312
GEORGETOWN                                111
GRÄFENBURG                            96, 233
GRAFTON                                   251
LANCASTER                                 106
LISLE                                     148
LOBT GOTT, IHR CHRISTEN (see also
  8.6.8.8.6.)                    132, 264
LORD, FOR THY TENDER MERCIES' SAKE        121
PELHAM STREET                              24

ROCHESTER                             50, 105
ST. ANNE                                   51
ST. MAGNUS                 98, 103, 122, 187
ST. STEPHEN                               261
SONG 67                               73, 157
TALLIS' ORDINAL                           133
THIS ENDRIS NYGHT                         291
WINDSOR                                89, 91

**C.M.D. (8.6.8.6. 8.6.8.6.  Iambic)**

ALL SAINTS NEW                            213
CAROL                                     287
CROSS OF CHRIST                 68, 112, 113
ELLACOMBE                                 236
FOREST GREEN                         304, 326
MATERNA                                   241
OLD 137TH                                  88
ST. MATTHEW                               255
SALVATION                        53, 155, 237

**L.M. (8.8.8.8.  Iambic)**

AFFECTION                                 275
DANBY                                      90
DAS NEUGEBORNE KINDELEIN                   76
DEUS TUORUM MILITUM                       305
DEVOTION                             183, 306
DISTRESS                                   64

DUKE STREET 43, 222, 235, 252
FESTUS 219
HAMBURG 146, 177
HAMILTON 57, 139, 320
ILLINOIS 59
KEDRON 114
LUCIS CREATOR 273
MEIN' SEEL', O GOTT 189
MELCOMBE 158, 171
MORNING HYMN 265
O JESU CHRIST, MEINS LEBENS LICHT 208, 250
O SALUTARIS 140
OLD HUNDREDTH 13, 18, 37
PUER NOBIS NASCITUR 125, 301
ROCKBRIDGE 147, 263, 271
TALLIS' CANON 85, 138, 186, 270
TRANSYLVANIA 38, 201
TRURO 54, 190, 243
VOM HIMMEL HOCH 42, 104, 108, 193, 221, 225
WAREHAM 99, 130
WAYLAND 217
WINCHESTER NEW 246, 253
WINDHAM 154

L.M.D. (8.8.8.8. 8.8.8.8. Iambic)
CREATION 47, 66
LONDON 116
MERTHYR TYDVIL 200
WER DA WONET 143, 262

5.5.5.4. D.
BUNESSAN 266

5.5.5.5. Iambic
COLE (Irregular) 134

5.5.5.5. Trochaic
MEADOW COVE 166

6.4.6.4.6.6.6.4.
BETHANY 126
DAWN 267

6.5.6.5. D.
ADORO TE DEVOTE (see also 10.10.10.10.) 292

6.5.6.5. D. with refrain
GRÂCE SOIT RENDUE 319

6.5.6.5. Triple
ST. GERTRUDE 215

6.5.6.5.6.6.6.5.
MONKS GATE 94

6.5.7.5.7.5.7.5.
EINTRACHT (Irregular) 46

6.6.2.6.
ART 135

6.6.4.6.6.6.4.
AMERICA 242
GOD SAVE THE QUEEN 244
TRINITY 26, 149

6.6.5.6.5.
FOUR SEAS 161

6.6.6.6.
CAMPIAN 2 107
LAMENT 314
MARIA JUNG UND ZART (formerly MAINZ) 92

6.6.6.6.6. Iambic
GANADOR 136

6.6.6.6.6. with refrain
PERSONENT HODIE 296

6.6.6.6. D.
MEIN SCHÖPFER, STEH' MIR BEI 210
O MENTES PERFIDAS 70

6.6.7.6.
VALLEY FORGE (Irregular) 302

6.6.7.7.8.8.
AMHERST 31

6.6.8.4. D.
LEONI 6

6.6.9.6.6.8.
SCHÖNSTER HERR JESU 14

6.7.6.7.6.6.6.6.
NUN DANKET ALLE GOTT 19
O GOTT, DU FROMMER GOTT 87

7.5.8.5.
BOURDILLON (Irregular) 164

7.6.7.6.
CHRISTUS DER IST MEIN LEBEN (see also C.M.) 260

7.6.7.6.6.6.3.3.6.
MOOZ TSUR 279

7.6.7.6.6.7.6.
ES IST EIN' ROS' ENTSPRUNGEN 298

7.6.7.6. D. Iambic
COMPLAINER 40
ELLACOMBE (see also C.M.D.) 309
ES FLOG EIN KLEINS WALDVÖGLEIN 181
FAR OFF LANDS (formerly BOHEMIAN BRETHREN
HYMN) 247
KING'S LYNN 214, 238
LANCASHIRE 316
MEIRIONYDD 1
NYLAND 115
PAEAN 9
PASSION CHORALE 311
ST. THEODULPH 20
THE SPIRITUAL SAILOR 240
WEBB 209, 282

7.6.7.6. D. Trochaic
TEMPUS ADEST FLORIDUM 321

7.6.7.6.7.7.6.7.7.6.
IN VERNALI TEMPORE 323

7.6.8.6. D.
LLANGLOFFAN 227

7.7.6. D.
ACH, WAS SOLL ICH 170

7.7.6.7.7.8.
INNSBRUCK 268

7.7.7.7.
ACH, WANN WERD ICH 163
THE CALL 123, 184
CAMPIAN 5 313
HASIDIM 175
HOPE 129
LYNE 162
LYNE (Irregular) 152
NUN KOMM, DER HEIDEN HEILAND 67
NUREMBERG 245
POSEN 33
SAVANNAH 60
VIENNA 172

7.7.7.7. with Alleluias
LLANFAIR 317
EASTER HYMN 318

7.7.7.7. with refrain
GLORIA 294

7.7.7.7.6. D.
STRUTHER 29

7.7.7.7.7.7.
DIX 12
NICHT SO TRAURIG 284

7.7.7.7.7.7.7.
DIVINUM MYSTERIUM 290

7.7.7.7. D.
ST. GEORGE'S WINDSOR 10, 278
SALZBURG 173
SPANISH HYMN 127, 308
WATCHMAN 283

7.8.7.8.7.7.7.7.
REUNION 258

8.5.8.3.
WOODLAWN 226

8.6.8.6.7.6.8.6.
ST. LOUIS 286

8.6.8.6.8.6.
CONSOLATION (see also C.M.) 203

CORONATION 36
   8.6.8.6.8.8.
O JESU, WARUM LEGST DU MIR 205
   8.6.8.8.6.
LOBT GOTT, IHR CHRISTEN (see also C.M.) 118
REST 119
   8.7.8.7. Iambic
ACH GOTT UND HERR 169
ICH DANK' DIR SCHON 204
   8.7.8.7. Trochaic
CHARLESTON 44
GUTER HIRTE 48
LOBT DEN HERRN, DIE MORGENSONNE 63, 80
SHIPSTON 272
STUTTGART 117
   8.7.8.7.3.3.7.
MEINE HOFFNUNG STEHET FESTE 35
   8.7.8.7.4.4.7.7.
CWM RHONDDA 27
   8.7.8.7.6.6.6.6.7.
EIN' FESTE BURG 16, 62
   8.7.8.7.8.7.
PICARDY 293
   8.7.8.7. D.
AN DIE FREUDE 168
AUSTRIA 248
EBENEZER 220
HYFRYDOL 192
HYMN TO JOY 11, 195
IN BABILONE 191, 239
PLEADING SAVIOR 198
VESPER HYMN 274
   8.7.8.7.8.8.7.
MIT FREUDEN ZART 15, 257
   8.7.8.7.8.8.7.7.
ERMUNTRE DICH, MEIN SCHWACHER GEIST 297
WERDE MUNTER, MEIN GEMÜTE 28
   8.7.9.8.8.7.
BESANÇON CAROL 281
   8.8.4.4.8.8.3.3.4.4.4.
LASST UNS ERFREUEN 23
   8.8.8.
BETRACHT'N WIR HEUT ZU DIESER FRIST 151
BOHEMIA 141
   8.8.8. with Alleluias
O FILII ET FILIAE 315
   8.8.8.4.
OLDBRIDGE 159
   8.8.8.8.7.
WAS GOTT THUT (see also 8.8.8.8.8.) 30
   8.8.8.8.8.
BRIDGEWATER 232
WAS GOTT THUT (see also 8.8.8.8.7.) 307
   8.8.8.8.8.8.
FILLMORE 8, 180, 256
LEICESTER 86, 102
MACH'S MIT MIR, GOTT 156
MISSTRÖSTA EJ ATT GUD ÄR GOD 310
VATER UNSER 32, 81
VENI EMMANUEL 280
   8.8.8.8. D. Trochaic
SCHMÜCKE DICH 145
   8.9.8.8.9.8.6.6.4.8.8.
WACHET AUF 17
   9.8.9.8.
LES COMMANDEMENS 97, 176
   9.8.9.8. D.
RENDEZ À DIEU 269
   9.8.9.8.9.9.
ST. PETERSBURG (Irregular) 56

   10.4.10.4.
ST. MARTIN 58
   10.8.8.12.
ALDWINKLE 185
   10.10.10.4.
SINE NOMINE 75
   10.10.10.6
PEACE 206
   10.10.10.10. Iambic
ADORO TE DEVOTE (see also 6.5.6.5. D.) 128
AINSWORTH 97 52, 120, 249
CLIFF TOWN 83, 174
CONGLETON 69, 100, 150, 216
COOLINGE 84, 324
ERFYNIAD 39, 212
EVENTIDE 79
FARLEY CASTLE 3, 178, 228
MAGDA 78
SONG 24 167
SURSUM CORDA 71, 82, 179, 322
WINDSOR FOREST 199
WOODLANDS 61, 65
   10.10.10.10. Particular
YGDRASIL 197
   10.10.10.10.10.
ADAM'S SONG 2
OLD 124TH 196
   10.10.11.11.
LYONS 25
   11.10.10.11.
GENEVA 51 109
   11.10.11.10. Iambic
DONNE SECOURS 72, 77
INTERCESSOR 55, 144
L'OMNIPOTENT 234
   11.10.11.10. Trochaic
KEITH 101
   11.11.11.5.
CHRISTUS URUNKNAK 303
   11.11.11.11. Anapestic
FOUNDATION 21
MILTON 194
ST. DENIO 41
   11.11.11.11. Iambic
GENEVA 119 (Irregular) 229
   11.11.11.11.11.11.
FOUR WINDS 202
   11.12.12.10.
NICAEA (Irregular) (see also 12.13.12.10.) 4
   12.11.13.12.
KREMSER 22
   12.12.12.12.
CRADLE SONG 276
   12.12.12.12.12.
WHEELOCK 182
   12.12.12.12.12.12.
BINYON 153
   12.13.12.10.
NICAEA 5, 254
   14.14.4.7.8.
LOBE DEN HERREN 7

IRREGULARS, CHANTS, PROSES
ADESTE FIDELES 288
ES MUSS DIE GANZE CHRISTENSCHAR 325
FAMOUS MEN 230
THE FIRST NOWELL 285
KINGS OF ORIENT 300
LUMINA 110
PIONEERS 211
PONT NEUF 137
SHALOM HAVAYREEM 160
STILLE NACHT 289

# TOPICAL INDEX OF HYMNS

**ADVENT**
| | |
|---|---|
| The morning hangs a signal | 1 |
| The soul wherein God dwells | 92 |
| *Advent* | 280–284 |
| Lift up your heads, ye mighty gates | 310 |

**ANIMALS**
| | |
|---|---|
| Praise, O my heart, to you, O Source of Life | 2 |
| Bring, O morn, thy music! night thy starlit silence | 5 |
| In singing till his heaven fills | 8 |
| We thank you, Lord of heaven | 29 |
| What is this life if, full of care | 183 |
| In sweet fields of autumn, the gold grain is falling | 276 |
| Lift your hidden faces | 319 |
| Now the spring has come again | 323 |
| O, give us pleasure in the flowers today | 324 |
| Pleasure it is to hear, I wis | 325 |

**AFTER BENEDICTION**
| | |
|---|---|
| Since what we choose is what we are | 108 |
| What else is wisdom? | 109 |
| Be ye lamps unto yourselves | 110 |
| O Light of light, within us dwell | 122 |
| Ours be the poems of all tongues | 138 |
| Man lives not for himself alone | 151 |
| Serene will be our days and bright | 158 |
| *Shalom havayreem* | 160 |
| Let all who live in freedom | 171 |
| This thought shall have our whole allegiance | 176 |
| Let all men living in all lands | 225 |

**ALL SOULS' DAY** (*see Prophets, Exemplars, Pioneers*)

**ANNIVERSARIES AND REUNIONS**
| | |
|---|---|
| Fair is their fame | 72 |
| O thou, to whom the fathers built | 116 |
| Let us now praise famous men | 230 |
| O God, beneath thy guiding hand | 235 |
| As tranquil streams that meet and merge | 253 |
| Bring, O Past, your honor | 254 |
| O Light, from age to age the same | 255 |
| Rank by rank again we stand | 258 |

**THE ARTS OF MAN**
| | |
|---|---|
| In singing till his heaven fills | 8 |
| Let the whole creation cry | 10 |
| We come unto our fathers' God | 15 |
| Now let every tongue adore thee | 17 |
| Give thanks for the corn and the wheat that are reaped | 21 |
| We sing now together our song of thanksgiving | 22 |
| Man is the earth upright and proud | 62 |
| From the first man to climb the hill | 64 |
| We journey with a multitude | 66 |
| Before the stars a man is small | 68 |
| Leave starry heaven behind | 70 |
| We cannot kindle when we will | 86 |

| | |
|---|---|
| We are all blind, until we see | 103 |
| *The Arts of Man* | 135–140 |
| One world this, for all its sorrow | 145 |
| Life of ages, richly poured | 172 |
| When we have ended searching | 181 |
| These things shall be: a loftier race | 190 |
| Wonders still the world shall witness | 191 |
| Let us now praise famous men | 230 |
| The art, the science, and the lore | 250 |
| The blessings of the earth and sky | 256 |

**AT THE OFFERING**
| | |
|---|---|
| We give thee but thine own | 131 |
| O ye that taste that love is sweet | 141 |
| Spirit of truth, of life, of power | 146 |
| Man lives not for himself alone | 151 |
| Let all who live in freedom, won | 171 |
| When thy heart, with joy o'erflowing | 226 |

**AUTUMN AND HARVEST**
| | |
|---|---|
| O Lord of stars and sunlight | 9 |
| Give thanks for the corn and the wheat that are reaped | 21 |
| When thy heart, with joy o'erflowing | 226 |
| *Autumn and Harvest* | 275–278 |
| Thou, earth, art ours, and ours to keep | 307 |
| Praise to God and thanks we bring | 308 |

**BEAUTY** (*see Nature; The Arts of Man*)

**BUDDHISM**
| | |
|---|---|
| Be ye lamps unto yourselves | 110 |
| It sounds along the ages | 247 |
| The art, the science, and the lore | 250 |

**CALL TO WORSHIP**
| | |
|---|---|
| The morning hangs a signal | 1 |
| Holy, holy, holy, Lord God almighty! | 4 |
| Let the whole creation cry | 10 |
| From all that dwell below the skies | 13 |
| We come unto our fathers' God | 15 |
| Now let every tongue adore thee | 17 |
| All people that on earth do dwell | 18 |
| We sing now together our song of thanksgiving | 22 |
| O God, in whom we live and move | 24 |
| O worship the King, all glorious above | 25 |
| Come, thou almighty King! | 26 |
| Heaven and earth and sea and air | 33 |
| O Life that maketh all things new | 54 |
| Man is the earth upright and proud | 62 |
| The harp at nature's advent strung | 93 |
| God is in his holy temple | 117 |
| Sovereign and transforming Grace | 127 |
| Mysterious Presence, source of all | 130 |
| Unto thy temple, Lord, we come | 252 |
| Ye that have spent the silent night | 264 |

**CELEBRATION AND PRAISE**
| | |
|---|---|
| *Celebration and Praise* | 1–45 |
| Who thou art I know not | 46 |
| The spacious firmament on high | 47 |
| O Life that maketh all things new | 54 |
| The light, my light, world filling light | 59 |

Let us wander where we will                    60
We journey with a multitude                    66
The harp at Nature's advent strung             93
I love all beauteous things                   137
We sing the rapture of the breath             139
Now give heart's onward habit brave
intent                                        178

## THE CHANGING YEAR
O Lord of stars and sunlight                    9
All hail, the pageant of the years            205
In sweet fields of autumn                     276
    *The Changing Year*                   303–308

## CHILDREN
In singing till his heaven fills                8
Let the whole creation cry                     10
We thank you, Lord of heaven                   29
Now I recall my childhood when the sun         82
Let not young souls be smothered out          150
Can a father see his child                    163
Consider well your ways and lives             262
Your little flame of life we guard            263
To make this earth, our hermitage             306

## CHRISTENING OR NAMING
    *Christening or Naming*              262–263

## CHRISTMAS
The soul wherein God dwells                    92
Sound over all waters, reach out from all
lands                                         202
Veiled in darkness Judah lay                  284
    *Christmas*                         285–299
We three Kings of Orient are                  300

## CHURCH OF THE FREE SPIRIT
O God, in whom we live and move                24
God of grace and God of glory                  27
O Life that maketh all things new              54
The harp at Nature's advent strung             93
O thou, to whom the fathers built             116
Life of ages, richly poured                   172
Rise up, O men of God                         218
O prophet souls of all the years              233
With joy we claim the growing light           246
It sounds along the ages                      247
Light of ages and of nations                  248
Gather us in, thou Love that fillest all      249
    *Church of the Free Spirit*         252–261

## THE CITY
Calm soul of all things                        85
What makes a city great and strong?           102
We are all blind, until we see                103
The people of the earth go down               112
Freedom is the finest gold                    170
Where cross the crowded ways of life          189
Hail the glorious golden city                 192
I saw the city of the Lord                    204
The voice of God is calling                   214

## COMMITMENT AND ACTION
A mighty fortress is our God                   16
God is my strong salvation                     20
Lord of all being, throned afar                38
Man is the earth upright and proud             62
Not always on the mount may we                 90
Who would true valor see                       94
Say not, "The struggle nought availeth"        97

The generations as they rise                  104
Since what we choose is what we are           108
They cast their nets in Galilee               111
God, though this life is but a wraith         114
O star of truth, down shining                 115
Our friend, our brother, and our Lord         121
O ye who taste that love is sweet             141
Spirit of truth, of life, of power            146
This is the charge I keep as mine             147
Let not young souls be smothered out          150
It is a piteous thing to be                   154
When Stephen, full of power and grace         155
Make channels for the streams of love         157
Men, whose boast it is that ye                173
This thought shall have our whole
allegiance                                    176
Wonders still the world shall witness         191
Hail the glorious golden city                 192
    *Commitment and Action*             211–226
Obedient they but to a dream                  228
Blest is that man who sets his soul's desire  229
We met them on the common way                 237
O God of earth and altar                      238
It sounds along the ages                      247
O Light, from age to age the same             255
Faith of the larger liberty                   257
Rank by rank again we stand                   258
Awake, my soul, and with the sun              265
High o'er the lonely hills                    267

## COMMUNION SERVICE
Dear Lord and Father of mankind       118, 119
O thou great friend to all the sons of men    120
Our friend, our brother, and our Lord         121
Come, my way, my truth, my life               123
O thou whose gracious presence shone          125
"Remember me," the Master said                165
For no sect elect                             166

## CONFUCIANISM
Let him who would excel                        161
The art, the science, and the lore            250
But for the cockerel calling the noon
hour                                          322

## THE COUNTRYSIDE
Give thanks for the corn and the wheat
that are reaped                                21
We thank you, Lord of heaven                   29
For flowers that bloom about our feet          30
The light, my light, world filling light       59
Let us wander where we will                    60
Truly the light is sweet                      136
We sing the rapture of the breath             139
Peace is the mind's old wilderness cut
down                                          179
What is this life if, full of care            183
Once more the liberal year laughs out         275
In sweet fields of autumn, the gold grain     276
I walk the unfrequented road                  277
Come, ye thankful people, come                278
'Tis winter now, the fallen snow              301
Bells in the high tower, ringing o'er         303
All beautiful the march of days               304
To make this earth, our hermitage             306
Thou, earth, art ours, and ours to keep       307
Praise to God and thanks we bring             308

Now once again the heaven turns 320
But for the cockerel calling the noon
  hour 322
Now the spring has come again 323
Oh, give us pleasure in the flowers today 324
Pleasure it is 325
The sweet June days are come again 326
I walk amidst thy beauty forth 327

COURAGE
Morning, so fair to see 14
A mighty fortress is our God 16
God is my strong salvation 20
God of grace, and God of glory 27
We sing of golden mornings 40
Though man, the fiery element, sink like
  fire 61
From the first man to climb the hill 64
Say not they die, those martyr souls 76
When courage fails and faith burns low 95
Say not, "The struggle nought availeth" 97
Not gold, but only men can make 98
To suffer woes which hope thinks infinite 100
The generations as they rise 104
O star of truth, down shining 115
It is a piteous thing to be 154
When Stephen, full of power and grace 155
Eternal spirit of the chainless mind! 167
When a deed is done for freedom 168
Through all the long dark night of years 169
Life of ages, richly poured 172
Men, whose boast it is that ye 173
We move in faith to unseen goals 200
You that have faith to look with fearless
  eyes 206
All the past we leave behind 211
Gird on thy sword, O man 212
God's trumpet wakes the slumbering
  world 213
Men go out from the places where they
  dwelled 216
God send us men whose aim will be 217
Blest is that man who sets his soul's
  desire 229
We met them on the common way 237

DEDICATION OF CHURCH
All people that on earth do dwell 18
O God, in whom we live and move 24
God of grace, and God of glory 27
O thou to whom the fathers built 116
May nothing evil cross this door 159
All are architects of fate 175
Light of ages and of nations 248
The blessings of the earth and sky 256
Faith of the larger liberty 257
Rank by rank again we stand 258
To cloisters of the spirit 260
One holy Church of God appears 261

DEDICATION OF ORGAN
We come unto our fathers' God 15
Now let every tongue adore thee 17
The art, the science, and the lore 250

THE DEMOCRATIC WAY OF LIFE
  (see Freedom; In Time to Come; Man;
  Nation and Nations)

DOXOLOGY AND ASCRIPTION
From all that dwell below the skies 13
All people that on earth do dwell 18
Praise God, the love we all may share 37
Rejoice in love we know and share 42
Earth arrayed in wondrous beauty 48
Ours be the poems of all tongues 138

EASTER
The morning hangs a signal 1
All creatures of our God and King 23
For all the saints who from their labors
  rest 75
Say not they die, those martyr souls 76
Easter 315–318
Lift your hidden faces 319

EPIPHANY
The first Nowell the angel did say 285
Heir of all the waiting ages 293
On this day everywhere 296
Joy to the world! 299
We three kings of Orient are 300

EVENING
Bring, O morn, thy music! 5
Let the whole creation cry 10
For the beauty of the earth 12
Brief our days, but long for singing 28
Who thou art I know not 46
The spacious firmament on high 47
One thought I have, my ample creed 50
Whether day my spirit's yearning 63
Abide with me, fast falls the eventide 79
Noiseless the morning flings its gold 89
Truly the light is sweet 136
Evening 268–274

EVOLUTION
Praise, O my heart, with praise from
  depth and height 3
A fierce unrest seethes at the core 53
Man is the earth upright and proud 62
We journey with a multitude 66
O sometimes gleams upon our sight 177

FAITH AND TRUST
Morning, so fair to see 14
A mighty fortress is our God 16
God is my strong salvation 20
O worship the King 25
God moves in a mysterious way 34
All my hope on God is founded 35
We sing of golden mornings 40
God makes a path, provides a guide 45
The Lord's my shepherd, I'll not want 49
One thought I have, my ample creed 50
O God, our help in ages past 51
In this stern hour 55
Abide with me, fast falls the eventide 79
Say not, "The struggle nought availeth" 97
Nearer, my God, to thee 126
Give me your whole heart 134
Put down your foot and you shall feel 156
O sometimes gleams upon our sight 177
Serene I fold my hands and wait 186
No longer forward nor behind 187
We move in faith to unseen goals 200

You that have faith to look with fearless
   eyes                                        206
God of the earnest heart                      224
In sweet fields of autumn                     276

FAMILY
Give thanks for the corn and the wheat
   that are reaped                              21
We thank you, Lord of Heaven                   29
For flowers that bloom about our feet          30
May nothing evil cross this door              159
Can a father see his child                    163
Peace is the mind's old wilderness cut
   down                                        179
'Tis winter now; the fallen snow              301

FORGIVENESS OF OTHERS
All creatures of our God and King              23
O brother man, fold to thy heart thy
   brother                                     144
When Stephen, full of power and grace         155
Turn back, O man, forswear thy foolish
   ways                                        196

FREEDOM
In singing till his heaven fills                8
Give thanks for the corn and the wheat
   that are reaped                              21
We sing now together our song of
   thanksgiving                                 22
O Life that maketh all things new              54
How happy is he born and taught                99
Since what we choose is what we are           108
The crest and crowning of all good            143
One world this, for all its sorrow            145
For no sect elect                             166
   *Freedom*                                167-173
These things shall be: a loftier race         190
Wonders still the world shall witness         191
With joy we claim the growing light           246
As tranquil streams that meet and merge       253
Faith of the larger liberty                   257

FRIENDS (*see Love and Human Brotherhood*)

FULFILLMENT AND INWARD
   PEACE (*see Here and Now; Hours
   of Insight*)

GOD (*see The Life that Maketh All Things
New*)

GOOD FRIDAY (*see Maundy Thursday and Good Friday*)

GRATITUDE (*see Celebration and
Praise; Thanksgiving Day*)

HANUKKAH (*see Dedication of Church;
Freedom*)
Rock of Ages, let our song                    279

HERE AND NOW
O God, in whom we live and move                24
Brief our days, but long for singing           28
Our God, our God, thou shinest here            36
Go not, my soul, in search of him              88
God is in his holy temple                     117
   *Here and Now*                          174-188
Where is our holy church?                     259
I walk the unfrequented road                  277
Oh, give us pleasure in the flowers today     324

HINDUISM
Give me your whole heart                      134
The art, the science, and the lore            250

HOURS OF INSIGHT
O God, in whom we live and move                24
God makes a path, provides a guide             45
One thought I have, my ample creed             50
The world stands out on either side            57
O Thou whose spirit witness bears              74
   *Hours of Insight*                       83-93
The people of the earth go down               112
Yet when the splendor of the earth            113
God is in his holy temple                     117
Dear Lord and Father of mankind         118, 119
Come, my way, my truth, my life               123
Immortal love, forever full                   142
Woe unto him that has not known the
   woe of man                                  153
No longer forward nor behind                  187
We pray no more, made lowly wise              188
From heart to heart, from creed to creed      251
I walk the unfrequented road                  277

IN TIME TO COME
We sing now together our song of
   thanksgiving                                 22
God of grace, and God of glory                 27
Man is the earth upright and proud             62
O thou, to whom the fathers built their
   altars                                      116
The crest and crowning of all good            143
O brother man, fold to thy heart thy
   brother                                     144
One world this, for all its sorrow            145
Through all the long dark night of years      169
Here on the paths of every day                180
   *In Time to Come*                       189-210
Forward through the ages                      215
Creation's Lord, we give thee thanks          221
Behold a Sower! from afar                      236
High o'er the lonely hills                     267
It came upon the midnight clear               287
Ring out, wild bells, to the wild, wild sky   305

JESUS
Joyful, joyful, we adore thee                  11
For all the saints, who from their labors rest 75
Prayer is the soul's sincere desire            91
The soul wherein God dwells                     92
They cast their nets in Galilee               111
Dear Lord and Father of mankind         118, 119
O thou great friend to all the sons of men    120
Our friend, our brother, and our lord         121
Come, my way, my truth, my life               123
O brother man, fold to thy heart thy
   brother                                     144
"Remember me," the Master said                165
Where cross the crowded ways of life          189
Now is the time approaching                   209
Hail to the Lord's anointed                   282
Heir of all the waiting ages                  293
Hosanna in the highest!                       309
O sacred head, now wounded                    311
Beneath the shadow of the cross               312
When my love to God grows weak                313
Now in the tomb is laid                       314
Past are the cross, the scourge, the thorn    315

## JOY AND SORROW

| | |
|---|---|
| In singing till his heaven fills | 8 |
| Joyful, joyful, we adore thee | 11 |
| For the beauty of the earth | 12 |
| We come unto our fathers' God | 15 |
| Now let every tongue adore thee | 17 |
| All people that on earth do dwell | 18 |
| All creatures of our God and King | 23 |
| Brief our days but long for singing | 28 |
| We thank you, Lord of heaven | 29 |
| The light, my light, world filling light | 59 |
| Nay, do not grieve though life be full of sadness | 77 |
| Abide with me, fast falls the eventide | 79 |
| Since I have felt the sense of death | 81 |
| Now I recall my childhood when the sun | 82 |
| To suffer woes which hope thinks infinite | 100 |
| It is something to have wept as we have wept | 101 |
| I love all beauteous things | 137 |
| We sing the rapture of the breath | 139 |
| Serene will be our days and bright | 158 |
| Love can tell, and love alone | 162 |
| Every night and every morn | 184 |
| Happy the man, and happy he alone | 185 |
| Serene I fold my hands and wait | 186 |
| Where cross the crowded ways of life | 189 |
| All the past we leave behind | 211 |
| When thy heart, with joy o'erflowing | 226 |
| Morning has broken | 266 |
| Once more the liberal year laughs out | 275 |

## THE KINGDOM OF GOD (see In Time to Come; Love and Human Brotherhood)

## LABOR

| | |
|---|---|
| Truly the light is sweet | 136 |
| We sing the rapture of the breath | 139 |
| We praise thee, God, for harvests earned | 219 |
| Let all men living in all lands | 225 |

## LENT (see Hours of Insight; Prayer and Aspiration; Wrong and Repentance)

## THE LIFE OF INTEGRITY

| | |
|---|---|
| Divinity is round us never gone | 58 |
| The Life of Integrity | 94–113 |
| God, though this life is but a wraith | 114 |
| Let him who would excel | 161 |
| Let all who live in freedom, won | 171 |
| Men, whose boast it is that ye | 173 |
| All are architects of fate | 175 |

## THE LIFE THAT MAKETH ALL THINGS NEW

| | |
|---|---|
| Praise, O my heart, to you, O Source of Life | 2 |
| Praise, O my heart, with praise from depth and height | 3 |
| Praise to the living God! | 6 |
| Praise to the Lord, the Almighty | 7 |
| O Lord of stars and sunlight | 9 |
| Let the whole creation cry | 10 |
| Joyful, joyful, we adore thee | 11 |
| O God, in whom we live and move | 24 |
| Lord of all majesty and might | 32 |
| God moves in a mysterious way | 34 |
| Our God, our God, thou shinest here | 36 |

| | |
|---|---|
| Praise God, the love we all may share | 37 |
| Lord of all being, throned afar | 38 |
| Immortal, invisible, God only wise | 41 |
| God of the earth, the sky, the sea | 43 |
| There's a wideness in God's mercy | 44 |
| The Life That Maketh All Things New | 46–60 |
| Man is the earth upright and proud | 62 |
| We journey with a multitude | 66 |
| Leave starry heaven behind | 70 |
| Let us be faithful to our passing hours | 83 |
| Where is your God? they say | 87 |
| Go not, my soul, in search of him | 88 |
| Mysterious Presence, source of all | 130 |
| Immortal love, forever full | 142 |
| Put down your foot and you shall feel | 156 |
| Love can tell, and love alone | 162 |
| Life of ages, richly poured | 172 |
| Seek not afar for beauty | 174 |
| The amplitude of space comes down to your own door | 182 |
| We pray no more, made lowly wise | 188 |
| Light of ages and of nations | 248 |

## LOVE AND HUMAN BROTHERHOOD

| | |
|---|---|
| Joyful, joyful, we adore thee | 11 |
| From all that dwell below the skies | 13 |
| Morning, so fair to see | 14 |
| We sing now together our song of thanksgiving | 22 |
| We thank you, Lord of heaven | 29 |
| There's a wideness in God's mercy | 44 |
| Though man, the fiery element, sink like fire | 61 |
| Man is the earth upright and proud | 62 |
| It is something to have wept as we have wept | 101 |
| What else is wisdom? | 109 |
| To Mercy, Pity, Peace, and Love | 132 |
| Love and Human Brotherhood | 141–166 |
| When a deed is done for freedom | 168 |
| Freedom is the finest gold | 170 |
| Men, whose boast it is that ye | 173 |
| The amplitude of space comes down to your own door | 182 |
| Where cross the crowded ways of life | 189 |
| These things shall be: a loftier race | 190 |
| Wonders still the world shall witness | 191 |
| Come, children of tomorrow, come! | 193 |
| Turn back, O man, forswear thy foolish ways | 196 |
| Let there be light, Lord God of Hosts | 201 |
| Sound over all waters, reach out from all lands | 202 |
| I saw the city of the Lord | 204 |
| All hail, the pageant of the years | 205 |
| Now is the time approaching | 209 |
| Rise up, O men of God | 218 |
| Let all men living in all lands | 225 |
| When thy heart, with joy o'erflowing | 226 |
| O'er continent and ocean | 227 |
| Not alone for mighty empire | 239 |
| Who is the patriot? | 243 |
| Gather us in, thou Love that fillest all | 249 |
| Winter is a cold thing | 302 |

Beneath the shadow of the cross 312
Oh, give us pleasure in the flowers today 324

MAN

The morning hangs a signal 1
Lord of all majesty and might 32
Who thou art I know not 46
The spacious firmament on high 47
A fierce unrest seethes at the core 53
In this stern hour when the spirit falters 55
The earth is home and all abundant 56
Divinity is round us never gone 58
*Man* 61–71
The crest and crowning of all good 143
Woe unto him that has not known the
woe of man 153
Creation's Lord, we give thee thanks 221
We met them on the common way 237
Where is our holy church? 259

MARRIAGE

May nothing evil cross this door 159
The night has a thousand eyes 164

MAUNDY THURSDAY AND GOOD
FRIDAY

They cast their nets in Galilee 111
O thou whose gracious presence shone 125
When Stephen, full of power and grace 155
"Remember me," the Master said 165
Eternal spirit of the chainless mind 167
Blest is that man who sets his soul's desire 229
We met them on the common way 237
*Maundy Thursday and Good Friday* 311–314

MEMORIAL AND FUNERAL SER-
VICES

The morning hangs a signal 1
Bring, O morn, thy music! night thy
starlit silence 5
Praise to the living God! 6
A mighty fortress is our God 16
The Lord's my shepherd, I'll not want 49
One thought I have, my ample creed 50
O God, our help in ages past 51
*Transience and Ongoing Life* 72–84
Who would true valor see 94
A noble life, a simple faith 106
Immortal Love, forever full 142
Let us now praise famous men 230

MORNING

The morning hangs a signal 1
Bring, O morn, thy music! 5
Let the whole creation cry 10
For the beauty of the earth 12
Morning, so fair to see 14
For flowers that bloom about our feet 30
*Morning* 264–267

MOTHERS AND FATHERS

Now thank we all our God 19
Now I recall my childhood when the sun 82
Can a father see his child 163

NATION AND NATIONS

Give thanks for the corn and the wheat
that are reaped 21
Not gold, but only men 98
One world this, for all its sorrow 145
Man's comradeship is very wide 148

My country is the world 149
Freedom is the finest gold 170
These things shall be: a loftier race 190
Hear, hear, O ye nations, and hearing
obey 194
God send us men whose aim will be 217
God of our fathers who hast safely
brought us 234
*Nation and Nations* 238–244

NATURE

Praise, O my heart, to you, O Source of Life 2
Praise, O my heart, with praise from
depth and height 3
In singing till his heaven fills 8
O Lord of stars and sunlight 9
Let the whole creation cry 10
Joyful, joyful, we adore thee 11
For the beauty of the earth 12
Morning, so fair to see 14
Give thanks for the corn and the wheat
that are reaped 21
All creatures of our God and King 23
O worship the King, all glorious above 25
Brief our days, but long for singing 28
We thank you, Lord of heaven 29
For flowers that bloom about our feet 30
Heaven and earth and sea and air 33
Knowledge, they say, drives wonder from
the world 39
We sing of golden mornings 40
Who thou art I know not 46
The spacious firmament on high 47
Earth arrayed in wondrous beauty 48
The earth is home and all abundant 56
The light, my light, world filling light 59
Let us wander where we will 60
Man is the earth upright and proud 62
We journey with a multitude 66
Before the stars a man is small 68
Leave starry heaven behind 70
We sing the rapture of the breath 139
Put down your foot and you shall feel 156
The amplitude of space comes down to
your own door 182
What is this life if, full of care 183

NONVIOLENCE

O brother man, fold to thy heart thy
brother 144
When Stephen, full of power and grace 155
These things shall be: a loftier race 190
Come, children of tomorrow, come! 193
Hear, hear, O ye nations, and hearing
obey 194
Turn back, O man, forswear thy foolish
ways 196
The sky has gathered the flowers of
sunset 197
Bend back the lance's point 207

OLD AGE

Since I have felt the sense of death 81
Now I recall my childhood when the sun 82
It is something to have wept as we have
wept 101
Serene I fold my hands and wait 186
No longer forward nor behind 187

## ORDINATION AND INSTALLATION

| | |
|---|---|
| God of grace, and God of glory | 27 |
| O thou, to whom the fathers built | 116 |
| Life of ages, richly poured | 172 |
| The voice of God is calling | 214 |
| God send us men whose aim will be | 217 |
| Rise up, O men of God | 218 |
| From heart to heart, from creed to creed | 251 |
| As tranquil streams that meet and merge | 253 |
| Bring, O Past, your honor; bring, O Time, your harvest | 254 |
| Faith of the larger liberty | 257 |
| One holy church of God appears | 261 |

## OUR WORLD-WIDE HERITAGE

| | |
|---|---|
| Father of all, in every age | 133 |
| Ours be the poems of all tongues | 138 |
| Life of ages, richly poured | 172 |
| O'er continent and ocean | 227 |
| From age to age how grandly rise | 231 |
| O prophet souls of all the years | 233 |
| *Our World-wide Heritage* | 245-251 |
| Faith of the larger liberty | 257 |
| One holy church of God appears | 261 |

## PALM SUNDAY

| | |
|---|---|
| They cast their nets in Galilee | 111 |
| Our friend, our brother, and our Lord | 121 |
| Once to every man and nation | 220 |
| Blest is that man who sets his soul's desire | 229 |
| We met them on the common way | 237 |
| O come, O come, Emmanuel | 280 |
| *Palm Sunday* | 309-310 |

## PASSOVER (see Freedom; Prophets, Exemplars, Pioneers)

## PATRIOTISM (see Nation and Nations)

## PRAYER AND ASPIRATION

| | |
|---|---|
| The morning hangs a signal | 1 |
| O Lord of stars and sunlight | 9 |
| O God, in whom we live and move | 24 |
| Calm soul of all things | 85 |
| Be ye lamps unto yourselves | 110 |
| *Prayer and Aspiration* | 114-134 |
| O brother man, fold to thy heart thy brother | 144 |
| We pray no more, made lowly wise | 188 |
| Gather us in, thou Love that fillest all | 249 |
| From heart to heart, from creed to creed | 251 |
| To cloisters of the spirit | 260 |

## PRAYER RESPONSE

| | |
|---|---|
| What else is wisdom? | 109 |
| Be ye lamps unto yourselves | 110 |
| O light of light, within us dwell | 122 |
| Give me your whole heart | 134 |
| Ours be the poems of all tongues | 138 |
| Spirit of truth, of life, of power | 146 |
| Man lives not for himself alone | 151 |
| For mercy, courage, kindness, mirth | 152 |
| Serene will be our days and bright | 158 |
| Let him who would excel | 161 |

## PROPHETS, EXEMPLARS, PIONEERS

| | |
|---|---|
| The morning hangs a signal | 1 |
| Praise to the living God! | 6 |

| | |
|---|---|
| We come unto our fathers' God | 15 |
| A mighty fortress is our God | 16 |
| We sing now together our song of thanksgiving | 22 |
| God makes a path, provides a guide | 45 |
| One thought I have, my ample creed | 50 |
| Fair is their fame who stand in earth's high places | 72 |
| For all the saints, who from their labors rest | 75 |
| Say not they die, those martyr souls | 76 |
| Away, O soul, hoist up the anchor now | 78 |
| He that dies shall not die lonely | 80 |
| Who would true valor see | 94 |
| Mysterious Presence, source of all | 130 |
| He presses on before the race | 140 |
| One world this, for all its sorrow | 145 |
| When Stephen, full of power and grace | 155 |
| Eternal spirit of the chainless mind! | 167 |
| Life of ages, richly poured | 172 |
| All the past we leave behind | 211 |
| God's trumpet wakes the slumbering world | 213 |
| Forward through the ages | 215 |
| Men go out from the places where they dwelled | 216 |
| *Prophets, Exemplars, Pioneers* | 227-237 |
| Who is the patriot? | 243 |
| It sounds along the ages | 247 |
| Light of ages and of nations | 248 |
| Faith of the larger liberty | 257 |
| Rank by rank again we stand | 258 |
| One holy church of God appears | 261 |

## REVELATION IS NOT SEALED

| | |
|---|---|
| The morning hangs a signal | 1 |
| Praise to the living God! | 6 |
| O Lord of stars and sunlight | 9 |
| We come unto our fathers' God | 15 |
| We sing now together our song of thanksgiving | 22 |
| Knowledge, they say, drives wonder from the world | 39 |
| God of the earth, the sky, the sea | 43 |
| Who thou art I know not | 46 |
| The spacious firmament on high | 47 |
| A fierce unrest seethes at the core | 53 |
| O Life that maketh all things new | 54 |
| Divinity is round us—never gone | 58 |
| We journey with a multitude | 66 |
| How little our true majesty is shown | 69 |
| O Thou whose spirit witness bears | 74 |
| The generations as they rise | 104 |
| O star of truth, down shining | 115 |
| O thou, to whom the fathers built | 116 |
| Mysterious Presence, source of all | 130 |
| He presses on before the race | 140 |
| When a deed is done for freedom | 168 |
| Life of ages, richly poured | 172 |
| From age to age how grandly rise | 231 |
| With joy we claim the growing light | 246 |
| It sounds along the ages | 247 |
| Light of ages and of nations | 248 |
| The art, the science, and the lore | 250 |
| From heart to heart, from creed to creed | 251 |
| Where is our holy church? | 259 |

SCIENCE

Knowledge, they say, drives wonder from
the world 39
I am a part of all that I have met 65
Before the stars a man is small 68
One world this, for all its sorrow 145
These things shall be: a loftier race 190
Wonders still the world shall witness 191

THE SEA

Praise, O my heart, with praise from
depth and height 3
Bring, O morn, thy music! night, thy
starlit silence! 5
Let the whole creation cry 10
There's a wideness in God's mercy 44
From the first man to climb the hill 64
Away, O soul, hoist up the anchor now 78
We praise thee, God, for harvests earned 219
God of our fathers, who hast safely
brought us 234
O God, beneath thy guiding hand 235

SERENITY

Dear Lord and Father of mankind 118, 119
Serene I fold my hands and wait 186
No longer forward nor behind 187
(See also Hours of Insight)

SOCIAL JUSTICE

God of grace, and God of glory 27
What makes a city great and strong? 102
God, though this life is but a wraith 114
Truly the light is sweet 136
Let not young souls be smothered out 150
It is a piteous thing to be 154
When a deed is done for freedom 168
Men, whose boast it is that ye 173
Where cross the crowded ways of life 189
These things shall be: a loftier race 190
Hail the glorious golden city 192
Come, children of tomorrow, come! 193
Turn back, O man, forswear thy foolish
ways 196
Quest of the ages, goal of men 203
God's trumpet wakes the slumbering
world 213
The voice of God is calling 214
God send us men whose aim will be 217
Once to every man and nation 220
Creation's Lord, we give thee thanks 221
God of the earnest heart 224
O God of earth and altar 238
Not alone for mighty empire 239
O beautiful, our country! 240
O beautiful for spacious skies 241

SPRING

O Lord of stars and sunlight 9
We sing of golden mornings 40
Thou, earth, art ours, and ours to keep 307
Spring 319–325

SUKKOTH (see Autumn and Harvest;
Thanksgiving Day)

SUMMER

O Lord of stars and sunlight 9
For flowers that bloom about our feet 30
The light, my light, world filling light 59

We sing the rapture of the breath 139
Thou, earth, art ours, and ours to keep 307
Pleasure it is 325
Summer 326–327

THANKSGIVING DAY

O Lord of stars and sunlight 9
We come unto our fathers' God 15
All people that on earth do dwell 18
Now thank we all our God 19
Give thanks for the corn and the wheat
that are reaped 21
We sing now together our song of
thanksgiving 22
All creatures of our God and King 23
O worship the King all glorious above 25
We thank you, Lord of heaven 29
When thy heart, with joy o'erflowing 226
God of our fathers who hast safely
brought us 234
O God, beneath thy guiding hand 235
Once more the liberal year laughs out 275
Come, ye thankful people, come 278
Thou, earth, art ours, and ours to keep 307
Praise to God and thanks we bring 308

TRANSIENCE AND ONGOING LIFE

Praise, O my heart, to you, O Source of
Life 2
Bring, O morn, thy music! 5
Praise to the living God! 6
All creatures of our God and King 23
Brief our days but long for singing 28
All my hope on God is founded 35
The Lord's my shepherd, I'll not want 49
One thought I have, my ample creed 50
O God, our help in ages past 51
Roll on, ye stars, exult in youthful prime 52
O Life that maketh all things new 54
The earth is home and all abundant 56
Though man, the fiery element, sink like
fire 61
I am a part of all that I have met 65
Man imperishably stands 67
Transience and Ongoing Life 72–84
It is something to have wept as we have
wept 101
Nearer, my God, to thee 126
All things are doubly fair 135
I love all beauteous things 137
The amplitude of space comes down to
your own door 182
Quest of the ages, goal of man 203
I saw the city of the Lord 204
Gird on thy sword, O man 212
Awake, my soul, stretch every nerve 223
From heart to heart, from creed to creed 251
O Light, from age to age the same 255
In sweet fields of autumn 276
O day of light and gladness 316

TRUTH

Praise God, the love we all may share 37
Lord of all being, throned afar 38
Knowledge, they say, drives wonder from
the world 39
Rejoice in love we know and share 42
When courage fails and faith burns low 95

The generations as they rise 104
Truth is the trial of itself 105
Be ye lamps unto yourselves 110
O star of truth, down shining 115
When a deed is done for freedom 168
Life of ages, richly poured 172
Gird on thy sword, O man 212
Once to every man and nation 220

VOCATIONS (see Ordination and Installation; The Arts of Man)

WHITSUNDAY
O God, in whom we live and move 24
Divinity is round us, never gone 58
Not always on the mount may we 90
Send down thy truth, O God 124
Sovereign and transforming Grace 127
Mysterious Presence, source of all 130
From age to age how grandly rise 231
O prophet souls of all the years 233
It sounds along the ages 247
Light of ages and of nations 248
Gather us in, Thou Love that fillest all 249

WINTER
We sing of golden mornings 40
In sweet fields of autumn, the gold grain is falling 276
Winter 301–302
Bells in the high tower, ringing o'er the white hills 303
All beautiful the march of days 304
Thou, earth, art ours, and ours to keep 307

WISDOM AND UNDERSTANDING
Knowledge, they say, drives wonder from the world 39
Wisdom has treasures greater far 96
How happy is he born or taught 99
We are all blind, until we see 103
What else is wisdom? 109

WORLD PEACE
God of grace, and God of glory 27
O brother man, fold to thy heart thy brother 144
One world this, for all its sorrow 145
When Stephen, full of power and grace 155
Peace is the mind's old wilderness cut down 179
These things shall be: a loftier race 190
Wonders still the world shall witness 191
Come, children of tomorrow, come 193
Hear, hear, O ye nations, and hearing obey 194
Not in vain the distance beacons 195
Turn back, O man, forswear thy foolish ways 196

The sky has gathered the flowers of sunset 197
Years are coming—speed them onward 198
The time shall come when, free as seas 199
Let there be light, Lord God of Hosts 201
Sound over all waters, reach out from all lands 202
Quest of the ages, goal of man 203
All hail, the pageant of the years 205
You that have faith to look with fearless eyes 206
Bend back the lance's point 207
Thy kingdom come, O Lord 210
Let all men living in all lands 225
O'er continent and ocean 227
Not alone for mighty empire 239
O beautiful, our country! 240
Who is the Patriot? 243

WRONG AND REPENTANCE
Dear Lord and Father of mankind 118, 119
Let not young souls be smothered out 150
Woe unto him who has not known the woe of man 153
Can a father see his child 163
Through all the long dark night of years 169
Men, whose boast it is that ye 173
Hear, hear, O ye nations, and hearing obey 194
Turn back, O man, forswear thy foolish ways 196
The sky has gathered the flowers of sunset 197
We move in faith to unseen goals 200
Let there be light, Lord God of Hosts 201
All hail, the pageant of the years 205
The voice of God is calling 214
Creation's Lord, we give thee thanks 221
O God of earth and altar 238
Not alone for mighty empire 239

YOM KIPPUR (see Wrong and Repentance)

YOUTH
The generations as they rise 104
Let not young souls be smothered out 150
When Stephen, full of power and grace 155
All the past we leave behind 211
God's trumpet wakes the slumbering world 213
Men go out from the places where they dwelled 216
God send us men whose aim will be 217
Obedient they, but to a dream 228
Blest is that man who sets his soul's desire 229
Feet of the urgent pioneer 232

# INDEX OF FIRST LINES AND TITLES OF HYMNS

(When they differ, a hymn's title, as well as its first line, is listed. Titles, then, are in capital letters.)

| | |
|---|---|
| A BLESSING | 263 |
| A fierce unrest seethes at the core | 53 |
| A mighty fortress is our God | 16 |
| A noble life, a simple faith | 106 |
| Abide not in the realm of dreams | 222 |
| Abide with me, fast falls the eventide | 79 |
| ABIDING PRESENCE, THE | 24 |
| AFFIRMATION | 69 |
| Again, as evening's shadow falls | 271 |
| All are architects of fate | 175 |
| All beautiful the march of days | 304 |
| All creatures of our God and King | 23 |
| All hail, the pageant of the years | 205 |
| All my hope on God is founded | 35 |
| All people that on earth do dwell | 18 |
| All praise to thee, my God, this night | 270 |
| All the past we leave behind | 211 |
| All things are doubly fair | 135 |
| ALL WITHIN FOUR SEAS | 161 |
| AMERICA THE BEAUTIFUL | 241 |
| amplitude of space comes down to your own door, The | 182 |
| Angels we have heard on high | 294 |
| art, the science, and the lore, The | 250 |
| As tranquil streams that meet and merge | 253 |
| AUTUMN FIELDS | 276 |
| Awake, my soul, and with the sun | 265 |
| Awake, my soul, stretch every nerve | 223 |
| Away, O soul, hoist up the anchor now | 78 |
| | |
| Be ye lamps unto yourselves | 110 |
| Before the stars a man is small | 68 |
| Behold a Sower! from afar | 236 |
| Bells in the high tower | 303 |
| Bend back the lance's point | 207 |
| Beneath the shadow of the cross | 312 |
| BETWEEN MIDNIGHT AND MORNING | 206 |
| blessings of the earth and sky, The | 256 |
| Blest is that man who sets his soul's desire | 229 |
| Break forth, O beauteous heavenly light | 297 |
| Brief our days, but long for singing | 28 |
| Bring, O morn, thy music! | 5 |
| Bring, O Past, your honor; bring, O Time, your harvest | 254 |
| But for the cockerel calling the noon hour | 322 |
| | |
| Calm soul of all things, make it mine | 85 |
| Can a father see his child | 163 |
| CAN I SEE ANOTHER'S WOE? | 163 |
| CANTICLE OF THE SUN, THE | 23 |
| CHANGES, THE | 303 |
| CHILDREN OF TOMORROW | 193 |
| CHURCH OF THE FREE SPIRIT | 254 |
| CIRCULAR SECRET | 70 |
| CITY OF THE LORD, THE | 204 |
| Come, children of tomorrow, come! | 193 |
| Come, my way, my truth, my life | 123 |
| Come, thou almighty King! | 26 |

| | |
|---|---|
| Come, ye thankful people, come | 278 |
| COMMUNION HYMN | 125 |
| COMPASS, THE | 156 |
| Consider well your ways and lives | 262 |
| Creation's Lord, we give thee thanks | 221 |
| crest and crowning of all good, The | 143 |
| | |
| Dark hills at evening in the west | 273 |
| Dear Lord and Father of mankind | 118 |
| Dear Lord and Father of mankind | 119 |
| Divinity is round us—never gone | 58 |
| | |
| EARLY SPRING | 322 |
| Earth arrayed in wondrous beauty | 48 |
| earth is home and all abundant, The | 56 |
| EARTH IS ENOUGH | 180 |
| ETERNAL, THE | 67 |
| Eternal One, thou living God (See: With joy we claim the growing light) | |
| Eternal spirit of the chainless mind! | 167 |
| Every night and every morn | 184 |
| | |
| Fair is their fame who stand in earth's high places | 72 |
| FAITH OF THE FREE | 257 |
| Faith of the larger liberty | 257 |
| FAITH'S FREER SHRINE | 255 |
| Father of all, in every age | 133 |
| Feet of the urgent pioneer | 232 |
| FIERY ELEMENT, THE | 61 |
| first Nowell the angel did say, The | 285 |
| FOR ALL THE JOYS THAT GREET US | 29 |
| For all the saints who from their labors rest | 75 |
| FOR CEREMONY OF NAMING | 262 |
| For flowers that bloom about our feet | 30 |
| For mercy, courage, kindness, mirth | 152 |
| For no sect elect | 166 |
| For the beauty of the earth | 12 |
| Forward through the ages | 215 |
| Freedom is the finest gold | 170 |
| From age to age how grandly rise | 231 |
| From all that dwell below the skies | 13 |
| From all the fret and fever of the day | 84 |
| From heart to heart, from creed to creed | 251 |
| From the first man to climb the hill | 64 |
| | |
| Gather us in, thou Love that fillest all | 249 |
| generations as they rise, The | 104 |
| GETHSEMANE AND CALVARY | 313 |
| Gird on thy sword, O man, thy strength endue | 212 |
| Give me your whole heart | 134 |
| Give thanks for the corn and the wheat that are reaped | 21 |
| Go not, my soul, in search of him | 88 |
| God is in his holy temple | 117 |
| God is my strong salvation | 20 |
| God laid his rocks in courses (See: To cloisters of the spirit) | |

God makes a path, provides a guide          45
God moves in a mysterious way          34
God of grace and God of Glory          27
God of our fathers, who has safely brought us          234
God of the earnest heart          224
God of the earth, the sky, the sea          43
God save our gracious Queen          244
GOD SAVE THE QUEEN          244
God send us men whose aim will be          217
God, though this life is but a wraith          114
God's trumpet wakes the slumbering world          213
GOLDEN HERESY OF TRUTH, THE          104
GROWING LIGHT, THE          246

Hail the glorious golden city          192
Hail to the Lord's anointed          282
HANUKKAH HYMN          279
Happy the man, and happy he alone          185
Hard is now the constant woe          129
harp at Nature's advent strung, The          93
HARVEST FESTIVAL          275
He presses on before the race          140
He that dies shall not die lonely          80
Hear, hear, O ye nations, and hearing obey          194
HEART'S REMEMBERING (Part I)          112
HEART'S REMEMBERING (Part II)          113
Heaven and earth and sea and air          33
Heir of all the ages, I          245
Heir of all the waiting ages          293
HERE BE NO MAN A STRANGER          260
Here on the paths of every day          180
HERESY INDEED          154
HERITAGE          250
High o'er the lonely hills          267
HOLD FAST THY LOYALTY          95
Holy, holy, holy, Lord God almighty!          4
Hosanna in the highest!          309
HOURS OF INSIGHT          86
How happy is he born or taught          99
How little our true majesty is shown          69

I am a part of all that I have met          65
I cannot think of them as dead          73
I love all beauteous things          137
I saw the city of the Lord          204
I walk amidst thy beauty forth          327
I walk the unfrequented road          277
IF MAN THINK THE THOUGHT ETERNAL          63
Immortal, invisible, God only wise          41
Immortal Love, forever full          142
IN QUIETUDE THE SPIRIT GROWS          89
In singing till his heaven fills          8
In sweet fields of autumn the gold grain is falling          276
In the lonely midnight          292
In this stern hour when the spirit falters          55
INDWELLING GOD, THE          88
INWARD WITNESS, THE          74
It came upon the midnight clear          287
It is a piteous thing to be          154
It is something to have wept as we have wept          101
It sounds along the ages          247

Joy to the world! the Lord is come          299
Joyful, joyful, we adore thee          11
JUNE DAYS          326

KNIGHT WITHOUT A SWORD          155
Knowledge, they say, drives wonder from the world          39

LARGER FAITH, THE          188
LARK ASCENDING, THE          8
LAW OF LOVE, THE          157
Leave starry heaven behind          70
LEISURE          183
Let all men living in all lands          225
Let all who live in freedom, won          171
Let him who would excel          161
Let not young souls be smothered out before          150
Let the whole creation cry          10
Let there be light, Lord God of Hosts          201
Let us be faithful to our passing hours          83
Let us now praise famous men          230
Let us wander where we will          60
Life of ages, richly poured          172
Lift up your heads, ye mighty gates          310
Lift your hidden faces          319
light, my light, world filling light, The          59
LIGHT          83
Light of ages and of nations          248
Lo, how a Rose e'er blooming          298
Lo, the day of days is here          317
Lo, the earth awakes again          318
Lord of all being, throned afar          38
Lord of all majesty and might          32
Lord's my shepherd, I'll not want, The          49
Love can tell, and love alone          162

Make channels for the streams of love          157
Man imperishably stands          67
Man is the earth upright and proud          62
Man lives not for himself alone          151
MAN-MAKING          103
MAN OF INTEGRITY, THE          99
man of life upright, The          107
Man's comradeship is very wide          148
May nothing evil cross this door          159
Men go out from the places where they dwelled          216
Men, whose boast it is that ye          173
MERCY, PITY, PEACE, AND LOVE          132
MIDDLE STATE, THE          68
MIND OF MAN, THE          71
MORNING CHORALE          264
morning hangs a signal, The          1
Morning has broken          266
Morning, so fair to see          14
My country is the world          149
My country, 'tis of thee          242
Mysterious Presence, source of all          130

Nay, do not grieve, though life be full of sadness          77
Nearer, my God, to thee          126
NEW PATRIOT, THE          243
night has a thousand eyes, The          164

No longer forward nor behind                187
Noiseless the morning flings its gold        89
Not alone for mighty empire                 239
Not always on the mount may we               90
Not gold, but only men can make              98
Not in vain the distance beacons            195
Now all the heavenly splendor               268
NOW AND HERE                                187
Now give heart's onward habit brave
    intent                                  178
Now I recall my childhood when the sun       82
Now in the tomb is laid                     314
Now is the time approaching                 209
Now let every tongue adore thee              17
Now, on land and sea descending             274
Now once again the heaven turns             320
Now thank we all our God                     19
Now the spring has come again               323
Now while the day in trailing splendor      269

O beautiful for spacious skies              241
O beautiful, my country                     240
O BEAUTIFUL, OUR COUNTRY                    240
O brother man, fold to thy heart thy
    brother                                 144
O come, all ye faithful                     288
O come, O come, Emmanuel                    280
O day of light and gladness                 316
O God, beneath thy guiding hand             235
O God, in whom we live and move              24
O God of earth and altar                    238
O God, our help in ages past                 51
O Life that maketh all things new            54
O Light, from age to age the same           255
O Light of light, within us dwell           122
O little town of Bethlehem                  286
O Lord of stars and sunlight                  9
O Love! O Life! our faith and sight
    (See: Our friend, our brother, and our
    Lord)
O MAN, ACCLAIM YOUR HERITAGE                 66
O prophet souls of all the years            233
O sacred head, now wounded                  311
O sometimes gleams upon our sight           177
O SOURCE OF LIFE                              2
O star of truth, down shining               115
O thou great friend to all the sons of men  120
O thou, to whom the fathers built           116
O thou whose gracious presence shone        125
O Thou whose power o'er moving worlds
    presides                                128
O Thou whose spirit witness bears            74
O worship the King, all glorious above       25
O ye who taste that love is sweet           141
Obedient they but to a dream, who went      228
O'er continent and ocean                    227
Oh, give us pleasure in the flowers today   324
On this day everywhere                      296
Once more the liberal year laughs out       275
Once to every man and nation comes the
    moment to decide                        220
One holy Church of God appears              261
One thought I have, my ample creed           50
One world this, for all its sorrow          145
ONLY HE EARNS LIFE AND FREEDOM              176

OPEN WAY, THE                               219
Our friend, our brother, and our Lord       121
OUR FRIENDLY HOUSE                          256
Our God, our God, thou shinest here          36
OUR KINDRED FELLOWSHIPS                     253
Ours be the poems of all tongues            138
Out of the dark the circling sphere         208

PAGEANT OF THE YEARS, THE                   205
PARLIAMENT OF MAN, THE                      195
Past are the cross, the scourge, the thorn  315
PAST, PRESENT, FUTURE                       116
Peace is the mind's old wilderness cut
    down                                    179
People, look East. The time is near         281
people of the earth go down, The            112
PEOPLE'S LIBERTY, THE                       172
PEOPLE'S PEACE, THE                         179
PILGRIMS, THE                               235
PIONEER, THE                                232
PIONEERS, O PIONEERS!                       211
Pleasure it is                              325
POET, THE                                   140
PRAISE FROM DEPTH AND HEIGHT                  3
Praise God, the love we all may share        37
Praise O my heart, to you, O Source of
    Life                                      2
Praise, O my heart, with praise from
    depth and height                          3
Praise to God and thanks we bring           308
Praise to the living God!                     6
Praise to the Lord, the Almighty, the
    King of Creation                          7
Praise ye, praise ye the Lord                31
PRAYER                                      114
PRAYER FOR THIS HOUSE                       159
Prayer is the soul's sincere desire          91
PRAYER OF THE PILGRIMS                      234
Put down your foot and you shall feel       156

Quest of the ages, goal of men              203

Rank by rank again we stand                 258
Rejoice in love we know and share            42
"Remember me," the Master said              165
Ring out, wild bells, to the wild, wild sky 305
Rise up, O men of God                       218
Rock of Ages, let our song                  279
Roll on, ye stars, exult in youthful prime   52

Say not, "The struggle nought availeth"      97
Say not they die, those martyr souls         76
Seek not afar for beauty; lo, it glows      174
Send down thy truth, O God                  124
SENSE OF DEATH, THE                          81
Serene I fold my hands and wait             186
Serene will be our days and bright          158
Shalom havayreem, shalom havayreem          160
Silent night, holy night                    289
Since I have felt the sense of death         81
Since what we choose is what we are         108
SING NOTES OF LOVE                          141
sky has gathered the flowers of sunset,
    The                                     197
SON OF MAN, THE                             189

SONG OF THANKSGIVING 22
soul wherein God dwells, The 92
SOUL'S SINCERE DESIRE, THE 91
Sound over all waters, reach out from all
    lands 202
Sovereign and transforming Grace 127
spacious firmament on high, The 47
Spirit of truth, of life, of power 146
Spring has now unwrapped the flowers 321
STILL, SMALL VOICE, THE 87
summer days are come again, The (See:
    The sweet June days are come again)
sweet June days are come again, The 326

Thank we now the Lord of heaven 290
There's a wideness in God's mercy 44
These things shall be: a loftier race 190
They cast their nets in Galilee 111
This is the charge I keep as mine 147
This thought shall have our whole alle-
    giance 176
THOMAS KEN'S EVENING HYMN 270
THOMAS KEN'S MORNING HYMN 265
Thou, earth, art ours, and ours to keep 307
Though man, the fiery element, sink like
    fire 61
THOUGHT OF GOD, THE 50
Through all the long dark night of years 169
THY BROTHER 226
Thy kingdom come, O Lord 210
THY SUMMER 327
time shall come when, The 199
'Tis winter now; the fallen snow 301
To cloisters of the spirit 260
To make this earth, our hermitage 306
To Mercy, Pity, Peace, and Love 132
To suffer woes which hope thinks infinite 100
TRANSIENCE 77
TRUE FREEDOM 173
Truly the light is sweet 136
Truth is the trial of itself 105
Turn back, O man, forswear thy foolish
    ways 196

Unheard the dews around me fall (See:
    Noiseless the morning flings its gold)
UNIVERSAL PRAYER, THE 133
UNREST 53
Unto thy temple, Lord, we come 252

Veiled in darkness Judah lay 284
voice of God is calling, The 214

WAITING 186
Watchman, tell us of the night 283
We are all blind, until we see 103

We cannot kindle when we will 86
We come unto our fathers' God 15
We give thee but thine own 131
We journey with a multitude 66
We met them on the common way 237
We move in faith to unseen goals 200
We praise thee, God, for harvests earned 219
We pray no more, made lowly wise 188
We sing now together our song of thanks-
    giving 22
We sing of golden mornings 40
We sing the rapture of the breath 139
We thank you, Lord of heaven 29
We three kings of Orient are 300
What else is wisdom?  What else man's
    endeavor 109
What is this life if, full of care 183
What makes a city great and strong? 102
When a deed is done for freedom, through
    the broad earth's aching breast 168
WHEN ABRAHAM WENT OUT OF UR 216
When courage fails and faith burns low 95
When in his thoughts the stars and
    planets roll 71
When my love to God grows weak 313
When Stephen, full of power and grace 155
When the gladsome day declineth 272
When thy heart, with joy o'erflowing 226
When we have ended searching 181
Where cross the crowded ways of life 189
Where is our holy church? 259
Where is your God?  they say 87
Whether day my spirit's yearning 63
While shepherds watched their flocks by
    night 295
Who is the patriot?  He who lights 243
Who thou art I know not 46
Who would true valor see 94
Winter is a cold thing 302
Wisdom has treasures greater far 96
With joy we claim the growing light 246
Woe unto him that has not known the
    woe of man 153
WONDER 39
Wonders still the world shall witness 191
world stands out on either side, The 57
WORLD-TREE, THE 197

Years are coming—speed them onward 198
Ye shepherd plains of Bethlehem 291
Ye that have spent the silent night 264
Yet when the splendor of the earth 113
YIGDAL 6
You that have faith to look with fearless
    eyes 206
Your little flame of life we guard 263